The Spiritual Anatomy
of Emotion

"*The Spiritual Anatomy of Emotion* is brilliant . . . comprehensive
. . . holistic."

STANLEY KRIPPNER, PH.D., EDITOR OF *ADVANCES IN*
PARAPSYCHOLOGICAL RESEARCH AND COEDITOR OF
THE VARIETIES OF ANOMALOUS EXPERIENCE

"*The Spiritual Anatomy of Emotion* is a landmark book that presents
a picture of consciousness that is far more majestic than anything
conceived in conventional neuroscience. Based in solid science, this
bold effort will challenge anyone who reads it with an open mind.
Highly recommended."

LARRY DOSSEY, M.D., AUTHOR OF
RECOVERING THE SOUL AND *REINVENTING MEDICINE*

"Jawer and Micozzi articulate one of the most profound understandings of consciousness since Descartes. The book brings Antonio
Damasio's 'feeling brain' into full embodiment. It is a monumental
contribution to understanding ourselves as human beings."

ALLAN COMBS, PH.D., AUTHOR OF *THE RADIANCE OF BEING*

"*The Spiritual Anatomy of Emotion* presents a unique and arresting
view of such topics as mind, body, memory, illness, perception, and
emotion. The authors show us an altogether novel way of understanding who we are and what we're about. There's more to being
human than we ever imagined, and this book is an excellent road-
map for anyone who wants to take that journey."

ERIC LESKOWITZ, M.D., DEPARTMENT OF PSYCHIATRY,
HARVARD MEDICAL SCHOOL

"Jawer and Micozzi have collected a unique body of data on environmental sensitivity, which has great relevance to human health and psychology. They put together this data with original ideas on emotion very persuasively in *The Spiritual Anatomy of Emotion*. I highly recommend this well-written and accessible book."

ERNEST HARTMANN, M.D., AUTHOR OF
DREAMS AND NIGHTMARES AND
BOUNDARIES IN THE MIND,
PROFESSOR OF PSYCHIATRY AT TUFTS
UNIVERSITY SCHOOL OF MEDICINE,
AND PAST PRESIDENT OF THE ASSOCIATION
FOR THE STUDY OF DREAMS

"I agree completely with the thesis in *The Spiritual Anatomy of Emotion* from what I have observed in the many case reports we receive from the general public; from a monthly paranormal experience group at our center; and from my experience as a clinical psychologist."

SALLY FEATHER, PH.D., DIRECTOR OF RESEARCH,
RHINE RESEARCH CENTER

"Jawer and Micozzi have come up with important findings that could open up a whole new field of research."

CARLOS ALVARADO, PH.D., ASSISTANT PROFESSOR
OF RESEARCH IN PSYCHIATRIC MEDICINE,
UNIVERSITY OF VIRGINIA

The Spiritual Anatomy *of* Emotion

How Feelings Link the Brain, the Body, and the Sixth Sense

Michael A. Jawer
with Marc S. Micozzi, M.D., Ph.D.

Park Street Press
Rochester, Vermont

Park Street Press
One Park Street
Rochester, Vermont 05767
www.ParkStPress.com

Park Street Press is a division of Inner Traditions International

Library of Congress Cataloging-in-Publication Data

Jawer, Michael A.
  The spiritual anatomy of emotion : how feelings link the brain, the body, and the
sixth sense / Michael A. Jawer with Marc S. Micozzi.
      p. cm.
  Summary: "A cutting-edge examination of feelings, not thoughts, as the gateway
to understanding consciousness"—Provided by publisher.
  Includes bibliographical references and index.
  ISBN 978-1-59477-288-7
  1. Emotions. 2. Consciousness. 3. Mind and body. I. Micozzi, Marc S., 1953–
II. Title.
  QP401.J39 2009
  616.89—dc22

                                                                        2009007861

Printed and bound in the United States by Lake Book Manufacturing

10 9 8 7 6 5 4 3 2 1

Text design and layout by Priscilla Baker
This book was typeset in Garamond Premier Pro with Gill Sans as display
typefaces

The authors can be contacted at **emotiongateway.com**.

Contents

———◆———

———◆———

Note for Readers

———◆———

Throughout this book, the term *neurobiology* is used to indicate the way the brain and the rest of the body operate together, in a connected fashion. This expands on the dictionary definition of neurobiology: "a branch of the life sciences that deals with the anatomy, physiology, and pathology of the nervous system." The authors do not restrict themselves to the nervous system, applying a more holistic approach given the ample evidence (cited throughout this book) that the mind is far more than the brain.

Foreword

---◆---

Isaac Asimov, the astonishingly prolific writer, professor of biochemistry, and author or editor of more than five hundred works of science fiction and popular science, once said, "The most exciting phrase to hear in science, the one that heralds new discoveries, is not 'Eureka!' (I found it!) but 'That's funny. . . .'"[1]

Asimov meant, of course, "funny" not as something humorous, but something strange or bizarre, something that does not fit in. In science, funny things are often consigned to the margins of respectability and ignored. Yet they provide a great service, because they are the outliers that challenge our comfortable notions of reality and the status quo. They are therapy for the mental sludge and sclerosis that clog our intellectual arteries over time. They are a major source of breakthroughs and advancement in any domain of human understanding, including science.

Michael Jawer, in *The Spiritual Anatomy of Emotion*, with Dr. Marc Miccozi, has taken a courageous leap into this region. His quarry: the funny happenings that defy our conventional concepts of emotion, feeling, mind, matter, space, time, and our place in the grand scheme of things. Why is it important to pay attention to this strangeness? "The scientific study of emotion," he writes, "—and of the energy that animates us—may, without our fully realizing it, be placing us on the verge of a vital new understanding of the human organism and its place in the universe."

Readers who bump into the ideas in this book for the first time might consider Jawer's assertion hyperbolic. This might even include scientists who, at least in theory, are supposed to be open to new findings. Why such resistance to the areas that are Jawer's concern?

A smug, arrogant presumptuousness is settling over the biological sciences, a sort of herd mentality in which it has become fashionable to focus on certain areas—brain function and genes get top billing these days—and ignore others. This willful ignorance is breathtaking, because it disregards experiences occurring in a huge proportion of the population, what Jawer calls "anomalous perceptions and odd, inexplicable happenings . . . [that] are part and parcel of life, not some detritus that ought to be ignored or carelessly explained away."

These anomalous experiences are commonly called paranormal events. But "paranormal" is a deceptive word, because, in view of their widespread occurrence, there is nothing "para" about such events. Neither, strictly speaking, are they anomalous, for the same reason: their pervasiveness in everyday life. Those who turn away from this area need a wakeup call, a reality check.

For decades, sophisticated surveys by organizations such as the University of Chicago's prestigious National Opinion Research (NORC) have documented that these happenings are practically the norm.[2] At the NORC, social scientists have surveyed Americans about their inner lives periodically since 1972. These face-to-face surveys involve a random sampling of English-speaking Americans ages eighteen and older, and have provided some of the best information we have in the entire area of social science. They find that two-thirds of us report some sort of extrasensory perception, and nearly half describe "contact with the dead."[3] About 30 percent of us have had "visions," two-thirds have experienced déjà vu, and one-third have seen things at a distance, beyond the reach of normal vision.[4] These individuals, representing most of the nation, have been largely written off by the scientific community as delusional, fatuous, uneducated, and weak-minded. The social scientists at the NORC conclude otherwise. "[P]eople who have tasted the paranormal," they state, "whether they accept it intellectually or not, are anything but religious nuts or psychiatric cases. They are, for the most part, ordinary Americans, somewhat above the norm in education and intelligence and somewhat less than average in religious involvement."[5]

Sociologist Andrew Greeley of the NORC tested people who had profound mystical experiences, such as the perception of being bathed in white light. When these persons were subjected to a standardized test measuring psychological well-being, the mystics scored at the top of the scale. University of Chicago psychologist Norman Bradburn, who developed the test, said that no other factor has ever been found to correlate so highly with psychological balance as mystical experience.[6]

So, dear reader, if you have experienced these sorts of things, give yourself a pat on the back, because you are likely to be well balanced, educated, and smart!

Some scientists who openly examine the issues Jawer raises will find them compelling.[7] Jawer cites the example of the respected science journalist John Horgan, a former senior writer for *Scientific American*. Horgan reports that in his recent explorations he has "encountered so many intelligent, reasonable people . . . who believe in [the paranormal] or do not rule it out" that he was forced to review his own preconceptions.[8]

In science, it is evidence—not authority, opinion, or belief—that ultimately counts. Jawer painstakingly puts his observations under the microscope and constructs a model that includes an expanded role for emotion, feeling, and the entire body, not just that darling research subject, the brain. He redefines what it means to be "sensitive," a telling word derived from the Latin *sentire*, meaning "feel." He proposes new legitimacy for the ancient idea of soul.

The mark of a good theory is its ability to weave together observations that previously seemed to be separate, unrelated, and out of whack. Jawer does just that. He shows how feelings, emotions, and sentience are a kind of Rosetta stone that helps us decipher the connections between a variety of illnesses, conditions, and strange happenings.

One of the most impressive qualities of *The Spiritual Anatomy of Emotion* is the deep respect Jawer shows for the scientific tradition. This book is the work not of some new-age barbarian storming the citadel of reason, but of someone who reveres empiricism and rational precision.

Jawer challenges all of us to open our eyes, expand what we're willing to engage, and cease our censorship of reality.

The Spiritual Anatomy of Emotion is an exciting romp through ideas on which we eventually will base our concepts of what it means to be human. It is a masterful achievement.

LARRY DOSSEY, M.D.

Larry Dossey worked as a pharmacist while earning his M.D. degree from Southwestern Medical School in Dallas in 1967. He helped establish the Dallas Diagnostic Association, the largest group of internal medicine practitioners in that city, and was chief of staff of Medical City Dallas Hospital in 1982. Dr. Dossey is also the former executive editor of the peer-reviewed journal *Alternative Therapies in Health and Medicine* and former cochair for the National Institutes of Health's panel on Mind/Body Interventions. Currently he is the executive editor of *Explore: The Journal of Science and Healing*.

Larry Dossey is the author of nine books and numerous articles on the role of consciousness and spirituality in healing, including the *New York Times* bestseller *Healing Words: The Power of Prayer and the Practice of Medicine.* His work has had a wide influence. Nearly eighty medical schools have instituted courses devoted to exploring the role of religious practice and prayer in health; whereas, before his book *Healing Words* was published in 1993, only three U.S. medical schools offered this type of study.

Preface

◆

Our scientific power has outrun our spiritual power. We have guided missiles and misguided men.

MARTIN LUTHER KING JR.

I soon realized that no journey carries one far unless, as it extends into the world around us, it goes an equal distance into the world within.

LILLIAN SMITH, AMERICAN WRITER

AND SOCIAL CRITIC

As I write this, man's baser instincts seem once again to be exploding out of control. In the corner of the world known as the Middle East—cradle of monotheism, spawner of Western civilization—men of differing nationalities fire missiles across their borders, wreaking indiscriminate havoc on the lives of innocents. Their passions—a perverse and highly volatile mixture of fear, pride, ambition, anger, and hurt—are ignited by pure masculinity. While women weep amid the charred remains of their families, the insults, enmity, and missiles continue to fly.

Around the other side of the world, we shake our heads and go about our business, simultaneously reassured that we have outgrown that primal nonsense and secretly wondering if our vibrant, democratic society might be overturned one day by a similarly toxic brew. We read of the latest scientific advances—especially concerning the functions of the brain—and consider ourselves fortunate to be above the fray. We're on to the things that really matter: a greater understanding of human evolution, an accurate picture of our neurology and physiology, a sense even of our place in the cosmos. The explosive traumas of the Middle East seem, by this yardstick, to be far removed.

Yet the contradiction refuses to be ignored. Consider that the 1990s were christened by the world's scientific establishment as the Decade of the Brain. An influx of research dollars poured into neural research, resulting in a massive increase in our collective appreciation of this most fascinating of all human organs. The future seemed limitlessly bright. Gerald Edelman, an eminent neuroscientist and Nobel Prize winner in immunology, put it this way: "We are at the beginning of the neuroscientific revolution. At its end, we shall know how the mind works, what governs our nature, and how we know the world. Indeed, what is going on now in neuroscience may be looked at as a prelude to the largest possible scientific revolution."[1]

The 1990s will go down in history for other, more venal reasons. President Bill Clinton, at the height of his popularity, succumbed to the entreaties of an intern and fell quickly into ill repute. The economic dynamo of the dot-coms generated unsustainable (and, in many cases, unsubstantiated) profits, eventually subsiding while casting millions out of work. The name Enron will register for future generations much as the Gilded Age's grotesqueries are remembered today. Meanwhile, glamour-hungry athletes bulked up on steroids, smashing records set by earlier, harder-working heroes. All of this makes up the legacy of the 1990s. While the Decade of the Brain was proceeding apace, leaders in numerous fields thoroughly embarrassed themselves.

Looking at ourselves today, we can see that our own Western follies—while paling alongside the intense, prolonged hatreds of the Middle East—are nonetheless on the same order. They spring from the same source. We are, each of us, what zoologist Desmond Morris termed "naked

apes." We are not misguided for wanting to better understand our humanity (indeed, we must do so if we wish as a species to survive), but we *are*
mistaken for putting our faith wholly in neural circuitry to puzzle ourselves out. We are more than that. Our intellectual, emotional, and spiritual lives—our appetites, our musings, our morals, our aspirations and
pursuits of various kinds—are fueled by the physical. Yes, the brain is
physical, but it is encased in a body that supports it and nourished by sensory input that, the more we learn about it, shapes the brain's activity as
much as supports it.

Of all the phenomena that beguile today's breed of philosopher and
neuroscientist, consciousness—that function presumed to originate in
the brain—beckons most fervently. It is today's Holy Grail, the subject
of innumerable conferences and research studies seeking to better grasp
the human mind. Consciousness can reasonably be defined as the subjective nature of one's experience—the composite of the feelings, sensations,
and related qualities of being you.[2] But what makes up consciousness?
Feelings, perceptions, sensory input—the *traffic of the body.*

Here's an analogy. If you wanted to understand the United States,
would you choose to concentrate on Washington, D.C.? True, that juris-
diction is its capital, the seat of its government, and its political nerve
center. But is the "real" U.S. located there? No more so than Wichita,
Kansas; St. Petersburg, Florida; Philadelphia, Pennsylvania; or Bismarck,
North Dakota—and perhaps less. To fathom the country as a whole,
you'd have to travel to a given city or town, stay awhile, get the "lay of the
land"—observe and ultimately interact with the inhabitants. Knowing
the nerve center of the nation would help, but it wouldn't fully explain
anything. A country is more than its capital. So, too, a person—and his
or her consciousness—is more than the brain.

Nonetheless, the idea that consciousness is a product of (or a feature
exclusive to) the brain is commonly held among leading thinkers today.
This is a mistaken presumption. A badly mistaken presumption, I assert,
considering how little it takes account of our bodily processes and the lavish sensory banquet of which we partake each and every moment. A philosophy that equates the brain with the self literally overlooks *common sense:*

that which informs our perceptions as well as what we take for granted. We would do much better to appreciate sentience, the bedrock awareness of being alive.

This book posits that feeling is part and parcel of sentience. The dynamics of feeling in the body and brain—more specifically, the degree to which the flow of feeling connects us organically—will be shown to be a defining characteristic of our individuality. Buttressed by cutting-edge research, this framework offers a new perspective on such topics as immunity, health and stress, and psychosomatic conditions. The approach also affords an unexpected bonus: the ability to better understand anomalous perceptions (e.g., apparitions, poltergeists, so-called out-of-body experiences) that have long been derided, ignored, or dismissed because of our inability to place them in any rational framework. While such anomalies may be the bane of consciousness researchers, they *can* be decoded in terms of feeling. This is my contention in *The Spiritual Anatomy of Emotion.*

Interestingly, only in the last ten to fifteen years (coinciding with advances in brain scan technology) has the study of emotion attained scientific respectability. For a phenomenon long regarded as merely subjective—and thus unworthy of scrutiny—emotion stands revealed as a complex brain/body interaction from which we have much to learn. Concurrently, much-needed light is being shed on perennial mysteries such as chronic fatigue syndrome, posttraumatic stress, and synesthesia (overlapping senses). Now is the time for even more perplexing anomalies of the mind to become understood. The body—*sentience itself*—holds the key.

One skeptical yet open-minded observer has remarked, "It is the study of anomalies that drives science forward. . . . The strange and compelling experiences that people have reported across the ages provide an important and fascinating field of study for psychologists, neurologists, anthropologists, and others. We can only expand our knowledge of [human] functioning . . . and extend our theories of cognition by coming to understand the genesis of such experiences."[3]

I agree fully with this assessment. Further, I'm willing to bet that what has been called promissory materialism—the idea that knowing how the brain works will reveal our true human nature—will inevitably fail to reach its lofty goals, because we are more than the sum total of our neural matrices. Through our bodies, "We are wild . . . energy wells up in us like a perennial spring, urging us to ramble and play, to poke about and learn, to seek a mate, join body to body, and carry on with the story."[4] Through a more complete understanding of sentience, we can live more fulfilling lives as individuals. Moreover, armed with a greater appreciation for the intricacies of our animal nature, we will be in a position to develop greater empathy for one another, coexisting more peaceably as neighbors on this increasingly small, restive, and fragile planet.

Through a variety of disciplines—biology, physiology, neurology, immunology, psychology, even anthropology—we have the knowledge base needed to revisit what it means to be human. What we find may be more sensible than expected and yet more intriguing than we can guess.

MICHAEL JAWER
WASHINGTON, D.C.

Introduction

———◆———

*Emotions are first and foremost experienced in relation to
the body, and it is via the body that they are expressed.*[1]
RHAWN JOSEPH, NEUROLOGIST

Seems self-evident, doesn't it? When you feel love for someone, you have
a warm, open feeling in your chest—perhaps over your entire body. But
when you feel fear, your breath becomes short, your stomach constricts,
and your arms and legs may tremble. When you're angry, you feel the
steam rising through your gut, neck, and shoulders until you're close to
bursting. In contrast, when you're exuberantly happy, your smile beams a
mile wide, your eyes sparkle, and you may even find yourself jumping for
joy. And when you get sorrowful news, your face becomes downcast, your
throat tightens, and tears pour from your eyes.

This is called being human.

Feelings—the perception of them, the decisions of what to do about
them, their roots, their consequences, and above all, their unparalleled
reality—are the stuff of our lives. They're also, undeniably, the stuff of
our bodies.

Contemporary neuroscience is making leaps and bounds in understanding feelings. Brain scan technology reveals flickering images that
show which circuits in your head are processing the electrochemical

messages that are the neural substrate of emotion. The more we learn, the greater the promise for controlling—or at least mitigating—long-standing demons that have plagued the human condition, such as depression, obsessive-compulsive disorder, schizophrenia, and epilepsy. Taking a broad view, our ability to peer into the brain is spawning a remarkable new discipline, neurophilosophy, which is concerned with answering the Big Questions that have long been the hallmark of Western philosophy. Questions like "What does it mean to be conscious?" "What are the roots of the self?" and "How are human beings different from the other animals?" Patricia Churchland, a professor at the University of California–San Diego, puts it this way: "What's so exciting is that the philosophical questions raised by the Greeks are coming within the province of science."[2]

Exciting indeed . . . but be careful what we wish for.

Emotions—that phenomenon of the body—are increasingly being seen through the lens of the brain. And the body is being given short shrift. That in itself is not surprising, since neuroscientists are doing the looking and, by dint of their profession, are concerned first and foremost with the brain. But the palpable truth of what happens *in our bodies* when we're upset, when we're joyful, when we're lustful, enraged, lonely, guilt-ridden, surprised, or terrified, is being relegated to an afterthought. So fascinated are neuroscientists with the functioning of the brain, they take the operation of the body as a *consequence* of brain activity. It's the servant yoked to its master, the faithful companion.

Case in point: in 2002, I attended a lecture at the Smithsonian Institution in Washington, D.C., by the eminent neuroscientist Rodolfo Llinas. His was an outstanding presentation. He made his theories, assumptions, and research accessible to a lay audience by stating them clearly, understatedly, and with a touch of humor. Throughout, Llinas's focus was on the brain: how various perceptions, misperceptions, and aberrations come about and how they might, someday, be corrected. Discussion of this kind was exactly why people had come to hear him. Nonetheless, during the question-and-answer session, a woman, perhaps seventy years old (and quite unlikely to be taken for a neuroscientist in training) asked, "Dr. Llinas, do you ever have to go to the bathroom? Get the call of nature in the middle of a presentation like this one?" Now, this was, shall we say, a bit off the wall. Llinas, not the least bit thrown, responded, "Sure, sometimes." "Then," the lady responded, "you know that it's not always the brain that does the signaling."

Here's another illustration of how the body *knows*. A year earlier, I had put on a high-level conference for about 150 people. As principal organizer, I worked behind the scenes, including signing up speakers and firming the agenda. The morning of the event, the room was filling, a faint buzz of expectation was in the air, and a less faint chorus of butterflies warmed up in my stomach. I was ready for "show time." A scant twenty minutes before the conference was to begin, my co-organizer heartily recommended that, in recognition of my labors, I ought to take the podium and present welcoming remarks. I was, of course, flattered—and also flabbergasted. Yet, keeping on my game face, I managed to gracefully agree. I then strode with the utmost urgency to a nearby chair, opened my portfolio, and scribbled some notes (since I am not the kind of speaker who is terribly comfortable being extemporaneous, especially not at the start of a program). Five minutes before the hour, I had my notes in hand and was ready to go. I felt excited, but also reasonably well collected. It was then that I walked past a colleague and she took me aside. "You look panicky," she said. "Calm down, you'll be fine." Thank goodness she said that, for the moment she did, I realized I'd been kidding myself. I *wanted* to feel calm and cool, but my face gave me away. Hearing from another about the state of angst I was in helped me gain perspective. Where my brain had been sending me messages of "A-OK," my face—and probably my entire body—spoke otherwise.

It is ironic that, in neurology's pursuit of the electrochemical processes of emotion, the role of the "host" body is being snubbed. For centuries, science has stressed the mechanical, the material, and the predictable. So Western scientists dissected cadavers to identify the placement and deduce the workings of the circulatory system and various bodily organs. Emotion itself was not considered a fit subject for investigation, given its ephemeral and apparently irreproducible nature.

Today, as magnetic resonance imaging (MRI), position emission tomography (PET), and similar methods are showing the precise pathways of emotional signals, the brain is worshipped as king. Not the entire Dominion—granted—but most powerful sovereign.

Consider the following statement, which seems to sum up this momentous shift, "The thoughts and emotions that seem to color our reality are the result of complex electrochemical interactions within and between nerve cells. The . . . feelings of worthlessness and self-hatred that accompany depression, although they seem to be based on reality, are no more than distortions in brain electrochemistry."[3]

Now, in contrast, consider some of the things you will say about your own (and others') feelings—and state of mind:

- "That scene in the movie made my skin crawl."
- "I was so moved by what you said."
- "He just makes my blood boil."
- "She's comfortable in her own skin."
- "That stinks to high heaven."
- "I'm shouldering a lot of responsibility."
- "Don't step on my toes!"
- "Get a backbone, will you?"
- "I can feel it in my bones."
- "He finally got that off his chest."
- "It left a sour taste in my mouth."
- "I just can't stomach that."
- "I must admit, I go all weak-kneed when I see her."
- "My heart is full."
- "That sure was a gut-wrenching experience."
- "What a truly breathtaking view."

Of course, these comments are metaphors, but they also reflect real, sensate bodily experience. Such experience—from the time we are in the womb onward—shapes our mental life, our perceptions, our judgments, our likes and dislikes, and our theories and ideologies—including, yes, our speculations on what consciousness is or isn't. Cognitive scientist George Lakoff, of the University of California–Berkeley, puts it as follows: "Our brains take their input from the rest of our bodies. What our bodies are like and how they function in the world thus structures the very concepts we can use to think . . . the mind is inherently embodied . . . this is what we have to have to theorize with."[4]

My contention in this book is that feelings are not merely manifestations of various brain states, but that they also exist in their own right as the product of interaction between raw sensation on the one hand and mental activity on the other. Put another way, we must first be *sentient* (capable of sensory perception) before we can be *conscious* (self-aware). As we will see, the premier component of consciousness is feeling—not, as you might guess, thinking. Feeling preceded thought in our evolution, and it continues to underscore most everything we ponder, chew on, react to, learn, extrapolate, and pontificate on. To be conscious requires that you notice, first and foremost, what you're feeling. And what you're feeling has much to do with the body, of which the brain is a part. A major part, to be sure—in many respects the lead actor—but a part, nonetheless, of the bodily troupe.

Now, why should you care about any of this? Aren't the arguments immaterial to your own life? They're a conversation among scientists and philosophers. What do you care if consciousness gets defined this way or that way? The world will survive.

Yes, the world will survive. But the guiding assumptions may not be to our liking. And the consequences may be distasteful, if not altogether bitter. By downplaying the reality of the body—or casting it as an extension of processes in the brain—something essential gets lost. Namely, *you*. Your feelings don't get hurt, they get shunted aside. Your aches, pains, stresses, insecurities, glories, conflicts, repressions, loves, fears, and exaltations get explained away neurologically. Or they get "fixed" pharmacologically. Or both. In that transaction, your body, which is the underpinning of your self, loses. It loses the stand-alone validity of its own feeling.

Something else stands to get lost. Something that has been held at the margins of science, something seemingly far removed from the topics at hand: emotions, the body, selfhood, and consciousness. I'm speaking here of a type of experience that people tend to have occasionally, all around the world, in every age and *at* any age, but are effectively told to ignore, doubt, or dismiss. These are the "anomalous" perceptions: the feeling of a presence nearby, or an image, a sound, or a scent that registers clearly but somehow intangibly. All of these vanish as quickly and as mysteriously as they arrived, leaving the person who perceived them baffled . . . shaken . . . or stirred.

What to make of such perceptions? Should we dismiss them out of hand? It's tempting. After all, like feelings, they come and they go. Generally they do no harm, and sometimes can be looked upon as helpful, meaningful, or spiritually uplifting. They're unsettling, though. We don't know their cause, and we don't know their purpose.

With the exception of a sympathetic friend or family member, anyone we might choose to confide in is likely to look down his nose at us, wince, or shake his head and sigh. What, are you a nutcase? Come on, get real. Back to business, TV, or whatever.

Because we have no real answers (and don't even know what questions to ask), such experiences understandably get marginalized. Out of step with the March of Science, anomalous perception gets labeled as superstition or stupidity, fable or delusion. It may be these things—or it may not be. In any event, it is a real feature of the human condition. Gallup surveys consistently show that anywhere from one-third to two-thirds of the American public say they've had mystical, apparitional, or extrasensory experiences.[5]

My contention is that new light can be shed on anomalous experience through our rapidly advancing brain science. Just as our knowledge (if not our understanding) of emotion will increase as we gather new insights about the brain, so too should we be able to gain much-needed awareness of what exactly is happening during anomalous perception. And not just awareness of what is happening in the brain. Ideally, we should also be able to determine what is happening in the body. Because, like emotion, anomalous experiences appear to be a product of body-based feeling and mental perception *combined*.

Again, why should you care, especially if you are someone who has never had such an experience? My reply: anything that helps us understand what it means to be human is ultimately beneficial. If it's not beneficial for me, then for you; if not for you, then for your friend, neighbor, or associate; if not for them, then for their children or for society at large. The gain is in the learning—and from that prospect we should not turn away.

Cognitive scientist Steven Pinker of Harvard University has remarked, "A lot of times there'll be these embarrassing facts that you tuck away, thinking there's got to be an answer to them if only you had the time to look into it. But what you don't realize is that sometimes those facts are the ones that hold the key to a mystery, and so you've got to take those facts seriously because they change everything."[6]

The "embarrassing facts" we ought to take seriously in this regard are the reports of anomalous experience by ordinary, sane individuals from every walk of life, around the globe, not all of whom can be hallucinating, mentally deficient, or lying. Might these people share some characteristics in the dynamics of their brain/body interaction that could help explain what they claim to be experiencing from time to time? You will see the answer is yes—and learn *why emotion holds the key.*

1

◆

Putting Emotion in a New Light

*[These] mysterious and dominant feelings which surge
up within us from unknown sources—are they not pure
perturbations of the "psyche"?*[1]

WALTER CANNON, PHYSIOLOGIST AND
PIONEERING EMOTION RESEARCHER

In any field, find the strangest thing and then explore it.[2]

JOHN WHEELER, PHYSICIST

Consider the following accounts. (Only the names of the people involved have been changed, with the exception of the final account, in which actual names are used.)

- Adam, a precocious 18-month-old, lounges in his bathtub after dinner. He loves the warm, soapy water and the relaxed attention of his parents. Suddenly he sits bolt upright in the tub, screaming,

8

"The men! The men! They're coming! They're coming!" His eyes appear fixed on some distant object, and for the moment, he seems unaware of where he is, even who he is.

When asked by his understandably concerned mother who "they" are, he replies with mounting hysteria about men in uniforms and guns who are coming to get him. His mother, a psychotherapist who is well aware of her son's precocious development (he learned to talk at three months and was reading by his first birthday), tries her best to assure Adam that he is safe in his own bathtub with his own mother and father.

Then, as suddenly as the episode began, it is over, with their son seemingly unaware that anything out of the ordinary had taken place.[3]

■ Susan, forty-four years old, is at home one night with the distinct feeling that someone is in the room with her. The next night, she wakes up with a strong sense of her father's presence in the room. She is unable to go back to sleep.

The following night, she wakes up with the same feeling, except now she seems to smell her father's hair tonic. Determining that she is fully awake, she sees her father standing at the door of her bedroom. He looks well and whole, not sickly as he did before he died. She has been bothered by the fact that her father had been alone when he died, but now she has the impression that everything is all right and she shouldn't worry.[4]

■ Something odd is taking place in Mary's home. She (age sixty-two), her mother Lillian, son Keith, and granddaughter Krista have been hearing rapping noises emanating from several walls within their house. Additionally, various small objects have disappeared, turning up later in unlikely places; strange cold spots and unusual smells are noticed; and, most distressingly, puddles of water have appeared in several areas.

Over the next month, the frequency and severity of the water "showers" picks up, with all the family members getting wet. Lillian seems to attract the most attention, being repeatedly soaked. She also is nearly hit by a large, gilt-framed mirror, which falls despite having been securely mounted over the couch for years. No obvious reason is found for this, as the wire and screws that had secured the mirror to the wall are intact.

The family decides to call in a plumbing contractor, but he finds no particular source that would account for the copious amounts of water. One of his workers, however, has his shirt thoroughly soaked while standing in the living room—which so alarms him that he leaves the premises and refuses to return. Another contractor is brought in to inspect the air conditioning system and cannot identify a cause either, but all three of his workers are wetted.

A parapsychologist arrives to investigate. Mary tells him that the disturbances occur only when eleven-year-old Krista is at home. The family members complete psychological profiles and are interviewed, revealing to the investigator a high level of unhappiness despite outward efforts to appear a "happy family." Tension is particularly evident between Krista and her great-grandmother. Krista appears both passive-aggressive and withdrawn (she has even written a suicide note), with Lillian constantly vexed at her great-granddaughter.

The investigator recommends that the family seek counseling to address this repressed hostility. Ultimately, the unusual manifestations of water abate—with the cause never identified.[5]

■ Ron, twenty-nine years old and a new father, dreams on two successive nights of his own father. In the dreams, his father is portrayed in a favorable light, despite the fact that he is an alcoholic who left the family when Ron was just an infant (the two have had almost no contact since). The two dreams, which he attributes to being a new father himself, strike Ron as peculiar.

The following day, Ron's uncle (with whom he also has had little contact over the years) calls to say that the father is dying in a

Veterans Administration hospital and urges him to go visit. Ron immediately blurts out, "Would he come and see me now if I were dying?" He tells his uncle he has absolutely no interest in going. But after wrestling over the rage this phone call has conjured up and the sad and bitter memories he has, Ron decides on making the trip along with his wife and infant son.

Arriving at the hospital, he hardly recognizes the man in the bed, ashen gray and with tubes connected to his head. Ron's anger and self-pity now dissipate. Instead, he feels an overwhelming sadness and says a tearful good-bye. That is the last time he sees his father, who dies a few days later. The night after the hospital visit, however, Ron dreams of an elegant old black car driving him up to his grandfather's house (where he had lived in his infancy). Although he can make no sense of this short dream, it is comforting.

Twenty years later, Ron comes across an old photo of himself, his father, and the black car and recalls that he had seen the photo in childhood. It is the only picture he has of the two of them together.[6]

■ Melanie, age twenty-one and a biology major at college, is jogging across a bridge when she's hit by a truck and hurled onto a concrete embankment. Around that same time, her parents are at a meeting on the other side of the continent when her mother jumps up and says to her husband, "Glen, something's just happened to Melanie." She is right—and since the interruption is recorded in the meeting minutes, the coincidence is memorialized.[7]

■ Ruth, twenty-five years old and a mother of three, sees apparitions of her father. She is living in England, and he is living in the United States. She has had no contact with him for several years, but he is an alcoholic and molested her when she was young. She now sees these apparitions at various times of the day and night. They are extremely lifelike: they talk to her and move as a person would, and she can even smell her father's perspiration. Sometimes her father's face is superimposed on that of her husband, who is with her at home. Neither he nor anyone else sees what she sees. Increasingly anxious and sleepless, Ruth turns to a psychiatrist.

Initially, the psychiatrist can find no obvious brain or sensory dysfunction with Ruth. He does, however, learn something interesting relating to the way Ruth's brain processes visual information. When Ruth claims to see an apparition, her retina registers a normal response to light—but somewhere in her brain, the signal is interrupted.

Together, Ruth and her psychiatrist decide that she will try to exert control over these apparitions by ignoring and/or confronting them. Over a period of months, Ruth succeeds in managing them. She talks back to her father's apparition, asserting it is not real and will not bother her. Ultimately, she is able to call up this vision of her father at will and dismiss it at will. She also develops the ability to create lifelike images of friends and relatives. She and her doctor consider the therapy successful.[8]

■ Passengers and crew on Eastern Airlines' L-1011 fleet of jets during 1973 and into 1974 see, hear, and speak to solid-looking apparitions of two crew members, Captain Bob Loft and Second Officer Don Repo, who perished following the crash of Eastern Airlines Flight 401 into the Florida Everglades on December 29, 1972. The apparitions are readily identifiable as Loft and Repo. "They . . . appear and disappear in front of pilots, flight engineers, or flight attendants completely unexpectedly, and usually in flight."[9] The reports cease in mid-1974, when Eastern Airlines removes all salvaged parts of Flight 401 that had been installed in sister ships of its L-1011 fleet.[10]

Emotion Is the Catalyst

The above accounts have two things in common. First, if they are taken to be truthful, we can soundly infer that something exceptionally strange is going on. Second, they all have elements of heightened emotion:

- Adam, relaxing in his bathtub, is suddenly and inexplicably frightened—so much so that he doesn't appear to know where he is.
- Susan, upon smelling her father's aftershave and then seeing him, is relieved of the guilt she had been feeling over his lonely death.
- Mary's granddaughter Krista is unhappy and withdrawn, and evidently antagonistic to her great-grandmother in particular. Tensions within the family—which has four generations living under one roof—are evident.
- Ron is enveloped by rage, bitterness, and self-pity when he is forced to consider visiting his dying father. These feelings give way to an overwhelming sadness as he witnesses the man's final suffering and bids him good-bye.
- Melanie's mother, attending a meeting three thousand miles away from her daughter, is suddenly distraught, certain that something unfortunate has befallen her child.
- Ruth is extremely anxious in light of the apparitions intruding into her life. Her relationship with her husband and children is being disturbed by the turbulent legacy of her childhood molestation.
- In the immediate aftermath of the crash of Flight 401 into the Florida Everglades, the captain and second officer know they are badly hurt. Almost certainly they feel pain, fear, and horror over what has happened to them, their plane, and their passengers.

Throughout my examination of purported anomalies, I've been struck by the number of times intense emotion appears to play a pivotal role. This is far from a lone observation; researchers into the paranormal have long noted the conspicuous presence of emotion in accounts given by the people involved. One such report—a hallmark among the early cases collected by the British Society for Psychical Research (SPR)—dates from 1863. In this case, a woman's anxiety about the fate of her husband seems to be crucial. As the husband related the story, he'd been on a transatlantic crossing from Liverpool to New York when the ship was overtaken by a severe storm that lasted for nine days. On the ninth day, the man dreamed of his wife, who was at that time in the

United States with their children, visiting her parents. In the dream, she appeared at the door of his stateroom in her nightdress, hesitated on seeing that another passenger was also in the room, then moved across to give him a kiss. When he awoke, the man was told by the cabinmate that, during the night, the cabinmate had seen a woman appear at their door and move over to kiss the man. The witness also alluded to being envious of such female attention!

When the ship reached its destination, the man rejoined his wife and family. Her first question when they were alone together was, according to this report, whether he had received a visit from her during the journey. She claimed that news of the storm, which had caused another ship crossing the Atlantic to sink, had made her extremely anxious. On the night in question, she had lain awake thinking about him, and later on it seemed to her that somehow she had crossed the expanse of ocean, found the ship, located her husband, gone to his side, and embraced him. She also impressed her husband by allegedly describing the ship and its stateroom accurately.[11]

Emotion's Role Overlooked

Over the years, researchers have compiled similar reports in which strong feelings—especially feelings *wrestled with or bottled up*—appear to be an important factor. Some investigators have speculated that a sort of "emotional footprint" or "emotional resonance" might be at work. In general, though, researchers have tended to focus either on attempting to generate anomalies in the lab or on taking measurements in the locations where the alleged phenomena were taking place (e.g., taking pictures of glowing orbs or recording fluctuations in room temperature).

Each of these approaches seems to tacitly accept two general assumptions—both of which downplay the possibility that emotion is a central player. Along the first path (laboratory testing), it is assumed that what cannot be examined in the lab and reproduced is not worth paying attention to. Emotion is certainly unpredictable and hard to either generate or track in a controlled setting—not to mention reproduce under identical conditions, which is the gold standard of scientific inquiry. Along the second path (field research), investigators intent on taking physical measurements of a space tend to focus on tangible proof, often taking insufficient account of the feelings, intuitions, and insights of the people who are intimately involved.

I have come across only one instance where emotion has been squarely examined as a potential "psychic trigger." Bernard Carr, a leading member of the SPR, gave a lecture on this topic back in 1985.[12] He presented some evidence but then raised an obvious question. Since strong emotions are part of everyone's everyday life, why aren't anomalous perceptions more common?

Take, for example, poltergeist occurrences. The literature is replete with examples of the observation that a disturbed adolescent (such as Krista in the third account above) is part of the picture. But surely *many* adolescents are disturbed, if by that we mean are overwrought, feel isolated or persecuted, are uncertain of their place in the world, or hate their parents. If emotional volatility—combined in adolescence with hormonal upsurges—gives rise to poltergeist cases, we should expect to see (as one wag put it) "whole school buildings [to] come crashing down by the dozens each year around exam time."[13] Similarly, why would apparitions of a deceased relative not be frequently experienced by those who are grieving? And shouldn't anomalous activity proliferate around crime scenes, in the aftermath of earthquakes and other natural disasters, and on every spent battlefield?

This is indeed a significant issue if we take strong emotion to be a key to unlocking the dynamics of the anomalous. Like all good questions, this one is bound to yield enlightening answers. But let's consider some preliminaries: What is an emotion, anyway? How is it different from a feeling? Why do emotions exist, and what do they do for us as individuals and as a species? What happens in the brain and body when we have a feeling? What is the relationship between emotion and cognition? An examination of these questions will take us into some very interesting mind-body terrain.

2

---◆---

Feelings and Emotions
The Key to It All

Imagine you are an actor or actress, looking to win a certain part on stage. Forget whether you've ever actually acted before. Just imagine you have a script in your hands, you're reading over the action, and you're assessing the characters. There's one particular person you're keen to play. Maybe you've been asked to take that part; maybe there's simply something about the character that appeals to you. In any event, you've completed reviewing the script and you're sitting back trying to figure out how to play this part. You think about the character, what he or she does over the course of the play. Your aim is not simply to mouth the words; that won't help you win the role. No, you want to impress, to take the director—and the audience—by storm. You want to get inside that character's head and, better yet, inside his or her heart. You think: What's my motivation here? What *drives* this guy or gal? What's he or she *about*? What kind of emotions am I going to need to show to make the character work? Those decisions will ultimately color your posture, your line readings, and your attitude—and will be reflected in all the energy you manifest on stage.

Did you get the part? Well, in this imaginative exercise, I hope you did (and that you wowed 'em every night). Just think, if you were to make the role a success, the reviews would go something like this: "[Your name] embodies [name of character]." "[Your name] makes [name of character] come alive." "[Your name] IS [name of character]." Those accolades would reflect an important principle: emotion is at the core of anyone's character, even someone fictitious. Further, emotion animates every one of us. Which is another way of saying that emotion is *of* the body and expressed *through* the body.

The late psychologist Paul Pearsall, in his book *The Heart's Code,* makes a similar point in an even more personal way. He writes, "As you read these words, take one hand from this book and point to yourself. Where is your hand pointing? Most people find their hand touching the area of their heart. . . . No matter how important it thinks it is, the brain that is coordinating the pointing movements seems to know where a major component of the self it shares with the body resides."[1]

Pearsall's exercise is telling because (a) you probably did point to your chest (even if you are a neuroscientist) and (b) the heart has long been regarded as the seat of emotions as well as the center of our humanity. That may not be to the brain's liking, but it's a cultural and historical reality, dating from ancient Egypt and Greece, if not much earlier in our evolution as hunter-gatherers.[2] So, if we're going to try to understand terms such as the "self," the "soul," the "ego," and the "conscious I," it makes sense to consider emotion first and foremost. Feelings may literally be at the *center of who we are.*

What Is Feeling?

Let's begin by distinguishing the term "feelings" from the term "emotions." The reason is pragmatic: I want to get at two different concepts. As we go on, I will use each term assuming you know what I'm implying by it. The differences may seem small, but they will be significant. Let's start on the bottom floor.

The body has various sensory perceptions, the five principal ones being taste, touch, sight, hearing, and smell. These are the faculties through which we become aware of the world (and aware of ourselves; take, for instance, the sound of one's own stomach growling). While we are most familiar with our five senses, there are probably others. The late author Guy Murchie gave the matter quite a bit of thought and ended up listing thirty-two, which he divided into five major categories[3]:

- The radiation senses, including sight (our eyes' sensitivity to visible light) but also a sensitivity to radiation other than visible light, a temperature sense, and a sensitivity to electric current as well as magnetism. An example of sensitivity to radiation other than visible light is human beings' ability—under experimental conditions or during spaceflight—to actually see cosmic rays as points or streaks of light.[4] Regarding electric current and magnetism, so many different species of animals have been found to possess sensitivity to these phenomena that one author has stated, "It would be more surprising to discover that Man . . . happened to be [electromagnetically blind] than to discover he was not."[5]

- The feeling senses, including hearing, awareness of pressure, sense of weight or balance, awareness of one's proximity to something or someone else in space, and what Murchie himself calls *feel:* "particularly touch on the skin . . . awareness of intra- and intermuscular motion, tickling, vibration . . . cognition of heartbeat, blood circulation, breathing, etc." (This turns out to be a particularly important sensory grouping, as we shall see elsewhere in this book.)

- The chemical senses, including smell, taste, appetite, thirst, and humidity. Smell and taste are closely linked, as demonstrated by the fact that when you get a cold, your ability to taste is often diminished simply because your nose isn't working so well. Likewise, "Much of what we experience as flavor is really an olfactory experience. This is why . . . connoisseurs prefer to sniff their wines, which, without their fragrance, would be fairly tasteless."[6]

- The mental senses, which encompass pain (and, I would add, its opposite, pleasure), fear and dread, sexuality, relaxation and sleep, a sense of humor or playfulness, time sense, territorial sense, an aesthetic sense (appreciation of beauty and the arts), and intuition.

- The spiritual senses, including conscience, the capacity to sacrifice, and the ability to experience ecstasy, religious bliss, and/or unity with the cosmos.

You may not agree with Murchie's scheme or his enumeration of the various senses, but assuming his major point is that humans possess more than the rudimentary five senses of which we are most aware, he presents a compelling case.

Taking my cue from his listing, I shall identify the term "feeling" as a subset of the sensory perceptions he has described—namely, those most closely associated with the body and its processing of sensory stimuli:

- Awareness of pressure and vibration
- Sense of weight or balance
- Awareness of one's proximity to something or someone else in space
- Touch on the skin
- Awareness of intra- and intermuscular motion
- Cognition of heartbeat, blood circulation, breathing, bowels, and so on
- Sense of temperature and humidity
- Sensitivity to radiation, electricity, and magnetism
- Hearing
- Smell and taste
- Appetite and thirst
- Pain
- Pleasure
- Danger
- Sexuality
- Relaxation and sleepiness
- Time sense
- Humor and playfulness
- Aesthetic sense
- Intuition

From the standpoint of common sense, we can probably agree that many of these do, indeed, represent a form of feeling. Let's look at some that aren't so evident, however—beginning with sensitivity to radiation, electricity, and magnetism. A prime illustration of why such a sensitivity deserves to be included is the *feeling* that a momentary shock of electricity creates in the body. It's none too pleasant. In a more pedestrian way, ambient light (a form of radiation) is not only associated with temperature but also with touch on the skin. Think of sunbathing here: you definitely get a feeling from sunbathing. This feeling is a result of the skin's reaction to the effects of the energy delivered by the light. (Hopefully, you don't overdo it lest that feeling becomes painful and your skin starts to peel.)

Another questionable item on my list is hearing. Why should hearing, which appears to be its own sense, be grouped with feeling? The first reason is that sound is literally a vibration. When a bass guitar is pumping, we can feel the sound waves on our skin. Second, hearing a sound gives us an awareness of our proximity to the source. (In the case of our stomach growling, that source may be ourselves.) Sound, therefore, has an intimate connection with the body, which, of course, is all about feeling. As Mona Lisa Schulz states in *Awakening Intuition,* "Our bodies are . . . bathed in music long before birth since we hear the beating of our mother's heart, the rhythmic pulses of her lungs filling and discharging air. Once we are born, musical sounds fill our ears . . . lull us to sleep. . . . Music can inspire us to clap our hands, snap our fingers, march or tap our feet . . . accelerate pulse rate, raise or lower blood pressure . . . and can influence our mood and emotional state."[7]

I have made a slight adjustment to Murchie's lexicon by substituting the term danger for "fear and dread" on my roster of feelings. The latter, to my mind, will fit better into the definition of an emotion.

As to some of the other feelings on my list, anyone who has ever felt turned on can agree that sex deserves to be there. The same is true with relaxation and sleepiness, which are forms of feeling (one might equally say "diminishment of feeling") that we have every day—or at least every evening. Less obvious is a time sense. Yet is there anyone alive who never *felt* that time was passing quickly, passing slowly, or seeming to stand still? Time's connection with the body is a fascinating subject and will be treated in some depth in a later chapter.

Finally, it might be argued that an aesthetic sense, a sense of humor or play, a territorial sense, and a sense of intuition are too mental to be considered feelings. But the body, I submit, does play a central role in these perceptions. Language can be of some value here. When taking in a painting, a piece of sculpture, or a musical composition, we tend to say things like "That's striking," "That's overwhelming," or "That just feels right." These statements are colored by our intellect, it's true, but they also reflect a feeling, gathered from years of experience, as to what *form* of stimulus we find appealing (or not). The aesthetic form—whether on canvas, emanating from a concert hall, or performed on stage—is what generates the feeling.

Here's an example. In the wake of the September 11 attacks on New York and Washington, a version of the traditional spiritual "We Shall Overcome," performed by Bruce Springsteen, quietly affected many people who tuned in to NBC's coverage of the aftermath of those horrific events. The song was subsequently played for ad hoc congregations of baseball fans who attended Mets and Yankees games shortly thereafter. In all cases, this recording, "so plaintive, so stirring, so terribly, terribly evocative" (in the words of an NBC producer), enabled people to reflect, crystallize their sadness, and summon up hope. "It has a peaceful tone," he continued, "rather than a saber-rattling, angry feeling."[8]

Even places can trigger a distinctive feeling. Some locations are meditative, conducive to reflection, or even considered spiritually uplifting or sacred. The Vietnam Veterans Memorial in Washington, D.C., is such a place. Its design, however, is the opposite of a cathedral reaching inspirationally to the heavens. Instead, this memorial slopes gradually downward, its inky black granite walls etched with the names of every American soldier who perished in that war. The effect is to hush people almost immediately, to quiet the mind in contemplation of the loss of life. Surely each of us can think of buildings that similarly move us in some manner. All art forms are, in this respect, equivalent. Renowned architect Daniel Libeskind puts it very well: "Music and architecture are much the same. Both are about tone, balance, and harmony."[9] According to neurologist Oliver Sacks, "One might equally well say that music is moving architecture," adding rhythm and symmetry as further qualities common to both.[10]

The tone or chord that any work of art strikes in the observer does indeed equate to feeling. Which makes sense, given that the very word "aesthetics" derives from a Greek root meaning "of or pertaining to feeling" (as does its opposite, "anesthesia," which means "the absence of feeling").[11] Ultimately, as one observer puts it, "Art is a bodily-felt experience manifesting in chills up our spines, in the heart-lifting effects of melody, the inspiration and exhilaration of a beautiful sentence."[12] He goes on to suggest that the better integrated or accessible a person's feelings are in his or her life, the more expressive and the better an artist he or she is likely to be.[13] Indeed, it could be argued that the long life enjoyed by some of our best known writers, sculptors, architects, composers, and conductors is due, at least partially, to their continual invigoration by art—to the healthful effects of marrying one's deepest feelings with high intellectual acumen. The artistic output of such people is often inspiring (literally, breathtaking), just as the creative process must be for them.

A comprehensive study of history's most creative individuals reveals that bodily feeling and emotional expression generally go hand in hand with thinking and imagination. In his book *Sparks of Genius*, Michigan State University professor Robert Root-Bernstein—himself the recipient of a MacArthur Fellowship—observes that "the process of invention is always emotional and sensual and the resulting ideas are translated into words or numbers [by great writers or scientists] only in order to communicate with other people." For any highly creative person, he says, "Ideas emerge in the form of feelings, emotions, movements, images, and patterns. When we truly understand something, not only can we describe or explain it in words, numbers, or art forms, but we can sense and feel it too." As one illustration, many creative people empathize with their subjects, "becoming" the tree or animal they are painting, the electrons, stars, genes, or viruses they are studying, or the characters in the novels they are writing. The process then entails *transforming* the images and feelings in one's being into words, equations, sculptures, dances, or any other language that other people can appreciate. And these forms of expression are often merely the sides of a coin. Root-Bernstein points out that poet e. e. cummings, like many famous writers, was a painter and that Albert Einstein, like many Nobel laureates, was a musician.[14]

For the rest of us, our use of everyday language hints at our underlying feelings. "My sides ache," you might say after a buoyant bout of laughter—and feel a good deal better for the release. "I'm in a playful mood today," expresses another feeling state (as well as a mental one). "I just feel so protective of her" or "I feel strongly that we've got to protect our turf" both reflect a body-influenced territorial sense. Even intuition is nothing if not bodily mediated, as in "I can't put my finger on it but . . . it just doesn't feel right."

To this catalog of feeling, I would add an important qualifier: *you* *may not be fully aware of your feelings*. They may be perceptions that your body recognizes but your brain—at least on a conscious level—does not. The best examples of this are heartbeat, blood circulation, and breathing. These activities are going on all the time—you surely wouldn't be alive if they didn't—but how often are you aware of them? Mostly they're happening underneath, in a neglected corner of your consciousness, but if these processes become disturbed for any reason (say, you experience shortness of breath), the realization will immediately surface. As my wife, who is asthmatic, likes to say, "Nothing gets your attention like an inability to breathe." The same is true for numerous other bodily processes that typically operate below the threshold of our conscious awareness.

Alternately, a given feeling may have occurred so fleetingly that it never registered in your consciousness. Or it may once have been conscious, but since moved out of the foreground. Each of us, for example, has been known to block out or repress unpleasant feelings, typically those associated with painful or horrific experiences. But the body ultimately recognizes *all* feelings. They are after all, its language, its stock in trade.

What Is Emotion?

An emotion, as I define it, is a feeling that makes its presence known through a need, desire, or tendency to express it: whether by laughing, crying, shouting, jumping, gesturing, fighting, fleeing, hugging, or kissing. Such expression can also be by artistic means: writing about a painful subject, for instance; drawing, painting, or sculpting something that holds meaning for you; creating a poem or musical composition; singing, marching, or dancing; and even confessing or atoning for something you did wrong. All of these are ways to express something you feel.

This definition makes sense when you consider the word "emotion." Just as it sounds, an emotion is a feeling *in motion* within your body. And the word "emote" conveys the need to express it to another person—or at the very least, acknowledge it to yourself. This act of emoting can be direct (talking to someone, squeezing their hand) or indirect (writing in a private journal, pummeling a speed bag, muttering to yourself, yelling to no one in particular).

The following is a list of emotions. It is not meant to be exhaustive or all-encompassing, nor is it presented in any special order. The important thing to notice is how these emotions—as opposed to the simpler feelings—imply both movement in the body and the need for expression in some way:

Anger	Hate	Contempt	Frustration
Worry	Regret	Surprise	Awe
Fear	Dread	Distress	Relief
Sadness	Loneliness	Grief	Empathy
Happiness	Exhilaration	Joy	Hope
Despair	Dejection	Thankfulness	Longing
Lust	Envy	Disgust	Pity
Desperation	Resignation	Rebelliousness	Pride
Embarrassment	Shame	Guilt	Ambivalence

As mentioned earlier, fear and dread are placed in the category of emotions because I believe they impel a person to action more directly than a sense of danger. Something can feel dangerous, yet you can choose to stay on that path. In contrast, fear or dread is more likely to impel you to change the status quo. Reasonable minds may disagree, but that is my rationale.

Additionally, I do not consider depression—a subject much talked about these days—to be an emotion. Depression is a condition, the result of emotions unexpressed. In that sense, it is an anti-emotion, an example of what can befall someone when powerful feelings are disowned, bottled up, or dissociated. In many cases—perhaps all—there is also a genetic component, a latent disposition. But none of that alters my assessment that depression does not—indeed *cannot*—qualify as an emotion.

Then, why, you might ask, is ambivalence on the list? An ambivalent person rarely acts on what he or she is feeling (for a nice Shakespearean illustration, think of Hamlet's endless equivocating). And ambivalence is sometimes linked to depression: depressed people seem, often enough, to be ambivalent. To my mind, though, ambivalence is the confluence of competing or contradictory emotions. So it could fairly be said that the person's natural inclination *is* to express something, even though his or her impulses counteract. Ambivalence is thus a state of emotional affairs. Most often, it's a state that is temporary; when resolved, the emotion with the greater sway gets expressed, albeit in an often tempered fashion.

By now it should be obvious that few emotions are simple, pure, and uncomplicated. Just as the vast majority of colors we perceive in the world are mixtures of primary colors, so most emotions can be understood as mixtures of more primary feelings. The most complex emotions are probably an amalgam of feelings that are contrary (or, at the very least, are not naturally harmonious with one another). To choose an example: loathing, in this case self-loathing. Among its constituent parts could be desire, longing, anxiety, desperation, and shame. The result would be one very complex emotion, the acknowledgement and expression of which could pose quite a challenge.

Of What Value Are Emotions?

Just as I distinguish between feelings and emotions, so too the value each of these concepts has for human beings is different. The core value of a feeling is self-preservation and self-direction. Any animal that has sensory pathways and a body *feels*. That creature may or may not be conscious, that is, self-aware. But it is definitely alive, definitely sentient—and its feelings allow it to navigate and survive in the world.

In contrast, an entity must be conscious to be able to recognize and act on its feelings. Here I distinguish between animals that simply respond to their biological urges or instincts and those that consciously choose to express an emotion. Human beings are the only creatures that we know for certain recognize feelings moving in their bodies and express them to their fellows (or acknowledge them to themselves). But there is strong evidence that chimps, dolphins, whales, and elephants—along with species even better known to us, such as cats and dogs—do the same.

So what purpose do emotions serve? The following list represents the major theories. We start with the most basic (biological) function and proceed to the more advanced.

1. **Emotions enable individuals to discriminate "us versus them" (the self awareness aspect).** From an early age, we are able to distinguish that which is interior and that which is exterior based on two complementary yardsticks: what is being felt at any given moment in response to external stimuli and what *reaction* other people have to our own expression of emotion. Thus, emotions—emanating from others as well as ourselves—help individuals form a sense of self. (Psychologists also refer to having readily demarcated boundaries. This is not only an important concept but a highly useful one that we shall turn to throughout this book.)

2. **Emotions enable the individual to react quickly and expeditiously to changes in his or her environment (the adaptational aspect).** Emotions, by definition, impel movement. This process clearly aids decision making. Author Piero Scaruffi notes, "If I am

afraid of a situation, it means it is dangerous: the [feeling] of fear has already helped me make up my mind about how to approach that situation. If I were not capable of fear, my brain would have to analyze the situation, infer logically what is good and bad in it for me, and finally draw a conclusion. By that time, it may be too late."[15]

3. **Emotions enable individuals to communicate something of importance to one another (the collectivity aspect).** Both individual integrity and group functioning are served when emotions are employed. Bodily messages that convey "I'm happy," "I'm distressed," "I want your banana," or "Watch out!" can be expressed quickly and unambiguously, making them ideal for communication.[16] Charles Darwin recognized, and was the first to document, the prevalence of emotion in signaling feelings and intent;[17] in fact, if Darwin "were not so well known as the author of *Origin of Species*, his book entitled *The Expression of Emotions in Man and Animals* would probably be much more widely recognized and appreciated."[18]

4. **Emotions cement bonds between people, especially between parents and children (the interpersonal aspect).** The psychological term "attachment" is used to describe the strength of identification, based on love and affection, between children and their caregivers. Feelings conveyed through the eyes, the tone of voice, and the quality of touch are crucial, developmental psychologists are finding, to the infant's sense of self, his or her evolving feelings of self-worth, and the ability, much later in life, to form and maintain close and meaningful attachments.[19] More generally, emotions facilitate *empathy between individuals* since each of us learns, early on, to associate the facial expressions and other cues we receive to decode what other people are feeling.[20]

5. **Emotions are integral to memory and learning (the continuity aspect).** As one feels and expresses emotion, brain chemicals (neurotransmitters) and hormones circulate throughout the body. These chemicals, in tandem with neural structures and bodily organs and musculature, literally create memory as patterns of brain activity and of movement (or lack of same) in the rest of

the body.[21] The given memory, of course, may be conscious or unconscious. That is, available to our thought and inspection or filed away so that it is relatively—but not necessarily completely—inaccessible. Memory and learning will also be strongly reinforced whenever an educational or instructional experience is accompanied by strong emotion. What the teacher conveys with great passion will be much more readily learned by his or her students.

6. **Emotions are a barometer of needs unmet or goals unfulfilled (the motivational aspect).** Fear, for example, can be seen as a measure of lack of safety. Sorrow or dejection can be seen as a barometer of loss. Anger and rebelliousness can be viewed as the counterpoint to a lack of satisfaction. Greed, hope, and longing can all be viewed as a drive toward pleasure.[22] A variation of this idea is that emotions serve, in a very basic way, to propel the individual toward acceptance or rejection of whatever external reality he or she is encountering.[23]

7. **Emotions facilitate socially acceptable behavior and serve as a powerful reminder when one fails to live up to standards, whether held internally or externally (the ethical aspect).** Author Willard Gaylin offers the prime examples of shame and guilt—two "social emotions" that reflect transgressions against codes of conduct. In his words, "shame and guilt . . . specifically define the human being, and are essential in the maintenance of civilized society. . . . They are the building blocks of conscience, the core of the moral animal."[24]

8. **Emotions are essential to personal development and self-actualization (the developmental aspect).** Much as a fever signifies that the body is fighting off an infection, painful or negative emotions inform us that we are in the midst of a difficult situation and that learning needs to occur if we are to grow.[25]

9. **The emotional feedback loop, which involves the recognition of what we and our fellow individuals are feeling, is the driver of our species' progress (the evolutionary aspect).** In contrast to the idea that human beings are a veritable blank slate—that experi-

ence merely fills in preset genetic paths—there is the concept that emotional interaction between human beings is the engine propelling our species' rapid intellectual and cultural development.[26]

10. **In tandem with thinking, emotions determine the quality, value, and, ultimately, the meaning human beings place on their lives (the qualitative aspect).** As will be shown later in this book, emotion informs intellect. Feeling preceded thought in evolution, and it is still essential today. Without emotion—that is, the perception and expression of feeling—higher brain functions would operate in a vacuum, if they would operate at all. Thus, any assessment of our lives must be grounded in emotional experience. Several commentators have expressed this idea beautifully. Gaylin says that emotions "most profoundly shape our personhood and are most central to being human."[27] Fellow psychiatrist Elio Frattaroli notes that "it is primarily in our awareness of feeling . . . that we can discover who we really are. . . . The simple act of paying attention to your inner world, to the finely attuned layers and qualities of inner experiencing . . . crystallizes the core meanings of your life."[28]

In any situation—as a person is experiencing a given feeling or set of feelings and expressing himself or herself emotionally—at least one of the above purposes is being served.

When you step back and consider all that emotions are and all that they do for us, individually and communally, it's truly a wonder. Can you imagine being human without them?

Two-Way Emotional Processing

Reasonable people can disagree about what sensory perceptions, feelings, and emotions are. This discussion simply provides a framework. But I believe it captures accurately how we human beings function while paying due respect to the body in which each one of us dwells, marvels, and conjectures.

Some further elaboration is necessary. To begin, it's plain that emotions don't solely arise out of an action or situation you're directly involved with: being the recipient of a surprise party, for example (eliciting elation and/or thankfulness); being goaded into an argument (anger, frustration); finding yourself saying something inappropriate (embarrassment, guilt); or merely witnessing a beautiful sunset (awe). They can also arise from inward, much less tangible sources, such as when you:

- Recollect something
- Think about something
- Hear some news
- Fantasize or daydream
- Dream during sleep

The question is whether a bodily perception (feeling) is necessarily triggered first in all these instances, or whether your brain might be the initial actor and then alert your body. You may think, "That's silly; who cares? It all happens so fast as to be indistinguishable." And you'd be right. The question doesn't matter in the real world, but it surely does in the worlds of neuroscience and neurophilosophy. The issue of "which comes first, bodily sense or thought?" is as old as the hills. Or as old as humans' appreciation of the fact that they are both physical *and* mental creatures. Theoretically, the ante is huge. The indisputable fact that feelings happen *both* in the brain and in the body means that the study of emotion could have a very large payoff as regards the ultimate answers about human nature. Our ever-increasing ability to hone in on emotional activity in the brain, using specialized instruments that can detect lightning-quick flashes of neuronal excitation, suggests that a definitive answer may be at hand.

A rising school of thought suggests that brain activity inevitably comes first. Chief among the investigators in this area are Antonio Damasio, of the University of Southern California, and J. Allan Hobson, of Harvard Medical School. Their general idea is that activity in the brain below the threshold of consciousness sets off bodily reactions, which in turn inform higher-level brain activity and, finally, a conscious perception of what you are feeling. The terminology used by Damasio and Hobson is the opposite of what I have employed. Emotion, for them, is the *background state of the brain*. It is an ongoing assessment, in other words, of a person's external environment and internal bodily condition. According to Hobson, emotion is "a constant flow of vital data from deep within ourselves . . . not just a reaction to the world, it is a spontaneous and constantly present component of our subjective experience . . . that others pick up, read, and describe as our personalities."[29] Thus, we are constantly broadcasting our emotional state (in the framework I prefer, our "background feeling" state) through facial expression, posture, and tone of voice. The end product—what Damasio and Hobson term "feelings"—is, in contrast, a private affair. Feelings, they assert, are what register consciously, what you gauge for meaning, and what you remember experientially and try to learn from.

These theorists have obviously given the matter much thought, presenting meticulously developed arguments and experimental evidence. Along with other pioneers such as Joseph LeDoux of Cornell University's Weill Medical College, their work has ushered in a new day in the study and appreciation of emotion. Yet I wonder if their training as neurologists does not predispose them to see the brain as the prime mover in all cases. Damasio, for example, consistently makes statements such as the following:

- "The brain induces emotions. . . ."[30]
- ". . . brain representations . . . constitute a feeling."[31]
- "Emotions are complicated patterns of chemical and neural responses."[32]
- ". . . neural patterns . . . eventually become feelings."[33]

While acknowledging that the body is "the main stage for emotions"[34] and doing his utmost to show the body as an integral part of the emotion-feeling loop, Damasio is nonetheless convinced there can be no initial feeling state in the body.[35] Hobson is more explicit, opining that emotion *cannot* reside in the body. His argument: that our dreams are laden with emotion, yet all bodily sensations are blocked during rapid eye movement (REM) sleep, which is the period of sleep characteristic of dreaming. If we literally cannot feel our bodies during a dream, how can those emotions, which are undeniably vivid, be about the body?[36]

On first inspection, this reasoning appears sound. There is an answer to it, however—an answer that, if correct, illustrates that emotional processing can occur two ways. Dream emotion, I assert, is both like and unlike the type of emotion we experience in our waking life. Here's the rationale. It hearkens back to my original proposition that (a) sensory perceptions are the raw material of feelings, and (b) feelings may or may not become conscious, but (c) feelings needing to be expressed—what I term emotions—do become conscious as they are made evident to ourselves and others. This is the first route of emotional processing, requiring bodily input first and foremost. The brain comes in later. This is the path typically taken when something tangible happens directly involving you. We've already given the examples of having a surprise party thrown for you, being lured into an argument, being overheard saying something inappropriate, or witnessing a beautiful moment in nature. In these cases, there is plenty of sensory input to trigger the process.

However, there are also plenty of times when emotions arise and your body is *not* receiving palpable stimuli. When the stimuli, such as they are, are intangible or internally generated. We've already provided the examples of recollecting or mulling over something, hearing some news, daydreaming, and dreaming during sleep. Here, the relative lack of bodily input suggests a second route of emotional processing—the brain-generated pathway elucidated by Damasio and Hobson. This second pathway is employed when we are mentally moved by an image. But where does the image come from? In the case of a memory, we are already familiar with it, having filed it away. In the other instances, we are effectively piecing together an image from familiar bits and pieces. Consider the following example. The other day, my wife reminded me of a song that she loved—and I hated—from about twenty years ago. In order, the following things rapidly occurred: (1) I heard what my wife said, (2) I thought of the song and the vocalist who sang the song,

(3) I grimaced almost involuntarily and heard myself say yecch, and (4) I realized all over again how much I hated the song.

That was Damasio's neural pathway of emotion at work. Likewise, recall how you felt on learning in 2002 that the space shuttle Columbia had disintegrated on reentry into the atmosphere. If you're like me, you had a quite visceral, sorrowful reaction. But how did that reaction come about? In my case, there was little or no tangible, bodily input involved as a radio announcer was heard straightforwardly stating what had happened. In essence: (1) you heard the news or saw TV footage, (2) you recollected the Challenger disaster of 1985 or some other vivid mishap, (3) you got a sinking feeling in your stomach or a tightness in your throat, and (4) you realized you felt sadness or loss and expressed this somehow.

In both these examples (the song and the space shuttle), we are emoting based on images already stored in our minds as well as the feelings previously linked with those images. But how did those images originally arise? They, or their forebears, had to have been created by the first route of emotional processing, namely the body-generated kind. We simply cannot create an image out of scratch. Any image must be based on some kind of experience—and experience springs from the physical, the palpable, and the sensory.

So, when a person is dreaming during REM sleep and mentally (though not physically) apprehending feelings, the brain is truly doing all the work. It doesn't mean, as Hobson infers, that feeling is never generated in the body. It simply means that dream emotion, such as it is, is summoned via the second pathway and not the first.

I frankly would take issue with the notion that the content of our dreams—or, for that matter, of our fantasies, daydreams, or anything chiefly having to do with images—is necessarily either a feeling *or* an emotion. If no bodily processing is associated with an image, it must be affect neutral. Put another way, if you don't get some kind of rise out of the image, a feeling can hardly be involved. And, in my conception of things, the feeling can only become an emotion if it gets expressed.

Here's what happens during dreaming. Our representations are literally in our head; they are neural patterns alone. On awakening, we remember feeling joyful, terrified, irritated, loving, desirous, guilty, anxious, or any other combination of feelings that we may or may not have expressed in the dream. But did we truly feel those feelings? No. They are amazingly accurate reproductions of the real thing. They are facsimiles or facades, but they are not feelings in the sense that I am using the term, and certainly not emotions.

The Primacy of Feeling

Regardless of what researchers (or anyone else) mean by the terms "feelings," "emotions," or "feeling states," we should all be able to agree that this aspect of being is not merely an essential component of consciousness. Our deepest feelings inevitably dictate who we are as individuals, what's important in our life, what we choose to do, and what we become. "For human beings," remarks one observer, "the reality that ultimately matters is the reality of their feelings."[37]

That reality is undeniably material. Feelings are *embodied* in many ways, including ". . . by myriad changes in the body's chemical profile; by changes in the state of viscera; and by changes in the degree of contraction of various . . . muscles of the face, throat, trunk, and limbs. . . . [Feelings] also cause other significant changes in the state of several neural circuits in the brain itself."[38]

Likewise, each of us is familiar with what ensues when feelings go unexpressed. "The muscles may fail to relax and are held in as well, and the musculature becomes tense and tight . . . intellectually and physically the ability to function effectively can become impaired. In consequence, those who suppress their feelings . . . often experience debilitating muscle, back, and head aches."[39]

The flip side is the pleasure, the satisfaction, or at the very least, the relief that comes with emotional expression. Who has not literally felt better finally telling that special someone that you love them, or felt a weight lifted off one's shoulders by confessing something you've felt you had done wrong? Everyone says there is no better feeling than sex: here they may mean orgasm, which is experienced as both psychological bliss and physical release, or they may mean intimacy (ask any woman). Think about the exhilaration you may get from public performance: that dance recital, concert, or impromptu stand-up routine at the office. These are the emotional and physical counterpoints to holding in, denying, or ignoring strong feelings.

The balance of this book will be concerned with how we come by our feelings, starting with what is known (or can be inferred) about our condition in the womb and moving through early childhood and into adolescence. We will learn how the self develops thanks to structures in the brain, hormones in the body, and touches on the skin. We will explore the concept of feelings as energetic, consider how healing occurs, and examine the intimate role played by our immune system in health, stress, and illness. We will examine the familiar phenomenon of electricity and the less familiar ways that it underlies mental and bodily activity. We will take up phenomena as different as environmental sensitivity (extreme susceptibility to allergies, migraine headaches, and the like), synesthesia (conjoined senses, such as hearing a color or tasting a shape), and absorption (the tendency to lose oneself in an intense, often imaginative, activity). We will assess the ways that memories are formed in the body and in the brain, and learn what happens during traumatic experience when the conscious mind dissociates; that is, when feeling is withdrawn and memory goes "underground."

Throughout, we will consider anomalies such as apparitions, telepathic dreams, and poltergeists—assessing how these could constitute bona fide perceptions and profiling the type of person most likely to have (or, alternately, trigger) such an experience. We will look at the enigmas of phantom pain and posttraumatic stress disorder as well as so-called out-of-body awareness, and shed light on these highly puzzling yet intensely felt experiences. We will assess such diverse conditions as autism, synesthesia, chronic fatigue syndrome, and fibromyalgia (chronic pain) in an entirely new light. Last but not least, we will consider that most baffling of phenomena: time and the various ways it manifests to human beings.

As we traverse this fascinating ground, we shall remember, as anthropologist Desmond Morris emphasizes, "We are . . . still very much a simple biological phenomenon. Despite our grandiose ideas and our lofty self-conceits, we are still humble animals."[40] We shall acknowledge that the most accurate and useful barometer of this nature is emotion. Without our feelings and their impulse toward expression, consciousness and intellect would not exist, and our strides toward understanding ourselves and the world we inhabit would be pointless.

Emotion, accordingly, is the touchstone of this book. Its dynamics will be shown to traverse and connect all the topics we explore, each of which is exciting in its own right but which together constitute a new understanding of what it means to be human.

I invite you to take the journey with me.

3

---◆---

Feeling as the Integrator of Brain, Body, and Self

Feelings bear witness to the state of life deep within.[1]

ANTONIO DAMASIO, NEUROSCIENTIST

"I think, therefore I am" is the statement of an intellectual who underrates toothaches.[2]

MILAN KUNDERA, NOVELIST

The sheer breadth of what we can feel—not to mention the ability to articulate and act on it—is astonishing. So is our breadth and depth of intellect.
But as enlightened figures such as the philosopher Baruch Spinoza have
understood down through the ages, feeling *informs* thinking. Great literature, for example, soaring poetry, even monumental declarations of political
ideals such as the Magna Carta, the Declaration of Independence, or the
United States Constitution: these are no mere intellectual exercises. The
people who wrote them had blood coursing through their veins, they felt
intensively and acted on their convictions. So it is for every one of us today.

What we feel forms the cornerstone of our perceptions, our dreams, our motivations, our reflections, and our values—*who we are.*

Given that they are so important, it behooves us to look more closely at feelings and emotions from an evolutionary perspective. Why do they occupy the central place they do in our psyche? We shall survey some of the things that happen in the brain and the rest of the body when we feel scared, sad, joyous, surprised, and so on. We'll venture into the brain/body connection to glimpse how we are unified beings in multitudinous ways. And we'll consider the important implications emotion must have for any conception of mind. All this provides a basis for tackling one of the biggest subjects around: *What makes a self?*

Emotions Have an Ancient History

Our species, *Homo sapiens,* is tens of thousands of years old, having evolved from a now-extinct mammalian primate line millions of years more ancient. In the first 97 percent of our species' existence, almost everything that is characteristically human came into being, whereas the entirety of recorded history constitutes perhaps the last 3 percent.[3]

In our early evolution, emotion must have been all about survival. Fear and anger mobilized our ancestors for flight from—or fight with—the animals that stalked them. Our neurology and physiology was originally geared to simple survival.[4]

Only during the past ten thousand years or so did humans settle into communities, learn to farm, and begin to domesticate animals. Ultimately, they found that their fellow human beings had taken the place of predatory beasts as the most complex and dangerous everyday challenge. The fairly simple feelings underlying flight or fight now needed to be augmented by abilities to apprehend, judge, and respond to other individuals' motivations.[5] Our species' success may ultimately be due to the fact that, as one writer puts it, "We are the most cooperative creatures on Earth . . . humans have long formed enduring bonds with people who start out as strangers and go on to become partners in intimate relationships" ranging from marriage to business alliances.[6] Within this context, a wider range of feelings must have evolved to provide the necessary gut-level insight to successfully determine who to trust or mistrust, and on the flip side, to convey through facial expressions, posture, tone of voice, and such the required shades of meaning to others.

Take, for instance, the play of emotion on the face. As noted by William Allman, author of *The Stone Age Present,* "The emotions that show in someone's face play a crucial role in how we judge a person's goals, intentions, mood, and reliability. . . . [Such] cues are so important to human survival that a universal grammar has evolved in facial expressions."[7] Charles Darwin was the first to note, in 1872, that human beings have certain facial expressions in common, some of which are also shared by primates and other animals.[8] More recent research conducted by neuroscientist Paul Ekman, of the University of California–San Francisco, has corroborated Darwin's observations. When people around the world, in cultures as primitive as those in New Guinea, were shown photos of individuals with certain facial expressions, the "messages" were immediately recognized. Ekman concluded that at least four facial expressions are universally human: fear, anger, happiness, and sadness.[9]

The Autonomic Nervous System

Emotions don't just communicate something of importance to our fellow human beings. They're also tied to physiological responses that, if we pay sufficient attention, tell us something important about what we're experiencing ourselves at any given time. Consider this insight about feelings of pain: "When we're in pain, the localized place hurts but the entire body responds. We grow sweaty, our pupils dilate, our blood pressure shoots up . . . the same thing happens when we're angry or scared. There is a deep emotional component to pain."[10]

Such physiological activity is controlled by the autonomic nervous system (ANS), which regulates basic bodily processes including respiration, blood circulation, heart action, digestion, elimination, glandular activity, and pupillary reactions. (The workings of the ANS are not under conscious control; they are involuntary, hence the word "autonomic.") The

ANS has two branches, known as the sympathetic and parasympathetic nervous systems. The former speeds up the body's processes; the latter slows them down. In situations of pain or threat (at least as perceived by the individual), the sympathetic branch, through the influence of its nerves directly on the adrenal glands, will mobilize one's resources to meet the emergency. The senses go on alert, the pupils dilate, the heart muscle is stimulated, the blood pressure is raised, and oxygen delivery and consumption are increased. On the opposite end of the spectrum, the parasympathetic branch (through the vagus nerve—more on that later) takes precedence when one is coming down from a stressful situation, or already relaxed and enjoying oneself.

These two branches of the ANS can be considered the *yin* and *yang* of the body (see figure 1.) We'll examine them more closely in the next chapter. For now, the important point to remember is how closely feeling is linked with autonomic function. Feelings can be conscious, of course; whenever we are emotional, our feelings are right there in the open to be perceived. But the root of feeling is very much biological, very much physiological, and at least initially, *un*conscious.

Feeling Underlies Consciousness

Feeling itself is the basis of consciousness and underlies higher thought. Now, this statement is contrary to what many human beings (especially those of an intellectual bent) prefer to believe about themselves, but it is becoming generally accepted. Here's a somewhat poetic image that, nonetheless, presents the truth of the matter: "Like a cork floating on the surface of the ocean, consciousness rises and falls with each wave of feeling that passes through the body."[11] Moreover, both feeling and thought have a common origin in bodily states or movements. The process has been described thusly: "When the nerve impulses, set off by body movements, reach [the lower brain] centers, a person becomes aware of feelings. The impulse doesn't stop at these lower centers, however, but passes on . . . to the cerebral hemispheres, where image formation and symbolic thought take place."[12]

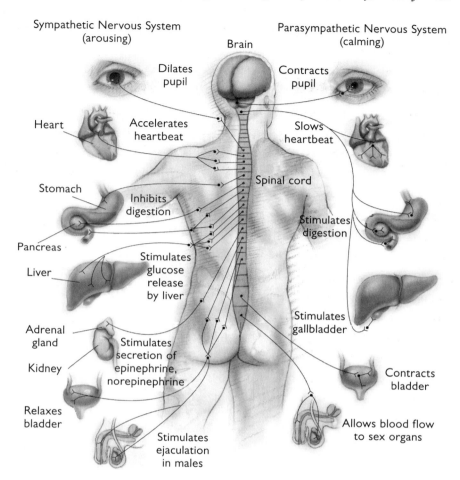

Figure 1. The autonomic nervous system.
Image provided by W. H. Freeman and Company/Worth Publishers.

Neuroscientist Antonio Damasio, who's been on the cutting edge of emotion research for two decades, argued the case eloquently in his break-through book *Descartes' Error: Emotion, Reason, and the Human Brain.* Feelings, he asserts, are intimately connected with the body—and con-stitute the basis for conscious thought. "Our minds," he writes, "would not be the way they are if it were not for the interplay of body and brain during evolution. . . . The mind has to be first about the body, or it could not have been."[13]

In a parallel way, evolutionary psychologist and philosopher Nicholas Humphrey presents two axioms:

1. Consciousness stems from the having of sensations.
2. The subject of consciousness, "I," is an embodied self.[14]

This is the *opposite* of what science and philosophy have held for hundreds of years. Since the time of Descartes, who postulated mind and body as being as being essentially two different things, philosophers have concentrated on the mind and scientists on matter. What is mental has been considered lofty or rarified—and limited to sheer speculation. What is *physical,* whether our bodies or aspects of the world around us, such as light, gravity, and so on, has been subject to robust scrutiny and experiment. Feelings, unfortunately, got lost in the shuffle. Although they are corporeal, they're clearly not material in the usual sense. And feelings like anger, envy, desire, and such were never considered sufficiently elevated to merit the attention of philosophers. In fact, quite the reverse: feelings and their emotional expression were seen as base, as animalistic, and as unworthy of serious investigation.[15] Descartes, after all, declared, "I think, therefore I am," not "I feel, therefore I am."[16] From the Enlightenment onward, researchers found it much more appealing, not to mention generally sanctioned, to explore everything from the circulation of blood in the body to the circulation of planets in the heavens. No doubt the ensuing accomplishments—by Harvey, by Kepler, by Faraday, by Watt—got a great many people excited. But to look into *excitement itself?* The motivation, not to mention the wherewithal, was severely lacking.

Accordingly, the past three hundred years have witnessed the study of consciousness without much attention to the fact that "there has never been a solidly established demonstration of a mind without a body."[17] That situation is finally being redressed. Humphrey, for one, points out that a mind requires boundaries. Consider, he says, that primitive animals—including our own ancestors—have all possessed some essential means to discriminate "me" from "not me." A physical boundary (skin or any other membrane) inevitably forms a threshold across which exchanges of matter and energy take place. Sensory stimuli are processed. Whether in terms of temperature, pressure, pain, or some other aspect, some forms of stimuli are beneficial for the organism, others harmful, and still others neutral. "Any animal that had the means to sort out the good from the bad—approaching or letting in the good, avoiding or blocking the bad—would clearly have been at a biological advantage. Natural selection was therefore likely to select for 'sensitivity,'" Humphrey writes.[18]

Over the eons, through elaboration of this discriminatory function, a basis for mind was formed. Some animals became capable, via their nervous systems, of storing, recalling, and reworking (as Humphrey puts it), "action-based representations of the effects of environmental stimulation on their own bodies."[19] Nature provided them with a means of not only answering the question, "What is happening to me?" but also of determining whether it was good or bad and what was to be done about it. Their decision-making apparatus necessarily reflected what was experienced; for example, you "hear" your thought enunciated in your head as you are thinking or reading.[20] The perception of sound—meaningful sound—becomes internalized.

The more advanced a species became, the better it was able to understand what was happening to it. It was able not just to receive the incoming stimuli, but to link them to their source, to be curious about that source, and to wonder what more broadly is "out there" and how that is distinct from, harmonious with, or anathema to what is "in here." At this stage, the "I" or the "me" is much more than the passive receptor of environmental stimulation: one becomes the witness of one's independent physical existence.[21] *Sentience transforms into consciousness.* One is a true self, capable of identifying ourselves, knowing that we exist in our own right. A personality can now take shape, and more abstract thought (e.g., symbolization, categorization) and creative expressiveness (e.g., language, art) is possible.

Alongside, we come to understand that sensations, feelings, and thoughts do not go on indefinitely: they each have a certain quality and a certain duration.[22] We know that we exist in time because *they* do. We perceive past, present, and future as applying to ourselves and the world in general. We "tell" time. And at the pinnacle of self-consciousness, we realize that we are bound to die.[23] This understanding makes our individual existence, and our commerce with our fellows, all the more precious.

None of this would be so, Humphrey argues, without embodied feelings. *Sentio, ergo sum* (I feel, therefore I am).[24]

The Old Brain

Today, we also know something important that earlier theorists, including Descartes, did not. We know that over millions of years of evolution, the brain actually grew from the bottom up, with its higher, thinking centers developing out of lower, more ancient parts.[25]

Take the most primitive part, the brain stem. Surrounding the top of the spinal cord, this is the seat of basic functions such as breathing, metabolism, instinct, and reflex. It is often referred to, somewhat disparagingly, as the reptilian brain. Yet, from this humble beginning emerged the emotional centers—and, more millennia later, the neocortex, or thinking brain. As Daniel Goleman, author of *Emotional Intelligence*, points out, "There was an emotional brain long before there was a rational one."[26]

The more we learn about the brain stem, the more germane to our humanity it becomes. Consider children whose cortex has been filled with cerebrospinal fluid instead of grey matter because of medical problems experienced shortly before or after birth. Neurologists expect that, in this condition (known as hydranencephaly), children will be in a vegetative state until they die. Not so. Observation of such children (ages one to five) discloses that not only are they alert, they also are happy, excited, sad, and pained—a whole palette of emotions. One observer noted that "a three-year-old girl's mouth opened wide and her face glowed with a mix of joy and excitement when her parents placed her baby brother in her arms." Another child, age five, "brightened upon hearing happy songs, but often cried during sad songs. . . . She disliked the loud noises of vacuum cleaners and hair dryers. She demonstrated understanding of a few words, including 'bunny rabbit' for one of her stuffed toys." Other of these children take behavioral initiatives such as learning how to switch on a toy.[27] These children aren't vegetables. They're conscious. Their brains may be severely impaired, but they can and do enjoy life. Perhaps, we might speculate, they possess some form of self-awareness as well.

Swedish investigator Bjorn Merker suspects that the brain stem plays a crucial role in what he calls "primary consciousness"—the ability to integrate sensations gleaned from the environment into behavioral decision making. In his words, "The human brain stem is specifically human." It is far more than a reptilian relic stashed in the brain's basement.[28]

Smell, Memory, and Feeling

Yet another primitive cortical structure lies at the roots of consciousness. The olfactory lobe, our "smelling brain," grew in tandem with the brain stem. Around the top of the brain stem, a layer of cells evolved to take in whatever the organism smelled and sort it into the relevant categories: edible or toxic, sexually available, enemy or meal. A second layer of cells sent reflexive messages throughout the nervous system so that appropriate action would be taken: taste, spit out, approach, flee, or chase.[29]

This discriminatory function developed even before our ancestors lived on land. Naturalist Diane Ackerman points out that, in the ocean:

> Many forms of sea life must sit up and wait for food to brush up against them or stray within their tentacled grasp. But, guided by smell, we became nomads who could search for food, hunt it, even choose what we were hankering for. In our early, fishy version of humankind, we also used smell to find a mate or detect the arrival of a barracuda. And it was an invaluable tester, allowing us to prevent something poisonous from entering our mouths. . . . Smell was the first of our senses, and it was so successful that in time the small lump of olfactory tissue atop the nerve cord grew into a brain. Our cerebral hemispheres were originally buds from the olfactory stalks. We *think* because we *smelled*.[30]

Today, our feelings—and memories of feelings—remain intertwined with our sense of smell. Furthermore, since only two synapses separate the olfactory lobe from the amygdala (a part of the brain critical to the perception of feeling, and one that we'll learn about momentarily), those memories tinged with smell carry a greater wallop than memories triggered by our other senses. Marcel Proust never knew this per se, yet he clearly understood the relationship between smell, memory, and feeling when he made an aroma central to the childhood recollections of his narrator in the novel *À la recherche du temps perdu (In Search of Lost Time)*.

A latter-day experiment will illustrate this. It was carried out by Rachel Herz, now at Brown University but then at the Monell Chemical Senses Center in Philadelphia. Herz's goal was to demonstrate that, if an odor were first experienced in an "emotionally salient" context, it would serve as an especially effective memory cue. Here's how her experiment worked. An equal number of male and female college students were divided into two groups. Students in the first group met with a researcher in a room that had a distinctive (and slightly unpleasant) ambient odor; students in the second group met the researcher in a room that had *no* ambient odor. After being greeted and asked to notice the conditions in the room (of which smell was one), the researcher played a trick on half of the subjects. Those unlucky students were told that, in a short while, they would have to give an impromptu speech—and that the speech would be of some importance *and* that they would be critiqued. This was intended to prompt anxiety. The other, luckier subjects were simply told to sit and relax. In each case, the researcher asked the person to rate how he or she was feeling, that is, the mood he or she was in. Shortly thereafter, all students were presented with a list of sixteen common English nouns that had no obvious emotional association (e.g., "pencil," "airplane," "key"). They were also asked to briefly describe an event that had happened to them that each word reminded them of. Everyone was then told to return in two days' time—which they did, either to the room in which the ambient odor was present or the room that was odor-free. This time, the researcher made no mention of ambient conditions and did not attempt to invoke any performance anxiety. Everyone was simply asked to try to recall as many words as they could from the first session, along with any associated memories.

What Herz found was that subjects who had rated themselves as anxious in the first setting *and* were in the odorous room recalled more words than students in the other groups. They did about 15 percent better than students who were not stressed and yet were still in the odorous room, and about 25 percent better than students who were anxious but had been in the odor-neutral room. This suggests that odor is a definite memory cue when an emotional state (and especially an unpleasant emotional state, such as anxiety) is involved.[31]

Even human beings' highest and most cherished thought process—belief—has been shown to activate a region of the brain associated with smell. Specifically, the research suggests that false assertions, such as "torture is good," trigger activation of the anterior insula, an area associated with the pleasantness or unpleasantness of odors. So when one reacts to a statement by saying "That sure smells fishy to me," something more than metaphor may be at work. The part of the brain that causes us to go "blecch" is in operation. This implies that our reaction to most any idea that strikes us as untrue is conditioned by neural circuitry drawing not only from long distant smell but from the closely associated *felt* memories. "When someone says something you disbelieve," comments neuroscientist Sam Harris, "it has a kind of emotional tone . . . [it] feels like something."[32]

This link with feeling suggests to me that our sense of smell has implications for the study of anomalous perception. Stay tuned! We'll return to this subject later in the book.

Evolution of the Neocortex

Over the eons, the brain evolved new layers. Bordering the brain stem, in close proximity to the olfactory lobe, grew the amygdala, the hippocampus (which is crucial in memory), and other parts of what is known today as the limbic system. (*Limbus* is Latin for ring, signifying this system's ringing, or circling, of the brain stem.) Also referred to as the mammalian brain—since this neural territory is thought to have come into being around the time of the first mammals—the limbic system added true emotionality to the brain's repertoire.[33] It is the seat of pleasure and pain discrimination, our most rudimentary feelings (e.g., surprise, fear, anger, disgust), and the memory of same. (Figure 2 shows some of the key elements of the limbic system, among others.)

From this region grew the two-layered cortex and the newest region of the brain, the neocortex. Here is the seat of thought: the neocortex contains the areas that put together and comprehend what our senses perceive and ultimately ascribe a meaning or value to those perceptions. Ideas, art, symbols, imagination, and morality—all of these emanate from the neocortex. Further, the neocortex adds nuance to our feelings. Love, trust, gratitude, even suspicion, bitterness and guilt—these and many

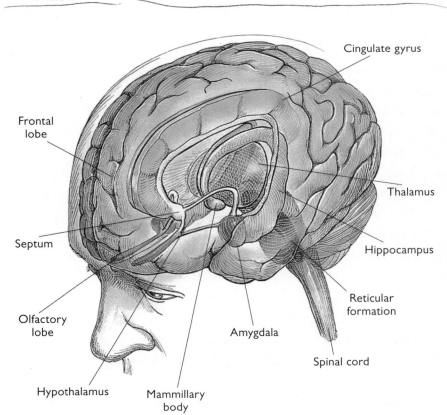

Figure 2. The limbic system.

Image provided by W. H. Freeman and Company/Worth Publishers.

other complex combinations of feeling and thought originate in this portion of the brain.[34]

The Amygdala: Emotional Sentinel

What happens, precisely, when a primal feeling such as fear is generated?
For the answer, let's turn to the amygdala, an almond-shaped cluster
(*amygdala* is the Greek word for "almond") near the bottom of the limbic
ring. There are actually two amygdalas, one on each side of the brain,
nestled toward the sides of the head. Evidence points to this structure as
the brain's specialist for processing elemental feelings. Animals that have
had their amygdala removed lack fear or rage and lose their urge to compete or cooperate. In these animals, demonstrations of emotion are well-
nigh absent.[35]

Neuroscientist Joseph LeDoux, of New York University has firmly
established the amygdala's role as emotional sentinel. Whether interpreting the emotional expressions of the people around us or monitoring for
perceived physical danger, the amygdala, he says,

> . . . scan[s] every experience for trouble. . . . "Is this something I
> hate? That hurts me? Something I fear?" If so—if the moment at
> hand somehow draws a "Yes"—the amygdala reacts instantaneously,
> like a neural tripwire. . . . When it sounds an alarm of, say, fear, it
> sends urgent messages to every major part of the brain: it triggers
> the secretion of the body's fight-or-flight hormones, mobilizes the
> centers for movement, and activates the cardiovascular system, the
> muscles, and the gut. Other circuits from the amygdala signal the
> secretion of emergency dollops of the hormone norepinephrine to
> heighten the reactivity of key brain areas, including those that make
> the senses more alert, in effect setting the brain on edge.[36]

These actions take only thousandths of a second. The "alarm" over-
takes a person before he or she is conscious of it, and before the neocortex can judge if the presumed threat is real, put it in perspective,

assess possible courses of action, and make a rational decision. The evolutionary value of this quickness must lie in the need for a split-second response if one is to survive an emergency, such as a predator poised for the kill.[37]

Recall, if you will, a time when you yourself panicked when you thought you perceived something dangerous. Was the movement suggestive of a spider? Was it something odd lying in the road, just barely ahead of your car? What about that soft sound like footsteps behind you, or a loud shot, or a boom? It's entirely possible that the amygdala scans for danger based on certain perceptions hardwired into us by evolution. We may react to such elements as size (as in a large, carnivorous animal), wingspan (reminiscent of the predators that once attacked human beings from the air), type of motion (as in the slithering of reptiles or crawling of poisonous insects), and certain sounds (such as growling or yelling).[38] In these and similar cases, our amygdala relies on first impressions, processing the overall picture or most striking aspects and reacting to a current threat as if it's identical to something faced before.[39]

It's important to note, however, that before a fight-or-flight decision is made, the individual freezes for a very brief interval, while revving the engines, so to speak. A temporary immobility is wired into us—indeed, into all mammals—before the sympathetic nervous system kicks into gear. This behavior, too, is governed by the amygdala. In some animals, like the proverbial deer stuck in the headlights, the immobility may be stark. We'll return to this transient freeze throughout the book as it presents truly fascinating implications.

Emotional Memory

The amygdala also plays a catalytic role in emotional memory. The more intense the alarm or the more vivid the encounter, the stronger the imprint. This is born out by the fact that experiences that scare, shock, or thrill us are among our most indelible lifetime memories.

These memories are whole-body recollections, but they start in the amygdala. It triggers the vagus nerve, which extends all the way from the brain to the adrenal glands atop the kidneys. (*Vagus* is Latin for "wanderer.") The adrenal glands, in turn, secrete the hormones epinephrine and norepinephrine, among many others associated with our flight-or-fight response. These surge through the body, priming it for an emergency. Signals from the body are carried back to the brain via the same hormones and nervous system.[40] The existence of this information loop—combined with the fact that the vagus nerve reaches almost all our internal organs—makes it understandable that our most vibrant memories are encoded not just cognitively in the brain, but also viscerally in the body.[41] Goleman points out that "many potent emotional memories date from the first few years of life, in the relationship between an infant and its caretakers. This is especially true for traumatic events, like beatings or outright neglect." The fact that the amygdala matures more quickly than other brain structures—being fully online at birth—indicates why such traumas would retain a special prominence.[42] This is the case even though one may have no conscious recall of the trauma. Interestingly, there appears to be a strong connection between childhood trauma and anomalous perception. We will explore this association in succeeding chapters.

More Complex Felt Perceptions

Human beings not only feel and react, of course; we also *know* that we feel and are, therefore, self-conscious. Thanks to our cortex and neocortex, we experience multiple types and shades of feeling, some of them (like admiration or trust) melded with judgmental thoughts or values. These more mental felt perceptions are produced in a very different way than those produced by the basic alarm system we have been considering. The difference is illustrated by Damasio.

Imagine, he says, how you would feel if you met a friend whom you had not seen in a long time, or if you were told that a person with whom you had worked closely had died. Recollections would be summoned up of those people and, depending on the content, your heartbeat might accelerate (in, say, receptivity) or your face pale (in shock). Associated chemical changes would be induced in various parts of the body and brain through activation of the endocrine system, which would release hormones into the bloodstream. Neural activity would also be directly modified by neurotransmitters released from the brain stem.[43] At some point you would likely become conscious of how you were feeling in response to the event. (Such conscious awareness wouldn't occur under the amygdala-driven alarm scenario, at least not until after the provocation had passed and you had a chance to reflect on it.) With greater involvement by the cortical centers, you would become aware of the feelings sooner, and they would likely be more complex.

This is the process that produces feelings such as embarrassment and pride, apprehension and regret, exhilaration and danger, hope and dejection. As opposed to our primal feelings—fear, anger, happiness, sadness—these are overlays or variations on a theme. Damasio offers his take: "Euphoria and ecstasy are variations of happiness, melancholy and wistfulness are variations of sadness, panic and shyness are variations of fear."[44]

Alternately, a person may consciously evoke a feeling, such as when jealousy is aroused by brooding on what one does not possess. Actors make professional use of this capacity when they imagine, simulate, or otherwise summon up the real thing.[45] Furthermore, a person may make a conscious appraisal, thinking "That taxi driver is cheating me," or "This baby is adorable," and a fitting emotional response will follow.[46] In a similar way, if one superimposes the value judgment of others, a socially tinged feeling such as guilt or shame may result.[47]

Function of the Insula

In recent years, neuroscientists have identified a structure in the cortex called the insula as the lead processor of these more complex felt perceptions. Its importance is pointed up by its large size in humans relative to other mammals, even primates.[48] The insula is now recognized as the wellspring of the kinds of social feelings mentioned above, such as pride and prejudice, gratitude and resentment, delight and disgust, guilt and shame. But if one needed an example of how such feelings remain rooted in the body, the insula offers a perfect illustration.

This part of the brain is, essentially, a receiving zone that reads the physiological state of the entire body via nerve receptors that detect heat and cold, hunger and thirst, aches and pains, tastes and smells, gut feelings, itches on the skin, and other visceral sensations. This information is transformed, in the front part of the insula, from mere sensory input into social feelings that are at the core of self-consciousness.[49] So while it's not part of the limbic brain, the insula nevertheless recasts bodily information into felt perceptions that undeniably register keenly with us.

Prefrontal Lobe Can Override Amygdala

In everyday situations when no threat is imminent, a series of circuits in the neocortex—in the prefrontal lobes just behind the forehead— effectively governs our behavior. This prefrontal area modulates the amygdala, allowing for discernment in emotional reaction. After considering what someone has said, for instance, we may realize we are offended or angry and develop a strategy to rectify the situation. The neocortex essentially performs a risk/benefit analysis of possible reactions and chooses among them.[50] Goleman calls this more purposeful processing route the "high road," as opposed to the "low road" of split-second, automatic response when our brains sense danger.[51] Sometimes the prefrontal area will even override an alarm generated by the amygdala in order to reappraise the situation, thus providing a measure of self-control and restraint of potential outbursts.[52]

The prefrontal cortex is the neural sector where most or all of the circuits involved in a felt reaction come together. Consider it something like a highway cloverleaf, with different branches connecting one to another. Especially influential in this convergence is an area called the orbitofrontal cortex. It forms the underside of the prefrontal cortex, sitting on top of the eye sockets. In *Emotional Intelligence*, Goleman explains, "This is the area that seems most critical for assessing emotional responses as we are in the midst of them and making midcourse corrections. The orbitofrontal cortex both receives signals from the amygdala and has its own intricate, extensive web of projections throughout the limbic brain. Through this web it plays a role in regulating emotional responses—including inhibiting signals from the limbic brain as they reach other areas of the cortex, thus toning down the neural urgency of those signals."[53]

I suspect that the dampening activity of the orbitofrontal cortex plays a role in actually producing anomalies. Keep this thought in the back of your mind; we'll explore it later.

Feelings within the Unified Organism

Whenever we feel a feeling, chemical changes take place within us. Hormones released into the bloodstream and neurotransmitters emitted from the brain stem reflect a continuously shifting state of affairs, but it's a state of affairs within a unified organism.

Just as our most vivid memories are clearly visceral as well as cognitive, the line between the brain and the rest of the body is really no line at all. Chemical messengers are crossing it all the time. Although science speaks of the nervous system or the immune system, we should note that the concepts are metaphorical. Scientists used to believe these were separate working systems, but not anymore.

The nascent field of psychoneuroimmunology is shedding light on the connections. And, the more that is learned, the more insight is gained on how extensive the overlap really is. The term "psychoneuroimmunology" reflects this interface: "psycho-" for mind, "neuro-" for the neural and endocrine (hormonal) systems, and "immuno-" for the immune system.[54]

That the body's immune system could be influenced by the brain—a truly seminal discovery—was first brought to light in 1975 by psychologist Robert Ader at the University of Rochester. He and his colleagues later advanced the idea that cells are lined with many specific receptors to which only specific molecules can attach themselves. These chemical messengers circulate throughout the body and are the vehicles through which the nervous, endocrine, and immune systems communicate.

Such communication goes well beyond the immediate physical connection of neuron to neuron. Within the entire body, a variety of "information substances" are constantly transmitting innumerable messages.[55] Among these substances are peptides, chains of amino acids that are themselves the building blocks of proteins. A given peptide's message is relayed through receptors—sites on the surface of nerve cells through which a given message is transmitted to the cell nucleus.[56]

Now, anyone who has ever noticed that one consequence of feeling "blue" for an extended period of time is the greater likelihood of catching a cold or infection has also noticed, perhaps without realizing it, how our state of feeling influences immunity. Stress likewise suppresses immune function through the action of epinephrine and norepinephrine (also known as adrenaline and noradrenaline), along with other substances released by the adrenal glands.[57] Psychoneuroimmunologists have found that such chemical messengers act reciprocally on the brain and the rest of the body—and that their receptors are most dense in the neural areas affecting feeling. Candace Pert, a molecular biologist formerly at Georgetown University, determined that the limbic portion of the brain contains upward of 85 percent of the neuropeptide receptors her team studied.[58] Furthermore, Pert and her colleagues noticed a high concentration of these receptors "in virtually all locations where information from any of the five senses . . . enters the nervous system." The entire body can thus be characterized, in Pert's view, as a single sensing and feeling organ: a far-flung, unitary, psychosomatic network.[59] Depending on the precise external or internal stimulus taking place at any given moment, a particular information substance will flow through our body and bind to specific receptor sites. When this binding takes place, we feel a given feeling, encode a given memory, or are prompted to emote a certain way.[60] Pert goes on to conjecture that our bodily organs store emotional memories based on the specific receptors they possess and the nature of the chemical messages they receive. Memory, she posits, resides in virtually every part of our body.[61]

A New Definition of Mind

As appreciation for the complex and integrated nature of our perception has grown, neuroscientists are realizing that the head is not at all divorced from the heart or the gut, and that our bodily feelings actually underlie and support more advanced thought processes. Damasio opines that "emotions and feeling provide the bridge between rational and non-rational processes, between cortical and subcortical structures."[62] Pert is inclined to put it in more metaphysical terms, asserting that emotions are "at the nexus between matter and mind, going back and forth between the two and influencing both."[63]

It is increasingly apparent that our very definition of mind must change. Science and society continue to speak of the mind-body relationship; that hyphen, alas, perpetuates the outmoded distinction assumed by Descartes. A view of mind and body as two divergent categories is not just inaccurate but decidedly unhelpful if we wish to truly progress in understanding the human animal. Ader puts it this way: "Nobody working in this field believes there's any separation between [mind and body]. It's all one."[64]

A comment here about the word "psychosomatic." In the past, it's been used pejoratively, as in "Those symptoms are all in her head; they're not really real—they're psychosomatic." Used this way, the word assumes that something either has material reality *or* is made up, irrational, imaginary. The false Cartesian duality is maintained. But "psychosomatic" literally refers to the whole of who we are: psyche (e.g., mental, emotional, psychological) and soma (e.g., molecular, bodily, material). Understood properly, it becomes clear that everyone is psychosomatic! *Psychosomatic is normal.*[65]

Ken Dychtwald, in his pioneering 1977 book *Bodymind*, expressed a concept that I wish to expand on.[66] The mind, let us say, is the combination of brain and body, including every aspect of us and everything we feel, think, know, intuit, remember, or have forgotten. Within this conceptualization, the body is central to the mind and so are feelings. I propose that feelings are actually paramount because, as Damasio so aptly expresses it, they allow us to "mind the body."[67]

Feelings are nothing less than the biological substrate of the mind. They are inseparable from our health and the quality of our lives—and absolutely essential to any consideration of what it means to be an embodied human being.

Given this recasting of the traditional notion of mind, I shall, from here on, be using Dychtwald's term whenever I wish to refer to the whole person. "Bodymind" will be shorthand for the amalgam of who each of us is physically, mentally, emotionally, and (as will become clear) spiritually.

The Brain of the Gut

To compellingly illustrate the bodily aspect of mind, let us now turn to the gut. Recall, if you will, the last time you were sick to your stomach: perhaps home with the flu but, in any event, sick as a dog. How well were you able to think? The answer is probably "not well." When a person is lying pitiably in bed, soaked with sweat and able only to throw up, the brain isn't of much use. Thinking becomes subservient to how we feel, how able we are to muster some energy or useful mental activity. So perhaps we should turn our attention to that part of us that seems to govern in such situations. It's the place also where we feel butterflies when we're nervous; a queasy, churning sensation when we're anxious; and a palpable, sinking sensation of dread. The gut, in other words: the pit of our stomach. What's going on down there?

The gut actually possess its own, self-contained nervous system, known as the enteric nervous system, which can operate in the complete absence of input from the brain or even the spinal cord. It is huge, encompassing more than one hundred million nerve cells in the small intestine alone. When you add the nerve cells of the esophagus, stomach, and large intestine, the result is that the bowel contains more nerve cells than the spine. This makes the enteric nervous system effectively our "second brain."[68] So what are all those nerve cells responsible for? As one journalist discovered, "When someone skips lunch, the gut is more or less silent. Eat a pastrami sandwich, and contractions all along the small intestines mix the food with enzymes and move it toward the lining for absorption to begin. If the pastrami is rotten, reverse contractions will force it—and everything else in the gut—into the stomach and back out through the esophagus at high speed. In each situation, the gut must assess conditions, decide on a course of action and initiate a reflex."[69]

Then, too, the enteric nervous system is a vast chemical factory within which is represented every type of neurotransmitter found in the brain. (Ninety-five percent of the body's serotonin is manufactured in the bowel, from whence it travels to the head.) Think of neurotransmitters as the words that nerve cells use to communicate. The lexicon of the brain, then, is fluently spoken by the bowel.[70] Indeed, the stream of messages between the two is so continuous that scientists have begun to refer to them as one entity: the brain-gut axis. Assisting in the dialogue is the vagus nerve. The fact that 95 percent of its fibers run from the gut northward suggests that the term "gut feeling" isn't merely a figure of speech.[71] The connection shouldn't be surprising when one realizes that both the gut and the brain originate, during fetal development, from the *same clump of cells.*[72]

Despite this intercommunication, the system of the bowel can and does operate on its own. The reason for this capacity is simple. Evolution decided that digestion—a fairly primitive function—shouldn't be a prerequisite for thinking. So the gut can run on autopilot, along with all other aspects of our autonomic nervous system. We're rarely aware of its functioning unless it's brought, for some reason or another, to our attention (e.g., cramps, ulcers, diarrhea, heartburn).[73] When we *are* made aware, it's generally compelling. The primitive gut holds the modern brain's attention.

Given this dual role (solo/copilot), we should consider that the enteric nervous system might develop its own psychosomatic maladies, which could then be apprehended and chewed on (you'll pardon the expression) consciously. Perhaps the sensations of fullness and uneasiness, and all shades in between, lend themselves to more complicated cognitions. This concept, "simplistic as it may be, is likely to turn out to be as revolutionary and hopeful as Copernicus's discoveries," in the words of anatomy professor Michael Gershon of Columbia University, who has devoted the greater part of his life to understanding the second brain.[74] Naturally, though, it's

the first one that fascinates, holding an army of neuroscient
"Every time I call the National Institutes of Health to chec
proposal," Gershon comments, "I become painfully aware of t
the brain has on the gut."[75] It is hardly an easy imbalance to a
field of neurogastroenterology—the study of the brain-gut connection—
is underway, mirroring strides being made in psychoneuroimmunology.
Both have to do with connections, and both promise to bring about a
much more comprehensive picture of what it is to be human.

Gut-Level Complaints

Casting our vision ahead a bit, it seems likely that the two fields will ultimately converge. Start with the fact that the gut is, of itself, a major immune
organ, containing more immune cells than the rest of the body combined.[76]
Add the latest findings that the aforementioned vagus nerve plays a major
role in immunity, too. All of the body's major organs (e.g., the heart, spleen,
liver, kidneys) are in contact with this nerve, and most cells of the immune
system work within the same organs. Although the communication is not
entirely understood, at least one experiment has identified the vagus nerve
as an electrochemical catalyst for the body's immune response.[77]

For a start, progress is being made in understanding one of today's
most common medical complaints—and most puzzling gastrointestinal conditions—irritable bowel syndrome (IBS). (Previous generations
knew it as irritable or spastic colon.) At any given time, about one-fifth
of Americans are affected by some form of IBS.[78] Like another malady
affecting a like number of people—depression—IBS has to do with serotonin (people with IBS tend to have too little of it). More generally, physicians are recognizing that many disorders of the gut involve changes in
the ANS and that connections with the immune system pertain as well.
During a stress reaction, for example, the first brain activates what are
called mast cells in the bowel, releasing histamines and other inflammatory agents. If the stress becomes chronic, inflamed tissue in the gut will
become tender, leading to problems.[79]

An ANS that is perpetually on alert will likely lead to a hypersensitive gastrointestinal tract.[80] As we'll gather in the next chapter, early trauma—in infancy, childhood, even *before* birth—programs the bodymind's stress activation system, known as the hypothalamic-pituitary-adrenal axis, which is part of the hypothalamic-pituitary-adrenal (HPA) system. This "set point" is lower in persons subjected to early trauma, prompting them to be hypervigilant and subject to all manner of debilitating conditions, such as migraine headache, chronic pain, and a variety of allergies. Evidence for such a link is widespread: many (perhaps most) patients treated for chronic gut disorders have experienced such childhood traumas as parental divorce, a major illness or accident, or the death of a loved one.[81] An overlap between generalized hyperreactivity and conditions such as IBS is also being established more systematically.[82]

Whether the root cause of these difficulties is considered to be more "nature" or "nurture" is of little consequence. The point is that both nature and nurture conspire to produce our personalities, our psychologies, and our physiologies. In the same way, our thoughts, feelings, and perceptions—whether conscious or unconscious—are linked to our physical and mental well-being, our immune function, and our very sense of self. The bodymind, complex as it is, acts substantially as one.

Emotional Energy

Some Asian practices (e.g., qi gong, t'ai chi, kundalini, and tantric yoga) emphasize that the lower abdomen is a reservoir for energy. Given what we now know of the enteric nervous system, surely the idea of the stomach's connectedness with the rest of us is sound.[83] But what about the concept that it's a storehouse for latent energy?

I do contend that feelings comprise energy (and shall elucidate in chapter 5). For the moment, simply summon up a vision of a time you became frustrated or angry and impulsively smashed a wall or some piece of furniture. Or consider how drained one can get after worrying about a loved one whose health has taken a turn for the worse. We might picture joy as radiating a person's happy energy out into the world, and despair as inhibiting energy when the individual recedes into himself or herself. Such contractions, by the way—especially if chronic or irreversible—surely endanger health. A person can waste away or die from sorrow; a "broken heart" is more than a turn of a phrase. In surveying such cases, one prominent cardiologist has observed, "The [heart] tissue is alive. *It's just not moving.*"[84] (Emphasis mine.)

The word "emotion" comes from the Latin *emovere,* meaning "to move from" or "to move out of." Recall that feelings originate from a change in bodily state and that an emotion (at least in my terminology) is a feeling expressed by the individual. Change connotes movement, and movement connotes energy. Take the energy released from crying or that liberated during sex. The amount of energy can be immense, and the effect of such releases is almost always beneficial. Tension in the body is reduced, and a healthier functioning restored.[85]

Beyond a measure of calories, perhaps, there is no way at present to measure emotional energy. However, an attempt to capture it linguistically has been made by many cultures and philosophers. The Hindus call it *prana,* the Chinese know it as *chi,* and Freud termed it the libido.[86] Some parapsychologists talk about psychic energy. In my estimation, they are all referencing the same thing.

Tears and Laughter

Two of the most potent forms of emotional expression known to humanity are crying and laughing. They are so universal that, it is safe to surmise, they must play a fundamental biological and/or behavioral role. We'll explore both those roles here—and find much that sheds light on what it means to be human.

Let's begin with crying. Not just any crying, but crying from joy, sobbing with relief, trembling with trepidation, weeping out of sorrow—in short, crying as a release for intense feelings. Did you know that the chemical content of such emotional tears differs from that of reflex tears produced, for example, when we're slicing an onion? Emotional tears contain more manganese and proteins, including the stress hormones prolactin and adrenocorticotropic hormone (ACTH).[87]

The result is often unmistakable. People tend to feel better after they cry, and not coincidentally, look better too.[88] In one survey, 85 percent of women and 73 percent of men reported feeling less sad or angry after crying.[89] A number of studies associate the ability to cry with improved health.[90] Tears and laughter, one researcher asserts, "are two inherently natural medicines. We can reduce duress, let out negative feelings, and recharge. They . . . are the body's own best resources."[91]

People differ quite a bit in their penchant for crying. Pioneering research done by William Frey, a biochemist in Minneapolis, shows that the frequency of crying in normal, healthy individuals ranges from zero to seven episodes per month for men and from zero to twenty-nine episodes per month for women.[92] The average is 1.4 times a month for men and 5.3 times a month for women.[93]

While fully half of the men surveyed said they never cry, only 6 percent of the women did. Contrary to what you might expect, Frey found that people who are depressed don't necessarily cry more than others and that women's crying doesn't necessarily correlate with their hormone levels.[94] It is true that the tear glands of the sexes are structurally different, leading women to cry more profusely when they do. And whereas men tend to tear up and cry quietly to themselves, women's weeping is a much noisier and visible affair.[95]

The following is a wonderful sketch I found highlighting the diverse circumstances under which people will cry: "A sick baby cries long and plaintively in the night. A young woman sobs in despair and disbelief at her husband's death in the September 11 attacks. Under cover of darkness, furtive tears swell in the eyes of a grown man watching the movie *Titanic*. As others grin and congratulate a bride, her mother weeps uncontrollably. Crying is at once among the most familiar and the most mysterious of human behaviors. . . ."[96]

Indeed, Frey's survey reveals that sadness accounts for 49 percent of people's tears, happiness 21 percent, anger 10 percent, fear or anxiety 9 percent, and sympathy 7 percent.[97] We can say with some assurance that crying originates in infancy as an indicator that something is amiss (not dissimilar from the young of animals and birds that also issue distress calls to alert their parents). One finding even suggests the b back to the womb.[98]

In any event, by adulthood, crying has plainly become a more con. plicated—and distinctive—affair. For one thing, the evidence is that only human beings shed emotional tears. (This is not to suggest that animals don't feel pain or other feelings, simply to note that their emotions aren't evident through tears. The one creature that has been observed to shed tears that might reflect sadness is the elephant—though no consensus exists on whether this is truly the case.)[99] Furthermore, although crying may well be done in front of other people, it is also done alone. One might therefore ask: is solo crying still carrying out a communicative function? I would answer yes. As author Tom Lutz observes, "Crying . . . occurs at times when we cannot put complex, overwhelming [feelings] into words. Tears can supplant articulation, which is why they offer release."[100]

When one cries to oneself, I would add, even more than a form of release it may be a way for the bodymind to convey a deeply felt message to ourselves about whatever is happening. A person won't be moved to cry, for instance, at a movie, a play, or a musical or narrative passage if that scene or passage doesn't resonate deeply within. In that case, weeping would be inauthentic. But a good cry will signal to whoever is around— and it may be only us—that something of importance is taking place. "Attention must be paid," as the wife of Willy Loman says repeatedly in the play *Death of a Salesman*. Our bodymind—our psyche—is speaking.

Love, death, abandonment, exaltation—these are the critical themes of our lives that often find expression in tears. Our feelings are there all along, but given a trigger—perhaps it is news that jumps out of an envelope, a beautiful natural vista, a moving piece of art or music, or the culmination of a personal investment of effort—our feelings spill out into conscious- ness. Consider how a Beethoven symphony can transport many people into a state of bliss. "What may be happening," comments one psychiatrist (and music lover), "is that Beethoven is giving [listeners] a language for powerful feelings they . . . hadn't been able to express. The [instantaneous] reaction is: 'That's it.'" Adult crying is thus a "declarative action of the body rooted in the subterranean movements of our hearts . . ."[101]

Consider this account from the sports world of tennis champion Rafael Nadal's first major tournament victory in the 2005 French Open:

> In a match filled with spectacular exchanges at dramatic moments, Spanish sensation Nadal beat an unseeded but unyielding Mariano Puerta. . . . "This is incredible," said Nadal, who turned 19 Friday. "It's a dream come true." The No. 4-seeded Nadal overcame three set points in the final set. . . . "I fight every ball, [he] said. . . . "When I have problems in the match, I fight, I fight, I fight every game."
>
> . . . after 3 hours, 24 minutes of tennis, he closed out the victory. Nadal collapsed to the clay, flat on his back, then rose and embraced Puerta at the net. "These moments are very strong," Nadal said. "It's something you can't explain. When you reach your goal, it's an extraordinary moment. For the first time, I cried after winning a match. It never happened to me before."[102]

If the bodymind were not able to send this message and effect this emotional release, it would not be as healthy. Sir Henry Maudsley, a founder of British psychiatry in the late nineteenth century, remarked, "Sorrows which find no vent in tears may soon make other organs weep." Charles Dickens had one of his characters in *Oliver Twist* suggest the following about the value of crying: "It opens the lungs, washes the countenance, exercises the eyes, and softens down the temper. So cry away!"[103] However, a person can weep profusely and *not* feel better. People who suffer from depression, for instance, can cry well nigh continuously with no relief—and possibly feel worse for the effort. This is because depression is a form of inner immobilization, permitting little assuagement or relief. In contrast, sadness comes naturally to our bodymind and reflects a state of inner vitality in which feeling can flow.[104]

Social Value of Crying

There is another prism through which to view the purpose of crying: that of social communication, intimacy, and bonding. When a person cries in front of another, the natural inclination is often to touch or hold the person who is crying, to seek to comfort him or her. And, between individuals who are especially close, weeping can be a signal that some aspect of their relationship is in jeopardy: that they are not understanding one another or are on the verge of parting company on some important matter. Psychologist Randolph Cornelius of Vassar College sees weeping in this sense as a search for resolution. People who are in need of being held, being reassured, or having differences patched up will cry not only to express this need to others but to try to gain some progress or resolution. If the resolution is not there, he says, they aren't likely to feel better.[105]

Regardless of which function of adult crying is being served at any given time, it can fairly be said that it is "our mind that's really crying, not just our tear ducts."[106] Crying gets to the heart of what concerns us, what we are invested in, and what ultimately *moves* us. If we have reason to cry but cannot or will not, the message our bodymind is sending will remain inside: neither we nor others around us will heed it. That loss of emotional expression is not just unfortunate, but it also has very real health effects. It may also have long-term psychic effects. Many ghosts, intriguingly, are said to be moaning or weeping—rather plaintively searching, one might infer, for resolution.[107] Whereas folktales suggest that these are lost souls mourning for something they left behind in this world, I suspect the process has to do with biology. A person in whom the energy of feelings is stopped up—bodily as well as through issues unresolved between the neocortex and emotional brain—constitutes a likely trigger for anomalous occurrences. We know that crying involves the interaction of advanced parts of the brain with more elementary structures that control our basic physiology (e.g., limbic system, brain stem).[108] The inhibition of crying must be at least as complex and could, in some extraordinary cases, be found to have serious consequences beyond those currently accepted.

A Good Laugh (and Not So Good)

Laughter is also an incompletely understood subject, although, like emotional tears, it is a quintessential human trait. (While chimps laugh in response to tickling, they evidently don't laugh when alone, nor in the immensity of circumstances in which human beings find cause to laugh.)[109] There are also some significant differences between laughing and crying. Whereas crying mutates into different forms from its genesis in childhood—and takes place in more varied contexts—adult laughter is probably very close in form and function to its childhood antecedent. Also, the reasons we laugh are not as numerous as for when we cry. We can laugh out of a sense of kinship, friendship, frivolity, hilarity, or absurdity, but not out of any stronger feelings, such as fear, anger, love, or elation. Nor do we laugh out of any aesthetic sense, for example, on hearing a powerful passage of music or being moved by the spirituality of a given place or experience. And while a good laugh is understood to be a valuable stress reliever, laughter per se is not nearly as deep as crying. It doesn't put us in touch with our innermost selves, in other words.

Nonetheless, laughter does cement social bonds. It is constantly taking place: around the water cooler, in the cafeteria, and at the family dinner table. It also betokens one's humanity: people without a sense of humor are considered cold, aloof, self-absorbed, and uncaring. This makes sense when one considers that laughter's origins are in early childhood, when one is often being tickled by parents and other close relatives. Laughter thus springs from touch itself.[110] People who weren't touched much as kids probably won't laugh as much nor have the "feel" for other people that they might otherwise.

Additionally, one literally feels better following a good belly laugh, after one's sides have stopped aching and the ruddiness has receded from one's face. The health effects are measurable, from muscle relaxation and lowered blood pressure to reduction of stress hormones and improved immune function. A good laugh is aerobic, providing a workout for the diaphragm and increasing the body's ability to use oxygen. The result is a feeling akin to being cleansed.[111] Indeed, the deep breathing promoted by frequent belly laughter expels residual carbon dioxide in the lungs and replaces it with oxygen-rich air.[112]

In later chapters, we'll see how breathing holds a key to hypnosis and how blood circulation relates to the workings of acupuncture. In both of these cases—as well as with laughing and crying—one's metabolism is being altered. The energy transmitted by cells is being redirected, with the brain and the rest of the body actively involved. All are truly *psychosomatic* phenomena. Thus, while laughter figures much less frequently in the parapsychological literature (there are fewer cases of supposed disembodied laughter than ethereal weeping),[113] I am not entirely surprised that it occurs.

The disproportion, I suspect, might roughly correspond to the degree to which laughter, as opposed to tears, reflects paramount concerns of the self. While we don't laugh out of the same deep reasons as we cry, we do laugh because we're able to recognize our own flaws (e.g., greed, arrogance, envy, pride, ignorance) in others whom we pillory. (The great comedians have always recognized this.) So it seems possible that reports of anomalous laughter could stem from the same process I have outlined elsewhere. The guffaws could be interpreted ironically, as the energetic equivalent of the realization that one has, unfortunately, failed to measure up to one's deeply held internal standards. Since laughter nearly always occurs in groups—anomalous laughter is no exception—the interpretation might be that one among the laughing party at one time felt deeply guilty even in the midst of frivolity. This would be a variation of the chronic inhibition of crying discussed above: a person who transmutes his or her sadness into joyless laughter. (You've no doubt heard the phrase "tears of a clown.") The result, however, would be the same: a bodymind with unresolved physical energy and ambivalent mental circuitry.

Feeling: Route to the Self

Descartes, as scientists and philosophers are coming to realize, was mistaken. The literal truth is "I *feel*, therefore I am." From the physical, feeling foundation of the mind stems not only the core human experiences of laughing and crying but all of our capacities on up to thought, insight, and advanced reasoning.

This spectrum equates to our bodymind, although that term refers to the generic human schematic. When speaking about particular individuals and their personalities, I prefer the commonly used word "self."

How does a self come about? Why do one person's character, disposition, habits, and tendencies differ so dramatically from someone else's? This is a challenging question, but one that we can address, armed with the understandings reached in this chapter.

The role of feeling will, as you might surmise, prove central to the puzzle. It will also prepare us to understand how anomalies could occur—and to picture who would trigger them, who would perceive them, and just why the *self* is inevitably involved.

4

♦

Selfhood

Sentience (Capable of sensory perception)

Its Origins in Sensation, Stress, and Immunity

The peepholes of life. Senses to detect the world. . . . The peepholes begin to open before birth. They are synonymous with life. . . . Throughout our lives, until the peepholes of the senses close, we are sentient beings, sensing the energy and chemicals and objects in our environments.[1]

JILLYN SMITH, SCIENCE JOURNALILST

We often don't appreciate just how wondrously complex we human beings are, or for that matter, the complexity of our animal friends, who share our planet and participate in life themselves. All of us are sentient: we perceive through our various sensory organs, we feel, and we react. There is great equality in sentience. While the capability of any given sense differs from species to species, the basic capacity to take in environmental information and literally make sense of the world is a trait common to every life-form on Earth.

Thinking, on the other hand, is not so widespread, nor is self-awareness. So many other creatures live their lives on instinct and reflex; for them, thinking is a rudimentary affair. The province of consciousness is rather narrow compared to the spectrum of sentience, which spans the animal kingdom. Sentience, of which feeling is part and parcel, characterizes all those—humans or animals—that we take to be individuals.

In the previous chapter, we established *sentio, ergo sum* (I feel, therefore I am). If this formulation is correct, it can be rephrased "I feel, therefore I am a *self*." In seeking the origins of selfhood, then, we ought to begin with the sensory foundations of feeling.

It's a common misconception that life begins at birth. While it is not my desire to open up the Pandora's box of precisely when life begins, clearly the human fetus—and the equivalent forms of other animals—is functioning well before birth, with sensory organs, circulatory and digestive systems, a nervous system, and other parts of its developing form. The more our technology is able to probe into the origins of individual life, the more we comprehend how extraordinarily complex and awe-inspiring these arrangements are. But how does the *self* actually emerge? By self, I mean the unique, composite organism that ultimately lives, ventures forth into the world, grows, and learns. The roots of selfhood are as fascinating as any subject we can imagine—and they begin with that most basic of sensory perceptions, touch.

Touch

The sense of touch is the first one to develop. At six months, when the embryo has neither eyes nor ears, its skin is comparatively well formed. If stroked lightly at this age, the embryo will bend away from the source of stimulation.[2] In the womb, enveloped by the mother's amniotic fluid, the skin of the embryo—and later the fetus—must "have the capacity to resist the absorption of too much water . . . to respond appropriately to physical, chemical and neural changes, and to changes in temperature."[3]

Skin is basic to our existence: without it, what would enfold us? Not only are we covered by skin, but our skin also turns inward to line such features as the eye, ear, mouth, nose, and anal canal. In that respect, it is the "mother" of each of the other senses.[4] The skin can further be said to represent the organism's external nervous system, since both the skin

Comfortable w/ in one's own skin

and the internal nervous system arise from the embryo's surface covering, the ectoderm. While the brain and spinal cord develop from the inward-turned portion of the ectoderm, the rest becomes our hair, teeth, and sensory organs. Ashley Montagu, the late anthropologist and author of a seminal work on touch—called, appropriately enough, *Touching*—observes that "from its earliest differentiation, [the skin] remains in intimate association with the internal or central nervous system."[5] He comments further, "The skin itself does not think, but its sensitivity is so great, combined with its ability to pick up and transmit so extraordinarily wide a variety of signals, and make so wide a range of responses, exceeding that of all other sense organs, that for versatility it must be ranked second only to the brain itself."[6]

Montagu coined the phrase "the mind of the skin," which captures this relationship.[7] His formulation anticipated the term "bodymind," which gained currency in the 1970s and, as we shall see, remains a highly accurate depiction of the interconnectedness of brain and body.[8] As we shall also see, this interconnectedness is mediated by our feelings.

In the typical adult, the surface of the skin has an enormous number of sensory receptors involved in the apprehension of heat, cold, pressure, and pain. A piece of skin the size of a quarter contains more than three million cells, one hundred sweat glands, fifty nerve endings, and three feet of blood vessels. It is estimated that there are some fifty receptors per one hundred square millimeters, giving a total of 640,000 sensory receptors.[9] Interestingly, the skin also conducts electricity. Its sensory receptors are electrically activated when stimulated; this process can be measured in so-called lie detector tests, which, in reality, do not measure a person's truth-telling so much as demonstrate his or her physiological reaction to a given thought, idea, or memory. The amount of electricity typically generated is in the range of 10–100 millivolts (a millivolt being one-thousandth of a volt).[10] As they do in other capacities, individuals vary in this one, with certain people appearing to manifest an ability to generate considerably more electrical charge. (This intriguing possibility will be explored in chapter 6.)

As one would expect, the areas of the brain that register and process tactile influences (not only touch per se, but also air movement, changes in pressure and humidity, and other sensations) are correspondingly large. The gross numbers similarly attest to the importance of this sensory organ in our lives. The skin of the average male adult weighs about eight pounds, or roughly six to eight percent of his total body weight.[11]

Here's another yardstick by which to measure the paramount importance of touch in our lives. That yardstick is language. The way we talk to one another is emblematic of how we perceive ourselves in the world. Consider the ubiquity of phrases such as:

- Reach out.
- Hold on.
- Get a grip.
- Lean on me.
- Let's be in touch.
- Don't be so thin-skinned.
- He's hard to handle.
- She's abrasive.
- Our agreement is firm.
- I need something tangible.
- It pains me to hear you say that.
- Don't be so touchy.
- Shake it off.
- She's tactful.
- He's heavy-handed.
- Don't you get it?
- He's cold.
- She's hot.
- It just feels right.

To further illustrate the preeminence of touch among our sensory perceptions, consider Helen Keller, who became blind and deaf in infancy but nonetheless led a full and exemplary life. Montagu notes that "a human being can spend his life blind and deaf and completely lacking the senses of smell and taste, but he cannot survive at all without the functions performed by the skin."[12]

Four centuries ago, the philosopher Thomas Hobbes put it well when he said, "The shape and form and space of the outer world of reality, its figures and the background from which they emerge, are gradually built by the infant out of the building blocks of its experience, entering through all its senses, always contingent, correlated, measured, and evaluated by the criterion of touch."[13]

So what is the infant's—and, going back further, the neonate's—experience like? A leading researcher, Sibylle Escalona, writes, "the baby's life is a succession of . . . touches, sounds, sights, movements, temperatures, and the like."[14] From a base of such experiences, the infant begins to differentiate itself from the world "out there." The baby reacts, is reacted to, and so on. He or she begins to acquire a sense of himself or herself as someone to whom things happen and who can make things happen.[15] This is the beginning of selfhood. The process is evident in infancy, but has its beginnings in the womb.

Smell

Just as touch is the first sense to develop in the individual, it was also, quite probably, the first such capacity to emerge in humankind's evolution.[16] Close on its heels had to have been the sense of smell. Why? Because the oldest form of communication on this Earth is chemical. The chemical senses—smell and taste—enable even the most primitive organisms to discriminate self from other and to identify potential food sources, mates, and friends apart from what could be poisonous, unfriendly, or simply irrelevant.[17] Territory, dominance, reproductive status, diet, and health are all conveyed through chemical signals, which are cheap in terms of the energy required to produce them and efficient because of the tremendous effect they can have, even in low concentrations.[18]

One estimate is that more than half a million odors are floating around in the world. Most of these have a biological origin and carry vital information intended for various species.[19] To make sense of them, though, you have to be the right species in the right place at the right time. Dogs, for instance, have a vastly larger olfactory capacity than humans, and they can sniff the breeze or the ground and learn the equivalent of one's morning newspaper. Along with other mammals such as lions and wolves, dogs can track extremely well and are able to identify individual human beings as well as others of their species by chemical signatures.[20]

Other animals get their news in other ways. Snakes and lizards flick their tongues in the air, gathering in wayward molecules and then inserting the tongue into a chemically sensitive structure in the roof of their mouth.[21] Smells emitted when an animal is threatened can also be telling. Antelopes are known to emit a musky smell when disturbed, and frightened house mice leave traces of concern so clearly on the surroundings that these paths of flight are avoided by other mice for up to eight hours.[22] Of course, the aromatic results of an upset skunk will be carried for miles around.

The chemical senses are, along with touch, known as the *proximity senses,* as contrasted with the distance senses of vision and hearing. The distinction is significant given that the most pleasing and most disgusting sensations we know are registered through touch, smell, and taste.[23] While "we can shut our eyes against a disturbing image, or cover our ears to avoid anything discordant . . . we have to go on breathing."[24] Similarly, we have to go on tasting, lest we die of starvation. And smells carry a particularly intense charge for us, due to the fact that the nose is directly linked via a nerve fiber pathway to that ancient part of our brain, the limbic system. The limbic portion is concerned almost exclusively with the "four Fs": feeding, fornicating, fighting, and fleeing. The rest of the brain evolved from this base.[25] Thus, smells of whatever kind are entwined with our instincts, our appetites, our emotions, our sexual behavior, and our response to stress.[26]

Discriminating odors is quite a complex business: "When we sniff, we inhale odor molecules, which then bind to receptors in the nose. There are at least three thousand molecules that we can distinguish and we have at least one thousand odor receptors in our nose. Different types of odor molecules activate different combinations of receptors, alerting us to what we are smelling."[27] This capacity is evident early on in newborns. At six days old, awake babies can discern the difference between their mothers and strangers.[28] The process began well before that, of course, in utero.

The same can be said for hearing. Between its own heartbeat, its mother's heartbeat, and the rhythm of her breathing, the fetus lives in a fluid world of syncopated sound.[29] It is also well known that the fetus is capable of responding to sounds outside of the mother's body, hence the trend toward playing classical music near pregnant women with the notion that it will enhance the baby's brain development. This idea, while probably misguided, does recognize the relationship between our sensory "peepholes" and the brain's decoding, interpretation, and recall of the information provided by them. Through the brain, raw sensation becomes perceptual.

Critical Junctures in Brain Development

To have perceptions at all—indeed, to realize that an "I" exists that is something more than the sum total of one's bodily sensations—a brain is necessary. The brain, of course, does not exist separately and in its own right. Its structure and capacities develop in tandem with sensory input. Activation of the senses stimulates nerve cells (also known as neurons) to grow and interact with one another.[30] And you have a staggering number of neurons! Your brain is made up of one hundred billion of them, each networked with thousands of others. Neurons, though, make up just ten percent of the cells in the brain.[31] The other ninety percent are support cells called glial cells.[32] While their function is not completely understood, one significant aspect of glial cells appears to be insulation of the "conducting cables," or axons, that carry electrochemical impulses between neurons. By surrounding, protecting, and nourishing those transmission pathways, the conglomerations of glial cells help speed messages within the brain.[33]

In its first year after birth, the infant's brain grows more than it ever will again, attaining seventy percent of its final weight.[34] By the end of three years, brain growth is up to ninety percent.[35] This remarkable development is exceeded only by the brain's spectacular growth in utero, when nerve cells are generated at the rate of 250,000 per minute during peak growth.[36] No wonder, then, that the fetal brain is highly susceptible to "environmental influences that may affect its developmental trajectory and, in worst cases, cause structural or functional damage that may not be evident for years to come."[37]

In the earliest phase of the brain's development, nerve cells are restlessly moving around, each heading for its unique location as designated by our genetic blueprint. But, as with blueprints for a house, elements of the final construction may differ from what the plans called for, depending upon the construction materials used, decisions made on site by the builder, the impact of intensive or unanticipated weather conditions, and so on.[38] In the same way, key factors such as the mother's diet, her habits such as smoking or drinking, her feelings about the baby, her stress level, and her general state of health or illness all stand to affect the developing fetus. Hormone levels, the concentration of oxygen in the blood, and the supply of glucose and other nutrients are all avenues by which the fetus can be influenced, for better or for worse. Peter Nathanielsz, a prominent researcher into prenatal development, uses the term "programming" to describe the long-term effects on biological functioning that can be dictated by external influences. He comments, "During fetal and newborn life, there are critical periods in the growth and development of each organ in our bodies. At these critical times, each individual organ is especially sensitive to challenges that have the potential to permanently alter the development of that organ and hence the whole body. . . . In addition, when a critical phase . . . is missed or even significantly delayed for any reason, the next step may be impeded . . . each milestone interacts with the next one. Timing is everything."[39]

Here is an example from the animal kingdom. If newborn female rats are injected with a single dose of male sex hormone on the fifth day of their life, they will *never* ovulate. Their reproductive brain centers will have been reprogrammed and permanently altered. However, if female rats are injected with the same hormone on the twentieth day of their life or later, they will be completely fertile once they reach puberty. The difference, in this case, is not the foreign hormone but its timing. By the twentieth day, the critical window of vulnerability—to this substance, at least—is past.[40] To take another example, the corn lily plant contains a toxin that causes deformities in the fetuses of pregnant sheep. Depending on what day of gestation a sheep ingests the corn lily, a different deformity can occur.[41]

In human beings, a variety of conditions can prompt permanent alterations in the development of the brain and spinal cord. Let us return to the case of nerve cells moving about the brain in its very earliest stage. If, for whatever reason, one set of cells is slow to settle into its particular location—or, worse, gets into the wrong place—the whole structure of the brain can be compromised.[42] As Nathanielsz describes it, the birth, connection, and activation of neurons is interlinked. If a cell makes a mistake, gets the wrong information, or doesn't reach its correct location, subsequent activities may not occur or may be carried out incorrectly. What holds true for neurons also holds true for their support system, the glial cells. The glial cells need to be properly developed in order to do their job. Neurons alone do not a brain make.[43]

Stress and Its Effect on the Fetus

The correlation between a mother's health and her baby's functioning is easy to understand given the obvious fact that, during pregnancy, the fetus is locked in a biological embrace with its mother via the placenta, an organ that acts as a lung (transporting oxygen), a gut (transporting food), and a kidney (removing waste). The placenta is a conduit between mother and child, protecting the latter from some harmful compounds, but alas, not all of them.[44]

When we look closely at the function of the placenta, at times when challenges and stresses of various kinds occur to the mother, we find it entirely possible that the mother's response to such challenges may program the developing baby's lifelong capacity to handle stress on its own. Such stress in the mother may also program the child's disposition later in life toward conditions such as depression, chronic fatigue, and alcoholism, not to mention a weakened (or, alternately, hypersensitive) immune system and tendencies toward shyness and sensory defensiveness (a condition characterized by extreme sensitivity to light, color, texture, noise and/or smell).

How can such wide-ranging effects be possible? The culprits are two biological systems that are involved in a person's (in this case, the pregnant mother's) response to stress. The first is the sympathetic nervous system, which links the brain to the other internal organs and regulates essential functions such as breathing, heart rate, and digestion. Normally the functioning of this system is unconscious (e.g., you don't normally realize you're digesting food unless you have gas pains or heartburn). But in a stressful or alarming situation, the system kicks into overdrive, diverting blood from the skin to the muscles for a fight-or-flight reaction, marshaling additional oxygen for respiration, causing your body to sweat so that your insides are kept cool, and reacting in other ways.

The brain trigger for these reactions is a structure called the hypothalamus. While the hypothalamus normally serves to regulate pleasurable functions such as eating, drinking, and sex, in moments of anxiety or threat it stimulates the adrenal glands (located on top of each kidney), causing them to release the hormones noradrenaline and adrenaline. A mildly stressful activity such as public speaking is known to elicit a 50 percent increase in the amount of noradrenaline circulating in the bloodstream and a 100 percent increase in the amount of adrenaline. People who suffer from chronic stress register persistently raised levels of both hormones, along with side effects such as high blood pressure, gastrointestinal problems, high levels of cholesterol in the blood, increased muscle tension, and headaches.[45] (Interestingly, there is evidence suggesting that more noradrenaline is produced in situations where the person can exercise a degree of control over the anxiety-provoking source, whereas uncontrollable fear or angst provokes a greater output of adrenaline.[46])

The second major player in the mother's stress response is the HPA system, which involves the hypothalamus and the pituitary and adrenal glands (hence HPA). When this system is activated, a similar cascade of changes takes place in the brain and body. The major difference from the action of the sympathetic nervous system is in the duration of the response. Whereas activation of the sympathetic nervous system occurs within seconds of the perceived threat, and its effects subside within an hour or so of that threat's passing, the HPA system takes minutes to get going, and its effects may persist for days, weeks, or longer.[47]

The HPA system's activity begins when the hypothalamus sends a hormone known as corticotropin-releasing hormone (CRH) to the pituitary gland, a pea-sized outgrowth of the brain located just below the hypothalamus. The CRH stimulates the pituitary gland to release a second hormone called adrenocorticotropic hormone (ACTH). This hormone is carried via the bloodstream to the adrenal glands, which, in turn, release a slew of other hormones. (See figure 3.) The most relevant of these for our discussion is cortisol, a kind of steroid akin to those used to treat allergies and inflammation.[48] Once in the bloodstream, cortisol prompts a multitude of changes. It prompts the liver to release glucose, a substance vital to rapid exercise, and acts to release fat, an excellent source of fuel for the body. It also acts inside the cell nucleus, instructing selected genes to increase or decrease their activity. The effect is typically an increase or decrease in the production of enzymes, which themselves regulate the rate at which various activities occur within a cell.[49] So the impact of cortisol

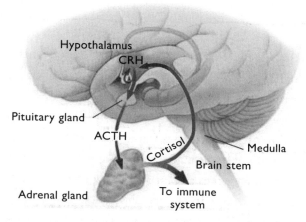

Figure 3. The HPA stress response system.
Image by Roberto Osti Illustrations.

[handwritten annotation: shortage of cortisol]

is quite wide-ranging, going to the core of cellular activity and the body's ability to marshal the energy it needs to respond to the perceived threat.

Both too much and too little cortisol in the blood can have adverse effects on health. Too little results in an inability to marshal energy in cases where a strong stress response is needed.[50] Also, with a shortage of cortisol the body's immune system can become overactive, prospectively leading to allergies or other types of autoimmune disorder. Too much cortisol has the opposite effect, with the immune system becoming suppressed and the individual becoming more susceptible to disease.[51]

Immune Suppression and Overactivity

Now the story becomes more compelling. Cortisol is one of a class of steroids known as glucocorticoids (hormones also released by the adrenal glands), which exercise a profound influence on the immune system. The immune system represents far more than the body's ability to ward off colds and infectious disease. In the words of behavioral biologist Paul Martin, it is ". . . a breathtakingly complex and subtle entity whose intricate workings are still far from being fully understood . . . one of the great wonders of nature, rivaled only by the brain in its intricacy and elegance of design. It is a multi-layered system of biological defenses . . . a highly complex and coordinated array of interrelated, interacting elements."[52]

More than one researcher has compared the workings of the immune system to those of a nation, a society, or an economy.[53] As with those entities, the immune system cannot be localized. Its components are located throughout the body: in the thymus (at the front base of the neck), the spleen (below and behind the stomach), the lymph nodes (clumps of tissue in the armpit, groin, neck, and elsewhere), the bone marrow, the tonsils, and especially the appendix. Immune cells—white blood cells, or leucocytes—are also found in the blood, where they travel anywhere they are needed, particularly to areas of injury or infection. The action of these cells produces the familiar inflammatory response as the blood supply is increased to the affected region and the blood vessels expand and surrounding tissues swell up.[54]

Most important in the immune response is a type of white blood cell called a lymphocyte. These, in turn, are subdivided into B cells and T cells: the former produce tiny proteins known as antibodies that attack bacteria, viruses, and other foreign invaders in our bodies; the latter attack the foreign invaders without producing antibodies. There are several classes of T cells, too. Helper T cells stimulate the B cells to produce antibodies, suppressor T cells shut off the others when enough antibodies are around, and natural killer cells go right to work by attacking the invaders.[55]

Seen in its entirety (figure 4), the immune system serves as a virtual map of the body, including the brain. But it is something more. Like a nation or a society, the immune system possesses its own identity. It recognizes what is foreign almost instantaneously. In this respect, it is quite like the nervous system, which detects and responds to stimuli in the outside world and forms a lasting memory of those stimuli. In this way, the brain learns; so does our immune system, not in a cognitive sense but physiologically. It is effectively our body identity just as the nervous

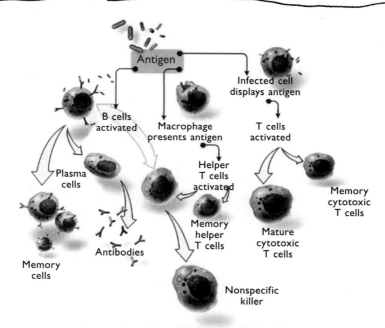

Figure 4. Immune Response System.
From Kiss of Death: Chagas Disease in the Americas, *University of Utah Press, 1998.*

system (which includes the brain) can be said to represent our cognitive awareness. Together, they make up our self.[56]

This biological reality of the self is further cemented by cumulative evidence of the extent to which the nervous system and the immune system communicate with one another. Their dialogue is constant. Forget the fairy-tale notion of the brain collecting data and barking orders. Sometimes it does that, but just as often it is on the *receiving end* of information and alerts. Of course, the communication is so rapid-fire as to render the issue of sender and receiver, for all intents and purposes, moot. The two systems, nervous and immune, speak the same language. The same two languages, actually. One is electrical, consisting of impulses conveyed across yards of nerve cell connections. The other is chemical, with scores of hormones, neuropeptides, and other messenger molecules.

These two languages are not spoken by accident. Consider that, in the first place, the nervous and immune systems are actually hardwired to each other. Nerve endings have been found in the tissues of the immune system: in the bone marrow and thymus gland, where immune cells are produced and developed, and in the spleen and lymph nodes, where those cells are stored. Next, consider that the vast array of chemical messenger molecules that were once thought to be restricted to the nervous system but are now known to be active within the immune system as well. Third, consider that changes in any part of the nervous system—whether produced by a brain lesion, a head injury, or abuse of drugs like alcohol, cocaine, amphetamines, and nicotine—can produce an increase or a decrease in immune function. Last, consider that changes in immune function are often accompanied by changes in nerve activity. An inoculation, for example, which purposely introduces foreign cells into the body in a bid to increase particular immune system activity, will produce changes in the electrical activity of neurons in the hypothalamus and other parts of the brain.[57]

The study of these linkages is called psychoneuroimmunology. As we saw in the last chapter, this pioneering field is making an ever more compelling case for the biological unity of self. Yet its assertions are hardly new. The renowned neurophysiologist Sir Charles Sherrington declared over fifty years ago that "it is artificial to separate [the physical and the mental] . . . they both are of one integrated individual, [who] is psycho-physical throughout."[58] Eastern religions and philosophy, of course, have a long tradition of emphasizing that essential unity.

Manifestations of Prenatal Stress after Birth

With all that as a backdrop, let us now return to the question of how factors that affect a pregnant mother can possibly determine her baby's lifetime capacity for handling stress and predispose that child to a range of challenging conditions. We've seen that the placenta intimately connects mother and child, preventing some harmful elements from passing through to the child but not denying them completely. In cases where the mother's adrenal glands are stimulated to produce copious amounts of the stress hormones noradrenaline, adrenaline, and—especially—cortisol (through activation of the sympathetic nervous system, the HPA system, or both), some of that cortisol will pass through to the fetus. In addition, the fetus itself is capable of secreting cortisol if it receives biochemical messages that all is not well. This constitutes its own stress response.[59]

A stressed fetus is more apt to be born early because the adrenal glands also issue biochemical messages that signal the beginning of the birth process. In effect, these babies may be saying, "Let's get on with it; outside might be better for me than inside right now." Similarly, the adrenal activity of a mother who encounters a significantly stressful event or condition—an upheaval in the family, for example, or loss of employment—may lead to premature labor.[60] Infants born prematurely, and whose nerve cell connections have not matured sufficiently, are prone to be more shy, anxious, and jumpier than average and to exhibit greater sensitivity to sound, touch, and other stimuli.[61]

On the other hand, being born one or more weeks *after* one's due date may predispose an individual toward allergies. The fetus, in no hurry to be born, can be viewed as sending the message, "Everything's hunky-dory in here; no stress to speak of." This relatively stress-free state may prompt *greater* immune activity. Current evidence implicates a disparity in the balance between helper and suppressor T cells—and the consequent number of circulating antibodies—as the cause.[62]

There is even evidence to suggest that schizophrenia is influenced by environmental programming. Because schizophrenia often runs in families, the standard inference is that its origins must be entirely inherited. The data, however, can be interpreted differently. In people with schizophrenia, brain size is about 2 percent less than normal, the hippocampus (a part of the brain associated with learning and memory) can be as much as 15 percent smaller, and the corpus callosum (the bundle of nerve fibers that connects the brain hemispheres) is thinner than it is in people who do not have schizophrenia.[63] Alternately, epidemiological data imply that schizophrenia could result from wintertime viral infections, as more people born in late spring and early summer come to suffer from the disease. Their mothers would have been pregnant with them during the winter months, when the flu and other viral infections are common. The jury is still out on this association, however.[64]

Still other evidence suggests that many people with schizophrenia suffered physiological complications at birth or in utero.[65] One study, for example, indicates that mothers with an elevated blood lead level are twice as likely to bear children who, decades later, go on to develop schizophrenia. The suspicion is that exposure to lead destroys nerve cells in a fetus's growing brain.[66]

The bottom line with schizophrenia, as with so many other conditions long thought to be exclusively genetic, is that while the disease undoubtedly has genetic *roots,* the sprouting of those roots depends on adverse environmental influences to which the developing baby's brain is exposed. This would explain why one identical twin may become schizophrenic yet the sibling does not.[67]

Alcoholism and drug abuse also demonstrate the significant effect of programming on the developing child. Once again, the key is stress. It turns out that glucocorticoids, in addition to mobilizing the body's resources in the face of a threatening situation, stimulate the same reward pathway in the brain that is stimulated by drugs of abuse. The reward is release of the neurotransmitter dopamine, which usually occurs in response to pleasurable events.[68] The effect has been demonstrated experimentally with rats (a species prone to considerable stress, almost all of it the result, seemingly, of encounters with human scientists). One study found that ". . . placing mother rats during their last week of pregnancy in narrow plastic cylinders three times a day caused their offspring to grow into adults that produced more [cortisol] during stress than rats that had not been prenatally stressed. The prenatally stressed rates were also regular drug fiends, sticking their nose through the cage hole to receive amphetamine infusions about two and-a-half times more than rats that had experienced a more relaxing time in the womb."[69]

Human beings, most likely, react in the very same ways, and not just because of experiences in utero. In a study conducted by the Centers for Disease Control and Prevention and Kaiser Permanente, it was found that children who experienced child abuse—an extreme form of stress—have double the likelihood in adulthood of becoming addicted to nicotine or alcohol, and astonishingly enough, *triple* the likelihood of becoming addicted to harder drugs.[70] Fortunately, not everyone programmed in such a way necessarily becomes an addict. The abiliy to control one's situation, or at least to cope with it, offers the prospect of minimizing the harmful effects of stress.

Infants and Touch

A mother or maternal caregiver can also counteract the effects of programming—and, in any case, promote optimum development of her newborn. The avenue is "hands on" maternal affection. As articulated by Montagu, the benefits of such closeness are undeniable. Mammals' widespread licking of their young, for instance, is probably designed to keep the sustaining systems of the both the mother's and the child's body "adequately stimulated . . . through the activation of essential hormonal and other changes."[71] Among domesticated or laboratory animals (e.g., sheep, monkeys, and the ubiquitous rat), numerous studies have confirmed that the "handling or gentling of [these] animals in their early days results in significantly greater increases in weight, more activity, less fearfulness, greater ability to withstand stress, and greater resistance to psychological damage."[72] Young rats that are petted (or "gentled"), but in every other respect treated identically to unpetted rats, learn and grow faster and show greater liveliness, curiosity, and problem-solving ability. The evidence of enhanced brain development is clear, especially in the formation of the fatty sheaths that surround nerve fibers—the glial cell conglomerations we mentioned earlier.[73]

The most famous experiments in this regard are the ones conducted on monkeys by psychologist Harry Harlow. He noticed that laboratory-raised baby monkeys showed a strong attachment to the cloth pads that were used to cover their cages. Whenever these pads were removed for cleaning, the monkeys would try clinging to them and then engage in violent temper tantrums. Harlow got the idea to build a terrycloth surrogate mother, with a light bulb behind her that radiated heat. The result was a mother "soft [and] warm . . . with infinite patience, a mother available 24 hours a day. . . ." Harlow then installed a second surrogate mother built entirely of wire mesh, without the terrycloth "skin" and hence lacking in contact comfort.[74] To complete the experimental set-up, some of the surrogate mothers were built to "lactate" (dispense milk) and others not. The lactating and nonlactating units were distributed equally among the terrycloth and wire-mesh mothers.

The results were clear. The baby monkeys clung to the terrycloth mothers far more extensively than to the wire-mesh mothers, even when the wire-mesh mothers dispensed milk.[75] Plainly, primate young overwhelmingly desire warm and nurturing physical contact.

Montagu writes that "the more we learn about the effects of cutaneous stimulation, the more pervasively significant for healthy development do we find it to be."[76] "Cutaneous stimulation" is a catchall term for touch, licking, and gentling. A study of orphaned children bears out his statement. These particular children hailed from Eastern Europe; they had been raised in crowded orphanages with not much cuddling from adults, but were later adopted by foster parents in the United States. Despite their settling in with loving families, these children were found to have lower levels of certain hormones (vasopressin and oxytocin) that are associated with attachment and affection. The researchers concluded that children who have been deprived of gentle, caring touch from an early age may never surmount that deficit, as some of the key connections in the brain may remain substantially underdeveloped.[77] Infants who *are* handled lovingly do not face this obstacle. They will also benefit, in the long run, through enhanced immune system functioning.[78]

The consideration of immune functioning brings us back to the topic of stress. Montagu suggests that the relative immunity to the consequences of stress exhibited by gentled animals might be due to a *less active HPA system,* which, as we have seen, exerts long-term effects on an individual's health, either suppressing or revving up immunity depending on how much cortisol and other stress hormones—especially CRH and ACTH—are produced.[79]

The experimental evidence with primates again supports this presumed mechanism. Charles Nemeroff, a psychiatry professor at Emory University and a leading voice on anxiety disorders, compared three groups of monkeys and their babies: [80]

> The young monkeys in the first group were reared in conditions in which there was plenty of good food available for their mothers. As a result, the mothers did not need to exert too much energy and mental effort in foraging. A second group of mothers had to work hard to find food. This high-foraging group was working at gathering food all the time. A third maternal group had a constantly changing availability of food, a very insecure situation that is difficult to adjust to. The infants of the mothers who had constantly to change their behavior were highly stressed. . . . [They] became pathologically shy when put in mixed social groups. Measurement of hormones in the [HPA] stress system showed that the levels were the same in the babies of the high- and low-foraging groups but were elevated in the variable foraging group.

Repeated findings from other such studies constitute, in the view of

Nathanielsz, an overwhelming body of evidence that early life experiences—especially maternal care—can alter the set point of the HPA stress axis.[81] In other words, the individual's inclination towards shyness, environmental sensitivity, jumpiness, and an exaggerated stress reaction will have been programmed for life.

Stress, Cortisol, and Depression

"We all know people," points out Nathanielsz, "who appear calm and collected under almost any circumstance. Stress certainly appears to be optional to them, or at least controllable to a level they can tolerate." On the other hand, we all "come across people who have a very short fuse and high anxiety levels."[82] The latter appear to have extra-responsive HPA systems.[83]

Excessive activation of both the HPA and sympathetic nervous systems is implicated in certain forms of clinical depression. People who are depressed tend to have higher levels of cortisol, adrenaline, and noradrenaline and, consequently, suppressed immune function.[84] The interaction of depression and the immune system also manifests in other ways beyond the brain. Cytokines, which are proteins produced by immune cells that, in turn, cause inflammation, are notably higher in people experiencing distress, grief, and depression. Inflammation is linked to heart disease, so increased cytokine production may be a factor.[85] By the same token, research has found that cytokine expression is reduced through laughter, that the arteries relax and blood flow is increased.[86] The terms "light hearted" and "heavy hearted," it seems, may be reasonably good descriptors, not just of mood but also of heart function itself.

Still, depression is primarily thought of as a mental illness—and the public associates a neurotransmitter, serotonin, with the condition first and foremost. Drugs such as Prozac, Zoloft, and Paxil raise serotonin levels by inhibiting the reuptake of serotonin that is released into neural synapses, thereby elevating the mood of people who are feeling down. (Interestingly, sunlight accomplishes the very same end.[87]) And while neurotransmitters are typically associated with the brain, 95 percent of

serotonin is actually found in the gut.[88] So we see that "being ...
really a whole-body problem, not one confined to the head.

This is far from the complete picture because other elements of th ...
immune system are more active in people with depression (making them
more susceptible to allergies); this implies an undersecretion of stress hormones versus the higher levels we've noted of cortisol, adrenaline, and noradrenaline. "Unscrambling the precise mechanisms whereby depression acts
on immune function is an immensely difficult problem," writes Martin.[89]

Chronic Fatigue and Immune Function

The puzzle of immune function is thrown into particularly sharp relief
in chronic fatigue syndrome (CFS). While the term "chronic fatigue syndrome" has come into use in recent decades, its cluster of symptoms (dis-
abling tiredness, muscle pain, inability to concentrate, skin rash, vision
problems, and sleep disorders) was first recorded in 2000 BC.[90] Near the
turn of the twentieth century, people with CFS-like symptoms were diagnosed as having "neurasthenia" or, just as frequently, hysteria.[91] These conditions were said to be diseases of upper-middle-class women in much the
same way that CFS was more recently derided as the "yuppie flu."[92] That
impression is only partially correct, however. While it is true that women
are predominantly affected, some research has found the illness to be widespread among members of lower socioeconomic groups, with Latinos exhibiting higher rates than Caucasians. Likewise, though CFS is rarely thought
of as affecting children, the results of at least one study done in the United
Kingdom suggests that its incidence among kids might be underreported.[93]

What is most striking is that the cause of CFS—*if* there is a single
cause—has steadfastly refused to reveal itself. Lacking a genuine physical basis for the illness, many medical professionals (and others) have
attributed CFS to psychological factors which, in their eyes, makes the
condition suspect. The fact is that many CFS sufferers have symptoms
that match the diagnostic criteria for psychiatric disorders *and* organic
disease.[94] Martin points out that the onset of CFS is often preceded by a
viral infection; the condition is also associated with a persistent, low-level

e system. These facts give credence to the organic
e same token, many people with CFS exhibit signs
hich sometimes seem to have preceded the onset.
:hological viewpoint.[95] The dichotomy only serves
ines such as psychoneuroimmunology and neuro-
ointing towards, namely, that mind and body are

Some symptoms of CFS, incidentally, parallel those of another chronic condition known as fibromyalgia. In the former, severe fatigue is the major complaint; in the latter, intensive muscle pain takes precedence.[96] As with CFS sufferers, people affected by fibromyalgia are not simply imagining their symptoms: research consistently finds that the spinal fluid of those with the condition is marked by high concentrations of a pain transmitting chemical called substance P and lower than normal levels of the pain-reducing agents serotonin and noradrenaline. Individuals affected by fibromyalgia also tend to be hypersensitive to touch.[97]

Fearful Personalities

Pain, whether chronic or intermittent, intense or negligible, is the feeling in the human catalog of feelings that is most closely associated with touch. A feeling that requires expression (as I have defined it) is an emotion. I now submit that, among all the emotions, there is none as primal as fear: none so vivid, so unmistakable in the body, or in such dire need of reactive expression. Fear requires a closer inspection, through the lens of neurobiology. In the process, we're bound to learn much that is essential to an understanding of selfhood.

Fear is the focus of Ned Kalin, professor of psychiatry and psychology at the University of Wisconsin–Madison. He also directs that school's HealthEmotions Research Institute, one of the few organizations in the world dedicated to illuminating the complex relationships between emotion and health. Kalin emphasizes that "fearfulness is one of the most basic . . . responses we can have. It supersedes everything because of its survival value."[98] But fear as the *dominant* aspect of someone's temperament—habitual fear, malingering fear, excess fear—is debilitating to a person and can ruin one's social relationships. Kalin and his colleagues, therefore, are probing the basis of what they term a "fearful disposition," one marked by inhibition, withdrawal, and other indicators of a high degree of stress. What they've found is elevated levels of the hormone CRH in the cerebral spinal fluid of monkeys who have fearful dispositions, as contrasted with monkeys who are characteristically less fearful. The pattern holds at the three junctures tested: at eight months, twelve months, and three years of age.[99]

As we saw earlier, CRH is produced in the brain's hypothalamus early on in the HPA stress response. CRH signals the pituitary gland to secrete another hormone, ACTH, in turn signaling the adrenal glands to produce cortisol to mobilize the rest of the body. That is the short-term effect of CRH. The long-term effect may be to influence a brain structure called the locus coeruleus, a tiny spot at the base of the brain that appears to direct the individual's attention to environmental events by virtue of its being networked with virtually the entire brain. Experiments with monkeys (different monkeys from Kalin's) demonstrated that the locus coeruleus becomes most active when the animals are presented with new and unexpected stimuli.[100] So, in tandem with the hypothalamus, this structure may be involved in setting the individual's set point for vigilance (i.e., what level of stimuli will inevitably trigger a stress reaction).

The evidence that CRH plays a major role in the HPA stress axis is compelling. First, when this hormone is injected into the brains of lab animals, their fear reaction lasts for hours (unlike reactions from other neurotransmitters). Second, CRH is less evident in the brains of rat pups whose mothers groomed and licked them than in rat pups whose mothers did not engage as much in this behavior. And monkeys who freeze in place when a person they don't know enters the lab have higher amounts of CRH as well as cortisol.[101] This *freeze response*—which is neither flight nor fight, but akin to both—may evoke its own particular pattern in the bodymind. We'll explore this possibility later on.

Until now, we've been discussing brain structures located in what is known as the limbic system, a region that evolved much earlier in our history than the neocortex, which is the modern, "thinking" brain. The limbic area is the brain's emotional center, evaluating sensory information in primitive terms of friend or foe, threat or attraction, pain or pleasure. The neocortex, in contrast, is a much more recent addition, literally surrounding the emotional core.[10] It is the part of the brain in which we engage in rational thought, mull over concepts, and make plans.

Kalin and his colleagues—principally Richard Davidson, also of the HealthEmotions Research Institute—have found that the right frontal part of the neocortex displays more electrical activity in monkeys that are characteristically fearful, whereas the left frontal portion is more active in monkeys that are less fearful. And it's not just evident in monkeys: the same pattern has been identified in young children. It is important to add, however, that not all children who are shy, hesitant, or fearful at an early age will necessarily remain that way. One study found that a majority of children who were timid at age two were no longer marked by timidity at age four. Another study found exactly the same vector between the ages of three and nine. So, in this case at least, biology is not destiny. By learning to be more extroverted, individuals will no longer display the right/left frontal asymmetry, nor have continuously elevated CRH and cortisol levels.[103]

On the other hand, a person who does not grow out of early shyness may well retain these characteristics. Davidson has noted consistent differences among adults in the way their frontal cortex is activated during emotional states like anger or pleasure. Using advanced brain scan technology, he says, "We can see that some people will have more right-sided response to the emotion, some will have more left-sided response, and that both responses will remain relatively constant over time in those individuals." In addition, he finds that people with increased left-side activation generally report being happier than people with higher right-side activation.[104]

This left-side/right-side distinction can be pictured via an analogy. Think of characteristic left-sided activity as a predisposition for *approach,* and a right-sided tendency as a predisposition for *avoidance.* The former conjures up descriptions such as openness, exploration, curiosity, boldness, enthusiasm, and resilience; the latter brings to mind associations with wariness, concern, anxiety, caution, negativity and, of course, shyness. Another way to sum up the differences is with the concepts *extroversion* and *introversion.*

Over the past three decades, Jerome Kagan, a psychology professor at Harvard University, has been studying introverted and extroverted children. He put forward the theory that arousal level (i.e., reactivity) is inherited, although learning can significantly modify its expression. One piece of evidence is that the anxiety levels in identical twins studied resembled each other far more than in fraternal twins.[105] And a leading measure of arousal—heart rate—is distinctively higher in fetuses that grow up to be inhibited children than the heart rate of other fetuses.[106] However, the evidence can just as easily be interpreted as supporting the view that environmental programming is at work. (It does not appear that Kagan and his associates probed for stressful influences on these children's mothers while pregnant.[107]) One conclusion that *can* be unequivocally supported is that the characteristics of self begin to coalesce before birth.

Another observation made by Kagan is that the introverted children he studied were more prone to hay fever and eczema—as were their relatives.[108] As has already been suggested, there is reason to believe that allergies (which represent an overactive immune system) should correlate with lower-stress pregnancies, delayed births, and lower than normal levels of cortisol. The flip side is that higher stress during pregnancy, elevated cortisol levels, and exaggerated reactivity should all be associated with immune *suppression,* not allergies. The tendency toward some forms of allergy among shy children, therefore, is puzzling. Perhaps the changes associated with birth—moving from a warm, nurturing environment into the bright, loud, cold environment of the hospital room—in some way reprograms their HPA set point, and hence their immune predisposition. Or perhaps the mothers of some of these children encountered a physical complication at birth, with attendant stress and the same effect. Or, maybe these children's early nurturing was so full of loving physical contact that their immune disposition was, again, counteracted. Or possibly all of the above had some effect. The whole subject of immune function is terribly complex, as we saw with depression, and is just beginning to yield its secrets. In any case, Kagan's findings are consistent with those of a host of others,[109] so an underlying mechanism needs to be found.

The Right Orbitofrontal Cortex

The portion of the brain that Kalin, Davidson, Kagan, and others have been focusing on—the right frontal cortex—is fascinating for yet another reason. On its underside is an area called the right orbitofrontal cortex. This critical region functions as a regulator of emotion, much as the hypothalamus serves to monitor and regulate basic needs such as food and sex. Neuroscientists—particularly developmental neuroscientists—are greatly interested in this region, since our development as rational, emotionally literate beings depends so much on the balance between our *expressing* feelings and *exercising conscious control* over them. As was noted in chapter 3, the orbitofrontal cortex is a major area of convergence in the brain, connected with the older, feeling structures as well as the newer, thinking areas.

Interestingly, no part of this region appears to be on-line at birth.[110] This probably owes to the fact that the fetus, while clearly experiencing feelings, is not able to express them terribly well in the womb. There simply is not much room to do so. Upon birth and release into the wide world, the possibilities for emotional expression literally open up. The right orbitofrontal cortex then has something to do—and what a job it is!

According to Allan Schore, a widely respected neuropsychiatrist at the University of California–Los Angeles, this part of the brain is not only central to our emotional life but, as a consequence, must figure prominently in any assessment of selfhood.[111] The infant's interaction with caregivers essentially feeds the orbitofrontal cortex, especially during the first two years of life. Major disturbances over this period "can lead to very different psychosomatic . . . and personality problems."[112] Child abuse or neglect would definitely qualify as one such disturbance. Another is accidents, particularly a head injury, since the orbitofrontal areas are susceptible to hematomas, contusions, and similar injuries.[113] There is evidence that such damage may lead to a whole range of sensory distortions in later life, including visual and auditory apparitions and phantom smells and tastes. Another consequence may be a disturbance of the immune system, because allergies are said to emerge or to worsen among children and adults with orbitofrontal damage.[11] This hearkens back to the question I raised above, namely why introverted children should exhibit allergies. Perhaps an overactive right orbitofrontal cortex is to blame.

Developmentally, the bottom line is that healthy activation of the entire right hemisphere depends on the relationship of the infant with his or her primary caregivers. Love and care bestowed on the child foster development of the brain's mechanisms for assessing, controlling, and expressing feelings. Not only that, but a growing body of evidence also shows that the right hemisphere is deeply connected with our ANS, which controls the short-term response to threat, and the HPA system, which keeps us "stressed" over a longer period of time.[11] *Our very sense of self evolves from the emotional bonds of childhood,* as rooted in the interwoven dynamics of the bodymind. Based on a firm neurobiological foundation, we become secure, attached people capable of discerning legitimate threats to our well-being, reacting appropriately, and ready to reach out to others with care and concern.

Mirror Neurons and the Foundation of Empathy

Now seems an ideal time to move into the subject of empathy, a quality without which civilized society itself would not be possible. In the last few years, researchers have discovered what they believe is the wellspring of empathy in the developing child and, for that matter, in the adult. That source is mirror neurons, brain cells whose role it is to reflect others' actions—reinforcing, in turn, the cues that underlie social behavior.

Mirror neurons were found, serendipitously, by a team of Italian researchers who were probing the brain of a macaque monkey. They noticed a group of cells that fired not only when the monkey performed an action but also when it saw the same action performed by someone else, hence the term "mirror neurons." These cells do more than reflect another's actions, however. Mirror neurons also fire when an individual sees someone else experiencing a distinct sensation or feeling, such as pain, embarrassment, fear, or elation. As such, the cells seem to be associated with—some would say they underlie—empathy. The association makes sense given that mirror neurons are much less active in children with autism and one of the red flags of autism is difficulty understanding the viewpoint or experience of another.[116]

Increasingly, researchers suspect that impeded development of mirror neurons in early childhood is a factor in attachment difficulties as well as a range of personality characteristics and even personality types. The Type C person, for instance (about whom we shall learn more later), is diffident and prone to anxiety. The person prone to become immersed in a task or an imagining—a trait known as absorption—could likewise be shaped by insufficient growth of mirror cells.[117] Alternately, a person who's insufficiently able to empathize and build mutually supportive relationships could become a loner or, just as easily, a domineering corporate CEO. In all these cases, mirror neurons whose growth was impeded could result in a mature personality that's less than ideal.

The function of mirror neurons, in combination with the individual's threshold for nervous system reactivity (what we've termed the HPA set point) probably explains how certain people are more apt to "catch" other people's moods or be overly affected by personalities or emotional attachments.[118] (In coming chapters, we'll examine such people in detail, as an inquiry into their neurobiology can, in turn, offer penetrating insight into the human condition.)

Neurobiologist Vilayanur Ramachandran, of the University of California–San Diego, goes so far as to predict that mirror neurons will "do for neuroscience what DNA did for biology" in shedding light on empathy, imagination, and "a host of mental abilities that have remained mysterious." Because these cells effectively "put ourselves in the shoes of another," the argument goes, they must be at the basis of feeling itself. "We start to feel [other people's] actions and sensations in our own cortex," says another researcher.[119]

This point of view, which I call the silver bullet theory of emotion, makes two mistakes. First, it implicitly accepts that feeling originates in the brain, ignoring the fact that what the cells are mirroring is not another brain but a *bodily action*—a movement, vocalization, or gesture—presumably indicative of what that the other person is experiencing. I say "presumably" because some people are quite adept at deceiving through their body language while others are ambivalent, camouflaging the truth from themselves as well as others. In any case, mirror neurons rely on physical cues, so it is debatable whether the empathy that is believed to result truly originates in the brain.

The second error the silver bullet theory embraces is that mirror neurons are somehow a phenomenon unto themselves—that *they* are the key to understanding emotion. This devalues the limbic region, which is universally acknowledged as the brain's focal point of emotional processing. I suggest that mirror neurons are not the enablers of empathy but rather the conduit to a fundamentally more important region of the brain. It is worth considering that our stored memories of how people tend to look or act in a given situation are relayed to the mirror neurons, enabling them to recognize certain actions within a given emotional context. The mirror cells would then take in what others are exhibiting more than decide, on their own, what is being felt.

Interesting though they may be, mirror neurons are probably not the home of deep-seated feeling. Instead, I propose, they are a sort of focusing device—binoculars, if you will—that trains our attention on other people. They are part of a system of emotional processing that itself is key to who we are as individuals. We are more than the by-product of our neural activity. The further we look into development in utero and in early childhood, the more this should become clear.

The Teenage Years

Throughout this chapter, we've been concentrating on the earliest stages of the formation of the self, particularly the months spent in the womb, followed by birth, infancy, and young childhood. Medical science and psychology used to hold that, by age five or six, one's basic personality characteristics were set because growth, at least neurologically speaking, was substantially complete. That view turns out to be mistaken. The preteen and teenage years are a time of remarkable tumult in the human brain and the endocrine (hormone) system—far more than was ever thought. The newest findings cast a different light on the emotional upheavals of puberty, showing adolescents to be "crazy by design."[120] Barbara Strauch, medical science and health editor of *The New York Times,* describes it this way: "The teenage brain . . . is still very much a work in progress, a giant construction project. Millions of connections are being hooked up; millions more are swept away. Neurochemicals wash over [it]. . . . The teenage brain is in flux, maddening and muddled. And that's how it's supposed to be."[121]

Many parents have observed that the period of adolescence rivals the "terrible twos" for sheer, excruciating change. "The tantrums, the slamming of doors, the fighting, the name-calling, the animalistic behavior" are all on display, as one parent expertly enumerated.[122] Teenagers themselves admit that their moods are all over the map and sweep over them suddenly, unbidden. Experts had thought the answer was simple: hormones. It is manifestly true that hormones cause more general discombobulation during the teenage years than at any other time in human development. Production of the sex hormones, testosterone and estrogen, begins as early as age eight in girls and age ten in boys. Over the next few years, the levels rise steadily, culminating in the onset of menstruation in girls at the average age of thirteen and the production of sperm in boys at around fourteen.[123] The impact of hormones is hardly limited to the bodily changes of puberty. In the brain, testosterone and estrogen (quantities of which are produced by both men and women, by the way) "can make brain cells and branches grow or disappear, make neurotransmitters excited or calm, and, working on the inside of the cell, turn genes in the nucleus on and off."[124] It's no wonder that teenagers seem, at various and sundry times, to be out of control: estrogen levels during adolescence, for example, are believed to increase anywhere from 650 to nearly 5,000 percent.[125]

Other hormones are at work, too. Dopamine, a dominant player in the brain's pleasure and reward pathway, is present at a fairly high level, inducing teenagers to engage in risk-taking, thrill-seeking behavior.[126] The bottom line is not only that teenagers' feelings *feel* more intense, but that their world may actually seem a brighter, more vivid, more compelling place than at any other time in their lives.[127]

Concurrent with this hormonal tide, the brain of every adolescent undergoes a massive remodeling, which affects everything from logic and language to impulses and intuition.[128] Neurons bloom exuberantly, with their axons and dendrites—their sending and receiving antennas—reaching out to connect with other neurons. In particular, the frontal lobes, which are the font of our thinking, planning, and self-regulation, peak in volume at about age eleven in girls and twelve in boys. Then a curious thing happens. After increasing to far beyond adult levels, "the gray matter in the adolescent brain . . . does an about-face and starts a steep trek back down."[129] At least 15 percent and in some regions more than 50 percent of the neuronal connections formed earlier are ultimately pruned.[130] The result: a leaner, meaner thinking machine.

Aiding and abetting this process are the glial cells, which, as you'll recall, outnumber neurons by a factor of 9 to 1. They increase their production of a fatty material called myelin, which insulates the neuronal antennae. Myelin production, in fact, doubles during the teenage years.[131] This results in improved communication between brain cells and a noticeable leap in cognition. As neuronal pruning occurs, those connections will become fewer but also faster and more efficient.

The significance of this shift cannot be overstated. The frontal lobes encompass the prefrontal cortex (the right side of which, as we have seen, is associated with introversion) as well as the orbitofrontal cortex (the right side of which has special prominence in the conscious control of emotional impulses). Thus, as teenagers' brain cells blossom and then are pared back, what is being fine-tuned more than anything else is the "inhibition machinery"—teens' ability to say no, to decide *not* to act impulsively.[132] Progress in this area is shown from experiments with young teenagers, whose amygdalas (which are central to the instinctual responses of fear and anger) show markedly greater activity than they will during later adolescence or adulthood.[133] As connections to the right orbitofrontal cortex become more fully wired up, young people can tether their feelings and choose a more reasonable course of action. They no longer feel at the mercy of their impulses, inclined to lash out or act on a whim. They are more focused and emotionally better controlled.

It is relevant here to point out that poltergeist outbreaks have historically been associated with teenagers and even preteens. The word "poltergeist" means, in German, "noisy ghost," and a poltergeist's characteristic activities—making a racket, throwing things—do indeed seem juvenile. I will return to this subject later on but, for now, let us consider that less than optimum connections between the limbic region and the neocortex may be responsible. Remember, too, that the sex hormones marking puberty begin to be produced in girls around age eight and in boys about age ten. Less well-known sex hormones, called androgens, appear as early as age six or seven. (Androgens emanate not from the testes or ovaries, but from the adrenal glands.)[134] If a hormonal imbalance is to blame for some poltergeist outbreaks, the age at which such effects might be seen would precede by several years the timeframe we customarily think of as adolescence.

Additionally, it may be significant that graphs of electrical activity outside the skulls of infants and children show spikes occurring roughly at ages four, eight, and eleven weeks; four, eight, and twelve months; and two, four, seven, eleven, fifteen, and nineteen years. Harvard University psychologist Kurt Fischer believes that these electrical patterns mirror leaps in cognitive development.[135] It would be interesting to determine how poltergeist agents match, age-wise, against this gradient, especially since odd electrical activity (e.g., lights, radios, and TVs turning on and off at random) is said to be yet another trick in the poltergeist's bag.

Regardless of whether changes in the preteen and teenage brain can explain this particular anomaly, it is plain that selfhood is a major theme of adolescence—not just metaphorically, but also biologically. The body and the brain are both busily engaged in "becoming what they will be."[136] In this regard, it may be significant that two of the conditions we touched on earlier—depression and schizophrenia—often burst on the scene during adolescence. (Think Holden Caulfield here, the troubled protagonist of *Catcher in the Rye*.) Is some fluctuation in hormonal activity responsible for the sudden onset of depression in some pubescent children? Is a dysfunction in the brain's pruning process to blame for schizophrenia, leaving affected individuals with too many neural connections bringing in too much extraneous sensory information? Both mechanisms have been proposed.[137] Regardless of what the correct answers turn out to be, adolescence is clearly a time when major changes are in gear. In every case, the development of an autonomous self will be brought to fruition.

Nature Works via Nurture

Our discussion of what exactly is happening with teenagers raises anew the fascinating question of how much selfhood is driven by nature and how much by nurture. Previously, I compared a human being's development in utero with blueprints for a house (i.e., one's genetic instructions). I noted that elements of the final construction may differ from what the plans specified based on any number of environmental factors, such as the construction materials used, variations decided on by the builder, and so forth.

Nowhere is this interplay more evident than in what is being learning about depression. It turns out that stressful life events are significantly more likely to trigger depression in people who have a genetic predisposition for it. In a study carried out by British researchers, more than eight hundred individuals were tracked over a five-year period as they lived through crises such as a death in the family, the loss of a job, or the breakup of a relationship. One-sixth of this group had a high-risk version of a particular gene, as evidenced by their being two-and-a-half times more likely to develop depression. The researchers concluded that nature works, in this case at least, via nurture. Stressful experiences, which happen to everyone, are like falling off a bicycle. It's the person's genes that determine whether he or she is wearing a helmet.[138] As New York University psychologist Gary Marcus puts it, "A gene is really not a dictator, but an opportunity."[139] Or, one might equally assert, a huge potential pitfall.

This type of approach, which emphasizes environmental factors at least as much as one's genetic blueprint, holds great promise for untangling the myriad factors that might explain why anomalies occur in a particular household or to a particular person. After all, the hormonal and neuronal tides of puberty affect every boy and girl, and yet it is just one out of millions who goes berserk and shoots classmates. Similarly, anomalous events such as poltergeist phenomena are extremely rare. By looking to the individual's neurobiology, as well as to the environmental factors that affect selfhood, we may be able to determine how and why such oddities occur.

The Self and the Other

In reviewing the course we have followed, this much should be plain: the roots of the self are planted well before birth, in sensation and in stress. Our nervous systems develop in response to sensory input, and our immune systems develop in response to perceived threat. To fully appreciate the picture, though, one further element must be understood. This element has been so basic to our discussion—hovering quietly behind virtually everything that has been said—that it may have gone unnoticed. But now it needs to be made unmistakable: *having a self requires distinction, separation from another.*

Are you familiar with the term "codependent"? It refers to two people who rely so much on each other, whose strengths and weaknesses counterbalance one another so completely, that their individual egos are, for all intents and purposes, intermingled. Saying that two people are codependent is not a compliment. The situation is not a healthy one for either party because they are too wrapped up in one another to grow sufficiently as individuals.

The early situation in the womb is something like that for mother and child. All of the neonate's needs are provided for and controlled by the mother. Existence is serene. If the situation were to continue indefinitely, the mother could be seen as little more than a host and the neonate as little more than a parasite. But the situation does change: the fetus grows. Through sensory input—touch and smell at first—it begins to distinguish what is "out there" from what is "in here." Its nervous system develops. Then, the inevitable variations in its mother's diet, sleep, sexual activity, health, and emotions—all of which stem from simply being human and not necessarily from any major stress or traumatic occurrence—begin to be noted. The fetus is better able to read and react to the chemical messages that are associated with the mother's varying states, whether minute to minute, hour to hour, or day by day. These variations are the earliest, and most beneficial, form of stress. Increasing, the fetus gains an appreciation of its surroundings and the fact that they *are* surroundings. And the feelings that it has are the precursor to emotions that can be expressed when the fetus finally leaves the womb and can kick, scream, coo, burble, smile, squeal, hug, and otherwise express itself. Thomas Verny, author of *The Secret Life of the Unborn Child,* puts it this way:

> . . . the unborn's ego begins to function sometime in [the second trimester]. His nervous system is now capable of transmitting sensations to his higher brain centers. . . . Say, for instance, that a woman's particularly hectic day has tired her [and her] unborn child. That tiredness creates a primitive feeling—discomfort—which brings the unborn baby's nervous system into play; his attempt to make sense of that feeling involves his brain. After enough of these episodes, his perceptual centers become advanced enough to process more subtle and complex maternal messages. (Like the rest of us, the unborn gets better with practice.)
>
> . . . Anxiety, within limits, is beneficial to the fetus. It disturbs his sense of oneness with his surroundings and makes him aware of his own separateness and distinctness. It also pushes him into action . . . he starts erecting a set of primitive defense mechanisms. In the process, his experience of anxiety and what to do about it slowly becomes more sophisticated. What began as a blunt, displeasing feeling . . . acquires a source (his mother), prompts his thoughts about that source's intentions toward him, forces him to conjure up ways of dealing with those intentions, and creates a string of memories that can be referred to later.[140]

This brings us back to a touchstone of this book: the body. Individual self-awareness, what Freud called the ego, is the perception of the bodily self.[141] Of course, this is what our immune system recognizes on an unconsciousness, physiological level. Moreover, whenever we feel or otherwise perceive something, we are simultaneously experiencing the division between self and other.[142] In this respect, we are creating finer and finer distinctions in a process that began in utero, accelerated sharply at birth, and has been continuing ever since.[143] Our lives—and, inextricably, our appreciation of space and time, form and substance, and all our other sensory experiences and feelings—are invariably lived in the body.[144] If we are "in touch with" ourselves, we are "in touch with" reality, and vice versa.[145] That means that we demonstrate and express our emotions.[146]

The very word "emotion" (built around the word "motion") alludes to the self becoming, not merely being. Life is constantly in flux, and so long as we are alive, so are we. Looked at a slightly different way, each of us is far more an activity than a thing. Consider that things are static, inanimate, but people are dynamic, constantly acting or reacting.[147] Furthermore, it can be argued that what individuals do—what we are ultimately about—is *constructing meaning*. "Experience is not what happens to you," remarked Aldous Huxley, "it's what you do with what happens to you." Each of us, naturally and fundamentally, seeks to understand what life is about, to construct meaning, and to make sense of it all.[148] Feeling and its outward expression from the body (emotion) is central to that process. Neuroscientist Antonio Damasio's landmark book, *The Feeling of What Happens,* captures this process in its apt title. Our selves are bound up with our bodies, our felt perceptions, and our active efforts to elicit meaning from life.

As we move on to consider other aspects of reality—consciousness, energy, and anomalies that appear to defy that reality—an understanding of selfhood and its basis in sensation, stress, immunity, and feeling will prove useful to always have in mind.

5

◆

Energy, Electricity, and Dissociation

Links to the Anomalous

Actor Mel Gibson trained, many years ago, at Australia's National Institute of Dramatic Arts in Sydney. He recalls just how much he thrived on being in front of a live audience: "When I did it, I was wired all the time. You couldn't switch it off when the curtain went down. You'd have to drink at least four pints of beer and hit yourself with a mallet to go to sleep at night. It was just too much energy. It was coming out of my ears!"[1]

This is one vivid example of the energy often felt in our bodies. All of us are familiar with similar highs: when we engage in an activity that's tremendously exciting or invigorating, when we achieve something that extends us beyond what we (or others) thought we could accomplish, or when we conjure up thoughts of a special someone who fires our imagination or our fantasy. The feeling runs throughout our bodies, seeming to carry our brains along for the ride. It may indeed seem like an uphill battle to contain (and maybe we don't want to contain it at all).

Here's a very different example, a profile of baseball pitcher Curt Schilling during the World Series. "Moments before Curt Schilling is about to pitch the ninth inning, he leans forward on the Arizona Diamondbacks' bench. He stares wide-eyed at the dugout steps, as if seeing some other world. . . . He has the look of a boxer coming out for the ninth round. . . . Schilling's intensity reaches a level beyond most of the best athletes. [He has an] extraordinary ability to find within himself a rare psychic energy. . . ."[2]

In this case, Schilling's energy is focused, contained, directed. He is, you might say, absorbed in what he is doing—or, more accurately, in what he's preparing to do next. Again, each of us has been in such a zone, where we marshal great mental concentration in order for our bodies to do our bidding. At the end of such experiences, we often feel completely drained, worn out, and spent.

Next, consider the following examples of two contrasting people. They could be anyone we know or have met before, even though the individuals being described are an elderly grandmother and a middle-aged accountant. Here's a description of the grandmother: "She really brightens up a room as soon as she walks in. My grandma is ninety-two years old but, whenever I'm around her, I feel younger, happier, and more energetic. There's just something about her."[3]

The accountant, on the other hand (and this is not meant to be a slur on accountants) ". . . is just a downer. We know he's down even before he walks in the door. Even the dog can feel him coming and hides. We say that he's PMS: pretty mean-spirited."[4]

Here is a final case, one that's probably less familiar although some of us may have had a similar experience ourselves or heard about one from friends or coworkers. This particular passage is from molecular biologist Candace Pert: "For years I had lectured and written on the power of healing techniques considered at best unorthodox and at worst quackish, which I had experienced in my own body as powerful and having merit despite the strong resistance . . . of conventional medicine and my own inability to explain them in the conventional biological paradigm. Feeling 'energy moving' is a common denominator in many of these techniques and I experienced this from my first encounter with acupuncture over 25 years ago. . . . I felt the appropriate movement before [the doctor] had even described it."[5]

Now, it is not the purpose of this book to provide evidence for acupuncture or any other alternative medical treatment. These approaches remain controversial, although some have garnered more credence than others.[6] I do strongly suspect that each of the above experiences has a common basis: in our neurological processes (what's going on in our heads), our physiological processes (what's going on in our bodies), and, most importantly, in the overlap between the two. This is where emotion resides.

The Energy of Life

What gets you out of bed in the morning? What revs you up, gets your juices going? Alternately, what is it that causes you to knuckle down when you need to, face facts, and do what needs to be done?

The answer, on its face, is simple enough: energy. Physical energy, mental energy, willpower, enthusiasm, motivation, determination, inspiration—call it what you like. But when you examine this obvious answer a bit, it leads to an appreciation of a much more complex phenomenon. For starters, the energy we're talking about is invisible. How can that be, especially for something that feels so tangible, something that literally *moves* us? If it's invisible, there's reason to believe it must be working on a microscopic level, and possibly on a macro-universal level as well, just like the force of gravity—another force we never actually see or touch, but that works on everything we know.

Whatever energy is, we clearly don't possess the same storehouse of it all the time. We feel it ebb and flow, hour to hour and day by day. Sometimes we're "up," wired, intense, or involved, and at other times we're "down," tired, out of sorts, or blah. Given our druthers, we'd much rather be the former. That's because "how energetic we feel is a major component of how happy, healthy, productive and creative we are. . . . With an abundant supply of body and mind energy, our world opens up as we expand our interactions with people, projects, and places."[7] According to the *Harvard Business Review,* the most essential quality for success in the business world—and doubtless this is true of most other settings—is "a high level of drive and energy."[8] Beyond the attainment of success, without energy there simply would be no joy, excitement, or pleasure—nor, for that matter, any of the other feelings we invariably experience as human beings.

It is probably misguided to think of energy as a static thing and more appropriate to conceive of it as a capacity or, better yet, a process or flow. As Guy Brown, a biochemistry fellow at the University of Cambridge, notes in his book *The Energy of Life,* the modern idea of energy is similar to that of money: "Money is a capacity to buy things. It comes in many forms—coins, notes, checks . . . bonds, gold—and it can be used to buy many sorts of things. . . . Now energy is a capacity for movement or change in a physical or biological system. It comes in many forms, such as chemical energy, electrical energy, or mechanical energy, and it can be used to 'purchase' many forms of change, such as movement, chemical change, or heating."[9]

An example will illustrate this analogy. Picture a rock balanced precariously on the edge of a cliff. One could calculate that, if it were to fall, a certain amount of energy would be released through the movement, noise, heat, and impact. In a similar manner, if a certain bill were to change hands, the value of that bill (say, $50) would buy a given amount of food, drink, or entertainment. And just as the rock could fall off the cliff (as opposed to standing still or even rolling backwards), the bill can be held, invested, or spent for various things.[10] So it's the *capacity* of both the rock and the money that's important as well as the *process or dynamic* of their falling or being spent (or not, as the case may be).

The analogy between energy and money isn't exact. There is one major difference: unlike a given financial transaction, the amount of energy used or expended in any activity will be conserved. Here's a case in point. If you pay $200,000 for a house one year and sell it for $210,000 or $190,000 the following year, without having done anything to the house, the $10,000 difference doesn't simply show up in another form. The two transactions are separate and distinct. Whereas the first law of thermodynamics states that energy is strictly conserved—a rock that falls will release exactly the same amount of energy as it took to raise it in the first place.[11]

Here's another key point. *The energy of living organisms is electrical.*[12]

Essentially, everything that happens in our cells is due to their molecules (more or less stable arrangements of atoms) bumping into each other and rearranging. This activity either requires or releases energy, depending on whether the new arrangement has more or less energy than the old. And energy comes in the form of electricity, in the force of attraction or repulsion within the molecule. Electrons within the atom carry a negative charge, and protons carry a positive charge. Opposites attract and likes repel. Depending on the number of these charges and how they come to be arrayed, the molecular energy will be more or less than that of the previous arrangement.[13]

Perhaps the most noteworthy thing about living organisms is that, so long as they are alive, they evidently defy the second law of thermodynamics, which states that, as the molecules of something randomly interact, their arrangement will, over time, become less and less ordered. This is also known as *entropy*. We see the operation of this law in the fact that things (e.g., a wheat field, a garden, a house) inevitably decay, degrade, and otherwise appear less orderly (without more energy being invested in their upkeep, that is). But the various forms of life (e.g., animals, plants, fish, birds) emerge into this world as highly organized individuals, growing and sustaining themselves *contrary to entropy*. Unlike wheat fields and houses, they can summon energy whenever needed to do the things they do (e.g., hunt, germinate, move about, communicate) as well as store that energy to be able to call upon it in the future.[14] Of course, when they die their substance returns to being governed by the second law. But what about when they are alive? No question will ever be more basic to medicine, religion, philosophy, or science.[15]

Energy Production in the Cell

To our eyes, the human body is solid and fairly simple: a few limbs for manipulating what it finds in the world and and a few orifices for getting things in and out. Put the body and its organs under a high-powered microscope, however, and the story spreads out. We can make out structures—and spaces within and between structures—that are reminiscent of lily pads on a pool of water. And this microscopic realm is one of almost unimaginable complexity.[16]

The basic unit of the structures we find there is the cell. A cell is, essentially, a bag full of water, but one in which lots of different molecules are floating around. These include sodium, sugars, amino acids (which make up proteins), proteins themselves, and fascinating bits called adenosine triphosphate (ATP). The cell is also crisscrossed by filaments, which are the transportation pathways. Through the food and oxygen our bodies take in each day (themselves a form of energy), the cell's many molecules vibrate and collide with their neighbors—anywhere from one million to one billion times a second, depending on the size of the molecule.[17] As a key part of this activity, ATP visits most parts of the cell every second, colliding with literally billions of other molecules. Picture ATP as a general-purpose energy source, a sort of bank that lets other molecules within the cell make deposits and withdrawals. The withdrawals fund the body's energy, and the process takes place continuously so long as we live.[18]

The workers in this buzzing, frentic cell "metropolis" include enzymes, transporters, and proteins. Think of these as machines, with enzymes serving to convert one kind of molecule into another, and transporters causing a molecule to move from one part of the cell to another. Each enzyme or transporter does its job over and over again, about a thousand times per second. Proteins are an equally important type of machine: they are akin to processors that drive across the cell's filaments, carrying various loads and transforming them in turn. The significance of proteins lies in the fact that they are responsible for the assembly and breakdown of every single molecule—including themselves, ATP, and deoxyribonucleic acid (DNA). While DNA gets more press (because it is a blueprint for the proteins and, by extension, for all the other microscopic components of life), proteins are far more vital to the moment-by-moment operation of the cell. There are ten thousand to twenty thousand different kinds of proteins, making up much of the cell's volume that is not water. And in the entire human body, there are one hundred thousand different types of protein—making them pretty darn ubiquitous but also a huge challenge to comprehend what, exactly, all of them do. We know that some of them comprise hormones and immune system antibodies, and that they make muscles contract. And that a single protein, called hemoglobin, transports and releases oxygen in the blood—a vital function, indeed. But there is much more about proteins that we don't yet know.[19]

Harnessing the Body's Energy

Your body may have quite a bit of energy available, but having the capacity and putting it to use are two different things. Again, let's use the analogy of money. You may have sufficient cash flow to buy a certain house, but the transaction is contingent on whether the owners of that house have closed on a new house yet themselves. So you have to wait until they do.

This state of affairs is somewhat similar to what happens in the body, where the creation and maintenance of energy encompasses a whole slew of steps, each of which can potentially put a brake on all the others if any kind of problem is encountered.

Furthermore, neither the cells nor the organs of which they are made "knows," intuitively, how much energy the whole organism requires at any given moment and, therefore, what their role should be in producing a certain capacity. They need a messenger to tell them. And here is where the hormones and neurotransmitters we first discussed in chapter 3 come in. Hormones travel through the bloodstream, circulating within the brain and the various bodily organs. Neurotransmitters follow a path traced by nerve cell connections. Regardless of which type of messenger is involved, the cells have receptors on their surface (thousands or even millions of them) that pass along whatever the message is inside. A given cell may be receiving hundreds of different messages simultaneously, so it must decide what to do based on what kind of cell it is and where in the body it is located.[20]

Given that your body contains a hundred thousand billion cells[21] and they are networked (especially in the brain) with hundreds or even thousands of others, we can see that the process of harnessing energy is extremely complex. Energy-limiting conditions such as depression, chronic fatigue, and even the common cold—all of which have connections with the immune system, itself a conglomeration of cells and organs—become more problematic the closer we look at the various factors that can produce them.

Electricity: The Dynamo of Life

As was mentioned earlier, electricity and life are virtually synonymous.[22] When we refer to cellular activity of whatever kind, we are talking about the interaction of molecules. Each of those molecules, proteins, ATP, enzymes, and so on, are arrangements of atoms. The atoms themselves are arrangements of electrons (negatively charged particles), protons (positively charged particles), and neutrons (neutral particles carrying no charge). When our bodies convert the energy of food and oxygen into internal energy, the "wet bags" of cells—and all of their molecular constituents—vibrate. Their atoms get shaken up and rearranged: they become new molecules. In so doing, energy is either required or released.[23] This energy, on the atomic level, is electric.

Water, which makes up 70 percent of cells, is a reasonably good conductor of electricity. As opposed to wires, however, which conduct an electric charge via movement of electrons, our "wet" cells conduct electricity in league with electrons, protons, and charged particles (ions) such as phosphate, potassium, chloride, and sodium.[24]

The key to this process is what's known as the cell's sodium pump. Located on the cell membrane, the sodium pump uses ATP (the energy bank we met earlier) to transport sodium ions (positively charged sodium) outside the cell. This pumping of charge produces an electric field across the cell membrane, the generation of which, simultaneously in cells throughout the body, powers countless different activities, including the functioning of muscles, heart, and nerves.[25]

Sodium electricity is not the only form of electricity produced in the cell, but it is the final one in a complex chain beginning with respiration and the intake of food. The food we eat is initially burned by particles within the cell known as mitochondria. These are ancient organisms, complete with their own DNA and similar to bacteria, that our cells have harbored for millions of years. About one thousand mitochondria reside per cell, and they alone convert the energy of food into the energy of ATP. Thus, mitochondria can be appraised as the true power stations of the cell.[26]

The entire process outlined above—from breathing to the final step of energy production—is termed *metabolism*. When we say that someone has a fast metabolism, this indicates that the person produces (and expends) energy more quickly than someone else whose cellular processes proceed at a slower rate.

Issues of Electricity

All living creatures are held together—and powered—by electricity. Of course, electricity holds together everything else that is made up of atoms, all the nonliving substances that exist in the world. So, if there is a "life force," electricity in and of itself could not qualify.[27]

Further, since all atomic interactions are, by definition, electric, science views the cellular processes described above as chiefly chemical, which serves to distinguish them from the simple conduction of electrons (i.e., flow of current) that occurs in metals and other nonorganic substances. This is because science was divided for quite awhile between two schools of thought: one that attributed living processes to phenomena that could be identified and explained, and another that believed that living things possessed an inherent and mystical life force. The latter school was called vitalism, and it had a tradition stretching back centuries. The discovery, in 1786, that a frog's leg muscle would twitch in response to an electric charge caused many people to believe that electricity was that force. The notion became prevalent around the turn of the nineteenth century, when a physician named Franz Mesmer hypnotized people (or "mesmerized" them) and attributed the healing that resulted to a force he called "animal magnetism," which was thought to permeate the universe as well as animals and people.[28] But in 1868, the discovery of how signals are carried between nerve cells put an end, for all intents and purposes, to the vitalist challenge.[29] Hence, today's dominant field is called biochemistry, not bioelectricity.

In this book, I have chosen to split the difference in terminology, referring to the propagation of nerve impulses from cell to cell as being electrochemical. This is accurate, encompassing, and nonpejorative. It also leaves open an intriguing possibility, proposed in 1941 by biochemist Albert Szent-György (who had previously won a Nobel Prize for his discovery of vitamin C). Szent-György suspected that the random shaking and colliding of molecules was too disorderly and slow to explain the speed and efficiency with which living beings react to environmental changes and summon the energy they require. He suggested that relatively large molecules, like proteins, could act as semiconductors. That is, they could resist or conduct the flow of electricity, depending upon conditions. (Semiconductors, such as silicon chips, characterize today's highly successful solid-state electronics. They can be switched on or off and controlled quite easily.)[30] He proposed that, the larger the molecule, the greater the likelihood that the electrons of constituent atoms would be arranged in close proximity—close enough to "belong . . . to the whole system." The molecule itself would then conduct current in the same way wires do. More than four decades later, in 1988, Szent-György put forward an equally interesting idea, that the space between molecules should itself be able to conduct electricity. In the cell, this means salt water.[31]

His proposals are not easy to test because the techniques used to explore the semiconductive behavior of solids do not readily translate to complex substances like cells and proteins.[32] Likewise, water is emphatically *not* a solid. Despite these limitations, some circumstantial evidence exists in support of his hypotheses, such as experiments demonstrating that bone growth can be stimulated and limbs regenerated through externally applied electrical charge.[33]

These theoretical mechanisms have received little in the way of consistent study for another reason: mainstream scientists tend to discount them. On the other hand, considerable progress has been made in understanding a mechanism known to aid electrochemical signaling between nerve cells. You'll recall that cell transporters cause a molecule to move, either within the cell or beyond it. One type of transporter is called an ion channel. Metaphorically, it is a gatekeeper, ushering positively charged sodium ions (any atom that has a charge is an ion) from one cell to another.[34] Ion channels have now been spotted, and scientists are excited because the closer we can visualize the workings of the cell, the greater the potential for treating transmission-related aberrations in the brain and heart such as epilepsy and arrhythmia, respectively.[35]

Before we leave this subject, consider that electrical energy exists not only *within* the body but also extends *outside of it,* as measured by electrocardiograms (ECGs) and magnetocardiograms (MCGs). The heart's energy, at least, reaches the perimeter of our physical selves and beyond. This is not altogether surprising, given that our circulatory system—with the heart (and its associated electrochemical activity) at its center—carries blood everywhere.[36] But did you know that the heart produces the strongest electrical and magnetic activity of any organ in the body, including the brain?[37] Measurements displayed on MCGs show the heart to be five thousand times more electromagnetically powerful than the brain.[38]

I believe the heart's traditional identification as the seat of emotions is in no way mistaken. When we feel love, it is a whole-body phenomenon, a feeling of joy and wonder radiating from our center. That is not our brain misinterpreting where the feeling comes from or assigning it, whimsically and metaphorically, to our chest. *It is a bodily reality.* The feeling, in turn, is energetic. The fact that it is grounded in electrochemical processes should not in any way diminish our appreciation for it. Nor should we make the mistake of underestimating the power of the emotions moving within us.

The Freeze Response

In chapter 3, we examined stress and the fact that it is a consequence of the fight-or-flight response of the body's sympathetic nervous system to a perceived threat. Let's very briefly reprise this subject, this time seeing the whole reaction in terms of the huge amount of energy being harnessed:[39]

- Adrenaline and noradrenaline are released, enabling you to speed up your thinking and reactions.

- The hypothalamus, amygdala, and other limbic brain structures dramatically increase their activity.
- Movement is frozen, and all the senses rivet on the perceived danger. (Eyes widen, ears prick up, and all else is ignored.)
- The heart beats harder and faster. (You can sometimes hear it in your ears.)
- Blood is diverted from the skin to the muscles. (You may look pale.)
- Respiration increases and blood pressure rises.
- The muscles are tensed.
- Sweating is increased to cool the body. (You may break into a cold sweat.)
- Appetite is suppressed and production of saliva stops. (You get a dry mouth.)
- The gut and bladder relax. (You may get "butterflies" or even, if stressed enough, wet your pants.)

Clearly, a great deal of energy is being called into service, with the underlying perception that the threat may persist and you will either have to fight or flee.

Let's focus on the period *before* fight or flight is decided on, however. Picture this: you've heard a strange noise, very close by and unexpected. Something about it seems ominous. Or perhaps you've caught sight of something—also unexpected and odd—out of the corner of your eye. Or else you hear a high-pitched siren, wailing uncomfortably close. Or you smell an acrid odor, again very close by and extremely unwelcome. What is the very first thing that happens? You startle; you freeze. This is an innate, reflexive response in mammals as they evaluate what to do next.[40] In energetic terms, your entire bodymind and its attendant cellular processes are poised for further action. Especially if the danger is perceived as a life-or-death situation, the stakes are raised to the highest possible level.

This freeze response and its immediate aftermath hold the key to unlocking issues of great import to the human psyche: trauma, dissociation, and certain types of anomalous phenomena. Bear with me as I proceed to explain the connections. We will be heading from a rock-solid basis in neurobiology into psychological and, ultimately, parapsychological terrain. In other words, from what is extremely well known and understood, to what is reasonably well comprehended, to what is gathered only murkily. On this journey, we'll leverage the biophysical knowledge built up in this and earlier chapters, namely, what is happening in the body and the brain when we experience terror, shock, dread, extreme stress, and strain. Experiencing those feelings (or any other feelings, for that matter) means, for our purposes here, a lightning-quick six-step process:

1. The sensory organs channel incoming perceptions.
2. They are processed in the body (feelings are felt), but beneath the level of consciousness.
3. The brain is alerted via hormones and nerves.
4. The brain sends out various neurotransmitters and other chemical messengers.
5. Energy is marshaled: respiration increases, the muscles are tensed, and so on.
6. The threat rises to conscious awareness, and the brain decides what the self will do.

In the conception of neuroscientists such as Antonio Damasio and J. Allan Hobson, this process runs somewhat differently, but with the same effects. With the brain in the vanguard, steps 2 and 3 disappear. While the sensory organs naturally do their thing, bodily processing occurs as a result of brain direction. Yet steps 4, 5, and 6 remain the same. So the key for us remains: What is to be done now that the body and brain are poised for action—and yet, contradictorily—are temporarily immobilized? What happens to all the energy that has been summoned up? Notice that no emotion, as I have defined it, has yet transpired. Because the individual is in "freeze frame," the feelings have not been expressed. And therein lies the significance.

Consequences of Being Immobilized

Peter Levine, a physiologist and psychologist practicing in Colorado, has written eloquently on the freeze response in his book *Waking the Tiger*.[41] The title references the animal kingdom, and Levine, in examining the behavior of predators and prey in the wild, draws contrasts with the behavior of human beings when they are physically threatened. He not only considers the initial freeze response but also the immobility that animals tend to exhibit after they have fled or fought and either been hunted down or overcome in combat. Nature has evolved this particular form of immobility, Levine says, for two sound reasons. First, by "playing possum," the prey might be able to surprise its attacker in an unguarded moment and manage to run for its life. Second, by immobilizing itself, the prey enters an altered state in which no pain is experienced; it will not have to suffer when being torn apart as the meal it is earmarked for.[42]

Lest anyone wonder if human beings have evolved the same response, here is the story of a Major Redside, a British hunter in the Bengal jungle back in the 1920s.

[He had] stumbled when crossing a swift stream, dropping his cartridge belt into the water . . . now out of ammunition, he noticed a large tigress stalking him. Turning pale and sweating with fright, he began retreating. . . . But it was already too late. The tigress charged, seized him by the shoulder and dragged him a quarter of a mile to where her three cubs were playing. As he recalled it afterward, Redside was amazed that his fear vanished as soon as the tigress caught him and he hardly noticed any pain while being dragged and intermittently mauled while the tigress played "cat and mouse" with him for perhaps an hour. He vividly remembered the sunshine and the trees and the look in the tigress's eyes as well as the intense "mental effort" and suspense whenever he managed to crawl away, only to be caught and dragged back each time while the cubs looked on and playfully tried to copy mama. He said that, even though he fully realized his extreme danger, his mind somehow remained "comparatively calm" and "without dread." He even told his rescuers, who shot the tigress just in time, that he regarded his ordeal as less fearful than "half an hour in a dentist's chair."[43]

Though I hope very few of us have ever had to experience it, this form of anesthesia is rather remarkable. I can attest to experiencing something similar when I was involved in a scrape in my twenties. I was returning to my urban apartment late one rainy night; as I approached the lobby entrance, I felt a rap on the side of my face, stumbled, and saw a man come into view demanding my wallet. I had never been mugged before, and realized immediately what was happening. Unlike the example with Major Redside, I had a weapon in hand (my umbrella) and did not feel completely overwhelmed. In fact, I felt anger rather than fear and summoned up a large and, for me, bellicose voice that spat invective at my attacker. In retrospect, this may not have been the smartest reaction because I quickly noticed a second man come into view on my left. It dawned on me to make a run for it when, to my great good fortune, a resident of the apartment building across the courtyard yelled down and both men took off. Struggling at this point with the reality of my close call but equally exhilarated with the outcome, I took the elevator upstairs and walked into the apartment I shared with my roommate with as much nonchalance as I could muster. He was not fooled, however, immediately looking aghast and asking, "What happened to you?" Not one for snappy repartee, I replied, "I was mugged," and then noticed what was patently obvious to him: my lip had been split and was oozing blood. I'd had no appreciation for that whatsoever during the conflict. Now that the threat was past and the stress hormones were not racing so fast through my system, I began to feel pain and realized the cut needed treatment. Ultimately, my roommate drove me to a downtown hospital and I received a dozen stitches—my only ones to date, thankfully.

The Need for Emotional Release

The point is that we *can* be anesthetized to different degrees under various kinds of duress. How we come out of these situations will determine whether or not they will be traumatic. While they may literally inflict trauma of the physical kind, our emotional reaction bears on whether the psychic trauma will be longer lasting. Here we return to the concept of energy associated with emotion. Levine puts it this way: "Traumatic symptoms are not caused by the 'triggering' event itself. They stem from the frozen residue of energy that has not been . . . discharged; this residue remains trapped in the nervous system where it can wreak havoc on our bodies and spirits."[44]

Levine indicates that, where the freeze response is concerned, humans are actually at a disadvantage compared to other animals.[45] Our bigger brains and highly evolved neocortex mean that we have the wherewithal (given sufficient opportunity) to consider options other than simply fighting or fleeing. We can conceivably employ tactics such as supplication, negotiation, subterfuge, bribery, and other strategies. Or we can dig in our heels and wait, either for help to arrive or for our assailant to weary of the impasse and leave. In humanity's history, after all, we have been both predator and prey. That duality continues: open up any newspaper and empathize with people caught up in wars, sieges, and threats of various kinds. Their response is rarely *only* to fight or *only* to flee. In contrast, animals have evolved little or no such capacity. They know when a predator has gotten the better of them and, like Major Redside, go limp when no escape is in sight.

That does not mean, however, that their energy has been completely shut down. No, their stress response and their stirred-up feelings are held in abeyance. Proof of this can be found in the fact that Major Redside (and others we will meet who are under duress) experience—and remember— their situations with crystal clarity. Because their systems are on high alert, their limbic brain structures and the potent mix of chemicals circulating in their bodies combine to form and record a vivid impression of what is going on. Time seems to slow down, so much so that seconds seem like minutes or hours.[46] The movies play on this fact when they show highly emotional scenes, such as battlefield heroics, in slow motion.

Levine draws an interesting comparison between the freeze response and ". . . what occurs in your car if you floor the accelerator and stomp on the brake simultaneously. The difference between the inner racing . . . and the outer immobility . . . creates a forceful turbulence similar to a tornado. . . . To help visualize the power of this energy, imagine that you are making love with your partner; you are on the verge of climax when suddenly, some outside force stops you. Now, multiply that feeling of withholding by one hundred, and you may come close to the amount of energy aroused by a life-threatening experience."[47]

The latter analogue is not only interesting but also compelling since, during orgasm, the heart rate more than doubles.[48] Everyone is familiar with how good that emotional release can feel. Likewise, we all know how much of a relief it can be to blow one's top in pent up anger—even if this makes things miserable, for a time, for someone else.[49] Humor is also a fine release. Scientists who have looked into what happens in the body when someone is having a good laugh have discovered that the biological changes are virtually the reverse of those that occur during a stress response.[50] Not surprisingly, then, humor has been found to enhance immune function.[51] I am reminded here that much classic comedy plays on the dynamic of tension and release. If you are an American, think of Jackie Gleason's blue-collar everyman Ralph Kramden. If you are British or otherwise a fan of Monty Python, think of John Cleese's manic hotel proprietor, Basil Fawlty. Both of these characters endured misstep after self-imposed misstep until they could no longer contain their frustration and lashed out comedically—to the audience's great relief and delight. Director Alfred Hitchcock famously employed a parallel process in his films, building suspense up to a pitch and then modulating it. Amusement park roller coasters do the same thing, though a bit more obviously. All of these methods work to release stress, although some of course seek to elicit it in the first place! That they are enormously effective can be seen in their legions of fans worldwide.

In real-life situations, this torrent of energy requires an outlet if trauma is to be avoided. Among wild animals, long-term trauma is virtually nonexistent since prey either are caught and killed or escape and undergo spontaneous shaking and trembling along with profuse sweating and deep breathing, forms of catharsis that enable them to dissipate the pent-up feelings and return to normal.[52] This spontaneous form of recovery has real survival value. One noteworthy experiment showed that, among three groups of chicks (two of which had been immobilized and a control group that had not), the group that had been immobilized but allowed to recover spontaneously had the highest survival rate when confronted with a new threat.[53]

In contrast, human beings who actively suppress the potent energy of their feelings, who pass it off as "no big deal," attempt to nullify it through drugs, alcohol, or sex, or unconsciously put it out of their awareness risk a variety of unpleasant consequences. The first law of thermodynamics is followed: energy is conserved. In this case, we are speaking of the energy of bodymind arousal (i.e., of feelings held in the body and prevented from emotional release). But the operation of this law is no more in doubt than it is with other forms of energy we're used to thinking about: heat and motion. In actuality, the neurobiology of stress is so well established there can be no doubt that energy, in the usual sense of the word, is harnessed and then held in abeyance.

Types of Energy Emergencies

Human beings' dual stress systems—the sympathetic nervous system and the HPA system—can be set off by any number of figurative challenges. Levine's catalog includes:[54]

- birth complications or trauma
- loss of a parent or close family member
- physical injuries such as falls or accidents
- abuse, whether physical, emotional, or sexual
- being the victim of or witnessing violence
- being the victim of or witnessing a natural disaster
- undergoing surgery or other medical procedures
- being anesthetized

▪ prolonged immobilization of a body part (for example, having a cast put on an arm or leg)

These examples all have one thing in common: being in a situation where the ill effects are overwhelming, irreversible, or both. Put another way, they are situations where one is on the receiving end of something threatening, harmful, or undesirable and one has little or no control over it. Because of this vexing combination, the younger a person is when he or she experiences such difficulties, the more problematic they are emotionally.

People viewing the above list, Levine obsereves, tend to be surprised by the final three items: undergoing surgery, being anesthetized, and having a body part immobilized. I can speak to the last of the three. If I sleep in an odd position and my arm falls asleep, I wake up with a start and am absolutely petrified at not being able to feel or move this body part as I normally do. Perhaps this is just me. But it makes intuitive sense that when one's body is put at a disadvantage—for whatever reason—we would be made uncomfortable at least and would exhibit a full-fledged stress reaction at most.

Surgery is no exception. Here, the reaction may be extreme because one is being assaulted, in a sense, albeit by a highly trained (we hope) professional who (again we hope) has obtained our permission to do this or that to our innards. Levine explains, "Even though a person may recognize that an operation is necessary, and despite the fact that [he or she is] unconscious as the surgeon cuts through flesh, muscle, and bone, it still registers in the body as a life-threatening event. On the cellular level the body perceives that it has sustained a wound serious enough to place it in mortal danger. Intellectually, we may believe in an operation, but on a primal level, our bodies do not."[55]

The Felt Sense

What does an overwhelmingly or irreversibly horrible event *feel* like? We have all had them, though often enough they recede into memory as we attempt to get on with our lives. Consider the following anonymous example, however, and put yourself into the place of the person describing it:

> My five-year-old son and I were playing ball in the park when he threw the ball a long distance away from me. While I was retrieving the ball, he ran into a busy street to get another ball he had spotted. As I reached to pick up the ball we had been playing with, I heard the tires of a car screech long and loud. I knew instantly that Joey had been hit by the car. My heart seemed to fall into the pit of my stomach. All the blood in my body seemed to stop circulating and fell down to my feet. Feeling pale as a ghost, I started running toward the crowd gathering in the street. My legs were as heavy as lead. Joey was nowhere in sight, yet with the certainty that he had been involved in the accident, my heart tightened and constricted, . . . fill[ing] my chest with dread. I pushed through the crowd and collapsed on Joey's still body. . . . His body was scratched and bloody, his clothes were torn, and he was so still. Feeling panic-stricken and helpless, I frantically tried to piece him together. . . . I tried to wipe away the blood . . . to pat his torn clothes back into place. I kept thinking, "No, this isn't happening. Breathe, Joey, breathe. . . ." A numbness began to creep over me as I felt myself pulling away from the scene. I was just going through the motions now. I couldn't feel anymore.[56]

Unfortunately, this event really occurred; it is not taken from a work of fiction. Despite (or because of) her wrenching feelings, the narrator was able to describe her intense physical reactions: "my heart seemed to fall into the pit of my stomach," "pale as a ghost, I started running," "my legs were as heavy as lead," "feeling panic-stricken and helpless," and finally, "a numbness began to creep over me . . . I couldn't feel anymore."

Each of these sensations is an accurate depiction of a physiological state, most of which is unconscious and yet can be discerned from what we can—or cannot—feel. For example, "pale as a ghost" refers to blood being diverted from the skin and into the muscles. Someone who is panicked may not only look white, but may also break into a cold sweat as the sympathetic nervous system acts to keep the body cool. Moving into anomalous territory for a moment (I will do so at length later), I find it more than coincidental that ghosts are often described as both pale and cold, or as inducing cold in the witness. This is no mere figure of speech. It is a clue as to what is going on.

Close awareness of our bodily state—of pressure and vibration, weight and balance, touch on the skin, breathing, heartbeat, blood circulation, temperature, smell and taste, appetite and thirst, hearing, pain, pleasure, alertness, and all the other bodily perceptions I catalogued as feelings in chapter 2—constitutes what Levine calls "the felt sense." A brief discussion of the felt sense will be essential before moving to our next subject, namely, what happens when feeling is *diminished* as a consequence of trauma, conflicted impulses, or extended mental concentration. Levine says, "The felt sense can be said to be the medium through which we experience the totality of sensation. . . . [It] blends together most of the information that forms your experience. Even when you are not aware of it, the felt sense is telling you where you are and how you feel at any given moment. . . . It is so integral to our experience of being human that we take it for granted, sometimes to the point of not realizing that it exists until we deliberately attend to it."[57]

In our rushing, whizzing, workaday world, the felt sense is indeed overlooked. It is the quality of self-perception and feeling that meditation and other "mindfulness" practices seek to restore. These practices all begin with intentionally slowing oneself down, breathing more deeply, and noticing our inner state—literally how we feel. It is the antidote to what ails modern society. The rock band the Eagles caught the essence of wanting to retrieve the felt sense with a song titled "Learn to Be Still." Stillness does indeed encourage mindfulness and, with it, an appreciation for ourselves as embodied individuals.[58]

Dissociation

Neglect of the felt sense in the midst of frenzied business is one thing. By consciously slowing oneself down, taking a deep breath, and similar steps, the felt sense can typically be recouped, regained, and resuscitated. But sometimes "getting that old feeling back" can be more of a challenge. This is because the brain may, under certain circumstances, *dissociate from the body,* in effect withdrawing conscious investment from the felt sense.[59] In milder forms of dissociation, we can feel spacey or forgetful, although in more severe forms, we may routinely delve into fantasy, come to believe our everyday world is flimsily unreal, or as with the woman who lost her child Joey, begin to feel divorced from one's own feelings, even one's ability to feel.

When an overwhelmingly negative experience causes one to dissociate, heart rate and blood pressure drop (as they do when one is in shock). Production of ATP in the cells is decreased, so there is less energy to call on.[60] A feeling of faintness may ensue. The person may be temporarily unable to speak, yell, or otherwise react. Even more curiously, time may be experienced in slow motion and events seen from an outside vantage point, as if the person undergoing the trauma were someone else. A sense of unreality ensues. Afterward, one's conscious memory of the event may be sketchy or lost altogether.[61]

Dissociation often functions as a defense mechanism, with the person drifting away in various ways whenever someone or something threatens to remind him or her of the initial event or series of events. When dissociation becomes a routine, characteristic way of living life, we say that person suffers from a dissociative disorder. This is not a good or healthy thing, as evidenced by some of these comments:[62]

- "I've been in a shell, and I feel empty inside."
- "The emotional side of me just shuts down under stress."
- "I couldn't remember whether it really happened or I imagined it."
- "My mind wanders, and I go in and out. I just go away to myself."
- "I'm like a filter, who on a particular day depends on what's coming into me and what's going out. I don't feel connected internally all the time."
- "It's not feeling real or feeling that I'm just doing things automatically."

- "It's like . . . watching a movie in my head. . . . And you forget who you are, where you are, what time it is, what's going on in your life."

By the same token, we *all* dissociate at various times and to different extents, because dissociation is actually a universal phenomenon. Becoming engrossed in a good book is a form of dissociation, as is daydreaming and fantasizing. In these cases, dissociation can be pleasurable—a welcome diversion from the hassles and worries of everyday life. Déjà vu, the odd sense that one has lived a particular moment before, is also a dissociative phenomenon, although not often appreciated as such.[63] Farther along the continuum, someone may bury himself or herself in work, a hobby, or a form of recreation as a more prolonged escape.[64]

At the far end of the spectrum lie such difficulties as recurrent amnesia, partial or complete identify confusion, depersonalization (an extreme sense of detachment, such as the feeling that one's actions are simply mechanical or that one's body or self is disconnected), derealization (the feeling that features of the environment are illusory), the creation of multiple personalities (clinically termed dissociative identity disorder), and out-of-body experiences.[65]

Anomalous perception in general is considered to be dissociative, though not abnormal, given that Gallup polls and other surveys consistently show that large numbers of presumably healthy people report having what are typically called psychic experiences.[66]

Dissociation can occur at any age, depending on the circumstance and the degree of control (both real and perceived) that the individual has over it. As stated earlier, children are more likely than adults to become traumatized because they are often and literally helpless—a critical factor in the dissociative response.[67] This should not, however, imply that adults faced with an overwhelming threat would not themselves freeze and then unconsciously put their feelings (and the tremendous energy associated with them) into storage, thus setting the stage for dissociation.

Bodymind Recall

It is noteworthy that memories of the original threatening event (or series of events) are usually more amenable to body recall than to conscious, verbal recall. In other words, it may well be more difficult to talk about the event and its ramifications than to realize that you simply *feel* uncomfortable on some level.[68] Likewise, your posture, body language, and interactions with other people may offer subtle (or not so subtle) hints that something is bothering you, has gotten under your skin. Because it has. Your limbs, muscles, ligaments, and bodily organs retain an unconscious impression of the memories in a fashion that the conscious, thinking brain struggles to comprehend.

Ample clinical evidence for dissociation can be found in brain scans performed on victims of abuse. Results include a reduced size of the corpus callosum (the bundle of two hundred million nerve fibers connecting the two hemispheres), a larger than normal amygdala (a structure integral to the brain's processing of fear), and a reduction in size and volume of the hippocampus (the key structure involved in memory).[69] Let's examine the first of these findings, as its implications go to the core of this book's concerns.

Brain Hemispheres and the Corpus Callosum

While capacities in general are spread across the brain, its left and right hemispheres each have some particular talents (see figure 5). Predominant left side activities include reason, analysis, sequence, space and depth perception, and language. The right side is occupied more with feeling, aesthetics, nuance, tone, and intuition.[70] Due to these specializations, some types of information dealt with by one half of the brain cannot be processed or even recognized by the other. So the right side may not only perceive a given subject differently but also have different memories connected to it, thus drawing conclusions entirely different from the left side—and vice versa. This is a major source of intrapsychic conflict but also the wellspring of creativity, because the transfer and synthesis of (literally) differing views leads to new perceptions, ideas, and insights.[71]

The less the highway between the two hemispheres is traversed by neural activity, the greater the possibility that one half of the brain will know something that the other half doesn't, or will know it in an entirely different way.[72] In adult victims of abuse, the reduced size of the corpus callosum suggests that memories and perceptions are more likely to remain in one hemisphere. These impressions associated with the threat or trauma will be stored on the right side, with the left side less able to decipher them and articulate that understanding in rational terms.

The difficulty can be especially pronounced for children, because the corpus callosum takes more than ten years to grow to maturity. Additionally, much of what infants and toddlers learn is assimilated and processed before language (a left-brain skill) is acquired and used extensively.[73] The upshot is that a traumatic childhood memory may be stored predominantly in the right hemisphere, and the individual, as he or she grows to adulthood, would be unable to access those body memories except through body experiences, e.g., exercise, somatic therapy, massage, yoga, and the like.

LEFT HEMISPHERE

Language

Computation

Logical reasoning

RIGHT HEMISPHERE

Spatial reasoning

Face recognition

Music

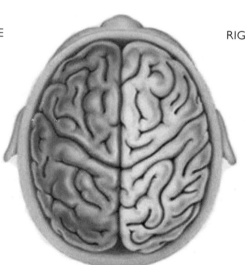

Figure 5. The two hemispheres.
Image from www.thebrain.mcgill.ca.

People who harbor such memories may dissociate more readily when faced with people, places, or things that are reminiscent of the traumatic episodes. In some cases, the tendency may become a major or even dominant aspect of their personality. Alternately, such people may betray their internal schism by becoming testy, anxious, fearful, or moody for no evident reason. They may acknowledge that something is amiss, or they may deny being bothered at all.[74] Sleep difficulties or nightmares may be experienced. And they may develop physical symptoms characteristic of the dissociative personality, including neck and back pain, gastrointestinal problems (e.g., ulcers, irritable bowel syndrome), premenstrual syndrome, asthma and allergies, migraine-type headaches, vertigo, chronic pain, and chronic fatigue.[75]

Neurologist Robert Scaer suggests that whiplash provides an especially useful example. People involved in even low-speed accidents, he says, clench their muscles and contract their bodies to protect themselves from an anticipated impact they cannot escape. The energy associated with this freeze response, if harbored internally, can lead to chronic muscular pain.[76] Scaer also notes that, among his patients with extended whiplash-type symptoms, 70 percent indicated they had a prior traumatic experience and one-quarter reported they had been abused as children.[77]

The above group of physical conditions is often, and correctly, termed psychosomatic. But this is not to suggest that they reside entirely in a person's head—far from it. As we have seen, they reside just as much in the body, and entirely in the mind when the mind is appreciated as the union of brain (nervous system) and body (organs, muscles, skin, circulatory system, digestive and eliminative systems, and immune system). As we saw in the last chapter and as we shall see yet more strikingly in upcoming discussions, the immune system in particular links the brain and the body, the head and the heart. And feelings influence immune function: less so if the person manages to express them and more so if they are held in.

The Person Unaware of Frozen Energy

Let us return to the mother who realized, desperately and tragically, that her young son had been hit by a car. In her words, "All the blood in my body seemed to stop circulating. . . . With the certainty that [Joey] had been involved in the accident, my heart tightened and constricted." Alas, her description is not only poignant but accurate, because as the immobility response takes hold, energy that in another instance would have been discharged through flight or fight does indeed become constricted and bound up in the nervous system. Shortly thereafter, realizing that her son has been gravely injured and there is nothing she can do about it, the mother's felt sense wavers and she experiences the first signs of dissociation: "A numbness began to creep over me as I felt myself pulling away from the scene. I was just going through the motions now. I couldn't feel anymore." In the long term, if the bound-up energy of her feelings is not given emotional or physical release, trauma is likely to occur and, with it, a propensity toward dissociation or psychosomatic illness.[78]

Ideally, a person who has undergone severe stress or confronted an overwhelming threat via the freeze response becomes aware of the held-in energy that requires discharge. Such awareness can arise from within, if one is sufficiently in touch with oneself, or can be pointed out by observant friends, relatives, and associates. The way this energy finds expression can be surprising, as can be the recognition of how much energy there is to express.

Frozen Energy and Reenactment of Traumatic Events

Now, what of individuals whose own stress reactions are frozen during a threatening event but who do not understand or appreciate the need to release all the pent-up energy? We have already seen how significant problems can result, including a tendency toward moodiness, anxiety or fearfulness, dissociative personality traits, sleep problems, and psychosomatic symptoms. All of these are the hallmarks of trauma. But I will go a step farther and suggest something startling: this vortex of energy in the body, when combined with issues or preoccupations held in the brain, can generate the phenomena we know of as ghosts, poltergeists, and similar haunts.

On the most superficial level, I have already noted that people undergoing fear or terror can go cold, clammy, pale, and white—and that these same adjectives have been commonly used in describing apparitions (and people's reactions to apparitions) through the centuries. Another, more compelling piece of evidence is that traumatized people are sometimes prone to act out the causal event or subconsciously put themselves into situations that resemble the causal circumstance. Their reason, as Levine points out (giving due credit to the observant Freud), is that these individuals wish to be free of their trauma, but they simply do not know how to go about it effectively. So they attempt to recreate the original situation, desiring, on an unconscious level, to somehow act differently so that the pent-up energy that has been playing havoc within them can be released. Unfortunately, they *cannot* act any differently if they dissociate, repress, deny, or otherwise fail to possess a full, conscious awareness of what happened to them during the original situation as well as what has happened to them since.[79] So we have the makings of what Freud called "repetition compulsion" and the ancient Greeks knew as tragedy: individuals who are consciously blind to the source of their problems (witness Oedipus), fatefully replaying the same events, the same relationships, without a satisfactory resolution.

Among the "often-bizarre reruns" cited by Levine is a Vietnam veteran who, every July 5, in the early morning hours, simulated the circumstances surrounding his buddy's death in a rice paddy by staging robberies—using nothing but a finger in his pocket as a gun. The man would remain at the scene, the police would arrive, and he would be taken into custody. Upon examining these reenactments, Dr. Bessel van der Kolk, a psychiatrist at the veterans' hospital where this man was taken the last time around, realized that "the vet had orchestrated the cast of characters needed to play the role of the Viet Cong. . . . Once he became aware of his feelings and the role the original event had played in driving his compulsion, the man was able to stop reenacting this tragic incident."[80] Levine comments, "If we look at this man's behaviors without knowing anything about his past, we might think he was mad. However, with a little history, we can see that his actions were a brilliant attempt to resolve a deep emotional scar."[81]

Levine views some instances of accident proneness as fitting this pattern, especially when the accidents are similar in some way.[82] He also notes the compulsively repeated play of traumatized children, a subject studied extensively by psychiatrist Lenore Terr.[83] As in the case of the Vietnam vet, he points out that reenactments can occur with the anniversary of the trauma-inducing event.[84] In all these cases, he concludes, "frequent reenactment is the most intriguing and complex symptom of trauma."[85]

It is also the hallmark of many reputed hauntings, where an apparition is said to mindlessly walk the same path or go through the same routine year after year, generation after generation. Many poltergeist outbreaks are likewise characterized by what appears to be irrational (but certainly persistent) behaviors such as rapping on walls, moving objects, making bizarre sounds, and even creating gushes of water. Poltergeist occurrences will be addressed more extensively in chapter 7. For the moment, I simply wish to point out that these two types of paranormal phenomena, which often seem to be primarily linked to a given place, can equally (and perhaps more appropriately) be seen as emanating from a disturbed personality—specifically, a personality characterized by unresolved trauma.

The Type C Personality and Susceptibility to Illness

We run into an apparent problem here, which is, very simply, that neither ghosts nor poltergeists appear, on the face of it, to be very "bodily." Quite the opposite: these types of occurrences seem entirely *discarnate,* earning a well-deserved reputation as spooky. How, then, can I be on solid ground in relating them, first and foremost, to thwarted biological stress reactions and the consequences of same?

Let us return, for a moment, to the fast-developing science of immunology. In recent years, a cluster of personality characteristics has come to be identified as the Type C personality, someone who is at heightened risk for a slew of afflictions, from colds to asthma to cancer. In contrast with the Type A person (who angers easily and has difficulty keeping feelings under wraps) and the Type B person (who has a healthier balance of emotional expressiveness), the Type C person is a *suppressor,* a stoic, a denier of strong feelings. He or she has a calm, outwardly rational, and unemotional demeanor, but also a tendency to conform to the wishes of others, a lack of assertiveness, and an inclination toward feelings of helplessness or hopelessness.[86] As we would surmise, however, their diminished emotional expressiveness does not in any way mean that Type C people feel their feelings any less. This has been revealed in experiments with infants. Those who were insecurely attached to their mothers showed increased pulse rates and higher cortisol levels when separated from them, despite remaining outwardly calm.[87] Associated changes in immune function also registered: fewer circulating lymphocytes and antibodies and lowered lymphocyte and antibody responsiveness.[88] In adults, researchers measured heart rate and also planted an electrode to measure tension in a muscle at the center of the forehead—a muscle often involved in headaches. When purposely agitated by the researchers, certain people who had high muscle tension said they felt fine and weren't upset, though the readout from their bodies contradicted them.[89]

This is the sort of personality that Canadian physician Gabor Maté has studied extensively. Over his years of family practice, Maté relates, he began to notice a pattern: individuals who were unable to express anger, who didn't seem to recognize the primacy of their own needs, and who were constantly doing for others, appeared to be the ones most susceptible to a slew of ailments, from asthma, rheumatoid arthritis, and lupus to multiple sclerosis and amyotrophic lateral sclerosis (ALS, also known as Lou Gehrig's disease). These conditions are all autoimmune disorders. Maté claims that, when an individual engages in a long-term practice of ignoring or suppressing legitimate feelings—when he or she is just plain too nice—the immune system can become compromised and confused, learning to attack the self rather than defend it.

Emotional expression, in Maté's view, is absolutely essential because feelings serve to alert the individual to what is dangerous or unwholesome—or, conversely, to what is helpful and nourishing—so that the person can either take protective action against the threat or move toward the beneficial stimulus. If someone never gets angry, this reflects an unhealthy inability or unwillingness to defend personal integrity. Such "boundary confusion" can ultimately become a matter of life and death. If someone just cannot say no, Maté argues, his or her body will end up saying it in the form of illness or disease.

Maté is careful to qualify that not everyone who has difficulty acknowledging or acting on feelings has such a fate in store. Hereditary and environmental factors surely play a role; perhaps, for many people, it's a more decisive one. But he *does* argue that how a person handles stress will, in some manner, affect his or her overall health because the brain, the body, and the mind are something other than separate entities. Together they constitute "one super-system of which the emotional centers, neurological pathways, hormonal glands and immune organs are all aspects. They are all wired together electrically by nerve fibers and they also speak the same chemical language. They do not and cannot function in isolation from each other."[90]

Maté agrees with the other authorities I've cited that the biology of potential illness arises early in life, with the brain's stress response mechanism programmed by the experiences of early childhood and infancy, if not earlier.[91] Over time, a person's unconsciously learned habit of dissociating feeling from awareness comes to be reflected in immune system dysfunction. It's as if the immune cells are just as confused about boundaries as the individual who fails, emotionally, to delineate them for himself or herself.[92] Autoimmune illness thus becomes the culmination of an insidious, lifelong process.[93]

The Chronically Dissociated Person

A fascinating case of just such a personality was presented by psychologist Ian Wickramasekera in a journal called, appropriately enough, *Advances in Mind-Body Medicine*. He reported on a man, using the pseudonym K. C., who was thirty-five years old at the time, married, and the father of two. Over the previous five years, K. C. had developed hypertension, uncontrollable flushing, severe headaches, and mild depression. His case was an immensely difficult one to understand or cure, mostly because of the patient himself. In Wickramasekera's words:[94]

K. C. was studied more than 20 times for extensive periods . . . at [three] famous medical school centers. . . . His health insurance company had spent more than 2 million dollars . . . on high-tech, biomedical studies. But only his headaches were moderately improved. . . . The other . . . symptoms were unaltered or had worsened. . . . Psychiatric interviews and conventional psychological testing . . . found no evidence of any significant psychopathology. . . .

K. C. . . . had quit work 3 years earlier and progressively had become, in his words, "an invalid." He felt that he was barely able to perform simple housekeeping and childcare activities. He also gained weight and increased his alcohol intake. Prior to his assorted symptoms, he had been an excellent student and a leader in college . . . on the fast track to a top executive position with a major national corporation. K. C.'s . . . invalid status enabled his wife to resuscitate her own promising professional career, which had been interrupted by the birth of the children. He reported some mild marital stress . . . but he denied any recent or remote significant distress at home, work, or in any social relationships. . . .

In spite of the adversities of the last several years, K. C. appeared cheerful, humorous, and socially outgoing. Nonetheless, he had a cold and wet handshake. . . . Even resting baseline measures indicated a sympathetically activated body. His most reactive systems were cardio-vascular . . . a high skin conductance . . . (a measure of sweat gland activity). . . . Hence, even under resting baseline conditions, K. C.'s body was on a "red-alert" status. But this apparently was a "secret" to him. During the measurements, he reported feeling calm. . . .

Because he was visiting our medical center, he spoke to his wife daily from his motel room. I asked him to measure and record his blood pressure twice before, during, and after speaking to his wife. His record indicated the same strong blood-pressure elevation while talking to his wife and a delay in blood-pressure recovery after the conversation. He also experienced the flushing across his face, chest, and back. In addition, he noticed a feeling of sadness and irritation. . . .

In the course of 3 weeks of intensive . . . psychotherapy . . . K. C. became aware of intense rage towards his wife who he perceived as "jealous" of his prior professional success because it left her "trapped" as a housewife. . . . He perceived her as very domineering and seeking to separate him from his children and parents. He felt she blamed him for the pregnancies that had interrupted her promising professional career, which was now slowly prospering during his illness.

At the conclusion of the 3 weeks of therapy, K. C.'s physician had withdrawn him from all blood-pressure medications . . . and the flushings had stopped. He recognized that he had very frustrated and angry feelings toward his wife . . . and that he now felt profoundly ashamed of what had become of his promising career. . . .

When he returned for a 3 months medical-psychological follow-up, all his . . . symptoms had declined in frequency and intensity by more than 80 percent. . . . He had separated from his wife, built a closer relationship with his children, and was contemplating divorce and another adult relationship. . . .

K. C. was extremely fortunate to have found, in Wickramasekera, a physician willing to look past the inconclusive medical data to the person suffering behind them and to be able to connect the dots that indicted the overall picture of the man's subtle but churning emotional physiology.

A patient with fewer means, less persistence, and perhaps, in less distress, would not have had the wherewithal to seek out the answers to his predicament and, ultimately, find ways to express and redirect the suppressed energy of his dissociated feelings.

Much as K. C. would have been left wondering, so too our society historically has wondered about the origin and manifestation of anomalous phenomena. We consider the paranormal to be occult (meaning obscured or hard to see), and this prevents us from considering that it could have fairly mundane, biological origins. The transmutation of an *internal,* unseen, but subconsciously registered stress reaction to the *external,* shadowy, but nonetheless sensate world of the anomalous is something exceedingly strange. I believe, though, that the connections to our own physical reality are there. As Sir Isaac Newton was able to infer the existence of an invisible force (gravity) from the known motion of objects, so it remains for us to discern the existence of a realm coincident with the one we take for granted. The gateway into that dimension is *emotional* and *energetic.*

Phantom Pain: A Parallel Phenomenon

The prospect of apparitions or poltergeists is truly no less occult than another extraordinary phenomenon that *is* being investigated by contemporary neuroscience. I refer here to the puzzle of phantom pain.

For hundreds of years, and probably well before, certain people who have lost a limb have been known to complain vociferously about strange sensations where their arm, leg, hand, or foot used to be. The sensations are said to be not just strange, but also uncomfortable and, in many cases, extremely painful. "Cramping," "itching," "burning," and "shooting" are the adjectives most commonly used. The patients' discomfort ranges from being occasional and mild to continuous and severe. Sometimes the phantom sensations occur immediately after surgery; sometimes they manifest after weeks, months, or even years. In some cases they abate, only to return later. As difficult as the phenomenon is to pin down, it is quite common, affecting upward of 70 percent of those who have had amputations.[95]

Phantom pain isn't limited to limbs. Pain in nonexistent breasts, teeth, tongues, and even penises is mentioned in the literature.[96] Even stranger, phantom pain is experienced by paraplegics—people who have had a complete break in their spinal cord and, therefore, should have no feeling in their body below the point of the break.[97] Strangest of all is the fact that phantom sensations are reported not only by people who *used* to have a body part but also by people who *never did.* In other words, by some individuals (approximately one out of five) who were born without the given appendage.[98]

A perspective shared in all cases is the compelling feeling that the phantom limb (or other body part) is actually there—invisible to the eye but nonetheless *a part of the self.* As described by one of medicine's foremost experts on pain, Ronald Melzack of McGill University, "A phantom foot is described not only as real but as unquestionably belonging to the person. Even when the foot is felt to be dangling in the air several inches below the stump and unconnected to the leg, it is still experienced as part of one's body, and it moves appropriately with the other limbs and with the torso."[99]

In public, this private reality becomes undeniable. One man, for example, felt his phantom arm extending straight out from the shoulder, at a right angle to his body. He "therefore turned sideways whenever he passed through doorways, to avoid hitting the wall." Another man, whose phantom arm seemed to be bent behind him, "slept only on his abdomen or on his side because the phantom got in the way when he tried to rest on his back." Phantom appendages may, in fact, seem to the person to be *more* substantial than an actual limb, especially if they hurt like the dickens.[100]

These cases are eerie indeed and, despite the advances of medical science, still unaccounted for. Like ghosts, they are apparitional—and their effects are perceived. Unlike ghosts, they relate to a specific body part that used to be (or could have been) part of the person. Ghosts, in contrast, seem to be a quasi-representation of a whole person, but one who is no longer coincident with a living body anchored in time and space. Science takes the anomaly of phantom pain seriously and has attempted to explain it neurobiologically, while environmental types of phantoms remain off-limits. But both, I propose, can be understood in energetic terms as being fundamentally *dissociative phenomena.* Before undertaking this explanation of phantom pain, however, let me present what medical science currently infers about the roots of phantom sensation.

Phantom Pain and the Neurosignature

Melzack, who has investigated this phenomenon more extensively than anyone else, proposes the following model. Phantom limbs, he says, must be generated in the brain. Whereas others have implicated particular regions or functions of the brain (such as the angular gyrus or the circuits that register sensation), Melzack points to a much more complex interplay of sensory pathways, emotional processing, and self-recognition. The information exchanged among these systems, he says, adds up to a "characteristic pattern of impulses indicating that the body is intact and unequivocally one's own." This pattern he calls the person's "neurosignature." If and when the systems underlying it are deprived of sensory input (as when a limb is lost), the neurosignature continues to register and one's former sense of oneself is retained.[101] Thus, "a person may feel a painful ulcer or bunion . . . or even a tight ring that had been on a finger. Such individuals are not merely recollecting sensations," observes Melzack, "but feeling them with the full intensity and detail of an ongoing experience."[102]

Because phantom sensations occur even among some individuals born without a given body part, the underlying neural matrix must be prewired, Melzack reasons. He cites a thirty-two-year-old engineer who was born without a leg below the knee. In this man, " . . . his phantom leg and foot remain vivid but vanish for several hours once or twice a week. He is always astonished and delighted when they return."[103] So, while aspects of the neurosignature may thus vary in intensity, the neurosignature itself is reasonably consistent and develops before birth, according to this theory.

The major lesson derived, according to Melzack, is this: the brain "generates perceptual experience even when no external inputs occur. *We do not need a body to feel a body.*"[104] [Emphasis mine.]

The above emphasis I have added with some incredulity. While other neuroscientists may differ on the "phantom" explanation itself, I presume they would more or less unanimously endorse this big-picture view of the brain's primacy over the body. It is an opinion we encounter again and again, and one I believe to be tragically misguided. Not that Melzack's explanation of phantom sensation must be off base; on the contrary, it makes great sense to me. But he ends up opining that the brain generates the experience of the body, as if one's sense of self is invariably a neural product. The difficulty with that position, as we have seen, is that the brain develops in conjunction with sensory input in utero. Without sensation and stress, there can be no brain to formulate the sense of self, which Melzack calls the neurosignature (and Levine has termed the felt sense). Whether or not a body part has been lost, the sense of self requires sensatory input in order to coalesce.

Melzack's position is rather like J. Allan Hobson's argument that emotion must be entirely due to the brain since, during REM sleep, feelings are experienced in the complete absence of bodily input. But the feelings in dreams are not true feelings: they are akin to phantoms because they are predicated on *memories* of feelings experienced in the body. Actual feelings are not being activated—they are being parroted. The same thing, I submit, is happening in the case of phantom pain. When a limb is lost (or the spinal cord is damaged), the brain "remembers" what that particular body part felt like, down to the particulars of a bunion on a foot or a ring on a finger. It then replicates that experience. In cases in which a person who never had a hand, foot, arm, or leg nonetheless feels the limb exactly where it should be, I presume that the brain is drawing upon the feeling of limbs that *are* there to generate the sense of ones that aren't. Perhaps the person's neurosignature, in these instances, is based on the original blueprint (i.e., the genetic plan for the individual that, for whatever reasons, was not carried out to the letter in utero).

The Role of Dissociation

Perhaps the most interesting question to ponder, with regard to phantom pain, is the same one we have posed for other anomalies: why does it happen to some people and not others? What distinguishes, for example, the 30 percent of amputees who don't experience phantom pain? Similarly, why should some people's sensations come and go while others' remain constant? The answer, I posit, has to do with the energetic flow of feeling in the given individual and his or her tendency toward the Type C personality traits we surveyed earlier: keeping a stiff upper lip, maintaining outward calm yet nonetheless reacting internally, seeking to fulfill others' wishes, and, at least occasionally, feeling hopeless or powerless.

My hypothesis is that the 70 percent or more of amputees who do experience phantom pain are individuals in whom the flow of energy is *slower or less direct*. It may well be that way because of dissociation. The loss of a body part, after all, must be among the most traumatic events a person could ever encounter. Who would want to part with an appendage if it could be avoided? Yet when illness, disease, conflict, or accident requires it, surgeons must perform the operation. I can well understand, before and after the fact, wanting to deny or distance oneself from this unfortunate reality. But the extent to which patients are able to accept the procedure—and the evolving self-image that must necessarily accompany it—is the difference, I would wager, in their likelihood of experiencing phantom sensation.

Consider the following two cases, reported by a psychiatrist who also considers himself an energy healer. In each case, he used his hands to identify areas of discomfort in the person's body (or areas that used to be part of his or her body) and draw out the pain. I make no inferences here regarding either the validity or the efficacy of such treatment, but simply present the reports, which I view as raising a provocative notion concerning dissociation:[105]

> Case 1. Mr. A., a 37-year-old cargo loader, lost his left leg just below the knee after suffering a massive crush injury when a cargo dolly jackknifed into his leg. He developed stump and phantom pain which was not responsive to two years of rehabilitation treatments. . . . Formerly an avid athlete, he appeared to withdraw from life due to the loss of his old self-image as a hockey player and "tough guy." He was also quite invested in a Worker's Compensation suit against his former employer, which consumed much of his emotional energy.
>
> He was offered [this alternate form of therapy] largely because no intervention during his multidisciplinary pain program had been particularly effective. Much to the surprise of Mr. A. and myself, we could both detect the contact of my hand with his phantom limb. Mr. A. had his eyes closed during the treatment, which made the experience all the more impressive to both of us. Steady movements

to draw the stuck energy out of his phantom leg caused a readily noticeable shift in his pain sensation, which he described as feeling like the pain was "draining" out of his leg. . . .

He described this process of releasing his pain as frightening to him. Somehow, he was holding onto the pain, and preventing it from totally leaving his body. He realized that if he could no longer feel any pain in his phantom leg, he would have to experience the true absence of his leg for the first time since his injury . . . doing so would also involve accepting the fact that he would never play hockey again. He stated quite clearly that he was not ready to proceed with further energy healing, because he wasn't yet ready to accept his disability. He was referred for a course of cognitive-behavioral psychotherapy to deal with this reconceptualization, but he made little further progress.

Contrast this patient's reaction and outlook with that of the following patient:[106]

Ms. B. was a 65-year old widow whose severe diabetic peripheral vascular disease necessitated a below-the-knee amputation of her right leg. However, she apparently misunderstood her surgeon's plans, because she went into surgery with the expectation that only two of her toes would be removed (the painful and gangrenous ones). Needless to say, she was shocked to wake up and find her lower leg missing. Within hours of her recovery from surgical anesthesia, she developed phantom pain of the two toes she had expected to lose. The pain was not responsive to multiple medications, and one month into her post-operative rehabilitation program, I was called to see her about a possible depression.

She proved to be a very feisty yet trusting woman who was primarily upset that her esteemed surgeon has so misled her. Part of her psychotherapeutic work with me involved venting her frustration, and also communicating her distress directly to her surgeon. These conversations allowed her to feel as though a load was lifted from her shoulders, but her pain persisted. More dramatic results came with the application of direct energy healing.

She too was able to feel my hand as it moved along the phantom limb, and she also felt as though the pain was a substance that could be guided to drain out of her foot. . . . [The sensation] was also accompanied by a vivid feeling of sky blue "relaxation" that flowed down her body. . . . As the phantom pain dissipated, she became more aware of the pain in her stump, and soon this too left. After our first energy healing session, she was pain free for the first time since surgery. However, the physical irritation of being fitted for a prosthetic leg and the emotional strain of a visit home led to a relapse of the pain. She then . . . learned to observe that her pain followed a predictable pattern. When she was tired or feeling stressed . . . her pain recurred shortly after each energy treatment. If she was well-rested and peaceful, she could be comfortable all day after the treatment.

The differences between these two instances are striking. Mr. A. desperately wished to retain his old self-image as the rough and ready hockey player, whereas Ms. B. was able, after venting her anger and frustration, to accept to some degree her predicament. If we picture Mr. A.'s feeling flow as being blocked given his particular trauma and Ms. B.'s as benefiting from the removal of an obstruction, we can likewise understand the persistence of the former's ghostly sensations versus the latter's diminished discomfort. To the extent that the individual is emotionally honest and healthy (not an easy task, especially under these circumstances), dissociation will be reduced, with genuine feeling flowing to all areas of one's actual body.

People who are affected by phantom pain are, I submit, suffering from the effects of dissociation. As in the examples we examined earlier in this chapter, they have suffered an overwhelming threat (or a perceived threat) to their safety and security. They involuntarily froze at some point out of fear and to protect themselves. The result was that a huge vortex of bodymind energy was marshaled but never released.

Now, instead of feeling being withdrawn from a given part of their body (or the person generally feeling spacey or numb in circumstances reminiscent of the original event), these individuals' energy stream is dammed up where the amputation occurred. This is felt as phantom pain, which can be lessened with appropriate attention to the whole person. This means attention not just to the symptoms reported, which a neurologist would typically focus on, but also to the person's feelings about the operation, about the hospital experience, about his or her self in general—the very types of things that an alternative therapist would be more likely to ask about.

Additional Factors in Phantom Pain

Eric Leskowitz, the physician and energy healer whose accounts of Mr. A. and Ms. B. were supplied here, points out that a person's distress *before* a scheduled operation has been shown to correlate with the severity of postoperative phantom pain. So, someone may fixate on a given sensation—say, the feel of a ring worn on a finger that won't be there after the operation—and that sensation may become incorporated into the phantom sensation ultimately experienced.[107] Instead of feeling being lost, here feeling is actually *magnified*. The body part is gone, but the bodymind awareness (synonymous with Melzack's neurosignature and Levine's felt sense) remains. Indeed, to quote Melzack once more, it is understandable that individuals would feel such sensations "with the full intensity and detail of an ongoing experience."

Leskowitz makes the interesting point that "such issues as incomplete mourning [for the lost appendage], suddenness of loss, [and] lack of adequate psychological preparation" could well contribute to a person's prospect of experiencing phantom pain.[108] At least as important, I suspect, are major personality traits such as:

- the person's overall degree of vitality and vigor
- the extent to which he or she is introverted or extroverted
- how the person handles stress

- the likelihood of engaging in fantasy or escapism
- how sensitive the person is to environmental stimuli
- his or her proneness to psychosomatic ailments
- the ability to recall dreams and likewise embrace subconscious material

The full import of these characteristics will be discussed in chapters 8 and 9. For now, suffice it to say that a whole range of factors—core personality traits as well as factors impinging more on the person's immediate situation—could be assessed for their relevance to phantom pain. We have seen a definite difference in the self-image and postoperative reaction of Mr. A. and Ms. B. *How else* are they dissimilar or, for that matter, alike? Has anyone systematically compared the 30 percent of patients who report no phantom pain against the 70 percent who do? What more about the dissociative process could such a study reveal? I, for one, would like to see it undertaken. The results, as a counterpart to brain-based investigations of phantom pain, would be most enlightening.

Posttraumatic Stress Disorder

We now come to a quite disturbing phenomenon that has attracted considerable attention since the end of the Vietnam War. While it is undoubtedly as old as the hills in human experience, medical science is just beginning to understand the condition that has been dubbed posttraumatic stress disorder (PTSD).

Among war veterans and other people who have survived extremely perilous circumstances (e.g., coming under enemy fire, confronting a natural or man-made disaster, repeated instances of child abuse), the details of the threat are revisited in PTSD. The events are not just passively reexperienced, but literally relived as current sensory input. A car horn, a shadow, or an odor can rekindle the very sights, sounds, smells, and feelings that the person experienced at the time of the original event. Inevitably, that original event was some kind of bodily attack or was at least interpreted as such: witness the development of PTSD in certain people following surgery or even following a difficult child delivery.[109] In any case, the original event causes a major disturbance to the individual's sense of integrity.

I use the word "integrity" purposefully since, on the one hand, not only is it true that a person's sense of self is disturbed in PTSD, but, on the other, that his or her memories of the traumatic event fail to be incorporated in the usual way. While the reexperience of the traumatic event is disturbingly vivid—complete with all the physiological shock and fight-or-flight reactions that the person had in the original situation— what is remembered and felt seems to exist *entirely on its own*. Each recreation is the same as the last; the threads, you might say, are not woven into the totality of what happened "back then." Although the individual may feel transported to the time and place of the trauma, nothing else in his or her life at that time is recalled, appraised, or factored in. In this sense, PTSD is not a time machine. The memories are fragmentary, standing on their own, and not integrated either into the past or current self.[110]

An authority on trauma, Bessel van der Kolk of the Boston University School of Medicine, has described PTSD as "speechless terror" reasserting itself.[111] Indeed, the memory seems to be all about feeling and perception, with the person unable to talk about or narrate what is going on as it is being reexperienced. Therapists know they are making progress when a patient with PTSD gradually comes to recognize that the experience is something that can be assessed as it happens.[112] A good part of the problem may be that individuals with PTSD show physical changes in the brain that impede memory, including a reduction in the size of the hippocampus, the corpus callosum, and the anterior cingulate (which plays a role in regulating emotion).[113]

People affected by PTSD also show many of the hallmarks of a dissociative disorder. They are often depressed or fatigued and bothered by headaches or chronic pain. They may have difficulty sleeping or be plagued by nightmares. Additionally, they are prone to feeling irritable, to being overtaken by sudden and inexplicable bouts of anger, and to displaying both hypervigilance and hyperarousal.[114] Changes in immune functioning have also been noted.[115] Yet the condition carries its own distinctive neurobiological trademark. Levels of the stress hormone cortisol, which is typically high in people suffering from acute and chronic stress (as well as those with major depression), are *low* in people with PTSD. This seems counterintuitive and, in fact, has come as a surprise to researchers, especially since levels of other stress hormones, such as adrenaline, are almost always increased in persons suffering from chronic stress, including those affected by PTSD.[116]

The question is, what does this finding mean? Why should some people suffering from trauma show all the symptoms we have come to expect— including an elevated cortisol level in the body—while others sharing a great many of those symptoms nonetheless develop the more spectacular disturbance of PTSD? Researchers have quite a task in trying to tease the dynamics apart. Consider that, of the entire population of traumatized individuals, a relatively small proportion—approximately 8 percent—lives with this condition. (Women are about twice as likely as men to develop PTSD, or at least to come forward and be diagnosed with it.)[117] Yet upward of three-quarters of both men and women with PTSD have an overlapping psychiatric disorder, most prominently depression.[118] Clearly, while threats to life and limb do engender trauma in predictable ways, not everyone responds to peril in the same way. It is these individual differences I find so fascinating. By understanding how different people react to similar crises, I believe we can learn much about the human mind: brain plus body.

Clues to the PTSD Riddle

Rachel Yehuda, director of the Traumatic Stress Studies Center at Mount Sinai Hospital, has proposed that individuals beset by PTSD may have characteristically low cortisol levels. Or, she acknowledges, it may be that cortisol takes a dip among certain people in the immediate aftermath of a threatening experience. The evidence seems to argue in favor of the latter—a clue I will address shortly. In any case, Yehuda suggests that the best way to look at PTSD is as a condition reflecting both individual differences and the neurobiology of trauma.[119]

I agree, and I further suggest that PTSD be viewed through the lens of brain/body connectivity. To begin, I propose that PTSD predominantly affects those individuals we previously termed high reactors, who are naturally more vigilant due to an altered HPA set point. Their experiences, therefore, are likely to be more intense and memorable than for most of us. This would, for instance, explain one combat veteran's remark that the smell of gunpowder inevitably makes him feel hot: "It's as if my whole metabolism changes."[120]

Indeed, Yehuda makes the point that "PTSD patients don't just have an image of [the traumatic event] . . . they also recall the physiologic response they had of fear, helplessness, or horror. They may even actually experience components of that physiologic response as they are remembering the event long after it occurred. So remembering the event becomes a traumatic experience itself for someone with PTSD."[121] I am going to further speculate that a diminished corpus callosum, previously noted as a characteristic of people with this condition, is a *preexisting feature* of their neural landscape. We have already seen that the fewer connections there are between the hemispheres, the greater the likelihood that the brain's "rational" left side will have difficulty interpreting and articulating the feelings processed by the right. People with PTSD, I conjecture, are less able than others to explain an event to themselves, to put it in perspective, and to calm themselves down—especially if the event in question is terrifying. Think about it this way:

Those individuals who are able to keep talking to themselves while a [potentially] traumatic event is occurring, and who keep planning for a possible future . . . still feel intense fear, but their left-brain approach to understanding prevents them from being overridden with terror.

[Other] individuals . . . experience the world from a more sensory, emotion-laden place. . . . They cannot, in the instant of terror, manage a sequential understanding of the event, nor can they decide in a rational or logical manner what to do next in order to protect themselves. They are, in other words, in a place of "speechless terror."[122]

An Illustration

Let us now consider the following scenario. Such a person is physically assaulted. Without being able either to flee or fight back, he or she is overwhelmed. Drawing on Levine's frozen energy model, we can say that the individual's torrent of stirred-up feelings is *held in suspension*. Those feelings, and the memory of those feelings, fail to be expressed outwardly; neither are they incorporated into the rest of the bodymind. They remain trapped, an obstruction in the stream. (Here it is worth noting one additional symptom of PTSD: circulatory and cardiovascular impairment. Beyond the numerous other characteristics of a bodymind disorder, this one effectively conjures up the image of a literal obstruction in the flow of feeling.) While another trauma survivor would "divest" feeling to the extent that he or she becomes disconnected, amnesiac, or depersonalized, in the case of a PTSD patient the energy surges back when sensory stimuli reminiscent of the original threat arise, effectively pushing the memory back to front and center. If we picture the original traumatic event as a stone in the body (rather than, in people with other dissociative states, a dam), we can imagine the current periodically sweeping the impediment to the surface, only to then let it drop back down until the next evocative sight, sound, or smell suddenly unleashes the process again.

Stones, unlike wood or other vegetative matter that we typically associate with a natural dam, are not apt to decay—at least not over our lifetime of mere decades. The traumatic memory thus exists on its own, unincorporated into the rest of the individual's recollection of that time, that slice of life. When such an obstruction is pushed to the surface, the person's highly activated HPA system ensures that the reexperience is as vivid and as frightening as the original event truly was.

In this connection, Australian psychologist Michael Thalbourne brings an interesting observation to light. He notes that people experiencing panic attacks (replays of traumatic events that are identical, for all intents and purposes, with PTSD outbreaks) say the attacks are sometimes felt as *energy surges*. People report feeling a bolt of lightning, as it were, emanating from their spine and running through their bodies. Thalbourne relates these energy surges to the kundalini power described in ancient Hindu texts.[123] In recent years, kundalini energy has undergone a reexamination, and Thalbourne's mention of it strikes me as not only theoretically interesting but perhaps also as a literal validation that an energy surge is involved in PTSD. Yet such upwellings (which are most often characterized as crackling electricity rather than gushing water) are not reported by everyone who has the condition. (To my knowledge, no one has ever done a survey to ascertain what the percentage might be.) I will venture to say that the individuals who do experience kundalini-like effects are most likely those who, neurobiologically, have the greatest degree of connectivity throughout their brain and body. (We shall meet these extraordinary people, who have been designated variously as having thin boundaries or being highly sensitive, overexcitable, or transliminal, in chapter 8.)

Personality Factors In PTSD

To round out our understanding of PTSD, we still need to inquire into patients' lowered cortisol level. This factor obviously constitutes a significant departure from the increased cortisol levels recorded in people who are chronically stressed, depressed, or otherwise suffering the fallout of trauma. Here I suggest that the "stone" contained in the bodymind of someone with PTSD is so compact, so self-contained, that the stream effectively learns to flow around it. Only during the occasional, horrific surges is the individual truly back on high alert. The rest of the time, the stone may be considered less an obstacle than an island the current moves past. So while a variety of psychosomatic symptoms are still experienced (after all, there is still a blockage in the system), the object itself is sufficiently isolated and worked around that cortisol levels drop. The threat has, in large measure, ceased to be active.

On the surface, this state bears some resemblance to the Type C personality we became acquainted with earlier. Such people, as you'll recall, are outwardly calm and unexpressive, preferring to keep their feelings under wraps. These individuals are often unassertive and tend to profess hopelessness when push comes to shove. Yet their bodily functioning betrays them. From heart rate to muscle tension to skin conductance, they show unmistakable signs of a bodymind that is still grappling with issues of feeling, that *wants* to discharge its ossified energy and acknowledge the full extent of its humanity. Recall that K. C., after noticing feelings of sadness and irritation after conversations with his wife, was led to discover still more potent feelings of frustration and rage, after which he separated from his wife and began building a closer relationship with his children.

Here is where PTSD parts company from depression, chronic fatigue, and the rest. The individual with PTSD is so ill-prepared, physically and mentally, to cope with the original threat that the memory of it is well-nigh segmented from the rest of his or her being. The terror or horror originally experienced is indeed speechless: it has little means of communicating with the rest of the bodymind, of becoming consciously known, of working itself out. And speechless it will remain, unless therapists and other caring medical professionals seek to kindly, gently, gradually intervene. In contrast with some other psychic wounds, time alone will not heal this one.[124]

Future Questions for PTSD

The framework I have proposed to try to understand PTSD is obviously unconventional. For that I make no apologies. As with dissociative identity disorder, phantom pain, and other such ailments, PTSD represents a truly baffling phenomenon. To further distinguish its etiology from that of other debilitating conditions, certain questions need to be asked.

It would be interesting to know, for example, to what extent PTSD "replays" coincide with phantom pain or other sensations, if they do at all. How many individuals with PTSD have a history of exaggerated reactions to everyday stimuli, be they sunlight, sounds, aromas, tastes, textures, or even the weather? What proportion report migraine headaches or the curious fact of synesthesia? Do they report apparitions any more or less than the general population? At least one fact is known: people with PTSD are extremely susceptible to hypnotic suggestion.[125] This finding supports my contention that PTSD develops in people who are innately sensitive, but obviously more evidence is needed. As it comes to light, medical science will be in a better position to appreciate how our bodymind functions— or, just as importantly, how it malfunctions.

Energy Expressed, Energy Retained, Energy Transmuted

You'll recall at the beginning of this chapter that we profiled several different people's experience of energy. There was Mel Gibson, who caught the acting bug big-time and whose youthful exuberance felt like "just too much energy" to be contained. Pitcher Curt Schilling's intensity seemed to place him in "some other world" as he prepared to take the mound. The ninety-two-year-old grandmother we saw simply radiated effervescence, whereas the middle-aged accountant we met was "a downer." And molecular biologist Candace Pert was one among many who've had a powerful feeling of "energy moving" in an acupuncture treatment.

We explored the concept of energy as a dynamic *capacity* or *process,* comparable to money, which can reside or be transmitted in many different forms. However, there was one major difference, namely, the first law of thermodynamics, which states that energy is conserved. In other words, so long as a given system has not changed (that is, energy has neither been added to nor subtracted from it), the amount released will be exactly the same as the amount invested—in a different form perhaps, but an identical amount.

The point is that emotional energy, just like any other form of energy, can be stored, focused, drained, or liberated. It can radiate out to others, for better or for ill; it can be vividly felt or left to work its own way in our bodies and nervous systems. But as physicist James Trefil points out, "There is no such thing as a free lunch. . . . All we can do with energy is exchange one form for another."[126]

Could dissociated bodymind energy play a role in the enigma of apparitions? Ghost stories are as old as the hills, and cover the gamut from prince to pauper. Here is one I came across quite by accident. It is taken from a reminiscence by Christopher Buckley, a former speechwriter in the Reagan White House who now satirizes politics through his novels. Buckley relates that, in 1983, he had the privilege of dining with the president and two royal princesses visiting from abroad. Discussion at one point turned to the Prince of Wales Room, where, in 1865, a partial autopsy and embalming were performed on the martyred President Abraham Lincoln. Buckley writes, ". . . Reagan turned to one of the princesses and remarked that his . . . spaniel, Rex, would begin barking furiously whenever he came into this room. There was no explaining it, Reagan said. Then he told about Lincoln and suddenly the president of the United States and the two princesses began swapping ghost stories and I was left openmouthed. . . ."[127]

Like many other history-laden buildings, the White House has long been rumored to be a haunted locale. Lincoln's ghost has reportedly been sighted (and nebulously felt) often. No less a pragmatist than President Harry Truman wrote to his wife, "I sit here in this old house, all the while listening to the ghosts walk up and down the hallway. At 4 o'clock I was awakened by three distinct knocks on my bedroom door. No one there. Damned place is haunted, sure as shootin'!" Over the years, Lincoln's presence (or some type of presence, at any rate) has also been remarked on by residents ranging from Eleanor Roosevelt and Ladybird Johnson to presidential daughters Susan Ford and Maureen Reagan as well as by notable guests such as Winston Churchill and Carl Sandburg.[128] Clearly, apparitions and other strange phenomena are not merely the province of the ignorant, the backward, and the lame.

Mindful, perhaps, of this aspect of the building's reputation, the White House marked Halloween 2003 by adding a page to its website featuring an interview with its longtime chief usher, Gary Walters, concerning some of the strange phenomena that staff members there have been privy to. In a video clip showing him to be entirely sincere (since taken down by the Obama administration), Walters gave a firsthand example:

"I was standing at the state floor. . . . The [two] police officers and I felt a cool rush of air pass between us and then two doors that stand open closed by themselves. I have never seen these doors move before without someone specifically closing them by hand. It was quite remarkable."[129]

It is often said that ghosts represent the spirit of someone who still had something to do in this life, who had an unresolved purpose (or perhaps a lingering regret), and who is either unaware of being deceased or unwilling to depart from earthly existence. Such superstitions, I posit, are not far from the truth—but the truth lies in the biochemistry of the brain and the body and in the emotional energy retained in our being. I will state my concept again: the frozen energy of the stress reaction, *combined with issues or preoccupations held in the brain,* can generate the phenomena we know of as ghosts, poltergeists, and similar haunts.

The Basis For Energy Medicine

Scientists, of course, have always been aggravated by superstition, and rightly so, since superstition impedes our rational understanding of the world. But superstition can, in some cases at least, contain a grain of truth. That kernel may not be presented in terribly scientific terms, fit neatly into the current paradigm, or be something that the average scientist wishes to hear. But if there is some underlying validity, the superstition (or, as some would have it, folk wisdom) persists. In a similar vein, scientists have been quick to discount or dismiss so-called healers who claim to feel energy moving in the course of their work, and likewise the reports of patients who have felt *something* in their bodies change for the better as a result of such treatments. One difficulty is that the language self-described healers use to describe how they work—which is mostly about *feelings and intuitions*—has failed to penetrate the Halls of Science because it is not the language that scientists use and does not reflect the concepts they have assimilated.

Consider, though, this intriguing observation by researcher Bernard Grad, who has studied people who seem to possess healing ability: "I have conducted experiments in which I obtained extraordinary results with people who made no claim to be healers but who *were in states of emotional arousal.*"[130] [Emphasis mine.]

Quite possibly, where the energetic processes of our bodymind are concerned, scientists and lay healers are not that far apart. The more that is discovered about the neurobiology of emotion, and of the interaction between the nervous and the immune systems, the more commonality I predict science will find with so-called energy medicine (and vice versa).

Grof's COEX Model

Remarks concerning emotional energy run throughout the literature of alternative medicine. One person who has made a dedicated effort to conceptualize what might be going on is researcher Stanislav Grof. His book, *Realms of the Human Unconscious,* describes his remarkable experiences in the 1960s conducting psychotherapy with the use of psychotropic drugs, chiefly LSD.[131] This was a time when the field of psychology was much taken with the topic of "human potential" and the idea that mind-altering drugs could elicit otherwise inaccessible material from the unconscious that might shed light on an individual's particular problems. Grof and his colleagues administered controlled doses of LSD; these sessions were followed up with sessions of traditional psychotherapy. Grof noted that the imagery that tended to arise "had a structure not dissimilar to that of dreams . . . it soon became obvious that LSD could become an unrivaled tool for deep personality diagnostics if its specific effects and symbolic language became better understood."[132] The imagery his patients reported—and its often close association with a string of traumatic memories—crystallized for Grof in a term he originated called "COEX," for systems of condensed experience. He writes:

> A COEX system can be defined as a specific constellation of memories consisting of condensed experiences . . . from different life periods of the individual. The memories belonging to a particular COEX system have a similar basic theme or contain similar elements and are associated with a strong emotional charge. . . . The

deepest layers of this system are represented by vivid and colorful memories of experiences from infancy and early childhood . . . up to the present life situation. Each COEX system has a basic theme that permeates all its layers and represents their common denominator. . . . Particularly important are COEX systems that epitomize and condense the individual's encounters with situations endangering survival, health, and integrity of the body.[133]

As Grof's patients proceeded through therapy, they inevitably touched on these interlinked memories, in some cases appearing to literally relive them. As they did, the emotional energy liberated was intense and its connection with the body beyond doubt. The "spontaneous shaking and trembling" noted by Levine among animals recovering from a freeze response occurred often, along with a headache, nausea and vomiting, and pain in various parts of the body.[134] These presumably represented a reconnection to the person's felt sense that had been dissociated at the time of the trauma. Ultimately, Grof observed that an "enormous amount of affective energy" had to be discharged before the individuals regained their composure and felt that they had fully recovered and integrated the experience.[135]

People can carry such calcified energy inside themselves for years, perhaps their entire life. One might say they are haunted by dissociated feelings and memories without consciously knowing it. If it is not released in other ways, that very energy is responsible, in my view, for the sort of hauntings we know as ghosts and poltergeists.

Why the Phenomena Aren't More Widespread

Let's say that you are now willing to grant credence to this view or, at the very least, recognize that it could have some merit. The question then arises, since so many people live through stressful, shocking, or traumatic experiences, either as children or as adults, why are anomalies not more common? Why, in other words, are the hauntings I am attempting to explain not in evidence every day, everywhere there is a Type C person walking around, unaware of the accumulating stresses in his or her body and out of touch with the memory of any traumas that may have occurred in childhood? As someone who is relentlessly skeptical of my own ideas, I realize this question needs to be asked—and answered—at least tentatively.

The first and most obvious response is that not every Type C person is carrying around the relics of trauma. Plenty of our fellow citizens are calm, courteous, unprepossessing, unassertive, and just plain nice without necessarily harboring the explosive emotional energy associated with an immobility response that never worked itself out. They may not be as aware of their moment-to-moment feelings as others who are more cognizant, but stoicism or emotional reticence do not necessarily equate to having a traumatic past. The converse is also true: someone who is prone to dissociate is not guaranteed to be shy and retiring in all circumstances. In situations that have little to do with the original trauma, the person may be emotionally articulate and expressive. In all but the most relevant (and therefore threatening) situations, such a person may appear to be anything *but* a Type C personality.

The second answer is that a person may be more prone to a slew of behaviors and personality traits—including dissociation and the harboring of energy in the body—due to the combined influence of genes and environmental factors operating before birth. As was described in chapter 4, this person may be constitutionally more anxious, more susceptible to stress, and more likely to experience the ill effects of a prolonged freeze response. Put another way, the person may be a more probable candidate for future energetic phenomena such as ghosts and poltergeists because of his or her particular neurobiology—a set of conditions extant at birth and subject (to a not unlimited extent) to later modification.

A third answer to the issue of why such phenomena are not more apparent is that *comparatively few people have the sensitivity to perceive them or the inclination to grant them their due.* Just as so many of us go about our business each day, taking less notice of the emotional cues coming from our colleagues (and even our spouses and children) than we should, I also suspect that the ability to really *notice* indications of frozen energy in people is relatively uncommon.

My final response to this all-important question is that energy harbored in the body is a necessary but not sufficient ingredient for the manifestation of psychic phenomena. Such energy must be accompanied by *an issue or pre-occupation held in the brain.* I will address this topic more fully in chapter 7, but for now, suffice it to say that the connection between the emotional (limbic) region of the brain and the cognitive (neocortex) region should draw our attention. Just as human beings, much more so than other animals, are likely to dissociate during and in the aftermath of an overwhelming threat, so too we are more apt to ponder what to do about a subject, especially one that holds emotional meaning, without achieving resolution.

Here's an example. A nurse, age fifty, was flying in a plane that suddenly lost an engine. Over those next turbulent moments of uncertainty, she recollected, "All I could think about was my garage. How I hadn't cleaned it, and how messy it would be when someone came in and saw it. It's crazy what you think about."[136] Why, indeed, would her mind—or anyone's mind—be drawn to such a comparatively trivial issue during a crisis? Perhaps, I submit, because it represented some kind of a lingering, emotionally resonant concern that she wished to resolve, if at all possible, in what could have been construed as her final moments.

The part of the brain where such decision-making is believed to occur is the right orbitofrontal cortex. As we saw in chapter 3, emotional expression is regulated there. This region is also critical in the development of selfhood, which begins shortly after birth and is programmed early on through interactions with one's primary caregivers.

A Personal Experience

The preponderance of ghosts and apparitions that not only repeat the same routines but are also said to be fruitlessly "in search of something" suggests to me a parallel, not just with people who unconsciously reenact a traumatic occurrence but also with others who find that they cannot consciously resolve a particular issue. A nagging doubt, a concern about the consequences of taking a given action, the propriety or the perceived guilt—any of these considerations amounts to the thinking brain overriding what the more primitive, emotional brain may wish to express, get out in the open, or have done with. This is the flip side of the dynamic I postulated earlier concerning what is necessary and sufficient for an anomalous experience to occur. The energy of dissociated feelings in the body represents the means, and the neurological "hang-up" in the right orbitofrontal cortex represents the motive. When the two converge with opportunity, the result can be disquieting.

Consider a striking experience my entire family had just a few years ago. It wasn't spooky in the customary sense—for one thing, it happened in broad daylight in our very own home—but the fact that it wasn't per- haps makes the theory I am proposing more amenable to examination.

What happened was this. The time was just before noon on a crisp, clear autumn day. A beloved family pet, Dalton the Great White Cat (as I liked to call him) had perished about ten days before, having been hit by a car just up the road from where we live. This came as a surprise, because he knew the neighborhood well and, at age eleven, was still rela- tively lithe and quick. As it happened, the neighbor who found Dalton had no nametag to identify him or his owner, since my feline had a habit of slipping it off and I wasn't always prompt in getting him a new one. So by the time I found out what had happened, my cat had been buried and I had no chance to say goodbye. A couple days later, my wife Bonnie, our two-year-old daughter Gabrielle, and I were informally gathered at the top of the stairs. Up to that point, we had decided not to tell Gabrielle defini- tively what had happened. The feelings of sadness were too strong, and both Bonnie and I were hesitant at hinting at death. But at that moment, my daughter had asked us pointedly, "Where's Dalton?" I got at eye level with her and started to explain that he had "decided to go somewhere special and wasn't coming back." As I began talking (with a definite lump in my throat) there was a series of knocks at the front door, just a few feet away. They were quite insistent, and Bonnie immediately went to answer them. She remarked that it must be a certain neighbor girl she had invited over. Oddly, the knocks seemed to me to be coming from a position lower down on the door than the average person (even someone small) would knock. In any event, scant seconds later my wife had opened the door—

and no one was there. Not a child, not an adult, not a mischievous teenager, not an animal. We thought fleetingly that it might have been a bird, but dismissed that possibility because the knocking was distinct from a mere pecking. Anyway, no bird had ever pecked at our door, nor had anything remotely similar ever happened to Bonnie or me.

This extraordinary incident took place at the very instant when a renewed sadness over the loss of our pet was welling up (read: energy) and both of us were struggling to break the news to our daughter (read: cognitive ambivalence). Our entire family heard an insistent knocking that arose out of the moment, the source of which defied conventional explanation, although the sound itself seemed commonplace enough. Strange but true and not, in my estimation, a coincidence.

Obsessive-Compulsive?

Far stranger occurrences have been reported throughout the annals of psychic literature. They can be more vivid, repetitive, or disturbing, presumably owing to the feelings involved being more dissociated, the associated energies being stronger and more deeply rooted, and the unresolved issues having greater import—though not necessarily. Some ghost stories come across as so odd that a variation on the model I have proposed may be in order. An account in the memoir of a noted parapsychologist, Nandor Fodor, is a prime example. He mentions the experience of a Lady Harris in England (no date given, but presumably from the late nineteenth or early twentieth century). An apparition appeared in her home, evidently searching for something. Fodor writes, "On making inquiries she found that the previous owner of the house had had a tremendous beard and when he retired for the night, he used to tie it up with an elastic. The crazy idea occurred to her that the ghost was searching for an elastic. She put one on the tallboy [British term for a high chest of drawers]. . . . The elastic disappeared and the ghost was no longer seen."[137]

Reports like this—speaking to evidently quite trivial personal matters—have, in the aggregate, given parapsychology a bad name. And why shouldn't they? After all, we would like to think that our lives matter in the grand scope of things, that we're here on Earth to learn, grow, and evolve, and that after we shuffle off this mortal coil, we have better things to do (if we have things to do at all) than to maintain our old, pointless habits. Ghost stories of this ilk seem even less worthy of scientific inquiry than the compulsive reenactments that I examined earlier and attributed to the unconscious striving to resolve some traumatic episode.

Yet is not the word "compulsive" just the right one to describe the behavior of the ghost in Lady Harris' house? It seems to me that a more consistent (and less judgmental) interpretation would be that the person's habit *itself* constituted the "issue or preoccupation" in the brain that I have posited as essential for phenomena of this type to occur. Perhaps the fact that the previous owner of the house chose to maintain an unusually long beard spoke to a more compelling issue, one related to family (a tradition among men in his family that he felt conflicted about), societal norms (that he felt intent on maintaining), or gender relations (were lengthy beards a turn-on or turn-off to women 150 years ago?). Alternately, perhaps this man's habit owed to what we now call obsessive-compulsive disorder, or OCD. While much about this syndrome is still unclear, OCD is gradually being illuminated as a neurobiological disorder. Already it has been linked to low levels of the neurotransmitter serotonin. Brain scans also show that patients with OCD burn energy more rapidly in the frontal lobe and the pathway connecting that lobe to the basal ganglia.[138] If I am correct, therefore, energetic processes in the brain and body will be shown to underlie even these very strange, almost inscrutable reports.

6

———◆———

Feeling and the Influence
of Atmosphere

*Do you remember how electrical currents and "unseen
waves" were laughed at? The knowledge about man was
still in its infancy.*

ALBERT EINSTEIN

*To know that we know what we know, and to know
that we do not know what we do not know, that is true
knowledge.*

COPERNICUS

The atmosphere is freighted with significance. The very air that we breathe
is the same medium through which we see, hear, scent, and feel touch on
our skin. The warmth of sunlight . . . a reassuring hand on the shoulder . . .
the smell of rain-drenched pavement on a muggy day . . . the pulsating bass
of a rock anthem . . . the sight and shout of a friend in greeting—these are
the incessant beckonings of sensation that we glean through the air.

So much information is conveyed about our environment through the air, which of course we are continuously sharing it with all the life on Earth that breathes in or out. But, for all that information—and that tangible connection with the rest of the planet—the air goes virtually unnoticed. Why? Because the atmosphere itself is invisible. The one possible exception: if you're unfortunate enough to live someplace where smog is prevalent. Otherwise, this constant of our existence is something we never actually *see*. Despite being immersed in it as thoroughly as are fish in the sea, the air, it is said, represents "the most outrageous absence known to this body."[1]

Yet it is never really absent; we are always enveloped by it. And, beneath the threshold of consciousness, our bodymind registers quite a lot—much more, I suspect, than has been dreamed of by our Western philosophy. For it is my contention that the terms we sometimes employ—and that serve as apt metaphors for what's happening in a given time and place— are sometimes *more* than metaphors. As an example, people will speak of a "frightened atmosphere," an "oppressive sadness," or an encounter that is "thick with danger." Often we say we wish to "clear the air" after an argument or disagreement. Clearly these statements are descriptive in the sense that one is noticing the body language and vocalizations of others: their facial expression, posture, and gestures, along with the volume, tone, and pitch of their voice. Odors are undoubtedly also involved; in the case of "electric" romantic attraction, it's pheromones. But *more* may be going on in the case of purportedly haunted locales. A statement recorded in the course of one recently published investigation affords an example: "I take my sleeping bag up the stairs and into the haunted room. It's horrible in here. It's as if the air is made of invisible sponge."[2] Another person felt that a particular room was somehow "fuller" than normal.[3] While I have not catalogued such mentions, I have come across them and made similar observations myself in locations where, for some reason, I felt oddly ill at ease. I have experimented with the lights, the placement of furniture, the operation of clock radios, and so on, and found that such variables do not appear to diminish the strange sense that the atmosphere itself contains something extra, that it is unquiet or amiss in some way.

For this reason, we shall explore in this chapter the form of energy that percolates through our world and the universe at large. It's the energy that opens up the world to our inspection: the phenomenon of *light*. Electromagnetic radiation—of which visible light is one aspect—is an elemental and pervasive force in our universe, connecting what *is* with the ability of sentient beings to apprehend what is. As we shall see, there is undoubtedly more to electromagnetism than meets the eye.

Let There Be Light

The most distinctive characteristic of light is the way it connects sentient beings with the objects of their perception. Light not only enables us to see our surroundings but also is reflected in the perceiver's own eyes. A glint in the eye indicates life and vitality. Shining or gleaming eyes indicate intelligence or depth of feeling. We speak of eyes looking cold or dead, that do not have that gleam, that sparkle, visible in them. And, of course, when someone's eyes "light up," we know they are feeling something special. We apprehend this thanks to the medium of light itself.

I've always been fascinated by words' origins, which can tell us a good deal about their latent meaning and the other words they're related to. The Indo-European root of the word "light" is the same as for the words "illuminate" and "luminous," all of which convey brightness, radiant energy, and the means to take them in via the eye. It's also noteworthy that "luminary" (from the same root) indicates not just "a celestial object that gives light" but also "a source of intellectual or spiritual light."[4] Spirituality and light are indeed linked, as we will glean shortly.

First, however, let us take up another relevant etymological insight. "Atmosphere" is certainly an important term to consider, given that light from our sun and the farther distant stars makes its way through the earth's atmosphere before reaching our eyes. "Atmosphere" derives from the Sanskrit word *atman,* which signifies not only "air" and "breath" but also "soul." This relationship has a parallel with other words, including "psyche" (which stems from the ancient Greek, meaning "breath" as well as "mind"), "animate" (derived from another Greek term meaning "wind"), and "aspire" and "inspire" (from the Latin, meaning "to breathe" as well as "spirit"). Another ancient language, Hebrew, offers a word, *ruach,* with a similar dual significance: "wind" and "spirit."[5] Such associations were held by many other cultures, such as the Lakota Sioux and Navajo peoples of North America.[6]

Well before our industrially advanced and technologically savvy era, a link between invisible air, the mind, and animate, respiring life was accepted as fact by people around the world. Their languages—the roots of our language—suggest that they were aware of a subtle, almost ineffable quality to the atmosphere. Today we may scoff at this notion, brushing it off as an outdated anthropological artifact, or we may choose to examine it further. I believe the latter course is warranted, given the vast amount of sensory information that acts on our minds via the medium of the air and, more fundamentally, the force of electromagnetism. Just as the brain and the body are increasingly appreciated as aspects of our unified mind, we would do well to reappraise our *selves* in light of that most universal influence on all life.

A Short Lesson

The place to start is with an overview of electromagnetism. It is, simply put, the force that acts between charges and magnets. It is also one of four elemental dynamics at work in the universe, the other three being the "strong force" (which holds particles together in the atomic nucleus and, at a deeper level, holds quarks together in a particle), the "weak force" (responsible for some radioactive decay processes), and gravity (the force of attraction that one piece of matter exerts on another).[7]

Matter itself is made up of atoms. Although atoms are composed of numerous smaller particles (such as electrons), the atom itself is the smallest unit of matter that retains its distinctive identity as a chemical element. The electrons in the atom, which orbit the nucleus, move in orbits at certain well-specified distances from the nucleus—a feature famously discovered by physicist Neils Bohr. An input of energy is required for electrons to move from a lower to a higher orbit, that is, to overcome the attractive force exerted on the electron by the nucleus. Conversely, if an electron moves from a higher to a lower orbit, there will be an excess, or discharge, of energy.[8]

Energy is constantly being exchanged because the constituents of matter are continually interacting with one another. When combinations of atoms collide, electrons are rearranged, moving into higher or lower orbits.[9] If the former, energy is *absorbed*. If the latter, energy is *emitted*. In either case, the difference in energy leaves the atom in the form of a photon. Such is the process by which an atom emits light and other forms of electromagnetic radiation.[10]

Visible light, radio waves, microwaves, and X-rays are all examples of electromagnetic radiation. Such radiation differs only in its wavelength, although this difference is considerable. For example, AM radio waves are hundreds of miles long, while microwaves are a matter of inches. Going farther along the electromagnetic spectrum (figure 6), infrared radiation is measured in wavelengths of thousandths of an inch, ultraviolet radiation in wavelengths of a few hundred atoms, and gamma radiation

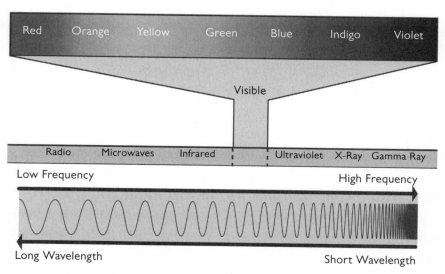

Figure 6. The electromagnetic spectrum.
Image provided by Eric Scafetta Design & Illustration.

in waves that span just one atom or less.[11] The frequency of a wave, by the way, is inversely related to its length. The shorter the wavelength, the higher the frequency, and the longer the wavelength, the lower the frequency.

The electromagnetic spectrum corresponds to a spectrum of energy as well. The shorter the wavelength, the more energy is being emitted. So, red light is the least energetic in the visible spectrum, while blue-violet is the most.[12]

The color of light we perceive depends, as you might imagine, on the wavelength—at least for starters. The longest wavelength our eyes apprehend is red, while the shortest is blue-violet. (Light that contains all wavelengths in equal proportion appears white.) Many other factors, though, are involved. The light entering our eyes triggers a complex chemical reaction in the retina, which translates to physiological processing in the rest of the eye, along with the consequent interpretation of nerve signals by the brain. So color perception turns not just on the radiation coming from *out there* but also on one's own cognitive capacities and even state of mind.[13]

Furthermore, we see colors based on light being absorbed and then reemitted *by the given material*. If two materials that are both illuminated by sunlight—let's say brick and grass—are differently colored, it's because the light being reflected by their atoms is a particular wavelength. We don't see the wavelengths of sunlight that are absorbed by their atoms, only those reemitted. This reflected light, as processed by our eyes and brains, is what gives the brick its orange-red quality and the grass its green.[14] The color of the given material is characteristic of the atoms that make it up, because each atom can only absorb and reemit certain energies based on the defined orbits of its electrons.[15]

Other parts of the body besides the eyes are involved in detecting electromagnetic radiation. When something is hot, for example, the atoms in it are moving around very rapidly. (The relative movement of the atoms is known as *kinetic energy*. Hot materials have more kinetic energy than cold materials, because the atoms of the latter are moving more slowly.)[16] When your hands feel heat being emitted, say from a stove, they are actually absorbing infrared radiation, the energy of which speeds up the movement of atoms in your hand—and your brain interprets the sensation as heat.[17] Your skin is likewise an effective detector of ultraviolet radiation, as a bad sunburn will attest.[18]

Electricity and Magnetism

Let's take a look now at the two components of the term "electromagnetism," beginning with the latter. We know that when electrons jump down into lower orbits within an atom, energy will be discharged. If the resulting charges are pushed through a wire, what results is what we call electric current—whenever electric current is flowing, a magnetic field is produced. The greater the current through a loop of wire (and, for that matter, the more loops there are), the stronger the magnetic field. The loop itself is an *electromagnetic circuit.*[19]

The relationship works in reverse, too. If you move a magnet near a loop of wire, an electric current will flow in the loop. Most electricity in our society is actually generated through this latter process, known as electromagnetic induction. In an electrical generator, some source of energy (e.g., burning coal, falling water) is used to make a shaft rotate. The spinning shaft is attached to a loop of electrical wire between the poles of a magnet, and the fact that the loop is spinning in a magnetic field means an electrical current will be produced in it. This current is then tapped and run through power lines, eventually coming into your house to run your lights, your stereo system, and the rest of your appliances.[20]

It should be noted that the sodium electricity produced in the cells of the body (see chapter 4) is different than the process outlined above.[21] *Externally produced* electrical charge is a basic property of matter. Think of a time you scuffed your feet on the carpet: static electricity was produced. The rubbing motion pulled electrons out of the carpet (which became negatively charged) and into your body (which became positively charged or, colloquially, "received a jolt").[22] The electricity "out there" undeniably produces an effect "in here."

Reversing the perspective, the energy produced by the brain and the heart extends outside the body. It can be measured by devices such as electrocardiographs (ECGs), magnetocardiographs (MCGs), and magnetoencephalographs (MEGs). Thus, electromagnetism is very much a two-way street. The ability of organisms to perceive electromagnetic energy—and the ways we might *interact* with that energy—shall attract our attention as we proceed.

Sensory Processing

Human beings, so far as we know, are unable to consciously perceive most forms of electromagnetic radiation because the frequencies, which are beyond those of visible light, fall outside the range of our sensory apparatus. (It should be added that such tuners as radios, TVs, and X-ray telescopes have effectively extended our sense of vision and hearing.) But suppose Guy Murchie, the author we met in chapter 1, is correct and humans possess a radiation sense that, at least theoretically, encompasses an ability to register electromagnetic radiation that lies *outside* of the normal range?

This might not be terribly far-fetched given that many of our fellow creatures seem to possess a radiation sense exceeding—or at least differing from—our own. For instance, evidence suggests that loggerhead turtles, which accomplish prodigious migratory journeys of thousands of miles, have an innate ability to perceive the direction and strength of the earth's magnetic field.[23] Furthermore, scientists have identified a molecule (found in the eyes of migratory birds) that seems to have the necessary structural and chemical features to serve as a veritable compass. The molecule reacts—under laboratory conditions, at least—to very weak magnetic fields, suggesting that the Earth's magnetic field lines might be plainly visible to these birds, like the dashed line in the middle of a road is to us.[24]

Certain of our fellow humans could conceivably draw on such an exceptional ability to process incoming stimuli. Consider the account of a reputable neuropsychologist concerning one of his patients. The man had come for a consultation because he was convinced that he could feel cell phone transmissions in his head—and the sensation was driving him crazy. The man's wife and all his previous doctors suspected he *was* crazy, but the neuropsychologist arranged a test. He had his assistant phone him sporadically during his meeting with the patient, in order to gauge if the patient would be disturbed by the calls. The patient *did* notice them, allegedly down to the second the calls were placed.[25] Another published anecdote suggests that a man could receive AM radio broadcasts through his teeth.[26] And some individuals literally hear radar as buzzes or hisses.[27]

Although sound is a form of vibration rather than electromagnetic radiation, it has been suggested that very low frequency sound (also known as infrasound, defined as having a frequency less than 20 Hz or cycles per second[28]) can cause feelings of anxiety and depression—even physical illness—in certain hypersensitive people. Dizziness, middle ear pain, respiratory difficulties, shivering, and nausea have all been reported. The effects of infrasound allegedly can also go beyond this: some people report the disturbing feeling of a presence nearby or even glimpse an apparition. These people may, concurrently, feel that their bodies are cold or that the room has gone cold.[29]

One such account was provided by a British engineer, the late Vic Tandy. Based on his profession and his native logic, he was skeptical on first hearing, in the 1980s, a report that his company's laboratory might be haunted. The report came from the onsite cleaning woman, a person who'd worked there many years and whom Tandy describes as "dependable . . . hardworking . . . and not easily flustered." Yet she literally ran into Tandy one night as she was bolting out of the lab. Pale and obviously distressed, she announced that she had seen a ghost. One evening the next week, working late at his desk, Tandy himself witnessed an apparition there, preceded by the palpable yet indistinct feeling of a presence. Although every bit the methodical engineer, he found himself panicked, sweating, and with his hairs standing on end. There was, he relates, "a cold chill and slight movement in my peripheral vision. Very slowly, this movement began to resolve into a grey figure that moved as if approaching me from behind and to my left. It was indistinct but moved as a person might. . . . As I sat up and turned, the apparition faded away. Nothing was out of place and, apart from my physical condition, it was as if nothing had happened."[30]

Attributing this experience to overimagination or overexertion, Tandy returned the next day and put a blade into a vice on a workbench. As he did so, he noticed the blade begin to move up and down. Fighting the panic this aroused, he considered that "there might be some energy involved in what I was seeing." He conducted a quick experiment, pulling out the blade and slowing moving it along the floor in an effort to ascertain where in the room the vibration would be greatest. The peak occurred "right next to the desk where I had been sitting the night before." The variation in movement suggested to him "the presence of a standing wave" of sound. Interestingly, the laboratory was of an odd configuration—30 feet long by 10 feet wide—as it had been constructed from two garages placed back to back. Taking these dimensions into account, Tandy proceeded to calculate the likely frequency of the wave at 18.98 Hz, which is within the infrasonic range.[31] Next, he sought to identify the source of the sound. This turned out to be relatively simple: a new exhaust fan had been installed in the basement just one week earlier. It was not only an odd collection of parts but was also so large "it would make the average office fan look like a toy."[32] The fan produced a huge excess of energy since, despite its size, the air movement was rather small. Switching the fan off had a curious result, as Tandy recalls. "[It] gave the laboratory a much lighter feeling. . . . It could almost be described as the feeling one gets when the windows to a stuffy room are opened. The stuffy feelings are not all that apparent until they are relieved." In contrast, when the fan was running it seemed to engender an "oppressive" feeling.[33]

In another case that Tandy presents—that of Coventry University's Information Center—people have reported "an intense feeling of presence" along with "a strange chill to the atmosphere." These people typically exhibit symptoms of intense fear, including pale complexion, goose bumps, chills, and feeling rooted to the spot. Interestingly, not everyone who visits the Center reports such feelings. At least some of the tour guides, who are quite familiar with the premises, do not.[34] This is significant, I believe. Differences in individual neurobiology are undoubtedly at work.

Stepping back, there are two striking commonalities among these reports. First is the feeling of fear: either of being "frozen" or of wanting to flee in a panic. In the previous chapter, we looked at the freeze response and its neurobiological consequences. In the next chapter, we will look more fully at fear in the context of anomalous experience. For now, I simply wish to note that a feeling of fear is paramount and suggest that it may not entirely owe to what we would expect logically, that is, that someone sensing an invisible presence will panic out of not being able to identify the source of the perceived threat. Undoubtedly the "not knowing" triggers anxiety—how could it not?—but the remarkable degree of fear relates to something else, I suspect. That "something else" is *outside the individual.*

The second commonality supports this proposition. In the lab, Tandy sensed a grey figure that seemed to creep up on him from behind. The color and apparent movement were identical to what the cleaning woman reported. Now, we might infer that, having listened to her story earlier, Tandy unconsciously lent these very characteristics to the locus of infrasound he encountered. That is surely a reasonable interpretation. He himself acknowledges that "fear needs a focus. . . . I knew something [in the room] was clearly wrong and was desperately seeking an explanation. . . . [I] had the cleaner's description of the apparition in my mind."[35] By the same token, I am struck by the similarity of reports from Coventry's Information Center, which hosts many foreign visitors unlikely to know of its reputation.[36] They describe apprehensions (in both senses of the term) and physical symptoms that take place *in exactly the same location:* the entrance to a cellar doorway. Tandy took measurements at the site designed to ascertain the frequency of the hypothesized infrasound. He came up with 19 Hz—a figure remarkably close to the level measured at his own company's lab.[37]

The recurring colors (typically white or gray) perceived by certain people in these situations suggest to me some sort of electromagnetic activity. Likewise, the similarity of description concerning shape, location, and movement indicates an external environmental source that, nonetheless, is interacting with the individual. My supposition is that the sources of infrasound—whether an appliance, a motor, or whatever—are effectively *tuners or amplifiers* rather than the ultimate cause of the discomfort.

Furthermore, the dimensions of any allegedly haunted space, along with the resonance of its walls, floor, and ceiling, presumably contribute to this tuning. I have noted in some of my own "site visits" that the rooms in question were elongated, like Tandy's lab, or jumbled, highly ornamented, or painted in garish colors. Possibly these aspects of a space are not only responsible for the overall ambience but also play a role in the operation of physical forces within.

A Place in the Sun

Let us now move outward, from a consideration of rooms and individuals, locations and neurobiologies, to a wider slant, namely the earth we inhabit and the sun that animates it.

Very simply, the earth is a magnet. As it rotates, its core of liquid iron rotates with it; this motion is believed to give rise to the earth's magnetic field. Whenever you see a compass needle pointing north, you are witnessing a force whose origin goes to the very heart of our planet.[38]

The sun, too, has a magnetic field. It is believed that, as the sun rotates, the motion of charged particles in its interior gives rise to its magnetic field.[39] And while the earth's magnetic field has been known to reverse polarity every so often (at least three hundred such reversals have taken place over several hundred million years), the sun's magnetic field seems to reverse itself every eleven years. The reasons are not well understood. It does seem, however, that sunspots are consequences of magnetic storms and magnetic phenomena under the sun's surface. These spots go through an eleven-year cycle, waxing and waning along with the magnetic field.[40]

The shining of the sun is, of course, its emission of electromagnetic radiation in the form of visible light. Beyond its heat and light—which, indeed, make life on Earth possible—the sun, like any star, effuses an extraordinary amount of gamma ray, X-ray, and ultraviolet radiation. This "solar wind" normally streams toward the earth at about one million miles an hour. Fortunately, Earth's own magnetic field extends out in space approximately forty thousand miles, shielding the planet's life from the deadly effects of these emissions. (This protective region is called the magnetosphere.) Especially energetic solar storms, however, can shoot billions of tons of highly charged atomic particles toward our planet at speeds of more than two million miles an hour. The effects range from beautiful displays of the aurora borealis in the skies above the Northern Hemisphere to the disruption of satellites (knocking out radio and TV transmissions) and the creation of electrical surges (overwhelming transformers and causing blackouts).[41]

Additionally, the earth is constantly being bombarded by cosmic rays generated by the sun and other stars. At this very moment, particles from these showers are passing through your body at the rate of about three a minute.[42]

Electromagnetic radiation is also produced by our own planet. High in the ionosphere, electrical storms rage; perhaps three or four thousand such storms are directing lightning all over the globe at any given moment.[43] Much lower down, the soil itself continually emits electrically charged particles (ions) into the air. On a clear, sunny day, the earth will have a negative charge and the atmosphere a positive charge, so that these electrons stream skyward from the soil and from plant life. But during stormy weather, the polarities are reversed, with the earth becoming positive and the bottom of the cloud base negative.[44]

Atmospheric Influences

As shown by the foregoing examples, the Earth's atmosphere conducts a good deal of electromagnetic radiation, whether in the form of visible light, ultraviolet rays, cosmic rays, lightning, or ions emitted from the ground itself. So it should come as no surprise that, just as some individuals are especially sensitive to inaudible infrasound, certain people are affected by other atmospheric influences. Have you heard of seasonal affective disorder (SAD), otherwise known as the "winter blues"? It's been the subject of growing attention, affecting as it does women more so than men and people in northern latitudes more than southern. Susceptibility to SAD may also be conditioned by heredity. It's logical that light should figure prominently in its treatment, with the use of special light boxes growing in places like Seattle.[45]

Other people are known to feel poorly before a thunderstorm breaks. The buildup of positive ions in the air is believed to raise levels of neurotransmitter serotonin in the bloodstream, bringing on such symptoms as irritability, nausea, blurred vision, and headache.[46]

Of relevance here is that a variety of creatures—ranging from dogs and cats to goats, chickens, horses, possums, rats, deer, elephants, cattle, and even the birds and the bees—are said to become agitated before natural disasters such as earthquakes, volcanoes, avalanches, and tidal waves.[47] Well-documented observations come from two recent disturbances, namely the earthquake and consequent tsunami that devastated East Asia in December 2004 and the tremor that struck Kobe, Japan, in January 1995.[48] One scientist in Japan thought it strange that, before the latter event, "so many earthworms dug themselves up in my small garden." Many of his neighbors noticed the same thing. He did not know, at the time, about the folktales concerning the meaning of a large number of emerging earthworms.[49] In fact, legends concerning odd behavior of a variety of animals—including earthworms—go back centuries.[50]

After the Kobe quake, this geophysicist, the late Dr. Motoji Ikeya, made it a point to study such evidence to determine if animal behavior can serve as an early warning system. He found that catfish were especially useful for this purpose.[51] His consequent book, *Earthquakes and Animals: From Folk Legends to Science,* proposes a new field of study: electromagnetic seismology. Ikeya offers an electromagnetic model for why animals may act peculiarly before a natural disaster, namely, that they are sensing electrical changes in the air. Neurotransmitters may be affected, and their body hair (if they have any) may also react. Ikeya points to his work with rats, which showed changes in blood plasma and brain fluid in response to a rock compression experiment simulating a seismic event.[52]

Such fracturing, deep in the earth, is presumed to cause changes in the polarity and concentration of airborne ions—the same source theorized for why certain people feel anxious before a thunderstorm.[53] Others have suggested that animals literally feel vibrations in the Earth itself or that they are reacting to gas released prior to a quake.[54]

Infrasound has also been nominated as the source of the animals' reactions. A number of animal species can hear below the 20 Hz threshold that distinguishes the lower limit of human hearing, among them elephants, hippos, giraffes, rhinos, whales, and alligators. Because infrasound can travel vast distances unimpeded by land, air, or water, it is thought that these animals are capable of carrying on long-distance communication.[55] Elephants, for example, are believed to pick up infrasonic messages through the ground courtesy of receptors in their feet;[56] this ability "can be noticed by the sudden reaction to lift their head from drinking, bathing, or eating, and act in a peculiar fashion."[57] The author of a book on this phenomenon, naturalist Katy Payne of Cornell University, first intuited what might be happening based on her reaction while standing near an elephant cage at the zoo one day and feeling a peculiar "throb and flutter" in the air. It reminded her of the deep bass notes she experienced as a girl in church—and a new research tack was born.[58]

Perhaps, one might speculate, Payne herself is especially sensitive. Or she might simply be expert at putting two and two together. In any event, numerous survivors of the 2004 Indian Ocean tsunami have suggested that not just elephants but many other species must have an infrasonic or similar early warning capacity since virtually no animal remains were found in the aftermath of the disaster—in contrast with the roughly two hundred thousand human bodies. In many cases, such as with elephants, the animals were observed fleeing to higher ground or (in the case of dolphins) moving out to sea.[59] Since infrasonic waves are produced by numerous kinds of natural disturbances—volcanoes, earthquakes, tornadoes, avalanches, hurricanes, and other sea storms—such ability would have an obvious evolutionary benefit.[60]

Other researchers aren't so sure. They point out that animals react to so many things—hunger, predators, mating cues—that determining if they are on the receiving end of any form of advance notice is nearly impossible.[61] It's also germane that the Chinese, who suffer many earthquakes and so have devoted themselves to this subject, have found that not every event seems to elicit unusual animal behavior. Furthermore, the anecdotes people report could predominantly reflect a *human* tendency: namely contributing significance to things that people would never have remembered or remarked upon absent a disaster.[62]

Still, it's well worth considering that human beings, at least in some extraordinary cases, could share forms of sensitivity that appear at first to be solely the province of our animal cousins. We might find that, just as every corner of the earth teems with life, the atmosphere, too, hosts a multitude of messages, although they remain unseen to our eyes. One researcher, emboldened by the vistas now opening up on infrasonic capacities in the animal kingdom, exclaims, "There is this unseen world out there. . . . I want people to know it exists."[63] It just might.

Audible Auroras

One intriguing example comes from the far north. Some people seem to have an unusual reaction to that most spectacular of all atmospheric displays, the aurora borealis, also known as the northern lights. Over centuries—and still documented today—a noise described as a hissing, swishing, rustling, or crackling has been reported in connection with the northern lights. Tales of spirits and spirit voices also abound in the myths of native people living in Alaska and northern Canada in conjunction with this phenomenon.[64] The sounds have been recorded and are the subject of ongoing investigation and theory.

Interestingly, the noise is not evident to everyone witnessing an aurora. One person might hear the popping and whooshing clearly while another, standing just a few yards away, hears nothing.[65] The explanation presumably owes to something other than imagination because several people have reported hearing auroral noise before seeing the display itself.

Four main explanations have been offered for this fascinating phenomenon.

1. The electrical nature of auroras (remember the charged particles of the solar wind) induces a discharge in objects on the ground, so that long, dry grass, frozen pine needles, and bushes literally crackle. This is known as the "brush discharge" theory.[66]

2. The people who hear auroral noise are not hearing anything that's actually originating from the outside environment; instead, they are getting their sensory signals crossed, with visual input from these spectacular atmospheric displays somehow translated into sound. There is precedent for this in the condition known as synesthesia, in which the senses overlap. People with synesthesia will see a color associated with a sound, or taste a shape, or experience other interesting combinations.[67] The possibility of sensory crossover is further implied by anecdotes that auroras may be accompanied by a sulfurous smell.[68]

3. Some as yet unknown mechanism is causing certain people to literally hear the electromagnetic radiation present in the form of auroras.[69] Here it may be relevant that women and young people evidently report the sounds more often than older people or men. If true, auroral noise—assuming it is literally heard—may turn out to be at the high-frequency end of the human hearing range.[70] On the other hand, professor Colin Keay at the University of Newcastle in Australia suggests that very low frequency (VLF) radio waves (i.e., radiation with a frequency between 3-30 kHz)[71] could be responsible. Such waves could become audible, he theorizes, through a person's hair or eyeglasses, which would serve as a sort of transducer, as could nearby brush.[72]

4. While it has never been proposed as a direct explanation, the fact is that auroras produce infrasound. Increased pressure resulting from electricity high up in the ionosphere causes air movement like that of a bow wave off of a ship. Geophysicists have recorded the infrasound thus created.[73] Since this sound is inaudible to human ears—by definition—it cannot be what people purport to hear. Nevertheless, there could be some kind of correlation.

It may be that no single theory adequately explains all cases of auroral noise, that various explanations apply when different cases or individuals are concerned. I wonder, though, whether the pronounced electromagnetic nature of auroras allows a parallel to be drawn with "haunted" locations where electromagnetic anomalies are so often recorded.[74] It is not only the general location of a haunt that is associated with electromagnetic variations; most often a particular *part* of the place (as in Tandy's examples) is implicated through both recurring ghost reports and on-site measurements.[75] While sound is not a form of electromagnetic radiation, I am yet intrigued by the anxious, unsettled, even sorrowful feelings reported by individuals exposed to infrasound—feelings that seem to have an analogue in the cautionary tales of the Eskimos attributing auroral sounds to "departed souls."[76] Ought we to write off such correlations as nothing more than coincidence, and the tales of people in northern latitudes as solely superstition? Before doing so, I believe that further appraisal of the mind-atmosphere interface will prove fruitful.

Temporal Lobe Lability

One prominent researcher looking into the likely overlap between natural forces and anomalous perception is Michael Persinger of Laurentian University in Ontario, Canada. His work focuses on electromagnetism's effects within the brain, particularly in the temporal lobes. Persinger proposes that some people have high temporal lobe lability; that is, they are prone to tiny, epileptic-like seizures. (The condition is also known as temporal lobe epilepsy.) This may come about, he suggests, if a person has been exposed to excessive amounts of electromagnetic radiation, either from man-made or natural sources. Such exposure lowers the amount of melatonin, a hormone secreted by the brain's pineal gland that induces sleep at night. Since melatonin is also an anticonvulsant, a deficiency of it will raise the chance of microseizures, especially in the right temporal lobe.[77]

Individuals who have high temporal lobe lability are, in Persinger's estimation, more artistic and more anxious than the general population, as well as more disposed toward anomalous perception. He speculates that electromagnetic radiation of extremely low frequency (i.e., waves with a frequency less than 3 kHz)[78] in the earth's atmosphere, acting via the pineal gland, influences the temporal lobes, producing feelings of flying, floating, or being out of the body, along with the sensation of voices, shadowy presences, and full-fledged apparitions.[79] Since the hippocampus (the brain's memory center) and the amygdala (its emotional sentinel) are located just below the temporal lobes, Persinger suspects that remembered images and feelings must be brought into play and misinterpreted as real.[80] When people have lost someone especially close to them—when they are bereaved—they are especially susceptible, he surmises.[81] The result is that vivid images of the loved one may well up that are indistinguishable from reality. And due to the drop-off in overnight melatonin, they will be woken up by these very apparitions.[82]

Persinger is also intrigued by geomagnetism, which examines the magnetic consequences of seismic activity beneath the earth's surface. He proposes that increased geomagnetic activity can induce temporal lobe microseizures just as atmospheric radiation can.[83] Tectonic stress, he has written, could elicit feelings of dread and the physical accompaniments of goose bumps and hair standing on end. He even ventures that poltergeist effects could be attributable to geomagnetic activity, with objects being levitated or thrown around depending on the magnitude and direction of the geomagnetic force. In support of this notion, Persinger and his associates have gathered evidence that both hauntings and poltergeists tend to manifest at times of high geomagnetic activity.[84] A team at the University of Iowa, working independently, affirmed this finding based on its own statistical analysis.[85] (A connection was also found between the solar wind and hallucinations,[86] although another Persinger study suggests that some types of anomalous perception correlate with *low* magnetic activity.[87])

Magnetic Pulses on the Brain

Much credit should go to Persinger for having the courage not only to theorize in so novel a way but also to actually test his assertions. In his lab, he aims magnetic pulses at the temporal lobes of volunteers to find out whether, and how often, haunt-type perceptions are produced. Sitting in a comfortable chair in a soundproof chamber, subjects put on an unwieldy looking helmet bedecked with electromagnetic circuits. The results, from more than a decade of research, indicate that magnetic fields do indeed produce curious perceptions (e.g., a felt presence, a sense of flying or floating) in a high percentage of people: 80 percent of the approximately one thousand people tested.[88] This is not to suggest that 80 percent of the population has high temporal lobe lability, but rather to show that magnetic fields have discernable effects on the individual. No other researchers have yet corroborated Persinger's data, however.[89]

Persinger is as open to the possibility that people with high temporal lobe lability are accessing "actual information that's in the environment" as he is to the possibility that the magnetic bursts to which they're exposed are producing figments of their imagination.[90]

My supposition is that both paths are not only possible, but taken by different people depending on their inherited neurobiology, their degree of sensitivity to external *and* internal stimuli, their life experiences, and the way in which they typically process the energy associated with feeling. To begin to tease out the strands, let's call on the testimony of consciousness researcher (and former parapsychologist) Susan Blackmore, who visited Persinger's lab circa 1990. Despite her avowed skepticism, she found her own experience highly unsettling:

> I was wide awake throughout. Nothing seemed to happen for the first ten minutes or so. . . . Then it felt for all the world as though two hands had grabbed my shoulders and were bodily yanking me upright. I knew I was still lying in the reclining chair, but someone, or something, was pulling me up. Something seemed to get hold of my leg and pull it, distort it, and drag it up the wall. I felt as though I had been stretched halfway up to the ceiling.
>
> Then came the emotions. Totally out of the blue, but intensely and vividly, I suddenly felt angry—not just mildly cross but that clear-minded anger out of which you act—but there was nothing

and no one to act on. After perhaps ten seconds, it was gone. Later, it was replaced by an equally sudden attack of fear. I was terrified—of nothing in particular.[91]

Two aspects in Blackmore's account strike me as especially note-worthy. First, she experienced highly convincing sensations and feelings, despite their not being prompted by any real physical attacks or emo-tional insults in the outside world. This gives credence to the idea that at least some bereavement apparitions, for example, can seem entirely real but remain just that: apparitions. (Moving observations to this effect are, sadly, available through the comments of those who have lost a child or sibling in the current Iraq War.[92]) Second, generalized feelings of fear and anger suddenly arose in Blackmore's mind. This is rather different than the effect produced by other experimenters who have stimulated particu-lar parts of the brain during surgery. In such cases (we shall survey them momentarily), the patients recalled images and feelings associated with particular people and events. This, I submit, bears considerably more sim-ilarity to haunts where people see or hear a lifelike individual—clothed in period garb, no less—and report fairly definite felt impressions.

Tapping into the Brain

Several experimenters before Persinger have stimulated subjects' temporal lobes and elicited a wide variety of feelings and images. For whatever rea-son, these researchers (Persinger included) have tended to be Canadian.

The first and most prominent was Montreal neurosurgeon Wilder Penfield. In 1933, while operating on a conscious patient who had epilep-tic seizures, Penfield applied an electrical stimulus to the temporal cortex and evoked what he took to be a vivid memory—much to his and the patient's surprise. During a subsequent surgery, one patient whose lobes were stimulated heard a tune being played and thought it was the radio. Another patient recalled his mother telephoning. Penfield believed he was summoning exact "playbacks" and noted that his patients perceived them less as memories than as reexperiences of the original event.[93]

Some thirty years later, an associate of Penfield's, neurologist José Delgado, along with colleagues at the Yale University School of Medicine, conducted a similar experiment. His conclusion, however, was different. Delgado believed that the patient was experiencing memories associated with what she had been speaking about, thinking about, or unconsciously tapping into immediately before the electrical stimulus. This patient did not believe she was reexperiencing events; instead, she was puzzled and sometimes frightened by the intrusion of unbidden words and voices, which were experienced as anomalous.[94] (Persinger draws on this theory to explain why people with temporal lobe lability are apt to see apparitions of their loved ones: he believes it is because they are thinking about them, either consciously or unconsciously, before they go to sleep.[95])

Further progress was made in the 1980s by another experimenter, the late Pierre Gloor of the Montreal Neurological Institute, in his work with patients who had temporal lobe epilepsy. Gloor's team found that the perceptions evoked depended on stimulation of limbic structures, particularly the amygdala and hippocampus. The phenomena produced included visual and auditory hallucinations, memory flashbacks, déjà vu, and emotions (predominantly fear).[96] One patient whose amygdala was stimulated "had seizures that started with a feeling of intense fear. . . . She let out a terrifying scream and her facial expression and bodily gestures were those of someone having a horrifying experience . . . the seizures started in the limbic structures of the right temporal lobe, particularly the amygdala. . . . In addition to this fear, the patient had a feeling of someone being nearby. She then distinctly saw a person who seemed to be standing in the sun. Upon questioning she identified this person as a former boyfriend."[97]

Another patient exhibited an impressive array of such perceptions but adding a particular smell:

When the right amygdala was stimulated . . . the patient immediately opened his mouth with an astonished look on his face, sat up, and said that . . . it was the feeling of being at a picnic. . . . "A kid was coming up to me to push me into the water. . . ." When questioned, he said that this had been a true event in his life which occurred when he was about eight years old. . . . A "big fellow" had pushed his head under the water at that time.

Later . . . the right amygdala was again stimulated. . . . He again became nauseated, felt that he was somewhere . . . he had been before, and felt that it was dark and raining. He was extremely frightened and pale. . . .

Left amygdaloid stimulation . . . produced an olfactory sensation, "something to do with animals," which the patient claimed he had experienced before.[98]

Gloor and his team found that *limbic structures appear to be key,* whether the feelings and perceptions evoked relate to things that actually happened to the person in the past or are more generalized. In the conclusion to their paper, Gloor and his colleagues adroitly connect the role of the limbic brain with the processing of sensation itself, stating that "whatever we experience with our senses . . . must ultimately be transmitted to limbic structures in order to assume experiential immediacy. Attaching some affective or motivational significance to the [perception] may be the specific limbic contribution. . . . This may be the precondition for the [perception] to be consciously experienced or recalled and may imply that all consciously perceived events must assume some kind of affective dimension, if only ever so slight."[99]

This important insight reflects what Antonio Damasio and other of today's consciousness researchers are beginning to acknowledge—that what we perceive is essentially the *feeling of what is happening to us.* Since we must be sentient (capable of sensory perception) in order to feel, it is the brain's role to sort through sensory input to determine what is paramount, what should be acted on, what should be ignored, and what should be transiently noted and filed away. The limbic circuitry of the brain is involved in sifting through such perceptions and assigning shades of feeling to them. The type and degree of feeling equates to the remembered meaning for the individual.

The Brain as Filter

Let's return to Persinger's conjecture that people with high temporal lobe lability, at least in some cases, might be tapping into information that is actually emanating from the environment.

Biologically, the function of the nervous system—of which the brain is the pinnacle—is to cull the most meaningful information from the environment. Our sensory organs are like slits, allowing in a limited range of frequencies among the span of electromagnetic radiation and sound waves that would otherwise inundate us. Our brains ultimately process only what our bodies and nerves deem relevant.[100]

Here's a down-to-earth analogy. Think back on the last crowded party you attended. Once or twice in the overall buzz of conversation, you heard your name being mentioned or something being said about you from a corner of the room. Although you were engaged in your own conversation, this mention of you stood out: you perceived it amid the din. Another example will be familiar to parents, especially mothers, who find themselves being awakened by a faint cry from their child in another room, while otherwise sleeping placidly through the muffled sound of traffic or, perhaps, late-night television.[101]

In both of these cases, our nervous systems are drawing attention to the most meaningful information. That information, of course, need not only be external. If you're in the middle of a conversation, say, and you suddenly feel a pain or remember an assignment you missed or something else you should be doing, you are being alerted to meaningful *internal* information. The principle is the same, though. One's internal and external milieus are constantly being filtered and appraised.

The limbic portion of the brain specializes in tagging sensory input (and recollected sensory input, or memories) with the appropriate shade and intensity of feeling. As Gloor and his colleagues surmised, this form of processing is required for anything we sense to gain experiential immediacy, to be perceived as relevant in any way, shape, or form. The relevance may be conscious or it may lurk about as unconscious. However, it always has an affective dimension.

Electromagnetic Sensitivity?

Human beings specialize in taking in the visible part of the electromagnetic spectrum. As Carl Sagan put it, "We're visible light chauvinists. That's the only kind of light to which our eyes are sensitive." But, he conjectured, "if our bodies could transmit and receive radio waves, early humans might have been able to communicate with each other over great distances; if X-rays, our ancestors might have peered usefully into the hidden interiors of plants, people, other animals, and minerals."[102]

Now, let's suppose that some individuals *can* apprehend electromagnetic radiation or other conveyors of information outside of the normal range. Recall the man who could allegedly feel cell phone transmissions, the people and animals who are manifestly affected by infrasound, or the people who possibly hear auroras. One suggestion is that the pineal gland (which we met before—it produces melatonin) may sense geomagnetism.[103] This tiny, pinecone-shaped structure near the middle of the brain has long inspired fanciful theories. Anatomists long ago thought it might be a valve that controlled the flow of memories into consciousness.[104] Rene Descartes, the influential seventeenth-century thinker, proposed that it must be the seat of the soul, based on its location deep in the head and due to its having no apparent division into left and right sides as most other brain structures do. (With the advent of microscopes, this observation turned out to be incorrect.)[105] It is true that lower-vertebrate animals have pineal-like structures that bear a strong resemblance to the photoreceptor cells of the human eye. Early in our own evolution, the pineal gland may have been located near the top of the head, where it could have measured light intensity.[106] Its current role as a secretor of melatonin attests to its continuing sensitivity to daylight: melatonin production coincides with nightfall and ceases around dawn.[107]

The late Robert O. Becker, a pioneer in the field of bioelectricity, suggested that the pineal gland may simultaneously sense geomagnetic changes.[108] He pointed out that the beaks of migratory birds contain traces of magnetite, which could allow these creatures to determine the direction of the earth's magnetic field.[109] Magnetite is found in bacteria and protozoa, as well as in mollusks, fish, and birds. It has also been discovered in human brain tissue.[110] Perhaps this betokens a latent human ability to sense geomagnetic information along with the manifest ability to process visible light. In Becker's opinion, it would be no more surprising that "life developed specific organs to sense the geomagnetic field and to derive . . . information from it than that it developed specific organs to sense and derive information from light."[111] Considering that roughly 90 percent of the molecules in the human brain remain to be understood, science may ultimately determine that humans, birds, and other animals have more capacities in common than we thought.[112] Experience has certainly shown that, once an oddball notion is translated into the *demonstrable* and the *quantifiable,* mainstream science can begin to accept it.[113]

More broadly, the radiation sense postulated by Murchie ought to be admitted into the realm of possibility. Let us differentiate, yes, the likely from the blatantly implausible, but let us not exclude by prejudgment, by effectively turning a blind eye or a deaf ear. This would be not only a mistake in principle but also would constitute a huge irony given that our subject here is *sensory* discrimination. The mind ought to be more open.

Light: From Sensed to Spiritual

Let's return now to the concept of atmosphere and its root association with air as well as with the soul. We understand that the invisible air that surrounds us is assuredly not a vacuum. It is the conveyor of electromagnetic radiation. And electromagnetic radiation provides the physical grounding for our ability to sense.[114]

Furthermore, since virtually all the energy employed by life on Earth comes from the sun, it must be said that electromagnetic radiation is the force that animates us. Nothing we know of could exist—let alone bring anything *else* to light—without it.[115] One scholar thus states: "No force other than electromagnetism so fully and intimately permeates and affects our lives and the global ecosystem. It provides the physical means by which humans can in turn sense the wonder of nature."[116]

According to the Bible, God said "Let there be light" and the universe sprang into being. Regardless of your belief in a higher power, the connection between light and creation is strong. According to cosmologists, the infant universe 14 billion years ago was almost incomprehensibly dense, with all of the forces of nature unified and indistinguishable. When the big bang occurred and the universe rapidly expanded, however, those forces—the strong, weak, gravitational, and electromagnetic—separated into the four we know. Today, the echoes of the Big Bang can be observed in the faint cosmic background of microwave radiation, an imprint still extant across the universe.[117] It can thus be said that electromagnetism not only connects creatures tangibly with one another via the sensed world but with their common origin in deep space and time.

This is why, I propose, the word "atmosphere" is bound in the lexicon with more spiritual terms connoting both breath *and* consciousness. People in ancient times were not wholly ignorant. Indeed, I would argue that, living so close to nature, our forebears were possessed with greater intuitive wisdom concerning the origins of life and mind. For them, the word "atmosphere" could encompass what, for us, are disparate meanings but which in those times were appreciated as varying aspects of the same thing: air, breath, psyche, and soul. The atmosphere might be invisible, but it was surely not empty. Nor could it possibly be devoid of the utmost religious and philosophical significance.

In our own modern culture, light retains an unmistakable symbolic importance. We learn that God spoke to Moses through the burning bush; understand that the halos painted around saints are intended to convey a vivid message; and gather that the Buddha was "enlightened." The concept of enlightenment—of being endowed with surpassing insight or wisdom—is something we still aspire to. In our secular, communal ceremonies, we observe the eternal flame at John F. Kennedy's gravesite and witness the torch being carried every four years to the site of the Olympic Games. Then, too, a still, small candle burning bright or a lighthouse on a rocky promontory are near-universal symbols of hope, radiance, and salvation.[118]

Light is also a recurring motif in near-death experiences (NDEs), which cannot be other than profoundly life shaking and spiritual. Many people who have had them report passing through a long, dark tunnel, which finally opens into the presence of a being of light who exudes unquestioned warmth and love.[119] Individuals who have undergone a mystical experience will similarly attest that they have "come into the light" in an intensely personal, psychophysiological sense.[120]

Light, therefore, is inextricably linked with spirituality and probably has been since the dawn of human consciousness. People have long regarded light as signifying the cosmic source of our animating energy as well as representing a manifest link to other living things.[121] Our ancestors—and indigenous peoples living close to the land today—may also have understood that light carried "messages" to other animals, even if unaware of the electromagnetic spectrum itself or the properties of electromagnetism. What I want to suggest next is that electromagnetic radiation may, under certain circumstances, contain *more* information than our philosophy currently admits.

Electricity: From Outside In

In the last chapter, I postulated that the energy of unexpressed feeling in the body—in tandem with a preoccupation held in the brain—is the flashpoint for anomalous occurrences. "Unrecognized," "dissociated," "dammed up," "insufficiently processed"—all such terms apply to the state of feeling frozen inside. Ghosts, poltergeists, and similar phenomena grow out of this neurobiology, we have considered. But how could such energy migrate, as it were, into the environment, much less be contained there?

One can only surmise that such a phenomenon must bridge the gap between energetic processes in the body that are chiefly biochemical, and the nonorganic electromagnetic radiation that we have been assessing in this chapter. For a start, we know that energy produced by the heart and the brain does extend beyond the body's confines. The amount of such energy, however, hardly approaches the level presumably involved in hauntings. There is yet another factor that may pertain, namely, that ordinary electric current conducts *one thousand times faster* than the brain's nerve cells do.[122] This differential, as we saw in the last chapter, puzzled biochemist Albert Szent-György, who sought to explain the speed and efficiency with which living beings react to their environment and mobilize the energy they require. He suggested that relatively large molecules, like proteins, could act as a semiconductor. (A semiconductor is a material that is neither a pure conductor nor a pure insulator, but in which a sufficient number of electrons are able to move around in response to an external charge, thus allowing electric current to flow through the material. Silicon is the best example of a semiconductor; silicon chips are ubiquitous in computers and other electronic devices.[123]) The larger the molecule, hypothesized Szent-György, the greater the likelihood of its conducting electricity just as a wire does. He further proposed that the space between molecules should itself be able to conduct electricity.[124]

We noted that there is some evidence to support this idea, for example, the way in which bone growth can be stimulated and limbs regenerated through externally applied electrical charge. An especially intriguing experiment took place in 2006, demonstrating that natural electric currents in tissue play a vital role in orchestrating wound healing in the skin by attracting repair cells to damaged areas. Researchers Josef Penninger and Min Zhao even identified the genes that seem to control the process. "We were originally skeptical, but then we realized it was a real effect," comments Penninger. "It's not homeopathy, it's biophysics."[125]

The experiment proceeded from a foundation we are familiar with, namely that cells and tissues function electrochemically, with positively and negatively charged particles flowing across cell membranes. This exchange creates electrical field patterns all over the body. When tissue is wounded, the flow is effectively short-circuited. Penninger and Zhao realized that the resulting alteration is what attracts and guides repair cells to the damaged area.

Here's how it worked. The researchers grew layers of mouse tissues in the lab. After wounding these tissues, they applied varying electrical fields to them, and found they could accelerate or completely halt the healing process, depending on the orientation and strength of the field. Next, they set about determining what genes might be involved. They looked at those known to make repair cells migrate and found that *the genes can be influenced by electric fields.* In one case, when a certain gene was disrupted, the repair cells moved 30 percent faster toward the wound. In another, the cells moved away from the wound. In a third test case, they stayed put.

The idea that the cellular director of all genetic information—DNA itself—conducts electricity is not a new one.[126] To my mind, it raises the intriguing possibility that some people's apparently exceptional sensitivity to electromagnetic radiation could have a genetic basis. But I wish to suggest something additional here. Namely, that the business of our bodymind—which boils down to the sifting of sensory input and consequent endowment of perceptions with feeling—can perhaps export itself to the electromagnetic environment if that environment is somehow conducive to feeling. We have surveyed a sufficient number of examples of people and animals affected in extraordinary ways by electromagnetic radiation (and by sound) that it seems fitting to wonder if, under extraordinary circumstances, the process might work in reverse.

From Inside Out

We don't yet know how the atmosphere might be a conveyance for repressed or dissociated feeling. But I am aware that poltergeist effects, to name the most energetic of all anomalous displays, have repeatedly been observed to decline with distance, indicating that some type of real-world radiation is involved.[127] We previously noted Persinger's theory, which is so far backed by findings, that geomagnetic activity is connected with poltergeists. Circumstantial evidence likewise suggests that electricity is involved in many poltergeist displays (e.g., lights flashing on and off, anomalous bursts of light around a poltergeist agent, tape recorders and video cameras malfunctioning).[128] William Roll, perhaps the world's foremost poltergeist investigator since the 1960s, coined the term "recurrent spontaneous psychokinesis" (RSPK) to connote the consistency that such bizarre effects seem to have from case to case.

Raymond Bayless, another prominent investigator, covered a case in

1980 of particular relevance. He inferred a mechanism very much like that proposed by Colin Keay, two decades later, for how auroral sounds can become audible. To wit:

> The phone and paging systems in a factory went dead or were drowned out by high-frequency sound when a young female worker was present. Her electric typewriter and calculator, and Bayless's own tape recorder also malfunctioned.
>
> The year before, another worker had experienced similar problems in the same setting. In this particular plant, electronic equipment generated strong radio waves and Bayless thought that the two women "modulated radio waves into a form that could be picked up physically on electronic equipment." In other words, the women had become electroacoustic sources which, in combination with the [ambient] electromagnetic energy at the site, caused the phone and paging [systems] to become electroacoustic transducers.[129]

While the general approach taken by both Bayless and Keay is consistent, one salient difference is important to note. In Bayless's conception, the women who were the poltergeist agents are *themselves electromagnetic sources*—or at least relay stations—whereas in Keay's framework for auroral sound, people are *passive receivers* whose clothing or eyeglasses just happen to transduce the externally produced radio waves.

Remarkable cases of RSPK, because they are few and far between, stand out in the parapsychological literature. A similar instance, investigated by Hans Bender in 1967, concerned disturbances to the electrical systems in a lawyer's office. For instance, a host of fluorescent tubes went out, and electricians found that these were almost completely unscrewed and ready to fall. The lawyer's telephone bills were also sky high. One showed that his office had called the automatic time service ninety-six times. He had the dial padlocked, but this made no difference. A young employee, Anne-Marie, was found to be the focal point of the disturbances: they did not occur when she was not in the office. It turned out she had been dismissed from several previous jobs because of similarly strange goings-on.[130]

Let's step back a moment to ask: Could individuals really produce sufficient electromagnetic radiation to begin to account for poltergeist phenomena? While the conventional answer is a resounding no, keep in mind two themes of this book that may be especially apt here. First, the body is a significant player in anomalous experience because the bodymind—not just the brain—is the seat of feeling. Remember that MCG measurements show the heart to be five thousand times more electromagnetically powerful than the brain.[131] Second, people's sensory thresholds differ substantially and so does their characteristic neurobiological processing. (We'll get into this more in chapters 8 and 9.) Thus, I propose that certain individuals may indeed possess the qualifications required for being a bona fide poltergeist agent. These qualifications are, at bottom, *emotional* and *energetic*.

Let's consider the energetic side first. An ingenious experiment conducted in 1990 demonstrated that self-described healers can apparently produce electrical surges of between 4 and 221 volts (the median in this study was 8.3 volts). The duration was not long (the median was 3.6 seconds), but the effect was noteworthy.[132]

It's interesting to relate how the experiment came about. Researchers had come across a mid-nineteenth-century reference to an obscure meditative practice by Tibetan monks in which the monks were electrically insulated while they sat in a dark room in front of a reflective copper wall and beneath a bar magnet. By staring at their image on the wall for periods of time, the monks were said to "develop lucidity." The implication for the late researcher Elmer Green and his colleagues was that an electrostatic charge might have built up in certain of the adepts. They proceeded to devise a procedure by which such effects could be detected.

Three basic types of tests were carried out. In the first type, an electrometer was attached to the meditator's body, while four wall electrometers operated simultaneously. Ten people who meditated regularly were chosen to be monitored during forty-five-minute sessions; during these periods, no electrostatic surge reached the level of 4 volts. In the second type of tests, the meditators were noncontact therapeutic touch practitioners; in contrast to the first group, they were classified as parapsychological "sensitives." These subjects produced the electrostatic surge results noted above. In the third type of test, the noncontact therapeutic touch practitioners actually performed therapy at a distance with patients who had complained of minor ailments such as tennis elbow, lower back pain, and such. Here, the therapist sensitives produced surges of between 4 and 190 volts—and did so more frequently than during solo meditation. In all cases, video cameras were employed to screen out the possibility of a meditator's motion causing an electrical effect. The investigators concluded that the surges were "anomalous because neither we nor our consultants (biomedical engineers, physicists, and physicians) can point to any known psychophysiologic mechanism by means of which high-amplitude voltage surges lasting a few seconds can be generated in the human body."[133] It would obviously be ideal for another team of scientists to try to replicate this experiment and its findings.

Going a bit farther back in the literature—and across continents—a famous Russian RSPK subject, Nina Kulagina, became well known in the early 1970s for, among other things, allegedly having a strong magnetic field around her and, by extending her hands, being able to remotely move small objects placed up to six or seven feet away from her. These observations were made exclusively by Russian researchers and conducted without an ideal set of controls. Subjects like Kulagina, nonetheless, raise the question of whether certain people are truly exceptional when it comes to electromagnetic effects.[134]

Further evidence that individuals might literally exude electricity—and, in turn, be unusually affected by it—is presented in the next chapter. For now, I wish to reiterate that our bodymind operates, first and foremost, on feeling. The relevance to poltergeist phenomena is perhaps best indicated via a startling anecdote reported by Roll. In one particular investigation, the focus of activity was a fourteen-year-old Ohio girl. Her parents had agreed to bring her to a university to conduct tests. By the time the researchers were ready, though, the incidents around her had fallen off. A psychotherapist who had been counseling the girl "suggested that hypnosis might evoke the bodily sensations that had been associated with the events and thereby [reactivate] the events themselves. *This led to a resumption of occurrences.*"[135] [Emphasis mine.]

Roll's conclusion is that RSPK may be an extreme form of normal processes in the bodymind, especially those involving emotion. For most agents, though, "the phenomena seem to be no more conscious than muscle spasms."[136] This is a highly meaningful inference in my estimation. Case researchers, Roll writes, have consistently identified emotional upset as a factor in presumed poltergeist subjects, but aggressive impulses are "directed not at . . . other people but at substitute objects" (i.e., the furnishings and possessions of the individual they are presumably upset with but unable to satisfactorily confront).[137]

It also bears noting that individuals such as Kulagina—assuming her RSPK proclivity to be at all genuine—are consistently observed sweating, hyperventilating, going pale, and becoming hoarse, all of which are indications that the sympathetic branch of their autonomic nervous system is activated and that considerable short-term energy is being marshaled.[138] But to what end? To move a cigarette lighter a few feet away? To bend a spoon? These seem rather trivial tasks to get worked up about, especially for an audience of hardened skeptics who aren't likely to be impressed anyway. My supposition is that the RSPK subject in such demonstrations is being called on to mimic a more genuine, if unconscious, form of feeling. The cigarette lighters, spoons, and so on are merely stand-ins for the people or events deep in the mists of memory that trigger such intense neurobiological arousal.

Roll's study of the Ohio teenager, interestingly enough, disclosed two neural abnormalities: one in the brain stem and another in the right temporal lobe. The girl had suffered a head injury when she was twelve and may, he postulates, have had a lowered threshold for microseizures. As an infant, the unfortunate girl had contracted pneumonia and—to add insult to injury—was abandoned by her birth mother. She was raised by an adoptive family with whom she was living at the time of the alleged disturbances. The activity apparently triggered by her was "regularly attended by headaches and fluttering feelings in [her] stomach," writes Roll.[139]

The conclusion these observations point to is that *the flow of feeling in poltergeist agents is constricted* due to a neurobiology that has been adversely affected by heredity and/or life circumstances. Possibly in conjunction with temporal lobe lability and geomagnetic influences, such a person becomes a generator of electromagnetic radiation or, at least, a transducer for energy in the immediate environment.

In connection with temporal lobe lability, it's worth noting that many presumed poltergeist agents over the years have displayed symptoms suggestive of epilepsy, such as seizures, convulsions, and fainting spells, or have actually been diagnosed as epileptic. Intriguingly, during these subjects' convulsions, the reported RSPK activity *ceased* in several cases.[140] Perhaps the seizure itself throws a monkey wrench, as it were, into the dynamic, much as a sneeze interrupts other, more typical, bodily activity.

Feeling and Electromagnetism

This chapter has documented the myriad ways that electromagnetic radiation, seismic waves, and sound waves affect man and other animals. We have also become acquainted with the evidence that, given a person's particular neurobiology, he or she may effectively displace the energy of repressed feeling into the surroundings.

If such a mechanism exists, it denotes a remarkably intimate interaction between human beings (some of them, in any event) and the atmosphere we live in. Electromagnetic radiation, I conjecture, is *conducive to feeling.* The energy that envelopes us in this universe—or at least some portion of the ambient electromagnetic spectrum—is, as Roll and Persinger put it, "both physical and psychological." Hauntings and other anomalies can then be seen as "physical phenomena with a human face."[141]

The human element is of paramount importance. In the next chapter, we shall delve into the anatomy that sculpts people's anomalous perceptions and return to explain the experiences of the six individuals (Adam, Susan, Mary, Ron, Melanie, and Ruth) and the one group case (the Eastern Airlines L-1011 apparitions) that were discussed in chapter 1.

7

◆

Anatomy of a Crisis

Rush (his real name) is sixteen years old and has just gotten his driver's license. On a summer Saturday night, he and four other guys pile into his best friend's car. He is in the front seat, passenger's side. They go cruising down a country road. Unexpectedly, the car of another friend, also packed with teenagers, passes them going the other way, then slams on its brakes, and does a quick U-turn. The chase is on.

The car Rush is in accelerates down the narrow road, headed toward a curve. Halfway around it, the car veers out of control and off the road toward a high dirt embankment. As he stares out the window, the embankment seems to move toward Rush in slow motion. He's frozen in his seat with an awful sinking feeling in the pit of his stomach, his pulse pounding in his ears. He is vividly aware of every blade of grass on that embankment. Time seems to slow down.

Then, with a loud bang, the car hits the embankment. The vehicle bounces in the air to the other side of the road and comes to a stop. Everyone piles out. Miraculously, no one is hurt. The same cannot be said for the car.[1]

Looking back on that night, Rush Dozier, author of *Fear Itself*, a book exploring the neurobiology of this most basic mammalian feeling, observes:

What I experienced was a classic fear reaction. . . . At that moment, I thought I was going to die. A series of automatic physical changes designed to maximize my chances of survival took place in my body.

Much of my blood was immediately diverted to my large muscles, particularly my legs, so that I would have the maximum energy necessary for a quick escape. . . . Perspiration oozing out of my pale, cool skin produced the sensation of a cold sweat. The pounding I heard was my overwrought heart at work and my skyrocketing blood pressure. Quick-energy hormones like adrenaline were pouring into my bloodstream and muscles. . . . The odd feeling in my stomach was my digestive system contracting and turning off as all non-essential systems shut down in preparation for the escape.

The momentary feeling of being frozen in place is also a characteristic reaction to fear . . . it forces you to concentrate on every possible avenue of escape. This concentration is accompanied by a dramatic sharpening of perception, stimulated by an instant flood of chemicals into the brain. . . . In my case, every detail of my surroundings came so sharply into focus that it seemed unreal. My very perception of time slowed.[2]

All of us harbor similar memories of a dangerous, thrilling, or life-threatening event. I present Dozier's account as an example of a chain of split-second bodymind events that accounts for, I propose, at least some phenomena long regarded as paranormal. By closely examining the dynamics of intense feeling within the bodymind, we may find that a scientifically supportable foundation exists for happenings that come across as surpassingly strange, yet might actually derive from our quintessentially human nature.

Energy in the Body, Preoccupation in the Brain

In chapter 5, I linked together the subjects of energy, electricity, and dissociation in seeking to explain how the bodymind's response to severe stress—at least in people prone to be stoic, unemotional, or unassertive—can produce anomalies. In the face of a life-threatening emergency, a vast amount of energy is summoned, although the person momentarily startles while the brain decides what to do. In the microseconds that a decision is being made, one's entire neurobiology is poised for self preservation—the proverbial fight-or-flight reaction. During these moments, the individual is in freeze frame as his or her feelings (and the energy so constituted) prepare for expression. But if this vortex of energy fails to be adequately discharged, it remains trapped in the nervous system. Traumatic symptoms—ranging from whiplash to PTSD—are among the inevitable results.

The problem is particularly acute if, owing to the extreme shock of a situation (and, likewise, the lack of control over it), conscious investment is withdrawn from the felt sense. People so afflicted come to feel divorced from their own feelings, even from their *ability* to feel. Individuals can carry such calcified energy—and the associated memories and feelings—inside themselves for years. That energy, I've argued, in tandem with issues or preoccupations held in the brain, is responsible for ghosts, poltergeists, and haunts.

Human beings are not only complex creatures but also unified beings whose neurology, physiology, and psychology are connected in myriad ways. When significant energy is held in the body *and* a significant matter is unresolved in the brain, we have what might be called a combustible juxtaposition. Within the brain itself, a given matter may be insufficiently processed between the limbic region, which recognizes feelings, and the prefrontal cortex, which modulates emotional expression and helps us decide, rationally, what is to be done. Such preoccupations effectively reside in a nether region below full consciousness. We may be somewhat aware of a lingering doubt or a nagging concern, but it remains, in a manner of speaking, out of view. When, however, such an issue has as its counterpoint energy that is frozen in the body, an anomalous occurrence is possible, given the appropriate trigger.

In the Nether Region

Let's return for a moment to the physiological activity that results from an alert sounded by the amygdala. The pupils dilate, the muscles tense, the blood supply is increased, and the heart rate and release of perspiration quicken as the sympathetic branch of our autonomic nervous system (ANS) kicks into high gear. Through the glands, hormones (especially adrenaline) are released into the bloodstream. Chemical receptors are activated along the vagus nerve, which runs from the heart (indeed, from most of the internal organs) to the brain. Additionally, neurotransmitters are sent directly into the brain from the brain stem. All this activity takes place unconsciously, before the neocortex has a chance to identify the nature of the emergency (whether life-threatening, joyful, or anything in between) and devise an appropriate response. Daniel Goleman, author of *Emotional Intelligence,* termed this avenue the "low road" of neural processing.[3]

Along the "high road," the neocortex will, a second or two later, assess the information procured from the senses. A cognition will thus form concerning the given situation—and the person's impetus to fight or flee may be modified or countermanded. More complex feelings may take the place of sheer anger or abject fear; these feelings can include sorrow, pity, amazement, relief, regret, embarrassment, frustration, or ambivalence.

When a basic feeling is modified or overridden, the directive comes through the *orbitofrontal cortex.* The variety of biochemical actions that primed the individual for fight or flight will now be ratcheted down as consciousness begins to regain control. Respiration, heartbeat, blood supply, and digestive functioning return to normal. The reservoir of energy amassed seconds before is now emotionally expressed via laughter, tears, sighs, a happy shout, or a scornful protest—as well as actions such as head shaking or foot stomping. (More broadly, zoologist Desmond Morris has observed that human beings "make use of virtually any trivial actions as outlets for our pent-up feelings." He lists such activities as pacing back and forth, tapping on a desk, smoking a cigarette, scratching our head, biting our nails, tugging at a beard or mustache, rubbing our chin, and twirling our hair.[4]) Regardless of how it is expressed, the energy immediately conjured up by our sympathetic nervous system's response to an emergency or surprise must follow the law that energy is conserved in a living system. Ultimately, too, the amygdala's warning light will be reset.

What may *not* be reset, however, is the hypothalamic-pituitary-adrenal (HPA) stress system. The actions of this system—such as the release and reabsorption of cortisol—are of considerably longer duration, especially if the threat is perceived to be overwhelming and/or chronic. What role can we infer the orbitofrontal cortex to have if the HPA axis is active for a prolonged period of time? In such a situation, rather than a basic feeling being either followed through, modified, or overridden, the individual's feelings will go underground, as in the case of phantom pain and PTSD. (Both, we have seen, are fundamentally dissociative syndromes.) This lack of resolution could well be mirrored neurologically, with associated concerns caught between the emotional brain and the prefrontal cortex. Or completely unrelated issues or preoccupations (e.g., half-understood compulsions, worries, guilt) could likewise remain insufficiently processed. In either case, I propose, when a set of circumstances in the *body* mirrors that in the *brain,* the stage is set for something bizarre to potentially occur.

Genetic Evidence

An intriguing piece of evidence for at least the neurological side of this scenario is to be found in the work of Stanford University geneticist Richard Myers. He and his colleagues were studying the preserved brain tissue of people affected during their lives by depression, bipolar disorder, and schizophrenia. (Some of the sample brain tissue also came from individuals affected by none of those disorders.) Myers's team was searching for the genes that might underlie the conditions. What they noticed, he relates, was that "the patterns of active genes fell into two distinct groups—depending on how the patients had died. The statistics were screaming at us. It was pretty remarkable." What emerged was that the individuals who had endured prolonged deaths, over hours or days, showed one pattern of genetic activation. Those who had died suddenly (e.g., from a heart attack, accident, or suicide) showed another.[5]

Myers thinks that his group inadvertently discovered a snapshot of dying brain tissue. But why would the genetic trail differ between those who had a quick exit or a lengthier demise? "During a prolonged illness," he hypothesizes, "the brain might be starved of oxygen and sugars, triggering it to switch on a whole suite of genes that help cells survive." But this process must run on low energy, because "the dying brain also seems to dampen down genes involved in energy metabolism." The picture we get is of a brain struggling to survive, low on fuel but doing its best. Such a struggle could be waged concurrently in the rest of the body, because the researchers speculate that proteins and other cellular components activated in the dying brain could filter into the blood.[6]

I find this discovery highly interesting, because it suggests that, when the brain senses that it is dying, certain genes switch on. Cellular processes are affected, perhaps throughout the organism. If a matter of concern *were* occupying the orbitofrontal cortex (the convergence area between the limbic region and the prefrontal cortex) and displaced energy *were* being held in the body, a prolonged demise would at least give the individual an opportunity to resolve the conflict. However, in the case of an extremely quick demise, such ambiguity could never be processed and the energy would remain trapped. My inference is that people who fit this bodymind profile and die *suddenly* are more prone to manifest as ghosts or ghostly phenomena than people who have some advance notice and, thus, the opportunity to make peace within themselves.

A View Overlooked

While researching this book, I came across a fascinating interview with a man named Nandor Fodor. He was a psychiatrist who, from the 1930s to the 1960s, made it his business to investigate alleged psychic phenomena. Like many of his time, he was a Freudian. Unlike Freud, however, he chose to devote considerable attention to the paranormal. Fodor investigated numerous cases and developed several theories to explain the reports he encountered. In an interview late in his life, he singled out the feeling of *anguish* as having a presumed connection with many of the strange circumstances he'd looked into.[7]

Now, the Latin root of the word "anguish" is *angustia,* meaning "straightness," "narrowness," or "constriction." The general concept could be said to mirror my own proposition of feeling energy being caught or constricted within the bodymind, including the half-processed concerns that may be held between the limbic brain and the neocortex. While the neurobiology of emotion had yet to be explored in Fodor's day, I suspect he instinctively knew what he was trying to describe. I mention this because it seemed an interesting take from a learned man whose line of work was quite distinctive and brought him face-to-face with some rather unusual reports.

Huge Energy—Psychic Outlet?

In chapter 5, we noted that a great deal of energy can be marshaled when one's sympathetic nervous system mobilizes to face a potential threat. It's been compared to flooring your car's accelerator—with *you* being the car. Now let's get acquainted with a bizarre phenomenon that will allow us to further appreciate just how much energy is truly involved.

Episodic dyscontrol is a rare condition that leads to sudden outbursts of violence in otherwise normal people. Often their condition is caused by a brain tumor, head injury, or epileptic seizure. In one instance, a man tried to decapitate his wife and daughter, becoming so violent the police had to bring him into the station wrapped in a fishnet. Elsewhere, a sixteen-year-old boy tore the door off a refrigerator. And, in a fit of rage, a 105-pound woman picked up a large upholstered armchair and threw it over a dining room table.[8]

"An attack of episodic dyscontrol," explains Dozier, "mimics the intense fear and violent anger any of us might feel if a stranger suddenly tried to kill us. But in this illness there is no actual threat, only a misfiring of the primitive fear system." This was demonstrated by the neurologist who examined Julie, a patient who had stabbed another woman when they brushed against one another in a ladies' room. By examining Julie's response to electrical stimulation of various parts of her brain, the neurologist determined that she was being affected by epileptic seizures in her right amygdala.[9]

Normal people, too, in intensely threatening situations, have been known to perform amazing feats of courage and strength. The energy is primarily due to the combination of adrenaline and noradrenaline, which speeds up the heart rate, increases lung capacity, fuels the muscles by producing new supplies of sugar, and boosts the oxygen content of the blood that flows into the muscles.[10] Dozier relates the following story, told by a teacher friend of his—a "petite woman" who was in college when the incident took place.

> Late one night at her sorority house a bunch of drunken fraternity boys began pounding on the front door, demanding to be let in. When she and several other women refused to open the door, there was momentary silence, then a huge crash against the door. The fraternity boys were back, this time using a telephone pole as a battering ram. A utility company was installing new poles in the area and had left a stack of them nearby. The house mother of the sorority came down to see what was going on just as the boys knocked down the door. Their momentum carried them through the doorway, pole and all. As they stumbled in, they dropped the telephone pole—right on the leg of the house mother. When they realized what they had done, they panicked and ran. My friend said she had never been so frightened in her life. She ran to the house mother, who was pinned with a broken leg under the heavy pole. Desperate, she grabbed the end of the pole and lifted it off the woman. She had no idea how she did it. When the police came, it took six men to carry the pole out the door. She said every muscle in her body was sore for weeks.[11]

I suspect that such latent energy will be found to account for the otherwise impossible movement of heavy objects in poltergeist cases.

Inevitably, the phenomena in these situations revolve around a particular person. (Investigators call that person the "agent" or the "focus.") I theorize that such people conform to the profile we have been discussing: the crossover of a significant matter unresolved in the brain with a torrent of energy held in the body.

Return to Seven Cases

To illustrate how this juxtaposition underlies anomalous occurrences, let's return to the examples of the six individuals (and one group case) presented initially in chapter 1.

- Passengers and crew on Eastern Airlines' L-1011 fleet of jets during 1973 and 1974 see, hear, and speak to solid looking apparitions of two crew members, Captain Bob Loft and Second Officer Don Repo, who died soon after Eastern Flight 401 crashed in the Florida Everglades. The reports cease in mid-1974, when the airline removes all salvaged parts of Flight 401 that had been installed in sister ships of its L-1011 fleet.
- Adam, a precocious eighteen-month-old, lounging in his bathtub, suddenly sits bolt upright yelling, "The men! They're coming!" His eyes seem fixed on something far away, and Adam appears temporarily unaware of where he is or *who* he is. He explains with mounting hysteria about men in uniforms and guns who are coming to get him. Then, as suddenly as the episode began, it is over, and Adam is back to normal.
- Melanie, a twenty-one-year-old college student, is jogging across a bridge when she's hit by a truck and thrown down a concrete embankment. At approximately the same time, her mother jumps up in the middle of a business meeting and says to her husband, "Glen, something's just happened to Melanie." She turns out to be correct.
- Susan, forty-four years old, home alone, feels one evening that someone is in the bedroom with her. On successive nights, she wakes up with a strong sense of her father's presence, smells his hair tonic,

and ultimately, sees him standing at the door. She'd been bothered by his being alone and sick when he died, but now he looks well.

- Ruth, twenty-five years old, sees vivid, lifelike apparitions of her father. These are frightening because he molested her when she was young. She's not had contact with him for several years; nevertheless, the images move, seem to talk to her, and even smell like her father. Later on, working with a psychiatrist, Ruth learns to exert control over the apparitions. She is even able to create lifelike imagery of friends and relatives.

- Ron, twenty-nine years old and a new father, dreams two nights running of his own father, an alcoholic with whom Ron has had virtually no contact since he abandoned the family. The next day, Ron learns that his dad is dying in a Veterans Administration hospital. After agonizing about whether to visit, he ultimately does. After his father dies, Ron dreams of an old black car driving him to his boyhood home. While the image is a cipher, twenty years later Ron finds a childhood photo of himself with his father beside the identical car.

- A multigenerational home is evidently harboring a poltergeist. Mary, age sixty-two, her mother Lillian, son Keith, and granddaughter Krista hear rapping sounds, household objects seem to disappear and then mysteriously reappear elsewhere, strange smells and cold spots are noticed, a large mirror falls over, and family members (as well as a plumber and air conditioner repair worker) are soaked by spontaneous water showers inside the house. Once the family obtains psychological counseling, the phenomena abate.

Let's reexamine these intriguing—and well-documented—cases one by one.

Flight 401

For well over a year following the crash of Eastern Airlines Flight 401 into the Florida Everglades, passengers and crew members on other Eastern flights reportedly saw and heard lifelike, three-dimensional apparitions of Captain Bob Loft and Second Officer Don Repo (most often the latter), both of whom died as a result of the crash. Passengers who did not know either of the men identified them without hesitation from photographs.[12]

At the time of the crash, Loft and one other crewman, First Officer Bert Stockstill, were at the cockpit controls. They had the plane at an altitude of 2,000 feet, diverting west from Miami because of an indication on initially approaching the airport that the landing gear in the nose of the plane might not be in the deployed and locked position. Repo, who was also the chief engineer for the flight, and another technical expert, Angelo Donadeo, had crawled down into a compartment underneath the cockpit floor in an effort to see whether the nose gear was, in fact, down.

Unbeknownst to all four men was the fact that the autopilot, while continuing to read 2,000 feet, had been inadvertently disengaged and the plane was actually falling at the rate of 500 feet every twenty seconds.[13] The blackness of the Everglades and the smoothness of the L-1011 Whisperliner's operation provided no indication of this rapid descent. There was no warning light in the cabin, and the one chime that did sound to report trouble was at such a low volume that none of the crew noticed it. The dark, still waters of the Everglades enveloped the plane with a terrifying suddenness when Flight 401 hit that night at 11:42 p.m.

The crash claimed ninety-nine lives. Incredibly, there were seventy-seven survivors—among them Donadeo. The soft mud and waters of the Everglades were credited for the high survival rate and for the prevention of fire breaking out in full force.[14] Of the other crew members in the cockpit, Loft and Repo were found badly injured but alive. Loft was apparently in shock but struggled, as if trying to get out of the plane. He was lucid enough to tell rescuers, "I am going to die." His struggle ended within an hour of being found. Donadeo and Repo were in the watery compartment underneath the cockpit, calling out that they did not want to drown. Repo, one rescuer noted, "seemed to be angry." He was flown to a hospital but died there thirty hours later.[15]

Several elements of this account are worth noting. First, Loft and

Repo did not perish instantly but were *conscious of their condition.* Despite the shock, they struggled. Repo, in particular, evidenced anger and a determination to fight. As we know, anger can mobilize a considerable reserve of energy in the fight for survival.

Second, each had a notable stake in his profession. Loft was an experienced pilot, fiftieth in seniority among Eastern's four thousand pilots. His colleagues described him as "conscientious, a perfectionist."[16] Repo had risen from aircraft mechanic to flight engineer and had a great affinity for the L-1011 aircraft.[17] It's likely that each man harbored a sense of responsibility for the fate of the plane and the well-being of the passengers and crew. Their injuries, however, prevented them from doing anything about it. This constitutes the sort of neural dilemma—with activity crossed between the fear- and anger-generating limbic system and the more deliberative prefrontal cortex—that is of interest to us.

Third, the fact that a great deal of electronic equipment was part and parcel of the plane may be relevant to the subsequent apparitions. Repo was in the nose wheel-well at the time of the crash, a compartment adjacent to the forward electronics bay.[18] Of equal import, many of the apparitions of Repo on sister L-1011s allegedly took place in the galley, adjacent to the section of the planes that carried electronic equipment.[19] While this may be a coincidence, it may also betoken something more. In any case, Eastern Airlines evidently decided to remove all the salvaged parts from Flight 401 that had been installed on other L-1011s.[20] Shortly thereafter, by mid-1974, the apparitions had ceased.

Young Adam

The account of eighteen-month-old Adam is fascinating for quite different reasons. Unlike the crew of Flight 401, he was in no danger. In fact, he was being given a relaxing bath one evening. Nor was he old enough to have the sort of highly developed cognitive system that we would associate with decisions to redirect or override particular feelings. Electronic gear is also plainly excluded from the picture.

We do note the presence of water, although in this instance it was helping Adam to relax, which may be significant in its own right. Investigators of the paranormal have often noted that relaxation appears to be conducive to extrasensory perception.[21] Indeed, Adam experienced other episodes such as this one, most often when he was in the tub, but at least one other time when he was playing with puppets.[22] In those circumstances, Adam evidenced an intense panic.

Who the armed men in his account were and who was doing the hiding are questions that understandably intrigued Adam's parents. They came to the conclusion that the former were German storm troopers and the latter were Jewish civilians. The issue remained puzzling, though, since his parents

> had never presented material about the Second World War to him, nor had [they] discussed Hitler or the Nazis in his presence. Although Jewish, they had not been directly affected by the Holocaust; both extended families lived in the United States during the war. In any event, [they] were quite sure that Adam had not heard war stories from grandparents, aunts, or uncles. The only remaining source was a babysitter who had occasionally watched him for an hour or two during this period. . . . Not surprisingly, after [these] episodes began she was very thoroughly questioned about how Adam had spent his time while in her care. Finally, she was asked directly whether she had ever talked with Adam about the Nazis. She replied indignantly that she certainly had not, adding that such a horror was no kind of thing to talk about with any child, and certainly not with Adam.[23]

It's possible that Adam was having his own odd kind of amusement, pulling their leg, but this seems unlikely given his extremely young age, the very real terror he appeared to be experiencing, and the bizarre nature of his explanation as to what was happening.

Terror, in the words of the late psychologist Alexander Lowen, is "a paralyzing emotion that freezes the body."[24] It is "a more intense form of fear than panic and develops in situations where any effort to resist or escape appears hopeless." When terrorized, "feeling is withdrawn from the periphery of the body. . . . It represents a flight inward."[25] This is precisely the mechanism that we have equated with *dissociation,* which is a disengagement from the felt sense.[26]

Just who was dissociating, however? For that matter, how could Adam, safe at home in the United States, possibly have accessed a memory of terrified Jewish civilians from a half-century earlier on an entirely different continent? The questions are difficult, but I will propose answers later in this book. For now, simply consider the possibility that terror—or for that matter any intense feeling not allowed adequate expression—could prove extremely problematic even if it has been part of an individual's personality and experience a world away.

Melanie and Her Mom

We've all heard accounts where a mother suddenly senses something is amiss with her child; a wife is certain her husband is in trouble; a sibling intuits that something has befallen her brother or sister; or someone gets the feeling that a friend is in dire straits. Inevitably, we hear that the hunch turned out to be correct, that the inexplicable concern was justified. Many, perhaps most, of these accounts can be chalked up to what's been called the "file drawer effect," that is, one remembers the suspicions that turned out to be valid, while forgetting all those that came and went unfounded. In Melanie's case, however, her mother's outburst during the business meeting was recorded in the minutes.[27] If this were something more than a coincidence, what could account for it?

Let's start by appreciating that such synchronicities are frequent enough that at least two terms have been developed to describe them: "telesomatic events" ("tele" as in distance, "somatic" as in body) and "clairsentience" (the presumed ability to feel another's pain or physical state, at a distance, in one's own body).[28] The recipient of the information apprehends it suddenly, without any particular expectation, and often feels something striking, poignant, or odd.[29] Some examples follow.

- A mother was writing a letter to her daughter, who was away at college. She started to feel in her right hand a burning so intense that she could no longer hold the pen. Less than an hour later, she received a phone call from the college telling her that her daughter's right hand had been severely burned by acid in a laboratory accident.[30]

- A man and his wife were attending a football game when the man got up and announced they had to return home because their son had been hurt. When they arrived home, they discovered that the boy had shot a BB into his thumb, which required immediate surgery.[31]

- A woman suddenly doubled over, clutching her chest as if in severe pain, and said, "Something has happened to Nell; she has been hurt." Two hours later the sheriff came, stating that Nell had died on the way to the hospital. She had been involved in an auto accident, in which a piece of the steering wheel had pierced her chest.[32]

- A registered nurse received a call after midnight concerning a patient she had been seeing weekly. The patient's daughter had already called 911. The nurse went to the patient's home and found her looking terribly ill, with low blood pressure, chest pains, and breathing difficulties. After the ambulance left with the patient, the nurse returned home to try to sleep. She was suddenly awakened by "a violent jerk that went through my whole body." As she was trying to figure out what had happened, the phone rang. The patient's daughter was on the line, saying that her mother had just experienced cardiac arrest but that the doctor had been able to "shock her back" to life.[33]

- All eight members of a farm family in upstate New York arose one morning, had their breakfast, and then dispersed to various points on the farm to begin their day's work. Later that morning, they each began to experience a strange feeling of foreboding. Thinking they were becoming ill, each one of them stopped working and returned to the kitchen, unaware of the feelings of the others. This unusual behavior coincided with the accidental death in Michigan of a son in the family.[34] (In a survey done by the late Ian Stevenson of the University of Virginia, more than one person experienced the same telesomatic symptoms simultaneously in approximately 6 percent of the reports collected.[35])

When such instances occur between mothers and their children, we tend to label them "mother's intuition," as if that folksy attribution can explain away the phenomenon. It does not. Attempts at explanation have focused on the mother-child connection during pregnancy and immediately after birth, when the two individuals are effectively one. A psychiatrist and student of anomalies proffers a suggestion.[36]

The baby is a direct extension of his mother's body image . . . she does "the doing" for him. She feeds him when he is hungry; she gives him warmth when he is cold. . . . His signals of distress, his whimper or cry, his kicking and flailing, send her scurrying to his aid.

[But] the neonate, while highly vocal, is nonverbal. His expressive movements can barely indicate more than distress or comfort, hunger or satiation. . . . Still, the efficacy of interaction between mother and baby seems to exceed the limited repertoire of whatever conventional signaling code joins them together as one functioning whole. [It must be] that in the preverbal or nonverbal phase signals are exchanged and a "mutual cuing" occurs in a way which runs far ahead of the infant's capacity to make himself understood. [The] mother seems to "understand" in a way which is difficult to account for in terms of the "ordinary" means of communication.

Three objections can be lodged against this approach. First, in light of what science is learning about mirror neurons, a psychiatric or telepathic explanation is unnecessary (if not merely fanciful). Second, if speech supersedes this supposed telepathic link, why would the link continue to operate after the child has become an adult? Third, siblings hardly share the same symbiotic relationship as mothers and children—nor do friends or even spouses—so what sort of "information transfer" could possibly allow for a person in such a relationship to suddenly feel ill at ease about the other?

Of relevance here is the Stevenson survey mentioned above. It indicated that, while a third of such cases involve parents and children, two-thirds do not. The upshot seems to be that emotional ties are more important to understanding the phenomenon than a mother-child link per se.[37]

Susan's Sense of Smell

In the case of middle-aged Susan, we recall that she initially had a feeling that someone was in her bedroom with her, woke up the following night with a strong sense of her father's presence, and then woke up on the third night smelling her father's hair tonic. She subsequently "saw" her father as healthy and got the impression that, although he died alone and sickly, he was now all right.

This account has a parallel reported in the book describing the reports of apparitions associated with Flight 401. Repo's wife told investigator John Fuller that she woke up one night "with an overpowering odor of Vitalis on the pillow next to her. Don had always used Vitalis, but there had been none in the house for over a year when this happened. The pillows were new and clean. But the odor was so strong that it woke her up . . . it did not disappear until well into the next day."[38]

These reports could be explained by Michael Persinger's theory of bereavement apparitions, in which a person's memories of a loved one are made tangible through the agency of the hippocampus. It is true that smell is among the oldest capacities of the human organism. As was noted in chapter 3, the olfactory bulb is located just above the brain stem in close proximity to limbic structures such as the amygdala and hippocampus. Thus, when we smell something, it very often conjures up a vivid association. As expressed so evocatively by naturalist Diane Ackerman, "Smells detonate in our memory like poignant land mines, hidden under the weedy mass of many years and experiences. Hit a tripwire of smell, and memories explode all at once. A complex vision leaps out of the undergrowth." She notes specifically that "when her lover is away, or her husband dies, an anguished woman goes to his closet and takes out a bathrobe or shirt, presses it to her face, and is overwhelmed by tenderness for him."[39] Perhaps, during sleep, the brain's ruminations on a loved one move in reverse, from specific associations (a face, a shirt) to the dearly departed aroma they are intimately connected with. The poignancy of this felt memory might then wake up the sleeper.

I'd like to venture an alternate possibility. We know that human beings are inherently social creatures and that an elaborate emotional toolbox evolved to enable us to survive among our fellows. If our predilection is to communicate—which means *receiving* a message as well as *conveying* one—we might be programmed to perceive emotional energy in the electromagnetic environment through the primitive limbic channels of the brain most closely connected to the sense of smell. A particular aroma might then imply the presence of emotional energy and the possibility of accessing it.

Thus, it may be that some residue of Don Repo's bodymind energy, or Susan's father's, was available to the individuals who were closest to them. How this could happen in apparent disregard of time and space is a topic I'll approach elsewhere in this book.

Ruth's Apparitions

As related by Dr. Morton Schatzman, an American psychiatrist practicing in London in the mid-1970s, a woman he calls Ruth came to him anxious and fearful over recurring apparitions of her father. In all other respects, she seemed normal. "She had no psychiatric disorder," notes Schatzman. "Nor did she have an illness of her body or sensory organs."[40]

A striking fact was how much fear and revulsion this apparition of her father aroused in Ruth. According to Schatzman, "When Ruth's 'father' appeared during her visits to my office, she was terrified. I have never seen anyone so overcome by fear. What kind of person, I wondered, could inspire such feelings?" The answer became evident during therapy. Ruth recalled that her father had attempted to rape her when she was ten.

He was often in jail or in a mental institution. He was also alcoholic and abusive.[41]

Ruth knew the perceptions were not real, yet they were lifelike in every respect. Today, I believe, she would be diagnosed as suffering from PTSD. In chapter 5, we saw how PTSD has been aptly described as "speechless terror" and "horror frozen in memory."[42] People who are high reactors— who have a low HPA stress reaction threshold—relive their traumatic experience as if it is happening *now*. The sights, sounds, smells, and fears fail to be incorporated into memory in the usual way. I've proposed that they are retained as a self-contained "stone" that is occasionally thrown up into consciousness by the currents and eddies of the bodymind.

That Ruth's peculiar neurobiological functioning was ingrained in her was demonstrated by an ingenious experiment performed by Schatzman and his colleague, Peter Fenwick. Using an electroencephalograph and an electroretinograph, they ascertained that whenever Ruth saw an apparition of her father, her retina responded normally to light but brain waves in her visual cortex were altered. A similar response was obtained for her hearing.[43] These results mirror more recent findings from brain scans run on people susceptible to hypnotic suggestion. They really do process reality differently.[44]

Yet Ruth's penchant for making the past (her abusive father) immediate and present ultimately allowed her to control the apparitions. Prompted by her highly supportive therapist—and slowly and painstakingly at first—she managed to tell the image of her father to "get lost" and quit bothering her. After a time, it did. Buoyed by this success, Schatzman asked Ruth if she could conjure up apparitions of other, friendlier people she knew. She found, to her elation, that she could. This capability, as we shall see later on, is characteristic of people who manifest what is called *psychosomatic plasticity*.

It's been estimated that less than 50 percent of what we see is actually based on information entering our eyes.[45] This figure isn't hard and fast, to be sure. At any moment, you or I can be surprised by the fact that we just drove through a stop sign, or we can issue a greeting to someone we see in a crowd, only to learn (to our chagrin) that it's a complete stranger.

What we hear, see, touch, taste, and smell can clearly vary based on what we're used to, what we want to experience, or what we expect to apprehend. For some of us, the correspondence between internal expectation and external reality is generally much higher than 50 percent. For others (the fantasy-prone individuals—more about them in chapter 8), the figure may be much lower.

The key point to appreciate here, however, is the importance of feeling in conditioning our internal imagery and our bodymind apparatus. In Ruth and other people who suffer from PTSD, experiences from months or years ago surface as immediate, intensely felt, rapid-fire images. This is because imagery is effectively our bodymind's language, and it is intimately connected with feeling. Ask any artist if you doubt the validity of this statement. Imagery especially appeals to the right side of the brain, which processes form (e.g., facial expressions, vocal expressions, posture) and feeling (e.g., music), more than the left. The language of imagery is rich, symbolic, and highly personal—but in everyone, it can be said to represent the brain's interface with the body.[46] As such, feelings that have been dissociated within the bodymind can nonetheless be accessed through imagery.

As we shall see, people like Ruth who, through a combination of nature and nurture are highly reactive, are the ones most likely to believe their imagery is real—as well as to be possess a bona fide ability to subliminally access the emotional energy of others.

Ron's Expanded Perception

Feeling and imagery are part and parcel of dreaming. They also connect to the anomalous, as demonstrated by Ron, the new father who dreamed of his long-absent father on two successive nights and was coincidentally informed that the man was on his last legs in a Veterans Administration hospital. After visiting his father there, Ron dreamed of an elegant old black car that, at the time, meant nothing in particular. Twenty years later, though, he came across a photo of his father holding him as a baby next to the same vintage automobile—and realized it was the only picture he had of the two of them together.

Ron's intense feelings are made quite clear in his account. Upon hearing about his father's status in the hospital—and initially deciding *not* to go visit—Ron was overcome with a potent mix of recollections.

> Rage, bitterness, and self-pity enveloped me like live steam. Where was he when I needed him? . . . Ferocious fights between my father and my mother, face scratching, me standing there in helpless fear saying "Mommy, I'll get you my hammer to hit him . . ."—all this washed over me. That rotten bastard! . . . He cheated me of a normal childhood. He would not even pay the $5.00 a week of child support awarded by the divorce court. . . . He never even sent me a Christmas card! Why did he screw me up like that? Let the son-of-a-bitch die by himself as he deserves!
>
> I wandered around all that beautiful fall day with hot tears streaming down my face, alternating between bitterness and sadness. Gradually I became torn about whether I should see him at all . . . I didn't know what to do.[47]

Ron notes that, aside from the two nights when he dreamed of his father, he hadn't recalled dreaming of him at all and had almost no contact with him. The dreams thus seemed odd, especially as they portrayed his father in a sympathetic light. He assumed they must relate to his becoming a father himself, yet their meaning remained unclear.

Before addressing this mystery, we must take a close look at the dream state itself. Surely the most defining characteristic of a dream is its blurring of reality, including the lack of a defined progression of feelings and events. "The laws of logic, physics, decency and common sense apparently are abandoned," writes author John McCrone, "as we cross over into a playground for the [subconscious]."[48] McCrone attributes this disconnectedness to one's conscious train of thought (which he terms the "inner voice") being sidetracked—so that memories, desires, feelings, associations, and impressions tumble together without benefit of a coherent, conscious narrator.[49] He concludes that dreams are "nothing more than a scrambled version of normal . . . consciousness" and not indicative, as

Freud and his followers would have it, of either repressed material or symbolic meaning.[50]

McCrone's assessment of the dreaming process strikes me as insightful, although I disagree with his conclusion. Surely our dreams navigate effortlessly among a wide range of perceptions, memories, and associations. Fleeting observations that were made during the day, barely registering in the waking mind, make their way to prominence during dreaming. Half-formed thoughts, inarticulate feelings, or an impetus never followed through may come to the fore during the night, allowing us (if we manage to remember the dream's imagery) to expand our awareness of what is affecting us and what we are feeling deep down. With the conscious narrator displaced, little-noticed stimuli can be attended to and either disposed of, filed away, or brought together with like memories and reflections. Details that may not have been apparent to us during wakefulness may surface, and connections between events or personalities of our present and past may be made.

Sometimes information known on an unconscious, bodymind level is perceived in the context of a dream. Robert Van de Castle, a professor emeritus at the University of Virginia who has studied dreaming extensively, states that "dreams can be sensitive indicators of biochemical or physiological changes."[51] It is well known that pregnant women often dream of buildings, rooms, or animals, which are images relating to the body, the womb, and the developing fetus. In his book, *Our Dreaming Mind,* Van de Castle cites numerous instances where "the unconscious mind of the pregnant woman seems able to monitor and detect biochemical imbalances, tissue abnormalities or structural defects in the uterine environment and communicate an awareness of disturbed functioning through dream imagery, which is sometimes fairly literal, sometimes symbolic."[52]

In other words, dreams may serve as a kind of nocturnal sonogram. The menstrual cycle can likewise affect dreaming. In one study, women tended to report different types of dreams after ovulation than before.[53]

Anyone—man or woman—can gain information about his or her body via dream imagery. In a type of dream that Van de Castle terms "prodromal," the specific images can reflect symptoms of a physical condition not yet perceived consciously. Such dreams have been observed going back to Aristotle, Hippocrates, and the second-century Greek physician Galen, who mentioned the case of a man who dreamed his leg was turned to stone and who developed a paralysis of this leg a few days later.[54] Van de Castle offers several modern-day examples:[55]

- A man who dreamed of eating pizza and then having his stomach break open, only to experience a perforated ulcer the following night.
- A woman who dreamed of "wiggly, incandescent worms of all colors" crawling over her eyelids, who developed an inflamed retina two days later.
- A girl who dreamed of being shot in the left side of the head, who woke up with a severe migraine headache on that side.

This type of case illustrates our dreams' ability to serve as a virtual X-ray. Given how entwined and continuous is the communication between our brain and body, it is not surprising that neural, hormonal, or glandular changes should come into awareness during sleep. This is, after all, when subliminal information is more likely to retrieved and assessed.

Could prodromal dreams possibly mirror an experience that *someone else* is undergoing? I should like to consider the possibility. Ron, for example, dreamed of his father immediately before learning that the latter was gravely ill. Perhaps this was more than coincidence. Such dreams are well known and either recognized or dismissed as being telepathic, clairvoyant, or paranormal. Inevitably, they deal with people or subject matter the dreamer knows well and with whom he or she has an important emotional connection.[56] What is happening, I suspect, is that the source of the imagery (in this case, Ron's father) is going through an *intensively felt* circumstance.

Consider that Ron's father was literally dying. Beyond the physical elements involved in the dying process, presumably he was reflecting at some level on his life and his abandonment of his family. Recall Myers' finding that the brain tissue of individuals whose death was prolonged shows a genetic pattern different from those who had died suddenly. I've inferred that the struggle going on in the dying brain is matched by cellular activity in the rest of the body. If significant issues or preoccupations were held in abeyance in a given person's brain and, concurrently, the energy of dissociated feelings is held in his or her body, perhaps something of this situation can be communicated via the electromagnetic environment to *someone else who is dissociating.* If the person undergoing the intensively felt circumstance has an emotional tie to the dreamer, then the dreamer would be even more receptive. We know that the more vividly felt an experience, the clearer the memory. In the limbic brain, the amygdala and the hippocampus are involved, but so is the vagus nerve, connecting what goes on cognitively to what goes on viscerally. Hormones, peptides, and other information substances travel throughout the bodymind, constituting a veritable psychosomatic network. Just think about where you were at the time of the assassination of John F. Kennedy, the space shuttle *Challenger* explosion, the death of John Lennon, or the September 11 attacks on the World Trade Center and the Pentagon. You probably remember a variety of small details that would never be recalled were the events not quite so significant. In a similar manner, people who fit the bodymind profile I have discussed might provide a veritable "snapshot" of their feelings that is accessible to certain others. The imagery, or at least the intuition, would be akin to what emerges during a prodromal dream.

The general concept—minus the neurobiology—is outlined by Michael Shallis, formerly a lecturer at Oxford University, in his book *On Time.*

Bodies do not stop at the skin but extend outwards into the space around them. Human senses reach out into the world, some farther than others, but even apart from the five senses man extends outwards. . . . When feeling happy and expansive I extend out in some way, I feel bigger. When I feel insecure I shrink down both psychologically and in the space around me. . . . If people extend in space why not in time as well? . . . When lives suddenly become involved in extreme drama and emotional tension then the extended selves may well reach out dramatically in space and time, and thereby be detected by people sufficiently aware of their own sensitivity to these things.[57]

Ron, of course, had conflicting feelings about his father (anger and resentment alongside love and longing). These were, in the main, suppressed and unacknowledged. This represents the nurture side of the nature/nurture equation I have proposed to account for certain individuals' increased sensitivity. For them, the background canvas of feeling can instantaneously coalesce into particular imagery. How such dynamics transcend the normal limits of space and time is an especially fascinating question that merits—and will receive—extended scrutiny in chapter 12.

The Jacksonville Poltergeist

Stranger than any account we've examined so far was a series of events described by two parapsychologists, Andrew Nichols and William Roll, that took place at a home in Jacksonville, Florida, between November 1996 and January 1997.[58]

To reprise: Living in the house were Mary Barton, age sixty-two; her mother Lillian, age eighty-seven; her son Keith, twenty-eight; and her granddaughter Krista, eleven. (All names are pseudonyms.) The house was a modern, seven-year-old structure in an affluent suburban neighborhood, with five bedrooms, three baths, and a swimming pool. Initially, rapping noises were heard, followed by the disappearance and reappearance of household objects, strange cold spots, and unusual smells. Sprays of water seem to emanate from nowhere, increasing in frequency and intensity. Puddles formed, and several gallons of water were said to splash spontaneously. Elderly Lillian seemingly got soaked most often; she was also jeopardized by a heavy, gilt-framed mirror that nearly hit her when it toppled over. The reports were corroborated by plumbing contractors brought in to identify the source of the water problem, which was never found. (One of the workers was so alarmed by being wetted that he refused to return to the site.)

In reviewing the family's claim for water-damaged furniture and carpet, the insurance company contacted Nichols and Roll. They proceeded to interview all of the witnesses and took photos as well as thermal, electrical, and magnetic gauges of the premises. Nichols and Roll pegged Krista as the focus of the strange events, which took place only when she was home. They noted that unhappiness in the entire family seemed high (which was understandable, with such bizarre events taking place), although Krista seemed particularly troubled. She had written a suicide note, and exhibited "an extraordinarily high aggression level." Krista's relationship with her great-grandmother Lillian appeared especially strained. Physically, the investigators found a marked difference in magnetic field strength at several locations where the phenomena were said to have occurred.

Nichols and Roll ultimately suggested that the family seek counseling. Their report concluded by noting "there has been no activity in the home since Krista entered psychotherapy. . . . It is uncertain if this is the result of therapy or because the phenomena had run their course."[59]

This case encompasses a variety of bizarre effects that have long been a staple of poltergeists: unexplained emissions of water (or, alternately, spontaneous small fires), electrical anomalies such as TVs and appliances turning on and off, objects moving of their own accord (often quite heavy ones), items disappearing and reappearing (sometimes with entirely new items being introduced), strange smells, and rappings and other noises.

The case also centered on Krista, an adolescent who fits the profile of what researchers term a poltergeist personality, meaning that he or she has a low tolerance for frustration accompanied by repressed feelings of hostility.[60]

We might begin to make sense of such phenomena by virtue of an account provided by a former poltergeist "focus" named Michael Talbot. His 1991 book, *The Holographic Universe,* was inspired from personal experience.[61]

When I was a child, the house in which my family had recently moved (a new house that my parents themselves had built) became the site of an active poltergeist haunting. Since our poltergeist left my family's home and followed me when I went away to college, and since its activity very definitely seemed connected to my moods—its antics becoming more malicious when I was angry or my spirits were low, and more impish and whimsical when my mood was brighter— I have always accepted the idea that poltergeists are manifestations of the unconscious psychokinetic ability of the person around whom they are most active.

This connection to my emotions displayed itself frequently. If I was in a good mood, I might wake up to find all of my socks draped over the house plants. If I was in a darker frame of mind, the poltergeist might manifest by hurling a small object across the room or occasionally even breaking something. . . . My mother tells me that even when I was a toddler pots and pans had already begun to jump inexplicably from the middle of the kitchen table to the floor. . . .

I do not make such disclosures lightly. I am aware of how alien such occurrences are to most people's experience and fully understand the skepticism with which they will be greeted in some quarters. Nonetheless, I am compelled to talk about them because I think it is vitally important that we try to understand such phenomena and not just sweep them under the rug.

I find Talbot's admission enlightening. His identification of an evident link between his feelings and the odd manifestations are articulate and, I strongly suspect, on the mark. (Alas, Talbot is no longer among the living, so he could not be consulted for this book. Roll, however, is one of the principals I did consult.)

Now, let's move on to the strange phenomena themselves. We have become familiar with the prominent place of smell in the emotional brain, so strange smells associated with a poltergeist might not be so inexplicable after all. As to rappings and other odd noises (explosions are sometimes reported), we noted in the last chapter how hissing, swishing, and crackling sounds are sometimes reported in conjunction with the aurora borealis. We also looked at the strange effects of low-frequency infrasound. I now posit that *the atmosphere itself* is similarly responsible for the sounds connected with poltergeist activity. If this is correct, certain people should be more highly sensitive to such radiations than others. The same people, presumably, would register the odd smells and, for that matter, cold spots that are often reported.

The issue begs a systematic inquiry into whether individuals who can be classified as high reactors on the basis of the functioning of their HPA stress system consistently report more anomalous perceptions; and specifically, in poltergeist cases, whether these people are the *only* ones reporting strange noises, smells, and temperature fluctuations or whether their perceptions are shared by other, less highly reactive people. In other words, how real (versus subjective) are such phenomena? My guess is that, for the few poltergeist reports each year that seem legitimate—and that are subjected to scientific scrutiny—the perceptions involved will be shown to be largely, though not completely, in the bodymind of the beholder.

This brings us to the three most impressive features of the Jacksonville case: the copious amounts of liquid (whether it was water is not completely certain), the movement of heavy objects, and the spontaneous appearance, disappearance, and reappearance of all sorts of household items. If these reports are not being fabricated, and if they're not due to a skilled magician, one gets the impression that a considerable amount of energy must be involved. I would, once again, look to the emotional brain. We have seen how the phenomenon of "episodic dyscontrol" can cause sudden, unprovoked bouts of violence in some people. Whether it's a teenager tearing a refrigerator door off its hinges, a 105-pound woman heaving an upholstered armchair over a dining room table, or a man who became so intensely violent that police had to wrap him in a fishnet, a limbic system gone haywire can harness tremendous energy.

I surmise that if the poltergeist focus is unwilling or unable to express his or her feeling energy outward through normal means, that energy may act on the immediate surroundings electromagnetically. In this connection, remember Gabor Maté's observation that the person chronically unable to stand up for himself or herself risks illness through a compromised immune system. The immune system will then reflect that person's own boundary confusion and the habit of dissociating feeling from awareness.[62]

The poltergeist personality exemplifies such difficulties to an extreme. Perhaps, in these cases, the individual's emotional processing is affected by an organic problem—a brain injury or a misfiring neural sequence akin to epilepsy—in conjunction with the vast hormonal changes that are characteristic of adolescence. We would need to conduct a brain scan of agents such as Krista to determine if this is correct. By the same token, since the phenomena at her house abated after she began psychotherapy, perhaps organic difficulties are less to blame than the way one learns from one's family to address feelings.

Since many—but by no means all—poltergeist agents are adolescents, we might likewise consider what features, among the numerous biochemical changes taking place at that stage, contribute most significantly. We know, for example, that estrogen levels rise exorbitantly. Are they so much more "off the chart" among poltergeist agents? What about the vast increase and subsequent large-scale pruning of cells in the frontal lobes? Between the ages of roughly ten and nineteen, the connections to the right orbitofrontal cortex, which has a great deal to do with impulse control, are being fine-tuned. Could some form of glitch in these massive changes be responsible for turning the flare-ups of the teen years into a poltergeist episode?

Associated questions arise and are posed in equal earnest. Does the neurotransmitter serotonin play any role? What about a buildup of positive ions in the air corresponding to hot or humid weather? Are patterns of local seismic activity possibly involved? The whole matter of poltergeists is, I submit, so strange as to offer an enormous opportunity to better understand both normal and abnormal human functioning.

Electromagnetic Interactions

The primary way human beings experience life is through feeling. Underlying each shade of what we feel is a complex amalgam of electrochemical activity throughout the bodymind. I have suggested that anomalous occurrences are the result of a disturbance in feeling. Such disturbances must be electrochemical and, it stands to reason, have an effect on the external environment as surely as our environment has an effect on us. But one ought to ask, does evidence exist to support this inference? It does.

In Great Britain over the last several decades, physician Jean Monro and electrical engineer Cyril Smith carried on remarkable work with individuals beset by apparent electromagnetic sensitivity. Their patients, it seemed, manifested an allergic reaction when exposed to particular frequencies. These people evidently also emitted electrical signals themselves. Comments such as "I'm no good with electrical things" or "I can't wear a quartz watch—they're always stopping" were their common complaints. Some reports stood out, such as the man who "had a robotic system in a factory completely malfunction each time he stood near it" or the individual whose car ignition failed "as soon as an allergic reaction was triggered by fumes from a diesel truck in front."[63] (Monro and Smith's subjects, in one respect at least, were in good company. Wolfgang Pauli, a giant in theoretical physics, was reputed to have such a consistently hazardous influence on finely calibrated equipment that his colleagues took to joking about the "Pauli effect."[64])

Smith's method of capturing the evidence was simple enough. His subjects would hold a tape recorder set to record but with no microphone connected. "If the subject is reacting strongly enough," Smith wrote, "there will be sufficient interference passing through the [unit] to be picked up by the amplifier circuits. A wide variety of signals may be obtained on replay and these vary not only from patient to patient but differ on different occasions with the same patient."[65]

Anecdotal evidence was also gathered during the 1980s by Shallis.[66] He sent a letter to twenty or so magazines inviting their readers to share any accounts of electrical sensitivity. Before long, he had received hundreds of replies, heard from numerous scientists and other researchers, and appeared on the BBC. He subsequently devised a questionnaire and conducted interviews. Among the results are the following:

- Seventy percent of Shallis's group reported that they were affected by allergies. The more severe their electrical sensitivity, the more severe the allergies were said to be.
- Sixty-nine percent claimed to have had an anomalous experience.
- Seventy percent reported that they had a surgical operation sometime during their life.

These points are intriguing, not just because of the association between electricity and perceived anomalies but also because of the mention of allergies and bodily insult (in the form of surgery). Shallis writes, "Hospitals figure quite a lot in the cases I have studied, possibly because people in hospital are frequently in a tense emotional or distressed condition."[67] (It could equally be said that if a person *isn't* tense when being admitted to a hospital, he or she is likely to become so, given the many challenges inherent in this institutional health care setting.) Likewise, his research features unconventional reports of strong feelings linked to apparent anomalies. One woman attested, for example, that light bulbs turned off in her presence when she was upset. Another person's problems with electricity supposedly began after her father had died. Still another stated that her bedroom light glowed blue, even when it was not turned on, during a time of great emotional upheaval. An especially striking (literally) anecdote involved a woman who said she'd walked out of her front door after an intense emotional experience "and a lightning bolt then struck the pathway at her feet."[68]

These sorts of statements may come across as preposterous. Are such people completely out in left field? Perhaps they're highly imaginative—or borderline delusional. Certainly the literature is replete with papers documenting that individuals who are highly suggestible, fantasy-prone, and so on will attribute highly improbable explanations to everyday occurrences.[69] People who experienced a difficult childhood or who have a family history of alcoholism or depression are also more likely to engage in "magical thinking."[70] Tests carried out on people who claim to be electrically sensitive have usually failed to verify such susceptibility.[71] And, highly germane to our purpose, it's been noted that hallucinations themselves "seem to be predominantly of images which arouse strong feelings."[72]

I do wish to hold the door open to the *possibility,* at least, that certain people—owing to a neurobiological predisposition—are legitimately prone to highly unusual perceptions and/or interactions with their environment that strike the rest of us as fanciful, implausible, or just plain bizarre.

Let's return for a moment to the type of energetic emergencies that have been the focal point of this chapter. An electric shock certainly qualifies—and, as might be expected, numerous people with supposed psychic ability are said to have suffered an electric shock as a child.[73] An interesting example is the United Kingdom's Matthew Manning. From a young age, he was the subject of scientific scrutiny; in his own books, he recounted a litany of extremely odd events that seemed to swirl around him much as a hurricane revolves around its eye. While Manning could not recall being affected by an electric shock, an investigator's conversation with his parents turned up the fact that his mother "had suffered such a severe electric shock three weeks before Matthew was born that she feared she might lose [him]."[74] Based on what we learned in chapter 4 about infants being affected by their mothers' experience, we might surmise that the shock to his mother's system set young Matthew's HPA axis to a low activation threshold. He might have also been "programmed" with an ability to summon up the energy of his feelings in unusual ways as well as the unwitting tendency to interact with electrical energy in the immediate environs.

In one of his reminiscences, Manning made this interesting comment about cars in which he was traveling.

> On several of the journeys I have made with my father . . . the engine cut out for no apparent reason, as if the ignition had been switched off. It seemed to be an electrical fault that stopped the engine; we could be traveling along, sometimes at a speed of 70 mph, when we suddenly would lose all speed and acceleration. The car would come to a halt and refuse to start again. The remedy we found after some experience of this was for me to get out of the car, after which the engine would start immediately. This has occurred in three different cars and has never happened when I was not a passenger.[75]

Manning's account—if truthful and not simply indicative of a series of mechanical coincidences—coincides with an observation made by Smith. Given that some of his electrically sensitive patients reported problems in automobiles themselves, Smith conjectured that "an extended metal surface near a reacting allergic patient, acting as a mirror for the patient's own electromagnetic emissions, [seems to] make these reactions worse."[76]

Sexual Expression

My surmise has been that individuals who fit a certain bodymind profile—those who harbor half-resolved issues in the brain and have a backup of unexpressed energy in the body—may find themselves acting on their surroundings in highly unusual ways. That such people would have severe or long-standing allergies is understandable given that the person's immune system may serve as a mirror of his or her boundary confusion in handling strong feelings (i.e., banishing them from awareness).

It would likewise be understandable if the lack of a sexual outlet contributed to this dynamic. Sexual activity, after all, has been known to provide an energetic release for strong feelings such as jealousy, resentment, and rage. Some would contend that, as often as such feelings get in the way of honest and loving sexual encounters, at other times sexual excitement is heightened through the liberation of underlying tensions.

At least one investigator has noted "a connection between sexual frustration and poltergeist effects . . . such effects cease when the [given person] leads a normal sex life."[77] Another intrepid paranormal researcher, the late Scott Rogo, detailed several interesting cases where a *monk* experienced strange goings-on. Monks are, of course, ascetic. But Rogo chose to concentrate on a psychological explanation—covert guilt—as the root cause of these alleged poltergeist outbreaks.[78] My perspective is that guilt *does* qualify as one of those matters that could easily lie half-processed between the limbic brain and the prefrontal cortex. More certain, however, is that sexual energy, when unexpressed, can wreak profound havoc.

The flip side is that sexual contact sets in motion a cascade of very real internal changes. Intercourse is all about touching and being touched—

and touch can have intimate and profound effects. During arousal, levels of the hormone dehydroepiandrosterone (DHEA) rise in the brain, as do the peptides vasopressin and oxytocin in the bloodstream.[79] At orgasm, oxytocin surges to as much as five times the norm, the heart rate doubles, and about two hundred calories get burned. Endorphins are released from the brain, giving sexual partners a literal high.[80] Having sex also deepens breathing, which in turn clears carbon dioxide from the blood.[81]

Within the past decade, science has trained its eye on this fascinating subject. We now know *where* in the brain orgasmic activity is generated: in the septum.[82] It's also understood that sex boosts immunity. Levels of immunoglobulin, an antibody, have been shown to be 30 percent higher in college students who engage in intercourse regularly than in those who do not. Additionally, frequent sexual activity is linked with a lower risk of breast cancer in women and prostate cancer in men.[83]

Orgasm can even be considered a form of "decongestant," clearing the skin of rashes and acne while diminishing stress and interrupting depression.[84] In all these respects, the afterglow of a satisfying sexual encounter confers verifiable benefits. Compromised sexual function, however, doubtless works in the reverse. Just as stultified feeling is a factor—perhaps the predominant one—in numerous psychosomatic conditions, pent-up sexual energy translates to tension harmfully retained within the bodymind. As with other forms of dammed up energy, I suggest that there may, at least in certain circumstances, be electromagnetic consequences.

Looking Ahead

I offer a final note. In the nineteenth century, talented psychics were often referred to as sensitives. As we'll see in the next chapters, this term turns out to have been right on the mark. It lacked any scientific basis but, in light of today's accumulating neurobiological evidence, it's as sound a way to describe a certain type of personality as one can conceive.

8

◆

Sensitivity, Personality Traits, and Anomalous Perception

I am psychic. . . . It is not something I have gone looking for. I have suppressed and denied it . . . and I have argued about it endlessly, but only with myself. . . . I am convinced that there is a silent group of psychics in our culture, ridiculed and confused, lacking reproducible data and waiting to come into the spotlight.[1]

LETTER (NAME WITHHELD) TO THE
EDITOR OF *NEWSWEEK*

Can you tell me someone who can spot after-shave at 50 paces—and it can set him off and give him migraines— has a psychological illness?[2]

JIM CHAMBERS, CONCERNING HIS SON JEREMY

Those who dance are considered insane by those who can't hear the music.

GEORGE CARLIN

In the last chapter, we assessed the dynamics within individuals—neurobiological, emotional, and energetic—that can prompt certain types of anomalous phenomena. Now we'll survey the *personality traits* that combine to make certain people susceptible to environmental influences that the rest of us rarely if ever notice. Put another way, we shall answer the question: Who is most likely to perceive apparitions, and why?

A Reminiscence

Let's begin with an interesting observation from the British parapsychologist Tony Cornell. He was recounting his 1967 investigation into a woman's report of an apparition at home. What struck Cornell was that, while he (as principal investigator) was unable to perceive anything odd around the premises, both the woman and an associate of his reported seeing the same ghostly figure, dressed identically, at the same time. So he wondered, "Why should one person see an apparition in sufficient detail to describe its dress while another person, at the same time and place, sees absolutely nothing? . . . Such cases as this one produce an element of contradiction of the kind that forever plagues psychic research."[3]

In this case, Cornell's associate suggested that the answer might be some form of telepathy by which the woman might have communicated her impressions to him. However, the associate had just arrived on the scene when he claimed to notice the apparition, whereas Cornell had been there for several minutes conversing with the lady. Why her telepathic vision would have singled out the newcomer instantaneously—and passed Cornell over—begged the question.

In this chapter, I propose a wholly different explanation, one that revolves around the concept of *sensitivity*.

What Is Sensitivity?

We're all familiar with the word, but what does it truly mean to be sensitive? The dictionary offers a four-part definition: (1) capable of perceiving with a sense or senses; (2) responsive to external conditions or stimulation;

(3) susceptible to the attitudes, feelings, or circumstances of others; and (4) registering very slight differences or changes of condition.[4]

The evidence points to a wide variability of sensitivity, both among individuals and within the different stages of a person's life. Some of the differences are well known. For a start, women exhibit markedly greater sensitivity across all five senses.[5] The perception of pain varies considerably from person to person,[6] as does acuity in taste, smell, and color perception.[7] Changes within a given person's lifespan are equally noteworthy, with sensitivity fluctuating due to the influence of hormones (e.g., a woman during ovulation), personal circumstances (e.g., an injury sustained or a disease suffered), preprogrammed genetic conditions (the onset of nearsightedness, for instance), and age (e.g., the acuity of smell declines as both women and men get older).[8] Additionally, it's widely recognized that individuals who are disadvantaged in one sense often enjoy greater sensitivity in another.[9]

The Author's Perspective

What difference does any of this make? For that matter, why should I—a regular guy who does not count himself as especially sensitive—go to the trouble of trying to explain why other people *are?* The answer stems from my professional experience in Washington, D.C., where I spent ten years representing commercial office building owners and managers. One of the central issues I was involved in was indoor air quality, which concerns the extent to which people are comfortable and productive (or *un*comfortable and seemingly ill) based on the quality of the air they breathe in their workplace. Now, at first glance, this must seem rather far from the subjects this book is concerned with: the basis of anomalies and anomalous perception in the neurobiology of human emotion. Yet there is a bridge.

I was tasked with working with the Environmental Protection Agency—and with the commercial real estate firms belonging to the trade association that employed me—to develop consensus guidance on how to maintain acceptable air quality inside buildings and how to go about solving complaints if they *did* occur. Everyone involved wished to avoid so-called sick buildings—instances where groups of people have ostensibly become ill while working in a given building. Once a building gets labeled as sick, it's a structure that no one wants to continue working in, and if no one wants to work there, its marketplace value obviously goes south. Hence, the enlightened self-interest of the association I was working for.

The symptoms that accompany questionable air quality in buildings are those typically associated with illnesses ranging from the common cold to chronic fatigue syndrome (e.g., headache, sore throat, dizziness, lethargy, watery eyes). Some of these symptoms can also be caused (or exacerbated by) stress. But they can also be triggered by mold, over- or underhumidified air, insufficient fresh air, and the chemicals emitted by new carpet, furnishings, paints, and cleansers. Occasionally, a person feels that he or she has been affected by poor indoor air quality and that the steps taken by building management to alleviate the presumed sources are insufficient. He or she may become, at that stage, an inveterate complainer and feel that it's no longer possible to be in the given workplace *without* feeling ill. In certain extreme cases, individuals have come to be regarded as hypochondriacs—sometimes by their families and peers in addition to their bosses. While others may view them as mentally or emotionally disturbed, such individuals typically view themselves as "environmentally ill." When no one believes them and their work situation can evidently not be remedied, they often become depressed, despondent, and all the more isolated.

This is the worst-case scenario for an indoor air quality problem. The question is, how much of the situation is due to the *built environment* and how much to the *felt environment* of the individual? As I spoke to office occupants who believed they had been made environmentally ill, I began to suspect that the issues were neither entirely in their mind nor entirely external. Indeed, several people related to me that they'd been sensitive to various things (e.g., smells, lights, even the radiation from video display terminals) for as long as they could remember. When a few individuals confided that they'd also had apparitional experiences, the wheels in my head started turning.

What if, I wondered, these people weren't entirely out in left field but harbored a threshold sensitivity level much lower than the rest of us? Wouldn't their impressions be difficult to accept and their challenges difficult to remedy? I thought of my wife—who is asthmatic and has been since age three—starting to wheeze in our downstairs study when I can be in that room for hours at a time without ill effect. While we remedied that problem through drainage work around the room's perimeter, my wife is still asthmatic. When she wheezes, it is a matter of the external environment interacting with her physiology. What if apparitional perceptions are something similar?

I decided to investigate the extent to which apparitional perception might coincide with various forms of environmental illness (e.g., long-standing allergy, migraine headache, chronic pain and fatigue, and the poorly understood variants of sick-building syndrome, multiple chemical sensitivity, and electrical sensitivity). This was circa 1995, and I had little sense of how to construct such a survey or how I might go about distributing it. But I resolved to look into the matter, entirely apart from my professional responsibilities.

I knew I would need to learn a great deal about neuroscience, biology, physiology, and related disciplines—and that the "ramping up" would take a few years. I also knew that the people I had been interviewing in order to develop indoor air quality guidance would have the ultimate insights. If I took their reports at face value (and yet not incredulously), I would have all the raw material I would need. If I aligned myself with serious and yet open-minded scholars in various fields, I could develop a framework to place such reports in a neurobiological perspective. I knew well that the study of emotion was rapidly gaining credibility. A formerly subjective experience—the province of poets and novelists rather than biologists or neuroscientists—was now a hot topic for objective study. The idea that a variety of *other* forms of hitherto subjective experience might share a common basis, revolving around the organizing principle of sensitivity, was enormously exciting. I decided to seek out as much relevant knowledge as I could, sound out as many broadminded academics as I might come across, and try to identify a sufficient number of "sensitives" as well as "controls," from whose testimony I could develop (and, ideally, test) applicable hypotheses.

This project has lasted more than ten years, but it has afforded me a truly unparalleled opportunity to learn about the human animal. In the process, I've gathered a solid appreciation of what it means to be sensitive.

Cases in Point

One woman wrote me that her son (no age given) has "hypersensitivities . . . [his] hearing is so sensitive he can hear small animals walking from inside the house and can hear trains a far distance that no one else can unless they turn off all noises and listen very carefully." While this sounds a bit like the character of Radar O'Reilly from *M*A*S*H,* she continued, "He also has experiences seeing shadows of people that no one else does. When little, he experienced seeing what he described as 'critters' when he was sick, which scared him. As a toddler, he was supersensitive. . . . I was thinking that he might just have been sensitive enough to see something that the ordinary person couldn't—since his other senses are so acute."[10]

Next, consider these sketches of four individuals I interviewed. Their names have been changed, and their accounts are paraphrased:

- Sally is sixty-two years old, divorced with three grown children. She has had allergies most of her life, as have others in her family. She considers herself to be sensitive to electricity and contends that computers and other electronic equipment do inexplicable things in her presence. Sally reports occasionally hearing voices, seeing lights, and having tactile experiences with no apparent source. These perceptions have occurred throughout her life to a greater or lesser extent, with one such period being when she was experiencing dissatisfaction in her marriage.

- Edward is a medical doctor in his midfifties, married with children. He is athletic and health conscious, having lived the past decade with multiple chemical sensitivity, a condition for which he was once hospitalized. Now he limits his exposure to cleansers, solvents, paints, pesticides, and even air fresheners and colognes and he runs a clinic for others with such sensitivities. Sometimes, Edward notices that computer screens and lights seem to flicker when he is near. He says that, occasionally, he feels a presence or sees an apparition. Some of his patients volunteer similar experiences.

- Betty is in her early sixties, also a medical doctor who is married with children. Earlier in her life, she suffered from headaches that were so severe she underwent surgery to try to alleviate them. Teflon implants and, later, titanium implants were used. These implants led to further chronic pain as well as, she asserts, multiple chemical sensitivity. Betty has learned to live with these conditions and believes that she can see and feel energy emanating from other people. She suspects she has always had this ability and now considers herself a healer—both vocationally and personally.

- Hank is fifty years old, a small businessman with one child. He has lived with depression as well as a sleep disorder for many years. When he was five, he was hit by a car and suffered a head trauma. From that time on, he claims, he has been aware that he can sense other people's feelings. Hank did not realize this was not normal until he met someone he considers telepathic, who helped him to hone the ability. Today, Hank has a circle of such friends—many of whom, he notes, seem to have problems with wristwatches, computers, and other appliances malfunctioning in their presence.

In conversations with these four people, I found them to be friendly, well mannered, and seemingly well adjusted. The themes that ran through their accounts, however—accidents or significant medical challenges, emotional upset and attunement, perceived sensitivity to chemicals or electricity, and anomalous perceptions—clearly stand out.

The Sensitivity Survey

In a 1995 meeting with Dr. William Roll, a parapsychologist, I related my interest in a possible parallel between environmental illness and apparitional experience. Roll suggested developing a survey to assess the various factors that might be involved, and I enthusiastically took him up on the idea.

I began by circulating a draft survey to several physicians who specialized in treating environmental illness, and then revised the questionnaire based on their responses. I also sought input from Roll and other parapsychologists who had experience giving surveys. The questionnaire that I ultimately went forward with covered fifty-four items, aimed at assessing the physical, mental, and emotional factors that might underlie various manifestations of sensitivity. The intention behind most of the questions (numbers 1–43) was to compile a composite picture of the individual's medical, emotional, and family history. Items asked about included:

- Gender, age, handedness.
- Weight and perception of body shape. (These items were included based on the observation that many notable mediums, especially those who are women, have been heavy.)
- Marital status, number of children, highest educational level attained.
- Self-assessment of temperament and tendency toward imagination.
- Birth order within the family, early or late arrival, if known.
- Self-assessment of childhood happiness.
- Incidence of remembered trauma. (In assessing this item, I judged an event as "traumatic" if it concerned a severe or protracted illness, a serious accident, major surgery, familial abuse, or being suddenly dislocated from one's home. I excluded the more common and less severe ups and downs of childhood, such as schoolyard taunting, being stuck in a tree, and so on.)
- Whether the person ever smoked or grew up in a smoking household. (This question was asked due to the possibility that environmental tobacco smoke might be a factor in the respondent's health later in life.)
- Satisfaction with the level of physical/sexual contact in one's life.
- Medical conditions such as asthma, allergies, migraines, sleep disorder or nightmares, depression or mood imbalance, eating disorders,

exhaustion or chronic fatigue, schizophrenia, epilepsy, alcoholism, and dyslexia.

- Perceived conditions such as electrical or chemical sensitivity, unusual sensitivity to sound and light, and synesthesia. (The latter two items, which I became aware of through completed surveys, were added midway through the project.)
- Severity and duration of any of the above conditions.
- Incidence of the above conditions in the person's immediate family.
- A trigger event, if any, that might be connected with a condition or conditions noted.
- Whether the person ever received a strong electric shock.
- Any seeming effect on electrical or mechanical devices.
- Medications taken and psychotherapy engaged in. (These questions were aimed at clarifying a person's experience of physical and emotional difficulties. If someone enters into therapy, for example, the issues at hand might make him or her more susceptible to stress or illness. Likewise, it is worth considering the possible influence of prescription medications on a person's perceptions and behavior.)

The remainder of the survey (questions 44–54) inquired whether the subject had ever had an apparitional experience, that is, the feeling or perception of something he or she could not verify was physically there. These questions did not ask about *other* unexplained perceptions in favor of zeroing in on this particular type. This set of questions was also intentionally open-ended, in contrast with items 1–43, which offered yes/no, multiple choice, and 1–5 scales for responding. The idea was to avoid leading respondents by using terms such as "ghost," "poltergeist," "presence," or "energy" and to, instead, allow the individual to describe, in his or her own words, what was remembered about the experience. (Some respondents did note an experience that was *not* apparitional, such as objects moving, precognition, or telepathy. Rather than exclude these mentions arbitrarily, I included them in the final tally.)

The survey was distributed to people who considered themselves either environmentally or psychically sensitive. I used three major avenues to identify candidates and get the survey into their hands: (1) promoting the project in newsletters or journals read by those with a likely interest in such matters; (2) requesting that environmental physicians and others with whom I had spoken circulate the survey to their patients and colleagues; and (3) referencing the survey in online forums devoted to environmental illness or paranormal phenomena.

Three professional journals ended up noting the project in their pages: the *Journal of Parapsychology,* the *Journal of the Society for Psychical Research,* and the *Journal of the Society for Scientific Exploration.* Three associations also did in their newsletters: the American Psychosomatic Society, the Bioelectromagnetics Society, and the American Academy of Environmental Medicine. The Center for Frontier Sciences at Temple University mentioned the project in its *Frontier Perspectives,* as did two offbeat but useful forums: *Fate* magazine and an e-mail list run by paranormal investigator Dennis William Hauck, author of *Haunted Places: The National Directory.*[11]

After several years of steady effort, I was able to obtain completed survey responses from 112 people: sixty-two from self-described sensitives and fifty from a control group of people who did *not* identify themselves as sensitive. I took care in the solicitation of responses from controls, making sure that as many as possible (in the end, all but five) were individuals who didn't know me personally. I also tried to ensure that control group respondents would be geographically dispersed, diverse in age, and predominantly women. (The last element was especially important because the sensitives were mostly women.) Interestingly, I received assistance on this phase of the project from the National Capital Area Skeptics, an organization in the Washington, D.C., area that is open-minded but duly skeptical about extraordinary claims. I remain grateful for their input and advice.

Hypothesis and Caveats

The core concept of my survey project was that sensitivity is a real—and demonstrable—neurobiological phenomenon. My supposition was that certain people are, from birth onward, disposed to a number of conditions, illnesses, and perceptions that, in novelty as well as intensity, distinguish them from the general population. This goes right to the heart of the dictionary definition of "sensitive," which is "capable of registering very slight differences or changes of condition." Individuals who are extraordinarily sensitive *should* exhibit greater susceptibility to allergies, chronic pain and fatigue, migraine headache, and environmental stimuli ranging from sights, sounds, and smells to further flung electromagnetic influences. Such people would also be expected to indicate a high degree of emotional sensitivity as well as a high incidence of anomalous perceptions.

The survey was designed to test this overall hypothesis. The instrument itself had a fourfold aim:

1. To gauge the extent to which individuals who describe themselves as sensitive appear to be affected by the factors mentioned above
2. To gather whether their immediate family members may have been similarly affected
3. To determine the extent to which environmental sensitivity parallels reports of apparitional perception
4. To compare and contrast these findings with similar questions asked of a sample of people who do *not* describe themselves as innately sensitive

As you will see, the results gathered were striking, demonstrating a statistically significant difference in several factors between sensitives and controls. My project, however, is clearly a starting point rather than any sort of final word. Consider that there are three fairly obvious limitations to this type of research. First, most of the survey questions were retrospective, with subjects being prompted for their recollections and self-assessment. Even assuming that every person responded to the best of his or her ability and with utmost candor (which may not be true, since outright fabrication is certainly one possibility), responses may still be colored by:

- poor or insufficient recall
- perceptions unsupported by objective, clinical criteria

- credulity, vivid imagination, or hypochondria
- the mere fact that the person might have been feeling stressed, anxious, or otherwise unwell at the time he or she was completing the survey

By the same token, it should be added that a person can harbor a legitimate illness and *not* feel unwell, at least in the early stages.[12]

A second limitation is the relatively low number of people in the control group. Controls for this type of exercise are difficult to come by because they don't have a motivating interest or stake in the survey. And the larger the control population, the better the inferences that can be made regarding the prevalence of conditions associated with sensitivity.

Third, beyond presenting a few self-assessment items (such as imagination, temperament, and childhood happiness) and one question concerning psychotherapy, my survey did not attempt to profile respondents according to scales common in parapsychological research. These include assessments of hypnotizability, proneness to dissociation, somatization (conversion of a mental or emotional problem into a physical complaint), magical thinking, and belief in the paranormal. I chose not to include these types of personality questions because they would have made my questionnaire unwieldy and diminished the likelihood that someone would take the time to complete it. (In the end, I strongly suspect that my survey touched on the above traits anyway. More on that later.)

Please note: the survey is available at www.emotiongateway.com, this book's website, where it can be downloaded and returned. My associates and I continue to be receptive to completed surveys by both sensitives and individuals who are not especially so. The more data we are able to compile, the stronger the investigation will be.

Previous and Parallel Research

This project certainly did not unfold in a vacuum. A growing body of research has been quietly accumulating around the notion that certain types of people are seemingly predisposed toward extraordinary sensitivity—and seeking to illuminate why. This research regards sensitivity from two equally valid perspectives: as a reaction to minute changes in a person's *internal state* and as responsiveness to changing conditions *outside* the individual. Let's begin our scan of the most relevant literature with the "inside" story.

Inborn Sensory Differences

"No two people live in the same sensory world," observes Paul Breslin, a neuroscientist at the Monell Chemical Senses Center in Philadelphia. "The world you see, the food you taste, the odors you smell—all are perceived in a way unique to you."[13] What tastes bitter to one person, for instance, another person may find exquisitely appealing. The differences are not just qualitative. Testing at the Monell Center has disclosed that a bitter chemical known as phenyltheocarbamide (PTC) can be tasted by some individuals at the vanishingly small concentration of 18 parts per billion. In contrast, if the concentration is high enough—say, 360 parts per million—everyone can taste it. This finding has its analogue in the realm of scent, where some people with cystic fibrosis can detect certain smells at levels ten thousand times weaker than the norm.[14]

Breslin and his fellow researchers are beginning to link such differences to our genetic inheritance. Taste, smell, and color perception have been found to vary according to the type, quantity, and configuration of individuals' sensory receptors. In many cases, the differences are huge. Take color blindness, a condition that occurs in approximately 8 percent of the population, mostly men. This is obviously a sensory deficit. On the other hand, some women possess an enhanced color vision, with the ability to distinguish between what, to the rest of us, seem identical shades of green. (Men, such as myself, may never fully grasp the concept of magenta, alas.) Thresholds of pain may also owe to genetic differences, a subject receiving increased scrutiny.[15]

The implications of this research are profound. When one considers that virtually everything we know about ourselves and the world is based on information obtained through the senses, the fact that objective differences exist in people's sensory abilities suggests that our consensus reality may encompass a far wider spectrum than previously appreciated.

Not only are we as individuals the product of our senses, but the way we experience facets of our own existence may differ meaningfully from that of our fellows.

High Sensitivity

Psychologist Elaine Aron has written extensively about highly sensitive persons (HSPs), a term she coined based on interviews or consultations with thousands of sensitives over a period of a dozen years.[16] Aron describes HSPs thusly:

> Highly sensitive individuals are those born with a tendency to notice more in their environment and deeply reflect on everything before acting. . . . They are also more easily overwhelmed by "high volume" or large quantities of input arriving at once. They try to avoid this. . . .
>
> Although HSPs notice more, they do not necessarily have better eyes, ears, sense of smell, or taste buds—although some do report having at least one sense that is very keen. Mainly, their brains process information more thoroughly. This processing is not just in the brain, however, since highly sensitive people, children or adults, have faster reflexes . . . are more affected by pain, medications, and stimulants; and have more reactive immune systems and more allergies. In a sense, their entire body is designed to detect and understand more precisely whatever comes in.[17]

Aron adds that HSPs are "unusually empathetic," feeling their own emotions and paying heed to others' more intensely than other people do. They also tend to have rich inner lives (with complex, vivid dreams) and come across as highly perceptive, creative, and intuitive when able to surmount what often is a natural inclination toward shyness, fearfulness, stress, and withdrawal.[18]

Aron believes that sensitivity has been built into human neurobiology for sound evolutionary reasons. Other species, she says, are made up of "roving" individuals and "sitting" individuals. The rovers boldly seek out such necessities as food, warmth, and shelter, while the more cautious sitters hang back. "There are enormous advantages," she writes, "to having a . . . minority who reflect before acting. They notice potential danger sooner . . . think carefully about consequences . . . and often insist that the others pause . . . and develop the best strategy. Clearly the two [dispositions] work best in combination."[19]

Two eminent psychologists at Harvard University, Jerome Kagan and Nancy Snidman, have done much to document that people do seem to fall naturally into these two groupings. In their book *The Long Shadow of Temperament,* Kagan and Snidman note that approximately one-fifth of the young children they've studied are "high reactors" who demonstrate high levels of discomfort or distress at novel stimuli or situations. The 40 percent who are "low reactors," in contrast, readily welcome and adapt to new experiences. This pattern typically extends into adolescence and, odds are, beyond.[20]

As we saw in chapter 4, infants with more electrical activity and blood flow in the right frontal part of their neocortex are characteristically fearful. Aron interprets this finding as reflecting the *inborn nature* of high sensitivity. It makes sense, she says, because the brain's "behavioral inhibition system," which is presumed to be especially active in HSPs, would be associated with the thinking (the "wait and see") part of the brain.[21] Given this predisposition for avoidance rather than approach, HSPs would be apt to intensively monitor and process incoming stimuli, whether aural, visual, olfactory . . . or, I might add, *emotional.*

Sensory Defensiveness

Aron speculates that as many as 15 to 20 percent of children are highly sensitive.[22] This estimate is shared by another researcher, Sharon Heller, an exponent of what she terms "sensory defensiveness." (Heller's book is arrestingly titled *Too Loud, Too Bright, Too Fast, Too Tight.*[23]) She agrees with the hypothesis that sensitivity often, although not always, originates in infancy. "For most adults," she relates, "hypersensitivity is a long-standing . . . problem. Their parents often recall that they were unusually sensitive during infancy—they may not have liked being cuddled, they may have started easily to noise."[24] However, she adds, "any trauma that disrupts the nervous system at any age can generate sensory defensiveness." Such trauma, she argues, can "alter brain chemistry and literally rewire the brain."[25] And sensory overload, however acquired, increases stress as well as vulnerability to illness.[26]

Heller cites the following as evidence for sensory defensiveness at an early age:

- Tactile-defensive newborns will resist snuggling by stiffening or pushing away.[27]
- Highly reactive infants show a faster heart rate when stressed and even when asleep.[28]
- Anecdotally, many sensory-defensive adults recall having an especially acute sense of smell as children, along with pronounced allergies.[29]

Over time, sensory defensiveness has a major effect on the body, according to Heller. She profiles a woman known as Sandra. Whereas Sandra "always had a weak immune system and a sensitive constitution," at age thirty-eight she still suffers from a veritable catalog of debilitating conditions: chronic fatigue, aching muscles, sleep difficulties, headaches, asthma, and allergies.[30] Why might this be so? Heller implicates the body's fight-or-flight system. In people who are sensory defensive, she says, this system is constantly in operation. Environmental stimuli that wouldn't trigger a stressful reaction in other people cause a chronic stress response in these individuals. Heller states that "eventually the immune system is depleted and the body succumbs and breaks down."[31] At that point, she notes, the stage is set for a variety of ailments, including chronic fatigue and depression, sleep interruptions and nightmares, decreased memory and ability to concentrate, high blood pressure, migraine headaches, irritable bowel syndrome, ulcers and gastrointestinal problems, allergies, skin disorders, and chronic pain.[32]

If Heller is correct, such people are susceptible to the environmental ills prominent in the profiles of the four individuals I sketched toward the beginning of this chapter: Sally, Edward, Betty, and Hank. An allergen or pollen of little consequence to most people—maybe even a low-level noise, a flickering light, or a stray aroma—could trigger or accelerate legitimate somatic challenges that most of us, thankfully, never encounter. In some instances, one might speculate, these challenges extend to even stranger anomalies.

Sensory Processing Disorder

High reactors, HSPs, and sensory defensives—these concepts (and neurobiologies) have penetrated public awareness through a new term that includes a requisite word for our time: "disorder." Sensory processing disorder (SPD) will seem familiar to anyone who's read through the previous sections. The difference, perhaps, is that it's attracted the attention of occupational therapists as much or more than psychologists. It also focuses squarely on children, who have come to occupy the attention of baby boomers who are now parents themselves.

A psychologist and occupational therapist, the late A. Jean Ayres, first described the condition in 1972 as revolving around difficulty handling information coming through the senses, including not just the five obvious senses but the equally critical proprioceptive and vestibular senses. The latter tell us, respectively, where our limbs are in relation to the rest of our body and how our body is oriented in space. Examples of such difficulties include:

- Being extremely sensitive to touch but not being able to tell *where* one is being touched
- Having shaky balance or inability to maintain an upright position (known as ataxia)
- Not using the left and right sides of one's body in a coordinated manner
- Being unsure how to carry out new or unfamiliar movements
- Bumping into people and things and being generally clumsy
- Having extreme reactions to sensory stimuli that the rest of us take for granted[33]

These types of problems, according to Ayres and her successors, reflect a neural shortfall—a disconnect between sensation itself and its translation into meaning and action. With these children, the brain might not automatically recognize where a given sensation is coming from or whether that sensation is important or trivial, dangerous or benign. It's a function that most of us take for granted, but kids with SPD feel overwhelmed, frustrated, confused, or tormented by stimuli on an ongoing basis. These feelings translate into problematic behavior, including irritability, jumpiness, and full-blown tantrums.

To their parents, teachers, and peers, this behavior occurs for no apparent reason. The children come across as some combination of withdrawn, inattentive, annoying, spacey, disrespectful, stubborn, unruly, or unpredictable. They are considered learning disabled or consigned as discipline problems. The inability to get through to such kids can cause the most dedicated of parents and other caregivers to feel frustrated or guilty themselves. Here is a case in point, as expressed by Dr. Karen Smith, the mother of a boy named Evan (and coauthor of *The Sensory Sensitive Child,* a book inspired by him): "[I came to understand that] Evan was not oppositional by nature. Nor had he been poorly parented. Instead, he was at the end of his rope, trying to meet the demands of his world without the necessary neurological foundation. He was trying—and failing—to please the adults at school and at home as we dragged him through his life, oblivious to the challenges he faced every day."[34]

One question that naturally arises is whether SPD overlaps with conditions such as autism and attention deficit hyperactivity disorder (ADHD), which present some of the same symptoms. The first answer is that the majority of children with SPD are not autistic because they don't experience breakdowns in the three areas that typify autism: language development, social affiliation, and empathy.[35] Research also suggests that SPD is a separate condition from ADHD.[36]

Through her work in the Brain Research Institute at the University of California–Los Angeles in the 1960s and 1970s, Ayres became convinced that the efficient organization, interpretation, and use of sensory information underlies every aspect of perception and behavior. She realized (as was described in chapter 4) that the brain thrives on environmental stimuli: with no stimuli, there is nothing for the brain to do. Sensory integration, according to Ayres, is the product of three component processes: *sensory modulation* (the brain's automatic adjustment to the intensity of incoming stimuli), *sensory discrimination* (the brain's ability to distinguish different sources and types of sensory experience and judge their relative meaning), and *motor planning* (the ability to respond to sensory input with organized, purposeful motor activity).

Ayres likened the breakdown of sensory integration to a "traffic jam in the brain."[37] A child who has trouble with any of the constituent processes will find moment-to-moment going a challenge. Recall the title of Heller's book: we can see that such children would indeed react to things as too loud, too bright, too fast, or too tight, as well as too hot, too cold, too crowded, too smelly, or too yucky. They may report puzzling things to their parents or teachers as follows:

"I'm allergic to things on my skin."
"I don't like that shirt. It's too spicy on the inside."
"The sound of the waves is making me crazy in my head."
"I'm bleeding on the inside!" (This last is one child's reaction to pain.)

Beyond the five senses we know and appreciate, Ayres drew special attention to two more: the vestibular and proprioceptive. The focal point of the former is the inner ear; vestibular input helps us maintain our balance by telling us whether we're at rest or in motion, how fast and in what direction we're moving, and what objects are moving around us. Proprioceptive input comes to the brain from all over the body, including the joints, muscles, and bones, to give us the sense of what our body *feels like* at any given moment and where it is in space. Together these two systems literally keep us grounded. They regulate our posture and muscle tone. They help us negotiate our distance from other people and things.

A child who has difficulty with either of these two senses will simply not have the same relationship with gravity, you might say, as a typical person. He or she may seem clumsy or disorganized. Motor planning challenges—such as learning to write, color in the lines, put puzzles together, hit a baseball, ride a bike—may arise as well.[38]

Based on such information, Evan's mom began to come to some realizations about her son.

> [He was] a boy who couldn't—*absolutely couldn't*—stop thinking about the seam of his sock or the waistband of his underwear or the tag on the back of his shirt. A boy who couldn't button his pants, zip his jacket, or fasten his seat belt because he wasn't able to tell which of his fingers were touching the things he was handling. A boy who constantly made noise in order to screen out noise. A boy who bumped into things and moved around a lot in order to maintain his balance. A boy who felt under attack by his skin, by smells, by noises. By his friends. By his father. By me. No wonder he was pushing back. His body was in a constant state of alert, and he was putting out tremendous effort just to get through each day.[39]

This reference to a "constant state of alert," or hypervigilance, should remind us of what we learned in chapter 3: that the bodymind can be programmed in infancy, in childhood, even before birth, to react at a lowered threshold. Highly sensitive persons and sensory defensives, as both Elaine Aron and Sharon Heller observed, have more reactive immune systems and a greater incidence of allergies. So it should come as no surprise that allergies and other immune issues plague many of children with SPD.[40]

It might not be a revelation to learn as well that at least some children with SPD report anomalous perceptions.[41] This can perhaps be understood based on the very term "sensory *integration*" and the fact that it is done effortlessly, outside of consciousness. With kids—or adults, for that matter—who have SPD, the integration does not, by definition, take place seamlessly. What happens, one might ask, in the gaps?

Remember Rush, the writer we met in the last chapter, whose high-speed car chase as a teenager nearly ended in disaster. Before his car hit an embankment and flipped into the air, one could say that his senses were perfectly well integrated—even (like his car's engine) "firing on all cylinders." But once that car flew dangerously out of control, his senses (particularly the vestibular and proprioceptive systems) jumbled. Fear was driving his bodymind, and his perceptions drastically altered. In such cases, I would argue that one's senses are dis-integrated and one's feelings temporarily dissociated. Could this situation effectively open a gateway whereby anomalous information becomes available? Likewise, for individuals for whom dissociation is a more or less permanent feature of their personality—or for whom SPD or its equivalent is a way of life—might anomalous influences creep through? Could Susan, the woman we met in chapter 1 who awoke at night with a strong sense of her father's presence (and his hair tonic) conceivably have been processing something primarily *external* rather than reacting with a start to an upwelling of her own deep-seated memories? I ask this question not with naïveté but with the intent of provoking serious consideration.

Thin Boundaries

The foregoing concepts fit very nicely under the umbrella of "boundaries," a personality construct developed by Ernest Hartmann, a psychiatrist and sleep disorder researcher at Newton-Wellesley Hospital in suburban Boston.[42] Throughout this book, I will stress the utility of Hartmann's concept and return to it often. This is because it enables us to assess, in terms of personal attributes and behavior we can *see*, the connections within each of us: the neural, hormonal, and immune linkages that make up our bodymind and characterize our self.

Hartmann asserts that everyone can be characterized on a spectrum of boundaries from thick to thin. He states, "There are people who strike us as very solid and well organized; they keep everything in its place. They are well defended. They seem rigid, even armored; we sometimes speak of them as 'thick-skinned.' Such people, in my view, have very thick boundaries. At the other extreme are people who are especially sensitive, open, or vulnerable. In their minds, things are relatively fluid. . . . Such people have particularly thin boundaries. . . . I propose thick and thin boundaries as a broad way of looking at individual differences."[43]

His framework (figure 7) is especially useful given the evolutionary lesson we learned in chapter 3, namely that, without our body—and especially without our bodily *boundary*—we could not be sentient, or conscious, or individuals.[44] And of course we could not have individual personalities.

Hartmann's approach is robust, with at least five thousand individuals having taken his boundary questionnaire since the 1980s and some one hundred papers referencing the concept. Some of the characteristics evident in the *thin-boundary* personality type are:

- A less solid or definite sense of one's skin as a body boundary[45]
- An enlarged sense of merging with another person when kissing or making love[46]
- Sensitivity to physical and emotional pain, in oneself as well as in others[47]
- An enhanced ability to recall dreams[48] but also a tendency to experience nightmares[49]

Hartmann believes that the boundaries concept is not just a useful way to describe different people but also will be shown to reflect actual neurobiological differences.[50] I agree and will be elaborating on his provocative premise in this and coming chapters.

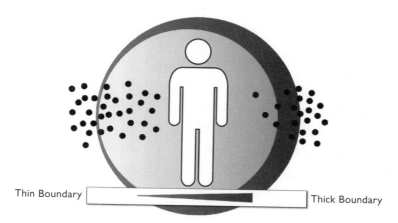

Figure 7. The boundaries concept.
Image provided by Eric Scafetta Design & Illustration.

Thin-boundary individuals, Hartmann proposes, are unusually sensitive from an early age, so they react—or recall reacting—more intensively to the usual traumas and difficulties of childhood.[51] In this vein, he draws on a fascinating study, "Unusual Sensitivities in Young Children," written by Paul Bergman and Sibylle Escalona and published in 1949.[52] Long before there was much attention to sensitivities, these researchers observed children ranging in age from three months to seven years old who were extraordinarily sensitive to stimulation (e.g., odors, sounds, colors, textures, temperatures) and whose feelings were also easily hurt. The children were observed rhythmically rocking themselves or covering their eyes and ears from unwelcome stimuli, which "seemed to have an extraordinarily intensive impact upon these children at a very early age. They were 'sensitive' in both meanings of the word: easily hurt, and easily stimulated. . . . Variations in sensory impression that made no difference to the average child made a great deal of difference to these children."[53]

Bergman and Escalona theorized that such kids start life with a high degree of sensitivity "against which they eventually succeed in building some defenses." However, if the defenses are invoked too early in the child's development—or if their formation is disturbed by some trauma—the stage could be set for psychological problems.[54] The researchers' surmise seems consistent with an observation made throughout the literature on environmental illness, namely that sensitivity and psychological challenges often go hand in hand.

Somatization

Similar associations have been made by Ian Wickramasekera, a psychologist intrigued by the psychosomatic nature of certain illnesses.[55] Wickramasekera turns the cause and effect around, however. Rather than assume that physical sensitivity predates or conditions the psychological consequences, he suggests that an individual's highly charged psychological issues can be *transmuted into physical symptoms* such as asthma and other forms of allergy, chronic pain and fatigue, and sleep disorders.

The process by which psychological distress engenders physical illness is termed somatization. "Put simply," Wickramasekera writes, "the [individual] is being . . . made sick by distressing secret perceptions, memories, or moods that [he or she] blocks from consciousness."[56] Despite the unconscious nature of somatization, the affected person can become manifestly hypersensitive[57] and even (in parallel with Hartmann's concept of thin boundaries) absorbed in the problems of others to such an extent that somatic symptoms develop out of this "surplus empathy."[58]

Overexcitabilities

A deep need for connections with other people is one of five areas of extreme sensitivity identified by Kazimierz Dabrowski (1902–1980), a Polish physician interested in personality development. Dabrowski studied "gifted" individuals and noted these recurring traits, which he called overexcitabilities:[59, 60]

- Psychomotor—surplus of energy, restlessness, curiosity
- Sensual—a strong reaction (either positive or negative) to sensory stimuli, aesthetic awareness
- Imaginational—strong visual thinking, vivid fantasy life, remembers dreams, enjoys poetry or metaphorical speech
- Intellectual—intense focus on particular topics, enjoys questioning and complex reasoning, problem solving
- Emotional—heightened emotional reactions, need for strong attachments, empathetic, difficulty adjusting to change

"Overexcitability," the translation of Dabrowski's term into English, is meant to convey the sheer abundance of energy possessed by gifted individuals and manifested in these areas. He believed that, by virtue of such energy, gifted children not only think differently from their peers, but they also register perceptions more intensively and feel things more deeply.[61] (Shades of Aron's HSP construct fifty years later.)

As one might expect, Dabrowski viewed overexcitabilities as the stuff of neuroses as well as giftedness. He theorized that individuals exhibiting these traits would inevitably undergo a series of developmental crises that, if navigated successfully, would enable a more distinctive and high-functioning personality to emerge.[62] The linkage is borne out in one therapist's comment that "years of experience with gifted children have convinced me that . . . heightened sensitivity is often at the root of various problems that bring gifted persons to counseling."[63]

Another counselor who works with gifted children notes an even more intriguing theme, namely the apparent past-life memories these children sometimes relate.

> When I am speaking to groups of parents and suggest that such memories . . . are common among . . . profoundly gifted children, I am bombarded by stories, which have become so plentiful now that they can no longer be dismissed as rare or even unusual. These children (particularly between the ages of 3 and 5) may speak of their "other mothers" from "before" when they lived someplace else. Or they may correctly (and often with intense feeling) identify photos of places they (or members of their family) have never been. They relate what they did when they "used to be a grown-up." . . . At varying ages they may tell of talking to relatives or friends who have died . . . they insist that these interactions are *real*."[64]

I note here that the Institute of Noetic Sciences (a research organization founded by former Apollo astronaut Edgar Mitchell) finds highly creative people to be more apt to demonstrate anomalous talents than any other group studied thus far.[65]

This is yet more evidence, albeit anecdotal, for a link between sensitivity and the anomalous. We'll be exploring such fascinating terrain more extensively as we continue. For now, suffice it to say that Dabrowski's work merits renewed attention because he captured certain key elements of sensitivity that more recent researchers are alighting on today.

Absorption

Recall that the proclivity for immersing oneself in something—whether a personal relationship, a memory, or a daydream—is said to characterize the thin-boundary person. This personality characteristic is termed absorption. As first articulated by Auke Tellegen and Gilbert Atkinson in 1974, absorption is "a disposition for having episodes of total attention . . . result[ing] in a heightened sense of reality of the attentional object, imperviousness to distracting events, and an altered sense of reality in general."[66] Some statements conveying this capacity are the following:[67]

- "The sound of a voice can be so fascinating to me that I can just go on listening to it."
- "While acting in a play, I have sometimes really felt the emotions of the character and have 'become' him or her . . . forgetting, as it were, both myself and the audience."
- "I can sometimes recollect certain past experiences in my life with such clarity and vividness that it is like living them again."
- "If I wish, I can imagine (or daydream) some things so vividly that they hold my attention in the way a good movie or story does."

It may not be entirely surprising to learn that one of our leading actresses, Meryl Streep, is an exemplar of this quality of absorption and, more generally, of high sensitivity and thin boundaries. "I have my antenna out, what can I say?" she explains in an interview. "That's my job as an actor. I'm hyper-alert to all signals. My boundaries are not so clear. I sort of bleed out into whoever I'm talking to."[68] Similarly, here is a revealing quote by impressionist David Frye, who was popular in the 1960s and 1970s, sending up presidents Johnson and Nixon. Frye describes the process whereby he would learn to mimic someone: "I would begin to believe I was that person. I would make his facial expressions, imitate his voice. I would get vibrations from just a brief meeting with [that] person . . . and hours later I would still be feeling them."[69]

Many actors and actresses—indeed, artists in general—may operate this way. Absorption is closely related to both hypnotic susceptibility and dissociation, which, as we've seen, connotes a lack of identification with one's immediate, felt sense.[70] Lines between what is manifestly real and what is imaginary become blurred as the person becomes immersed in some reverie or experience.[71] Such deep experiences are sometimes perceived as mystical or transcendent.[72]

In my view, environmental sensitivity may well be a precursor of the tendency toward absorption. In their paper, Bergman and Escalona note that one of the children they observed (called Berta, a pseudonym) would sit entranced while listening to certain symphonies. Likewise, she would become absorbed in experiences of touch.[73] From their description, it appears that Berta—and other children like her—chose to escape certain noxious stimuli by delving into certain pleasing ones. The private world they entered into could be construed as a crucible for introspection and fantasy-proneness. As we'll see in the next section, this dissociated world is also the entryway into anomalous perception.

Fantasy-Proneness

One of the seminal papers relevant to these topics is "The Fantasy-Prone Personality," written by Sheryl Wilson and Theodore Barber and published in 1983.[74] The authors described a group of fifty-two female subjects "who fantasize a large part of the time, who typically 'see,' 'hear,' 'smell,' 'touch,' and fully experience what they fantasize."[75]

These women engaged in vivid fantasizing from an early age. Imaginary companions and imaginary worlds were experienced "as real as real," while the awareness of actual surroundings tended to recede. Much of this ability appears built on a *profound involvement with sensory experience*.[76] A typical account is as follows: "I loved touch best and smell next best—the feel of my grandmother's skin, soft but wrinkled, the smell of grandpa's pipe and the perfume of a woman who was a friend of mother's, the smell of Sunday morning's roast in the oven, outside after the rain, the woods in autumn, smelling the crushed leaves and hearing them, too, my soft velvet dress when I was six, running in the rain, cold drops, shivering. . . ."[77]

Wilson and Barber suggest that vivid sensory experiences (and the vivid memories associated with them) are the precursors of fantasy-proneness, providing the raw material from which the person goes on to construct his or her remarkably lucid fantasies.[78] This makes sense in light of Aron's conjecture that highly sensitive infants and children have a more highly developed implicit memory (the kind of memory that relies on raw experience rather than words) than their less sensitive counterparts.[79]

Furthermore, while involvement in fantasy ebbs for the great majority of children by adolescence, fantasy-prone individuals carry their intensive involvement into adult life—some saying that they "practically live their lives in fantasy."[80] For example, a person will see, hear, smell, taste, and feel what is being described during a conversation—an ability remarkably close to synesthesia. Or that person may, while "watching a bird or looking at a tree . . . suddenly lose the sense of their body and feel they are the bird or the tree."[81] Such strongly dissociative experiences have more than a hypnotic quality. They are more like full-fledged hallucinations since "imagined aromas are sensed, imagined sounds are heard, and imagined tactile sensations are felt as convincingly as those produced by actual stimuli. . . . When [fantasy-prone individuals] recall an event, they are able to see, hear, and feel it again in much the same way as they did originally. . . . They sometimes feel that their fantasy world is real and that the actual world is a fantasy."[82]

It's equally noteworthy that the imagery arises automatically *in response to the person's thoughts and feelings.*[83] In chapter 7, we noted how imagery is the bodymind's native tongue—a language intimately connected with feeling. That fantasy-prone people have such a fluid (and florid) connection with their unconscious suggests that they may also be able to harness their feeling energy in unusual, transformative ways.

The balance of Wilson and Barber's remarkable study details the extent to which fantasy-prone people "see themselves as psychic or sensitive and report numerous [anomalous] experiences." Perceptions of this type include telepathy, precognition, out-of-body experiences, and seeing or hearing apparitions, not to mention the sense of having a palpable influence on electrical appliances.[84]

The perception that one affects lights, watches, and so on—along with virtually every other trait distinguishing the fantasy-prone person—would strike most people who are *not* fantasy-prone (or not thin-boundary) as delusory. However, Wilson and Barber concluded that their subjects were not pathological. "The overwhelming majority of fantasy-prone individuals," they write, "seem to fall within a broad range of normal functioning, and it is thus inappropriate to apply a psychiatric diagnosis to them. [Most] work, love, and socialize within the broad average range of adjustment."[85]

Work done by another pair of researchers, Steven Lynn and Judith Rhue of Ohio University and the University of Toledo, respectively, agrees with that assessment. Lynn and Rhue replicated the earlier study by casting an inquisitive eye on twenty-three fantasy-prone individuals whose characteristics distinguished them from a pool of more than fourteen thousand fellow college students.[86]

There's yet one more piece of evidence that fantasy-proneness is not a pathological condition: the many adults who, as children, had realistic imaginary companions yet grew out of this phase naturally. Indeed, it's estimated that up to two-thirds of all children may have entertained at least one imaginary companion (IC).[87] These kids—of preschool or elementary school age—reflect several of Dabrowski's overexcitabilities (imaginational, intellectual, emotional) at this stage in their life.[88] Contrary to popular supposition, they are no more shy than their peers (they may actually be more outgoing) but perhaps harbor more anxiety about their social interactions.[89] The IC may appear because the child is dealing with something trying (e.g., difficulty in making friends, the imminent arrival of a younger sibling) or attempting to come to grips with challenging feelings ranging from anger to fear to loneliness.[90] However, an IC may equally reflect the child's capacity for vivid imagination and his or her interest in fun and companionship,[91] an inference supported by the fact that ICs are typically abandoned when real children are around.[92] Children with an IC are well able to distinguish their imaginary playmates from real;[93] they also have no greater difficulty than their peers in making or keeping real friends.[94] In any event, the IC will usually disappear by age ten.[95]

A minority of kids with ICs, however, will extend their penchant for vivid fantasy and their strong connection with bodymind feeling and imagery into adolescence and beyond. They become the fantasy-prone adults described earlier. Not only do they continue to experience vivid imagery but they evidence a higher than usual awareness of their moment-to-moment internal state.[96]

Transliminality

The idea that certain people have an exceptionally direct *connectedness within* has a distinguished history. An early exponent was psychologist William James, who, along with his colleagues at the turn of the twentieth century, was very much taken with what was called "subliminal consciousness." Today the concept is advanced by Michael Thalbourne, formerly at the University of Adelaide, who has updated and refreshed it. Thalbourne writes about transliminality, which is the tendency for psychological material to cross thresholds in or out of consciousness.[97] (See figure 8.) People who display a high degree of transliminality "might . . . be expected to have erupt into consciousness, from the preconscious, experiences that we variously know . . . as psychic, mystical, and creative," he asserts. "Conversely, persons low in transliminality would be expected to . . . rarely if ever report [such] experiences."[98]

Studies done by Thalbourne and his associate Peter Delin have documented nine aspects of the highly transliminal person.

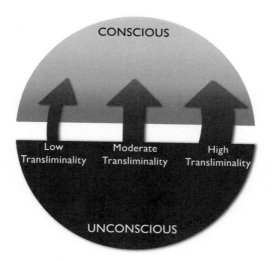

Figure 8. The transliminality concept.
Image provided by Eric Scafetta Design & Illustration.

- a creative personality
- mystical or religious experience
- magical thinking (i.e., believing that one can or does influence external events not normally susceptible to influence)
- manic-like experience
- absorption
- fantasy-proneness
- paranormal belief and experiences
- an interest in dream interpretation
- a heightened sensitivity to environmental stimulation

Additionally, there are indications that highly transliminal people are more likely to experience synesthesia (conjoined senses). This would make sense if we suppose that synesthesia reflects a higher degree of neural and sensory interconnectedness.[99] (This likelihood will be taken up at greater length in the next chapter.)

Context-Induced Experiences

A key question that arises with regard to fantasy-proneness and high transliminality is: what, exactly, is crossing into awareness? To what extent is the imagery or perception an accurate representation of what's in the external environment versus a reflection of one's internal feelings or pre-occupations? Put another way, how likely is it that this type of individual is so empathetic, so suggestible, that legitimate external stimuli prompt his or her internal imagery machine to *manufacture* an experience that becomes as "real as real"?

Apparitions can certainly be provoked by an intense need for something: think of island castaways conjuring up a realistic rescue ship or parched nomads visualizing an oasis in the desert.[100] More prosaically, people can fairly easily be tricked into sensing that which does not exist. This was memorably demonstrated on BBC Television one April Fools Day, when viewers were told by a respected professor that it was now possible to broadcast smells and that the aromas of onions and coffee could be perceived by anyone concentrating sufficiently on his or her end of the television. Hundreds of viewers wrote in to say that they had, indeed, picked up those particular scents (along with a few others not mentioned).[101]

In assessing such examples, the late Gordon Rattray Taylor, in his book *The Natural History of the Mind,* notes that "the production of imagery is going on all the time in the older, primitive part of the brain, but is normally ignored or shut off by the cortex. . . . Only when the cortex is numbed or inhibited—or when the fantasy is strongly amplified by [need or expectation]—does it break through into consciousness."[102]

Additionally, it's clear that some people, given sufficiently ambiguous stimuli, are likely to misinterpret what's going on in their environment. Useful work has been done in this area by James Houran and Rense Lange (both associated at the time with the University of Illinois–Springfield). In one experiment, a couple reported unusual events in a perfectly unhaunted house after simply being told the location was haunted.[103] Beyond simple suggestibility, Houran and Lange assert that people who are most comfortable with deciding quickly what's going on rather than taking their time to evaluate something strange, new, or different are more likely to report anomalous experiences.[104] This process is intensified, the investigators found, if the situation arouses anxiety or fear.[105] In such cases, people will misinterpret normal stimuli (e.g., sounds, smells, lighting, object movements) for presences and the like.

Other Causes of Hallucinations

I don't doubt that Houran and Lange are correct. Nor, for that matter, do I doubt Richard Wiseman, a popular British psychologist who's made a name for himself by investigating reportedly haunted locations and noting a variety of situational factors (e.g., lighting levels, ceiling height, acoustics) that might lead to apparitional perceptions.[106] Nor do I dispute that imagery can be produced by any number of other factors.

Sensory deprivation and extended isolation, for instance, are well known to generate apparitions. A variety of adventurers over the years—balloonists, sailors, and pilots, including Charles Lindbergh on his famous trans-Atlantic flight—have reported being joined by, and even conversing with, phantom companions.[107]

An organic condition known as Charles Bonnet syndrome can also produce quite interesting imagery. It is most common in elderly people.[108] As an example, an eighty-eight-year-old man, in full possession of his faculties but losing his sight, begins to see small cartoon characters that are, to all appearances, lifelike. The hallucinations are believed to result from his brain becoming "bored" by the lack of incoming visual stimuli; it fills in the blanks by allowing a potpourri of remembered images and details to resurface.[109] This is an unusual phenomenon, to be sure, but there is nothing necessarily anomalous about it.

Nor is there any doubt that illusions can and do arise from numerous other sources, whether psychiatric illness (e.g., schizophrenia), neurological disorder, traumatic head injury, seizures, strokes, migraines, macular degeneration, neurodegeneration, sleep deprivation, or the use or abuse of certain drugs or medications.[110] People afflicted by temporal lobe epilepsy are known to experience not only visual hallucinations but also auditory, olfactory, and gustatory (taste) hallucinations. In these people, smells can suddenly arise that are rotten or sickening, and tastes can occur that are vividly bitter, sweet, or salty.[111] A condition known as phantosmia, possibly caused by nasal polyps or damage to olfactory or gustatory nerves, causes still other people to perceive unsettlingly strong phantom smells.[112] A temporal lobe seizure can occasionally trigger a synesthetic experience,[113] as can the ingestion of hallucinogenic drugs.[114] Brain lesions or severe head injuries can result in individuals seeing "vague forms moving at the periphery of their vision when no one is there," hearing "nonexistent muffled music in the next room," smelling "both pleasant and unpleasant smells that are not present," and having "strange tastes in their mouths."[115] A Swiss neurosurgeon was even able to conjure up the perception of a "shadow person" mimicking his patient's movements by electrically stimulating a region in her brain called the tempoparietal junction. The woman found the experience to be unsettling, even scary, although she knew full well the stranger behind her was not real.[116]

Furthermore, a certain percentage of the population (my wife, for one) occasionally experiences vivid imagery during the drowsy state before sleep (when it is called hypnagogic imagery) or in the period before fully waking up (hynopompic imagery). The perceptions are generally visual and/or auditory. Sometime they relate to past events, ranging from childhood memories to activities undertaken earlier in the day. A person may appear to be bending down in a garden, for example, or overhear snippets of conversation. On other occasions, the imagery seems altogether foreign, from another time or place. The experience can be enthralling as much as it can be downright puzzling.[117] Explanations tend to suppose, as did Rattray Taylor, that sensations, memories, and feelings are constantly being processed beneath our conscious awareness. In drowsy, somnambulant states, some of this material floats toward the surface, where people sometimes become aware of it.[118]

How many people experience hallucinations? The numbers are larger than you might expect. For a start, surveys have found that anywhere from 19 to 28 percent of the population experiences sleep-related hallucinations.[119] A poll of some thirteen thousand Europeans disclosed that as many as 40 percent report at least an occasional hallucination. However, this same survey indicated that those who report *recurring* hallucinatory perceptions are far fewer: perhaps 11 to 12 percent.[120]

Presumably, this subset of individuals is fantasy-prone and, at root, highly transliminal. If their hypnagogic or hypnopompic images are especially bizarre or frightening, they might be mistakenly attributed to the paranormal.[121] In support of this mechanism, it's noteworthy that many of Wilson and Barber's fantasy-prone subjects *did* report frequently experiencing vivid imagery before falling asleep or when waking up. As opposed to the many people who are able to realize that the images are not really there, the fantasy-prone group tended to feel that what they were viewing had its own, independent existence. This class of fantasy-prone people can evidently call up imagery equally well with their eyes open or closed.[122]

Metachoric Experiences

This type of real-as-real fantasy has been termed *metachoric* by psychologist and philosopher Celia Green.[123] It is essentially, she says, a waking dream—one that can be entered into and left off with no obvious discontinuity *and* where the person's surroundings appear as immediate and realistic as the normal, physical world. Green has examined numerous accounts of apparitional and otherwise uncanny experiences, including out-of-body travels and lucid dreams, and believes "a good many of them [are] completely hallucinatory."[124] In some cases, she notes, the person is observed carrying on a conversation or engaging in a routine activity, whereas that person perceives himself or herself to be doing something completely different. At such times, the individual is literally in a world of his or her own. Sometimes the discontinuity is marked (e.g., the person snapping out of it is somewhat shaken), but sometimes he or she slips into and out of the metachoric experience unaware, indeed, *preferring* the internal experience over the more mundane, everyday world. The experience is evidently akin to an absorbing motion picture, except the person is *in* the movie.[125] Sometimes the movie is summoned consciously, but other times it runs spontaneously.[126]

Shared Perceptions

If one accepts that highly transliminal, absorption-prone, and fantasy-prone people account for most reports of the paranormal, one difficulty remains: namely, the cases where two or more people report a *shared* vision or sensory perception of some kind. Of relevance here are several well-documented investigations into reportedly haunted locations, involving subjects regarded as sensitive as well as controls. In these cases, certain parts of the locale (e.g., a hallway, a bedroom) are consistently identified as sources for the unusual perceptions.[127, 128] This trend recurs regardless of whether the subjects are told beforehand that the location is reputedly haunted.

A trio of explanations has been proposed. First is the idea advanced by Houran and Lange that normal surroundings can elicit offbeat perceptions in more than one person so long as *each* of those individuals is (take your pick) suggestible, anxious, fearful, prone toward magical thinking or paranormal belief, or simply uncomfortable with ambiguity. If two such people are together in the same setting, they might then mutually reinforce those misperceptions. Second, Wiseman's research points toward certain *environmental elements* being the culprit when more than one person reports an anomaly. And third, remember neuroscientist Michael Persinger's assertion, in chapter 6, that electromagnetic perturbations—along with a sensitized temporal lobe—are responsible for anomalous perceptions.

These theories undoubtedly apply in many, perhaps most, instances. But they fall short of accounting for the observation made by Cornell at the beginning of this chapter. How could a person who has just arrived on the scene purport to see the exact same imagery as someone else with whom he was completely unfamiliar? One might reply, "He was simply fabricating," or, "He just wanted to lend credence to the subject's description." Both are surely possibilities, but I return to the literature on innate sensory differences—high sensitivities, sensory defensiveness, overexcitabilities, thin boundaries—as the more likely (and scientifically supportable) explanation.

My own proposal is that *some* especially sensitive individuals may legitimately be reacting to *some* external influences in *some* situations. If these people fit a particular pattern—if they react to known environmental allergens, for instance—then we have bona fide physiological evidence for the possibility that they may react exceptionally to *other* stimuli as well. I suggest that environmental sensitivity may thus be a neurobiological marker for anomalous influences, assuming they do exist.

Hints of Extreme Sensitivity

It is tempting to chalk up reports of extraordinary sensitivities as instances of mental illness. But, given our ever-increasing ability to pinpoint the neurobiological foundations of behavior and perception, these susceptibilities may turn out to be just that—susceptibilities. Consider this provocative example, offered by psychiatrist William Philpott, of a patient known as Karl.

Karl had been under treatment for paranoid schizophrenia. . . . The morning of his first day in the hospital he exhibited his usual symptoms; however, he also complained of smelling gas. Based on my psychiatric training, I reasoned that this was another of Karl's delusions. I had seen many schizophrenics who said they smelled various things; I always assumed their ideas to be delusions. But . . . I began to look for a source of gas, for I knew that any person with a lowered biochemical homeostasis with a prior record of . . . allergic reactions to either food or chemicals would be [highly] sensitive to the incriminating substance. . . .

It turned out that . . . around the corner from his room was a stairway leading to the kitchen. I opened the door to the stairway, and to my surprise I, too, smelled gas. They had just cooked break-fast on a gas range below. He was right! He did smell gas; his hyper-sensitivity at detecting the presence of natural gas was acute because he was allergic to this substance. . . .

His history revealed that three years before, while driving a propane-filled fork truck in an apple warehouse cooler, he was over-come by the fumes from the truck. . . . It was after this that he devel-oped his psychosis, and these attacks had always coincided with his driving the fork truck in the apple cooler. He also reacted to several foods, but only gas fumes made him delusional.[129]

It would be interesting to know what other factors in Karl's background—his particular combination of nature and nurture—might have predisposed him to this unusual form of sensitivity. This is precisely the kind of information I aimed to collect in my own survey, the results of which are discussed in the next chapter.

What's Out There to Take In

Before we head there, however, I wish to offer two other intriguing findings, which suggest that human beings in general take in much more than they are consciously aware of. The first, reasonably well-known example is referred to as "Gorillas in our Midst"; the experiment was developed by psychologist Daniel Simon.[130] Here's how the exercise went down in a huge conference room of psychotherapists—although it consistently goes the same way, regardless of the audience. Here, the therapists were being shown a videotape of two teams (three players on each team), one dressed in white shirts and one in black shirts, passing around a basketball. The session facilitator was Jon Kabat-Zinn, the author and advocate of mindfulness-based meditation.

"Watch the team in white," instructed Kabat-Zinn, "and count how many times they pass the ball." As the tape played, both the white and black team members slowly wove in and out of each other, methodically passing their basketball. After a minute or so, Kabat-Zinn stopped the tape, cautioning the few in the audience who'd erupted into somewhat mystifying laughter not to say anything while he asked everyone else how many passes they'd counted. The estimates varied considerably. "Now I'm going to play the same tape again," he said, "and, this time, don't count the passes. Just watch." As the tape played, more bursts of startled laughter erupted around the hall. "How many of you saw something unusual?" he asked, and now about half the audience raised their hands. "I'm going to play the tape one more time," he said, "and watch the right corner of the frame."

This time, everyone finally got it. Waves of laughter rolled through the audience as they finally noticed someone dressed in a gorilla suit walking slowly through the teams, pausing in the middle of the frame, looking right at the camera, beating its chest a few times, and then walking out of the frame. Why had everyone missed it the first time?[131]

Actually, not *everyone* missed it—a few did get it the first time the tape was played. And therein lies the kernel of my argument about sensitivity. I suspect that, if Hartmann's boundary questionnaire were to be given to the therapists in that very room (or, for that matter, to any large enough audience), we would discern a trend. Namely, the people who see the gorilla early on are *thin-boundary individuals*. In the words of Elaine Aron, such highly sensitive people "notice more in their environment. . . . Their entire body is designed to detect and understand more precisely whatever comes in."[132]

While the rest of us are often afflicted with what's called inattentional blindness (the tendency not to notice the gorilla), for certain people it *jumps right out.*

Animals, Children, and Autistics

Interestingly, animal psychologist Temple Grandin believes that individuals who are autistic will naturally see the gorilla because they perceive the world in a fairly concrete, holistic manner. Most other people, she suggests, are too busy deciphering visual and other incoming stimuli through their neocortex. Their brains "use the detailed raw data of the world to form a generalized concept or schema, and that's what reaches consciousness. Fifty shades of brown turn into just one unified color: brown."[133] It's an entirely autonomic process, out of our control. So most of us end up seeing what we expect to see in any given situation—and who would expect a gorilla to come sauntering through a basketball game?

In contrast, Grandin proposes that animals would "get" the gorilla, because they resemble autistic people in their information processing ("You can't get anything past a cow," she quips).[134] Both animals and people with autism may well experience the world as a "swirling mass of tiny details."[135] (We might similarly infer that children—especially younger children—would pick up the gorilla because they haven't yet become accustomed to seeing, or excluding from sight, based on fixed conceptualization.) Grandin makes some strong arguments and, in this sense, perhaps at least some individuals who are autistic (and young children, for that matter) can be said to resemble non-autistic people with thin boundaries.

Speaking of autism, science is beginning to catch up with the parents of autistic children, many of whom have insisted for years that the condition is not solely brain based. Bringing firsthand observations of compromised immune systems to the fore, they have attempted to train physicians' attention on the same clues.[136] The accumulating data indicate a *whole-body explanation,* with one potential cause being exposure to environmental toxins. Given that the condition often improves when children are put on a more careful diet, one prominent researcher comments that "it can't just be genetic, prenatal, hardwired, and hopeless." Pediatric neurologist Martha Herbert, of Massachusetts General Hospital and Harvard Medical School, goes on to state that she no longer sees autism as a disorder of the brain, but as a disorder that *affects* the brain. She comments, "What I believe is happening is that genes and environment interact, either in a fetus or a young child, changing cellular function all over the body. . . . And it's the interaction . . . that leads to altered sensory processing and impaired coordination in the brain."[137]

Her theory is consistent with the fact that many autistic kids have a history of food and airborne allergies, repeated ear infections, and eczema. The research is certainly suggestive: a study of more than seven hundred families with an autistic as well as a normal child found a significantly different profile of antibodies (also known as immunoglobulins) and other proteins (cytokines) that, beyond their immune effects, may influence brain proteins.[138] Additionally, a team at the University of California–Davis identified eleven genes governing natural killer immune cells that are much more active in autistic children. The kids studied had 40 percent more natural killer cells and 20 percent more B cells. The researchers' hunch now is that immune differences in a mother's bloodstream might predict whether she'll have a child with autism.[139]

Just as we saw with depression in chapter 4, autism is undoubtedly a complex condition caused by an interplay of immune, genetic, and environmental factors.[140] A child's immune system—or the mother's—may be the trigger for what's seemed, up until recently, to be a solely *neural* condition.

Of particular relevance to the thesis of this book, author William Stillman—who himself has Asperger's disorder, considered to be a mild form of autism—has collected numerous accounts of anomalous sensitivities among persons with autism.[141] Eight years before Stillman, author Donna Williams wrote of her own psychic experiences, such as out-of-body journeys and allegedly clairvoyant dreams.[142] Intriguingly, Williams muses throughout her book on why she is the way she is, invoking two

factors that will not seem strange to readers of this book: sensory sensitivity and thin boundaries. She describes being continually flooded with
sensory information and intensively registering other people's physical or
emotional pain "as though their energy [were] affecting me . . . whether
they displayed it or not."[143] She recalls "losing herself" in her surroundings at age six months (an impressive feat of recollection itself if true): this
remark is perfectly in keeping with the thin-boundary trait of absorption
that we surveyed earlier.

Absorption, in turn, reflects *dissociation,* i.e., a lack of identification
with one's immediate felt sense. The disconnect is evident in Williams'
contemplations regarding her very sense of self. As a child, she regarded
her body as something less than a tangible home and continues to question whether her selfhood has ever truly resided there. Perhaps due to her
many out-of-body perambulations, she has always identified bodily feelings as separate from the self, from the "I."[144]

Sense of self, it seems fair to say, constitutes a major distinguishing
factor in autism. Consider this striking report indicating that people
with a high-functioning form of autism (e.g., Asperger's disorder) have a
weaker sense of self than normal individuals.[145] The experiment, devised
by P. Read Montague Jr., a neuroscientist at Baylor University's College of
Medicine, was ingenious. He and his colleagues simultaneously scanned
the brains of mildly autistic teenagers and normal teenagers as they played
what Montague referred to as a "trust game"—a computer simulation
wherein two players receive an amount of money and then send whatever
amount they choose back and forth to the other player. Based on previous
research, Montague had identified a neural signature betokening the sense
of self: a pattern of activity in the cingulate cortex. The earlier research
(also carried out by Montague and his colleagues) had shown that, when a
person who is not autistic views someone else performing an activity (such
as athletes playing sports or ballet dancers dancing), he or she will show
increased blood flow in the cingulate cortex. This is not entirely surprising, because the cingulate cortex is known to be active during social
interactions—even virtual ones. It seems to track who is responsible for an
outcome during a social exchange.[146] During the trust game, however, the

autistic players showed this response far less than the normal subjects did.

"It was the first time an autistic kid had been scanned in a social exchange," observes Montague. "They cognitively understood the game. It's not that they [didn't] understand . . . it's that there is a very low level of 'self' response. It's impaired in them and the degree to which it is missing correlates with their autistic severity. The more you are missing the self response, the more autistic you are."[147]

I will venture to say that individuals with autism who are high functioning are thin-boundary people, whereas those who have a more severe form of the condition are thick-boundary people. The concept of boundaries in this case refers to the relative lack of connectivity across brain regions in autistic people and the relative overconnectivity within local areas.[148] An autistic person's sense of self, I propose, reflects this state of affairs.

While the evidence suggests that many or most people with autism are highly sensitive,[149] it is their *sense of self*, I believe, that determines whether they are high functioning or more significantly impaired. Those with a poorer sense of self (as Montague indicated) can be said to have thicker boundaries. When they dissociate, their displaced energy is likely to trigger anomalous occurrences—whereas Stillman, Williams, and other thin-boundary autistics are likely to *perceive* anomalies, and in a characteristic jumble of detail.

This distinction makes sense when we take a second look at Matthew Manning, the focus of any number of bizarre events whom we met in the last chapter. Manning most likely had thick boundaries from the beginning. As a child, he was "an introvert who . . . absolutely refused to talk to strangers. When scolded for mischievousness, he would withdraw into a corner and remain there, sometimes for hours, curled up in total isolation." Some years later, the headmaster of his boarding school described him as "a loner and rather lethargic." Even when being interviewed on television, he could appear aloof and self-absorbed.[150] One shrewd observer, the late psychiatrist Jan Ehrenwald, suggested that Manning was autistic. His family dynamics probably contributed, as the teenager seemed "locked in a muted conflict with his no-nonsense father" and the poltergeist activity that swirled around the younger Manning "seemed to defy the pedantic, law-and-order routine of the . . . household." Anomalous events "subsequently wrought havoc in the study rooms and dormitories of his prep school—one of the last citadels of unchallenged paternal authority in the British Isles."[151]

One further indication of Manning's pronounced autism as well as his displacement of felt energy springs from a period in his life (ages 15–16) when he produced remarkable automatic writing and drawing. The former was written both in English and in several foreign languages, including Greek and Arabic, which he could not speak. The drawings "seemed to be a striking mimicry of Albrecht Durer's, Leonardo da Vinci's, Pablo Picasso's, or Aubrey Beardsley's works. Even though flawed in some technical detail, [the drawings'] style and execution faithfully mirrored the original model."[152] This facility is reminiscent of the deeply withdrawn idiot savants of the type dramatized in the movie *Rain Man*. Such individuals present some extraordinary capacity—whether it's reciting entire pages of a phone book from memory or producing incredibly intricate artwork—that is so unexpected and self-contained that it is difficult to fathom. Of course, parapsychological manifestations are equally difficult to account for. When someone such as Manning evidences *both*, it's appropriate to consider that they might be related.

What Is Normal?

Autism, as currently understood, is not a single condition: it's a group of disorders with behavioral, language, and cognitive symptoms that bear some relation to each other. Asperger's disorder, as a mild form of the condition, is thus one of several autism spectrum disorders (ASDs). What people with these conditions have in common are many of the following (to varying degrees):[153]

- challenges with language and imagination, such as being extremely literal
- difficulty recognizing nonverbal communication (tone of voice, facial expression, and so on)

- motor skill problems, such as clumsy or uncoordinated movements
- repetitive or restrictive patterns of thought and behavior
- impaired ability to empathize and carry on social interactions
- abnormal sensitivity to sensory stimuli, such as light, sound, smell, texture, and taste

No doubt you noticed the last bullet point especially. (Additionally, it should also be noted that, for reasons that are as yet unclear, men are four times as likely as women to have an ASD.)[154]

Certain people you know are likely to qualify. Engineering, physics, mathematics, music, art, computing—speculation is that these and other professions are home to at least some, possibly many, people with Asperger's disorder or another ASD. Historically, figures such as Isaac Newton, Albert Einstein, and Vincent van Gogh might well have been somewhere on the autism spectrum. In our own time, the late chess champion Bobby Fischer probably had a severe form of the condition; another Asperger's candidate might be Microsoft founder Bill Gates.[155] Having an ASD seemingly presents no barrier to success.

Estimates are that ASDs affect from one to three people in five hundred, with the incidence being far greater for children the younger they are. As many as one out of every 150 children born today may fall somewhere on the autism spectrum. That's double the rate of ten years ago, and the diagnosis is increasing 10 to 17 percent each year.[156] Such an increase prompts many observers to declare it an "epidemic." What's unclear is whether the prevalence of ASDs is truly increasing or whether the difference can be explained by a wider awareness of these conditions, more and better studies, and a greater number of parties with a vested interest in diagnosis and treatment.[157] Roy Richard Grinker, a George Washington University professor and parent of an autistic child, views the rise in diagnostic rates as "a sign that we are finally seeing and appreciating a kind of human difference that we once turned away from and that many cultures still hide away in homes or institutions or denigrate as bizarre."[158] Morton Ann Gernsbacher of the University of Wisconsin says amen: "Abnormal is defined only in relation to normal, and the definition of normal, like beauty, often lies in the eyes of the beholder."[159]

This is a critical realization. Human differences, including those that incline some people to high sensitivity, fantasy-proneness, or dissociation, are a source of knowledge about who we are biologically and how we've evolved as a species. Denigrating or dismissing people who are in any way autistic is as shortsighted as neglecting or deriding individuals who claim clairvoyant, precognitive, or otherwise anomalous perceptions. The thick-to-thin boundary continuum could be as useful a concept as the autism spectrum in describing personality types and the neurobiology on which they stand. What is needed is to put aside our preconceptions and to look and listen with an open mind.

Sensory Integration: An Additional Clue

We noted above that people with ASDs often have a pronounced sensitivity to sensory stimuli or have an unusual reaction to the way things smell, taste, look, feel, or sound. (Interestingly, they can be somewhat *insensitive* to pain.)[160] Their sense of balance, awareness of themselves in space, and sensory integration can also be impaired. This is what it's like, in the words of one such person: "[The] knack of knowing where my body is does not come easy for me. . . . I do not know if I am sitting or standing. I am not aware of my body unless it is touching something. . . . Your hand on mine lets me know where my hand is. Jarring my legs by walking tells me I am alive."[161]

His description, while reminiscent of the individuals we met earlier with sensory processing disorder, indicates how profoundly compromised is the *bodily sense of self* in people with more pronounced forms of autism.

The good news is that many parents of children who have ASDs are trying sensory integration methods of treatment—and that more than nine in ten have found these methods helpful. Furthermore, children with ASDs who undergo sensory integration therapy show demonstrable progress over children with ASDs who receive standard treatment.[162] While the research hasn't yet looked at the efficacy of such therapy for kids at distinct points along the spectrum of ASDs, it's entirely possible, in my view, that differences will be found based on high-functioning types (equating to the thin-boundary personality) and those with more severe forms of autism (thick-boundary personality). Perhaps effects will ultimately be noticed in the extent or manner in which individuals register anomalous perceptions or—in the extreme case of poltergeist agents—in the frequency or intensity of the anomalous events associated with them. Recall that, in the last chapter, such occurrences ebbed once eleven-year-old Krista started psychotherapy. If a poltergeist agent's *sensory stimuli* were to become better modulated and integrated, perhaps similar benefits would be realized in other cases.

Blindsight

Let's return to the notion that people in general take in far more sensory information than they realize. While thin-boundary individuals will inevitably notice more (i.e., the gorilla strolling through the basketball game), how do the rest of us know we might be seeing such things, too?

Here's a rather startling experiment written up in 2005 for the *Proceedings of the National Academy of Sciences.*[163] A team led by Tony Ro, a psychology professor at Rice University, induced temporary blindness in volunteers by using magnetic pulses that affected their visual cortex, the area in the back of the brain that processes what our eyes see. During this momentary blindness, the volunteers stood before a computer screen, on which flashed either a vertical or horizontal line. In a second test, a red or green ball was shown on the screen.

When the subjects were asked what they had seen, all reported they'd seen nothing, and indeed, they should not have been able to see anything. But when asked to guess which way the line was oriented, they were right 75 percent of the time, and they were correct 81 percent of the time on the color of the ball. By chance, these figures should both have been roughly 50 percent.

Some of the volunteers said they'd been guessing randomly, but others reported "having a feeling" about what was on the screen. Their higher confidence tended to correspond with a more accurate guess.

What was going on? Ro and others suspect that we have ways of processing information *unconsciously,* well outside of awareness. Visually, this phenomenon is known as blindsight. It has not been proved but has been the subject of much theory and investigation. The brain is always assumed to be the prime actor in blindsight, the source of cognitive routes beyond those already well documented. But what of the eyes? Or the ears, the nose, the skin, for that matter? Why should we arbitrarily distinguish neural processing from the sense organs bringing in the stimuli?

The answer is that we shouldn't—but that our brain disposes us to. As was covered in chapter 6, the brain (and the nervous system as a whole) keeps us from becoming overloaded with sensation. Each of us comes equipped, as long as we live, with our own, very essential filter. The mechanism of these filters differs quite a bit, so that thin-boundary people process more. Their version of the world is denser and more complex and vastly more challenging to deal with. As Aron puts it, "Most people walk into a room and perhaps notice the furniture, the people— that's about it. Highly sensitive persons can be instantly aware, whether they wish it to be or not, of the mood, the friendships and enmities, the freshness or staleness of the air, the personality of the one who arranged the flowers."[164]

Animals' Extreme Abilities

In this respect, the capabilities of such individuals probably bear some resemblance to the information-processing capacity of many animals— and animals have long appeared to possess some pretty remarkable abilities. From dogs that hear high-pitched sounds to bats that can pick out objects far away in complete darkness, elephants that communicate with each other over long distances through low-frequency underground vibrations, birds that migrate to and from precise locations across the hemispheres, and even ants with their fulsome "language" of smell, many creatures have an extended sensory apparatus that often appears, to our sensibilities anyway, to defy explanation.[165]

To take one pedestrian example, my wife and I have a cat that is wonderfully friendly—almost like a dog in this respect—but practically impossible to put in a carrier whenever we plan on taking her to the vet. Instead of climbing all over us and purring, as she is wont to do, on these occasions she simply cannot be found. How does she read our intentions so accurately? Presumably, she is supersensitive to body language and scurries out of reach as soon as my wife or I give the slightest unconscious indication that we intend to put her in the box.

To offer a far more striking example, some dogs are able to "predict" when a person is about to suffer a seizure. Whether they do this through their remarkably keen smell, their attentiveness to the person's bodily signals, a combination of these, or some other way isn't yet known.[166] Other dogs have been able to "smell" cancer in a patient before the medical diagnosis was made.[167] And in one of the most remarkable cases on record, a cat named Oscar, who lives in the advanced dementia unit of a nursing home in Providence, Rhode Island, correctly "predicted" the passing of twenty-five patients by choosing to curl up with them in their final hours. Oscar's track record is more accurate than that of the trained professionals who work there. No one knows how he selects the patients to keep company with: whether he notices telltale scents or perhaps reads something into the behavior of the medical staff. Oscar is not an especially friendly cat, so his lying next to a patient for hours at a time is out of character. But "he doesn't make too many mistakes," and his case has been written up in the prestigious *New England Journal of Medicine*.[168]

Grandin calls such abilities *extreme perceptions* and says that certain people have them, too. She notes that a student of hers, Holly, who is severely dyslexic, "has such acute auditory perception that she can actually hear radios that aren't turned on . . . [She] can hear the tiny little transmissions a turned-off radio is [still] receiving. She'll say, 'NPR is doing a show on lions,' and we'll turn the radio on and sure enough: NPR is doing a show on lions. Holly can hear it. She can hear the hum of electric wires in the wall. And she's incredible with animals. She can tell what they're feeling from the tiniest variations in their breathing."[169]

Similarly, Grandin mentions that many autistic people claim to actually see the flicker in fluorescent lights. Holly is evidently one of them and can "barely function" under fluorescent lighting.[170]

Kreskin and Extremely Sensitive Perception

Reading Grandin, I was reminded of a quite different sort of person: the Amazing Kreskin. Billed as a mind reader, Kreskin himself claims nothing of the sort. What he does maintain is that he possesses ESP—defined by him as "extremely sensitive perception." He is convinced that the more that is learned about anomalous talents, the less anomalous they will turn out to be.[171] This obviously differs from the standard notion of ESP as "extra" sensory. Let us recall here that author Guy Murchie suggested that human beings might have as many as thirty-two senses, which he organized into five major groupings (the radiation senses, the feeling senses, the chemical senses, the mental senses, and the spiritual senses). So, what Kreskin taps into is probably not extrasensory in point of fact, but merely beyond what we take our presumptive five senses to encompass.

In his act, Kreskin demonstrates a talent similar to what is commonly referred to as telepathy or clairvoyance. Even offstage, he will sometimes guess something correctly out of the blue, not knowing himself how or why. These instances are often trivial, like stating what someone is going to say before her or she says it. On one memorable occasion, however, Kreskin stopped a performance short because he was convinced that a woman in the audience with whom he'd interacted during the show was planning to commit suicide. "I had sensed it," he relates, "almost the way one feels sick to one's stomach, an actual, physical sensation of queasiness that was immediately and consciously associated in my mind with death."[172]

Kreskin is interested in the paranormal (as are many accomplished magicians). This interest has been lifelong because, from childhood, he clearly possessed certain remarkable abilities. In his twenties and thirties, he served as a medical intuitive to an established physician, and the anthropologist Margaret Mead later suggested that "sensitive" was an apt description for him.[173] Thus, Kreskin always wondered how his particular aptitudes relate to standard notions of the psychic. He has become convinced that what he's honed to a fine art—and a handsome living— is the propensity to "recognize physical characteristics that telegraph the thought that produced them." But, he adds "there's a great deal more to extremely sensitive perception, although I don't know what, precisely."[174]

In this book, I am proposing that what still confounds Kreskin— indeed, what puzzles *all* true sensitives, the people close to them, and the people who study them—can best be explored through the lens of feeling. Inborn sensory differences (thin boundaries, sensory defensiveness, overexcitabilities, call them what you will) clearly begin to explain how some individuals perceive life so differently from those around them. Still other personality constructs (high transliminality, absorption, fantasy-proneness) apply as we seek to explain certain people's strong interest in, and pull toward, the anomalous. But I suspect the brain/body dynamics of *feeling* represent the missing piece in this puzzle.

By directly questioning people who are highly sensitive, we have a down-to-earth way of beginning to fathom those lessons. In the process, we stand to learn much more about the nature of perception, the nature of cognition, and how we as human beings impinge on—and interact with—our environment. The emotional nature of our surroundings is an overlooked fundamental of our existence.

9

◆

Environmental Sensitivity
Attesting to the Bodymind

*Man has no Body distinct from his Soul; for that call'd
Body is a portion of Soul discern'd by the five Senses, the
chief inlets of Soul in this age.*

WILLIAM BLAKE, *THE MARRIAGE OF HEAVEN AND HELL*

If sensitivity is a bona fide neurobiological phenomenon, one would expect various forms of it to coincide within particular individuals. The makeup of their bodymind would dispose them toward any number of conditions, illnesses, and perceptions that the rest of us would probably consider ourselves at a loss to cope with. Minus the illnesses, though, these peculiar susceptibilities could well be considered to add spice to life. As we shall see, people who are synesthetic (i.e., who experience blended senses such as feeling a sound or tasting a shape), for example, value their perceptions highly and, by and large, can't imagine experiencing the world any other way!

Overlapping Sensitivities

Before we get to the results of my survey, I should like to point out that the circumstantial evidence for overlapping forms of sensitivity is plentiful—and it's increasing. For starters, four conditions seem to be clustered: migraine headache, depression, chronic pain (clinically termed fibromyalgia syndrome), and chronic fatigue syndrome (CFS). People with chronic pain often experience moderate to severe fatigue, people who suffer from depression are more likely to get migraine headaches (and vice versa), individuals with chronic pain are more likely to be depressed, and so on. In each case, women are disproportionately affected. Additionally, fibromyalgia, migraine, and depression appear to run in families, suggesting that a genetic predisposition may be present.[1]

That certain people are demonstrably sensitive is affirmed by a variety of neuroimaging data. For instance, individuals with irritable bowel syndrome (IBS), a dysfunction often linked to CFS and fibromyalgia, demonstrate greater activation of a particular region of their brain than control subjects.[2] People who are highly hypnotizable evidence a more extensive pattern of blood flow in the brain following a hypnotic suggestion, compared with when they are *not* being hypnotized.[3] For synesthetes who "hear" words in color, electrical activity takes place in the brain's language and visual areas concurrently, whereas only the language area lights up when words are heard by ordinary individuals.[4] Synesthesia, not surprisingly, is also closely associated with environmental sensitivity,[5] and there is a tantalizing link with anomalous perception, at least for some people with this condition.[6]

Survey Results

As was mentioned in the last chapter, my survey project had four major aims.

1. To gauge the extent to which individuals who describe themselves as sensitive appear to be affected by various conditions, as well as to what degree these people share certain demographic factors, personality traits, and kinds of experience
2. To gather whether their immediate family members might have been similarly affected

3. To determine the degree to which environmental sensitivity parallels apparitional perception
4. To compare and contrast these findings with similar questions asked of a sample of people who do *not* describe themselves as innately sensitive

Here are the findings. Afterward, I'll focus on some of the significant results and have a crack at what they might imply.

Base Demographics

Out of the sixty-two sensitive respondents, forty-four were women and eighteen were men (a ratio of 2.3 to 1). The average age of this group was 41.4 years. The control group encompassed fifty individuals: thirty-three women and seventeen men (a ratio of 1.9 to 1). Their average age was 43.4 years.

A large proportion (62%) of the sensitives stated they were firstborn or only children, this figure being higher for the women (66%) than the men (53%). Among the control group, 52% indicated they were first-born or only children. This number was the same for the women and the men.

With regard to marital status, 26% of the sensitives reported they were single, 52% that they were married or in a long-term partnership, and 18% that they were divorced or separated. Among the control group, a smaller percentage (18%) said they were single, a larger proportion (70%) that they were married or in a long-term partnership, and 6% indicated that they were divorced or separated.

Nearly all of the sensitive respondents (93%) said they had taken some college classes, graduated college, or gone on to postgraduate work. The figure was slightly lower for controls (88%).

Other Characteristics and Experiences

With regard to handedness, 73% of the sensitive group said they were right-handed, with no major difference between the sexes. Twenty-one percent indicated they were ambidextrous; this figure is slightly higher for the women than the men. Among the control group, 88% said they were right-handed, with only one respondent (2%) saying she was ambidextrous.

Twenty-four percent of the sensitive respondents indicated they were born prematurely or were late arrivals, and 10% said they were adopted. This compares with 18% of the control group who said they had been born prematurely or were late arrivals and 3% who said they were adopted.

Twenty-six percent of the sensitive group indicated they had smoked at one time, with 35% saying that smoking was commonplace in their homes growing up. The percentages were higher among controls, with 40% saying they had smoked at one time and 48% noting tobacco smoke as prevalent in their households growing up.

When asked about psychotherapy, 45% of the sensitives reported they had been in therapy at some point in their lives (50% of the women and 33% of the men). This contrasted with just 26% of the control group who said they had ever been in therapy (33% of the women and 12% of the men). Less contrast was evident in responses to the question, "Have you ever taken any type of medication for more than six months?" Here, 62% of the sensitive group said yes (73% of the women and 44% of the men), along with 60% of the control group (70% of the women and 47% of the men).

Individuals' Self-Assessment

Concerning self-assessment of imagination, 53% of the sensitive group (58% of the women and 47% of the men) described themselves as highly imaginative. This contrasts with 38% of the controls (42% of the women and 29% of the men).

The item on self-assessment of temperament (introversion/extroversion) yielded several differences. Female sensitives were four times likelier than female controls to rate themselves as introverted/restrained. (The proportions were 36% and 9%, respectively.)

No such difference was evident among the men. A virtually identical ratio of male sensitives (44%) and male controls (47%) characterized themselves as introverted/restrained.

Overall, the men in my survey, regardless of which camp they were in, were more likely than the women to view themselves as introverted/ restrained. This contrast was especially pronounced among the male controls, nearly half of whom said they were introverted/restrained but only 6% of whom said they were extroverted/emotive.

Among sensitive respondents, the men were more likely—by a factor of 3.5 to 1—to characterize themselves as being introverted or restrained, whereas no such difference was apparent for the women. Among controls, the men similarly described themselves as introverted or restrained but by a much larger ratio (8 to 1). Women in the control group, on the other hand, were more inclined to see themselves as extroverted/emotive (by a 5 to 1 ratio).

On self-assessment of body type, sensitives of both genders were more apt to perceive themselves as thin, this being more true for the men (who indicated "thin" three times as often as "wide") than the women (who were only twice as prone to indicate "thin"). Among controls, this trend was reversed in the men (who saw themselves as "wide" 1.5 times more frequently than "thin") but not among women (who were still twice as prone to indicate "thin").

The survey also inquired into satisfaction with the level of physical/sexual contact in one's life, with controls rating slightly higher satisfaction than those in the sensitive group. Thirty-seven percent of the sensitives (38% of the women and 33% of the men) rated their satisfaction high, whereas 25% rated their satisfaction low (24% of the women and 28% of the men). This compares with 51% of the control group who rated their satisfaction high (53% of the women and 47% of the men) and 23% who rated their satisfaction low (22% of the women and 27% of the men). Looked at on a scale of 1 to 5 (1 equating to "unsatisfactory" and 5 to "ideal"), female sensitives scored 3.5, compared with female controls at 3.6; male sensitives scored a relatively low 3.0, compared with male controls at 3.4.

Female controls were more likely than their sensitive counterparts to remember their childhoods as happy. Among the control group, 54% (56% of the women and 53% of the men) said their childhoods were "wonderful," with just 10 percent rating their childhoods as "unhappy" (6% of the women and 18% of the men). In contrast, 23% of the sensitives (19% of the women and 33% of the men) reported that their childhoods were wonderful, while 35% rated them as unhappy (40% of the women and

22% of the men). Evaluated on a 1–5 scale (1 equating to "wonderful" and 5 to "extremely unhappy"), female controls scored 2.0, compared with female sensitives at 3.5; male controls scored 2.5, compared with male sensitives at 2.4.

Sensitives were also more apt to note a traumatic event in their childhood, at 55%, compared with 18% for the control group. Among female sensitives, 57% recalled a traumatic event, compared with 18% of female controls. The difference was similarly pronounced among men, with 50% of men in the sensitive group recalling a traumatic childhood event, compared with 18% in the control group.

Environmental Sensitivity/Medical Conditions—Individual

Below are the percentages of people who checked off medical items and the percentage indicating that their condition is or was severe:

TABLE I. RESPONDENTS' MEDICAL SELF-PROFILE

	Checked		Self-Rating as Severe	
Condition	Sensitives	Controls	Sensitives	Controls
Allergies	63%	34%	24%	6%
Depression	57%	20%	20%	4%
Migraine headaches	45%	14%	17%	4%
Exhaustion/chronic fatigue	43%	4%	12%	4%
Chemical sensitivity	40%	0%	13%	0%
Sleep disorder/nightmares	40%	6%	7%	0%
Electrical sensitivity	30%	0%	13%	0%
Asthma	26%	16%	6%	4%
Mood imbalance	25%	2%	3%	0%
Eating disorder	18%	2%	7%	0%
Dyslexia	15%	0%	2%	0%
Alcoholism	7%	0%	3%	0%

One of the items added midway through the survey project—"Unusual sensitivity to light or sound"—was checked frequently, to the point where it would have ranked near the top had the item been included in the survey from the beginning. Twenty-six percent of those in the sensitive group marked this line, compared with just 2% of the controls.

Two other items added midway were nightmares and synesthesia. The former was checked by 11% of those in the sensitive group and 6% of those in the control group. The latter was checked by 6% of the sensitives and none of the controls. Again, extrapolation suggests that nightmares could be experienced by one-fifth of self-described sensitives and synesthesia by upward of 10%.

Environmental Sensitivity/Medical Conditions—Family

Below is the total number of close relatives (i.e., parents, children, siblings, grandparents, aunts, and uncles) who respondents believed were affected by each condition.

TABLE 2. FAMILY MEMBERS' MEDICAL PROFILE (ATTRIBUTED)

Condition	Sensitives (62 in sample)			Controls (50 in sample)		
	No. of Relatives	Female	Male	No. of Relatives	Female	Male
Alcoholism	42	14	28	10	1	11
Depression/mood imbalance	42	24	18	19	16	1
Allergies	31	20	11	8	4	4
Migraine headaches	25	22	3	10	5	5
Asthma	15	8	7	7	6	1
Sleep disorder/ nightmares	9	4	5	3	2	1
Chemical sensitivity	7	4	3	0	0	0
Electrical sensitivity	7	5	2	0	0	0
Schizophrenia	5	4	1	1	1	0
Dyslexia	5	1	4	1	0	1
Exhaustion/chronic fatigue	3	3	0	1	1	0

Note: Percentages were not used for the above tally as respondents could indicate any number of close relatives (or none) they believed to be affected.

Unusual Experiences

Fourteen percent of the sensitive respondents indicted that they had been struck by lightning or otherwise suffered a severe electric shock. This item was checked by a higher ratio of women than men (by 2 to 1). In contrast, none of the controls indicated that they had ever been struck by lightning. (Fact: the approximate chance of being struck by lightning in a given year in the United States is estimated at 1 in 700,000.[7])

A much higher number—37% of the sensitive group (42% of the women, 29% of the men)—claimed that their presence affects computers, lights or appliances in an unusual way. Only 6% of the controls (evenly divided among men and women) checked this item. When asked if the presumed electrical effect might have been triggered by any identifiable event, condition or circumstance, most sensitive respondents were unsure.

The final section of the survey asked about experiences where the respondent might have perceived something that could not be verified as being physically present through normal means. Nearly three-quarters (74%) of the sensitive respondents said they had had such an experience (82% of the women and 55% of the men). Virtually no one said they were unsure. This result contrasts with 16% of the controls who said they had had an apparitional experience (21% of the women and 6% of the men). However, another 14% of the control group indicated they were unsure.

When asked to briefly describe these experiences, sensitives checked the following perceptual modes (with multiple categories being more the rule than the exception):

Perception	Women	Men	Overall Number of Mentions
Visual	28%	59%	23
General "presence"	35%	29%	21
Auditory	30%	12%	15
Olfactory	28%	12%	15
Lights/energy	21%	18%	12

Perception	Women	Men	Overall Number of Mentions
Objects moving	19%	6%	9
Emotional	12%	18%	8
Tactile	14%	6%	7
Precognition	9%	18%	7
Telepathy	5%	12%	5

The percentages were quite different for the control group. (Dashes indicate the item was not mentioned at all.)

Perception	Women	Men	Overall Number of Mentions
Visual	-	-	-
General "presence"	21%	6%	8
Auditory	9%	0%	3
Olfactory	6%	0%	2
Lights/energy	3%	0%	1
Objects moving	-	-	-
Emotional	-	-	-
Tactile	-	-	-
Precognition	3%	0%	1
Telepathy	-	-	-

Little indication was provided that apparitional experiences are apt to take place at any particular time of the day or season of the year. Of sensitive respondents volunteering such information, 37% indicated that the perceptions took place during evening hours or overnight, 28% recalled they had taken place during daylight hours, and the other 35% noted no discernable trend. Among the handful of controls who responded to this item, half said the experience had taken place during evening hours or overnight, and the other half noted no discernable trend. Neither was there any pattern to the season of the year when respondents said their perceptions had occurred.

Finally, 59% of the sensitive group (53% of the women and 80% of the men) indicated that someone they knew—even a pet—had reacted similarly to the alleged occurrence. Among controls, 88% said someone they knew had reacted similarly. Sensitive respondents (but not controls) mentioned pets having shared these experiences as often as they did immediate family members.

Major Connections

The survey results support the hypothesis that certain people are much more susceptible to allergies, illness, depression, migraine headaches, nightmares, and other conditions than the general population. The same is evidently true of those in their immediate families.

The findings also support the contention that environmental sensitivity may encompass an anomalous aspect, because the sensitive respondents were 3.5 times as likely, on average, to assert that they'd had an apparitional experience. Sensitives were also 2.5 times as likely to indicate that an immediate family member was affected by similar physical, mental, or emotional conditions.

That such links should appear is not surprising in view of the fact that, in order to gain participation, the survey was presented as examining both environmental *and* psychic sensitivity. Additional investigation is needed to determine more precisely what demarcation may be found between people who consider themselves to have (or better yet, are actually *diagnosed* as having) some form of environmental illness versus those who consider themselves psychically sensitive.

While no single factor in a person's background is likely to distinguish him or her as sensitive, six demographic or personality factors stand out as statistically significant.

1. Being a woman
2. Being ambidextrous
3. Appraising oneself as an imaginative thinker
4. Appraising oneself as introverted

5. Recalling a plainly traumatic event—or series of events—in childhood

6. Asserting that one's presence causes televisions, lights, computers, and other electrical devices to malfunction

Two other factors—being a firstborn or only child and being single—were more prominent among sensitives but not overwhelmingly so.

Independent Corroboration

These findings are intriguing—and suggest that underlying neurobiological differences may be at work. Further research is needed, however, to corroborate the results. If future investigators uncover the same sorts of connections, it might follow that sensitive persons could register (either consciously or unconsciously) anomalous influences in the environment that bypass most other people. This possibility is well worth looking into. Since the publication of my study, dozens more individuals have stepped forward to say that they, too, are sensitive and that the six-item profile presented above describes them well.

Independently, a trio of researchers asking people similar questions (one using an adaptation of my survey) has uncovered similar associations. Like mine, the surveys undertaken by two of those researchers (David Ritchey and Dean Radin) focused on people who self-identified as sensitive.[8] This approach, while valuable in and of itself, necessarily limits the utility of the results.

The third researcher (Brandon Massullo) took a different tack.[9] He surveyed 251 volunteers who were visiting Mary King's Close, a historical site in Edinburgh, Scotland, reputed to be haunted. Prior to beginning a tour of the premises, the participants completed a thirty-item questionnaire based on my survey. Participants were later categorized as sensitive based on their response to certain key questions. (Sixty-seven of the 251 participants, or 27%, rated as sensitive. Of that sensitive group, nearly three-quarters were women; this compares with 61% of the non-sensitives.)

Groups of between 5 to 17 individuals proceeded to tour the site, accompanied by guides who knew of the experiment but who were blind to the details. Unbeknownst to either them or the people touring, ten rooms in which the participants were asked to stop had previously been assessed, using sophisticated monitoring equipment, for ambient electromagnetic radiation. Five of these rooms had been designated "high EMF" rooms based on the readings obtained, with the other five rooms designated "low EMF" rooms. (The former had magnetic field readings nearly three times as high as the latter.) The participants were asked to spend a few minutes in each room and write on a standardized checklist any unusual perceptions they might notice in that location.

The results were provocative. Sensitives reported significantly more anomalous experiences than non-sensitives. The most frequently reported perception was "change in temperature" (noted by 29% of participants), followed by "dizziness/headache" (reported by 16% of subjects) and "sense of a presence" (reported by 9%). By a ratio of greater than 2 to 1, women reported more unusual perceptions than men. Most interestingly, while significantly more anomalous experiences were recorded in the high EMF rooms, *the difference pertained to sensitives only.* Non-sensitives reported no major difference between the two types of rooms, leading Massullo to suggest that the sensitive individuals could have been registering subtle EMF-related effects.

One possible explanation, of course, is Richard Wiseman's "situational" perspective, which proposes that ambient conditions (e.g., lighting levels, room dimensions, and acoustics) lead people to conclude that a room is haunted. Massullo tested this hypothesis within his experiment. He asked members of the Mary King's Close staff, who knew the premises well, to rank the ten rooms, at the outset, from least haunted or eerie to most haunted or eerie. (For good measure, they also rated the rooms according to which they supposed had the lowest magnetic field strength through the highest magnetic field strength.) The results showed little correspondence, either between the staff's collective ranking of "hauntedness" with the number of anomalous experiences subsequently reported in the rooms, or between the staff's estimate of magnetic field strength with the measurements actually taken.

294 Environmental Sensitivity

A second skeptical explanation for the study's results draws from the considerable evidence, surveyed in the last chapter, that people who are environmentally sensitive are also likely to have a fantasy-prone personality and are therefore prone to manufacture anomalous perceptions. The results, however, were contradictory on this point. While one of the survey questions found sensitive participants more likely than non-sensitives to view themselves as imaginative thinkers, another question found no significant difference between sensitive and non-sensitive participants on the issue of having had an imaginary friend as a child, which, as we've seen, can serve as a barometer of a vivid creative life.

The major skeptical argument remaining relates to sensitives' belief in the paranormal. While Massullo's study found that environmentally sensitive subjects scored significantly higher for paranormal belief than non-sensitive subjects, this does not explain the clustering of reported anomalous perceptions in the high EMF rooms.

Overall, the results indicate that sensitives may be able to register differences in electromagnetic radiation not noticed by other people and that such differences are, at least to some extent, independent of paranormal belief or situational cues. An open question is whether, as Houran and Lange have proposed (see last chapter), individuals who believe in the paranormal *and* are suggestible *and* who don't tolerate ambiguity well might instantaneously transmute an unexpected stimulus (e.g., a tingling sensation owing to a high EMF location, or a flickering light or a stray odor) into a full-fledged anomaly. More sophisticated studies are surely needed to adequately investigate these interesting possibilities. However, considering this was the first time the Environmental Sensitivity Survey (or rather a variation of it) had been put to use in an allegedly haunted location, a promising start has been made.

Branching Out

What is needed now is a broad and ambitious effort to learn the extent to which various forms of sensitivity are reported in the general population—and the extent to which certain people who do not consider themselves sensitive nonetheless qualify based on their responses to a consistent set of questions.

There is a noteworthy precedent for this type of approach. In 2005, the Centers for Disease Control and Prevention announced that CFS—a condition historically derided as being "all in the mind" of patients—is a biologically real condition that probably has a genetic basis. This determination was made through a far-reaching evaluation of more than two hundred individuals with chronic fatigue syndrome.[10] They were tested in any number of ways as well as questioned through surveys. As has been found with other oft-dismissed phenomena, from fibromyalgia and IBS to hypnosis and synesthesia, when enough people purport to be affected by something in repeatable ways, the science generally follows. Anomalous perception, I propose, is no different. In time, it will be found to have a bona fide neurobiological basis that opens it up to the light of day. The data are now before us; we have only to inquire seriously and give due credence to what people tell us they're experiencing.

Discussion of Specific Trends

Accordingly, I want to probe more deeply into some of the more interesting findings of my own sensitivity survey. The results turn out to be in accord with (or at least not in blatant opposition to) a great deal of research and theory. The correlations suggest that sensitivity may, indeed, be a multifaceted phenomenon—and that anomalous perceptions could be rooted in the same neurobiological ground.

Bodymind differences, in other words, could explain quite a lot. Remember that no two people live in the same sensory world. How each of us is arrayed to process incoming stimuli—and especially, I would wager, the characteristic way we process *feeling*—will tell a highly individual tale.

Gender Differences
The first and most readily apparent survey result is the preponderance of women sensitives, an extremely high percentage of whom reported apparitional perceptions. Interestingly, while the percentage of control

participants who said they'd had an apparitional experience was obviously much lower, the proportion of women controls who indicated so was even higher than among those in the sensitive group! Why might this be?

While it's possible that women are simply more interested than men to respond to a survey concerning subject matter of this kind, the evidence is compelling that the female of the species is *innately different* from the male. For a start, women are markedly more sensitive than men in taste, smell, and hearing, with differences evident from prepubescence through old age.[11] While men consistently show greater visual acuity, women's eyes adapt faster to the dark and, conversely, tolerate brightness better.[12] Tests also point to a fascinating difference in what the sexes are quicker to recognize in their field of vision: women see human figures more readily than objects, whereas men perceive objects more readily than people. This distinction has been noted in infants as young as five months.[13]

With regard to touch, women are, once again, more sensitive. This includes awareness of pain, where women demonstrate a greater reactivity across all ages.[14] (Of potential relevance to the debate over electrical sensitivity, one study has shown that electrical conductivity of the skin in neonates is considerably higher in females than in males.)[15]

Women are also vastly more susceptible to a range of autoimmune diseases.[16] This difference may owe in part to the way the sex hormones, such as testosterone and progesterone, influence the respective gender's immune system.[17] Furthermore, the metabolic processes of men and women likely work at a different rate, influencing the course of health and disease. Thousands of genes have been found to express themselves differently between the genders, leading to the inference that tissues, organs, even the brain itself, are all programmed to work at a different pace or level of specialization.[18]

Speaking of the brain, many of its structures differ in size between the genders. The hippocampus, for instance, is larger in women, with the amygdala being larger in men. Production of neurotransmitters differs noticeably, too. For example, serotonin levels have been measured as 50% higher in men.[19] Of equal or greater import, the back portion of the corpus callosum—an elongated bundle of nerve fibers that carries information between the brain's two halves—is wider and larger in women than in men. This difference exists not just in adulthood; it has been found in utero.[20]

This discovery about the corpus callosum supports the idea that, throughout their lives, women may boast greater communication between the hemispheres. Quantitative evidence is provided by the finding that women's rate of interhemispheric blood flow is generally about 15% higher than men's.[21] Moreover, while men have 6.5 times the amount of grey matter in their brains (relating to information-processing capacity) than women, women have nearly 10 times the amount of white matter (representing connections between processing centers) than men.[22]

Given the very different way the sexes' brains are organized, a biological basis may exist for the oft-noted observation that men have more of a predilection for symbolic thinking, visual-spatial tasks, logical reasoning, and objects, while women have a greater affinity for language, communication, emotional-verbal activities, relationships, and people. The former rely on the activity of a single hemisphere (the so-called left brain), whereas the latter connote a greater degree of connectivity with the right brain.[23]

Not surprisingly, women are more adept at remembering emotionally tinged information. This was demonstrated by an experiment in which participants' brains were scanned while they rated a series of photographs from neutral (e.g., fire hydrants) to highly negative (e.g., mutilated bodies). Three weeks later, the participants returned to look at another series of photos that was slightly different, as new images had been interspersed with the ones viewed before. The subjects' brains were again scanned as they were asked to state whether they remembered the given image, whether it only seemed familiar, or whether it was new. Women recalled the images better than men and also rated them as more emotionally arousing. Furthermore, activity was evident throughout the women's brains. The experimenters concluded that the female brain is wired to remember emotional content and events better than the male brain.[24]

Undoubtedly, evolution played the key role in fomenting these crucial neural differences. Neuroscientist Rhawn Joseph traces their origin to the divergent roles of men and women that emerged thousands of years ago with the onset of big game hunting and the organization of family and communal life.[25] In the now rather traditional anthropological view, men became specialists in hunting and, over time, adroit at the visual-spatial tasks (e.g., direction, depth, and distance perception) required to search for and kill prey. Bands of roving men also needed to maintain a stealthy silence for extended periods to successfully stalk large game.

In contrast, women accounted for most of the gathering and other domestic tasks, which called for them to become skilled in the use of tools for digging out plants, grinding food, sewing garments, and so on. The use of tools then provided "the neural substrate for the temporal-sequential and grammatical aspects of what would become spoken language." Unlike the men, women were free to talk as they went about their business, with language lending itself to social exchange and bonding.[26] The myriad resulting differences in brain organization and function are evident today.[27]

Clearly, gender is not just a basic biological difference: the more we look at it, the more fundamental it becomes.

First-Born or Only Child

Given that first-borns represent just 35 percent of all children in the general population today,[28] the tilt toward respondents (both sensitives and controls) who are first-born or only children may owe to these individuals being more conscientious than later-borns and hence more likely to respond to surveys. However, some evidence suggests that first-borns are more likely to suffer from asthma, eczema, and various allergies because they have a greater susceptibility determined in utero.[29] Additionally, it is perhaps relevant that many children who have imaginary companions also tend to be first-born or only children.[30] This aspect of my survey, in other words, may have turned up something worth exploring.

Being Single

The survey showed that sensitives are nearly twice as likely as controls to be single, divorced, or separated, and (the flip side) less likely to have ever been married. One interpretation is that sensitives tend to have personal issues that make marriage more problematic for both them and their partners. Alternately, since the average age of the control group was slightly higher than that of the sensitive group, it could be that some of the sensitive respondents are approaching an age at which they will get married, rather than being married already.

Self-Assessment as Imaginative

The fact that sensitives (both men and women) rate themselves significantly higher on imagination makes perfect sense if we remember that sensitivity is likely associated with being a thin-boundary person who is fantasy-prone, inclined to absorption, and highly transliminal. These perceptual and personality styles should indeed equate to viewing the world (not to mention oneself) quite differently. Do they see themselves as imaginative, creative, and artistic? You bet.

Self-Assessment as Introverted

The survey item on self-assessment of temperament (introversion/extroversion) yielded an interesting gender difference. Sensitivity is evidently conducive to the self-perception of introversion—but only for women. Men, especially among controls, apparently consider themselves introverted or restrained as a matter of course. This discrepancy, I'd venture, has at least as much to do with learned style as innate biology.

Being Ambidextrous

Ten times more sensitive respondents than controls indicated they were ambidextrous—a highly significant difference. Given what we know of the corpus callosum, it's a distinct possibility that a greater degree of interchange exists between the hemispheres in people who are sensitive. This would explain not only why women are disproportionately sensitive but also why sensitives have a greater tendency to use both hands rather than preferring one.

Interestingly, the study of handedness and brain laterality is moving toward an approach where individuals are evaluated according to the degree they are "strong-handed" or "mixed-handed" rather than being assigned to the fixed categories left-handed, right-handed, or ambidextrous. This trend builds on decades of research showing that many people who think of themselves one way are actually mixed-handed to a degree. Strong left-handedness, in fact, occurs in only 2 to 3 percent of the population. *Degree,* then, not direction, may be the most useful barometer of hemispheric cross-communication.[31]

This approach offers some intriguing insights. It has been found, for example, that mixed-handers tend to do better than strong-handers on memory tests; they remember events more accurately and farther back into their childhood. This makes sense given that memory is encoded across the hemispheres and that mixed-handers may benefit from a wider corpus callosum. The differences go beyond what one might expect, however, with mixed-handers showing more openness to being persuaded (some would call it gullibility), a greater preponderance toward magical thinking, more proneness toward accidents and hypochondria, a higher likelihood of experiencing déjà vu, and a greater benefit from placebo treatments. Researcher Stephen Christman at the University of Toledo speculates that these personality traits are manifestations of "hyperconnectivity" in the mixed-handed brain.[32] Christman takes a broad view, which I think not only is warranted but also will be shown to be consistent with an expansive characterization of sensitivity.

Synesthesia

One of the intriguing survey findings was the proportion of sensitives who said they were synesthetes. While the percentage was not very high, no one in the control group indicated that they had synesthesia and it is notably rare in the general population. (Estimates over the last decade have ranged from 1 in 2,000 to 1 in 23. The measured prevalence has increased greatly as researchers have progressed from a reliance on self-selected samples, e.g., a group of people responding to a newspaper solicitation, to random population surveys.[33])

Synesthesia is the blending of senses that, in most people, are separate and distinct. (The word is derived from the Greek *syn,* meaning "together," and *aesthesis,* meaning "sensory perception." A related word is "anesthesia," which means "no sensation.")[34] While nonsynesthetes may say metaphorically, "This wine tastes wonderfully dry" or "I sure feel blue today," the synesthete actually experiences such perceptions. For him or her, a taste can be round or pointy, a word can taste like potatoes, the sound of a violin can be felt on the face, and a letter or number or even a smell can have its own vivid and recurring color. By far the most common evocation is color, whether it occurs in tandem with words, phrases, numbers, letters, music, or sounds. Nearly half of synesthetes, however, experience more than one mode of the condition.[35]

One recently discovered form is known as mirror touch synesthesia. Individuals who see someone else being touched sense that they themselves are being touched. This might be considered empathy in the extreme, with the mirror neurons we learned about in chapter 4 on virtual overdrive.[36] Given the centrality of touch in our sense of self, this type of synesthesia has especially intriguing connotations.

In the aggregate, what makes synesthesia remarkable—besides its obvious difference from typical sensation—is its automatic and vivid nature. Richard Cytowic, author of *The Man Who Tasted Shapes,* writes, "In addition to being involuntary, [the overlapping sensory perceptions are] regarded by the synesthete as real, often outside the body, instead of imagined in the mind's eye. . . . Its reality and vividness are what make synesthesia so interesting."[37]

Synesthetes are known to retain the same sensory associations (the sweet sound of a trumpet, for example, or the redness of the number 4) throughout their lives. Someone else with synesthesia may see the number 4 as purple and be surprised to learn that others perceive it differently.[38] Many synesthetes have excellent memories, which (like fantasy-prone people) they attribute to their unique and unforgettable sensations.[39] The phenomenon's *constancy* is also noteworthy. Nearly all synesthetes say they grew up with conjoined sensory impressions, in some cases presuming that their families and friends experienced the world the same way.[40] Indeed, the phenomenon is known to run in families, suggesting that it is inherited—although no particular gene or neurotransmitter has yet been found.[41]

Synesthesia is demonstrably real. Neuroimaging data, such as positron emission tomography (PET) scans and magnetic resonance imaging (MRI) reveal activity in both the language *and* visual areas of the brain in persons who see colored words, whereas activity registers solely in the brain's language areas for ordinary individuals, when members of both groups hear words being spoken.[42] Of course, the same has been demonstrated with schizophrenics who have auditory hallucinations: when they hear voices, parts of their temporal lobes light up, just as they would if the people were listening to an actual conversation.[43] This leaves open the question of what is happening in synesthesia to make the experience distinctive.

Of special interest to us, the condition has an oft-noted relationship with hypersensitivity. Women, who are far likelier than men in many respects to be sensitive, are also believed to predominate among synesthetes. The estimates vary considerable, from a ratio of 6 to 1[44] down to 2 to 1 or less in investigations conducted more recently.[45] (The difference may owe to a reporting bias, with far fewer men than women having disclosed their synesthesia in earlier surveys.[46]) One well-known synesthete, Carol Crane, puts it this way: "Like many synesthetes, I have a heightened appreciation for all kinds of sensory phenomena. . . . I tend to get overloaded quickly: like there's just too much sensory perception coming in at one time, and I have a hard time sorting it out and coping with it. . . . Shopping can do it. Being in a store where there's a lot of noise, colors, smells—it's just too much."[47]

At least one prominent researcher, Peter Grossenbacher (formerly with the National Institutes of Health), is looking into this association, noting that the link with "certain kinds of sensitivity . . . is an active area of research with us."[48]

The phenomenon has feeling associations as well. Manhattan artist Carol Steen notes, for example, that touch figures prominently in her form of synesthesia. The pain she experienced during a root canal came across as a vivid orange.[49] Other synesthetes see auras around the faces of certain people or perceive colors in connection with certain words. The colors evidently reflect the individual's feeling about the person or the word in question.[50] Researcher Jamie Ward, of University College London, notes that darker colors tend to be associated with negative feelings whereas brighter colors have more upbeat connotations. (This has a parallel with sound, where lower-pitched notes tend to be perceived as darker and higher-pitched notes as brighter.)[51] Synesthetes can likewise perceive music as round, wavy, or jagged, or a person's mood can come across as soft, warm, or pointy.[52]

Not surprisingly, synesthesia is associated with creativity: artists, musicians, and scientists seem to be disproportionately represented among its ranks. Novelist Vladimir Nabokov, composers Franz Liszt and Alexander Scriabin, physicist and inventor Nicola Tesla, physicist Richard Feynman, and contemporary artist David Hockney were (or are) synesthetes.[53, 54, 55] This bent toward creativity recalls Kazimierz Dabrowski's study of gifted individuals and the "overexcitabilities" he identified: restlessness, sensory and aesthetic awareness, imagination and fantasy, dream recall, intense intellectual focus, and heightened affect. Cognitive scientist Vilayanur Ramachandran, of the University of California–San Diego, suspects that such creativity may be the result of extraordinarily dense connections in the brain, especially between areas that process sensory information.[56]

Two other explanations have gained currency. As with Ramachandran's idea, these imply that synesthesia is part and parcel of the infant and, later, adult brain.[57] The *cross-modal transfer theory* proposes that infants are capable of recognizing objects via one sense (e.g., sight) if they have previously apprehended them through another sense (e.g., touch). The *neonatal hypothesis*—proposed by Daphne Maurer of McMaster University—goes further, suggesting that all babies are born perceiving across sense modalities and that they learn to differentiate senses *in reaction to* the cognitive confusion synesthesia inevitably causes. Evidence exists for both ideas, such as the finding that nonhuman neonates (kittens and hamsters) have links between diverse sensory areas of the brain. If such a premise were to be proved in human beings, it would refute child psychologist Jean Piaget's long-accepted principle that sensory systems are independent at birth and gradually integrate with one another over the course of a child's development.[58]

Synesthesia could also represent a breakdown in normal maturation of the adult brain. This is the model set out by Simon Baron-Cohen, professor of developmental psychopathology at the University of Cambridge.[59] He notes that some forms of synesthesia cause their owners "massive . . . stress, dizziness, a feeling of information overload," and that such sensory combinations are "clearly maladaptive." The thought is echoed to some extent by Grossenbacher, who points out the "awkward kinship" between synesthesia and hallucinations, while nonetheless distinguishing the former as "predictable, consistent, enjoyable rather than scary, and definitely not a disorder."[60]

Awkward indeed. Cytowic has advanced the notion that synesthetes might be more prone than the general population to anomalous perception, which *is* often viewed as pathological.[61] Could common neurobiological mechanisms be involved? It seems entirely possible. Not only are fantasy-prone people capable of experiencing synesthesia (simultaneously seeing, hearing, and feeling what is being described to them during a conversation, for instance),[62] but so are people with self-reported electrical sensitivity[63] as well as individuals who have had a near-death experience (NDE).[64] (Parenthetically, interviews conducted by psychologist Kenneth Ring suggest that at least some people who've had an NDE subsequently perceive sensations of energy or electricity, which is occasionally quite intense, moving through their bodies.[65])

We should consider one other possibility. Perhaps synesthesia—along with other forms of sensitivity—reflects an archaic form of neural processing. Recall Joseph's conjectures about the origin of differing neural aptitudes in men and women. Women may have been equipped, well back in our evolution, to notice subtler aspects of their environment than men, not just through the five individual senses but via an overlay of sensory impressions. Women, after all, held (and continue to hold) the key to our species' survival. If there are no healthy children, there is no future.[66] From an evolutionary vantage point, then, perhaps hypersensitivity was a good thing, whether in the form of synesthesia, sensory defensiveness, or just plain shyness.

This perspective is advocated to some extent by neurobiologist Jerre

Levy of the University of Chicago. She believes that women's built-in emotional and social sophistication, combined with their penchant for reacting instantaneously to sources of threat in the environment, is at the root of another phenomenon long associated with sensitivity: female intuition. This is "the ability of women, which men think illogical, to respond to a danger sensed rather than perceived—my baby's in trouble—or to produce a complete character analysis, later often proved right, of someone they've met for only ten minutes."[67] Here, it is worth recalling Elaine Aron's concept of rovers and sitters. Hundreds of thousands of years ago, if our female predecessors were indeed the sitters (gatherers) as contrasted with the roving males (hunters), these functions might well have become engrained in our respective neurobiologies, explaining why women predominate among sensitives even today.

Of course, it's also possible that each of us, man *or* woman, is secretly synesthetic.[68] The drugs LSD and mescaline can produce overlapping senses (as well as out-of-body perceptions), suggesting that everyone possesses the bodymind connections necessary to experience the world much differently than we normally do.[69] Perhaps, as Cytowic has suggested, synesthesia represents a far more basic form of perception than we realize.

Regardless of which explanation (or combination of explanations) turns out to be correct, the resurgence of interest in synesthesia holds the promise of shedding light on other forms of anomalous experience. After all, synesthesia was once considered bizarre, a condition that flouted the known laws of neuroanatomy and psychology.[70] Yet nature reveals itself by its exceptions. Just as synesthesia is bound to yield remarkable insights into the nature of perception and cognition,[71] so too connections will surely be found with a variety of other phenomena.[72] The association with sensitivity, in my estimation, merits the greatest share of attention.

Migraine

The prominence of migraine headache among sensitive survey respondents should perk our interest. Like synesthesia and unusual sensitivity to light and sound, I knew relatively little about this condition prior to undertaking the project. Learning more about the dynamics of migraine should enable us to discern its commonality with other forms of sensitivity.

In the United States, 12 percent of the population suffers from migraines. Women are three times as likely as men to be affected, although the disparity is not lifelong: it holds between the onset of puberty and the occurrence of menopause.[73] The prevalent theory is that individual sufferers have a more sensitive nervous system than most.[74] Australian headache expert James Lance, for example, believes that "the pain control system and the related neurotransmitters are different in [patients with migraine], being more sensitive to changes in the body itself or the outside world."[75]

Factors that can bring on a headache include stress, noise, glare, certain odors or foods, and even weather conditions. "Cold, rainy days are the worst for me," says one woman. "During the summer, when it's hot and humid, I can't even leave the house," says another.[76] A study by the New England Center for Headache found that the majority of its patients—just over 50 percent—were, indeed, affected by changes in temperature, humidity, and barometric pressure.[77] Warm, dry winds are likewise known to affect some people. Researchers at Hebrew University in Israel in the early 1970s found that winds such as the Santa Ana of Southern California and the Sirocco of the Mediterranean were associated with depression, irritability, and headache.[78]

This phenomenon bears some resemblance to the observation noted in chapter 6, namely, that certain people feel anxious hours before a thunderstorm, when the ionization of the air is presumed to raise the level of the neurotransmitter serotonin in their blood.[79]

More recently, Canadian neuroscientist Werner Becker found that the Chinook wind, which blows into Alberta province from the Rocky Mountains—sometimes at speeds approaching one hundred miles per hour—can trigger migraines.[80] Seventy-five headache patients were asked to keep a daily diary of their symptoms over a two-year period, noting whether they got a headache on a given day and, if so, what the symptoms were and when they came on. Thirty-two of the seventy-five patients, it turned out, were more likely to report symptoms during the period in question. Fifteen of them seemed to react to high wind speed, while seventeen more reacted to conditions *between* windy days. For some individuals, it turns out, migraines may even be prompted by local seismic activity.[81]

So, what happens to bring on a migraine? Two steps are involved: the lead-up to the migraine and the migraine attack itself. In the first phase (when people tend to feel depressed, irritable, or restless), serotonin levels are unusually high, constricting blood flow. Then, when the migraine hits, serotonin levels drop precipitously and the blood vessels dilate.[82] While migraines appear to be vascular in nature, the blood vessels are actually reacting to neural messages conveyed by the brain based on particular sensory input.[83]

Interestingly, biofeedback has been found to lessen migrainous pain in some patients. One form, known as temperature biofeedback, "is based on the notion that, as you become more anxious and uptight, your fingertip temperature falls. The blood vessels in the fingertips are responsive to . . . sympathetic nervous system activation. So the more aroused you get, the cooler your hands get." Patients who have a temperature feedback device placed on their fingertips can learn to warm their hands, effectively reducing their level of arousal. Certain people are better at it than others.[84] What they're able to do is actually alter their blood flow, decreasing the supply to vessels in the brain that are dilated, thereby reducing pain.

Acupuncture is suspected to work similarly. A study conducted by Bruce Rosen of the Harvard Medical School showed that, immediately after acupuncture needles were applied to points on the hand that are linked to pain relief in traditional Chinese medicine, blood flow decreased in certain areas of the brain. "When there's less blood, the brain isn't working as hard," Rosen observes. He goes on to suggest that any treatment that results in altered blood flow—including placebos—could be useful in alleviating pain and addictions.[85]

The usefulness of biofeedback or acupuncture in loosening the grip of migraine indicates that certain people aren't just extraordinarily sensitive to their surroundings, they're also extra sensitive to their own, *internal landscape of feeling.* Of relevance here is that the dynamics of migraine effectively parallel those of emotion. Consider that, in migraine headache, we have a remarkable confluence of factors: gender (women being over-whelmingly among those affected),[86] heredity,[87] and emotional style.[88] In support of this view, I cite the following anecdote from Lance:

> A patient of mine was having a heated argument with a girlfriend about the rebellious attitude he had toward his father when he had been a teenager, a subject that had distressed him in later years. At the height of the argument his vision started to blur, and soon he could see only the centre of objects. This tunnel vision lasted for about 10 minutes, after which his characteristic migraine headache developed. Some weeks later he was attending a cinema and found that the film dealt with the same problem of the father-son relation-ship that had always troubled him. Within a few minutes his vision misted over, and tunnel vision was again followed by a headache.[89]

An equally fascinating account comes from psychoanalyst Stephen Appel, who writes of his own longtime acquaintance with migraine, and one experience in particular.

> In a co-therapy session Rebecca, a vivacious young woman, paraple-gic after an accident that occurred after she got married, was con-fronting her husband yet again: "Why don't we have sex any more? I'm still interested." Yet again, her husband hung his head, saying little. Then a sudden change: he raised his head, looking directly at his wife and out poured a stream of cruel, cold truth-telling. "I'll tell you why. You think you're normal, but you're not. You won't hear this, but you're disabled. You just lie there, I have to do all the work. Do you know what it's like having sex with a handicapped person? It's not fun, I can tell you." . . . And so on for some considerable time. Then a tearful silence, broken eventually by Rebecca in her characteristic upbeat, appealing voice. "Yes, but that's just an excuse, we can try can't we?" The session came to an end, and as the couple left the room I was struck by a powerful and debilitating migraine.

Here the pain, rage, humiliation, sweetness, desperation, frustration, fear, horror, and heartbreak in the room became too great for me to handle. Taken aback, I identified with everything, it seems: his feelings about living with a paraplegic spouse, her hurt at hearing herself described in this way, and his desperation at her denial. Stunned into silence by the suddenness and the sheer magnitude of this emotional load, I was unable to relieve it. . . . I got a migraine for my troubles.[90]

Appel contrasts this episode with another in which he was listening to a patient discuss a breathing difficulty, which the patient believed was brought on by stress. The patient explained that the symptom was becoming less debilitating because he now realized *when* he was becoming stressed and was able to take a few deep, curative breaths. At the start of the session, Appel recalls that he had developed a pain in his left temple, but gradually, as the patient reported feeling calmer, "my [own] migrainous sensation lessened, then disappeared, accompanied by a sense of well-being."[91]

What do these examples demonstrate? The renowned neurologist Oliver Sacks asserts that migraine is "conspicuously a psychophysiological event . . . an oblique expression of feelings which are denied direct or adequate expression."[92] In other words, when a person is caught unaware by powerful feelings and has no suitable way to discharge the inner agitation, a migraine may result. (Sacks is hardly the first expert to have made this association. Psychiatrist Alfred Adler, a disciple of Freud in the early twentieth century, considered migraine an expression of unconscious rage—one of many instances he described of the mind provoking physical symptoms. Another psychoanalyst, Franz Alexander, literally wrote the book on psychosomatics in 1950. These pioneers would undoubtedly be gratified that, decades later, their insights concerning the interconnectedness of the bodymind have come to be validated through the field of psychoneuroimmunology.[93])

Appel understands his own tendency toward migraine as being "blindsided, mugged if you like" by the onset of strong feelings. It is akin to the instantaneous mobilization of energy during the fight-or-flight response, except the subject of the migraine is unaware of the enormity of the

buildup. Once the person is able to acknowledge the arousal (and, if possible, express his or her feelings), the migraine will, like a wave, crash over
and recede. In fact, suggests Appel, attending to the waxing and waning
of such symptoms may help "measure the extent of [one's] repression and
denial, or insight and relief." It seems to have worked in his case because
Appel says he has come to "recognize the early signs . . . [and] transform
these into feelings," and so no longer suffers from migraine.[94]

One fascinating side note is that Appel at one point chose the term
"poltergeist" to describe this underlying mechanism. He notes that powerful feelings expressed by others can immediately work themselves into
one's own system. He likens their transmittal to a poltergeist.[95] I find this
particular analogy consistent with the core concept of this book, that feelings held in the body lead to a variety of bodymind phenomena, including
anomalous ones.

Perceived Electrical Sensitivity

One of the survey's most interesting and statistically significant results is
the extent to which people who consider themselves sensitive claim that
their very presence affects lights, computers, and other electrical appliances in an unusual way. This could, of course, be viewed as an extension of the idea that such characteristics as fantasy-proneness, absorption,
suggestibility, and transliminality lead certain people to attribute highly
improbable explanations to fairly typical occurrences.[96] However, because
an unusually high percentage of the sensitive respondents indicated that
they had been struck by lightning or otherwise suffered a severe electrical
shock (a memorable and potentially verifiable event), I wish to propose
that electrical sensitivity represents a bona fide aspect of sensitivity.

Recall from chapter 7 that Michael Shallis surveyed hundreds of people in the United Kingdom—80% of them women—who claimed to be
electrically sensitive.[97] As with my survey, certain links jumped out: allergy
(70% of Shallis's sample, 63% of mine); susceptibility to loud sounds and
bright lights (70% of Shallis's sample; question added to my survey midway through the project); the claim to have been struck by lightning (23%
of Shallis's group, 14% of mine); to be affected by advancing thunder-

storms (60% in Shallis's survey, question not asked in my survey at the time); and to have had a psychic experience (69% of Shallis's group, 74% of my own sample).

Shallis himself deduced a connection between strong feelings, electrical sensitivity, and reported anomalies. He acknowledges that we don't know what we don't know, remarking that electromagnetism—"the physical force most apparent to us at the level at which we perceive the material world"—may be the vehicle for life forces that, at present, we simply do not comprehend.[98]

It bears mentioning here that, since ancient times, a variety of native peoples have noted the powerfully transformative effects of lightning. Anthropologist Mircea Eliade's classic text, *Shamanism,* outlines their understanding. Being struck by lightning constituted a way of being called to be a shaman, since it was believed to release the power to heal, along with other extraordinary abilities. Such capabilities did not just operate on humans; the wood of a tree that had been struck by lightning also was said to have its own power, which shamans were advised to take advantage of in constructing their ritual drums. Even if it resulted in death, lightning was believed to confer power. A person killed by lightning was to be buried as a shaman and was imagined as flying to a home in the sky. Such descriptions resound in the folklore of tribes from around the world.[99, 100] In our modern, hard-pressed, nature-deprived world, who is to say those ancient authorities were necessarily mistaken? A thorough investigation into the anomalous claims of people who report suffering a powerful electrical shock might yield fascinating dividends.

Perception of Apparitions

Yet another intriguing survey result concerns a gender difference in the *type* of anomalous perception. Male sensitives checked the visual mode twice as often as any other, whereas the response by female sensitives was much more varied. What this may imply is unknown, but it surely deserves further study.

In previous surveys of apparitional experience, vision was the predominant perceptual mode—much more so than in my survey.[101] In these other studies, hearing was the second most prevalent perceptual category, with touch and a general sense of a presence following. Among the sensitive participants in my survey, hearing was frequently indicated, but so was smell, followed by lights/energy (a category evidently unreported in the other inquiries).

Survey results are bound to differ given the varying demographic of their participants. Gender and age, I suspect, will be shown to be major factors conditioning individuals' anomalous perception. In the final analysis, a rigorous and, above all, consistent approach will be needed to address these hurdles.

Shared Apparitional Experience

One very surprising finding was the higher proportion of controls than sensitives (by nearly 50 percent) who assert that their unusual experience, if they had one, was shared by someone: a relative, a friend, even a pet.

At first glance, this isn't what you would expect. I myself would have imagined that Joe or Jane Q. Public, having perceived something strange, would either shrug it off as a figment of the imagination or, if there were someone else in the room at the time, ask that person to affirm that he or she wasn't perceiving the same anomaly. But perhaps my scenario is slightly off. Avowed skeptics who have reviewed my survey findings suggest that the reason this "sharing of experience" item is higher for controls is that ordinary (as opposed to sensitive) people are *more* apt to seek out affirmation from others nearby that they weren't alone in perceiving something strange. According to this view, sensitives are more accustomed to anomalous experience in the first place and so don't need to ask as much.

Role of Recollected Trauma

An especially noteworthy distinction between sensitives and controls (by a 3 to 1 ratio) relates to the recall of a traumatic event in childhood. The readiest explanation is the higher attribution by sensitives (by approximately the same ratio) of an immediate family member who suffered from alcoholism, depression, or mood imbalance. If we assume that parents who are in the grip of these conditions are likelier to mistreat their children—

or go into funks that precipitate a family crisis—then it only makes sense that these children should recollect traumatic experiences.

However, this is not the only applicable explanation. An overarching question, it seems to me, goes to the very heart of the nature/nurture continuum. To what extent is sensitivity shaped by trauma, as opposed to innate sensitivity conditioning the perception of trauma? Let us posit (as I have in this book) that some individuals are, by virtue of their HPA set point, more excitable, more reactive, and more easily stressed than other people. Would these same children not be more likely to be adversely affected by events that might not seem traumatic to other children who are not so sensitive?

Remember, in the last chapter, how young children have been observed reacting intensely to certain sounds, colors, aromas, textures, or temperatures.[102] It's reasonable to assume that, if a given sensation were pleasing to such children, they would delve into it; if it were noxious, they would seek an escape route. Recall here Bergman and Escalona's poignant evocation of early defense mechanisms, with children rhythmically rocking themselves, retreating from an environment perceived as harsh and unwelcome. It seems entirely possible that the private world these children entered into is effectively a crucible for introspection and dissociation, spawning the later personality traits of shyness, absorption, and fantasy proneness.

In other words, *innate environmental sensitivities could be the driver of adult personality.*

This doesn't indemnify the nurture side of the equation, though. Numerous investigators have established that magical thinking, belief in the paranormal, and anomalous perceptions are all conditioned by trauma, particularly chronic childhood abuse.[103] Their view is that fantasy and imagination serve as a defense against abusive treatment that the child cannot possibly alter. The illusion that the child holds some special, invisible capacity to influence people or events is reassuring, and from the comfort of this fancy flows a willingness to believe in strange powers generally. Over time, the child grows into an adult who is not only interested in things psychic but also believes that he or she actually experiences them.[104]

Cases in point are provided by Lenore Terr, a psychiatrist who is among the foremost investigators of early trauma and its consequences. She has profiled children who, in the aftermath of their horrific experience, "realized" that one or more omens had been present beforehand. If only they had paid attention to these signs, they imagined, the frightening episode could have been averted. In some cases, these kids came to believe that they harbored psychic powers and could predict future events—prospectively saving others from a similarly dire fate. Their "total sense of helplessness," Terr comments, was assuaged by this coping mechanism.[105]

Other children just learn to go away, deadening their bodymind. Terr offers this striking account of a boy known as Frederick, age seven, whose "stepfather had been throwing him against walls while [his mother] worked the evening shift." Here is how he reacted:

> Frederick glanced down at the playground pavement one day and saw blood. After several seconds of searching for a wounded companion, Frederick realized that it was *he* who was bleeding. The boy realized he could feel no pain.
>
> In a psychotherapy session I asked Frederick how he could make this sort of thing happen. "It jus' happens now," he said. "I used to pretend I was at a picnic with my head on Mommy's lap. The first time my stepdaddy hit me, it hurt a lot. But then I found out that I could make myself go on Mommy's lap [in imagination], and [his stepfather] couldn't hurt me that way. I kept goin' on Mommy's lap—I didn't have to scream or cry or anything. I could *be* someplace else and not get hurt."[106]

Unquestionably, childhood trauma does condition dissociation. One study of fantasy-prone people found signs of mental disturbance in approximately one in four, owing to such causes as harsh and repeated punishment during childhood.[107] Magical thinking has been demonstrated as characteristic of some children of alcoholics[108] as well as some people who consider themselves electrically sensitive.[109] Likewise, women (who made up 71 percent of my sensitive survey population) have been shown to be about twice as susceptible as men to somatization disorder,[110] the clinical term for the process whereby distressing memories and other psychological issues bring on physical illness.

The more that the neurobiology of trauma is studied, the more it becomes plain that the effects of chronic or intensive stress are significant— and lifelong. The consequence of such stress is to *block the formation of new neurons* in the brain. The brain thus becomes less plastic, less able to learn and adapt. Permanent memory loss may also result through damage to the hippocampus.[111] The more often an individual experiences threats, further- more, the more habitually sensitized his or her stress-handling system will become.[112]

Just how pronounced these and other bodymind effects will be depends on three factors: what stage of development the child is in when the particular trauma is experienced, his or her inherited neurobiology, and the ability of his or her primary caregivers to handle stress effectively themselves. Take the first factor: the younger the child, the more mallea- ble the central nervous system obviously will be. Its impetus is to organize sensory input, to quite literally make sense of the world. If that process is interrupted or threatened, a permanent toll is likely to be exacted. Indeed, the research into dissociation suggests that this involuntary form of bodymind "surrender" is more likely to become characteristic the younger the person is. But it also depends on the child's gender (girls are more likely to dissociate than boys), the degree to which the situation is physi- cally painful or injurious, the extent to which the child is truly powerless to respond, and whether models are available to him or her for coping without being overwhelmed.[113] Not everyone faced with a perceived life threat inevitably freezes, surrenders, or opts out via dissociation.

As I suggested earlier, the tendency to dissociate need not owe entirely to trauma. One's inherited neurobiology is crucially a factor. Consider that an infant can have no control over his or her inborn sensitivity to bright lights, loud noises, intrusive smells, or harsh tactile sensations. Dissociative personality traits could easily evolve from the simple urge to take refuge from such environmental influences.

Terr herself makes a telling observation. Some of the children she's examined, *"the ones, perhaps, who have an innate ease of hypnotizability,"* spontaneously discover that they can successfully retreat into a private world.[114] The emphasis in her quote is mine, because I believe it deserves to be highlighted. Trauma and innate sensitivity are not mutually exclusive; indeed, they reinforce one another.

Kenneth Ring holds a similar view. He surveyed people reporting NDEs,[115, 116] who also volunteered a greater incidence of childhood abuse and trauma than controls. On psychological profiles, too, they manifested greater dissociative tendencies. Ring's opinion is that these individuals are "sensitives with low stress thresholds" who, through "their difficult and in some cases even tormented childhoods . . . have come to develop an extended range of human perception."[117] Nature as well as nurture plays a role in anomalous perception, he proposes.

Another theory germane to this discussion is *cognitive immaturity*.[118] Timothy Yates and James Bannard, two Canadian researchers writing in 1988, suggested that children experiencing stressful circumstances may be more apt to develop hallucinations (e.g., to see ghosts or carry on with imaginary companions) because, in essence, they have thin boundaries. In their mind, "sensations, perceptions, hallucinations, dreams, fantasies . . . are not sharply distinguishable from one another." So the children see what they wish to see, or what they imagine they see, rather than what is manifestly there.[119]

Ernest Hartmann, the originator of the boundaries concept, offers credence by noting that, as children grow older, the brain normally prunes its synapses so that kids "become more serious and organized and lose some of the imagination, vivid imagery, and spontaneous creativity" they possessed earlier in life. The development of thin-boundary children, he proposes, lags during that period. The result: as adults, they are adaptable and creative but also retain "the vulnerability of the young child," tending to have vivid memories of their childhood and to identify with their remembered feelings.[120, 121] This conjecture is surely consistent with the evidence, yet not *in*consistent with the possibility that highly sensitive persons can legitimately apprehend stimuli in the external environment that bypass the rest of us who are more cognitively mature.

Topics for Further Investigation

"Scientists are always excited at things they don't understand. It means they're on the verge of discovery." So observes of Alan Lightman, a physicist at the Massachusetts Institute of Technology and a popular science essayist.[122] Carrying that spirit into my own investigations, I've sought to draw from the best research, constantly question my assumptions, and continually improve the quality of my information gathering. This approach is especially important given the controversial conjectures to which those findings have lead me, and the subject matter itself, which many people consider dubious. Nevertheless, like any professional scientist, I'm excited by what is coming to light—and seeking to explore further.

The results of my survey project were gathered during a five-year period, from 1999 to 2004. Based on constructive feedback gained from a variety of interested parties since then, I've refined the questionnaire, which now presents seventy questions (up from fifty-four in the original version). New questions include:

- An item asking the respondent's hair and eye color. (Along with handedness, these may be useful indicators of genetic influence.)
- A question on whether the person was delivered by C-section (to assess any link between this less-natural form of birth and later sensitivity).
- An item asking the respondent to rate the quality of his or her close personal relationships (to fathom to what extent the person has a supportive social network).
- A question on whether the respondent had an imaginary companion growing up (to probe for early indications of fantasy-proneness).
- An item asking if the respondent plays a musical instrument or engages in art (to gauge the extent of any association between sensitivity and creativity).
- Items asking whether any of the respondent's senses functions below normal and whether he or she has experienced any signs of poor sensory integration.
- Questions about a number of conditions that can be checked in the

inventory of medical self-reports: whether the individual has experienced a rash or persistent skin condition; whether he or she is prone to panic attacks or flashbacks; whether the person has autism or Asperger's disorder; and whether he or she suffers from hyperactivity, attention deficit hyperactivity disorder, seasonal affective disorder, irritable bowel syndrome, or hypertension.

- Items asking if the respondent has actually been diagnosed with any of the conditions he or she checks—and whether close family members who are claimed to have had the conditions were ever diagnosed themselves.

- A question on whether the individual is physically affected in advance by changing weather.

- A question asking whether he or she has ever had a major surgical procedure (and, if so, what age he or she was at the time).

- An expanded section looking into childhood trauma, asking the person to indicate whether the reported situation was a one-time event, sporadic, or frequent; his or her age at the time; and what the respondents' feelings were (e.g., terror, sadness, anger, resignation, hysteria, determination to fight back).

I hope that the survey instrument—not to mention the overall purpose of seeking data on sensitivity from the individuals most affected—will be judged as valuable and taken up by still other researchers. One worthwhile path would be to determine the extent to which people who are sensitive also have thin boundaries. The presumption, based on Hartmann's theory, is that they do—but it would be instructive to have sensitive individuals take Hartmann's boundary questionnaire to determine the overlap. I would also ask investigators who use the boundary questionnaire to give my sensitivity survey to the individuals they study. Comparing and contrasting the respective findings would be most illuminating.

Furthermore, the incidence of synesthesia among sensitives offers a tremendous opportunity to explore the respective roles of nature and nurture. If, as has been theorized, synesthesia results from the retention of early neural connections, the role of environmental factors in sensitivity could be more precisely sketched based on the extent to which childhood trauma, especially, is indicated in the completed surveys of synesthetes. It is also possible that different forms of synesthesia correlate differently with other survey items, most importantly the self-reports of apparitional perception. The questionnaire now asks synesthetes to note the particular form of the condition they have.

It would also be interesting to broaden the survey population by asking people known as dowsers to complete the questionnaire. (Dowsing is an ancient practice whereby a person attempts to locate underground water sources, buried metals, or other lost or hidden objects using a twig or rod held in the hand, or without such a tool at all.) Dowsers are said to possess a degree of electromagnetic sensitivity that aids them in their pursuits, yet it's also claimed that anyone can learn to dowse. Use of the Environmental Sensitivity Survey with a cross-section of this population could help to untangle this apparent conundrum of nature versus nurture.

Ultimately, it would be most enlightening to expand the investigation beyond individuals who attest to various forms of sensitivity. We need to assess the degree to which the factors presumed to underlie extraordinary sensitivity are extant in the general population. With a farther reach, we will have better data and be able to draw more supportable conclusions regarding a neurobiological basis for anomalous perception. If you would like to take the survey yourself, go to www.emotiongateway.com to download a copy. Your participation is encouraged and appreciated—whether or not you consider yourself sensitive.

A Genetic Basis for Sensitivity

I'd like to close this chapter by looping back to the way it began, with a nod to the likely genetic basis of sensitivity.

Several pieces of recent research stand out. The first was authored by Carla Shatz, a neurobiologist now at Stanford University. She's shown that a particular protein molecule—previously thought to be solely a part of the immune system—plays a critical role in early brain wiring.[123] While her discovery was made in mice, the same might be found to apply to people. In fact, Shatz notes that the gene associated with this protein in humans is located on a chromosome segment that has been implicated in a number of neurological disorders, including dyslexia. "It is time for people to think out of the box," she observes. "All bets are off when it comes to how these immune molecules are functioning in the brain."[124]

Dyslexia, while not among the medical conditions most frequently noted by my survey respondents, was nonetheless indicated by 14 percent of the sensitive group versus none of the controls. A relationship between dyslexia, migraine headache, and allergies was postulated by the late Norman Geschwind, who was interested in the apparent link between autoimmune disorders such as allergies and hemispheric functioning.[125] His nephew, Daniel Geschwind, who directs the neurogenetics program at the University of California–Los Angeles, is extending that work. His premise is that "genetic contributions to the development of brain structures are fundamentally related to human behavior."[126]

Another researcher, Lisa Boulanger of the University of California–San Diego, is exploring whether the seeds of autism might be planted in babies whose mothers are affected by viral infection during a particular juncture in their pregnancy.[127] Could it be, she wonders, that an overstimulated immune system at just that point could affect the developing baby's brain? (This line of inquiry hearkens back to the model proposed in chapter 4.) Boulanger notes, as others have, that autism is often accompanied by sensory overload, and sees this as a clue: perhaps the children of mothers who had challenges to their immune system during pregnancy lack the ability to filter out extraneous sensory information. A test of the startle response in at least some people with autism (as well as schizophrenia) shows that their filter may not be working well. "All of these things are just correlated in a very interesting way," she observes.[128]

Speaking of interesting, a remarkable inherited difference has been found for, of all things, dancing. An Israeli study of eighty-five dancers and advanced dancing students found that they have variants of two particular genes whose activity has been linked to both spiritual experience (via levels of the neurotransmitter serotonin) and social communication (via another brain chemical, vasopressin). This sets them off from the general population. "People are born to dance," says the researcher, Richard Ebstein. "The genes we studied are . . . related to the emotional side of dancing—the need and ability to communicate with other people and a spiritual side to their natures that not only enables them to feel the music but to communicate the feeling to others via dance."[129]

Memory, too—or at least certain forms of it—appears to have a genetic basis. People with a particular gene variant have been found to be twice as good at remembering emotionally charged events as individuals with the more common version of the gene.[130] This has obvious implications for sensitivity as conditioned by trauma.

It's likewise been found that people with variations in a particular stress-related gene appear to have been affected more strongly by abuse at an early age than comparable individuals *without* this particular genetic variation. This terrible legacy evidently persists into adulthood in the form of PTSD. Other gene variants yet to be found are probably also contributing, surmise the researchers.[131] Even if the susceptibility to debilitating trauma is inherited, whether or not a person actually comes to suffer from PTSD still hinges on early life experience.[132]

My inference from the bulk of the evidence surveyed in this chapter is that anomalous perceptions have a genetic basis, programmed down the ages to serve an evolutionary purpose. Women, for a variety of reasons, predominate among the sensitive population. As with migraine and synesthesia, associations exist between the tendency toward apparitional perception and such factors as ambidexterity; hypersensitivity to light, sound, and smell; and susceptibility to allergies, chronic pain, and chronic fatigue. These linkages constitute the *neurobiology of sensitivity* that, I argue, underlies reports of anomalous experience occurring across societies and throughout history.

Perhaps most intriguing of all—though by far the least explored aspect—is the bridge between anomalous perception, heightened emotional reactions, empathy, and (as Ebstein alluded to) spirituality. We shall traverse more of this fascinating territory in the next three chapters. Count on it being eye opening!

10

---◆---

Psychosomatic Plasticity and the Persistence of Memory

"I am too much of a skeptic to deny the possibility of anything."

T. H. Huxley

Let's try an experiment. Think back on a particular time when you were caught blushing. Really try to picture the situation: the setting, who you were with, what was happening. Now, what was said to make you blush? Did someone else say it, or did you hear yourself say something that gave you pause? What were you thinking at the time? What images or memories caused you to blush? What were the ensuing feelings? Can you bring them into the present moment and relive them?

Now think of a wonderfully tasty food: a dessert, maybe. Picture it on your plate. Get down really close to it. See the color, the texture; take a whiff and imagine what it will taste like. Mmmm. Now, have you begun to salivate or is your stomach rumbling, perhaps?

Here's one more experiment to try. Conjure up in your mind a vision of the most appealing person that you might ever want to go to bed with. What does he or she look like? What is that person wearing (or not wearing, as the case may be)? Notice the face, the body, his or her attraction to you or your own attraction back. What is going on between you? What do you *want* to go on? Let that fantasy play out a little longer. Now, notice how you are feeling. Has your heartbeat quickened? Has your mouth gotten dry? Have you had any other physical reactions?

Okay, calm down . . . back to quiet reading. Each of these examples illustrates an important biological principle: mere thoughts and feelings can generate a real physical reaction.[1] As in the above examples, the triggers may be embarrassment, hunger, or desire. Of course, nearly any thought—if it is connected with a feeling—and nearly any *feeling* may bring about a particular set of simultaneous physical perceptions (what Peter Levine calls the felt sense).

This is true not just for passing reactions but more lingering ones. Take the common ulcer. Some people react to stress—and to not being able to remedy the cause of that stress—by developing ulcers. An ulcer is produced when the sympathetic nervous system kicks into gear. The adrenal glands, signaled by the hypothalamus, release the hormones adrenaline and noradrenaline. The stomach, in turn, secretes more acid while reducing blood flow to the lining.[2] Now, it must be said that most ulcers can be traced to a bacterium, *Helicobacter pylori,* that lives in the stomach. Drugs targeting this bacterium have reduced the incidence of ulcers quite dramatically. However, only about 10 percent of people infected with *H. pylori* develop ulcers, and about 15 percent of ulcer patients don't harbor the bacterium. Some other factor—most likely stress—must be playing a role.[3] Then again, others of us react to feeling pressured, anxious, and stuck with *different* symptoms.

The Effect of Emoting on Stress and Immune Function

The fact is that threat of any kind elicits a bodily stress reaction. It matters not whether the subject in question is in the past, present, or future. Demonstrable effects on immunity often will follow. A fascinating experiment done at Ohio State University bears this out. The team of Janice Kiecolt-Glaser and Ronald Glaser collected immunological data from medical students before, during, and after their final exams. A number of changes in immune function were evident. The exam period brought about a decline in the activity of the students' natural killer cells, which fight viral infection. The production of another immune system chemical called gamma interferon, which stimulates the growth of natural killer cells, decreased by as much as 90 percent. And the responsiveness of the students' T cells (a type of white blood cell, also known as a lymphocyte) declined markedly. Accordingly, the students reported more illnesses (mainly minor respiratory infections) during the exam period than at other times during the year. Could these changes have been the result of exam-related alterations in the students' eating and sleeping habits? The researchers found no evidence for this, only for the effect of exam-related stress itself.[4]

Immune function has been found to vary not just during stressful periods but also on a daily basis, concurrent with mood.[5] At the other end of the scale, prolonged stress produces longer-term effects on immunity. To demonstrate this, the Glasers studied individuals who were caring for a parent or spouse with Alzheimer's disease, a tragically debilitating illness that gradually robs a person of his or her memory and other cognitive functions. During the study's thirteen-month period, these caregivers showed a reduction in three immune system measures. They were ill for more days than members of a control group and had a higher rate of depression.[6] The Glasers have found similar results in their study of married couples. Those in conflict-ridden marriages take longer to heal from all kinds of wounds—from minor scrapes to major surgery—than do happily married couples. Those who are outright hostile in their dealings with one another take 40 percent longer to heal and have poorer immune function.[7]

Further compelling evidence regarding stress and immunity comes from research on that most mundane of illnesses, the common cold. In a landmark British study, more than four hundred healthy men and women were asked about the significant life events they had experienced over the previous year (e.g., a new residence or job change, serious injury, pregnancy, birth or miscarriage, wedding or divorce, illness or death of a close family member, problems at work, child leaving home, retirement, major change in finances) as well as their *current* emotional state and an assessment of how well they typically cope with stress. These volunteers were then exposed to a standard dose of cold virus. The result: individuals with the highest stress ratings were six times more likely to become infected than those with the least perceived stress and twice as likely to actually develop a cold. This connection held up after the data were adjusted for factors including age, gender, prior health, allergies, smoking and drinking habits, sleep and exercise patterns, weight, diet, and education.[8]

As one might expect, significant life events have a direct bearing on stress and, by extension, on immune function. The death of a spouse, partner, or close family member is the most significant, followed by divorce and separation. The impact is perhaps most noticeable in young children, whose immune systems (indeed, whose entire neurobiology) is still developing. One study documenting this tracked hundreds of newborns until the age of six. Those whose parents had divorced or separated had increased concentrations of a particular cytokine related to the occurrence of allergic reactions.[9] Natural disasters and major accidents have an undeniable effect as well—and not just on kids. A case in point is the accident at the Three Mile Island nuclear facility in Pennsylvania that took place in 1979. Six years later, residents living near the damaged reactor had fewer immune cells circulating in their systems than control subjects living farther away. They reported continued high anxiety, as evidenced by higher-than-average pulse rates and higher levels of the stress hormones adrenaline, noradrenaline, and cortisol.

The adverse impact of *any* situation or event is greatest when the given situation is prolonged or the events are severe, undesirable, and follow on the heels of one another. That much reflects common sense, and the data demonstrate so. A persistent reduction in natural killer cell activity, for example, can lead not only to viral infection but also to autoimmune disorders such as allergies.[10] However, life events typically account for just 10 to 15 percent of the total variation in illness among people. Many of us who are exposed to stressful situations become ill, but many do not.[11] Acute stress can actually *enhance* the functioning of a person's immune system.[12] Even a chronic condition such as depression presents a mixed bag: while a decrease in immune function often accompanies depression, so can some forms of *increased* immune activity.[13] How it all works will vary from individual to individual. People born with a predisposition to be shy, anxious, or environmentally sensitive have their own characteristic immune responses. So will people prone toward a Type C personality (e.g., stoic, repressive, slough it off, grin and bear it). A variety of other factors—chief among them the quality of one's close relationships and the degree of social support received—also exert an influence.

This has been demonstrated by another Glaser study. They found that medical students who were lonely or socially isolated had weaker immune function than their peers.[14] The flip side is that having supportive personal relationships can *strengthen* immunity. And even if a person does not have optimum social support, one can be his or her own best friend. For instance, one study showed that divorced people who had the most negative feelings about their separation or the most difficulty "letting go" had the greatest downturn in immunity.[15] Similarly, in a group of women diagnosed with breast cancer, those who displayed a fighting spirit fared better in combating the disease than others who simply accepted their plight or gave up. Fifteen years after this group of women was first surveyed, 45 percent of those who fought against the disease were still alive and cancer free, compared with 17 percent of the women who had initially reacted with a sense of helplessness or resignation. Psychological response proved to be a better predictor of survival than a number of other factors, including the size of the tumor, the person's age, and the type of treatment.[16]

Desirability of Expressing Emotions

The above research is highly significant because it demonstrates the value of expressing emotions. Additional evidence comes from research conducted by psychiatrist David Spiegel at Stanford University. He and his colleagues found that women with advanced breast cancer survived twice as long if they took part in group therapy. By confronting their fears and venting their emotions (and, not coincidentally, via the support they received from the medical team and fellow sufferers), these women extended their lives as well as improved their *quality* of life. A similar result was obtained by immune researcher Fawzy Fawzy at the University of California–Los Angeles. There, ninety minutes of therapy once a week helped cancer patients reduce their fear, improve their coping skills, manage their stress, and bolster their social support. The patients' immune function was strengthened and, most important of all, their mortality rate was reduced by a third.[17]

The value of emotional expression is nowhere more evident than in a study done by the Glasers and psychologist James Pennebaker of Southern Methodist University. In this experiment, students who wrote about their feelings in a journal had better immune system functioning and fewer visits to the university's health clinic. Here's how it worked:

> . . . 50 healthy undergraduates were asked to write either about personal and traumatic events or about trivial topics for 20 minutes a day during four consecutive days. The 25 students randomly assigned to the "trauma" writing group took the assignment seriously; the topics they discussed were personal . . . ranging from problems with homesickness after coming to college, loneliness, and relationship conflicts, to parental problems such as divorce, family quarrels and family violence, and the death of a loved one. The "trivial" group had an assigned topic each day, such as descriptions of the shoes they were wearing or of a recent social event.
>
> Although there were no immunological differences between the two groups before they began the writing assignment, differences emerged by the end of the study. Immune system cells from students who wrote about traumatic events showed greater activity . . . than did cells taken from the blood of the other students. . . . Students who wrote about traumatic events [also] showed a drop in [health] clinic visits, relative to those who wrote about trivial events.[18]

Dozens of other studies have yielded similar results, whether the participants were college students, grade school children, or nursing home residents.[19] Even the simple act of naming an angry-looking face as "angry" has been shown to cause diminished activity in the brain's emotional alarm area, the amygdala. At the same time, an area associated with language processing lights up. Being able to articulate a feeling or recognition thus begins to transform the threat reaction to something potentially more nuanced.[20] Ultimately, says one researcher, "Writing gives you a sense of control and a sense of understanding. To write about a stressful event, you have to break it down into little pieces, and suddenly it seems more manageable."[21]

It's all the more noteworthy, then, that certain people fail to derive benefit; indeed, for them, diary writing makes them feel worse off.[22] How can this be? The explanation may relate to the dynamics of depression. Individuals who are prone to depression are distinguished, first and foremost, by a tendency to dwell on their problems or misfortunes.[23] This tendency reflects a bona fide neurological (perhaps even a genetically encoded) underpinning: brain circuitry that lacks a sufficient capacity to edit anxious thoughts.[24] When asked to keep a diary, then, people who are prone to depression will naturally return to what is troubling them rather than "giving it up" on paper. They ruminate rather than release. For them, expressive writing is not the best bet—but exercise, sincere forgiveness, or some other form of personal expression might be.

Still, the salient point here is that a stressful life experience need not be traumatic even if, on its face, it connotes the possibility, even the likelihood, of trauma. Acknowledging one's feelings and finding a way to express them—emoting—is essential to a healthy reaction. Not just immunologically but, I would add, psychically. As we have seen, a person's immune system is part and parcel of his or her *sense of self* as well as being closely connected with all of the body's functioning—including its production and storage of energy. The flow of feeling outward, into articulation and expression, represents a healthy flow of energy in which all the systems of the body are communicating harmoniously. "Let it flow and let it go," in the words of one psychotherapist, is the ideal.[25]

Human beings may not be the only animals that work this way. Evidence has been found that even rats seem to sigh with relief. If this is not a form of emotion, it might at least be a form of stress release. Researchers in Poland trained the rats to expect an electrical shock, but when a signal was given that the shock would not be administered, the rats often took a deep breath.[26] This result obviously needs to be replicated, but it seems believable given that all mammals possess the same basic stress-regulating neurobiology. Orphaned elephants, for example, whose parents were cruelly killed by poachers and who were deprived as youngsters of maternal affection, are observed as adults to manifest the very symptoms associated with human PTSD: an exaggerated startle response, asocial behavior, and depression. Trauma may, in fact, affect all mammals similarly.[27]

Different Boundaries, Different Connectedness

Let's return to the first three examples of feeling offered in this chapter, namely blushing, hunger, and sexual excitement. In the first instance, the bodymind is recognizing that an unexpressed feeling (even if associated with a memory rather than the immediate situation) is at odds with some internally acknowledged notion of propriety. The result is a blush, a visible indicator of social embarrassment. It may not be an emotion in the usual sense of the term, but the fact that one is blushing expresses something all the same. In the second instance, you envision a luscious dessert you have enjoyed immensely in the past, and salivating or tummy rumbling follows quickly. In the third case, the physical barometers of sexual desire are easy enough to pinpoint. Although they may not be visible to anyone else, our inclination is always to express or at least acknowledge to ourselves these feelings of longing. Like a blush (and most other indicators of feeling), they are certainly hard to ignore. When expressed in a rarified way (think here of the medieval troubadours or Cyrano de Bergerac), they become poetry, song, or fable. When expressed in a puerile way, they become pornography and media trash.

While each of us blushes and experiences the hallmarks of sexual desire, the flow of feeling is quicker in some people and slower in others. Here, it would be helpful to imagine a stream of clear, cold water, rippling over rocks, in continuous motion. Imagine also that the stream has various sources and tributaries fed by springs and empties into various channels and pools. That stream is the flow of feeling in the human body. Its sources are all the cells that, in combination, transform food and oxygen into the body's energy; its course is nerve fiber and the bloodstream; its tributaries are the muscles, organs, and the skin. The most important organ, the heart, is actually not a tributary but a central pump and a way station for the flow of feeling. As I have pointed out before, our everyday language recognizes this state of things in observations such as "Her heart really didn't seem to be in it," and "Their rejection left him heartbroken."

The thin-boundary people we met in the previous chapters—those inclined toward fantasy and absorption, sensory defensiveness, and forms of hypersensitivity such as allergies and migraines—have a greater connectedness among their bodies' various systems (nervous, immune, gastrointestinal, circulatory, respiratory, digestive, reproductive, endocrine, and glandular). This connectivity develops in the womb and is arrayed at birth, although life experience (especially early experience) inevitably modifies it. The result is a more rapid and direct flow of feeling. In contrast, the personalities and behavior of thick-boundary people—those who come across as stolid, rigid, implacable, or thick skinned—reflect a lesser degree of connection among their bodily systems and a less rapid, less direct flow of feeling.

What is the relation of all this to anomalous experience? In a nutshell, thin-boundary people are more likely to be psychically sensitive along with their other forms of sensitivity. Thick-boundary people are more likely to be the *cause* of psychic manifestations. The odds of anomalies developing dramatically increase when dissociation and an unresolved freeze response occur (i.e., when the energy of feeling fails to be expressed and dams up in the body). If such tension is harbored, various odd effects, including electrical ones, are possible.

It seems relevant here to point out that numerous investigations of hauntings and poltergeist phenomena have highlighted the emotional dynamics of a family gone awry rather than one person in isolation. As the saying goes, it takes two to tango, and often there is some shared family trauma or tension that a thin-boundary person and a thick-boundary person will each deal with in his or her own way. The group psychodynamics inevitably reflect the individuals' disparate neurobiologies.

It is likewise interesting to note how frequently such psychic outbreaks take place in households where three generations live together. In these cases, the complexity of the family's interactions is upped considerably. Of course, not all families with a shared trauma or all families with three generations living under the same roof experience anomalies. The vast majority, presumably, do not. Whether such outbreaks occur is a function of the flow of feeling and its unique form of processing within each individual. Most people, of course, are somewhere in the middle of the spectrum from thin-boundary to thick-boundary. Where the "outliers" meet is the most fertile ground for anomalies—especially if that ground has been seeded through trauma, dissociated feeling, and stored-up tension.

Psychosomatic Plasticity

Now let's take a look at an especially intriguing capacity of the thin-boundary person, namely, the ability to generate bona fide *physical reactions* to a thought, idea, or suggestion. Ernest Hartmann, whom we met in chapter 8, found that thin-boundary individuals do this much more readily than thick-boundary types. He instructed a small group of subjects to imagine that they were sitting by a fire with one hand near the fire and then that they were holding an ice cube in that hand. The thin-boundary subjects produced a significantly greater change in their hands' skin temperature than those with thick boundaries.[28]

The researchers Sheryl Wilson and Theodore Barber, whom we also met in chapter 8, echo Hartmann's observation by stating, "A striking characteristic [of] fantasy-prone subjects is that their vivid fantasies and memories are at times associated with physical concomitants."[29] Examples include:

- Spontaneously becoming ill upon seeing violence on television or in the movies
- Being affected by imagined heat and cold in the same way as actual heat and cold
- Experiencing an orgasm purely as a result of one's sexual fantasy

Barber gave this remarkable trait a name. He estimated that approximately 4 percent of the population has what he called "'psychosomatic plasticity'—an extreme capacity to turn suggestions . . . into bodily realities."[30] Psychosomatic plasticity, I suspect, might not be far from the neural plasticity evidenced by those who experience synesthesia. The difference would be that the first form of plasticity is a whole-body phenomenon, whereas the second reflects primarily sensory and brain processing.

Many of us, of course, are acquainted with psoriasis, another condition that may be related to psychosomatic plasticity. This skin disorder is not fully understood, but one thing is clear: it tends to get worse with stress.[31] A lot of that stress—as well as major hormonal changes—takes place during adolescence, when pimples, blackheads, and zits are at their most discomfiting. At least 40 percent of skin disorders generally (and this includes disorders in adults) are believed to have an emotional component.[32] Lesions, welts, rashes, boils, and the like may indicate the presence of conflicts underlying the skin that displays them.[33] The skin is extraordinarily sensitive, and as we have seen, it can fairly be said that the skin is the outward side of our internal nervous system. Anthropologist Ashley Montagu has further pointed out that "the skin, as we know from human faces, carries its own memory of conditions experienced in the remote and immediate past."[34] Just as weathered or smooth hands connote the sort of work experiences that people have had, so the uniqueness of our faces hints at the totality of our life experience. The process is entirely unconscious. Thus, it is not unreasonable to suppose that husbands and wives who are married for decades do, in fact, come to resemble each other—for better or for worse.

Hypnosis: Plasticity on Display

Plasticity comes in other forms. When one hears of individuals who cure themselves of some craving, raise hives, or cause a wart to disappear, it is often attributed to hypnosis. But hypnosis doesn't work for everyone: some people are more susceptible to hypnotic suggestion than others.[35] I am going to propose that hypnosis is a form of psychosomatic plasticity, and that hypnotically suggestible people are thin-boundary types. Consider

that, when hypnosis works, it evidently does so because the given suggestion ("You are getting sleepy . . .") is taken seriously by the person being
hypnotized, who proceeds to put it into effect physiologically and neurologically. In other words, suggestible people believe what they hear and
their bodymind acts accordingly.[36] Placebos, which are dummy drugs that
patients are told are the real thing, presumably work the same way, being
a more effective form of treatment for some people than for others. In
many cases, in fact, placebos work as effectively as the real medications.

Like the placebo effect, hypnosis is now being studied in some fairly
august quarters. Stephen Kosslyn and William Thompson, two researchers at Harvard University, found that certain individuals are, indeed,
"highly hypnotizable." They estimate that about 8 percent of the population qualifies (double the Wilson and Barber estimate). The highly hypnotizable group contrasts sharply with people who scored especially low
on Kosslyn and Thompson's tests. Results from that low-hypnotizable
group were "just garbage," as the scientists put it delicately.[37]

What tests separated the men from the boys, so to speak? Subjects'
brains were monitored by a PET scanner as they were being hypnotized.
A computer screen overhead presented them with a pattern of yellow, red,
blue, and green rectangles. The participants were then given the suggestion
to "drain" the color from what they saw on the screen. In another exercise,
the rectangles were presented in various shades of grey and participants
were told to see them in color. The result was that, under hypnosis, *both
sides* of the subjects' brains showed the relevant activity, whereas when they
were not hypnotized, only the right hemisphere lit up. Kosslyn and Johnson
theorize that the right side, which was active in both cases, "tweaks" the
left during hypnosis to look past what is actually seen, substituting the
imagined.[38] This makes sense given that the right side of the brain is more
imaginative than the left, which is given to logic and reason.

While the brain under hypnosis is a fascinating subject, it begs the
question of what the *body* is doing. Barber studied hypnosis at length and
concluded that individuals who are highly hypnotizable are able to alter
their blood flow. In his view, they effectively take suggestions, beliefs,
and imaginings "to heart" and change the blood supply to certain organs

and tissues, with noticeable bodily changes as the result.[39] And what does blood carry? Oxygen, answers John Sarno, professor of clinical rehabilitation medicine at New York University Medical Center. Sarno points out that the autonomic nervous system controls the body's involuntary functions, including blood flow. When an individual perceives a threat, his or her breathing becomes shallow and blood flow is altered to facilitate the fight-or-flight response. While Sarno does not use the term "dissociation," his thinking appears to be that, at certain times, the brain will divest blood from a particular set of tissues.[40] If this process becomes chronic, the given area of the body (e.g., neck, back, shoulders) will experience pain rather than the more genuine feeling that typically resides in that part of the body. This can be described as "compartmentalized dissociation," the term applied by Levine to a localized interruption in, and distortion of, the felt sense.[41] Activities that serve to deepen breathing and *increase* the blood (and lymph) supply, such as exercise and massage, tend to reduce pain, Sarno notes, at least temporarily.[42]

Deep breathing is a fundamental component of yoga, meditation, and other stress-reduction techniques. It should be added that good sex and a good belly laugh both deepen breathing, so they should likewise help to alleviate pain and stress. Universally, they are acknowledged to do just that.

Heart Rate Variability and Respiration

You'll recall that children who are characteristically shy or fearful have more electrical activity taking place in the right frontal part of their neocortex, whereas children who are more outgoing and confident display more activity in the left frontal portion. The pattern, as we noted, may or may not extend into adulthood: it depends on the person's accumulating life experience. A corollary may be found in another, even less well appreciated physiological factor: heart rate variability. This refers to the naturally occurring, beat-to-beat changes in a person's resting heart rhythm. Once thought to be monotonously regular, it is now known that the rhythm is variable, owing to the simultaneous influence of the two branches of the ANS: the sympathetic branch (which acts to slow heart rate) and the parasympathetic (which serves to speed it up).[43]

Along with blood pressure and the skin's electrical conductance, heart rate variability represents a way to gather how a person is feeling—at one particular time as well as over a period of time. It is, in that sense, *characteristic* of an individual, a rough barometer of the state of his or her physiology. Respiration, I submit, may likewise be characteristic. A person's pattern of breathing—which takes place mostly beneath awareness—may reflect his or her heart rate variability, and vice versa.

Just how important is breathing? Montagu puts it aptly:

> The urge to breathe is the most imperative of all man's basic urges, and the most automatic. . . . Under conditions of stress many persons go into labored breathing. . . . Yet, in spite of its automaticity, breathing or respiration is under voluntary control . . . for short periods of time, as any person who has ever taken singing lessons knows, [or] for very durable periods of time, as every yogi knows. This control is actually exerted during the ordinary activities of everyday life, such as speaking, swallowing, laughing, blowing, coughing. . . . Breathing, indeed, is not simply a physiological process but a part of the way in which an organism behaves.[44]

One could say that, as we breathe, so goes our physical state. This is literally true since oxygen (and food) are converted into the cellular ATP molecules whose incessant activity, in turn, produces the sodium electricity that powers our muscles and nervous system. So, without oxygen, no ATP. Without ATP, no energy. And without energy, no flow of feeling, no animation.

Cogitate on this. If we had to direct attention to our breathing at each moment—commanding ourselves to breathe in, then out, back in, then once again out, and so on—we would have difficulty devoting energy, time, or attention to anything else. How would we ever sleep if breathing needed to be a conscious, self-directed act? The situation might be stated thus: we don't breathe as much as we are breathed.[45]

It's no wonder that breath has been central to the concept of life since the earliest times, as well as closely identified with energy itself. Breath energy was known as *thymos* and later *pneuma* in ancient Greece, as *ka* in ancient Egypt, *atman* and later *prana* in India, *ruach* to the Hebrews, and *qi* to the Chinese.[46] These concepts also relate to the soul, spirit, or psyche. Our word "spirit," for instance, is descended linguistically from the Latin *spiritus* (breath) and is related to respiration, inspiration, perspiration, and such. The idea that a person might be in high spirits on a given day or, alternately, dispirited, speaks to the idea of how animated, how energetic they appear. Likewise, the word "animate" is derived from the Latin *animus,* meaning "mind," "soul," or "breath," and is related to words such as "magnanimous," "animosity," and of course, "animal." An exciting activity can leave you breathless, and changes in one's emotions are often accompanied by changes in breathing associated with yelling, panting, gasping, or sobbing.[47]

One must remember that oxygen is not the only molecule transported and released throughout the body via the bloodstream. So are a multitude of hormones, including cortisol, ACTH, prolactin (which stimulates immune activity), and substance P (implicated in fibromyalgia). And we shouldn't forget the white blood cells (also known as leukocytes), which are the immune cells, seeking out and attacking viruses and other invaders. If respiration and blood flow are crucial to hypnosis, then people who are hypnotized—or just highly suggestible—should be able to influence their own immune reactions. This is exactly what the research has found, time and again. Hypnotized subjects can develop an allergic reaction when they come into contact with a substance that is not truly allergenic but which they are *told* is; conversely, they can avoid an allergic reaction when told that a substance is not allergenic but it actually *is*.[48]

Thin-boundary people can provoke this same type of psychosomatic plasticity in other ways. In one well-documented case, a woman who was an experienced meditator was able to voluntarily reduce her immunological reaction to a skin test for a period of three weeks and then bring it back up again.[49]

Emotion as the Gateway

Just as I've suggested that the dynamics of emotion serve as a gateway into the anomalous, so too the flow of feeling constitutes the key to plasticity. Neurologist Antonio Damasio, one of the foremost theorists of emotion today, provides a wonderful example in his book *The Feeling of What Happens.* He relates an encounter between himself, his wife Hanna (also an emotion researcher), and the pianist Maria João Pires.

> When she plays, under the perfect control of her will, she can either reduce or allow the flow of emotion to her body. My wife . . . and I thought this was a wonderfully romantic idea, but Maria João insisted that she could do it and we resisted believing it. Eventually, the stage for the empirical moment of truth was set in our laboratory. Maria João was wired to the complicated psychophysiological equipment while she listened to short musical pieces of our selection in two conditions: emotion allowed, or emotion voluntarily inhibited. Her Chopin *Nocturnes* had just been released, and we used some of hers and some of Daniel Barenboim's as stimuli. In the condition of "emotion allowed," her skin conductance record was full of peaks and valleys, linked intriguingly to varied passages in the pieces. Then, in the condition of "emotion reduced," the unbelievable did, in fact, happen. She could virtually flatten her skin-conductance graph at will and change her heart rate, to boot. Behaviorally, she changed as well.[50]

In other cases, the feelings allowed—or reduced—are not nearly so pleasurable. Yet they illustrate the same principle, that the energy of feelings conditions psychosomatic plasticity. The following examples are taken from a remarkable book by behavioral neuroscientist (and medical intuitive) Mona Lisa Schulz (who seems herself to be electrically sensitive).[51] Here are thumbnail descriptions of some of the cases she describes. They all portray women, who, as we've seen, make up the vast majority of sensitives.

- A young woman who had just gone off to college "went to her first class but found she couldn't walk into the room. For some reason she was terrified. Her hands started shaking, her palms got sweaty, and she felt a nameless dread." Schulz intuitively "read" the girl's emotional life and saw that she'd had a strict upbringing. At a time of conflict between her parents, she had been sent away to an ultrarestrictive school. "There she had a lot of unpleasant experiences, from being rapped on the knuckles for misbehaving to being barred from lunch for not noticing that the collar of her uniform was askew. . . . She lost a lot of weight and became very ill." Her parents reunited for the sake of her health. She came home and put her boarding school experience behind her—or so she thought. "Walking into her first college classroom evoked in her body . . . the same fears she had experienced as a child."[52]

- A woman with dissociative identity disorder had once been abused by her father. Only one personality "knew" about the abuse. "Whenever this personality emerged, burn marks would appear on the woman's arms. When she flashed out of that personality, the burn marks would go away."[53]

- Another woman's skin would break out in large hives whenever she was around someone domineering. "Most of her problem involved her mother-in-law, with whom she had a difficult relationship. . . . Whenever she had a memory involving her mother-in-law, she would break out in hives." This included going to the mailbox and finding a letter from her. "And when she talked about her mother-in-law in the psychiatrist's office, [he] would watch the boils form on her skin right in front of him."[54]

- A still more unfortunate woman was regularly beaten up by her husband. "As her sons grew up, they prevented the father from beating their mother. He then began to attack her with words. Whenever he unleashed a barrage of verbal abuse . . . bruises and black-and-blue marks would appear on her skin in the very places where she had previously received bruises from her husband's beatings. . . . A psychiatrist watched the bruises appear on the woman's arms right before his eyes when she talked about the verbal abuse."[55]

- When hypnotized, a woman proved able to raise blisters on the back of her left hand only, and always in the same place. When questioned later, she indicated that "the area where the blisters had formed coincided exactly with an area of her hand that she had burned six years earlier with hot grease."[56]

- Another woman featured what was described as a "florid" facial rash that had steadfastly resisted all forms of treatment tried over a five-year period. She was referred to a psychiatrist, who asked her flat-out, "What has been the most difficult thing in your life over that period?" She quickly answered, "My husband's illness," but added, "I keep a brave face on it." The psychiatrist drew her attention to a possible link between her rash and the brave face. In their following session, the woman had a "cathartic opportunity for her bottled up feelings, and within ten days from her first assessment her rash had gone."[57]

Author Gordon Rattray Taylor, in his expansive survey of bodymind phenomena, *The Natural History of the Mind* (remarkably prescient for 1979), expressed amazement that "a local body memory . . . [could] endure . . . indefinitely," with wounds such as the above appearing so specifically that "areas . . . a few millimeters away [are] unchanged."[58] Yet that is where the evidence leads us. More recently, healer Julie Motz has used the phrase "body haunting" to describe cases in which a person's intense emotional experience is encoded in a powerful body memory that can arise many years after the original episode.[59] Her term may not sound terribly scientific— and may not, therefore, capture the attention or interest of scientists—but I believe it is an accurate representation of what is going on.

All of the above examples involve intense but dissociated feeling— plus the action of the immune system. Remember that, in every one of us, the elements of the immune system are in constant communication with those of the nervous system, and vice versa. We have seen that the two are actually hardwired to each other, communicating via nerve fibers and neurotransmitters. They also exchange information through hormones and other messenger molecules. In this manner, everything in the body is connected: brain, gut, glands, organs, muscles, bones, nerves, head, and heart. So the energy of feeling flows *throughout* the body. It flows the same way in all of us, although the passage is slower for some (thick-boundary people) and faster for others (thin-boundary types). And for everyone, blood, oxygen, and feeling pass through and are pumped by the heart. It is to this most essential and fascinating of all organs that we turn next.

Straight from the Heart?

"Research on the heart is now where brain research was decades ago," remarks writer and educator Joseph Chilton Pearce. Not only have neuropeptide receptors been located in the heart that provide a means for the brain to communicate instantaneously with this most vital of organs, but it's also known that the process can work in reverse. The heart's atrium area produces a peptide known as ANP (atrial natriuretic peptide) that acts on the hypothalamic-pituitary-adrenal (HPA) stress system, affecting secretion of the hormone ACTH by the pituitary gland.[60] Studies cited by the Institute of HeartMath (whose express purpose is to advance biomedical research on the heart) suggest that the communication is electromagnetic as well, with the heart's electromagnetic output changing in tandem with the state of bodily feeling. To members of the Institute, the traditional view of the heart as harboring its own, distinctive intelligence is not merely metaphorical, it is increasingly backed up by science. "With each beat, the heart continuously communicates with the brain and body . . . the messages the heart sends . . . not only affect physiological regulation but can also profoundly influence perception, emotions, behaviors . . . and health."[61]

The extent of this influence is beginning to be documented. The late Paul Pearsall, a psychologist and psychoneuroimmunologist, authored a remarkable investigation described in his book, *The Heart's Code.*[62] Like Candace Pert and an increasing number of others, Pearsall's focus is on the overlap between the brain and the body, thoughts and emotions, health and illness, and the immune and nervous systems. His book presents some truly remarkable stories told to him by heart transplant recipients and their families. In the aggregate, these seem to indicate that the heart (and perhaps other organs as well) carries within it a memory of the person from whom it came. Given the stunning—and well documented— accounts of psychosomatic plasticity offered earlier, this notion may not seem so far-fetched. Presuming that Pearsall's subjects (seventy-three heart transplant patients and their families, sixty-seven other organ transplant recipients, and eighteen donor families) were not entirely deceitful, the subject is worth at least assessing on its merits.[63]

Here are a number of accounts culled by Pearsall and his associates. In each case, information about the donor and recipient was verified by family or friends. The often-striking personality changes noted in the recipients preceded any contact with the donor's family or friends. For instance:

- A seven-month-old boy received the heart of a sixteen-month-old boy who had, tragically, drowned. Four years later, the recipient met the donor's mother. "When [he] first saw me, he ran to me and pushed his nose against me and rubbed and rubbed it. It was exactly what we did with [our son]. . . . When he hugged me, I could feel my son. I mean I could feel him, not just symbolically. He was there. I felt his energy." The recipient's mother reported that her son acted much differently in the presence of the donor's mother. "He is very, very shy, but he went over to her just like he used to run to me when he was a baby. When he whispered 'It's okay, mama,' I broke down." Similarly, when the families went to church together, her son "let go of my hand and ran right to [the donor's father]. He climbed on his lap, hugged him and said 'Daddy.' We were flabbergasted. How could he have known him? Why did he call him dad? He never did things like that. He would never let go of my hand in church and run to a stranger. When I asked him why he did it, he said he didn't. He said [the donor] did and he went with him."[64]

- "It's really strange, but when I'm cleaning house or just sitting around reading, all of a sudden this unusual taste comes into my mouth. It's very hard to describe, but it's very distinctive. I can taste something and all of a sudden I start thinking about my donor, who he or she is, and how they lived. After a while, the taste goes away and so do the thoughts, but the taste always seem to come first."[65]

- "I never really was all that interested in sex. I never really thought about it much. Don't get me wrong, my husband and I had a sex life, but it was not a big part of our life. Now, I tire my husband out. . . . When I told my psychiatrist about this, she said it was a reaction to my medications and my healthier body. Then I found out that my donor was a young college girl who worked as a topless dancer and in an out-call service. I think I got her sexual drive, and my husband agrees."[66]

- "I never told anyone at first, but I thought having a woman's heart would make me gay. Since my surgery [though], I've been hornier than ever and women seem to look even more erotic and sensual. . . . I think I've got a woman's way of thinking about sex now." This man's wife concurs. "He's a much better lover now . . . he just knows my body as well as I do. He wants to cuddle, hold and take a lot of time. . . . And one more thing, he loves to go to museums. He would never, absolutely never, do that. Now he [goes] every week. Sometimes he stands for minutes and looks at a painting without talking. . . . Sometimes I just leave him there and come back later."[67]

- After an appearance on a television program where he spoke about changes in a transplant recipient's personality following surgery, Pearsall received a letter from a psychologist indicating that the man had received a new kidney and "despite his dislike of spicy foods, now craves tacos and burritos and has taken a class to learn to speak Spanish." The man added that he had "just found out [his] donor was a young Hispanic man."[68]

- A forty-seven-year-old white foundry worker received the heart of a seventeen-year-old black male student who had been the victim of a drive-by shooting. He commented in an amazed tone, "I used to hate classical music, but now I love it. So I know it's not my new heart, because a black guy from the 'hood wouldn't be into that." However, according to the donor's mother, "Our son was walking to violin class when he was hit. . . . He died right there on the street, hugging his violin case. He loved music and the teachers said he had a real thing for it."[69]

- "When I got my new heart, two things happened to me. First, almost every night, and still sometimes now, I actually feel the [auto] accident my donor had. I can feel the impact in my chest. . . . Also, I hate red meat now. I can't stand it. I was McDonalds' biggest money maker, but now red meat makes me throw up."[70]

- A fifty-six-year-old college professor received the heart of a thirty-four-year-old police officer who had been shot while attempting to arrest a drug dealer. The recipient remarked, "A few weeks after I got my heart, I began to have dreams. I would see a flash of light right in my face and my face gets real, real hot. It actually burns."[71]

- A forty-seven-year-old man received the heart of a fourteen-year-old girl with anorexic and bulimic tendencies. He commented, "I feel like a teenager. I actually feel giddy. . . . I have this annoying tendency to giggle that drives my wife nuts. And there's something about food. I don't know what it is. I get hungry, but after I eat I often feel nauseated and that it would help if I could throw up."[72]

- A nine-year-old boy received the heart of a three-year-old girl who drowned in the family pool. The boy's mother reported, "The one thing I notice most is that [her son] is now deathly afraid of the water. He loved it before. We live on a lake and he won't go into the backyard. He keeps closing and locking the back door. He says he's afraid of the water and doesn't know why."[73]

- A five-year-old boy received the heart of a three-year-old boy who had fallen from an apartment window. The recipient took to calling his donor Timmy, saying "He's just a little kid. He's a little brother about half my age. He got hurt bad when he fell down. He likes Power Rangers a lot, I think, just like I used to. I don't like them anymore, though." In fact, the donor's name was Thomas, although his family called him Tim. Even more striking, according to the recipient's mother, was that their family had only recently learned that Tim "fell trying to reach a Power Ranger toy that had fallen from the ledge of the window. [Our son] won't even touch his Power Rangers any more."[74]

- A little girl, age eight, received the heart of a ten-year-old girl who had been murdered. She started screaming at night about her dreams of the man who had killed her donor. She told her mother she knew who it was. After she had several sessions with a psychiatrist, the latter "could not deny the reality of what this child was telling [her]." The mother and the psychiatrist together decided to call the police. Using the descriptions provided by the little girl, the murderer was found and convicted. "The time, the weapon, the place, the clothes he wore, what the little girl he killed had said to him . . . everything [she] reported was completely accurate."[75]

I came across a somewhat similar account myself a few years ago in the course of my research. A man in his fifties received the heart of a college student who had gotten drunk at a sorority party and died from a fall down a flight of stairs. For three nights following the transplant, the man had nightmares of falling down a flight of stairs. Then the nightmares stopped and the recipient had no further symptoms that appeared to be connected to the donor.[76]

Still other anecdotes are related by Louisa Young in her *Book of the Heart.*[77] For example:

- A white man received the heart of an urban teenager he "assumed" was black. Although he had grown up racially prejudiced, in the aftermath of the transplant, he found that his prejudice fell away. He developed a crush on one of the black nurses and started listening to news about Africa.[78]
- In a famous case, transplant recipient Claire Sylvia said she became vastly much more energetic, more assertive, and more flirtatious. She sweated more and "found herself admiring shorter, rounder,

blonder women, where before she had admired tall, dark, slender ones. Being propositioned by a lesbian made her wonder what signals she was giving out." (She knew that her heart had come from a man.) She developed a taste for chicken nuggets and green peppers. She wanted to wear green and blue, rather than the red and hot pink she had formerly favored. Five months after the operation, she said she dreamed of a young man named Tim. Tracking down the donor's family, it turned out that his name was just that. "And he'd had chicken nuggets under his jacket when he died. He loved green peppers. He was incredibly energetic. He had a short blond girlfriend."[79]

It's hard to know what to make of such reports according to our current medical and scientific knowledge, but a variety of commonsense explanations do present themselves. One obvious possibility is that, although patients typically have no *conscious* awareness of who their donors were, how they had died, or what kind of personality, tastes, or habits they had, the transplant recipients could have overheard nurses or other hospital staff speaking among themselves. Another easy-to-buy-into explanation is that, when older organ recipients report feeling younger and friskier, they really do: they've been reinvigorated with someone else's younger, stronger heart. They consequently benefit from improved circulation *plus* a burst of well-founded enthusiasm. A third conjecture is that the medications administered to patients to reduce the odds of organ rejection act in the same way as, say, LSD, prompting them to vividly imagine things that just aren't so or to recall scattered memories from their own past and attribute these to their donor.[80] Another explanation is that the transplant process is inherently stressful, with psychiatric symptoms arising in as many as 50 percent of transplant recipients.[81] Depression is common, and so is survivor guilt. As one person has commented, "Imagine: a hospital has agreed, at least in principle, to rip the heart and lungs out of your body and replace them with the heart and lungs of somebody who has just died. And for this you're being congratulated?"[82]

Most powerful of all, perhaps, the heart retains age-old symbolic associations that make "swapping" this organ with anyone else's extremely problematic. For millennia, the heart has been regarded as the source of courage, wisdom, love and, yes, personal identity. So should it be surprising that many transplant recipients wonder "who am I now" in the aftermath of their surgery? How much of their "old self," their unique set of likes and dislikes, their cumulative life experience, is still with them, and how much might be conveyed from their now deceased donor? Are they still themselves—or some sort of strange, new amalgam?[83]

I have no doubt that these explanations, separately or in combination, are sufficient to address at least some cases where a transplant recipient comes to believe that he or she has inherited personality characteristics or memories from the donor. But do such explanations always hold? I am going to suggest not. The cases cited earlier—especially taken in the aggregate—are very difficult to ascribe to any rational mechanism short of complete fabrication. Given the corroboration of spouses, siblings, and friends, they appear far too strange—and strangely *accurate*—to explain away.

Now, I ascribe some importance to Pearsall's mention that the most commonly reported memories described by heart transplant recipients are new smells and tastes.[84] This could be chalked up to medications used during or after the operation, as well as to biomedical side effects that are not yet fully understood. But as we saw much earlier in this book, smell and taste—our chemical senses—relate to an ancient form of perception, the most basic form of discrimination among organisms. The emotional brain literally grew out of the brain's olfactory bulb, with a direct connection maintained even today between the nose and the limbic structures. A vivid memory of a given time and place, and a closely associated set of feelings, can thus be called up simply through an aroma. Similarly, it would be a mistake to entirely dismiss a transplant recipient's account of reinvigorated sexuality. Procreation is an extremely strong biological urge, and sexual feeling itself can be intense and highly pleasurable. So if we imagine for a moment that smells and tastes could be "recovered" from organ donors, why not sex drive? Smell and taste are, after all, as much essential components of intercourse as desire itself.

Cardiosensitives

Pearsall's findings correspond to those of another researcher, Dr. Benjamin Bunzel at the University Hospital of Vienna. Bunzel assessed the accounts of forty-seven heart transplant recipients. Of these, 6 percent reported a distinct change of personality due to their new hearts, which they attributed to the memories of their donor.[85]

Six percent is not a huge number, but it is not a tiny one, either. The figure recalls the estimate of fantasy-prone and highly suggestible people (4 percent) given by researchers Wilson and Barber. Intriguingly, Pearsall found that the heart transplant patients he interviewed seemed to have numerous personality traits in common, which he took the trouble to not only catalog, but also to apply a label to: *cardio-sensitive*.[86] Making up his composite sketch are the following attributes (recognizable from earlier discussions in this book):

- Nearly all cardio-sensitives are women.
- Most reported a vivid, active fantasy life prior to their transplant.
- They are easily able to conjure up and share visual images.
- They are hyperalert to their environment.
- Many have allergies.
- Long before they became ill and had a transplant, most reported extensive dreaming and interest in the significance of their dreams. Following their transplant, most reported dreaming of their donor.
- Most say they are highly sensual and tuned in to their body. Many are athletes, musicians, and dancers.
- They are described by family members and friends as being psychic or very sensitive, and are said to have shown this sensitivity long before their illness was diagnosed and their eventual transplant.

Claire Sylvia is a case in point. As a dancer and choreographer, "she was very aware of her body and its connections to her mind and spirit." In the wake of her transplant, she considered that "emotionally, being reborn was painful and terribly difficult."[87] Presumably she evidences sensitivity in any number of ways.

The concept of transliminality shows special promise, in my opinion, for understanding how these cardio-sensitives function, both within themselves and within the world. Let us begin with the premise, supported by the above evidence, that these individuals were highly transliminal prior to their organ transplant, perhaps for their entire lives. Their reaction to the operation, and their sense of what their donor's personality must have been like, would then reflect their "tendency for psychological material to cross thresholds in or out of consciousness." Alas, that only sheds light on bodymind processing: the question of what, exactly, is crossing into awareness remains open. Could such material *really* be acquired from an external source?

The Persistence of Memory

Let us return to the premise that the body, and the energy of intense feeling *in* the body, is at the core of anomalous experience. Correlating that to an unresolved freeze response, along with the characteristic dissociation, ups the ante considerably. Could that energy, and the attendant information known by the bodymind, be conveyed elsewhere? Put another way, could dissociated memories (or *any* memories, for that matter, if linked strongly enough to feeling) be transplanted outside of the body at the demise of the individual who possessed them?

I shall cite some intriguing evidence that such might be possible. The immune system, so essential to the identification and maintenance of the self, is once again involved in these reports. We begin with the following item drawn from the *Archives of Internal Medicine*:

> A liver transplant may have saved the life of a 60-year-old Australian man—but it also nearly killed him. The liver came from a 15-year-old boy who had died from an allergic reaction to peanuts. But his nut allergy was never officially diagnosed, and doctors were unaware of it. So the day after the liver recipient returned home from the

hospital, he ate a handful of cashews. Fifteen minutes later, he had a life-threatening allergic reaction. The man was rushed to the hospital, where he recovered after drug treatment. . . . Subsequent blood tests showed that he'd developed an allergy to cashews, peanuts, and sesame seeds—the same allergies his donor had had.[88]

This account is revealing precisely because there is nothing anomalous about it. All we have is a life-or-death drama stemming from an allergy—but an allergy that came from someone else. The organ of conveyance in this case is the liver. Our livers play a key role in the body's metabolic processes, breaking down substances taken from the bloodstream (such as alcohol) and manufacturing and storing still other substances (such as sugar). So one can imagine that a transplanted liver might transmit an allergy (or, for that matter, an immunity) from donor to recipient. I am suggesting that the heart, and other organs as well, may do the same.

Next, consider a finding about what used to be known as multiple personality disorder and is now called dissociative identity disorder (DID). In such cases, one personality may have characteristics (e.g., an allergy or drug reaction, migraine headache, right-handedness or left-handedness, better or worse eyesight) *distinct from other personalities in the same individual*. What this suggests is that a whole raft of bodily functions, including immune function and various other indicators of sensitivity, are influenced in quite distinct ways when an individual dissociates into discrete "personalities."[89] This makes sense when we consider that the bodymind is a far-flung network encompassing all the organs, nerves, glands, muscles, and pathways in the body, not to mention its underlying cellular processes. Based on our understanding of dissociation—that conscious awareness of our bodily state (the felt sense) is interrupted and blood flow altered under conditions of massive stress—it would follow that the *energy* of these processes would also be significantly diverted.

Recall here our analogy of a stream, continuously in motion. It has its sources (all the cells that furnish energy), it follows a course (via the nerve fibers and the bloodstream), and flows into tributaries (the muscles and organs). When a person experiences an overwhelming threat, the bodymind's stress systems (the sympathetic nervous system and the HPA stress system) kick in, with all their attendant energetic changes. If this process becomes chronic, that is, if the immobilization response becomes patterned and dissociation becomes characteristic, particular tissues and functions are bound to be affected. This is because the underlying energy is literally bound in—in abnormal and unhealthy ways. Later, if a given body part is removed and transplanted (the ultimate form, I might add, of dissociation), the energy bound in that organ—with all its accompanying characteristics and memories—will be transferred to the recipient. Staying with our stream analogy, we might envision memories as the leaves floating along with the stream. Thus, where the stream goes, they go. And where the stream pools, they stay. If a given set of tissues (e.g., a heart, a lung, a kidney) is removed and transplanted, the memories that are part and parcel of the tissue will go along with it.

Here is another intriguing example, which might now be explained according to our model. A woman, who had suffered from DID for years, developed a severe infection in her left arm that could not be cured. Ultimately, the arm had to be amputated. Following the amputation, the woman was no longer beset with multiple personalities.[90] I infer here that the arm itself—the bed of the stream, one might say—was at the root of her problems. Having developed a severe infection (which could itself be taken as evidence of dissociation that was compartmentalized in that limb), the woman cast off at least one form of her troubles.

Memory Externalized

Could anything be more extraordinary that the examples we have already seen? In a word, yes. There are cases that I, for one, would interpret as evidence that memory within the bodymind might be conveyed *beyond* the individual who originally owned it. Consider the extremely odd finding that unusual birthmarks (and, to a lesser extent, birth defects) have been identified in one-third of children who claim to remember previous lives. The late Ian Stevenson of the University of Virginia, a true pioneer who devoted himself to investigating such reports, commented, "The birthmarks on these subjects are only rarely the simple . . . moles of which nearly every-one has one or more. The majority of them are depressed . . . in relation to the surrounding skin; they are usually hairless and often puckered and scarlike . . . [they] are usually larger than 'ordinary' [moles] and frequently occur where such [moles] never occur, such as the head or legs and feet.[91]

These markings are said to correspond to the location of wounds suf-fered by the deceased person whose life experience a given child claims to recall. Over his career, the intrepid Stevenson traveled extensively to countries such as India and Sri Lanka, where the concept of reincarna-tion is accepted, and he examined and interviewed some 2,500 children and their families. Where possible, he attempted to determine if their accounts could be verified. In most of the cases where the child in ques-tion had such a birthmark, Stevenson found "correspondences in loca-tion [with] the birthmarks and wounds . . . on the body of the concerned deceased person." When the person was said to have died from a gunshot wound, for example, the child would often have *two* birthmarks, perhaps corresponding to a bullet's entry and exit. Likewise, Stevenson interpreted many of the birth defects as corresponding to sword cuts, blade marks, and other such injuries. Based on this and a good deal of other evidence shown by these children (e.g., particular phobias, unusual games played, precocious interests), he proposed that previous lives may, at least some-times, be remembered.[92]

Such cases don't occur only among children halfway around the world. Physical injuries and emotional traumas are also a recurring theme among American children who puzzle over *their* predilections. One man with the gumption to put his musings into print is William Falk, editor of the national news magazine *The Week*.

As a child, I was fascinated by the Civil War. By age 10, I had read dozens of books on the war; I knew which generals fought at Chickamauga and Antietem and Chancellorsville, and how many soldiers had died, and how it all looked, and smelled, and felt. For hours, I'd arrange my plastic Union and Confederate soldiers on battlefields in my basement, painting enamel blood on the wounded, sawing off a few limbs for verisimilitude. It was an obsession that seemed to come from nowhere. Many years later . . . I paid $20 to a psychic who claimed to be able to "read" people's past lives. With no prompting from me, she announced that in a past life, I'd been a doctor working in the Union Army. The suffering and death I'd witnessed, she told me, had left a deep imprint. . . . I didn't take any of this too seriously, but it gave me something to chew on for a while.[93]

Reincarnation is a tricky concept because it implies that an *entire personality*—encompassing everything about the deceased—has somehow been incorporated into a new body. Further, it implies that the current person is an outgrowth, a follow-on, a natural extension of the previous personality (or chain of personalities). The mechanism I am hinting at is much different. It is an embellishment of the known, bodily processes of stress, immobility, and dissociation. It encompasses the physical and feeling knowledge that is stored unconsciously when shocking, painful, or otherwise overwhelming experiences become traumatic and the course of the emotional stream is diverted or dammed up. The latent energy conveyed will relate to the experience itself and the parts of the body most directly involved, comprising a virtual snapshot of what was being perceived at the time of the threat. I won't posit that the entire personality is reborn in a new body—only that the emotional energy that went unreleased in its time obeys the first law of thermodynamics and, through unknown means, is effectively transferred to a new residence. In this conception, what survives is the *impulse to express intense feelings* that have been frozen, held in, or repressed.

One might speculate, as I have earlier, that the people most likely to transmit such residual emotional energy are thick-boundary, Type C individuals—and the people most likely to apprehend it are thin-boundary sensitives. It might even be that the energies involved *predispose* certain individuals to be environmentally sensitive. If emotional energy were indeed conserved and conveyed under the special circumstances I have outlined, it might well affect the development of another self in utero (just as the liver of the Australian youth with a peanut allergy caused the identical form of allergy in the recipient of that organ transplant). The resulting self would be a distinct personality, not merely the extension of some "chain of being," but would nonetheless bear some hallmarks (or birthmarks, as the case may be) resulting from the earlier stressful and emotionally intense experience.

To test this proposition, at least indirectly, it would be useful to administer my sensitivity survey to members of three particular groups:

- People who have received organ transplants
- Children or young adults who claim to remember details of a previous life
- Children who are gifted or prodigies

With the first group, a start has been made in this direction by Pearsall, although his observations of cardio-sensitives are just that, observations rather than the results of a survey specifically designed to illuminate the factors contributing to sensitivity. With the second group, Stevenson's work raised some intriguing questions but he never looked at environmental sensitivity specifically.[94] Concerning the third group, attention has focused, to my knowledge, almost entirely on how the considerable mental abilities of prodigies develop—although an exceptional work on the subject, *Nature's Gambit* by David Henry Feldman of Tufts University, does present some quite riveting accounts of anomalous sensibilities manifested by two young prodigies. Of the first, it was observed that the boy demonstrated, from infancy, a "heightened sensitivity to others' emotional states." Until the age of five, he also related memories of his own birth and impressions of a prenatal state.[95] This sort of information begs the question of what a systematic inquiry into the subject of sensitivity would yield.

The accounts of the second boy (supplied by his parents in informal and very trusting conversations with Feldman and his wife) raise definite goose bumps. One of them has already been related in this book: how the boy (given the pseudonym Adam in the account) sat bolt upright in his bath at the tender age of eighteen months and shouted in terror about "the men" approaching in boots with guns. Similarly out of the blue, at age two-and-a-half he was playing in his mother's office with a puppet theater he had played with many times before, when he suddenly began screaming that he recognized that theater. After she took him out of her office and calmed him down, he related that the theater was in Göttingen, where he had studied medicine "before the war." His stunned parents later went to the library, looked up the town of Göttingen, and found that it is located in Germany's Rhine Valley, that its university was established in the eighteenth century, and that its town square is distinguished by a statue not unlike the one depicted in the backdrop of the toy theater their son had been playing with.[96]

On another occasion, Adam announced that he had lived in England (a place his current family had never visited) and had "especially enjoyed the countryside when the stickle bushes were in bloom." His parents had never heard of stickle bushes and again did some research. It turned out they grow in southern England, where they are popularly used as hedges, and bloom with a distinctive flower.[97] Like the first boy, Adam seemed to have memories of his own birth, including his reaction to the bright lights of the delivery room and the placement of a suctioning bulb into his nose. He also related apparently prenatal memories, such as the sound of his mother's singing and "the walls closing in on me—they hurt." What makes this latter point so remarkable is that his mother's pregnancy was beset by numerous complications, including uterine contractions that threatened to terminate the pregnancy from the fourth month onward.[98]

Finally, and perhaps most amazing of all, were Adam's comments at age four during the funeral service of a great aunt he had never met. I relate Feldman's account word for word; pseudonyms are used for Adam's mother (Fiona) and father (Nathaniel):[99]

Fiona and Adam sat alone in the anteroom, talking about this and that, while Nathaniel attended the funeral service. After a while, Adam interrupted their conversation. Looking across the room, he asked his mother who the two ladies were who had just joined them in the room. Fiona looked up, but saw no one. She asked him which ladies he meant, and he replied "The ones standing by the clock." Puzzled, Fiona told Adam that there weren't any ladies standing by the clock; no one was in the room except the two of them. Adam demurred, insisting that he saw two old ladies standing by and talking by the clock. He thought they might be waiting for the lady who had just walked into the room. Adam asked whether the newcomer mightn't be Aunt Bessie. Flustered, puzzled, and concerned, Fiona replied that she didn't see any old ladies in the room, unless he wanted to include her.

Undaunted, Adam described the three women's dress and what appeared to be a brief conversation among them. He observed that the first two ladies seemed to escort "Aunt Bessie" up a flight of stairs at the end of the room, stairs which were visible only to Adam. Once they ascended he matter-of-factly resumed his earlier conversation with an astonished Fiona.

As the service ended both Fiona and Adam were joined in the anteroom by mourners perceptible to both mother and son. Eventually Nathaniel also returned to collect his family. As a dutiful nephew and son, he had remained after the service for the family viewing of the coffin. Somewhat hesitantly Fiona asked Nathaniel to tell them how Aunt Bessie had been laid out. Not surprisingly, Nathaniel was taken aback at Fiona's unusual request, but when he realized she was serious he described Aunt Bessie's general appearance as best he could recall. It matched Adam's description of the invisible old lady escorted up the phantom stairs by her two equally imperceptible friends.

As perplexed and genuinely distressed as they were over incidents such as this, Adam's parents gradually came to the conclusion that "he was just geared to perceive and receive the world differently from . . . the rest of us." Feldman wonders whether prodigies "might not . . . be particularly sensitive" based on their family trees being stocked (as they often are) with surpassing talent and intensive focus. Not all families that produce prodigies boast such lineage, though. Nor do anomalous reports surface in all families of prodigies; they did in just two cases out of six that Feldman researched. Nonetheless, he suggests that "this whole realm of mystical experience is a significant part of the prodigy phenomenon" and one that merits further scrutiny.[100]

Plasticity: More Discoveries Ahead

As plasticity (which is all the rage in neuroscience circles) is studied further, I predict the concept will grow to encompass not just brain-based phenomena but bodymind phenomena as well.

One key may turn out to be the brain's glial cells. *Glial* is Greek for "glue," and, historically, it was believed that these cells serve as figurative spackle and caulk for the neurons they surround. Recent evidence, however, indicates that the predominant type of glial cell, known as an astrocyte, is the "missing link" between neuronal activity and cerebral bloodflow. Astrocytes receive signals directly from the neurons and cause nearby capillaries to dilate. The increased bloodflow that brain scans take as indicative of neural activity is, therefore, regulated by the astrocytes. Without this type of glial cell, the "food for thought" needed by the neurons—the oxygen and glucose carried by the blood—would not be delivered. Far from being bit players, astrocytes are crucial for understanding cerebral communications, declares Mriganka Sur, head of the research team at the Massachusetts Institute of Technology (MIT) that made the discovery.[101]

The relative lack of knowledge about glial cells—contrasted with their ubiquity in the brain—moved several noteworthy thinkers to speculate on their role. The work of the late biologist Robert Becker suggests that glial cells might not only support the neurons but also direct them electrically based on receipt of information from outside the body as well as within.[102] A somewhat similar idea was proposed fifty years ago by mathematician and philosopher Lance Whyte. He suggested that the neuronal activity of the brain might be less significant than a hypothesized flow of electricity that would invoke neural activity, starting with proteins in the cell.[103] Proteins, as we saw in chapter 5, are the cell's most basic constituents, synthesizing and breaking down every molecule in the human body—including ATP, the cell's energy "bank."[104] The protein known as hemoglobin transports and releases oxygen in the blood, a function that takes on added importance in light of what we've learned about the relevance of breathing to the experience of pain and stress and its bearing on tendencies ranging from hypnotic suggestibility to dissociation. The other interesting thing about proteins (at least for our purposes here) is that some of them comprise hormones and immune system antibodies.[105] So when we talk about the bodymind, proteins are the "building blocks" driving the communication.

Bloodflow itself is being reevaluated in scientific circles today. Christopher Moore, of MIT's McGovern Institute for Brain Research, questions the conventional wisdom that assumes the primary purpose of bloodflow is metabolic, i.e., to deliver fuel and oxygen within the brain. Instead, Moore proposes that "blood actively modulates how neurons process information." Localized changes in bloodflow, he suggests, affect the activity of nearby neurons, priming them (or, alternately, diminishing their capacity) to register a stimulus or otherwise transmit or encode information. The mechanism, presumably, is what his colleague Sur has identified—glial cells. A change in bloodflow, surmises Moore, could trigger astrocytes to release various hormones or neurotransmitters. Since blood circulates throughout the body (via the heart), the circulatory system itself would take on vastly greater importance as we come to understand the genesis of our thoughts and feelings.[106] It's a short step to intuit that feeling flow is a key to plasticity.

My hunch is that more evidence will be found to support these concepts. That evidence, in turn, might support the long-held contention of energy healers and medical intuitives that they can "read" symptoms of physical illness and emotional distress. It will become plausible to relate healers' electrical sensitivity to the flow of feeling we have posited or, more accurately, to chronic distortions in that flow. Given an enhanced awareness of the electromagnetic signals emanating from our bodies—especially from the center of blood flow and feeling, our heart—the diagnostic value of magnetocardiograms and the like should come to complement the value we now place on brain imaging techniques such as MRI and PET scanning.

Immune Conditioning

It's important to emphasize that the evidence is far from clear-cut that people who claim to be electrically sensitive actually are.[107] The strongest correlation may turn out to be between perceived electrical sensitivity and factors such as magical thinking, depression, and hypochondria. Some evidence already points in this direction.[108]

Furthermore, no discussion of electrical sensitivity—or any other possible type of bodymind sensitivity—would be complete without mention of a fascinating phenomenon called immune conditioning. This works akin to behavioral conditioning, the process whereby Pavlov's dogs famously learned to salivate at the sound of a bell that had previously signaled food. In the same way, a person's immune system can learn to associate a neutral stimulus (such as a smell or taste) with something that does affect immunity.[109] In one experiment healthy volunteers were injected with adrenaline, which increases immune activity. The injections were paired with a rather offbeat stimulus: a combination of white noise and a sweet taste of sherbet. Afterward, the ambient noise/sherbet combination was sufficient to evoke an immune response in the volunteers. In another instance, experimenters conditioned an allergic reaction to pollen and dust mites through a novel-tasting soft drink.[110]

This phenomenon goes a long way toward explaining reports such as one from the nineteenth century in which a doctor claimed to be able to induce an allergic reaction in a patient who was allergic to roses, simply by placing an artificial rose in front of him. In another case, a patient who merely looked at a hay field was overcome by a severe attack of hay fever. In the present day, the hospital environment itself can serve as the co-stimulus; patients can become behaviorally conditioned and start to feel sick in mere anticipation of returning there.[111]

Immune conditioning might explain certain instances of purported electrical sensitivity. A person could believe in all honesty that he or she is hypersensitive to electricity and yet, outside of the location that has come to be associated with the response (e.g., the workplace, the kitchen), the person would not produce an allergic reaction. The link often noted between emotional upheaval and electrical displays might also be explained this way—as could even odder associations, such as dowsers' claims that they can sometimes find water by simply looking at a map or casting their hand over one.

The Genetics of Plasticity

Discussion of immune conditioning recalls two other topics raised earlier in this chapter: hypnosis and the placebo effect. Both, we saw, are examples of a suggestion being made real in the bodymind of a sufficiently thin-boundary person. It would make sense if immune conditioning were found to affect certain people more than others. I trust that exploration, sooner or later, will move in that direction.

The likelihood is also that a genetic basis exists for psychosomatic plasticity. Toward the end of the last chapter, I mentioned some of the evidence supporting a genetic basis for sensitivity in general, such as the proclivity for remembering emotionally charged events, the impetus to express emotions and spirituality through dance, and the inability to filter out extraneous sensory information. Now (perhaps unsurprisingly), scientists have identified a gene linked to the placebo effect itself.

A team in Sweden did the research. They recruited more than a hundred people with an exaggerated fear of embarrassment, otherwise known as social anxiety disorder. Participants had to give a speech at the beginning and end of an eight-week treatment. This "treatment" consisted of a sugar pill for twenty-five of the participants, none of whom (or their doctors, for that matter) knew they were being given a placebo. Ten of these subjects responded much better than the rest. By the end of the experiment, their anxiety scores had halved, whereas scores of the other fifteen stayed the same. Brain scans also showed a noticeable reduction in amygdala activity in the subjects who benefited from the placebo. A further test disclosed that a double copy of a gene responsible for making serotonin was part of the makeup of most of the individuals in this group. (The double copy of the gene in question is suspected of enabling people to be less anxious, although other genes may turn out to play a role.)[112]

On the weight of such evidence, I strongly suspect that a genetic basis will be found for all types of high sensitivity and for all forms of psychosomatic plasticity. What is needed is innovative, rigorous, and sustained testing. The capacities some people have for "tuning in to" both their internal milieu and their external environs—and for translating what's there into extraordinary phenomena—will be proved, I believe. In good time, at any rate. And *time* is a fitting subject unto itself.

11

───◆───

Time, Energy, and the Self

"If science searches the universe—as it does—for certain kinds of truth, then these are inevitably the only ones it will find. Everything else will slip through the net."[1]

DAVID DARLING, ASTROPHYSICIST

Bonnie, my wife, looks into the mirror and singles out a few strands of gray hair. We were in our bedroom late one evening, talking about preschool starting up again for our daughter, age four, and son, almost two years old. Gabrielle, heading into pre-K, will surely enjoy the experience, as she always has. It will be an entirely new one for Bradley, but because of that, it's bound to be "growthful." Now Bonnie and I are reflecting on how far they've come—and how far we've come as parents. The realization is gratifying but somehow startling, especially when we muse on the knowledge that it has been twenty years since *we* were in school. In retrospect, twenty years seems like a short time, although it sure didn't as we were going through so many experiences: our first real jobs, serious (and not so serious) relationships, stepping up the professional ladder, getting engaged, getting married, working things out between us, traveling, a couple health scares, then having kids, learning to be parents, and trying our best to be *good* parents. The cursory look in the rearview mirror now prompts Bonnie to walk over to the real mirror. It also prompts her rhetorical question, "Michael, we're so old. How did we get so old?"

"Mature," I tell her. "You mean mature." But my commentary begs the question: How *did* we get so . . . mature? For that matter, when we look back on ourselves ten years from now, what will we see, both literally and figuratively? What further changes will we have gone through? Will our families still be in good health? How will our children have fared? It's exciting to imagine all that they will have learned, but a bit unnerving to think on how much less innocent, how much less carefree they will be. To them, ten years will have seemed like a lifetime, but to their parents, a decade will surely appear to have raced past at breakneck speed. That's the most unnerving realization of all. I take solace, though, by recalling a verse of Paul Simon's song "The Boxer."

> *Now the years are rolling by me, they are rocking evenly*
> *I am older than I once was, but younger than I'll be*
> *That's not unusual*
> *No it isn't strange*
> *After changes upon changes we are more or less the same*
> *After changes, we are more or less the same.*

Many things have been written and sung and said about time. In my humble opinion, Simon's song is among the most wise. It's simply an observation, not rendering a judgment nor placing a value. As we *are,* so time just *is.* We seem to be born into it; our passage through it and our ultimate demise are inevitable. And, precisely because the clock is ticking, life becomes infinitely precious.

Our impressions along life's journey, however, can vary considerably. A single intense experience can be over in an instant, whereas in boredom, anticipation, or dread, mere moments stretch out unbearably. During dreams (where we spend a fair amount of our lives), time is entirely inconsequential: images transpose themselves, scenes shift, and feelings come upon us so fleetingly that everything seems to be out of time completely. And, as pointed out above, our experience of time in childhood and youth is considerably different than that of maturity and old age. As we age, time seems to compress. What's that about? Indeed, what's any of it about? What are the implications for our experience of life—and of the unforeseen anomaly?

The answers may surprise you. Suffice it to say, time is not just a mental phenomenon. Far from it. Let's begin where nearly all these chapters have begun: with the body.

Time and Biochemical Energy

A fundamental relationship exists between time, energy, the body, and the brain. As we can easily verify from our everyday experience, time appears to pass quickly in certain situations; for example, when we are actively involved in a project or concentrating our attention. Similarly, upbeat feelings (e.g., enjoyment, happiness, elation) seem to make the clock tick faster. On the other hand, if we feel listless or find a situation dull and uninteresting, time will appear to drag. Time also feels prolonged during periods of intense emotion, whether the situations are pleasurable (e.g., a nighttime for two lovers lasting "forever"), mournful (e.g., a single day spent in grief seems like an eternity), or dreadful (e.g., moments of trepidation or panic that stretch out). There is no disputing these contrasts, but *why?*

Recall from chapter 2 that author Guy Murchie counted a time sense among the thirty-two types of sensory perception he discerned in human beings. I subsequently listed time sense in my own catalog of feelings because time is usually felt as passing slowly, quickly, or at some intermediate rate. The feeling is less palpable than some others, but I do believe it qualifies as a feeling, all the same. And that brings us back to the body.

Different individuals have different metabolic rates, that is, the speed at which energy is produced and cellular processes proceed in their bodies. Our metabolic rate when at rest and not having eaten anything for twelve hours is between 60 and 100 watts: the same amount of energy as produced by a typical household light bulb. If we were to just rest for an entire day and do nothing, our energy *output* would also be low—approximately 1,600 calories. When we are performing a modicum of activity, such as working in the office, our metabolic rate is around 50 to 75 percent higher than the resting rate. It doubles when we are excited or fearful and our sympathetic nervous system is causing adrenaline and noradrenaline to circulate. Manual labor can push it still further, up to two or three times the resting rate. And during peak exercise, our metabolic rate will increase up to tenfold.[2]

This explains why, when we are intensely emotional or are putting forth a strenuous effort, time appears to slow down. Our metabolism in these cases is elevated, with more "happening" internally than the clock seems to bear out externally. As an example, athletes at the peak of their game sometimes report being "in the zone": the flow of the contest slows down; things around them get quiet; they see everyone on the field, court, or rink with crystal clarity; and the ball seems much larger than it normally is. The zone represents an optimum level of arousal, with the heart rate between 115 and 145 beats per minute.[3]

When a person is under extreme stress, however—when the heart is beating fast, sweating is profuse, muscles are tensed, and hormones such as adrenaline and cortisol are pulsing through our system—time slows to a crawl. A riveting illustration was provided at the beginning of chapter 7, when Rush Dozier recounted his teenage automobile accident. Here's another case in point, recounted by a policeman in a life-or-death encounter with a criminal suspect:

> When he started toward us, it was almost like it was in slow motion and everything went into a tight focus . . . all my senses were directed forward at the man running at us with a gun. I couldn't tell you what his left hand was doing. I have no idea. I was watching the gun. The gun was coming down in front of his chest area, and that's when I [fired] my first two shots.
>
> I didn't hear a thing, not one thing. . . . We stopped shooting when he hit the floor and slid into me. Then I was on my feet standing over the guy. I don't even remember pushing myself up. . . . Time

had returned to normal by then, because it had slowed down during the shooting. That started as soon as he started toward us. Even though he was running at us, it looked like he was running in slow motion. Damnedest thing I ever saw.[4]

Evidence for this slowing down of time is actually available experimentally, through an ingenious trial arranged by psychologist David Eagleman, now at Baylor University's College of Medicine. He asked a volunteer to perform a backward free fall from a tower 33 meters (108 feet) high. (The base was thoroughly cushioned to ensure that no one would get hurt.) Eagleman's assumption was that, for the volunteer (a man named Jesse Kallus), time would slow—but how in the world could this be measured?

[Eagleman came up with the] "perceptual chronometer," a wrist-watch-like device which flickered blindingly fast between two [lighted] screens. Normally the flicker would be so fast Jesse could only see a blur. But if time slowed down for him, he might be able to discern the two different screens and read a random number on one of them.

"There's no way to fake this test," says Dr. Eagleman, "because if time is not running more slowly, [the volunteer] can't see the sequence."

All Jesse had to do was jump, and read. . . . When [he] landed, he noted he had seen "98." Dr. Eagleman checked. In fact the number was 96. Not quite spot-on, but the two numbers look very similar on a digital screen. . . .

Further jumps got similar results—all suggesting that time did seem to slow down for Jesse during the jump.[5]

Now, Jesse might be blessed with exceptionally keen eyesight or just grace under duress. But his experience in this high-pressure situation mirrors, I believe, the way time slows for *anyone* during periods of high stress, emotion, or physical exertion.

It should be noted that these perceptions, while remarkable, remain subjective (unless they are being measured by a perceptual chronometer, that is).[6] Another person at that very moment in another place, who is doing something relaxing, enjoyable, or invigorating, will be experiencing time in a completely different way. Yet clock time will proceed equally for all concerned.

In contrast, *thinking* requires less energy than you might imagine. When we think hard, our metabolic rate hardly changes.[7] So when we devote ourselves to a primarily mental activity, time seems to pass quickly. The same can be said of bouyant emotions. When we laugh our heads off at a show and later find that a whole three hours have passed, it's because we did not need to summon up that much energy to enjoy the proceedings. On the other hand, one might think that boredom and lack of engagement would equate to low energy and thus quicker time passage. But the reality is that, when we feel bored or lonely, we are dissatisfied— and dissatisfaction is a vacuum we wish to fill. So we pace back and forth, try to imagine a better situation, and so on. These activities call forth energy as an antidote to that which we do not wish to prolong.[8]

This correlation between metabolism and subjective time sense has been borne out by experiments showing that, as one's body temperature rises (and metabolism increases), time seems to pass more slowly. The reverse is also true: when body temperature lowers, time feels as though it is moving faster.[9]

Additionally, babies and children have higher metabolic rates than adults. This verifies our common observation that the littler ones among us have more energy. In fact, they do breathe faster and their hearts beat faster, their moods change more rapidly, and their thoughts and attention flit like butterflies. As experienced through their revved-up system, the world appears to be moving relatively slowly, but as they (and we adults) age, the metabolic rate decreases. Our activities, thoughts, and moods are subject to less fluctuation—and time seems to speed up. Hours, days, and years whiz by when contrasted with the sense of time in our childhood and adolescence.[10] Add to this the fact that the older we get, the more time we have "under our belts." Expecting a five-year-old to wait a half hour is simply not possible; for that child, a half hour constitutes a much higher proportion of his or her life lived to date than it would for a fifty-year-old man or woman, who can easily (and routinely) be made to wait three times that long in a doctor's waiting room.

In a somewhat related way, this explains why, when we drive a given route for the very first time, it seems to take longer than when we drive back or when we drive the identical route the next day. The difference is not the traffic; it is our familiarity with the route, the signposts, and the scenery we pass. One day it is novel and seems relatively fresh as we follow the directions and seek the new route, but the next day it is less so. If we drive the same route every day, it becomes routine and we hardly notice the travel time at all, unless something unexpected occurs, such as an accident or a detour. The analogy with children and older people is as follows. For children, most everything is new and interesting; as we age, however, the novelty rubs off and routine sets in, little energy is called for, and time passes uneventfully.

Earlier, I proposed that thick-boundary and thin-boundary people (as well as everyone in between) have different degrees of connectedness among their bodily systems as well as different rates of feeling flow. Thin-boundary types have a more rapid and direct flow of feeling, and thick-boundary people have a less rapid, less direct flow. Because this would correspond to their metabolic rate, it might be reasonable to infer that thin-boundary individuals, with their higher metabolism, typically experience time as passing more slowly than do individuals with thick boundaries.

Philosophies of Time

Of all the subjects known to humanity, time is perhaps the most inscrutable, hence, the one that has attracted the most attention from philosophers down the ages. Until the relatively recent emergence of science as its own domain and "scientist" as a stand-alone profession, philosophers served as generic thinkers into topics such as beauty, truth, and goodness and as natural scientists, seeking to understand the way the world worked and, indeed, what it was possible for anyone to know. Many of the concepts and observations they pioneered provide a context for what I shall call "biological time," that is, one's subjective experience of time based on metabolism, age, and energy level.

Biological time, I posit, is the most relevant of all perspectives to the explanation of anomalies, many of which appear to violate our expectation that time always moves from past to present to future. But just as our subjective experience of time may differ from what we see measured by a clock, so anomalous manifestations can and do diverge from time's forward flow. I should add that, as immediate and convincing as biological time feels to us, the fact that we experience it does not render clock time obsolete. Nor would an individual's anomalous experience—impressive and memorable as it may be—negate the fact that, during the anomaly, clock time continues to tick at the rate it always did (or, I should say, at the rate we choose to measure it).

I shall present a few points about time made by various philosophers, drawn from a venerable collection of essays titled *The Voices of Time*.[11] The selections, of course, are my own. These philosophers, as well as others not mentioned, each wrote a great deal and thought through these issues well beyond what I am prepared to mention. I shall, however, add a number of my own thoughts and amplifications that seem relevant in light of what we have learned about feeling, emotional expression, and the body.

Aristotle

This Greek philosopher was far more pragmatic than his teacher Plato, interested in how things actually worked rather than "ideal forms" that are not present to the senses. As such, he's a particular favorite of mine. Aristotle made the trenchant observation that *time can be equated with movement*. Anything that moves, moves in time. His exact words were, "Time is a measure of motion and of being moved."[12]

Aristotle's observation can be presumed to encompasses any movement: physical, mental or emotional. Included, then, are the cellular processes that power us, enabling us to perceive, feel, think, act, and *know* that we do these things. In this respect, a thought, an impression, a recollection, or a dream is indeed a movement in time. So is an emotion, which as we have seen, represents bodily energy proceeding outward toward expression. On the other hand, if a feeling were to get "stuck" internally and the accompanying energy chronically dissociated from a given part of the body, how would time be experienced for that particular organ? Try picturing a stream with a certain channel that's dammed up; the stream's flow goes *around* the portion that's stagnant, leaving the pebbles, leaves, and other debris deposited there untouched. This is one image Aristotle probably never considered and one question he presumably never asked. My inference is that, while time proceeds for the rest of the stream (i.e., the rest of the organism), it does *not* for that portion in which there is no movement.

Interestingly, the very process of aging—wherein cellular processes deteriorate and ultimately cease altogether—is itself a series of movements. In tandem with every sunrise and sunset and the changing of the seasons, we watch ourselves and those we know and love grow inexorably older.

Aristotle also postulated that time could not be experienced by someone in a deep, dreamless sleep because that was considered a virtual cessation of movement.[13] Today, of course, we know that the body is far from inactive during sleep: rest simply affords an opportunity to recoup energy. Indeed, some people (including myself) can program themselves to awaken at a particular hour. This indicates that our body's monitoring of our physiology continues all night and, with it, our sense of time.

Finally, Aristotle observed that, just as a thing in motion maintains its essential identity from one place to the next, so too a body in time ought to retain its intrinsic identity from past to future and all points in between.[14] That's not to say that we never change at all, which of course we do as we travel from place to place and from time to time—just that the essential "us" remains. In that sense, our procession through time can be seen as a kind of evolution. Just as travel is said to broaden a person, our journey through time should also connote learning, growth, and development. Identity in relation to time is a highly relevant subject, one we'll revisit in this chapter.

Immanuel Kant

This renowned eighteenth-century thinker believed (in sympathy with Aristotle but against what Plato and Isaac Newton supposed) that time *does not exist in itself.* Instead, he argued, time is a built-in property of our minds, of the way we perceive and experience the world. As we would inevitably see things being red upon wearing glasses with red lenses, so we must also view the world and everything in it temporally. Concepts like "succession" and "duration" make sense to us because that's the way our brains operate. We are born with red glasses, you might say, and we wear them as long as we live.[15]

Implicit in Kant's framework is the idea that other creatures that are sentient but whose minds are organized differently (e.g., birds, fish, insects) cannot perceive the flow of time as people do. While we know that they react to temporal changes, such as the shift from day to night and back again, they presumably lack the cognitive capacity to form an independent sense of time. Their behavior is entirely instinctual. Some mammals, on the other hand, by virtue of possessing a higher degree of consciousness, may be able to perceive time and its passage in a manner approaching that of human beings.

A Danish philosopher who came on the scene a few decades after Kant, Søren Kierkegaard, put it a bit differently. "Time," he commented, "does not exist without unrest; it does not exist for dumb animals who are absolutely without anxiety."[16] Anxiety, in his view, exists for man not only because he is sufficiently evolved to permit it, but also because he is aware of his own mortality. Kierkegaard was generalizing about animals; while some show no indications that they feel anxiety, others certainly do. Additionally, some creatures seem to evidence an understanding that they are about to die. If they *are* aware of their own mortality, we might speculate that they do possess some concept of time in and of itself. This will be germane as we explore animal consciousness in the next chapter.

The most important aspect of Kant's idea—presuming you accept it—is that, apart from the mind, time is nothing.[17] This has two significant implications for us. First, as modern neuroscience has traced the development of the brain from the older emotional regions to the neocortex, the processing of feeling has been understood to form the foundation for thought. Time, therefore, cannot exist apart from our *capacity to feel*. Second, our definition of the mind encompasses the brain plus the body, so having a body must also be essential to time. Neither having a body nor a capacity to feel is sufficient for a time sense, just an essential ingredient. This causes me to conclude that machines will never be able to experience or comprehend time, although they can surely be employed to monitor and count it.

Henri Bergson

Bergson was a French philosopher much concerned with the subjects of time, memory, and perception in general. He lived in the latter half of the nineteenth century and through to 1941—approximately the same period as Sigmund Freud.

Bergson took Aristotle's concept of time in a different direction by focusing on the continuous transition of mental states that we experience as "time passing."[18] This allows a greater appreciation of how differently we perceive time when our energy levels vary: how time flies by when we are enjoying something and how it seems to drag when an activity bores us. Bergson saw these changing internal states as a more appropriate metaphor for the succession of temporal moments than the movement of an object or a body in space, because the former seem to blend together and the latter, in contrast, appears more sharply delineated.[19]

In a major innovation, he also viewed time as a vehicle for personal growth, stating, "Suppose that I am trying to decide between two possible actions. . . . As I reflect on these alternatives, my self grows, expands, and changes. Just as . . . the present contains memories of the past, so my self 'lives and develops by means of its very hesitation' . . . this is what we mean by saying, when we speak of a free act, that the contrary action was equally possible."[20]

Free will has always been among the leading concerns of philosophy. Today it is one of the hotter topics among neurophilosophers as more is learned about brain mechanisms and the extent to which our behavior may be genetically encoded. In that context, Bergson's philosophy offers a hopeful antidote to the idea that there is no such thing as free will but that our thoughts and actions stem entirely from preprogrammed biochemistry.

Husserl and Heidegger

Edmund Husserl and Martin Heidegger were of the school of philosophy known as *phenomenology*. This approach considers how consciousness, (i.e., one's subjective experience) results from phenomena (i.e., sensory stimuli and qualities of the presented world). Husserl, who was a contemporary of Bergson and Freud, pioneered this school of thought. Heidegger, thirty years his junior, was both influenced by and diverged from Husserl. Nonetheless, both were concerned with the mechanisms of conscious perception.

Both also viewed the present as something other than a fixed moment in between the past and the future. The present, Husserl held, is "thick" because it arises from and looks back on the past (our memories and felt associations are perfect examples of this) as well as anticipates the future (through our hopes, desires, and expectations). Heidegger likewise regarded the present as uniting the past and future, so that every lived experience *spans these contexts.*[21]

One's felt perceptions provide an illustration of this—trauma particularly so. An intensely traumatic experience can become so deeply imprinted in memory that it is always "present." Indeed, for the traumatized person the future can lose its prospective meaning and become nothing more than a forum for remorseful repetition.[22] Even for someone grappling with garden-variety sorrow or dejection, the future can become drained of opportunity and promise.

On the positive side, a joyous event can fill us with such happiness, hope, or gratitude that the future cannot come too soon. If it is relied on too much, however, one might be accused of "living in the past." In any case, our very sense of self would seem to be inseparable from our perception of time. Whether we are mired in grief, propelled by elation, or feeling anything in between, such perceptions are inevitably *bodily.*

Before moving on, let it be noted that the perspective we are developing

—that time is tied to the human mind and stretches across identity—will be essential for understanding how the strang alies can seem to defy both space and time. This conjunction of and time is the province of our next eminent philosopher.

Samuel Alexander

Alexander, who lived in the same stimulating period as Bergson and Husserl, produced what has been called "the [single] most comprehensive and painstaking analysis of the idea of time."[23] What made it unique was his notion of not just space, and not just time, but overlapping space-time. All matter, he declared, springs from this fundamental property of the universe: space and time united, from the very beginning, into a single whole. "Space is in its very nature temporal and time spacial," Alexander stated. He illustrated this in the following way: Consider a point as something fixed in time. Picture a moment or an instant, likewise, as something fixed in space. A point would then *occur* at a certain instant and an instant would *occupy* a given point in space. Neither would exist without the other.[24]

If we accept a space-time overlay, we must consider this idea (or this fact of the universe) in light of Aristotle's earlier observations on identity. Remember Aristotle's contention that, just as a thing in motion maintains its essential identity from one place to the next, so too a body in time ought to retain *its* intrinsic identity. Now let's update this statement to reflect Alexander's thesis: just as a thing in motion maintains its essential identity from one space-time coordinate to the next, so too a body in time ought to retain its intrinsic identity from one space-time coordinate to the next.

This gives us a basis for evaluating a typically perceptive remark made by Murchie, namely that "time seems to be essentially the relationship between . . . things that have a common identity—between, say, a boy and a man grown from that boy—while space is the relationship between things . . . without common identity—as between a man and another man."[25] In other words, as we live our lives and proceed through space-time, we view time in terms of identity *continuity,* and space as a matter of identity *difference.* (One can add that Murchie's observation works equally well for societies and cultures as for individuals. As a nation proceeds through space-time, we view it, from the time side of the coin, as essentially the same country: the United States in 1883 or 2003. It is the same with the Chinese civilization or the Roman Catholic Church: they represent continuities.)

However, when an entity ceases to exist, its place in the space-time fabric is gone, too. As Murchie puts it, "Consider how, when a man is alive, there is an identity between his body (there then) and his body (here now), indicating that he exists in time. But after his death, the identity decreases between his body (there then) and his disintegrating body (wherever whenever), indicating that his body at last is loosening its bond with time."[26]

This analogy is something Alexander would likely have agreed with. He seems to have anticipated our current concept of mind as encompassing both brain and body because he referred to "the body-mind complex" as akin to his space-time correlation.[27]

Now, with regard to our bodymind moving through space-time, a fascinating possibility arises. When our emotions are being expressed (i.e., expanding into space), our experience of time should also be in some sense greater. This may explain instances of clairvoyance and precognitive dreams, where people geographically removed from an emotional event appear to nonetheless receive impressions of that experience in time. Conversely, if the flow of feeling is limited (i.e., if it is constricted within us), our experience of time should be diminished. In this respect, it would be instructive to know if telepathic, precognitive, or clairvoyant perceptions have ever seemed to relate an *un*emotional event, someone just eating his lunch, for example. One never hears of such instances, if they ever do occur. Maybe they do and, because they are so undramatic, are unreported. But if they *never* occur, it would tend to validate my theory of emotion.

Before we move on, here are two riveting examples of precognitive dreams. Each points to the distant struggle of another, not just against the tide of an intensively stressful event but also in defense of that person's very survival. The accounts are taken from a wide-ranging book on dreaming authored by psychologist Robert Van de Castle, whom we met in chapter 7:[28]

- At age twenty-three, long before he became famous as Mark Twain, Samuel Clemens dreamed he saw a metal coffin resting on two chairs in his sister's sitting room. As he approached the coffin, he saw the body of his brother Henry. One detail in particular caught his attention: a bouquet of white flowers, with one crimson flower in the center, lying on Henry's chest. A few days later, a Mississippi riverboat blew up and many of the passengers and crew were killed. Henry had been one of the crewmembers. When Clemens rushed to the scene of the accident, in Memphis, he found his brother lying unconscious on a mattress in an improvised hospital. There was some hope that his brother might pull through, but on the sixth night he died. When Clemens arrived at the room that was being used as a temporary morgue, he found that most of the dead were lying in plain wooden coffins, but there was one metal coffin lying on two chairs. Henry's struggle to survive had inspired such interest among the Memphis ladies that they had taken up a special collection and bought a metal casket for him. As Clemens approached his brother's casket, an elderly woman entered the room carrying a large bouquet of white flowers, in the center of which was one crimson rose, and laid them on Henry's chest.

- On October 21, 1966, a massive coaltip slid down a mountainside and engulfed the Welsh mining village of Aberfan, killing 144 people, mostly schoolchildren. In response to an appeal the following week in a national newspaper, an English psychiatrist by the last name of Barker obtained a large number of reports from respondents who felt they may have received anomalous information concerning this tragedy. After all claims were carefully checked out, thirty-five cases remained that Barker considered worthy of confidence. In twenty-four cases, the respondents had related the information to someone else before the landslide occurred. In one, the dreamer saw, spelled out in large, brilliant letters, the word "ABERFAN."

In another, a telephone operator from Brighton talked helplessly to a child who walked toward her, followed by a billowing cloud of black dust or smoke.

If time is, indeed, about the continuity of identity, it should not surprise us too much that death—the ultimate dissolution of identity (at least as far as we know)—is a theme of the most striking precognitive dreams. One noteworthy feature of the second dream above is that another identity, that of the village Aberfan, was evidently made known to at least one of the percipients. Here we have a *collective* identity being asserted through the minds of the people assaulted by this awful tragedy.

I do not know whether anyone in the United States, following in the footsteps of Barker, solicited people's reports concerning possible anomalous notice of the September 11, 2001, terrorist attacks against the World Trade Center and Pentagon. I did, however, come across this one anecdote published shortly thereafter. Take it for what you will.

I'm usually out of bed early. But on Tuesday, September 11, I just didn't want to get up. I slept past my five o'clock alarm. I slept past [my wife's] six o'clock alarm. I didn't wake up until 8:20; this was later than I'd slept in years. As I shuffled to the bathroom, I recalled bits and pieces of the unsettling dream I'd just had. I was in a big city, its skyline dominated by a towering skyscraper. I heard a huge explosion and, looking up, saw the top of the tower enveloped by a mushroom cloud. I raced into the lobby to find out what had happened. People were running frantically in all directions. A reporter told me the explosion was the work of a religious cult. That's when I woke up. I had no idea what the dream meant. I took a shower and got dressed. I turned on the radio.[29]

Most Americans who remember the aftermath of September 11 and the country's foray into Afghanistan will also recall the video footage obtained of Osama bin Laden, who masterminded the attacks. In addition to his gloating over the terrorist "success," the transcript revealed a curious preoccupation with dreams that several of his henchmen had had prior to the attacks, in which they allegedly saw planes smashing into the World Trade Center. As these particular underlings were not aware what particular attacks were planned, bin Laden worried that, if other people had access to the same dream information, his plans might be uncovered in advance.[30]

Now, my narrative returns to an earlier, less apocalyptic time. Namely, the beginning of the *past* century.

Sigmund Freud

As the father of modern psychiatry, Freud not only theorized the existence of the subconscious but also tried to elucidate how threatening thoughts and feelings might be kept there (i.e., repressed). While his concept of personality and personality development dominated the middle of the twentieth century, it has since come into question as objective knowledge of the brain and nervous system has replaced speculative formulations of the id, ego, and superego. Freud's views have also been shown to be exaggerated, if not erroneous, concerning the relevance of sex to children's early development (e.g., their interest in genitalia, their supposed desire for the parent of the opposite sex). Nonetheless, Freud was a groundbreaker who managed to construct a unified theory of human nature in the absence of much scientific knowledge about the brain. If he were alive today, he might not be disappointed by the fact that his light has dimmed, given his expressed desire to have his psychoanalytic concepts either affirmed or replaced by improved knowledge of brain biology.[31]

Freud was intrigued by dreams and what they might reveal about the mind. He noticed that in dreams, time is portrayed much differently than we normally experience it, with past, present, and future juxtaposed and the duration and order of events distorted.[32] He noted, too, that memories, urges, and other thoughts and feelings that have been repressed seem unaffected by time's passage: they exert just as powerful an influence thirty years after the fact as thirty days after.[33] Freud was also familiar with hypnosis and the altered time perception characteristic of that state.

A person who is hypnotized and told to perform a certain task, for example, will often grossly under- or overestimate how long it took to carry out the suggestion.[34] And, while Freud himself did not regress individuals to their childhood under hypnosis, it would not surprise him to learn that it can be done and that someone in such a hypnotic condition can believe he or she is living at that earlier stage.

Based on all of this evidence, Freud concluded that the subconscious does not care about time, that its processes are not altered by time and do not bear any relation to time at all.[35] This conclusion parallels my own, in the sense that the energy of dissociated feeling can be held in the bodymind indefinitely. So long as it is frozen, the problem is pathological. (I might add that the very word "pathology" is derived from the Greek word *pathos,* meaning "feeling," "that which arouses feeling," and more particularly, "suffering.")

The subconscious may be less in vogue these days, but that does not mean the concept lacks value or that the subconscious as a virtual realm of our bodymind does not exist. I believe that it does, and much of this book has endeavored to demonstrate as much. However, many cognitive scientists prefer the anatomical term "right brain" when describing the mind's proclivity for producing symbolism of the kind evident in dreams, which, they would agree, definitely do not conform to our waking experience of time. As we've seen, the right side of the brain processes information more holistically than the left and is much more concerned with emotion, relationships, and nuance than with analysis, logic, and cause-and-effect.[36] The former, you will note, are emphatically *nonlinear.* Thus, to say the right brain dominates during dreaming is equivalent to saying that the subconscious does so.

Freud was also interested in what he called "the uncanny," by which he meant anomalous perceptions that seem at once strange and familiar. The phenomenon of déjà vu is one such experience. In chapter 5, I noted that déjà vu could be classified as a kind of dissociative symptom. That is, when facing a situation reminiscent of something threatening or traumatic that occurred earlier in one's life, a person might experience the faintest of recalls but immediately have that recollection severed by the conscious mind, which wishes the memory to lie dormant. That vague and momentary recall would be experienced as déjà vu. Freud proposed something similar: that déjà vu represents the momentary recall of a memory deeply repressed from childhood or infancy.[37]

Carl Jung

Jung was a prominent disciple of Freud, but the two ended up parting company. Jung was far less interested in sex as a driver of personality development and more interested in what he termed the "collective unconscious," a kind of primordial, universal mind that, he postulated, underlies each person's subconscious. He did agree with Freud that one of the hallmarks of the subconscious is its apparent timelessness, and he sought to investigate that quality. Jung traveled around the world and lived among several indigenous cultures to learn firsthand about their myths and participate in their rituals. He was intensely interested in mystical experience and its relationship both to the individual subconscious and the collective unconscious. He noted that cultures such as that of the Australian aborigine featured myths about the "dreamtime," a timeless and spaceless realm out of which dreams, visions, ecstasies, and mystical experiences are said to occur, and which corresponds roughly to our concept of the unconscious.[38]

Jung realized that feelings have "a sort of latent psychic energy."[39] The deeper the feelings, he said, the more energy and import they contain. Feelings and images emanating from a person's subconscious would carry significant psychic energy; feelings and images issuing from the collective unconscious would carry even more. Jung termed the latter "archetypes" and identified what he saw as evidence for them in themes recurring throughout the world's mythologies as well as in individual dream symbolism. (The idea of archetypes, while provocative, has not been accepted into mainstream psychology or sociology. Similarly, the concept of the collective unconscious has been largely discarded as a relic of Jung's Teutonic heritage.)

He was also fascinated by what he termed "synchronicities," or meaningful coincidences. For example, a person dreams of someone he or she has not seen for years and, the following day, encounters that very person. Or a particular motif—a sunflower, for instance—is presented again and again in a short time and in completely different contexts. Such an unlikely conjunction is, by definition, a coincidence, but Jung viewed such correspondences as potentially meaningful and believed that they offered the person experiencing them an opportunity for development. He explained synchronicities as reflections of what he called the *unus mundus,* an overarching reality that encompasses both the physical and the psychic, the objective world and our subjective experience.[40]

Quasimystical Revelations

Jung's ideas are obviously difficult to test empirically, but there is one aspect we can examine, namely, the sense of total illumination that sometimes dawns on people in the midst of a mystical or quasimystical experience. Similarly relevant is any sudden realization or understanding of a matter long puzzling to us, typically punctuated by a cry of "Aha!" or a bemused utterance of "How in heaven's name did I come up with that?" These experiences are literally wonderful. We may be awestruck or, alternately, struck dumb and disbelieving our own good fortune. The process could be explained as the brain putting together information carried separately in its right and left hemispheres, with the long-awaited synthesis then dawning on us. No doubt that is the case in many such situations, especially where ideas or intellectual discoveries are being synthesized.

But there is another sort of "Aha!," one in which a person's deeper feelings and memories are uncovered and drawn together. Consider the following example, reported by a person who had, ostensibly, an out-of-body experience but which, by any measure, involved quite a bit of recollection as well as catharsis. Her pseudonym is Barbara, and her experience took place in a hospital bed as she was recovering from an operation:

> I saw myself in bed, crying . . . only I was a little child. And my mother was there and my father was there. . . . This was such an intense experience, it was like I was there again. Everything was the way it was when I was that small child. . . . I was picking up aromas.

I was picking up all the physical sensations of my mother hitting me again, yet, at the same time, besides my feelings, I understood her feelings and I understood my father in the hallway. . . . I was saying "no wonder." No wonder you are the way you are, you know? Lookit what's being done to you at such a young age. . . . I could see it from all angles now as an adult but at the same time I was experiencing it at maybe the age of four or five. . . .

It was like the most healing therapy there could be. . . . Years and years of intense psychoanalysis, of the most intense type of external therapy, could not have brought me through what I was experiencing rapidly. . . .

When I came back from [the purported out of body experience], I really understood. . . . I knew at that point that I had met myself.[41]

Barbara's experience—especially as highlighted in that last statement—is clearly about identity. Through her anomalous, "uncanny" recollection, she discovered the person she was at a particularly traumatic juncture of her life. Time shifting, in this case and, as I shall argue, in all such cases, is chiefly about identity: the bodymind's movement through time-space as an evolving continuity. Barbara (here, now) encountered Barbara (then, there). As present-day philosopher Jacob Needleman has remarked, "In such moments a witness has appeared within us—and it is we who are being witnessed."[42]

Applicable, too, is psychiatrist Stanislav Grof's concept of systems of condensed experience, or COEX. Recall his definition of a COEX system as a group of highly emotional, highly meaningful memories, all relating to a similar theme but drawn from various and sundry times throughout an individual's life. Especially prevalent are memories relating to any situation that threatened (or seemed to threaten) survival, health, or bodily integrity.[43] So it seems apropos that Barbara had this revelation while hospitalized.

Barbara's time shift also qualifies as a COEX type because it was experienced extremely vividly, just as if she were indeed back in her childhood bedroom. Finally, her experience fits the COEX model since it entailed a profound personal transformation or, at the very least, a first step toward such a transformation. She relived her particular memory in a quite visceral way (complete with smells) while simultaneously assessing it from a more objective, adult perspective. She was herself as a child, but she was also herself as a grownup. To a certain extent, we all live in the past and the present while re-experiencing memories, but in Barbara's case, past and present merged in a particularly meaningful way. She is, I would wager, a thin-boundary person.

Ernest Hartmann, who originated the boundary concept, has noted that people with thin boundaries retain strong childhood memories and remain identified with their childhood feelings. His choice of the word "identified," although presented in an entirely different context, is apt. Time is indeed about the self and thus about our *evolving identity*. I strongly suspect that thin-boundary individuals, as they do in so many other respects, experience time differently than the rest of us. They must experience time as more mutable and less subject to the strictures of past, present, and future—and as seeming to pass more slowly, given their more intense internal experiences.

Biological versus Linear Time

It should by now be evident that our experience of time is intimately related to the body's flow of feeling and the amount of energy we are marshaling at any given moment. One key is metabolic rate, a measure of energy production and of cellular activity in general. Metabolic rate differs among people based on their age, what they are engaged in (or disengaged from), to what extent their systems are revved up, and even the time of day. We are all familiar with morning and evening people, that is, those among us who consistently feel more energetic and capable at one time of the day than another. This is no mere turn of phrase: the phenomenon relates to a very real individual disposition. (One might say it's "constitutional" in the sense of our physical makeup.)

You may object that biological time is not "real" time, or linear time, which we identify with the clock. True, it is not clock time—but the fact that biological time is experienced subjectively makes it no less real. It could be argued that biological time is *more* real, the *most* real perception of time, because it is based in our bodies and rooted in real biological processes. Clock time, on the other hand (pardon the pun) can be seen as mainly a convenience, a social standard, a device based on the rotation of the Earth and its revolution around the sun, processes that matter less to us than our own biology.[44]

Does linear time exist outside of humanity's ability to conceptualize it? I submit that it does not. Hearkening back to Kant, time is nothing if not a concept, and one needs a feeling body, a thinking brain, and (probably) a limited lifespan in order to fathom it. This is not to say that, if self-conscious creatures didn't exist, the universe wouldn't carry on without us. Clearly it has done just that for billions of years, with galaxies forming, stars exploding, comets zooming, and planets spinning. But, unless there are mindful creatures to witness these developments, time would be a moot point. Only through the particular organization of our mind does time come into existence. And "existence" must be qualified: time does not live; it is a notion, a precept, a useful way of assessing our lives and the world we inhabit.

The key is to recognize that one mode of perceiving time can exist *alongside* another. Biological time is the mode most relevant to our internal experience, whereas clock time provides a way to reckon time's passage publicly, as a standard for everyone. Individuals gauge their own experience according to both internal and external modes.

Roots of Time in the Self

The predecessor of each person's sense of time is the maternal heartbeat heard by the fetus in utero. That rhythm—mainly steady, but speeded up during strenuous activity as well as times of stress—is the first temporal sequence we perceive. It is felt as a thumping as well as a sound, thus providing a foundation for the enjoyment we later find in music, dance, and marching.[45]

Later on, in infancy, the time it takes for the mother to respond to the infant's needs will help form his or her concepts of time, gratification, patience, and self-worth. Responses to a baby's cries to be fed, to be held, to have its diaper changed, and to be put down for a nap all contribute, as do the patterns followed in the given household as the child matures (e.g., routines followed, not followed, or followed sporadically).[46] Orders to the effect that "I want this done now!" contrast quite a bit with "Oh, that can be done whenever."

Time, as we noted earlier, is bound up with our sense of identity. Schizophrenics, whose hold on their sense of self is often tenuous, have been known to complain of a lack of temporal continuity. For them, time does not flow as it does for most others: it moves spasmodically, unreliably.[47] This is probably because, in schizophrenia, the individual suffers from a disconnection with the body. (The "schizo" in schizophrenia literally means "split.") While knowing that he or she *has* a body, the person does not know what he or she feels, and hence does not feel much connected to other people.[48] This illustrates again the mooring that *feeling* provides to our experience of time.

No discussion of selfhood would be complete without reference to the brain, which is, presumably, the main organ that allows us to judge the passage of time, whether biological or linear. (We must realize that, for neuroscientists or anyone else who believes in the primacy of the brain over the rest of the body, that last sentence must seem ridiculous. "Selfhood? Why should we consider anything *but* the brain?" Perhaps by now this attitude will appear to the reader as what it is: shortsighted and unfortunate.) One question scientists are debating is whether the brain harbors a specialized timekeeping mechanism or whether our awareness of time's passage results from the operation of more generalized faculties, such as sensory processing and memory. Supporters of the former view implicate the basal ganglia, a collection of small structures linked to the cortex by looplike nerve circuits. The time it takes for an electrical pulse to flow around the loop is effectively a tick of the clock, they suggest. Other neuroscientists argue that humans' time sense emanates from the way our brains recognize and process sensory stimuli. They point out that, in the brain's visual centers, many cells will fire only if an object is moving or changing in some way. So temporal processing doesn't rely on a special neural relay, they contend.[49]

The latter view is more consistent with the approach we are developing here, that whole-body processes—not merely neural ones—give rise to the perception of time. In this concept, the relevant circuitry is located throughout our bodymind. We are not distanced from external (nor internal) events by a "clock watcher" on high but rather are part and parcel of what we immediately experience. In that context, the energetic flow of feeling is paramount.

One of the brain structures that deserves a close look is the hippocampus, known to be critical to memory formation as well as the encoding of new information.[50] The hippocampus is also a key player in emotional memory because it is located next to the amygdala and directly connected with the olfactory nerve. This is a potent combination that, as we've seen, enables emotional memories tinged with aroma to be effectively recalled.[51] The power of this neural lineup to recall vivid memories, preserved over many years, is illustrated by John Kinge, a member of the Olfaction Research Group at Warwick University in England.

> [He works with the elderly] in a program he calls "reminiscence therapy," using a nostalgic aroma pack designed to evoke smells of the early 1940s. Trigger odors are held in stoppered vials containing pads soaked in scents identified simply as "Old Teapot," "Washday" or "Air Raid Shelter," each of which is capable of conjuring up long-forgotten information. After a sniff of an old-fashioned disinfectant in the sample labeled "Field Hospital," one veteran found to his astonishment that he could still rattle off his wartime rifle number.
>
> Group sessions with the aroma pack are even more productive. The unique odor of a teawagon that once belonged to a wartime women's auxiliary service catalyzed a recollection-fest among several women in their nineties. "It's amazing," said one. "With a single sniff you start to think again about all sorts of things. Memories come pouring out of the back of your mind. It was such a treat."[52]

Music exercises a similar sway on memory. Hearing a tune that was popular at a particular time in one's life can prompt a cascade of recollections. Music can even work around neural roadblocks. Neurologist Oliver Sacks writes of one of his patients who suffered from a brain tumor and so had not been able to form any new memories since the 1970s. "But if we talk about or play his favorite Grateful Dead songs, his amnesia is bypassed. He becomes vividly animated and can reminisce about their early concerts."[53] As opposed to smell, which follows a definite neural pathway, and smell-related memories, which are generated from the limbic region of the brain, music and musically associated memories appear to be whole-brain phenomena, with the right hemisphere involved in recognition of melody and timbre and the left in rhythmic pace and the sequence of lyrics.[54] Evidence of this can be found in brain scans of musicians who began their training in early childhood. In these individuals, the corpus callosum—the bridge connecting the two hemispheres—is as much as fifteen percent larger than in nonmusicians.[55] It has also been found that different parts of the brain are activated when one is listening casually versus paying close attention to a musical score, and when one is focused on harmony versus a straightforward melody or rhythm section.[56] Different regions of the brain also come into play when the music heard is pleasant or unpleasant.[57] Furthermore, it seems likely that music can affect the level of various hormones that travel throughout the body, including cortisol (a critical component in stress reactions), testosterone (which is involved in aggression and arousal), and oxytocin (a factor in nurturing behavior as well as, interestingly enough, labor contractions). Music can likewise trigger the release of natural painkillers known as endorphins.[58]

What smell and music have in common is that, under their influence, our "remembrance of things past" (as Marcel Proust put it) is dramatically enhanced. This is accomplished not so much in biological time as in, we might say, "emotional time" because both types of memory have a distinct emotional corollary. Therein lies the key to the highly curious time alterations apparent in many types of anomalies.

Anomalous Time: Setting the Stage

For a given experience to be considered paranormal, it must defy conventional explanations that rest on straightforward cause and effect. But if linear time is only one mode of perceiving and other modes—ones we are less familiar with—are also operating, then anomalous events may in fact occur. They will, however, forever remain a mystery, obscured and inscrutable to us unless we can chart their flow using other baselines. "The laws that govern such experiences may not be those that govern normal consciousness," comments neuroscientist Robert Ornstein. "The experience of the night is not that of the day."[59]

What happens in our bodies and brains during intensely stressful or emotional experiences is a veritable Rosetta stone. Understand the following factors and you have a basis for comprehending how anomalies arise:

1. Our built-in stress-response systems
2. The electrochemical basis of bodymind energy
3. The difference between feelings constrained and feelings expressed
4. The tumult of energy short-circuited during a freeze response
5. The myriad of neural and immune system interconnections within us
6. The psychosomatic, or bodymind, nature of memory
7. The difference between thin-boundary and thick-boundary dynamics
8. The self as a living entity moving through space-time

Throughout this book, I have endeavored to show how factor 7—different neurobiological sensitivity—relates to these other factors and prefigures anomalous perceptions. Now we come to the last relationship, between factor 7 and the astonishing composite of personal identity, time, and space that is factor 8.

The Overlay of Emotional and Biological Time

Think back on the many anomalies we have examined in this book: eighteen-month-old Adam's sudden fear (in the middle of a bath) that men in uniforms are approaching; Susan's smelling her late father's aftershave late at night, followed by a full-fledged apparition; the bizarre poltergeist effects taking place around Mary and her family; new father Ron's dreams of his absent father, followed by the news that his father is dying and a last visit with him in the hospital; Melanie being hit by a car at about the same time as her mother, three thousand miles away, senses that something is amiss; Ruth's lifelike visions of her abusive father—visions she eventually learns to control; the recurring apparitions of two crew members from doomed Flight 401; the memories and personality traits sensed by heart transplant recipients of their donors; the apparently precognitive dreams concerning Samuel Clemens's brother; the doomed children of a Welsh mining town; the terrorist attacks of September 11; Barbara's transformative (and transpersonal) experience while in the hospital; and finally, the same Adam, now four years old, pointing out to his incredulous mother that he sees his recently deceased aunt conversing with two other spectral women.

In these various cases, things are perceived as happening that *cannot* happen according to the everyday laws of physics. The customary recognition of space-time is tossed on its head, and consequently, the people involved are quite shaken. But the fact that they are shaken because the givens of space-time are changed should not trump the manifestly *emotional* nature of what is happening. Emotion is central to both the situations themselves (their internal dynamics) and the alterations of space-time that are evidently taking place.

When someone's feelings are being expressed, the energy is literally conveyed from the body into space, or more properly, from one set of space-time coordinates to another. Bear in mind that the former set of coordinates is *us*. So the energy moving out into space-time carries something of us with it. Our emotions are wrapped up with who we are, what we're feeling, and what memories are associated with what we're feeling. Think again of the stream analogy. An unobstructed flow of feeling outward is not only healthy, it is honest. Emotions, indeed, are the most honest emissaries of selfhood—far more so than words, which can be twisted, shaded, cloaked, and misunderstood. Even the feelings we keep inside ourselves are valuable representatives of the self. They (and their associated memories) may have overwhelmed the conscious mind and become dissociated from the felt sense, but they are still part of us and need to be brought to conscious awareness if we are to be whole and healthy individuals.

In the most intense encounters (such as a COEX experience), "time, space and motion fuse," writes the late psychiatrist and energy therapist John Pierrakos.[60] The catalyst for such alteration of our customary experience is the self. Not only is the bodymind operating in biological time, with our metabolism raised and time appearing to slow down, but we are also operating in *emotional time,* with the energy of feeling being channeled and expressed outward. A mental dip into the past may also take place, with memories germane to the feeling being uncovered and reviewed. So it is the overlay of biological and emotional time that lends itself to what I call *anomalous time.* In every case, something core about the self is at issue—if not for the person perceiving the anomaly, then for the person whose energy, spilling into the surrounding space-time, triggers it in the first place.

Ultimately, the way individuals perceive anomalous time depends on where they are on the thick-to-thin boundary spectrum. Real differences in neurobiological functioning will produce different forms of experience—though anyone can either encounter or generate an anomaly so long as intense emotions and issues of identity are involved.

In all cases, we cannot help but feel that the anomalous experience has a transcendent quality because, of course, it does. Our common experience of time, space, and identity is surpassed, overridden, temporarily replaced. It is not just a figment of our imagination or, as many neuroscientists would have it, an illusion produced by an odd form of neurological activity. Something at once deeper and more deeply felt is going on. Something important about someone's self is being expressed. It is, as Freud identified, uncanny. It is also profound. In the suspension of then and now, there and here, someone is trying to make his or her feelings known, to become more than he or she was, to become (even if not consciously aware of it) a more fully actualized person. Anomalies point to the validity of Kant's surmise that time and the human mind are inseparable. In living our lives, in feeling our feelings, we do not just perceive the passage of time, we are also capable of *influencing it,* albeit in extraordinary circumstances. Our selves, our emotions, and time itself are actually part of the same universal fabric.

Seen from this vantage point, the age-old question, What is time? can only be answered with another question, equally ancient and even more challenging: Why are we alive at all?[61] To this I can only propose: to become, via our intellect, our learning and not least, our emotional expression, the best realized people we can possibly be.

Is There a Self at All?

Throughout this book, my operating assumption has been that individual human beings have selves and that those selves are primarily neurobiological. That is to say, our characteristic ways of thinking and feeling, of acting and responding, stem from our physical makeup and the manner in which our brains and bodies work as one. Everything from our personality and memories to our threshold sensitivity and immune function depends, in my view, upon the self. Who we are and what we become thus has a tangible basis. The self is anything but illusory.

Yet there is a trend among neurophilosophers to pry the concept of self apart—to see it in oddly minimalist terms or to deny the possibility of its existence altogether. A few examples follow:

- Neuroscientist Joseph LeDoux proposes what he calls the "synaptic self," where the individual is the result of his or her pattern of connections among the brain's neurons. "You are your synapses," he proclaims.[62]
- Daniel Dennett of Tufts University, a leading figure among neurophilosophers, vigorously questions whether self is an appropriate concept. He cites research (famously performed by the late Benjamin Libet at the University of California–San Francisco) showing that the brain fails to register awareness of a conscious action—indeed, does not even register the *intention* of taking action—until after

its "readiness to act" (as measured by an electroencephalograph, or EEGs) is betrayed.[63] (Libet's findings have since been affirmed by a team at the Max Planck Institute for Human Cognitive and Brain Sciences in Germany.[64]) This seems to suggest that we are not the authors of our destiny, that decisions somehow precede conscious thought.

- In a similar vein, eminent neuroscientist Michael Gazzaniga of Dartmouth College points out that the brain's two hemispheres do very different things and perceive the world very differently. Our seemingly integrated sense of self is just that, he notes—a *seeming* integration. Our sense of continuity derives from the brain's articulate left hemisphere, a veritable "spin doctor" that interprets our perceptions and experience and convinces us we have a self, even though we do not.[65]

- Daniel Schacter, a professor of psychology at Harvard University, conceives of one's *memories* as the core determinant of self. Our memories are selective for the very reason that this process helps maintain a consistent sense of self—which would, in turn, break down were it not for our continually (and unconsciously) rewriting the past.[66]

- Psychologist Susan Blackmore contends that, just as our physical bodies are products of our genes, our behaviors and personalities are the products of "memes." This term, originally used in this context by evolutionary biologist Richard Dawkins, refers to units of culture that are mimetic, spreading themselves via imitation. (The word "mimetic" comes from the root word "mime.") Ideas, names, fashions, principles—these are memes, which replicate by passage from one person to another like a virus. Blackmore suggests that our minds are a conglomeration of these memes and that the very notion of an individual self is an illusion established by the memes so they themselves can be perpetuated. Human beings are, in her words, "meme machines."[67]

- An equally interesting view is held by astronomer and science writer David Darling. Akin to Ralph Waldo Emerson and the nineteenth-century transcendentalists, he suggests that the self is an illusion, preventing us from knowing the universe as it really is. Both our sensory apparatus and our nervous systems, Darling asserts, are designed to reduce and crystallize information coming in from the world around us. What we see and hear, what we taste and smell, and what we ultimately take for reality are mere *slivers* of that reality, never the entire picture, according to Darling. The sound and light waves that we process internally are necessarily changed as they are brought into focus and, ultimately, interpreted by the brain. This filtering function means that all of our perceptions are, in some manner, false. It also means, in his view, that our very sense of self is based on falsehood and amounts only to a delusion.[68]

With all due deference to these learned individuals and their provocative ideas—which carry weight and are undeniably fascinating to think about—I do believe they are barking up the wrong tree. Our sense of self, as grounded in the body, is *tangible*. This tangibility coalesces early on in life and is maintained as long as we live. Consider that whenever we look to our surroundings, we almost always see some portion of our bodies in the frame, as it were. As I'm typing right now I see my shoulders and arms, my hands (of course), the outline of my glasses, and my torso extending underneath the keyboard. This frame of reference develops primarily through vision, though our view of ourselves, but it is also formed through contributions by the other senses. Such body centrality is so ubiquitous as to be overlooked.[69]

Our sense of self, therefore, is unlikely to be dictated by memes (though alas, no one could ever prove it isn't). It underlies conscious thought and awareness, being first and foremost about our aliveness as individuals, about being sentient. Thus, the problem of the brain manifesting its electrical potential for some action before evidencing awareness of the action is really no problem at all. We do not need to be conscious to be alive. We do, however, need to be *embodied*. The issue is put most elegantly by evolutionary psychologist Nicholas Humphrey, who has done a great deal of thinking on these subjects. In his view, sentience—

and all the glory of bodily sensation—makes "a self worth having."[70]

I further assert that the higher up the evolutionary ladder one goes, the more advanced the self becomes. Self-conscious creatures, such as ourselves, are just that: *self* conscious. I do not believe our perceptions are in error or the result of spin, meme control, or illusion. Our selves are manifestly real—representing not just who we *were* and who we *are* but who we have *yet to become.* Biological time provides the constant and vital framework for such experience to take place, and clock time provides the consensus benchmarks. Emotional time betokens our energy of feeling being directed outward: a process of self-discovery and actualization. And our occasional, bizarre encounters with anomalous time indicate instances when that process is thwarted—when the continuation of self is in peril or when a person is unable to satisfactorily express some fundamental emotional truth. Anomalies in general, I posit, are saying nothing more (and nothing less) than "I am here now at this important juncture" or "I was there at a particular key place in my life." Most poignantly, they are saying (in the words of Marlon Brando's frustrated boxer in *On the Waterfront*), "I coulda been somebody."

Those caught in the throes of anomalous time fail to realize, literally, what their selves are about. Their evolving identity is at an impasse. But (and this is the most important thing) the "somebody" they wish to be is not illusory. It is not a chimera, a trick of the brain, or a joke played on us by the universe. It is sensate, integrative, and invaluable—the amalgam of all that is within us as well as our connection with the whole of nature. First and foremost, it is *bodily.* And in this regard, you must know that no esteemed scientist, no pioneering neurophilosopher, could ever weave theories on the *non*existence of the self if he or she were not well-fed, well-clothed, and materially comfortable. These are the physical prerequisites for our ability to speculate that our selves might not exist after all.

Time, Body, and Nature

I will close with a reminiscence. It is not my own, although it certainly does resonate. Presumably you've had a similar experience at some point in your life. Or at least I hope you've had, because this convergence of perceptions is notably pleasant, peaceful, and meaningful in an unconventional yet decidedly memorable way:

> I am fifteen years old; it is a brilliant October day; flaming maples and oaks line the street; the sky clear, crystalline blue; early morning. I am walking to school. Alone. Cars and trucks are beginning their morning hum. Cool autumn air, pure and sweet on my face and in my nostrils. Suddenly, for no apparent reason, I stop. I stop cold—or so it seems. But my legs continue to move, my arms are swinging rhythmically at my side. . . .
>
> At the same moment, with startling clarity, *I say my name aloud.* I don't recall *intending* to say my name like that, aloud, in strong and even tones—yet the saying of it is filled with intention and will, an intention of a kind I have never known before. I say my name: *Jerry.* And I say, with it: *I am Jerry. I am here. I am alive.*[71]

At times such as this, we find ourselves feeling "out of time"—our consciousness somehow expanded, our awareness of self enlarged and enhanced. Such experiences often arise spontaneously during childhood and adolescence, which makes sense given that, earlier on in our life, the world and all it offers have not yet been taken wholly for granted. Often enough, sensation itself is the trigger for such breakthroughs—impressions of a leafy glade . . . a moonlit night . . . a babbling brook . . . or the purity and coolness of a fall day, as for Jerry.[72] The brain may *process* such sensory perceptions, but it does not originate them. They arrive at the brain through the body. In this way, our experience of time and the self is influenced by being at home in nature.

We who have become time-pressed urbanites, working and dwelling in artificially conditioned environments, spending more time gazing at computer screens than outside our office window, should find reassurance in that lesson.

12

◆

Evidence for the
Emotional Gateway

It is only with the heart that one can see rightly; what is essential is invisible to the eye.

Antoine de Saint-Exupéry, *The Little Prince*

Men love to wonder, and that is the seed of our science.

Ralph Waldo Emerson

Of all the things that make us human, emotion poses by far the most obstacles to serious study. Only within the past twenty or so years, as medical imaging techniques have allowed researchers to see precisely what goes on in the brain when certain feelings are experienced, has science made any kind of leap in understanding this most fundamental of subjects. But what a leap it has been! So intoxicating are these glimpses of electrochemical energy dancing through the brain that many neuroscientists are convinced emotion must both originate and reside there. This book, of course, argues that the reality is wider, that we must take account of the entire body and the *self* of which the body is inextricably part. Further, I have proposed that emotions, by their very nature, seek expression from the bodymind and that emotional energy can, under certain circumstances, be transferred into the electromagnetic surroundings and held there indefinitely.

These ideas, especially the latter, are at odds with today's received wisdom. Yet it should be clear by now what power unexpressed feelings can exert within us: how they can alter immune function, create or aggravate illness, and produce psychosomatic symptoms. These are accepted facts, part of mainstream science and, indeed, the core of a vigorous young branch known as psychoneuroimmunology. As recently as 1985, the *New England Journal of Medicine* dismissed the possibility that the mind played any substantial role in health, editorializing that the "belief in disease as a direct reflection of mental state is largely folklore."[1] At that time, mind-body-health connections *were* largely in the realm of folklore—but research rapidly altered that state of affairs. Likewise, the most current research into the workings of the brain demonstrates its latent plasticity, its ability to change and grow, "a fact astonishingly contrary to a century of neurologists' dogma."[2] Now the pendulum is swinging the other way. As one neuroscientist jokingly observes, "Every year the brain gets more plastic than the year before."[3]

This is how science itself grows and develops: through tantalizing hints and offbeat anecdotes, false starts and cold trails, some initial momentum, expressions of interest, complementary research, sustained progress, and finally, a new consensus. Given sufficient time, the formerly heretical idea can become fashionable. However, as in most other realms of human endeavor, people tend to resist ideas that truly "push the envelope." Often their attention is trained within their own familiar discipline. They may be willing to incorporate advances if they seem relevant and not too threatening, but will dismiss ideas—even ones backed by evidence—that contradict their understanding of how things are. This is not to imply that all new ideas, all big ideas, or even all discarded concepts have innate merit. But it is to suggest that, when logical argument is advanced and provocative evidence marshaled, an idea should not be rejected out of hand simply because it calls long-standing suppositions into question.

To this end, I have cited a wealth of evidence indicating that certain individuals are sensitive, that their sensitivity has a neurobiological basis, and that, consequently, they may be able to perceive anomalous stimuli that the rest of us do not. This is definitely pushing the envelope but is still, I submit, somewhere in the "postal service." More problematic is the notion that intense feelings can be transmitted to others in nonordinary ways and can be harbored in the electromagnetic environment. What studies have inquired into these possibilities? Indeed, what research pertains to other key questions relevant to the thesis of this book, such as:

- Do animals perceive (or contribute to the perception of) anomalies?
- What accounts for out-of-body experiences?
- Could feelings ever be felt outside the body?

In this chapter, I shall cite some of these studies and the fascinating ideas they entertain. The selection is my own. It cannot claim to represent a cross section of the research; rather, it is intended as a sampling of some of the types of studies being done. One must give them their due as pioneering efforts while evaluating them critically as well as with an open mind.

Can Emotions Affect Random Event Generation?

The first experiment we'll look at sought to determine whether the emotions expressed by patients during psychotherapy could affect the output of a random event generator. (A random event generator is a machine designed to generate a sequence of numbers or symbols that lack any pattern. It's basically a more sophisticated, electronic-age method of doing what card shuffling and coin flipping have done since ancient times.) The patients agreed to be videotaped as the test was being conducted and have the therapist take notes on their expression of emotion. A computer, time-synched to the camcorder, collected the random event data. Output was evaluated when a given patient spoke with little or no emotion versus his or her spontaneous expression of sadness, anger, frustration, and anxiety. Only an emotion actually expressed (as opposed to a person saying, for example, that she felt like crying) counted toward the result. A statistical analysis revealed that the generator's output was higher than normal during periods of anger, lower than normal during periods of sadness and anxiety, and average during periods of neutral talking.[4]

Several weaknesses are apparent in this study. First, it was conducted by a single therapist, so his notes, videotapes, and conclusions are the only documentation available. Second, this particular therapist was trained in a school of psychology known as bioenergetics, where it is theorized that certain emotions correlate with a contraction of bodily energy and others with an expansion of bodily energy. These assumptions could also have unconsciously biased the investigator's reading of the results from the random event generator. Third, the investigator's own feelings could have influenced the detection of energy by the equipment. Fourth, the number of patients involved in the experiment (twelve) was relatively small.

Nonetheless, if the results are to be believed, emotional expression can have an effect on an adjacent electrical device. Not only that, but different emotions seem to have different effects. Anger was associated with a marked upward shift in the random event generator's output, whereas sadness, anxiety, and frustration seemed to evoke a distinct downward shift. As with the other research we'll become acquainted with, this deserves further investigation.

Are Body Image and Self-Conception Relevant to Extraordinary Sensitivity?

Two experiments suggest that body image and self-conception are involved in people's perception that they have obtained information or insight anomalously. In the first study, subjects were asked to envision their bodies as either permeable or presenting a barrier. The individuals who had a higher subsequent ESP score were significantly more likely to have conceptualized their body as permeable than were those with lower ESP scores.[5] In a second (unrelated) study, people who participated in a weeklong series of "psychic development" exercises took Ernest Hartmann's boundary questionnaire, which assesses personality along the thick-to-thin boundary continuum—not only overall but also according to a dozen subscales. The individuals who believed, by the end of the week, that they had been successful in psi reception were likely to be at the thin end of the boundary spectrum, especially along the emotional subscale.[6]

These experiments, while interesting, share one manifest weakness. Participants in both were believers in the paranormal or at least were open to the possibility of information being obtained in anomalous ways. And although the first study made an attempt to objectively measure ESP scores, the second relied entirely on participants' self-assessment. If a link between ESP and body image and boundary type is to be pursued, a better mix of people who do and *do not* believe in anomalies should be obtained, with a greater effort made to gauge success by strictly objective criteria.

Can Feelings Be Conveyed Telepathically?

Various studies have sought to determine, in a controlled fashion, whether feelings associated with given subject matter can be conveyed to someone at another location. A typical example is the following: Participants designated as "senders" looked at a dozen drawings intended to arouse a feeling of unpleasantness, mixed with a dozen drawings intended to elicit no feeling whatsoever. As each drawing was viewed, other participants designated as "receivers" were asked to report whether they were getting a picture of something neutral or unpleasant. The experimental focus was on unpleasant feelings because the researchers assumed that people naturally respond more strongly to a threat than to a reward. They also recognized that many spontaneous psychic experiences seem to be connected with unpleasant emotional events, such as serious illness or injury. The results were exactly what would be expected by chance, with a 50 percent hit rate for each type of drawing.[7]

Similar experiments have been conducted using emotionally intense photos depicting victims of crime and war, as contrasted with considerably more upbeat pictures. Senders were told either to simply concentrate on the feeling they got from viewing these slides *or* to try to telepathically transmit the feeling to receivers in another room. The results of such studies have uniformly been nonsignificant.[8]

It should not be surprising that this research has found no evidence for emotion being communicated anomalously. Two major handicaps are evident. First, none of the studies actually examined emotion, as I have defined it. Emotion requires genuine bodily feeling as well as the expression of that feeling. These experiments, in contrast, limited participants to mentally concentrating on feelings superficially elicited from visual stimuli. At most, senders were allowed to make faces or say certain words or phrases to themselves—highly controlled responses, unlike genuine emotion. The second flaw is that these studies, by definition, are laboratory experiments. Real feeling is part of real life, and real life is spontaneous and unpredictable. The laboratory, try as researchers may, is anything but.

What is needed is a more true-to-life approach, which would constitute a more accurate barometer of whether intense feeling can bring about anomalous events or impressions. The problem is a thorny one: how to conduct such an inquiry in a systematic and potentially reproducible way?

One method would be to "take the mountain to Mohammad"—that is, conduct tests in a more natural setting such as the subject's home. Another approach follows from the random event generator experiment profiled a few pages ago: make measurements when the subjects are doing what they are prone to do. In other words, when they are genuinely acting rather than play-acting—and ideally, when they are not cognizant of being observed. The fact that teenagers have been wired to a brain imager while playing video games (and this type of naturalistic experiment is more and more common) suggests applicability here. Finally, more reliance should be placed on having individuals document their perceptions *immediately after* a supposedly anomalous impression. Given a sufficient number of such reports by any one person, they could be subjected to content analysis, which would allow for a more systematic appraisal and the ability to flag any recurrent imagery that seems especially noteworthy. For me, the bottom line is to place greater faith in people's real-life experience and their documentation of the same. Trust, but by all means available, verify.

Can Feelings Be Perceived Precognitively?

In the last chapter, several dramatic examples were given of apparently precognitive dreams. A theory was also presented as to how such anomalies could arise. In a nutshell, I proposed that time is a construct of the human mind and is, therefore, subjective. Further, I suggested that different types of time coexist: biological (metabolic), emotional (which draws on memory), and linear (consensus or clock time). Anomalous time, as defined here, is the overlap of biological and emotional time. Temporal anomalies result from a person's emotional energy radiating outward, carrying with it something essential concerning that person's self. At another point in space-time, another individual (or even the same person) can perceive the anomaly—especially if he or she is predisposed to such reception through innate sensitivity or identifying with similar core issues of selfhood.

Without reference to this theoretical framework but in agreement that precognition ought to be possible, two researchers framed experiments designed to demonstrate how feelings can be experienced "before the fact." The first of the two, parapsychologist Dean Radin, wired subjects to a device (similar to a lie detector) that measured electrical conductivity of the skin before, during, and after they viewed a random series of pictures, some calming (e.g., pastoral scenes and household objects) and some graphic (e.g., erotic and violent scenes). In essence, the subjects' reaction time was being measured—and an interesting correlation was obtained with the graphic pictures. Reaction to those scenes kicked in shortly after the participants pressed a button signaling that they were ready to view a given photo, but *before* the photo was displayed. On average, the participants' reaction to the graphic photos was two seconds ahead of their reaction to the calm photos—more a "preaction" than a reaction. This, Radin concludes, is a demonstration of presentiment and an indication of how "intuitive hunches, especially bad feelings about upcoming decisions or actions, may be due to unconscious precognitive glimpses of future emotions."[9] Unfortunately, it is unclear from Radin's paper whether the individuals most inclined to "preact" shared any particular personality

402 Evidence for the Emotional Gateway

characteristics or whether, for that matter, their reaction time to *all* the pictures was shorter than their fellows.

The second experimenter, the late Theo de Graaf of The Netherlands, based his exercise on a premise very similar to the COEX concept of Stanislav Grof. The idea was that highly emotional events in a person's childhood can sensitize him or her to experiences that bear a certain resemblance—either concrete or symbolic—to the original occurrences. An event remote in space-time, according to de Graaf, if sufficiently momentous, may stand in for an experience in the person's own life, giving rise to such anomalous phenomena as crisis telepathy, precognition, or even poltergeist-like disturbances.

The twelve participants in de Graaf's experiment were first asked to guess the sequence of symbols in a randomly arranged deck of one hundred cards. Each card had one of five symbols on it. Next, the subjects completed a questionnaire meant to ascertain the level of trauma in their childhood. Finally, they viewed a series of pictures and wrote down whether they found each picture "shocking," "comforting," "indifferent," or "arousing mixed feelings." Unknown to the participants, these pictures had been keyed numerically to the deck of cards. De Graaf and his associates found a correlation between individuals' trauma scores and their likelihood of having correctly identified the cards keyed to shocking scenes. This seemed to suggest that certain of the participants were anticipating knowledge that they did not possess until later in the study.[10]

Three weaknesses in the experiment make themselves apparent. First, the participants were a small and uniform group of university-educated mental health professionals. Second, they had listened to a seminar on parapsychological research given the day before by de Graaf himself and so might have been favorably disposed to his ideas from the start. Third, the study was by no means double-blinded. That is, while the order of the cards was not known to the subjects, it *was* known to the experimenters— and the latter could have cued the former in the initial symbol guessing.

It seems to me that approaches such as those undertaken by Radin and de Graaf ought to be pursued in earnest by others interested in the odd time shifts that human beings can evidently experience. Interestingly, mainstream researchers *are* seriously investigating a similar phenomenon known to everyone—not a time shift exactly, but a gut feeling or a hunch. Investigators such as Antonio Damasio, who are primarily interested in emotion, believe that a particular part of the brain may be responsible for making conscious decisions based on unconscious awareness—in other words, for intuition.[11]

Damasio and his colleagues conducted the following experiment: Sixteen subjects were given $2,000 each in fake money, presented with four decks of cards, and told to turn over cards from any deck. They would lose or win money depending on the cards they turned up. Unknown to them, however, two of the decks were stacked so that players would ultimately lose if they picked from those decks—even though the two decks would produce payoffs *at first.* While the other two decks paid off less at first, they were set to produce winners over the long run. The key element in the test was that six subjects had damage to a part of their prefrontal cortex (the ventromedial sector) known to be involved in making decisions. People with this condition have normal intelligence and memory, but tend to display little emotion and have trouble making sound decisions. The other ten participants had normally functioning ventromedial sectors.

Sensors were attached to each participant in order to detect any sign of anxiety. Periodically, the researchers would stop the game to ask each person whether he or she had become aware of the best strategy to win. The results were intriguing. After losing a few times, the normal subjects began to show signs of anxiety *before* picking cards from the losing decks. They began avoiding those decks well before they gave any conscious indication that the decks were stacked against them. But around their fiftieth draw, these participants began to express a hunch that two of the decks were riskier than the others. By their eightieth turn, seven of the ten normal subjects had decided to avoid selecting from those decks. The other three hadn't formed the conscious awareness, but they still chose advantageously, showing that their intuition was working.

In contrast, the subjects who had ventromedial damage never sweated or showed other anxious responses, never expressed a hunch that some decks were losers, and continued to pick from those two decks. Clearly their intuition wasn't working very well—or maybe not at all.

Damasio and his colleagues concluded that intuition must be a brain-based phenomenon. In normal individuals, they posit, the ventromedial sector coordinates unconscious awareness (including prior emotional experience) and uses this information to reach a sound decision. I suspect this model makes sense when the stimulus—in this case, a card game—is primarily mental. When the stimulus is physical, however, my intuition is that the body acts first, with feeling-tinged information *leading* the brain to decide. In either case, we have here an interesting example of emotion researchers looking at an experience that, at least on the surface, could be called precognitive.

Does Infrasound Account For Apparitions?

In chapter 6, we noted that infrasound—sound waves below the 20 Hz threshold of human hearing—may be implicated in at least some instances where individuals are suddenly bothered by inexplicably strange feelings. I say "where" because proximity to defined infrasound sources has been linked with dizziness, middle ear pain, chills, nausea, and even, as we noted, the disturbing feeling of a presence or the apparent sighting of an apparition.

Infrasound has intrigued quite a few people over the years, most recently a team of musicians, acoustic engineers, and psychologists in England. In 2003, they framed a remarkable experiment testing the notion that infrasound is the cause of these peculiar feelings. They constructed a huge "infrasonic cannon" and placed it in the back of a concert hall in South London. The 750 people in the audience were asked to record their impressions as four separate pieces of music were played: two of them laced with infrasound and two of them not. The audience was not privy to which was which, and the infrasound was masked by the music in any case. (As a side note, the concert goers were not drawn from the paranormally inclined. A questionnaire administered beforehand disclosed that 42 percent were "believers"—a number slightly less than that of the entire British public.[12])

The results affirmed that infrasound can, in certain people, trigger shivers down the spine, a sense of going hot and cold, an increased heart rate, a heightened sense of smell, headache, an odd feeling in the stomach, a feeling of compression around the head and neck, and other physiological reports. Emotional complaints included feeling anxious, panicked, excited, and sorrowful as well as "a sudden memory of emotional loss." Up to 62 percent of the audience members recorded such perceptions.[13]

What I find particularly revealing is how many of the responses leaned toward the physiological as opposed to the overtly emotional— and that nary an apparition was reported. The infrasound didn't even heighten people's emotional responses to the music they were listening to! This is surely counter to what the researchers expected since the rumbling of pipe organs in church has been linked to spiritual feelings. But no one reported the sort of overwhelming fear that would have caused a person to bolt from the hall. Nor did a single concertgoer complain of feeling a presence lurking about. And just one audience member recalled an especially vivid memory of the sort that neurosurgeons have been able to elicit on the operating table.

This "apparition gap," as I'll call it, is odd considering that one hypothesis behind the infrasound-ghost connection is that apparitions are caused by the low-pitched sound literally vibrating the eyeballs.[14] Was the infrasonic pitch of this experiment too low? (It was just 2 Hz below the 19 Hz level identified by the intrepid Vic Tandy in two locations he investigated.) For me, the results of this superbly designed and controlled experiment indicate that something more is at work in haunted locations than just infrasound. I suspect that the infrasound acts as a tuner or amplifier for other environmental influences that trigger more profoundly emotional reactions. Perhaps such anomalous influences, if they are found, could be characterized by the infrasonic "trace" they make. Further dedicated and innovative research is needed to ferret out the interplay.

Can Electromagnetism Affect the Perception of Feeling?

In chapter 6, I proposed that electromagnetism, while not synonymous with feeling, might nonetheless be a *conveyance* for it. Specifically, that the Earth's atmosphere might harbor the energy of intense and dissociated feelings, affecting those individuals sufficiently sensitive to perceive the information. Both the accessing and the inherent *meaning* of the information would be felt by the witness as something uncanny.

Some evidence exists to support this hypothesis. To begin with, we noted that many of our fellow creatures seem to possess a radiation sense beyond what we take for granted. Loggerhead turtles, for instance, are able to perceive the direction and strength of the Earth's magnetic field. Numerous anecdotes support the proposition that many kinds of animals—both wild and domestic—react to impending natural disasters, whether through infrasound or other, possibly electromagnetic, means. But human beings may not be completely outclassed in this regard. Bees, dolphins, and people are among the species that have magnetic material *within them:* in our case, our brains contain the mineral magnetite; and bones in our sinuses contain deposits of ferric oxide.[15] So when some people occasionally tune into a radio broadcast through their dental work, hear radar as buzzes or hisses, or apprehend swishing or crackling sounds in conjunction with the northern lights, they are manifesting an extreme form of electromagnetic sensitivity.

Furthermore, science has known for some time that behavior can be modified by zapping the brain with electric or magnetic pulses. As an example, electroshock therapy has long proved successful in remedying depression (though precisely why remains a mystery). As we have seen through the tests of Michael Persinger in Canada, magnetic pulsations directed at the brain can induce a host of curious perceptions—including sensed presences—that subjects react to in bewilderment, anger, or fear. Taking a much different research tack, neuropsychiatrist Mark George of the Medical University of South Carolina—a leading proponent of transcranial magnetic stimulation (TMS)—believes that modest stimulation of neural circuitry holds great promise for enhancing learning and memory, not to mention overall well-being.[16]

It would be ideal if neuroscientists could expand their vistas to devise experiments that take into account individual differences in electromagnetic sensitivity and the way that feelings might be influenced by the application of different types of radiation. One researcher interested in such matters is Paul Stevens of the University of Edinburgh. He exposed subjects to low-frequency magnetic fields while they rated certain images for their feeling content (either "unpleasant," "neutral," or "pleasant"). The participants did not know when the fields were operating and when they weren't. At the same time, the electrical conductivity of their skin was measured so that their arousal levels could be compared with the images being viewed. Two interesting results were obtained. On the one hand, when the magnetic fields were operating—and contrary to Stevens' expectation—participants tended to rate the pictures more positively. At the same time, the skin conductance of most subjects (48 percent) *decreased*. Of the balance, 34 percent of the subjects exhibited no apparent reaction, and the skin conductance of 17 percent *increased*.[17] Distinct individual differences were thus observed.

An important side note: those 17 percent of the participants whose arousal level increased tended to rate the images more negatively. Stevens considers the individuals so disposed to have what he calls a "labile physiology," akin to what we mean by thin boundaries. He infers that one's neurobiology must play a key role in the way feelings are assessed.[18]

Do Animals Contribute to Anomalies?

At the end of chapter 5, I related a remarkable experience my family had a couple of weeks after our beloved cat, Dalton, had left this existence. At precisely the time I was kneeling down next to my daughter, summoning the resolve to tell her what had happened, all three of us heard a series of knocks at the front door, just a few feet away. My wife immediately went to open the door but found no one there: not a child, not a salesman, not a mischievous teenager, not an animal. We were completely at a loss for an explanation, but were struck by the coincidence with the situation at hand. Nothing remotely similar has happened before or since.

Since animals are sentient and share many biological characteristics with human beings, it seems possible that the same anomaly-producing

dynamics we have considered in this book might well apply to animals—
at least some of them. The following would be necessary:

1. The animal would have to have a higher-level thinking and reasoning center in its brain (similar to our orbitofrontal cortex) that, at
   least on occasion, could countermand inputs from the emotional
   portion.
2. The animal would need to forego the catharsis (that is, the energy
   release that takes place through spontaneous shaking and trembling, profuse sweating, and deep breathing) that is characteristic
   of creatures in the wild after they have escaped a life-threatening
   encounter.

Presumably only mammals have the bodymind configuration and
neural apparatus required to hold dissociated energy in the body along
with an issue or preoccupation in the brain. If the creature were capable
of experiencing the more complex or nuanced combinations of thought
and feeling that characterize human beings—such as embarrassment,
guilt, pride, apprehension, or regret—then such a psychosomatic state of
affairs might be possible.

Much evidence can be seen to support this conjecture. Start with
the commentary that "group-living mammals with complex brains lead
rich emotional lives." This statement issues from no less qualified a
source than famed primatologist Jane Goodall.[19] She offers two examples:
"Young animals, human or otherwise, show such similar behavior when
they are well fed and secure—frisking, gamboling, pirouetting, bounc-
ing, somersaulting—that it is hard not to believe they are not expressing
very similar feelings. They are, in other words, full of *joie de vivre*—they
are happy. [Additionally], I have watched chimpanzee children, after the
death of their mothers, show behavior similar to clinical depression in
grieving human children—hunched posture, rocking, dull staring eyes,
lack of interest in events around them. If human children can suffer from
grief, so too can chimpanzee children."[20]

It's bad biology to argue against the existence of feelings in other animals. After all, Charles Darwin's ideas about evolution suggest that differences among species are differences in *degree rather than kind.* Emotions, he believed, have evolved everywhere to carry out the same functions as they do in humans, for example, as a catalyst and regulator of social interaction.[21]

Mammals, in particular, are quite likely affected by stress in the same manner as we are and are similarly impelled to express their emotions. Remember, in chapter 10, how even rats seem to sigh with relief and elephants can be affected by a condition resembling, if not identical to, PTSD. If we presume that feelings in mammals comprise energy as they do in human beings, then these animals might be subject to the same internal dynamics we have conjectured for humans, whose own feeling energy short-circuits, dissociates, or is held in abeyance.

Consider the following anecdotes regarding dogs and cats and the role they appear to play in anomalous occurrences:

- A couple had owned an Irish setter for nearly fifteen years when he died. Three days after they buried Red, the woman awoke from a realistic dream of seeing Red running across hills to hear a characteristic barking. Her husband, who had also been awakened, heard the same thing; it sounded exactly like Red. On three more occasions the wife would awake from dreams of Red to hear the barking, and her husband would also hear the sounds (although he had not been dreaming of Red). A short time later, the couple brought a German shepherd puppy into their home and, from that day forward, the mysterious barking ceased.[22]
- A husband and wife each saw a medium-sized house cat in their new home. In one case, it raced by the wife and darted into an adjacent room; in another, it sat by the refrigerator as if anticipating a meal. In both instances, the cat vanished after a moment or two. At the time, neither spouse had spoken to the other about their sightings.[23]
- A woman whose dog had died heard him whining and crying all night long. This continued periodically over the next two months;

her husband said that he would hear Butch barking loudly at the back door. A neighbor (who knew Butch was deceased but not about the alleged sounds) told the couple about a dream wherein the dog was crying at the door wanting to be let in. Additionally, the owner related that she would hear a floorboard outside the bedroom squeak in the same way, and at roughly the same time, as it did when Butch was alive and wanting to be let out in the morning.[24]

- A dog brought into a supposedly haunted house refused to go up a flight of stairs. His fur stood on end, he growled, and he gave other indications of being frightened or agitated. A group of human investigators went up the stairs themselves, and several felt dizzy or affected by other strange sensations before they reached the top.[25]

- Both dogs and cats have been described as refusing to stay in certain rooms where someone has died or where a deceased person used to live.[26]

- A man woke from a nightmare involving a desperate struggle as if he was drowning, and he felt an apprehensive sense of terror and despair. He then had a second dream involving his dog, Bob, who seemed to be lying in water near some brush. The dog's body was subsequently found. He had been hit by a passing train while on a bridge that crossed over water.[27]

- A mother and daughter were having dinner when they became aware of a large, white cat under their table. They stood up and pulled back one of the chairs; the cat obediently walked out from under the table and down a hallway, where it stopped and looked at both women. It then seemed to dematerialize. A year later, the pair was surprised to see the same white cat when they were visiting the daughter's sister's house. As before, it walked in front of them and then watched them before dissolving from view.[28]

- A cat that died of feline leukemia still "visits" her owner at various places in her home and can be felt jumping onto the woman's bed in the mornings.[29]

- Speaking of felines, I can relate one other personal anecdote. When

I was single, I was up late one night reading in bed. At some point I got the feeling of a presence in the room, about ten feet in front of me. About this same time, Dalton, who had been laying on the bed, looked in the same direction, jumped onto the floor, and scooted underneath the bed. (He had never acted that way before, nor did he after; he was always the ruler of the roost.) The uncomfortable feeling persisted for nearly a half hour. To help it abate, I put on a Walkman radio and sang along to the music. I came to notice that the oppressive feeling had passed, and as if on cue, Dalton reappeared from under the bed.

- Unseen animals—or something akin to them—figure in many poltergeist cases. Bedding is reportedly moved as if by a small creature, and sounds are sometimes heard that are similar to a dog's panting.[30]
- Pet owners sometimes relate that their cat or dog seems to know when a family member has been hurt or has died off the premises. A poodle, for instance, was said to have become frantic at about the time that its family's eldest son was seriously injured in a car accident. Another report suggested that a Siamese cat began to cry in distress at exactly the time that his German shepherd companion died on the operating table at a veterinary hospital.[31]

It's interesting to note that, in about a third of these cases, the person involved perceives the pet *through a dream*. I suggest that the same bodymind process we examined in chapter 7—prodromal dreaming—might serve to convey an animal's feeling state to a human (or even another animal) with whom it has, or had, an emotional connection. The conscious "flip side" to this concept, we learned, goes by the moniker telesomatic, which is intended to describe a person's presumed ability to register another's pain or other intense physical state, at a distance, in his or her own body.

Veterinarian Michael Fox has coined the term *empathosphere* to describe a "universal realm of feeling that can transcend both space and time." He suggests that animals are more empathic than people and that their sensitivity exceeds our own.[32] If this is so, I presume it's because animals' consciousness is what has been termed primary: they are aware of themselves and their environment but less burdened by complexities such as reflection and rumination that typify human consciousness. They live "closer to the bone," one might say, than we do.

One animal ethologist, Jeffrey Moussaieff Masson, has remarked that animals possess feelings of "undiluted purity and clarity" (at least at times), compared with the "seeming opacity and inaccessibility of human feelings."[33] A former psychoanalyst, he wonders if the human ego doesn't get in the way of our experiencing feelings as directly and in as undistilled a way as other animals do. Animals, Masson says, ". . . [demonstrate] their feelings constantly. Annoy them, they have no hesitation in showing it. Please a cat, it purrs and rubs itself against you. What could appear as contented as a cat? A dog wags its tail and looks more genuinely pleased to see you than any human. What could appear as happy as a dog? Could anything seem as peaceful as a cow?"[34]

Beyond the ego itself, Masson provocatively suggests that *language* might be a sort of curse to our species as well as a blessing because "language sets [feeling] at a distance, that the very act of saying I am sad with all the connotations that the words have, pushes the feeling away a little, perhaps making it less searing and less personal."[35] He concludes that animals may well feel things more intensely than we do. If this is so, I can't help but wonder whether their feeling *energy* might consequently be greater.

As an example, Masson draws attention to some animals' capacity to express pure, unbridled joy. Take birdsong: anyone who has awoken to hear birds twittering on a spring day catches a sense for what feeling might be present beyond any communications function or territorial pronouncement. Thus, naturalist Joseph Wood Krutch conjectured, "Perhaps certain of the animals can be both more joyful and more utterly desolate than any man ever was." (He also opined, "Whoever listens to a bird song and says, 'I do not believe there is any joy in it,' has not proved anything about birds. But he has revealed a good deal about himself.")[36]

With regard to the "desolation" to which Krutch referred, I clearly recall a lion my daughter and I once saw imprisoned within a rather small chain-link fence: it was pacing back and forth monotonously and with an evident degree of frustration (one might even say misery). An animal denied the use of its natural abilities—to hunt, to soar, to climb, to dash—is almost surely forced into a pathos made worse by its inability, through language, to explain its predicament to itself.[37]

Darwin, in his book *The Expression of the Emotions in Man and Animals,* was unafraid to speculate on what animals might feel. More than one hundred years later, evolutionary and behavioral scientists are giving credence to what he observed and intuited. Evidence has accumulated of many species (e.g., dolphins, dogs, wolves, horses, chimpanzees, baboons) feeling sorrow, grief, or dejection. Elephants may even understand—and be moved by—the concept of death. Indeed, scholars consider elephants the "poster species" for animal emotions. Studies indicate with a fair degree of certainty that they have intense experiences comparable to human feelings of joy, anger, love, exuberance, delight, compassion, and alas, sorrow and grief.[38]

Just as remarkably, embarrassment or shame may be felt by species as diverse as chimps and macaws, and guilt by dogs. (Anyone who has ever owned a dog can surely attest to the latter.) The evidence of shame and guilt is highly significant because these emotions, at least in humans, connote not just an awareness of self but also a sense of having deviated from the social norm. This, in turn, suggests at least the possibility of a *reflective capacity* in these creatures.[39] If that is the case, the nuanced combinations of thought and feeling that characterize human experience (e.g., regret, longing, jealousy, melancholy) may be within their purview—and, with them, the sort of intrapsychic conflict that I've implicated in human-created anomalies.

We know, too, that biochemicals such as oxytocin, epinephrine, serotonin, and dopamine—which manifestly influence human feelings—are found in other animals as well. And of course the more primitive parts of the human brain, including the limbic portion that mediates feeling, have their counterparts in other animals' craniums and nervous systems. Recognizing these associations, Voltaire—who did not know about the limbic system—in the 1700s trenchantly addressed himself to "you who believe that animals are only machines. Has nature arranged for [an] animal to have all the machinery of feelings only in order for it not to have any at all?" Today, neuroscientist Jaak Panksepp, widely known for his research into the neurobiology of emotion, declares that "the evidence is now inescapable: At the basic emotional level, all mammals are remarkably similar."[40]

Another correspondence between human beings and other animals we should expect to see is empathy. Let's begin with the fact that mirror neurons—those cells in the brain that fire in response to the same actions one has performed being performed by someone else—were discovered not in humans but in macaque monkeys. Mirror neurons play a key role in empathy. Ergo, we have scientists' observations of empathetic behavior in species from monkeys to mice.[41] I have plainly seen a touching display of empathy on the part of my wife's cat Persephone who, several years ago, whirled around me in evident alarm and concern after I tumbled down a flight of steps and landed in a painful heap.

It would seem that the sentient world is connected, as Fox has proposed, in an empathosphere—especially if one accepts the possibility, outlined in the previous chapter, that intense, dissociated feelings can reach out through space-time. In this regard, let's consider man's best friend and ask why dogs seem to recur as apparitions far more frequently than do other animals.

First, it's a given that dogs—at least some of them—harbor terrific feeling energy, as their seemingly boundless delight and undisputed dejection will attest. Second, dogs are pack animals, used to living in groups and attuned to all the emotional signals and expressiveness that communal living entails. When denied the opportunity to develop as part of a canine pack, they will project similar associations onto their human families. Third, dogs and their owners display a "strong reciprocal social bond . . . clearly based on mutual respect and feeling."[42] When you add these elements up, you get high feeling energy in tandem with loyalty and devotion: the same characteristics that exist between blood relatives, close friends, even fellow soldiers. Dogs tend to become part of our families, as much because of the love they are able to impart as the care and affection bestowed on them. It's very much a two-way street. So it shouldn't be surprising that a dog could both apprehend feeling energy in the external environment and contribute to anomalies itself. I could easily interpret a dog's unwavering loyalty to its owner as a "preoccupation held in the brain," which is one of the two ingredients that I have defined as necessary to produce anomalous effects.

Raymond Bayless, the author of *Animal Ghosts*, wrote, "The question . . . of both human and animal haunting is fundamentally one and the same problem."[43] I regard his observation as correct. One might even entertain the heretical thought (perhaps not so astounding at this point) that, to the extent any creature manifests as a ghost, it bears a neurobiological similarity (as a species) to human beings and holds a close emotional tie with one or more of its human family members.

Ultimately, we homo sapiens would do better to ask, as Voltaire did four hundred years ago: Is there any reason to suppose that another species doesn't feel x, y, or z? Rather than: Can we prove that they do?[44] A fuller understanding of what feelings other animals experience—in tandem with the underlying brain/body dynamics—will, I suspect, prove far more meaningful than ascertaining solely what their cognitive capacities are.

What Accounts for Out-Of-Body Experience?

Now we come to what may be *the* most puzzling of all perplexing anomalies: so-called out-of-body experience (OBE). While readers may be familiar with Raymond Moody's groundbreaking 1975 book *Life After Life*,[45] the documentation of ostensibly out-of-body perceptions actually began some twenty years earlier with Hornell Hart, a Duke University sociologist. Hart analyzed about one hundred cases where people had claimed not only to depart from their bodies but also to manifest to others as apparitions. His work was followed up by Robert Crookall, a British geologist, in the early 1960s. Crookall was interested in any and all out-of-body accounts and eventually collected over one thousand of them. Two other researchers became active in the late sixties: John Poynton, a university professor in South Africa, and

Celia Green, a British psychologist. Poynton analyzed some 120 accounts and Green five times that many.[46]

So by the time *Life After Life* was published, a fair amount of investigation had already been conducted regarding OBEs. Consensus points included the following:

- While many individuals recounted their OBEs as having occurred while in a relaxed state, others said they arose under conditions of stress, illness, accident, or surgery.[47]
- People variously felt themselves in some sort of body, in no body at all, enshrouded by a mist, light, or fog, or at one with the mist, light, or fog.[48]
- Most everyone emphatically distinguished their OBE from a dream. Nonetheless, OBEs often occurred when a person was dozing or beginning to wake up—periods that, as we have seen, are conducive (in some individuals, at least) to the sudden onset of subconscious imagery. In the semiconscious state, these hypnagogic or hypnopompic images appear quite strange and with no obvious tie to the person perceiving them. In some cases, however, the imagery can evidently develop into an OBE. Indeed, some people claim to be able to induce an OBE through their "lucid" awareness of, and control over, such dream-like imagery.[49]
- In their out-of-body state, some people may decide to travel to a place and suddenly find themselves there, whereas others will experience the trip itself, passing effortlessly through walls and doors that normally impede the embodied traveler.[50]
- Individuals undergoing an OBE may claim to manifest as an apparition to people they know, or to be completely invisible and incommunicado. For example, in experiments tried informally, certain people claimed to have been seen as an apparition without their "subject" being tipped off that they would try.[51] In the absence of anything plainly visible, a feeling of a presence may still be reported. ("It was an indescribable feeling of the room being 'full' as opposed to 'empty,'" one observer commented.)[52] A set of

experiments at Duke University during the 1970s indicated that the person attempting to manifest through an OBE apparently had a calming effect on his pet cat, although his efforts with human observers were inconsistent.[53] In one especially intriguing case, a husband challenged his wife (who had a history of OBEs) to "visit" him during the night; he reportedly woke up suddenly toward dawn to see his wife's figure, "wearing a nightdress, its face . . . extremely pale, almost white," moving about at the same time as his wife was in bed, sound asleep.[54]

- People sometimes claim to have had a physical interaction with their environment during an OBE, such as picking up a flower, dropping a vase to the floor, or even kissing a loved one.[55] Occasionally their accounts are affirmed by an observer on the scene, but at least as often the claim of having carried out some verifiable physical action during the OBE turns out to be mistaken.[56]

- People who report OBEs often relate that they undergo a momentary blackout at the moment they perceive they are leaving or reentering their body.[57]

- Sometimes when "outside" of the body, a person may see, hear, and otherwise sense the same reality as usual, while in other cases that reality is distorted in color, shape, or content.[58] For example, an individual who had frequent OBEs reported, on one occasion, seeing his living room furniture rearranged, although it had not been.[59] Other people report that their sight is blurry.[60]

- Just as interestingly, the quality of perception seems to be independent of distance. An individual claiming to have traveled two thousand miles, for example, may report his or her surroundings with the same level of accuracy (or inaccuracy) as someone else purporting to travel two miles.[61]

- Individuals who have been monitored during an OBE show a marked dampening of electrical activity in the brain, while heart rate and other indicators of their autonomic nervous system remain normal.[62]

- OBEs are far more common than one might think. In a European study of some thirteen thousand people, almost 6 percent indicated they'd had an OBE.[63] A 1974 survey of the adult residents of Charlottesville, Virginia, plus students at the University of Virginia, disclosed much higher numbers. Fourteen percent of the townspeople and 25 percent of the students claimed to have had at least one OBE. Most startlingly, 83 percent of those who reported having an OBE said the experience had occurred *more than once*.[64]

Now, let's bring this data down to earth a little bit. The following pair of accounts will convey, first, what a spontaneous OBE is like (not as scary as you might think), and second, how one husband reacted to his wife's planned out-of-body excursion (and to him it *was* scary). First, here is the spontaneous report:

> One night while lying in bed I became gradually aware that a roll of what I will call "mist" was gathering against the ceiling and wall directly above my bed. It was stirring, very gently, in a somewhat rocking motion. . . . I could feel its presence and its motion as though I, Helen, *was* the mist. . . . I was not asleep. I was not dreaming. I could see it there, but not with my bodily eyes. . . . There was no fear, no questioning—simply a quiet acceptance of the fact that I was outside my body, hovering over it. There was a sensation of pushing against the ceiling, lightly, and of being stopped by it, as a toy balloon which has got away would be stopped. . . . [The experience] ended when I was aware of being back in my body.[65]

Next, an account of a wife's "purposeful" OBE as described by her baffled and concerned husband. He is watching from a couch as she meditates on their living room floor.

> I saw my wife's face begin to elongate, and then a vapor-like substance began to rise above her, taking on the resemblance of the shape of her face and shoulders. . . . I wanted to stop her but was too

stunned to move . . . this substance rose higher, very slowly. . . . It then stopped almost as spontaneously as it began. The whole occurrence took only about 15 or 20 seconds, but it was enough to scare the hell out of me.[66]

This whole subject came to the fore publicly as a result of Moody's book. *Life After Life* focused on one category of out-of-body awareness, that of near-death experiences (NDEs). Moody identified themes common to many peoples' perception of floating out of the body as a result of life-threatening accidents or severe medical emergencies. The typical pattern included the following: looking at one's body from above; hearing the commentary of the doctors, nurses, and loved ones immediately present; going through a dark tunnel; meeting deceased friends and relatives; encountering a being who emanates love, comfort, and understanding; conducting a "life review" wherein all the major and minor episodes in one's life seem to replay instantaneously; realizing that it is not yet time to "cross over"; returning to one's body; and proceeding to live life with a broader perspective—greater calm, less fear, renewed wonder—than the person did before.

Since Moody's book, many others have appeared, describing not just *spontaneous* perceptions (typically associated with major stress, accident, or illness) but also *intentional* out-of-body journeys in which the practiced individual travels more or less immediately where he or she wishes to go. Opinion on the validity of these reports is, as one would anticipate, split down the middle. One camp embraces the possibility of life after death, while another attributes such perceptions to fantasies generated by the brain.

Just where in the brain such fantasies might be generated is the subject of current research. One team of investigators has implicated the parietal lobe, located in the upper and rear part of the skull, as the guide for the body's orientation in space. When this area is running smoothly, they find, "there is a sharp distinction between self and non-self." But when inputs to the region are minimized, "that division breaks down, leading to a blurring of the lines between feeling in-body and out-of-body."[67] A variety of mystical and religious experiences, in which people perceive themselves at one with nature and the universe, are attributed to a quieting down of this "orientation area."

Attention has also focused on the temporoparietal junction (TPJ), on the right side of the cortex. In 2002, Swiss neurosurgeon Olaf Blanke fixed on this area in a most unexpected way. As he was preparing a forty-three-year-old woman for epilepsy surgery, he inadvertently triggered an OBE. The woman reported that she was "sinking into the bed," then "falling from a height." With stimulation of the angular gyrus—a spot just behind the TPJ—she could "see myself lying in bed, from above, but I only see my legs and lower trunk." Another occasion prompted "an instantaneous feeling of lightness and floating . . . close to the ceiling."[68]

Blanke, who practices at University Hospital in Geneva, subscribes to the theory that OBEs are the result of a breakdown in the brain's integration of sensory signals. The TPJ normally weaves together information about our body's location and balance, registering where one body part is in relation to another at any given moment. Disruption of this process can induce the sense of floating so often reported in OBEs, he surmises.[69]

Other researchers have pointed to oxygen deprivation and the drugs used in anesthesia. Both can trigger elements of the OBE—as, for that matter, can recreational drugs such as LSD, mescaline, and ketamine. The latter is often cited by researchers seeking a material explanation for OBEs. Ketamine was used as an anesthetic during the Vietnam War but was discontinued after soldiers complained about sensations of floating above their body. Subsequent experiments showed that it could produce the various features cited by people who report NDEs. If ketamine or other drugs can produce such perceptions, goes the argument, then other OBE reports must be similarly hallucinogenic. Here's the rub, though: people under anesthesia but not close to death have far fewer OBEs than individuals who come close to death without being under anesthesia. So, how can the drugs themselves be the source?[70]

The bigger question—at least for OBEs that take place when a person is clinically dead—is: How can a person whose brain has ceased functioning have any perceptions at all? Such people have no pulse, no respiration, and "flatlined" brain waves during this period of time—but their remembered experiences are highly structured, easily recalled, and clear. In the words of Sam Parnia, a critical care physician at the University of Southampton, the brain "should not be able to sustain such lucid processes or allow the formation of lasting memories."[71] Consider this analogy: such people are like a computer with its power source unplugged. Such a machine "couldn't hallucinate; it couldn't do anything at all."[72]

Is the Brain the Entire Issue?

This interest in attributing OBEs to a particular spot in the brain—or a certain chemical—is reminiscent of the desire of certain neuroscientists to link phantom pain to specific neural circuitry. Both quests miss the boat, in my opinion. They inevitably confuse *process* with *cause* and ignore the much more intriguing question of what psychosomatic (i.e., bodymind) conditions these phenomena could be arising *from*. Consideration tends not to be given to the possibility that some persons might be more apt than others to have such experiences. Researchers proceed from the unspoken assumption that anyone can—indeed, will—have an anomalous experience under the right circumstances. Debate then shifts to what the perceptions might mean.

This burgeoning field of inquiry goes by the provocative name of *neurotheology*. Its tenet is that out-of-body perception, including expansive spiritual and meditative experiences, is the inevitable result of brain wiring.[73] Of course, just because an experience has a distinctive pattern of brain activity does not mean it is solely a perception, having no external reality. Radiology professor Andrew Newberg, of the University of Pennsylvania, draws an analogy with, of all things, a pie. The fact that an industrious neuroscientist could produce a brain scan of "your brain on apple pie" doesn't mean there is no pie. According to Newberg, "There is no way to determine whether the neurological changes associated with spiritual experience mean that the brain is *causing* those experiences . . . or is instead *perceiving* a spiritual reality."[74]

Intriguing as that question is, we artificially limit ourselves with a brain-based explanatory framework. We should look, instead, to the entire bodymind and its energetic processes. These are, after all, what propel any OBE, NDE, or mystical experience. No one has these perceptions without at least starting from a foundation of physical existence. And we should begin with the incontrovertible fact that not everyone who is near death will have out-of-body perceptions. Estimates of the percentage of people who do range from 8 to 12 percent.[75] The latter figure comes from a landmark study published in the prestigious international medical journal *The Lancet*. A Dutch team followed 344 patients who were near death and then died clinically (i.e., were not breathing, had flat EEGs showing no electrical activity in the cortex and fixed, dilated pupils indicating no brain stem function). If one considers that a "crisis" OBE is caused by the dying brain, then every one of these people—all of whom subsequently revived—should have reported such perceptions. Just 12 percent did, however.[76] The leader of the team, cardiologist Pim van Lommell, ponders the implications.

> How can a clear consciousness outside one's body be experienced at the moment that the brain no longer functions during a period of clinical death? . . . Near-death experience pushes at the limits of medical ideas about the range of human consciousness. . . . The current concept . . . states that consciousness is a product of the brain. [But] could the brain be a kind of *receiver* for consciousness and memories, functioning like a TV, radio, or a mobile telephone? What you receive is not generated by the receiver, but rather electromagnetic informational waves . . . that are always around you and are made visible or audible to you by the brain and your sense organs.[77]

This speculation may be a bit premature. For the moment, let us examine more closely the 8 to 12 percent of individuals who do report varieties of OBE. What is known about them? First, they seemingly fit no demographic pattern, nor did they receive any particular type of medical treatment.[78] Their psychological makeup, though, is another story. Research on individuals who tend toward mystical experience suggests that their personalities are open-minded, fantasy-prone, dissociative, and perhaps transliminal (i.e., having a propensity for unconscious material to cross over into consciousness).[79]

Psychologist Kenneth Ring has interviewed and administered personality surveys to hundreds of people who report having had at least one OBE. He links their experience to "a history of child abuse and trauma," "development of a dissociative response style," and "the trait of psychological absorption." Ring further characterizes these individuals as "psychological sensitives with low stress thresholds" who were "already oriented that way as children." He finds that many "appear to cause a veritable epidemic of electrical mishaps," an observation seconded by other near-death researchers.[80] In some cases, these people experience synesthesia; many more of them suffer from migraines.[81]

Near-death researcher P. M. H. Atwater—who herself claims to have undergone three such experiences—says that, of the three thousand near-death survivors she has surveyed, nearly three-quarters report incidents of electrical sensitivity and fully 80 percent say they've become unusually sensitive to light and sound. Over half report they've become more allergic, especially to chemicals.[82] Additionally, they cite an accelerated metabolic rate, enhanced creativity, and a penchant for becoming absorbed in things more easily.[83] All these are indications, to my mind, of a thin-boundary personality. It will come as no surprise that Atwater's survey respondents also reported a high incidence of perceived psychic ability and anomalous goings-on.[84]

In assessing the evidence, I am in accord with Ring. It seems that people who have an OBE—especially those prone to multiple OBEs—fit the profile of the thin-boundary, environmentally sensitive personality to a "T." The constitutional makeup of these individuals is not merely altered by an out-of-body journey; rather, their neurobiology *predisposes* them to have it. We might speculate that the various factors that shape this personality type (e.g., heredity, prenatal influence, traumatic experiences in infancy or childhood) ultimately make certain people more likely to have a range of exceptional experiences: deeply religious, spiritual, or out-of-body. In a similar way, sensitives are also inclined, from an early age, to highly visual thinking, vivid and lifelike fantasy, hypnagogic imagery, absorption, and dissociation.

Previously, I suggested that apparitional reports lie along a continuum from the more readily explained to the extremely baffling. It is likewise probable that out-of-body perceptions fall along an axis from the purely internal to the partially external. By purely internal, I mean the type of personally generated hallucination that an individual so disposed can slip into without realizing that he or she is not actually perceiving the normal, physical world. These episodes are what Green termed "waking dreams" or "metachoric experiences" (as was discussed in chapter 8). Such perceptions could readily be taken for an OBE—and, if a person were on an operating table or otherwise facing a crisis, for an NDE.

Indeed, one researcher has advanced the novel idea that people who report NDEs aren't truly brain dead, but rather their neural activity is so minimal it goes undetected.[85] Neurologist Kevin Nelson of the University of Kentucky suggests that, when certain people are near death (or facing any kind of life-threatening emergency), they evoke a crisis response wherein their rapid eye movement (REM) state—which normally produces dream imagery when asleep—intrudes on and essentially hijacks perception. Evidence for this mechanism comes from interviews Nelson and his colleagues conducted with people who'd had a NDE. They tended to report visual or auditory hallucinations in their transition from wakefulness to sleep or vice versa. Given that the arousal system controls sleep-wake states and vigilance in general, Nelson and his team contend that some individuals are predisposed to out-of-body perceptions by way of REM intrusion. When in peril, such people will dissociate and, as part of that *fearful or highly stressed response,* mistake the imagery produced for the real thing.[86] The brain is still active, according to this theory, although our current technology judges the individuals as dead—and they themselves believe they *were* dead when they later recover.

Still, I am bothered by several recurring features of NDEs that suggest they have something other than an exclusively neural association:

- First is the sense of calm, even *elation* that so many people who have NDEs report when they are "back." This seems at odds with the numbness typically produced by dissociation as well as the overwhelming anxiety inherent in life-threatening emergencies.

- Second, people who have NDEs will often state that their perception was greatly expanded from normal—that they could see everything in the operating room at once, or in enhanced detail, or look into other locations simultaneously.[87] The vantage point is typically from above, from a corner of the room. If drawn solely from our experience—or even our imagination—this is a rather strange perspective to harbor. Shouldn't one see oneself at eye level, which is how we typically appear when we look in a mirror or at a photograph of ourselves (not to mention the way we view virtually everyone else)? Even if one accepts that a malfunction in the brain's TPJ is to blame and that our customary sense of self gets twisted around, why do people so frequently report seeing all manner of other activity from ceiling height as well?

- Third is the frequency with which people who are near death report meeting deceased friends and relatives. It might simply be that persons who are gravely ill wish or expect to become reacquainted with loved ones from an earlier time in their life. Yet surely some of us would wish to converse with Elvis, or John F. Kennedy, or Marilyn Monroe, or Kurt Cobain. I am being tongue-in-cheek here, but not by much. The preponderance of appearances by ex-loved ones seems to me quite remarkable. Why not meet Thomas Edison if you are an inventor? Richard Feynman if you are a physicist? Katharine Hepburn if you loved all her movies? Or your beloved Jack Russell terrier that departed this life twenty years ago? The list goes on and on.

- Fourth and perhaps most notable of all is the seminal and often life-changing nature of NDEs. In the unanimous opinion of those who've reported one, this experience is distinct from fantasy—even the vivid, real-as-real kind. Fantasy-prone people may lose themselves in their conjured-up worlds, but people who undergo NDEs are likely to feel profoundly transformed: psychologically, emotionally, spiritually.[88] Not only do such individuals say that it was not merely a dream or hallucination, but they often go further, relinquishing the fear of death and appreciating life all the more.

One might chalk all this up to a REM-driven fantasy, yet our dreams—as fantastic and free flowing as they are—rarely bestow such peace, convey such memorable "here's-looking-at-you-from-above" detail, or create such lasting inspiration. I therefore propose an *external aspect to the bodymind continuum*. A person may, in certain cases, dissociate to such an extent that he or she not only takes leave of the normal senses but becomes open to genuinely anomalous perception.

This "spectrum" approach would explain the many inconsistencies in OBE reports noted earlier in this chapter. There must be points within the middle of the continuum where someone suitably sensitive apprehends something other than the usual external stimuli while *also* being influenced by internally generated imagery. His or her perceptions will then differ from out-of-body experiencers who are perceiving primarily internal imagery as well as those who are registering mostly external impressions.

A fascinating idea along this line has been advanced by parapsychologist Michael Grosso. Rather than talking about specific personality traits like fantasy proneness, absorption, and transliminality, he looks at the largest possible picture: the extent to which a person is identified with his or her body. In other words, he looks at the degree to which a person either feels fully embodied (on one end of the spectrum) or feels disembodied and depersonalized (at the other end of the spectrum). He hypothesizes that different people are "placed" differently along this continuum at various points in their lives, depending on their particular neurobiology as well as what is happening to them at any given moment. For example, a woman meditating quietly may at first be attuned to her felt sense and reasonably embodied (e.g., by being mindful of her posture, her breathing, the feel of clothing on her skin, and sounds coming from nearby). But, as her meditation progresses, she may become more contemplative, paying less attention to the external world—even to her own feelings—and focusing more and more on thoughts and mental images. At this stage, says Grosso, she is less embodied and more dissociated. As the felt sense diminishes, the possibility of having an OBE increases.[89]

Grosso believes that a person having an OBE may be "a spatially extended entity, occupying and then slipping out of the body, like a hand-kerchief plucked from a vest pocket." Even more radically, he suggests that we should think of the body as being in an extended field of conscious-ness. Remove our accustomed bodily awareness, he proposes, and the uni-verse opens up to our inspection.[90] This idea, you will note, is not too dissimilar from van Lommell's speculation that the embodied brain is a kind of receiver for consciousness and memories. In a corresponding way, David Darling (who we met in chapter 12) posits that the very fact of our being embodied—with brains that reduce and modulate the flow of sensory experience—prevents us from apprehending the universe as it is. Through either an NDE or actual death, "the barrier between ourselves and the universe disappears," Darling projects.[91] All of these concepts hearken back to traditional religious belief that the body is a repository for something akin to soul.

"Soul," of course, is a term never used in science, medicine, or even the nascent field of neurotheology. "Consciousness field"—not quite the same thing—has taken its place. The newer term still engenders suspicion, if not outright hostility, on the part of neuroscientists. And understandably so, since the further we move from what we *know* in our typical daily exis-tence (e.g., sensory perceptions, feelings, thoughts), the odder things seem to get. What we know, the neuroscientists assert, is shaped, focused, and brought into definition by the brain. Therefore the brain must know *all*. But, as I have contended, the brain does not know all. Some types of sen-sory influence operate beyond the threshold of awareness. Then, too, when we dissociate, awareness is literally withdrawn from our felt sense. We sim-ply *observe* as our normal sense of time and space is held in abeyance.

The following is a case in point. It was reported by a young racecar driver whose car had been thrown thirty feet in the air during an accident.

Everything was in slow motion and it seemed to me like I was a player on a stage and could see myself tumbling over and over in the car. It was as though I sat in the stands and saw it all happening . . . but I was not frightened. . . . Everything was so strange. . . . I remember being upside down and looking backwards. And I saw the man who won the race pass under me. The guy looked up, and I remember that he had an amazed look on his face.[92]

What is happening here? Clearly the racecar driver is dissociating. Some would say that *all* he is doing is dissociating and that, in and of itself, explains the resemblance to an OBE.[93] But there is more. In the face of overwhelming shock or terror, the energetic processes of the driver's bodymind have short-circuited. It is ironic for someone who is used to exceptional speed, but he is now immobilized. His normal flow of breath, of blood, of feeling, and of energy spiked at such a high level that normal conscious awareness has given way to a sense of detachment, unreality, and disembodiment. The driver's perceptions have become strikingly similar to those during an OBE. For all intents and purposes, they *are* an OBE. That is because his normal neurobiological boundaries have been disrupted. His perceptions, you might say, are transcendent. His guard is down; he is temporarily sensitive to all manner of influence. For a few seconds, he is farther to one side of the scale of embodiment than he has probably ever been in his life. Depending on how the situation resolves itself, his feeling flow (remember our stream analogy) will either resume its course, be altered locally, or be rerouted more drastically and chronically. If the driver is lucky, he will return to being fully embodied. But if such an emergency occurs more than once—or if his constitution is naturally a thin-boundary type—his life will be forever altered. Anomalous influences are then apt to intrude, for which he may or may not have an explanation.

In this regard, let us consider an interesting study done by psychiatrist Bruce Greyson, who directs the Division of Perceptual Studies at the University of Virginia. He questioned sixty-nine people who had a history of anomalous experiences including at least one NDE. A whole host of perceptions—being out-of-body, encountering apparitions, having lucid dreams, seeing auras around people, and more—were reported to be significantly more frequent after the NDE than before. Greyson duly notes that his finding does not rule out two possibilities: that these people were more prone to extraordinary perception from the start or that, following their life-altering experience, they began deluding themselves about having psychic ability. Quite possibly either explanation could apply in a given case, with some individuals, at least, becoming more sensitive to all manner of influence than they were formerly.[94]

Now take another illustration, that of schizophrenia. Some cases, where a person's body image is distorted, have parallels with OBEs. Grosso cites one person with schizophrenia as saying, "When I am ill I lose the sense of where I am. I feel 'I' can still sit in a chair, and yet my body is hurtling out and somersaulting about three feet in front of me." Likewise, drug-induced mind-altering experience represents a form of depersonalization, according to Grosso. Someone on LSD will describe the experience as "getting high," "being spaced out," or having one's "mind blown." These correspond, he submits, to the transcendence of an OBE.[95]

Dreaming, too, is a dissociative process, Grosso contends—if for no other reason than the brain is disconnected from bodily sensation during REM sleep. We depersonalize nightly, but dismiss the phenomenon because it's a recurring fact of life. Occasionally we are stunned by a strangely telepathic or precognitive dream, which seems to indicate that our private dream world can extend out in time and space—much like an OBE. As Grosso notes, some dreams seem to share yet another characteristic with out-of-body perception: that curious overlap of privately generated imagery with consensus reality. Furthermore, in both OBEs and dreams, a person can become more lucid as to what is being perceived, even coming to *direct* where he or she goes and engaging in seemingly conscious interaction.[96] (Personally, I would wager that the more sensitive a person is—the thinner his or her boundaries—the more interest he or she is likely to have in lucidly influencing the course of a dream or an OBE. Actually *doing so* probably becomes a matter of practice.)

Grosso is careful to point out that he doesn't mean to "equate the average dream with the more striking type of OBE." He does, however, propose that "we are dealing with a group of interrelated phenomena . . .

which derive from a fundamentally similar mechanism."[97] From the vantage point I have presented throughout this book, I tend to agree. The evidence presented by lucid dream researchers offers yet more affirmation.[98]

Can Feelings Be Felt Outside the Body?

No inquiry into out-of-body perception would be complete without consideration of a final, most difficult question. If at least some OBEs *are* more than the sum of internally generated imagery—that is, if they betoken some form of bodily transcendence—how is it that people who have undergone such an experience report that they *sensed?* That they saw and heard what was taking place near their body as they hovered above? And further, that they *felt* the full range of feelings one normally does?

Research pertinent to this topic has been conducted by Emilio Tiberi of the University of Verona. He interviewed fifty-four subjects who claimed to have had an OBE. Half said they had been in reasonably good health when their experience occurred; the other half had been literally near death. They variously recalled feeling pain, hunger, thirst, heat, cold, curiosity, fear, surprise, joy, love, peace, sadness, frustration, anger, boredom, stress, anxiety, depression, embarrassment, and even sexual desire. Amazingly, some people reported that they even had sex during their out-of-body journey! (I am not sure whether people in this group felt curiosity, joy, embarrassment, or all three.) Notwithstanding the similarity of these feelings to normal, embodied existence, the subjects were unanimous in stating that what they'd experienced was different from a dream or a hallucination. Overall, one-third of the group stated that feelings were the *main feature* of their OBE. In surveying these responses, Tiberi opined that "the extraordinary power of out-of-body emotions signals the objective reality of the [experience]."[99] (This finding by Tiberi has been corroborated by van Lommell, whose team found that, among sixty-two patients relating near-death perceptions, more than half said they experienced "positive emotions."[100])

Now, consider something even more remarkable. When asked the origin of their out-of-body feelings (which are not emotions according to my definition), nearly half of the respondents answered "the out-of-body environment." This category was one of several they could have checked, and they were free to indicate more than one. Another third said that their feeling had been prompted by someone they encountered during their experience (such as a man who had felt sad upon seeing his wife crying), a third credited their own thoughts as the primary trigger, and a quarter attributed the feelings to their own abandoned body.

Here's the conundrum with these findings. If Grosso is correct and individuals undergoing such an experience are at least partially out of their body, how can sensory perception—and feeling itself—play such a prominent role? Shouldn't the dissociating person *lose* consciousness? Shouldn't "out-of-bodyness" be experienced as a formless, indistinct void, with the person unsure of where he or she is, or even *if* he or she is?

The difficulty at first appears insolvable, recalling nothing so much as the mind-body dichotomy that has so long plagued us in the West. But hold fast. Science is coming to embrace the view that there is no hard and fast distinction between the brain and the body. The skin, after all, is the nervous system turned outward. Hormones and neurotransmitters travel throughout the brain and body, linking it all in a psychosomatic network. The immune system, acting on an unconscious level, recognizes us as *us* more fundamentally than we could ever hope to do consciously. And thin-boundary sensitives are capable, as we have seen, of manifesting this indivisibility in far-fetched and yet quite palpable ways. They not only live, a good amount of the time, in fantasy, but when given a hypnotic suggestion or encountering something merely reminiscent of an earlier trauma, also are apt to change their own physiology in remarkable and unsettling ways. They raise welts. They develop—or sidestep—allergic reactions. They flatten their skin conductance, flush their complexion, alter their heart rate, and change their body temperature. Occasionally they exhibit dissociative identity disorder, creating multiple personalities with unique voices, attitudes, memories, habits, and yes, allergies. Sometimes they recall memories apparently not their own at all, complete with phobias or birthmarks supposedly corresponding to a different life. And every once in a while they meet themselves (or someone else) in time, stepping outside of our consensual public clock to confront *someone's* lifetime issues of identity and meaning.

There is a word for all this: "plasticity." It's not just neural plasticity, not just bodily plasticity, but plasticity of the self, of the ego, of the psyche. Use whatever term you like; the point is the same. I am talking about fluidity, permeability of what makes us who we are. The associated phenomena are made possible, as we have seen, by the energy of feeling. And that energy can be displaced into space-time, taking us—our selves, our memories, our feelings, our modes of perceiving—into the surrounding environment.

Recall that, when asked the origin of their "extrasomatic" feelings, half of the individuals in Tiberi's survey cited "the environment." I might add that a woman involved with another study offered this provocative comment: "I found that the physical body actually *keeps emotions from getting in.*"[101] [Emphasis mine.] Are these people simply in error? Feverish? Out of their minds? To the latter I would answer, along with Michael Grosso, yes. These people were literally out of their minds—their *bodyminds,* that is. Not everyone is able to do it. Not everyone would want to do it. Not everyone welcomes it or is heartened by it. But certain people are literally out of their minds, at least for a time. It is as if their energetic stream has, under extraordinary circumstances, overflowed its banks, carrying feeling out into the electromagnetic environment. This is the realm of ghosts, of poltergeists, of at least some OBEs, of time travel, extraordinary emotional communications, and identity overlap. It is what I have termed the *emotional gateway.*

Further evidence accrues from the truly remarkable fact that the majority of people who report NDEs say that they "returned" with an ear for melodious music: either classical compositions (from whatever musical tradition) or ambient, natural sounds. Many attest that they heard beautiful music when they were separated from their bodies.[102] One such man, an orthopedic surgeon named Tony Cicoria who was struck by lightning at age forty-two, was interviewed by the esteemed neurologist Oliver Sacks.[103]

When initially jolted out of his body, Cicoria recalled, he had "the most glorious feeling I have ever had" before "slamming back" into physicality with the sensation of searing pain from the burns the lightning produced. Weeks later, he developed "this insatiable desire to listen to piano music," which was completely out of character with anything in his past. He sought out Chopin recordings and had such a strong desire to play them that he taught himself. Close on the heels of this impulse, he started hearing music in his own head, which would intrude into whatever he was doing. The music would often come "in an absolute torrent" of notes with no breaks and overwhelm him. Cicoria became inspired—not to mention possessed—by what he began to call "the music from heaven." He also became much more spiritually inclined, reading every book he could find on NDEs, lightning strikes, and high-voltage electricity. He acquired "a whole library" on Nikola Tesla, the inventor of alternating current (who, by his own description, was extraordinarily sensitive).[104] Additionally, Cicoria thought he could sometimes feel emanations of light or energy around people's bodies.

Reflecting on this case, Sacks remarks that an NDE must be fraught with terror, inducing neurobiological upheaval and "alterations of consciousness and emotion that . . . are very profound." He considers the sudden onslaught of music in Cicoria's life—and in that of other patients he has studied—to equate to "a surge of emotionality, as if [feelings] of every sort were being stimulated or released."[105] I agree with this comparison, but relate it as much to the *emotionally conducive universe* I suspect we live in as to the neural changes that undeniably are produced by a shift as sudden, bizarre, and frightening as an NDE. Cicoria's boundaries, I suggest, not only thinned internally but externally as well. For a brief time, his dissociated energy and sense of self extended into his surroundings— and he returned with a musical "endowment" befitting the feelings woven into the very fabric of our existence.

This is also why thin-boundary, environmentally sensitive people so often perceive that they affect, and are affected by, electricity. As we saw in chapter 5, electricity is not the life force, but it is operating whenever we move a muscle, think a thought, or dream a dream. It's not exactly *what* moves us, but rather the *currency* of what moves us. We are clearly electromagnetic creatures, living in a universe whose most salient characteristic is its abundant electromagnetic energy. The people most affected by that energy are those the rest of us find the most difficult to understand.

Michael Shallis, writer of the unjustly neglected *The Electric Connection,* comments that ours is "a realm that we inhabit but do not recognize."[106] I believe that is true. The world is marvelously complex, and our place in it still subject to a good deal of uncertainty. Even the most ardent neurocentrist should not be immune to wonder, nor dismissive of new possibilities. Most of all, he or she should not cordon off the body from the map of evolving inquiry. On the contrary, the body—and all it can teach us—should be the renewed focus of our investigations. Because we are unified selves, with brain supported by body, thought underpinned by feeling, and conscious perception arising from unconscious processes, so neurophilosophy, neurotheology, and all the other nascent neuro- disciplines would be well advised to embrace the body. The feelings it encompasses could be the key to vast new understandings—if we remain open to them.

In the end, perhaps the skeptic, anomalist, and just plain Joe and Jane can agree that "there is no paranormal or supernatural; there are only the normal and the natural—and mysteries yet to be explained."[107]

13

———◆———

The Mind Reconsidered
A Meditation on Who We Are and Where We're Headed

*A new view of nature is emerging, which encompasses
both galaxies and neurons, gravitation and life, molecules
and emotions. As a culmination of centuries of studying
nature, mankind has been approaching the thorniest
subject of all: ourselves.*[1]

PIERO SCARUFFI, COGNITIVE SCIENTIST

*Until we bring sensory affect back into consideration, we
shall be fishing for consciousness in an empty pool.*[2]

NICHOLAS HUMPHREY, EVOLUTIONARY PSYCHOLOGIST

Slowly but surely, science is figuring it out; realizing that it's all connected; that "out there" cannot truly be separated from "in here"; that hard and fast distinctions between our brain and the rest of our body ultimately do a disservice to the entire organism. And that just as human beings are indivisible from the rest of creation, so our own consciousness—our awareness of being alive and our ability to think about our place in the universe—is ultimately one with our biology and our feelings.

435

For all the books that have been written on the primacy of the brain, and for all the lectures and news reports tacitly acclaiming neuroscience as king of the disciplines, glimmers appear now and again indicating that the body and its senses are actually master of the realm. More accurately, they hint that our mind is equally brain and body, thought and feeling, certainty and intuition, thorough realization and raw sensation. The mind is all of those things put together, an aggregation of capacities whose sum total is matched only by our ability to marvel. This, the most cutting-edge science is beginning to apprehend.

Consider a news item headlined "Bruised Egos Said to Cause Physical Pain." It seems that researchers at the University of California–Los Angeles wired up volunteers playing a group computer game. These volunteers were happily playing along when suddenly it appeared they had been maliciously blocked from further participation. The shock and distress of this rejection registered in their anterior cingulate cortex, a part of the brain that also responds to physical pain. This indicates that a hurt feeling, while instantly noticeable neurologically, is indeed a feeling of hurt—a visceral reaction. The physical and the mental reactions are two sides of the same coin.[3]

Here's another intriguing demonstration of that fact. Researchers at University College London found that the brains of people who are empathizing with others' physical pain also register pain themselves. The subjects in this case were women whose partners received an electric shock to the hand. The women were allowed to see the shock being administered but not their partner's facial reaction (eliminating a significant emotional cue). Magnetic resonance imaging scans showed that the women's brains lit up in the same areas as if a shock had been administered to them personally. The reaction appeared to be greatest in those who had the strongest emotional bond with their partner.[4] The results remind us of the fine line that exists between the physical and the mental—with feelings dancing along it constantly.

"In an interesting turnaround," it has been noted, "scientific, rational, mechanistic Western medicine is now taking the part of the respected elder statesman and everything 'nonscientific,' that of the revolutionary young pioneer."[5] Indeed, as Canadian physician Gabor Maté points out, among the general public, who are "ahead of the professionals in many ways and less shackled to old orthodoxies," there is little resistance to the concept that repressed emotion is a factor in illness.[6] "Intuitively, [it] fits with people's experience," he says. But the difficulty remains that clinicians, "who are into their head—by training, by inclination, by the nature of their work"—continue to resist not just the notion but also the evidence.[7]

The Dalai Lama: Case in Point

Despite the very real challenges, inroads are being forged. Consider one very illuminating dialogue taking place between West and East. The Dalai Lama, best known as the face of Tibetan Buddhism, has, for almost twenty years, been meeting with prominent neuroscientists to compare concepts of emotion, volition, consciousness, and mindfulness. This is not by accident: the Dalai Lama is fascinated by science and technology and has pushed for these meetings as much as the Western organizers. In recent years, the discussions have gone public. What is evident is that both camps have much to learn from each other as they contrast their assumptions about the mind and their knowledge of science and spirituality. A 2003 conference held at the Massachusetts Institute of Technology—and which attracted an audience of more than thirteen thousand people— thus opened with the observation that while our ability in the West for measuring, describing, and explaining the physical world is unparalleled, Tibetan Buddhism has, over 2,500 years, achieved its own insights into human nature through its emphasis on meditation and introspection.[8] Perhaps the time is near when such insights can be melded into a wider conception of how we human beings operate.

To that end, I was struck by an observation made by psychologist Paul Ekman concerning the Dalai Lama; specifically, the *feeling* Ekman got during an encounter with the latter, who, it should be mentioned, is commonly called Kundun (the presence) by his fellow Tibetans. His presence did indeed make an impression on Ekman, who considers the experience so uniquely moving as to be life altering. At one of the scientific dialogues, Ekman and his daughter had gone up to the Dalai Lama to ask him a question. In answering, the Dalai Lama took both their hands and rubbed them affectionately. Then, says Ekman, "I was inexplicably suffused with physical warmth during those five to ten minutes—a wonderful kind of warmth through my body and face. It was palpable. I felt a kind of goodness I'd never felt before in my life, all the time I sat there."[9]

The same observation is made by Marc Kaufman, a *Washington Post* writer on the sciences. He recalls that, when traveling abroad in the late 1980s, he had an opportunity to meet the Kundun.

> I remember that it was a cool day, and that I had spent some time in a chilly windowless waiting room. By the time I was ushered into the Dalai Lama's chambers, I was freezing.
>
> I was greeted by a smiling man in a sleeveless robe. He took one of my hands with both of his and slowly rubbed it. Despite the cold, despite his lack of sleeves, his hands were remarkably warm, and the warmth traveled into and through my hand and up my arm. It didn't transform my life, but it sure made me wonder how he did it.[10]

As one who has never met the Dalai Lama, I nonetheless humbly submit that it is more a matter of *who he is* than how he does it. His neurobiology, his constitutional makeup, his integrated personality—all these terms come to mind to represent the idea that the connectedness of one's heart and one's head, of one's thinking and feeling, is what is most important. Warmth connotes blood flow. Blood flow connotes the heart. The heart connotes feeling. And radiant feeling connotes a personality so comfortable in its own skin, so able to marshal and direct impulses, that the result can indeed be appreciated as a "presence."

This trait runs along the lines of charisma, but is deeper and more genuine. I remember feeling it in my contacts with the rabbi at the synagogue where I grew up. He was a rotund man with a deep, engaging voice.

His look and his manner conveyed a solidity of belief and a fidelity of word with action. Yet he was not above playfulness, as betokened by a twinkling in the eye and the occasional bear hug. And as serious as he was theologically, he had a down-to-earth interest in the welfare of his congregants, as evidenced by an outgoing manner and, yes, personal warmth. I myself felt drawn to him and always left a conversation feeling as though I had derived something important in his presence. Surely others felt the same.

I have argued that this sort of bodily grounding—one might say incarnation—is essential to any understanding of what it means to be human. The body is our terra firma, the foundation for all of our activities, be they primarily physical or predominantly mental. By this point, I hope to have shown that the neurobiology of feeling provides a link between subconscious perception and conscious thought. There is a bonus as well: variations in the neurobiology of feeling are, as we've seen, responsible for experiences and phenomena long considered anomalous. Their status as mere anomalies, scientific curiosities, or cul-de-sacs may at last be at an end.

Principles of a Revised Understanding

If these concepts are shown to hold water, the prospects are exciting indeed. The scientific study of emotion—and of the energy that animates us—may, without our fully realizing it, be placing us on the verge of a vital new understanding of the human organism and its place in the universe. This expanded view would reflect the following precepts, which I have discussed in the foregoing chapters:

1. Anomalous perceptions and odd, inexplicable happenings deserve serious investigation. They are part and parcel of life, not some detritus that ought to be ignored or carelessly explained away.
2. The brain and the body together make up the self, with myriad communications taking place throughout the organism every millisecond. Health and illness, feeling and mood reflect the

integrity of the self at any given moment, and immune function is inextricably tied to identity.

3. Formation of the self begins well before birth, although the process hardly stops there. The self comes to be through the cumulative influence of sensation, stress, and the *feeling* reaction to same. Touch is particularly important, serving as an integrator of various stimuli. The capacities of thinking, reflecting, and deciding come later and are built on an innately physical foundation.

4. Feelings, and their expression as emotions, are the bedrock on which human life exists and meaning is derived. To the extent that feelings are consciously recognized and given release, the individual is healthy; to the extent that they remain subconscious and bottled up, various forms of illness will result.

5. The body's production of energy serves to maintain the organism's vital functions, of which feeling is paramount. Bodily energy can be envisioned as a stream of feeling that flows to every tissue via the heart. The heart is, consequently, the mediator of feeling—consistent with the role attributed to it over millennia.

6. For each of us, conscious perception lies along a continuum. We are constantly being influenced by factors within (e.g., memories, felt associations, unconsciously generated imagery) as well as by external stimuli. What we consciously perceive sometimes owes more to the internal factors; at other times, the influences from within are virtually nil and we take in the world predominantly "as is." The middle part of the spectrum is most interesting as it concerns anomalies: it is a mistake to write off a given person's uncanny perceptions as nothing more than internally generated.

7. People vary in the degree to which they are sensitive to both the external environment and their internal, feeling state. Personality is thus predicated on neurobiology.

8. Thin-boundary or highly transliminal individuals with strong, dissociated feelings are more likely to manifest certain forms of chronic illness, while thick-boundary or low-transliminal people whose feelings are similarly dissociated will evidence other types

of illness. These conditions are not merely physical: they are psychosomatic because they reflect the energetic feeling state of the whole person.

9. Highly sensitive people are most likely to register anomalous influences, while thick-boundary individuals are more likely to be involved in the *creation* of anomalies.

10. Human beings are animated by electricity. Electrical oddities and distortions can betoken a disturbance in an individual's feeling state.

11. People who are highly sensitive (i.e., have a speedier and more direct flow of feeling) are more likely to demonstrate psychosomatic plasticity. This refers to the body spontaneously evidencing a memory of traumatic events or a person being able to conjure up a demonstrable physical reaction to thoughts or suggestions. In some extraordinary cases, plasticity may actually be evidenced across generations.

12. Just as our brains and bodies—the mental and the physical—are interlinked, so too the boundary between "in here" and "out there" is something other than hard and fast. The Earth's atmosphere, which seems to our eyes invisible, is actually a conveyance for electromagnetic radiation and infrasound beyond our threshold of awareness. The former may be influenced by strong, pent-up feelings; electromagnetism may also carry emotional information accessible to those who are sufficiently sensitive.

13. Finally, time is as much a component of energetic anomalies as people and places are. When the continuance of personal identity is at stake (i.e., when the self is threatened and energy marshaled to meet that danger) the stage is set for temporal aberrations. These may range from flashbacks and déjà vu to hauntings and precognitive dreams. Such distortions of time always relate to individuals, because time exists solely through our awareness of biological processes.

I am aware, of course, that many of these precepts represent a departure from today's mainstream. And that's fine, because not everything that's in the mainstream at this very moment was necessarily there a decade or two ago. Go back to the early 1980s and you'll find that the study of emotion—terrain upon which Antonio Damasio, Joseph LeDoux, Daniel Goleman, and a host of others have built their careers— was a scientific outland.[11] The whole field of neuroscience has exploded over the past decade, with our understanding of the brain being remade in the process. Similarly, our appreciation of the immune system in all its stunning complexity continues to expand thanks to pioneers in the field of psychoneuroimmunology. Why not turn the laser focus of science on the perennial conundrums of the anomalous? Surely society at large would benefit from an explanation, beyond the usual dismissals and cavalier putdowns.

We live in an incredible world. As one wit so aptly put it, "The fact that we live at the bottom of a deep gravity well, on the surface of a gas-covered planet going around a nuclear fireball 90 million miles away and think this *normal* is obviously some indication of how skewed our perspective tends to be."[12] In the same adventuresome spirit, at least one current observer of science—a writer who is squarely in the mainstream— has, in his recent explorations, "encountered so many intelligent, reasonable people . . . who believe in [the paranormal] or do not rule it out" that he was forced to review his own preconceptions.[13] As more presumed barriers between disciplines are broken down and once-sacred cows overturned, it seems quite rational to reassess our society's resistance to the anomalous and seek to evaluate what might be happening in fresh, inventive ways. What is called for, as scientists investigating the mind are coming to agree, is a sense of "skeptical enthusiasm," wherein new ideas are welcomed but tempered by serious scrutiny.[14]

The Presumptuousness of Neuroscience

But there is an impediment. Neuroscience, by its very nature, focuses on what is happening in the brain rather than what is manifest in the body. It begins with the assumption that neural activity is paramount: the crucible of our experience and the raison d'être of our lives. Neuroscientists literally look inward, to mental processes made up of neurons and synapses. They believe that if the parts can be understood and explained, then the whole can be also. They appreciate full well that the brain is an energy hog, using 20 percent of the body's blood and the same percentage of all the oxygen we breathe to nourish its one hundred billion neurons.[15] But they appreciate less fully that the heart's electromagnetic output exceeds the brain's by a factor of 5,000 to 1. As the late Paul Pearsall put it, "My brain tells me that . . . the mind is just a manifestation of itself. . . . Even discussing the possibility that the brain may not be the sole proprietor of our human essence can cause the arrogant brain to recoil."[16] Yet we have ample evidence that the immune system, with its multitudinous components located throughout the body, is at least as integral to an understanding of self.

Still, the neurocentrists are leading the charge. Leave it to one of them—the late Sir Francis Crick, distinguished Nobel Prize recipient for his codiscovery of DNA—to propose that there is not, never was, and never could be a soul.[17] The mind, in his view, is synonymous with the activity of our brains.

Now, I've no qualm whatsoever with the observation that "the three-pound human brain is the most wonderfully complex piece of matter on earth."[18] Or that its boundless intricacies are anything other than essential to any understanding of how we experience ourselves in the world. But a conclusion that the soul (or something akin to what we think of as soul) cannot exist represents an unjustified leap of scientific certitude— a leap of faith, one might even say. Equally dubious is the suggestion of some cognitive scientists that the brain may be the *very seat of the soul*.[19] This latter assertion, while tacitly acknowledging the soul as a possibility, may actually be the more arrogant as it appropriates the very term "soul" to lavish on the brain. Their tactic is rather more astonishing than what Crick called his own "astonishing hypothesis."

A word here about scientific presumptuousness—or presumptuousness in any endeavor. While a little knowledge is a good thing, and more knowledge is even better, presuming to know *all* the answers is asking for trouble. Yet, as historians of science readily acknowledge, claims are often accepted as true not so much because they are but because the given culture, at that point in time, is receptive to them.[20] In today's brain-driven, information-based, technologically avid society, we seem particularly susceptible to such dubious claims.

Perhaps this spasm of scientific "soul searching" is simply an excess of enthusiasm, an indication of how much we are learning about the brain at an ever more rapid pace. If so, we have a counterpart era to look back on. During the Age of Enlightenment, philosophers such as Thomas Hobbes and anatomists such as William Harvey (who elucidated the heart's circulation of blood) greatly advanced the knowledge of what makes human beings tick. It was an era of great activity, substantial promise, tremendous reliance on reason, and no small measure of pride. The English poet Margaret Cavendish, in 1653, puckishly characterized the emerging—and smug—consensus of the times: "That all sound, sent [*sic*], sight is created in the Braine. . . . That the blood goeth in circulation. . . . That all passions are made in the head, not in the heart. That the soul is a kernal in the Braine. That all the old Philosophers were fooles, and knew little. That the modern Philosophers have committed no errours."[21]

As if to confirm that human nature never changes, some on the scientific front lines today will state, unequivocally and beyond the shadow of a doubt that "the idea of love residing in the heart as opposed to the head will [one day] seem as absurd as bloodletting. . . . Like all emotions, love originates in the brain as surely as brilliant mathematical theorems do. We feel the passions of love because our brains contain specific neurochemical systems that create those feelings in us. We are not torn between the heart and the brain but rather between different parts of the brain. . . ."[22]

Yet others of a different bent would argue that one's brain—indeed, one's entire physical being—must be subservient to the soul, that our complex neurobiology does not stand alone, that it must be "the hardware to the soul's software."[23] I cannot agree with this stance either, because it merely begs the question, what could the soul *be*?

Sensation, Nature, and the Soul

If we have a soul (in addition to manifestly having a self), my supposition is that it would connect us with the whole of nature. The late psychologist Alexander Lowen expresses this idea as follows: "The soul of a man is in his body. Through his body a person is part of life and part of nature. . . . It is in our bodies that we appreciate the freshness of a stream, the sweet taste of pure water, the sight of blue sky, the song of a bird, the smell of a flower, and so on. . . . If we are identified with our bodies, we have souls, for through our bodies we are identified with all creation."[24]

A "gorgeous fever" is the lush description naturalist Diane Ackerman gives to our bodily life of sensation. Despite our highly developed mental capacity, she observes, "We still ache fiercely with love, lust, loyalty, and passion. And we still perceive the world, in all its gushing beauty and terror, right on our pulses." But the brain itself "is silent, the brain is dark, the brain tastes nothing, the brain hears nothing."[25] It is our body that directly takes in all the world has to offer. If human beings have souls, therefore, maybe it is more about *sentience* than consciousness. The following statement captures the idea nicely: One doesn't have a soul, one *is* a living soul.[26]

As natural creations, we delight in the plethora of sensations that is Nature. A warm breeze, a rippling stream, the hum of insects, the smell of pine trees—we easily take comfort in the natural world. If we can be considered "ensouled" creatures, then it's a short step to imagine that we're tangibly connected to the Earth itself and that our spiritual nature derives from this connection.[27] After all, spiritual life begins with a sense of wonder and awe, an experience built into our relationship with the natural world.[28]

This concept is expressed in the term "biophilia," coined by Harvard University biologist Edward O. Wilson. The Greek roots, *bio* and *philia,* together mean "love of life" or "love of living systems," which alludes, according to Wilson, to "the connections that human beings subconsciously seek with the rest of life."[29] Examples of biophilia include:

- Humans' interest in wild animals (through nature preserves and zoos)

- The appeal of house pets and companion animals
- Our attraction to baby animals—baby mammals in particular
- Our interest in gardening and keeping plants in our homes and offices
- The value of taking a stroll in the woods or getting more vigorous exercise outside
- The appeal of viewing a natural scene—in a painting or, better yet, out one's own window

Accumulating evidence suggests that, when we indulge our biophilia, we derive tangible benefit. People who own pets, to begin with, tend to have lower blood pressure and cholesterol levels than people who don't own pets.[30] Exposure to unthreatening natural settings can heal and revitalize, lessen stress, and promote recovery from illness.[31] European researchers determined that joggers who exercise in a natural setting feel better than people who burn the same amount of calories inside in a gym.[32] In one widely cited study, postoperative patients with a view of trees from their hospital rooms were found to have had a shorter stay, needed less pain medication, and made fewer negative comments to their nurses than patients whose view was merely of a brick wall. Another study showed that prisoners whose cells faced inward to a prison courtyard made 25 percent more visits to the health clinic than those who had a view of farmland.[33] In a school setting, classrooms with windows were found to enhance learning, based on a rise in student test scores. Merely being able to see the sun confers a benefit, since exposure to sunlight elevates the production of serotonin, which, in turn, can reduce pain.[34] (If you still doubt that a view to the outdoors is consequential, think of your typical office building and how workers will compete for an office with a nice view. Those who have to content themselves in a cubicle will often compensate with potted plants and/or nature-themed screen savers on their computers.[35])

None of this represents a startling new insight. After all, in the Bible, Psalm 23 relates, "He maketh me to lie down in green pastures, He leadeth me besides still waters. He restoreth my soul." And Henry David Thoreau spoke of the "tonic of wilderness."[36]

Those writers, and many others, knew that other life on Earth is literally our kin. Human beings, along with insects, flowering plants, and just about everything else except bacteria and other microorganisms, are believed to have descended from a single ancestral population of cellular organisms that lived in the oceans about 1.8 billion years ago. (Those ancient seas still flow in the salt water electrolyte solution that makes up the fluid component of our blood.)[37] Much later, our anthropoid ancestors spent their lives in intimate contact with nature. "They needed," says Howard Frumkin of Emory University, "to have a good sense for how nature worked. They needed to be able to smell the water, feel the wind."[38] Prehumans also lived in close proximity to animals, relying on them for food, clothing, hunting assistance, and (just possibly) companionship.[39] But Wilson and his writing partner Stephen Kellert of Yale University suggest that our kinship is innately emotional as well as plainly biological. Consider that even though there are certain creatures you may not love, you're not likely to be indifferent about them. Snakes often evoke fear, spiders apprehension, cockroaches revulsion, and so on. So it is with the rest of creation. Our hearts may go out to kittens and puppies, we may be awed by the majesty of lions and tigers, we may be envious of birds in flight, and we may feel happy under an aromatic magnolia tree or peaceful in a quiet meadow. These are very definite *feelings*.[40]

Now, consider how we use the word "soul" in common parlance. We may speak of a "vast, soulless" corporation. Or we may describe a certain ballplayer as the "heart and soul" of his team. Or we listen to "soul music" that conveys a mood and gets us swaying. Or we confide to a lover that we want that person "body and soul." In each case, we are associating soul with feeling. Not just any feeling, but deep feeling, core values, that which is vitally important or just plain moves us. These are not mere figures of speech, but reflections of true meaning, what our soul (if we "are" one) identifies with. As Damasio acknowledges "Feelings form the basis for what humans have described for millennia as the . . . soul or spirit."[41] This is not only historically accurate, I submit, but bodily true.

Other philosophies (e.g., Asian, shamanic, naturalistic) suggest that the energy of nature is at play within us, animating us while we live and residing in a number of levels of the biological self. The skeleton, it is proposed, constitutes the densest and deepest domain, removed generally from our conscious awareness and control. Through the bones, it is said, an individual is grounded to the foundation of life. Other energetic pathways are believed to conduct feeling through the muscles, nerves, and organs. Closer to skin level, it is suggested that each person has a semipermeable boundary through which environmental and psychological influences are either permitted or prevented from entering. The living body, in this view, possesses its own consciousness, which may or may not be apprehended by the thinking self or ego.[42]

Notwithstanding what you may think of such concepts, it's hard to argue with Wilson's point that nature is the "matrix in which the human mind originated and is permanently rooted."[43] So, of course our feelings will be deep-seated—and as ensouled creatures, we will likely feel a spiritual affinity with the natural world. Or at least we should. Kellert asserts that, if this "deep and enduring urge to connect" is imperiled or insufficient (as individuals or as a species), our spiritual well-being will suffer.[44] What he's referring to is alienation. If a person has little or no feeling for nature, it's a safe bet that one's bodily based feeling for oneself has gone awry—and, with it, the ability to empathize and care for others, whether those others are our fellow creatures or the planet that sustains us all.

Biophilia and Boundaries

The study of such connections—the inner and the outer—is known as *ecopsychology*. Among its foremost exponents are thinkers Theodore Roszak, James Hillman, Lynn Margulis, Dorion Sagan, Wendell Berry, Ursula Goodenough, and the late Paul Shepard. Hillman, in an essay titled "A Psyche the Size of the Earth," offers this provocative statement:

> There is only one core issue for all psychology. *Where is the "me"?* Where does the "me" begin? Where does the "me" stop? Where does the "other" begin? . . . The human subject has all along been impli-

cated in the wider world of nature. How could it be otherwise, since the human subject is composed of the same nature as the world? . . . An individual's harmony with his or her own "deep self" requires not merely a journey to the interior but a harmonizing with the [ecology]. . . . Perhaps killing weeds on my lawn with herbicides may be as repressive as what I am doing with my childhood memories. . . . Treatment of the inner requires attention to the outer.[45]

A similar point is made is made by psychologist Chellis Glendinning when she notes, "Regarding our minds and bodies as disconnected in health and disease, or thinking that radioactive waste buried in the Earth won't eventually seep into the water table, are symptoms of . . . fragmented thinking."[46] Another way to regard such an entrenched disconnect is, I suggest, to see them as emblematic of thick boundaries. A thick boundary viewpoint might be inclined to separate "me" and "my consciousness" from "my unconscious" and, equally, from "the world's creatures" and "the world's problems."

Thin-boundary people, on the other hand, are more likely to accept—by virtue of how they are constituted—a sense of the self in accord with what Wilson, Kellert, Hillman, and their colleagues are postulating.[47] Not only that, but some exceptionally thin-boundary individuals literally feel the world's pain. Psychotherapist Miriam Greenspan is one. In her book *Healing through the Dark Emotions,* she relates how she not only feels her clients' concerns in her own aches and pains during therapy but has also become aware of "more and more women who feel, in their bodies, the connections between the harming of the planet and their own emotional and physical ailments."[48]

Another woman puts it this way: "The Earth speaks to us through our bodies and psyches. She often cries, and many of us feel her tears and see her pain. I experience it as a force of nature entering me, like light."[49]

Such perceptions should not be taken lightly, waved away, or pathologized by those of us who don't (or can't) share the perception. We might, instead, consider the possibility that such thin-boundary people are a kind of natural bellwether as their neurobiology tends to blur distinctions between the core self and the world "out there" that the rest of us take for granted.[50] The ecology—of other people, of animals, of families, of societies, of the planet—lives in them. That ecology is fundamentally emotional.[51]

Ultimately, environmental degradation and an impoverished spirituality are intertwined. Our bodies, which have "formed themselves in delicate reciprocity with the manifold textures, sounds, and shapes of an animate earth," are our foundation for understanding that relationship as well as our surest vehicle for charting needed change.[52] The self and its fate—and the world and its fate—both depend on feeling.

A Closer Look at a Common Bias

Let us return now to the account first mentioned in the Introduction, namely, the time I was tapped "on the fly" to present welcoming remarks at a well-attended conference. While my head thought I was taking the challenge in stride, my facial expression (and probably posture as well) conveyed otherwise. My body knew what my conscious awareness had not yet apprehended. The balance of this book has been an attempt to describe other real-life situations—ones all the more remarkable and sometimes even bizarre—and to place them within a framework that literally makes sense, that is, a framework keyed to the body.

At least neuroscientists are not excluding the body, prima facie, from their explorations. Though they view the body as indispensable to the awareness of feeling (and the creation of mind), they steadfastly maintain that the brain is what triggers emotional states and that continues to be the ruling paradigm. Meanwhile, a similar worldview is conditioning futurist Ray Kurzweil's conjecture that human beings are destined to evolve into a union of man and machine, so that the resulting blend of biology and technology can do everything the brain can do, only better.[53] The Internet powerhouse Google is attempting, through its ever more efficient search engine, to bring such a change about sooner rather than later. Its cofounder, Sergey Brin, has remarked "You'd be better off . . . if you had all the world's information attached to your brain."[54] In these conceptions, the body is all but eclipsed, with feelings reduced to by-products of logical, intentional action.

Why should neuroscience operate from this basis—or, one might equally say, from this bias? Earlier, I suggested that the preoccupation with looking inward at the minute processes of cognition is simply the nature of the beast. But another factor may be at work. Most neuroscientists are men, and men are "wired" much differently from women. As we've seen, in almost every case, men have a higher sensory threshold; they literally take in less than their female counterparts. Their brains are also less holistic, with a narrower pathway between the hemispheres. Additionally, men's evolutionary heritage as hunters has undoubtedly put a premium on qualities such as analysis, planning, competition, and achievement. (One sees the same attributes on display in any sporting event anywhere in the world.) Women, in contrast, generally evidence a more highly developed emotional intelligence, a greater facility for language and communication, and a penchant for sensory cues that may elude the typical man. Thus it has been male philosophers, yogis, and others who have historically promulgated the idea of transcending the body, of attaining a "pure" mental or spiritual state where bodily feelings and earthly desires are left behind.[55] Such ideas are anathema to most women.

This is not to suggest that women would never venture into neuroscience, neurophilosophy, or related fields. In fact, this book has referenced several prominent women in those disciplines, and there are many more. I simply mean that the discoveries about emotion, which are being made predominantly by men, are bound to appear somewhat less consequential to the distaff side, which has a greater familiarity with them in the first place. In this regard, I think back to a lecture I attended at the Smithsonian Institution, where a lucid and enthusiastic Professor Damasio had just finished expounding on his theory of emotion and the latest evidence supporting it. I was walking out of the hall when I heard a couple conversing just ahead of me. "What did you think?" the man asked. There was a thoughtful pause. "Well, I guess it makes sense. I just don't understand what's so new about it," said she.

Kurzweil's vision of human beings evolving into "spiritual machines," it seems to me, could only be conceived of and championed by a man. It springs from the same fundamentally male orientation as the minds that brought us Dirty Harry, the Terminator movies and much more ominously, the Holocaust. Consider this: Who could have been more resolutely "rational" than the men who engineered the death camps in all their awful, mordant precision? The Germany of that era certainly did not lack for enlightened psychology, philosophy, or medicine. Yet the Jews—who were viewed as being subhuman, as having less than full and worthwhile selves—were systematically slaughtered.[56] So were members of other objectionable minorities, including Gypsies, homosexuals, and people with mental illnesses or deficiencies. This is the fate we risk when the thinking brain is extolled over the feeling body. These are the stakes along a slippery slope as leading thinkers contemplate that the self may not exist.

Beware the mind that places less value on feeling—literal feeling, in all its varieties and nuances—than on the notion of progress as something planned, implemented, and judged by the brain. Such ideas may begin as mere conceits, but carried out, they can become extremely dangerous. They would neglect the body's needs and the body's reality, forsaking what is most basic, what is quintessential to us. Just as no one would ever equate a disembodied brain with a person, so common sense suggests that no machine, regardless how intelligent, could be human. Machines are simply not embodied—yet embodiment is the foundation of who and what we are.

Caring for the Embodied Person

Now, a caveat. I comment, of course, as a man. One who, yes, enjoys the gladiatorial spectacle of NFL football (not to mention NHL hockey). So I am not antimale, nor am I antiprogress, especially when the progress heralds an alleviation of debilitating conditions such as depression, obsessive-compulsive disorder, posttraumatic stress disorder, Alzheimer's and Parkinson's disease, schizophrenia, and more. These afflictions wreak untold havoc on people's lives. If drugs or magnetic fields that work on the brain can reduce this suffering, it is all to the good. My concern is rather that medical science, in its zealousness for technological advancement, not overlook or devalue what is essential about the patients it is treating—namely, their humanity.

Depression, in particular, stems from a complexity of sources. While the person who is depressed may indeed be helped by drugs such as Prozac and Zoloft (which elevate and regulate the level of serotonin in the brain), those medications do nothing to address issues of feeling in the body. In fact, one consequence of their use is that feeling may actually be numbed, a development not always welcomed by the sufferer. On the other hand, the emotional issues that inevitably figure prominently in depression (e.g., traumatic experiences when young, relationships with parents, spouses and siblings, concepts about the value of a person's life) are matters *primarily* of feeling, having at least as much to do with the heart as the head.

The point is made with special urgency by Elio Frattaroli, a psychiatrist at the University of Pennsylvania, who argues that making people "better" is not just a matter of medication. Like physical pain, he notes, the symptoms of depression are signs that something is amiss inside. They should "serve as a wake-up call, forcing us to pay attention to [our] deeper needs."[57]

We have seen how intimately connected feeling is with bodily energy, with immune function, with the sense of self, with memory, imagination, dreams, and time itself. A purely neural approach, which views the individual as a set of symptoms rather than as a unified being, not only misses the big picture, but is bound to fall short in truly solving the world's problems. By that I mean not just the challenges experienced by individuals as presented to their doctors, but our planet's seemingly intractable difficulties. Fear, hunger, disease, war, oppression . . . these are elemental, primal, bodily realities. They originate from disturbances in feeling (e.g., greed, anger, bitterness) among those who are the aggressors, who then wreak emotional—and very real physical—damage on others. Those unfortunate others ultimately bear the burden, as attested by the vital things they lack (e.g., food, shelter, medical care, personal liberty) as well as the emotional reverberations in their own lives and those of their families over generations.

A more integrated conception of mind, which ranks the body and brain as equal partners, would do much better for humanity in the long run. I can think of five corollaries that would flow from this general principle. Consider, if you will, the value of each.

- A wider appreciation for the significance of feeling equates to greater import being placed on empathy in our daily lives. We would be more likely to "love thy neighbor as thyself," in other words.
- A fuller cognizance of the value of feeling one's feelings—of being consciously aware of them—translates to the resolve to experience life mindfully as well as to express one's emotions, so long as other human beings will not be injured.
- A greater understanding that anomalous perceptions have a tie to bodily reality means that the esoteric or paranormal should exert less pull on those who seem to need some transcendent "spark" to their existence. Ideally, people would be persuaded to simply live their lives, without seeking the anomalous for its own sake.
- The fact that some people are manifestly more sensitive than others—and the realization that such differences have a bona fide neurobiological basis—calls for individuals to recognize that the experience of others, while perhaps much different from their own, ought nonetheless to be given credence and stand on its own merit.
- Perhaps most important, the awareness that influences on (and insults to) the self begin before birth—and that so many of the bodymind's systems remain malleable through adolescence—requires us to treat our children well. Compassion, concern, and a decent respect to their opinions, experience, and welfare must all be part of the equation. Unless this dictum is followed, no meaningful changes are possible in the way that people (or nations, for that matter) treat one another.

The Head and Heart: A Unified View

If we are ever to achieve such aims, notes educator Joseph Chilton Pearce, a crucial distinction must be made, a distinction between *intellect* and *intelligence.* He writes, "Intellect is that impulse within us to solve problems, generally of its own making. . . . Intellect involves the brain while intelligence involves the heart. Intellect may be likened to a 'masculine' side of mind perhaps—analytical, logical, linear, inclined to science, technology, the search for external novelty and invention; while intelligence is more a 'feminine' side, open to the intuitive and mysterious interior of life, seeking balance, restraint, wisdom, wholeness, and the continuity and well-being of our species and earth."[58]

While this is an excellent point, I would argue that the choice so often presented to us, that of following the head versus following the heart, is a false dichotomy. The challenge in every age has been to integrate what we know, what we sense, what we feel, and what we intuit. Only then can we be fully human. If we allow ourselves to arbitrarily accept today's conventional wisdom—that the body exists to be led by the brain and that the glories of neuroscience will abolish suffering—then we will have succeeded only in bisecting ourselves. Just as nature is said to abhor a vacuum, so too the mind (what the Greeks termed the psyche) is not meant to be divided against itself. Psychic phenomena, which are so often derided as unreal, are actually the manifestation of processes in the bodymind that have been short-circuited. For those experiences that are genuine, the term "psychic" is accurate, because they stem from perceptions and knowledge that seeks to be made conscious and brought into the open. A dis-integrated mind is one that is ripe for psychic (one might equally say psychosomatic) disturbance.

The Anomalous Is an Open Door

Here I differ from those who intimate that anomalous perception must be, in some respect, the wave of the future. That the apparent proliferation of near-death and out-of-body experiences, or the vast increase in autoimmune disorders or in autism diagnoses somehow presages extraordinary abilities or cosmic consciousness about to be accorded the human race.[59] This seems unlikely, because in the words of psychologist Robert Ornstein:

[Human beings have] evolved to suit the conditions of a different world, a world that ended at the latest 20,000 years ago. We have not changed much during that period, although it seems a long time to us. . . . We are quite accustomed to thinking that [current-day] humans in Western society are very different from those living in remotest antiquity—cave dwellers, hunter-gatherers. . . . But to anyone who is aware of the recent discoveries in human evolution, our own time scale must be reset. Human beings, and our predecessors, evolved over a period lasting hundreds of millions of years. . . . The last 20,000 years are an insignificant amount of time. . . . We are the same people who were "designed" to live when our species . . . [roamed] the savannas of East Africa.[60]

So, neither do I side with those suggesting that mystical or transcendent experiences point humanity toward grand new vistas, nor with those who conclude, on the other side of the spectrum, that the paranormal "tells us nothing about consciousness."[61] On the contrary, I have argued that the anomalous reveals much about the building blocks of consciousness: sensation, perception, feeling, identity, cognition, and emotional expression. If this is correct, then aberrations of consciousness—repression and dissociation, to name the two foremost—can also be fathomed through the understanding of anomalies.

What is needed is an openness on the part of both camps, believers and naysayers, to the possibility that what has resisted explanation may yet be worth exploring. Those who embrace "energy medicine," who believe they possess an extraordinary capacity for intuition and healing, and who consider themselves highly sensitive or psychically gifted must realize that their abilities will not be accepted by the scientific community without systematic investigation, hard questions, and alternative scenarios. Likewise, mainstream scientists must at least recognize the possibility that some uncanny experiences may be authentic and devote to them a fair measure of rigorous yet open-minded investigation. In the words of author Louisa Young, we need a "kind of science . . . which balances what it sees with what it knows, and isn't afraid of either."[62]

For too long, accounts that baffle the mainstream have been ignored, put down, or explained away. This, of course, reflects the operation of human nature. People who do not walk a mile in another's shoes (or even a few yards) have little reason to give them much accord. We need only think of the mysterious "syndromes" evidenced by Vietnam War and Persian Gulf War veterans—from the initial incredulity on the part of government officials, to the sustained challenges to the presumption that these veterans' very physical complaints must owe to some mental or emotional disturbance, and to the conclusion that their conditions *did* have a bona fide etiology. Likewise, people who have fibromyalgia and chronic fatigue syndrome are learning that their illnesses have a basis in discernable neurobiology, and the same may eventually be said of people with clusters of other poorly understood symptoms. What is unconscionable, it seems to me, is attributing to pathology the reports of people whose perceptions are notably different than one's own (presuming one is in the mainstream).

The problem here is captured by Kathleen Noble, a psychologist at the University of Washington–Seattle who also works with "gifted" women in her private practice.

> . . . giftedness involves an affective awareness. Not one hundred percent of the time, but a lot of the women have intense radar; they're very psychic, and that can intensify introversion, if you withdraw from crowds because you always feel raw, or pick up too much energy. . . .
>
> Giftedness, per se, has often been described as pathology. I've had a lot of clients who come to me who have been told they are "too sensitive," "too empathetic," "too smart," "too verbal." . . .
>
> One of my clients is a physician who's extremely intuitive: when she was in medical school, she could make diagnoses that she hadn't the knowledge yet to be able to make, but she could read the body. And of course, what did her professors tell her? "You're so weird."[63]

As I was researching this book, I contacted many psychologists, neuroscientists, and psychoneuroimmunologists. Every single one was gracious in corresponding with me, a novice. Some voiced enthusiasm for my project, while others seemed oblivious to the implication of these ideas. Perhaps most telling, though, was a letter I received back from a prominent neurobiologist. "Let me state at the outset," she opined, "that I do not believe in the existence of paranormal phenomena. But I very much believe in the great sensitivity of sensory systems to detect information outside conscious awareness."[64]

My reaction to this assertion was twofold. First, I appreciated her candor and agreed, in principle, with her distinction between the paranormal and the extremely subtle. Upon reflection, though, I wondered why she found it necessary to disclaim the possibility of any plainly extraordinary occurrences. Presumably it owes to her standing in her profession; it is not expedient to reference the anomalous, and in fact, repeated mentions can endanger funding and jeopardize tenure. But I found myself returning to her phrase "do not believe." Why should the validity of nonordinary awareness be subject to—or automatically rejected by—personal belief? Perhaps the situation shall change if what is currently regarded as anomalous is brought, at least partially, into the realm of what we know, accept, and live with every day.

To that end, we may agree with Crick that only "time, and much further scientific work, will enable us to decide" if the mind is something more than myriad interactions in the brain.[65] I look forward to the day when neuromaging of self-described sensitives is done with the same purposefulness, eagerness, and frequency as that carried out today on teenagers playing video games, musicians playing difficult passages, and couples having sex. Yes, these experiments are actually taking place. Who would have imagined, just decades ago, that such investigations would be considered worthwhile? Yet they are. The scientific enterprise continues to evolve, and all of us who are interested in and concerned with being human should welcome its elaboration.

Perhaps then we shall be able to answer Thoreau's vexing question: "With all your science can you tell how it is, and whence it is, that light comes into the soul?" The problem may be intractable—but it is supremely human of us to want to try.

Acknowledgments

———◆———

Since this book has been ten years in the making, it's my great good fortune to have many wonderful people to thank.

First are the researchers and writers whose work has not only informed and inspired my own but who have aided me in many and sundry ways. They include: Larry Dossey (whose willingness to write this book's Foreword has meant so much and who generously offered to publish a paper of mine in his journal, *Explore*); Ernest Hartmann (a gentleman and scholar whose boundary concept provides this book's underpinning); Stanley Krippner (a man of wide-ranging interests whose enthusiasm first signaled that I might have a thesis worth publishing); the late Lyall Watson (whose intrepid forays into the biology of the unconscious I've enjoyed over the years and who sent along a message that was particularly welcomed); Joseph Chilton Pearce (whose humane discourses I've likewise followed and who provided one of this volume's first and most enthusiastic endorsements); Rupert Sheldrake (who took the time to meet with me and whose adventurous spirit of science is an inspiration); Kenneth Ring (whose engaging e-mails offered valuable feedback during the book's early going); Michael Thalbourne (whose concept of transliminality parallels my own thinking and whose correspondence over the years has provided continual encouragement); Allan Schore (whose willingness to converse with me is so much appreciated given his own trailblazing efforts in the fields of neuropsychiatry and attachment theory); Elaine Aron (whose focus on highly sensitive people pointed me in a helpful direction early on); James Hillman (who kindly corresponded with me when he didn't know me from Adam); Peter Grossenbacher (who patiently conversed on synesthesia and other issues, suggesting many useful ideas along the way); Colin Ross and Lenore Terr (who contributed valuable perspectives on dissociation and trauma, respectively); Mohammad Yunus (whose willingness to discuss sensitivity with a complete stranger was gracious and thoroughly appreciated); Elio Frattaroli (whose book on psychiatry in an age of medication opened up a cogent frame of reference); and Miriam Greenspan (whose work on the "dark emotions" offers intriguing food for thought).

Next are the parapsychologists, skeptics, and "fellow travelers" who have done much to illuminate a fascinating but neglected corner of individual experience—and who have helped me a good deal in my pursuit. They include: Bill Roll (whose suggestion it was that I undertake a sensitivity survey in the first place, and whose willingness to include me in one of his field investigations opened up a remarkable window); Sally Rhine Feather (whose invitation to speak at the Rhine Research Center I was gratified to accept and who can be relied upon for helpful responses to most any question); Lisette Coly (whose foundation provided me with the D. Scott Rogo Award, a grant that I was delighted as well as humbled to receive); James Houran (whose review of my first published paper, invitation to join a field investigation, and general good counsel have all been gratefully received); Chris Roe (whose editorship of the *Journal of the Society for Psychical Research* allowed me to publish my survey findings in one of the field's flagship journals); Caroline Watt (who sent me several papers and supported one of her graduate students in conducting an onsite investigation using the sensitivity survey); Brandon Massullo (that very student, who creatively adapted my survey and shared his findings); Christine Simmonds-Moore (who familiarized me with her research that draws on a similar theoretical base); Paul Stevens (who corresponded on electromagnetism and its possible relation to feeling); the late Ross Adey (who offered a wise perspective based on his study of bioelectromagnetics); Michael Grosso (whose intriguing speculations into the anomalous never fail to hold interest); Stephen Appel (whose open-minded correspondence on sensitivity I much enjoyed); Rick Leskowitz (whose desire to know more about phantom pain and energy healing is impressive); Cyril Smith (whose dedicated research into electrical sensitivity I have valued); Anne Silk (who generously shared materials relating to the same form of sensitivity); Albert Budden (who presented his intriguing take on a connection between allergies and electrical sensitivity); Dean Radin and Marilyn Schlitz (who passed along relevant information from their vast knowledge base at the Institute of Noetic Sciences); Bruce Greyson (who contributed many helpful comments from his own extensive experience); David Ritchey (who compared notes with me based on his project on anomalous sensitivities); Doug Richards (who shared his paper relevant to boundaries); Charles Tart (whose comment "You might be on to something" captured the refrain I heard from so many other valued sources); Stephen Braude (whose correspondence never failed to tickle in some way); Berthold Schwarz (a veteran psychical investigator who cheered me with his comments); the late Theo de Graaf (who kindly wrote to me concerning his research into trauma and its parapsychological import); Allan Cooperstein (who shared his work on exceptional forms of healing); Michael Piechowski (who shared his expertise concerning gifted children and "over excitabilities"); Diane Corcoran and P. M. H. Atwater (who provided a number of helpful responses on issues of near-death and out-of-body experience); Elly Brosius (who gave me the opportunity to speak to her Northern Virginia CFS-FMS Support Group and volunteered many good ideas concerning outreach); Gary Stone (who coordinated my talk to the National Capital Area Skeptics); Robert Forman (whose correspondence I enjoyed and who helped publicize the survey in its latter stages); Bill Stillman (who opened my mind to a possible link between anomalous perception and forms of autism); Bill Stoney (who provided wonderful historical background on parapsychological research); and Kreskin (with whom I conducted a fascinating—and, yes, entertaining—interview).

I wish to further express appreciation to a number of people who critiqued my work at various stages and without whom, frankly, the project would have built neither credibility nor momentum. They include John Palmer, Carlos Alvarado and Nancy Zingrone (whose conversations also helped familiarize me with the parapsychological community), James McLenon, Ruth Reinsel, Joanne McMahon, Roger Nelson, John Knowles, Linda Leblanc, Henry Bauer, George Hansen (who imparted one particularly sage piece of advice), Bob Bourgeois, Lucinda Grant, Louise Kosta, Mike Epstein, Jessica Utts, Paul Jaffe (who also guided members of the National Capital Area Skeptics to participate in my survey as controls), Michaeleen Maher, Gertrude Schmeidler, Nancy Didriksen, Gerald Ross, Patricia Norris, Roy Fox, and the late Marilyn Ferguson.

The following individuals helped publicize the fact that I was conducting a sensitivity survey. Their efforts were invaluable in attracting participation: Nancy Kolenda (editor of *Frontier Perspectives*); Marsha Sims (then-editor of the *Journal of Scientific Exploration*); Peter Johnson (secretary of the Society for Psychical Research); Dennis William Hauck (creator of the Haunted Places listserv); and all the other newsletter and magazine editors who publicized my appeal for survey participants.

No acknowledgment can be complete without a nod to the many sensitives who took the time to complete my survey and, in many cases, spent time with me on the phone filling in the picture and providing a vantage point I'd never had before. I can't thank them enough for their time and their trust. I hope they find the final product worthy of their exceptional experience. For that matter, I appreciate the key contribution made by people who don't consider themselves especially sensitive and yet made the effort to complete my survey in the interest of open-minded science.

I'm also grateful to the researchers who responded to my queries—and occasionally went beyond the call of duty in discussing issues or making suggestions. They include: Paul Plotsky of Emory University (who was extraordinarily gracious with his time); Jim Jones of the Centers for Disease Control and Prevention (a pioneer in the identification of chronic fatigue syndrome); Esther Sternberg (a leader in psychoneuroimmunology at the National Institutes of Health); Catherine Stoney of the National Center for Complementary and Alternative Medicine at NIH; Jackie Wootton of the Alternative Medicine Foundation; Peter Fenwick of the United Kingdom's Institute of Psychiatry; Mary Ann Cooper of the University of Illinois; Robert Henkin of the Taste and Smell Clinic;

Alan Hirsch of the Smell & Taste Treatment and Research Foundation; Barnard Baars of the Neurosciences Institute (who, in gratifying fashion, invited me to contribute an essay to his online *Science & Consciousness Review*); Thomas Ramsøy, managing editor of *Science & Consciousness Review;* Michael Corballis of the University of Auckland; Stephen Christman of the University of Toledo; James Rubin of King's College London and Ben Greenebaum of the Bioelectromagnetics Society (both of whom shared their knowledge of the state of research into electrical sensitivity); Chris McManus of University College London; Stephen Kosslyn of Harvard University; Kevin Nelson of the University of Kentucky; Jonathan Davidson of Duke University; Nicholas Humphrey of the London School of Economics; Robert Root-Bernstein of Michigan State University; Lawrence Marks of Yale University; Joseph Glicksohn of Bar-Ilan University; Ronald Melzack of McGill University; Joel Katz of York University; Mark Johnson of the University of Oregon; Jerre Levy of the University of Chicago; Simon Baron-Cohen of the University of Cambridge; synesthesia researcher Richard Cytowic; Gordon Claridge of Oxford University; Jaak Panksepp of Washington State University; James Pennebaker of the University of Texas-Austin; Robert Cloninger of Washington University; Leonard Jason of DePaul University; Judith Herman of Harvard University; Richard Loewenstein of Sheppard Pratt Hospital; Erik Jarlnaes of the European Association of Body Psychotherapy; Jane Koomar of Occupational Therapy Associates; Lucy Miller of the Sensory Processing Disorder Foundation; Karen Gouze of Northwestern University; and popular science authors Deborah Blum, John Horgan, and Mary Roach. I also wish to extend special thanks to neurologist Oliver Sacks, whose writings provide the peerless example of humane scientific inquiry.

Additionally, my thanks to the following individuals who helped this project attain final form: Jon Graham (acquisitions editor at Inner Traditions); Jeanie Levitan (managing editor); Erica Robinson (invaluable assistant to Jeanie); Chanc VanWinkle-Orzell (project editor); Jeff Lindholm (line editor); Claudia Bourbeau (indexer); Bill Gladstone (literary agent); Diane Arcangel (who directed me to Bill); John White (who preceded Bill as my agent, representing me faithfully even in semi-retirement); Allan Combs (who directed me to John); Brian Becker and Dena Jaffee (associates of Andrew Weil); Kelly Bulkeley (an outstanding author in his own right who graciously recommended a publishing contact); Edward Kelly (ditto); Roberto Patarca-Montero (who lobbied yet another publisher on my behalf); Sandra Schulman and Andrea Hurst (who saw sufficient promise in the project to read portions of the manuscript); Donna Thomson (who provided highly constructive criticism); Connie Shaw (who extended a welcome publication offer, but before the time was quite right); Art Pomponio, Georgia Hughes, and Lori Stone (who weighed the book seriously for their respective firms); Stephanie Tade (who, wearing her marketing hat, offered numerous valuable ideas); and Jessica Kingsley (who got the concept as clearly as anyone).

I next want to acknowledge several people who have helped publicize my work. They include Betsy Robinson (who wrote an article in *Spirituality and Health*); Kaja Perina (whom I corresponded with at *Psychology Today*), Lee Bowman (who published a piece for the Scripps Howard News Service); Michael Kell (host of the *Mind Brain & Body* streaming radio show on Voice America); Tacy Trump (the show's producer); Rick Berger (who communicated the survey findings within the Parapsychological Association); Annalisa Ventola and Maura Elizabeth Manning (who wrote about them on their blogs); and newsletter editors Steve Klein and Patrick Huyghe.

For permission to reprint illustrations in this book, I thank Joseph Bastien of the University of Texas-Arlington, Roberto Osti of Robert Osti Illustrations, Nancy Walker of W. H. Freeman and Company/Worth Publishers, and Bruno Dubuc of Vidéotron/McGill University. I'm also grateful to Paul Simon Music for permission to excerpt lyrics from the song "The Boxer."

I should also like to express my abiding appreciation to the following friends and family members. Some of them heard quite a lot about this project over the past ten years and indulged me by letting me talk about it for that long. Each supported me with friendship, enthusiasm, and constructive comments—and many with love besides. They include: my parents, Helene and Robert Jawer; my sisters, Anne Jawer and Judy Jawer; my brother, Bruce Jawer and my sister-in-law, Margo Vandrovec; my brother-in-law, Nick Vermont; my in-laws, Sandra and Arnold Wald; our treasured family friend Helen Fedder; my aunts, Shirley Silverman and the dearly departed Nancy Gordon; our good friend, the late Paynie Patterson; my chums Richard Aboulafia, Neil Pohl, Todd Birkenruth, Karen Suhr, Steve Hochman, Sheila Margeson, Brock Hansen, Mark Smith, Margie Jervis, Shawn Bohner, and Terri Zofer; my website designer, Eric Scafetta; my former bosses, Gerry Lederer and Paul Lynch (who were willing to grant me a leave of absence to work on the manuscript), and my current boss, Reese Meisinger (who allowed me to take time to work on the edits). My kids, Gabrielle and Bradley, also provided exemplary and loving support. One day they will realize that not every book requires a decade for a daddy to produce!

I want to express a special debt of thanks to two people in particular. The first is Marc Micozzi, medical editor for this volume. Marc is perhaps the best associate anyone could hope to have: steady, supportive, deeply knowledgeable of the history and practice of complementary and alternative medicine, pragmatic, and with a disarming sense of humor besides. I've been privileged to partner with him over four years now; we've kept the faith and made this happen.

Finally, this book is dedicated to my loving spouse, Bonnie Wald. More than anyone, she has been a nonstop booster of this venture—from the first hazy outline, presented over dinner at an Italian restaurant through the countless hours and hard slogging of research, writing, and editing. Bonnie is my confidant, life partner, patient and constructive critic, and utterly trustworthy friend. Were it not for her unwavering support over the past ten years (and all the late nights they have entailed), this book would not be in your hands. Along with my love, I hope this volume carries with it a sense of what we have accomplished together.

If anyone deserving has been left out of these acknowledgments, they have my assurance that it was inadvertent. My memory is an imperfect instrument; diligence makes up for some lapses, though, alas, not all.

Notes

◆

Foreword

1. Isaac Asimov, quoted in *Journal of the American Medical Association* 291 (1) (2004): 2350.
2. James A. Davis, Tom W. Smith, and Peter V. Marsden, *General Social Surveys, 1972–2004* (Chicago: National Opinion Research Center, 2005).
3. Michael Kearl, "Americans' Sense of Connection with the Dead," Trinity University, www.trinity.edu/mkearl/spirits.html.
4. Andrew Greeley, "The Impossible: It's Happening," *Noetic Sciences Review* 2 (Spring 1987): 7–9, www.noetics.org/publications/review/issue02/main .cfm?page=r02_Goleman.html.
5. Ibid.
6. Ibid.
7. Elizabeth Lloyd Mayer, *Extraordinary Knowing: Science, Skepticism, and the Inexplicable Powers of the Human Mind* (New York: Bantam/Random House, 2007).
8. John Horgan, *Rational Mysticism* (Boston: Houghton Mifflin, 2003), 103.

Preface

1. Gerald Edelman, *Bright Air, Brilliant Fire: On the Matter of the Mind* (New York: Basic Books, 1992), xiii.
2. Baroness Susan Greenfield, interviewed on *The Naked Scientists* radio program, June 22, 2002, www.thenakedscientists.com/HTML/podcasts/older.
3. James E. Alcock, "Science, Pseudoscience, and Anomaly," *Behavioral and Brain Sciences* 21 (2) (1998): 303.
4. Scott Russell Sanders, "Body Bright," *The Sun,* February 2000, 10.

Introduction

1. Rhawn Joseph, *The Naked Neuron: Evolution and the Languages of the Brain and Body* (New York: Plenum Press, 1993), 75.
2. Michael Lemonick, "Glimpses of the Mind," *Time,* July 17, 1995, 44–52.
3. Michael Lemonick, "Your Mind, Your Body," *Time,* January 20, 2003, 63.
4. Edge, "Philosophy in the Flesh: A Talk with George Lakoff," March 9, 1999, www.edge.org/3rd_culture/lakoff/lakoff_p1.html.
5. David Lukoff, "From Spiritual Emergency to Spiritual Problem: The Transpersonal Roots of the New DSM-IV Category," *Journal of Humanistic Psychology* 38 (2) (1998): 21–50.
6. "Pinker and The Brain," profile in *Scientific American,* July 1999, 34.

Chapter 1. Putting Emotion in a New Light

1. Walter Cannon, quoted in James J. Lynch, *The Language of the Heart* (New York: Basic Books, 1985), 261.
2. John Wheeler, quoted in V. S. Ramachandran and Sandra Blakeslee, *Phantoms in the Brain: Probing the Mysteries of the Human Mind* (New York: William Morrow, 1998), xi.
3. David Henry Feldman, *Nature's Gambit: Child Prodigies and the Development of Human Potential* (New York: Basic Books, 1986), 195–96.
4. Raymond Moody and Paul Perry, *Reunions: Visionary Encounters with Departed Loved Ones* (New York: Villard Books, 1993), 137–38.
5. Andrew Nichols and William Roll, "The Jacksonville Water Poltergeist: Electromagnetic and Neuropsychological Aspects," in *Proceedings of the Parapsychological Association* (forty-first annual convention, August 6–9, 1998, Halifax, Nova Scotia), 97–107.
6. Victor Mansfield, Sally Rhine-Feather, and James Hall, "The Rhine-Jung Letters: Distinguishing Parapsychological from Synchronistic Events," *Journal of Parapsychology* 62 (1) (1998), 3–25.
7. Mona Lisa Schulz, *Awakening Intuition* (New York: Harmony Books, 1998), 106–7.
8. *Phantom Encounters* (Alexandria, Va.: Time-Life Books, 1988), 100–101.
9. John Fuller, *The Ghost of Flight 401* (New York: Berkley Publishing Corp., 1976), 179–80.
10. Lyall Watson, *The Nature of Things: The Secret Life of Inanimate Objects* (Rochester, Vt.: Destiny Books, 1992), 168.
11. Michael Murphy, *The Future of the Body: Explorations Into the Farther Evolution of Human Nature* (Los Angeles: Jeremy P. Tarcher, 1992), 112–13.

12. Bernard Carr, "Is Emotion the Psychic Trigger?" (audiotape of lecture) Society for Psychical Research, February 12, 1985, London, England.

13. Richard S. Broughton, *Parapsychology: The Controversial Science* (New York: Ballantine Books, 1991), 231.

Chapter 2. Feelings and Emotions: The Key to It All

1. Paul Pearsall, *The Heart's Code: Tapping the Wisdom and Power of Our Heart Energy* (New York: Broadway Books, 1998), 23.

2. Louise Young, *The Book of the Heart* (New York: Doubleday, 2003), xxiv–xxv, 15; Marc Micozzi, *Postmortem Change in Human and Animal Remains: A Systematic Study* (Springfield, Ill.: C. C. Thomas, 1991), 23–29.

3. Guy Murchie, *The Seven Mysteries of Life* (Boston: Houghton Mifflin Co., 1978), 178–80.

4. Gerald L. Wick, "Cosmic Rays: Detection with the Eye," *Science* 175, February 11, 1972, 615.

5. Henry H. Bauer, *Science or Pseudoscience* (Urbana and Chicago, Ill.: University of Chicago Press, 2001), 130 (quotation by Robin Baker of the University of Manchester).

6. Rhawn Joseph, *The Naked Neuron* (New York: Plenum Press, 1993), 52.

7. Ibid., 325, 331.

8. David Hyman, quoted originally in the *Allentown, Pa. Morning Call,* www.peteseegermusic.com/peteandbruce.html.

9. "Intersections: Building the Soul of New York City," *Morning Edition,* National Public Radio, July 5, 2004.

10. Oliver Sacks, personal correspondence with author, Sep. 12, 2005.

11. William Morris, ed., *American Heritage Dictionary of the English Language* (Boston: Houghton Mifflin, 1981), 21.

12. David Lauterstein, "Touching Heaven: Bodywork and the Realm of the Incredible," *Massage and Bodywork* (December/January 2004), www.massageandbodywork.com/Articles/DecJan2004/TouchingHeaven.html.

13. David Lauterstein, "The Heart's Evolution," *Massage Today* (May 2003), www.massagetoday.com/mpacms/mt/article.php?id=10714.

14. Robert Root-Bernstein and Michele Root-Bernstein, *Sparks of Genius: The Thirteen Thinking Tools of the World's Most Creative People* (New York: Houghton Mifflin, 2000); Michigan State University press release, "New MSU Book Explores the Roots of Creativity," December 10, 1999.

15. Piero Scaruffi, "The Nature of Emotions," *Thymos: Studies on Consciousness, Mind and Life,* www.thymos.com/science/emotion.html.

16. Ibid.

17. Susan Greenfield, *The Private Life of the Brain* (New York: John Wiley & Sons, 2000), 48.

18. J. Allen Hobson, *The Chemistry of Conscious States* (New York: Little, Brown and Company, 1994), 160.

19. Richard O'Connor, *Undoing Perpetual Stress* (New York: Berkeley Books, 2005), 83–90.

20. Alison Gopnik, profiled in "Tears, Tantrums and Other Experiments," *The Guardian* (January 26, 2000), Features section, 8, www.guardian.co.uk/education/2000/jan/26/parents.familyandrelationships.

21. Candace B. Pert, *Molecules of Emotion: Why You Feel the Way You Feel* (New York: Scribner, 1997).

22. Piero Scaruffi, "The Nature of Emotions," *Thymos: Studies on Consciousness, Mind and Life,* www.thymos.com/science/emotion.html.

23. John C. Pierrakos, *Core Energetics* (Mendocino, Calif: LifeRhythym, 1987), 77.

24. Willard Gaylin, *On Being and Becoming Human* (New York: Penguin Books, 1990), 78.

25. Mona Lisa Schultz, *Awakening Intuition* (New York: Harmony Books, 1998), 76.

26. Stanley Greenspan and Stuart Shanker, *Diane Rehm Show,* National Public Radio, September 1, 2004, http://wamu.org/programs/dr/04/09/01.php, discussing their book, *The First Idea: How Symbols, Language, and Intelligence Evolved from Our Primate Ancestors to Modern Humans* (New York: Da Capo Press, 2006).

27. Willard Gaylin, *On Being and Becoming Human* (New York: Penguin Books, 1990), 78.

28. Elio Frattaroli, *Healing the Soul in the Age of the Brain* (New York: Viking Penguin, 2001), 19, 350.

29. J. Allen Hobson, *The Chemistry of Conscious States* (New York: Little, Brown and Company, 1994), 150, 157.

30. Antonio R. Damasio, *The Feeling of What Happens* (New York: Harcourt Brace & Company, 1999), 60.

31. Ibid., 279.

32. Ibid., 51.

33. Ibid., 52.

34. Ibid., 287.

35. Ibid., 283.

36. J. Allen Hobson, *The Chemistry of Conscious States* (New York: Little, Brown and Company, 1994), 155.

37. José Antonio Jáuregui, *The Emotional Computer* (Oxford UK and Cambridge, Mass.: Blackwell, 1995), as quoted in www.scaruffi.com/mind/j.htmls.

38. Antonio R. Damasio, *The Feeling of What Happens* (New York: Harcourt Brace & Company, 1999), 282.

39. Rhawn Joseph, *The Naked Neuron* (New York: Plenum Press, 1993), 76.

40. Desmond Morris, *The Naked Ape: A Zoologist's Study of the Human Animal* (New York: McGraw-Hill, 1967), 240.

Chapter 3. Feeling as the Integrator of Brain, Body, and Self

1. Antonio Damasio, *Looking for Spinoza: Joy, Sorrow, and the Feeling Brain* (New York: Harcourt, 2003), 140.

2. Nicholas Humphrey, *A History of the Mind* (New York: Simon & Schuster, 1992), 192.

3. Carl Sagan, *Billions and Billions* (New York: Ballantine Books, 1997), 32.

4. Willard Gaylin, *The Rage Within: Anger in Modern Life* (New York: Simon & Schuster, 1984), 166.

5. William F. Allman, *The Stone Age Present* (New York: Simon & Schuster, 1994), 19–20.

6. Ibid., 21–22.

7. Ibid., 94.

8. Candace B. Pert, *Molecules of Emotion: Why You Feel the Way You Feel* (New York: Scribner, 1997), 131.

9. Daniel Goleman, *Emotional Intelligence* (New York: Bantam Books, 1995), 290.

10. Diane Ackerman, *A Natural History of the Senses* (New York: Random House, 1990), 108.

11. Alexander Lowen, *Pleasure: A Creative Approach to Life* (New York: Penguin Books, 1970), 235.

12. Ibid., 133.

13. Antonio R. Damasio, *Descartes' Error: Emotion, Reason, and the Human Brain* (New York: G. P. Putnam's Sons, 1994), xvii.

14. Nicholas Humphrey, *A History of the Mind* (New York: Simon & Schuster, 1992), 115.

15. Susan Greenfield, *The Private Life of the Brain* (New York: John Wiley & Sons, 2000), 16.

16. Gerald Edelman, *Bright Air, Brilliant Fire: On the Matter of the Mind* (New York: Basic Books, 1992), 3.

17. Ibid., 1.

18. Nicholas Humphrey, *A History of the Mind* (New York: Simon & Schuster, 1992), 40.

19. Ibid., 42–43.

20. Ibid., 116.

21. Ibid., 45.

22. Ibid., 137.

23. Ibid., 191.

24. Ibid., 115.

25. Daniel Goleman, *Emotional Intelligence* (New York: Bantam Books, 1995), 9.

26. Ibid., 10.

27. Bruce Bower, "Consciousness in the Raw," *Science News Online* 172 (11) (September 15, 2007), www.sciencenews.org/articles/20070915/bob9.asp.

28. Ibid.

29. Daniel Goleman, *Emotional Intelligence* (New York: Bantam Books, 1995), 10.

30. Diane Ackerman, *A Natural History of the Senses* (New York: Random House, 1990), 20.

31. Rachel S. Herz, "Emotion Experienced during Encoding Enhances Odor Retrieval Cue Effectiveness," *American Journal of Psychology* 110 (4) (Winter 1997): 489–505.

32. David van Biema, "My Nose, My Brain, My Faith," *Time,* January 21, 2008, 47.

33. Daniel Goleman, *Emotional Intelligence* (New York: Bantam Books, 1995), 10.

34. Ibid., 11.

35. Ibid., 15.

36. Ibid., 16.

37. Ibid., 291.

38. Antonio R. Damasio, *Descartes' Error: Emotion, Reason, and the Human Brain* (New York: G. P. Putnam's Sons, 1994), 131.

39. Daniel Goleman, *Emotional Intelligence* (New York: Bantam Books, 1995), 292–95.

40. Ibid., 20–21.

41. "Vibrant Memories Have Visceral Origins," *USA Today,* December 22, 1998.

42. Daniel Goleman, *Emotional Intelligence* (New York: Bantam Books, 1995), 22.

43. Antonio R. Damasio, *Descartes' Error: Emotion, Reason, and the Human Brain* (New York: G. P. Putnam's Sons, 1994), 134–39.

44. Ibid., 149.

45. Ibid., 142.

46. Daniel Goleman, *Emotional Intelligence* (New York: Bantam Books, 1995), 293.

47. Alexander Lowen, *Pleasure: A Creative Approach to Life* (New York: Penguin Books, 1970), 174.

48. Sandra Blakeslee, "Humanity? Maybe It's in the Wiring," *New York Times,* December 9, 2003, F1.

49. Sandra Blakeslee, "The Small Part of the Brain That Makes Us Human," *International Herald Tribune,* February 7, 2007.

50. Daniel Goleman, *Emotional Intelligence* (New York: Bantam Books, 1995), 25.

51. Stephen Kiesling, "Wired for Compassion," interview with Daniel Goleman, *Spirituality and Health,* September/October 2006, 50.

52. Daniel Goleman, *Emotional Intelligence* (New York: Bantam Books, 1995), 26.

53. Ibid., 313.

54. Ibid., 167.

55. Candace B. Pert, *Molecules of Emotion: Why You Feel the Way You Feel* (New York: Scribner, 1997), 139.

56. Candace B. Pert, Henry E. Dreher, and Michael R. Ruff, "The Psychosomatic Network: Foundations of Mind-Body Medicine" *Alternative Therapies* 4 (4) (July 1998): 30–41.

57. Daniel Goleman, *Emotional Intelligence* (New York: Bantam Books, 1995), 168.

58. Candace B. Pert, *Molecules of Emotion: Why You Feel the Way You Feel* (New York: Scribner, 1997), 133.

59. Ibid., 143, 185.

60. Allen Schoen, *Kindred Spirits* (New York: Broadway Books, 2001), 44–45.

61. Candace B. Pert, *Molecules of Emotion: Why You Feel the Way You Feel* (New York: Scribner, 1997), 141–43; Richard O'Connor, *Undoing Perpetual Stress* (New York: Berkley Books, 2005), 331.

62. Antonio R. Damasio, *Descartes' Error: Emotion, Reason, and the Human Brain* (New York: G. P. Putnam's Sons, 1994), 128.

63. Candace B. Pert, *Molecules of Emotion: Why You Feel the Way You Feel* (New York: Scribner, 1997), 189.

64. Marina Pisano, "Mind-Body Connection," *San Antonio Express-News,* March 21, 2004, Life section, 1.

65. Richard O'Connor, *Undoing Perpetual Stress* (New York: Berkley Books, 2005), 330–32.

66. Ken Dychtwald, *Bodymind* (Los Angeles: Jeremy P. Tarcher, Inc., 1977), xii.

67. Antonio R. Damasio, *Descartes' Error: Emotion, Reason, and the Human Brain* (New York: G. P. Putnam's Sons, 1994), 159.

68. Michael Gershon, *The Second Brain* (New York: HarperCollins Publishers, 1998), xiii.

69. Harriet Brown, "The *Other* Brain, the One with Butterflies, Also Deals with Many Woes," *New York Times,* August 23, 2005, D5.

70. Michael Gershon, *The Second Brain* (New York: HarperCollins Publishers, 1998), xiii.

71. Chris Woolston, "Gut Feelings: The Surprising Link between Mood and Digestion," Health Articles & News Update, www.healtharticles.org/mood_digestion_081104.html.

72. Sandra Blakeslee, "Complex and Hidden Brain in Gut Makes Stomachaches and Butterflies," *New York Times* (January 23, 1996) http://query.nytimes.com/gst/fullpage.html?res=980CE0DF1F39F930A15752C0A960958260.

73. Ibid., xiv.

74. Ibid.

75. Harriet Brown, "The *Other* Brain, the One with Butterflies, Also Deals with Many Woes," *New York Times,* August 23, 2005, D5.

76. Maia Szalavitz, "Gut Thoughts," KIWIterapi, www.kiwiterapi.dk/whiplash/gutthoughts.htm.

77. Jamie Talan, "Found: A Brain-Immunity Link," *Newsday* (New York), September 23, 2004, A25.

78. Michael Gershon, *The Second Brain* (New York: HarperCollins Publishers, 1998), xiii.

79. Harriet Brown, "The *Other* Brain, the One with Butterflies, Also Deals with Many Woes," *New York Times,* August 23, 2005, D5.

80. Ibid.

81. Ibid.

82. Svein Blomhoff and others, "Perceptual Hyperreactivity to Auditory Stimuli in Patients with Irritable Bowel Syndrome," *Scandinavian Journal of Gastroenterology* 35 (6) (June 2000): 583–89; Howard Mertz and others, "Regional Cerebral Activation in Irritable Bowel Syndrome and Control Subjects with Painful and Nonpainful Rectal Distension," *Gastroenterology* 118 (5) (May 2000): 842–48.

83. Sandra Blakeslee, "Complex and Hidden Brain in Gut Makes Stomachaches and Butterflies," *New York Times* (January 23, 1996), http://query.nytimes.com/gst/fullpage.html?res=980CE0DF1F39F930A15752C0A960958260.

84. Jessica Ebert, "A Broken Heart Harms Your Health," *Nature News,* February 9, 2005, as reprinted on BioEd Online, Baylor College of Medicine, www.bioedonline.org/news/news-print.cfm?art=1558.

85. Alexander Lowen, *Pleasure: A Creative Approach to Life* (New York: Penguin Books, 1970), 77, 112.

86. Candace B. Pert, *Molecules of Emotion: Why You Feel the Way You Feel* (New York: Scribner, 1997), 276.

87. Susan McCarthy, "As Tears Go By," Salon.com, May 17, 1999, www.salon.com/health/feature/1999/05/17/emotional_tears.

88. Victor A. Parachin, "Have a Good Cry," Cyquest, www.cyquest.com/good_cry.html.

89. William H. Frey II, cited by Paula Becker, "The Healing Power of Tears," Cyquest, www.cyquest.com/motherhome/healing_power_of_tears.html.

90. William H. Frey II with Muriel Langseth, *Crying: The Mystery of Tears* (Minneapolis, Minn.: Winston Press, 1985), excerpted in "The Truth About Tears," www.yourstressmatters.com/stress9ab.htm; Lucy Hoe, "Tears Are the New Prozac," www.tribuneindia.com/2002/20021208/spectrum/main2.htm (citing work by Tom Lutz).

91. Victor M. Parachin, "Have a Good Cry," Cyquest, www.cyquest.com/good_cry.html.

92. William H. Frey II with Muriel Langseth, *Crying: The Mystery of Tears,* (Minneapolis, Minn.: Winston Press, 1985), excerpted in "The Truth About Tears," www.yourstressmatters.com/stress9ab.htm.

93. Charles Downey, "Toxic Tears: How Crying Keeps You Healthy," Cyquest, www.cyquest.com/toxic_tears_article.html.

94. Susan McCarthy, "As Tears Go By," Salon.com, May 17, 1999, www.salon.com/health/feature/1999/05/17/emotional_tears.

95. Charles Downey, "Toxic Tears: How Crying Keeps You Healthy," Cyquest, www.cyquest.com/toxic_tears_article.html.

96. Silvia H. Cardoso and Renato M. E. Sabbatini, "The Animal That Weeps," *Cerebrum* 2 (4) (Spring 2002): 7–22.

97. Victor M. Parachin, "Have a Good Cry," Cyquest, www.cyquest.com/good_cry.html.

98. Amy Norton, "Babies Show Signs of Crying in the Womb," WebMD Medical News (September 9, 2005), www.webmd.com/baby/news/20050913/babies-may-start-crying-while-in-womb.

99. Jim Moore, "Aquatic Ape Theory: Sink or Swim?" www.aquaticape.org/tears.html (first parenthetical statement); Silvia H. Cardoso and Renato M. E. Sabbatini, "When Elephants Weep," *Cerebrum* 2 (4) (Spring 2002): 106–9 (second parenthetical statement, re: elephants).

100. Lucy Hoe, "Tears Are the New Prozac," www.tribuneindia.com/2002/ 20021208/spectrum/main2.htm (citing work by Tom Lutz).

101. Steven Wynn, "Moved to Tears," *San Francisco Chronicle* (June 11, 2002), www .sfgate.com/cgi-bin/article.cgi?f=/c/a/2002/06/11/DD214485.DTL.

102. Steven Wine, Associated Press, "Teen on Top: Nadal Wins French Open," *The Examiner* (Washington, D.C.), June 6, 2005, 41.

103. Lucy Hoe, "Tears Are the New Prozac," www.tribuneindia.com/2002/ 20021208/spectrum/main2.htm.

104. Jeffrey Kottler, quoted in Judy Foreman, "Sob Story: Why We Cry and How," *Boston Globe,* October 21, 1996, C1.

105. "Laughter and Tears," *The Health Report,* hosted by Robin Hughes, Australia Broadcasting Corporation Radio National, April 15, 1996, transcript at www .abc.net.au/rn/talks/8.30/helthrpt/hstories/hr150401.htm.

106. Ibid.

107. Dennis William Hauck, *Haunted Places: The National Directory* (New York: Penguin Books, 1996).

108. Silvia H. Cardoso and Renato M. E. Sabbatini, "The Animal That Weeps," *Cerebrum* 2 (4) (Spring 2002): 7–22.

109. Steven Johnson, "The Brain + Emotions: Laughter," *Discover,* April 2003, 63–68.

110. Ibid.

111. "Therapeutic Benefits of Laughter," *Holistic Online,* www.holistic-online .com/humor_therapy/humor_therapy_benefits.htm.

112. Paul McGhee, "Humor and Health," *Holistic Online,* www.holistic-online .com/humor_therapy/humor_mcghee_article.htm.

113. Dennis William Hauck, *Haunted Places: The National Directory* (New York: Penguin Books, 1996).

Chapter 4. Selfhood: Its Origins in Sensation, Stress, and Immunity

1. Jillyn Smith, *Senses and Sensibilities* (New York: John Wiley & Sons, 1989), 2–3.

2. Ashley Montagu, *Touching: The Human Significance of the Skin,* 2nd ed. (New York: Harper & Row, 1978), 2.

3. Ibid., 2.

4. Ibid., 1.

5. Ibid., 2.

6. Ibid., 230.

7. Ibid., 1.

8. Ken Dychtwald, *Bodymind* (Los Angeles: Jeremy P. Tarcher, Inc., 1977).

9. Ashley Montagu, *Touching: The Human Significance of the Skin,* 2nd ed. (New York: Harper & Row, 1978), 4.

10. Ashley Montagu, *Touching: The Human Significance of the Skin,* 3rd ed. (New York: Perennial Library, 1986), 409.

11. Ashley Montagu, *Touching: The Human Significance of the Skin,* 2nd ed. (New York: Harper & Row, 1978), 4.

12. Ibid., 8.

13. Ibid., 197.

14. Ibid., 196.

15. Ibid., 200.

16. Ibid., 1.

17. Jillyn Smith, *Senses and Sensibilities* (New York: John Wiley & Sons, 1989), 7.

18. Ibid., 100.

19. Lyall Watson, *Jacobson's Organ and the Remarkable Nature of Smell* (New York: W. W. Norton & Company, 2000), 10.

20. Jillyn Smith, *Senses and Sensibilities* (New York: John Wiley & Sons, 1989), 101.

21. Ibid.

22. Lyall Watson, *Jacobson's Organ and the Remarkable Nature of Smell* (New York: W. W. Norton & Company, 2000), 118.

23. Ashley Montagu, *Touching: The Human Significance of the Skin,* 2nd ed. (New York: Harper & Row, 1978), 249.

24. Ibid., xi.

25. Rhawn Joseph, *The Naked Neuron* (New York: Plenum Press, 1993), 19–20.

26. Jo Durden-Smith and Diane deSimone, *Sex and the Brain* (New York: Arbor House, 1983), 217.

27. "Sense of Smell," *The Infinite Mind* radio program, produced by Lichtenstein Creative Media, week of October 17, 2001, quoting Dr. Stuart Firestein of Columbia University, summary at www.lcmedia.com/mind268.htm.

28. Jo Durden-Smith and Diane deSimone, *Sex and the Brain* (New York: Arbor House, 1983), 218.

29. Ashley Montagu, *Touching: The Human Significance of the Skin*, 2nd ed. (New York: Harper & Row, 1978), 137.

30. Jillyn Smith, *Senses and Sensibilities* (New York: John Wiley & Sons, 1989), 3.

31. Guy Brown, *The Energy of Life* (New York: The Free Press, 2000), 139, 142.

32. Michael Abrams, "Can You See with Your Tongue?" *Discover,* June 2003, 55.

33. Peter W. Nathanielsz, *Life in the Womb: Origin of Health and Disease* (Ithaca, N.Y.: Promethean Press, 1999), 193–94.

34. Ibid., 339.

35. Ashley Montagu, *Touching: The Human Significance of the Skin*, 2nd ed. (New York: Harper & Row, 1978), 45.

36. Brenda Patoine, "Prenatal Peril: Some Psychiatric Illnesses May Have Origins in the Womb," *Brain Work* 11 (5) (September–October 2001): 1–2.

37. Ibid.

38. Peter W. Nathanielsz, *Life in the Womb: Origin of Health and Disease* (Ithaca, N.Y.: Promethean Press, 1999), 10.

39. Ibid., 4–5.

40. Ibid., 5–6.

41. Ibid., 201.

42. Ibid., 198.

43. Ibid., 194.

44. Ibid., 24.

45. Paul Martin, *The Healing Mind* (New York: St. Martin's Press, 1997), 131; Kenneth Pelletier, "Between Mind and Body: Stress, Emotions, and Health," in *Mind-Body Medicine,* ed. Daniel Goleman and Joel Gurin (Yonkers, N.Y.: Consumer Reports Books, 1993), 21.

46. Paul Martin, *The Healing Mind* (New York: St. Martin's Press, 1997), 133.

47. Ibid., 133.

48. Ibid., 132.

49. Ibid., 123.

50. Peter W. Nathanielsz, *Life in the Womb: Origin of Health and Disease* (Ithaca, New York: Promethean Press, 1999), 125.

51. Paul Martin, *The Healing Mind* (New York: St. Martin's Press, 1997), 135.

52. Ibid., 66.

53. Daniel Goleman, ed., *Healing Emotions* (Boston: Shambhala, 1997), 54; Paul Martin, *The Healing Mind* (New York: St. Martin's Press, 1997), 66.

54. Paul Martin, *The Healing Mind* (New York: St. Martin's Press, 1997), 66–67.

55. Janice Kiecolt-Glaser and Ronald Glaser, "Mind and Immunity," in *Mind-Body Medicine,* ed. Daniel Goleman and Joel Gurin (Yonkers, N.Y.: Consumer Reports Books, 1993), 42–43.

56. Paul Martin, *The Healing Mind* (New York: St. Martin's Press, 1997), 68–69; Daniel Goleman, ed., *Healing Emotions* (Boston: Shambhala, 1997), 49, 52–55.

57. Paul Martin, *The Healing Mind* (New York: St. Martin's Press, 1997), 76–79; Janice Kiecolt-Glaser and Ronald Glaser, "Mind and Immunity,"

in *Mind-Body Medicine,* ed. Daniel Goleman and Joel Gurin (Yonkers, N.Y.: Consumer Reports Books, 1993), 58–59.

58. Guy Murchie, *The Seven Mysteries of Life* (Boston: Houghton Mifflin Co., 1978), 271.

59. Peter W. Nathanielsz, *Life in the Womb: Origin of Health and Disease* (Ithaca, N.Y.: Promethean Press, 1999), 125.

60. Ibid., 235–36.

61. Ashley Montagu, *Touching: The Human Significance of the Skin,* 3rd ed. (New York: Perennial Library, 1986), 62–63; Peter W. Nathanielsz, *Life in the Womb: Origin of Health and Disease* (Ithaca, N.Y.: Promethean Press, 1999), 239.

62. Peter W. Nathanielsz, *Life in the Womb* (Ithaca, N.Y.: Promethean Press, 1999), 240.

63. Ibid., 213.

64. Ibid., 213–14.

65. Thomas Verny with John Kelly, *The Secret Life of the Unborn Child* (New York: Dell Publishing Co., 1981), 105.

66. Helen Pearson, "Lead Linked to Schizophrenia," *Nature News,* February 2004, as reprinted on BioEd Online, Baylor College of Medicine, www.bioedonline .org/picks/news.cfm?art=802.

67. Cheryl Clark, "UCSD Will Lead Effort to Fathom Schizophrenia," *San Diego Union Tribune,* June 3, 2003, A1.

68. Steven Stocker, "Stress Has Hormonal Link to Alcohol, Drug Abuse," *Washington Post,* September 3, 2001, A9.

69. Ibid.

70. National Safety Council, "Experts Link Child Abuse to Disease Later in Life," *Family Safety & Health,* Winter 2002–2003, 5.

71. Ashley Montagu, *Touching: The Human Significance of the Skin,* 2nd ed. (New York: Harper & Row, 1978), 18, 114.

72. Ibid., 20.

73. Ibid., 187.

74. Ibid., 29–30.

75. Ibid., 30.

76. Ibid., 19.

77. Kate Ravilious, "Lack of Cuddles in Infancy May Affect Development of Brain," *The Guardian* (London), (November 22, 2005), 8, www.guardian .co.uk/uk/2005/nov/22/research.science.

78. Paul Martin, *The Healing Mind* (New York: St. Martin's Press, 1997), 134–35.

79. Ibid., 24–25.

80. Peter W. Nathanielsz, *Life in the Womb: Origin of Health and Disease* (Ithaca, N.Y.: Promethean Press, 1999), 131–32.

81. Ibid., 130.

82. Ibid., 126–27.

83. Paul Martin, *The Healing Mind* (New York: St. Martin's Press, 1997), 136.

84. Ibid., 96.

85. Amy Coombs, "A Matter of the Heart," *Nature Medicine* 14 (3) (2008): 231–233, www.nature.com/nm/journal/v14/n3/full/nm0308-231.html.

86. "University of Maryland School of Medicine Study Shows Laughter Helps Blood Vessels Function Better," *Science Daily* (March 19, 2005), www.sciencedaily.com/releases/2005/03/050309111444.htm.

87. "Sunlight and Serotonin," *BrainWork* (Charles A. Dana Foundation) 13 (1) (2003), 11; Joan Arehart-Treichel, "When Sunlight Dwindles, So Do Serotonin Transporters," *Psychiatric News* 43 (21) (November 7, 2008), 20, http://pn.psychiatryonline.org/cgi/content/full/43/21/20.

88. "Where is the Mind?" *The Infinite Mind* radio program, produced by Lichtenstein Creative Media, May 10, 1999, summary at www.lcmedia.com/mind9913.htm.

89. Paul Martin, *The Healing Mind* (New York: St. Martin's Press, 1997), 96–97.

90. Rosamund Vallings, "AACFS 6th International Conference," Alison Hunter Memorial Foundation, report at www.ahmf.org/aacfs_vallings03.html.

91. Guy Brown, *The Energy of Life* (New York: The Free Press, 2000), 115–16.

92. Ibid., 19–20.

93. Jill McLaughlin, "ME/CFS Fact Sheet," Alison Hunter Memorial Foundation, www.ahmf.org/infosheet.htm.

94. Paul Martin, *The Healing Mind* (New York: St. Martin's Press, 1997), 21.

95. Ibid., 22–23.

96. Christopher J. Gearon, "Learning About Fibromyalgia," *Well Times* (U.S. Public Health Service, Federal Occupational Health), November 1999, 14.

97. Anne Underwood, "Fibromyalgia: Not All in Your Head," *Newsweek,* May 19, 2003, 53.

98. Harvey Black, "Research: Investigators Pinpointing Fear's Activity in the Brain," *The Scientist* 12 (13) (June 22, 1998): 10.

99. Ibid.

100. Guy Brown, *The Energy of Life* (New York: The Free Press, 2000), 144.

101. Harvey Black, "Research: Investigators Pinpointing Fear's Activity in the Brain," *The Scientist* 12 (13) (June 22, 1998): 10; Christine Mlot, "Probing the Biology of Emotion," *Science* (May 15, 1998): 1007.

102. Guy Brown, *The Energy of Life* (New York: The Free Press, 2000), 137–38.

103. Harvey Black, "Research: Investigators Pinpointing Fear's Activity in the Brain," *The Scientist* 12 (13) (June 22, 1998): 10.

104. Marc Kaufman, "Scientists Probe Origin of Emotions," *Washington Post,* November 2, 2000, H12.

105. Guy Brown, *The Energy of Life* (New York: The Free Press, 2000), 131.

106. Sharon Heller, *Too Loud, Too Bright, Too Fast, Too Tight* (New York: Harper-Collins, 2002), 95.

107. Jerome Kagan, *Galen's Prophesy: Temperament in Human Nature* (New York: Basic Books, 1994).

108. Ibid., 161.

109. Sharon Heller, *Too Loud, Too Bright, Too Fast, Too Tight* (New York: Harper-Collins, 2002), 152–53.

110. Carol Schneider, "The Right Orbitofrontal Cortex—Master Regulator of the Brain and Body," *Bridges* (International Society for the Study of Subtle Energies and Energy Medicine), 8 (1) (Spring 1997): 8.

111. Charles Stroebel, "Neurobiology of the Self: Location, Development and Mechanisms," *Bridges* (International Society for the Study of Subtle Energies and Energy Medicine) 8 (1) (Spring 1997): 1.

112. Ibid., 11.

113. Carol Schneider, "The Right Orbitofrontal Cortex—Master Regulator of the Brain and Body," *Bridges* (International Society for the Study of Subtle Energies and Energy Medicine), 8 (1) (Spring 1997): 1.

114. Ibid.

115. Allan N. Schore, "Attachment, Affect, Regulation, and the Developing Right Brain: Linking Developmental Neuroscience to Pediatrics," *Pediatrics in Review* 26 (6) (June 2005): 204–17.

116. Carey Goldberg, "We Feel Your Pain . . . and Your Happiness Too," *Boston Globe*, Dec. 12, 2005, www.boston.com/news/globe/health_science/articles/2005/12/12/we_feel_your_pain_and_your_happiness_too/.

117. Daniel Siegel, comments presented at "Parenting from the Inside Out," a program sponsored by PEP Encouragement Program, Bethesda, Md., November 10, 2005.

118. Stacey Colino, "That Look—It's Catching!" *Washington Post,* May 30, 2006, H1.

119. Sharon Begley, "How Mirror Neurons Help Us to Empathize, Really Feel Each Others' Pain," *Wall Street Journal,* March 4, 2005, B1.

120. Barbara Strauch, *The Primal Teen: What New Discoveries about the Teenage Brain Tell Us about Our Kids* (New York: Doubleday, 2003), xiv.

121. Ibid., 8.
122. Ibid., 5.
123. Ibid., 130–31.
124. Ibid., 132.
125. Ibid., 128.
126. Ibid., 94.
127. Ibid., 133.
128. Ibid., 13.
129. Ibid., 16.
130. Ibid., 137, 191.
131. Ibid., 53.
132. Ibid., 31–32.
133. Ibid., 67–69.
134. Ibid., 154.
135. Ibid., 112.
136. Ibid., 8.
137. Ibid., 191–92, 197–98.
138. Shankar Vedantam, "Variation in One Gene Linked to Depression," *Washington Post,* July 18, 2003, A1.
139. Edge, "Language, Biology, and the Mind: A Talk with Gary Marcus," www.edge.org/documents/archive/edge133.html.
140. Thomas Verny with John Kelly, *The Secret Life of the Unborn Child* (New York: Dell Publishing Co., 1981), 64.
141. Ashley Montagu, *Touching: The Human Significance of the Skin,* 2nd ed. (New York: Harper & Row, 1978), 88.
142. Ibid., 100.
143. Ibid., 199.
144. Ibid., 201, 203.
145. Ibid., 206.
146. Ibid., 207.
147. Robert Kegan, *The Evolving Self* (Cambridge, Mass.: Harvard University Press, 1982), 7–8.
148. Ibid., 11.

Chapter 5. Energy, Electricity, and Dissociation: Links to the Anomalous

1. Dotson Rader, "'Even the Bad Times Make You Better' (Actor Mel Gibson)," *Parade,* July 28, 2002, 8.

2. William Gildea, "An Intense Experience: Sense of Purpose Keeps Growing as Schilling Keeps Going," *Washington Post,* October 25, 2001, D1.

3. Paul Pearsall, *The Heart's Code* (New York: Broadway Books, 1998), 29.

4. Ibid.

5. James L. Oschman, *Energy Medicine: The Scientific Basis* (Edinburgh, U.K.: Churchill Livingstone, 2000), ix.

6. Marc Micozzi, ed., *Fundamentals of Complementary and Alternative Medicine,* 3rd ed. (St. Louis, Mo.: Elsevier, 2006).

7. Guy Brown, *The Energy of Life* (New York: The Free Press, 1999), x.

8. Ibid., quoting *Harvard Business Review.*

9. Ibid., 2.

10. Ibid., 3.

11. Ibid., 2.

12. Ibid., 24.

13. Ibid., 5.

14. Ibid., 6–10.

15. Chip Brown, *Afterwards, You're a Genius* (New York: Riverhead Books, 1998), 60.

16. Guy Brown, *The Energy of Life* (New York: The Free Press, 1999), 14.

17. Ibid., 15–16.

18. Ibid., 11, 16.

19. Ibid., 17–20.

20. Ibid., 62–63.

21. Ibid., ix.

22. Ibid., 24.

23. Ibid., 4–5.

24. Ibid., 25.

25. Ibid., 35.

26. Ibid., 30, 32, 38–39, 44.

27. Michael Shallis, *The Electric Connection* (New York: New Amsterdam Books, 1988), 109.

28. Ibid., 116–17.

29. Ibid., 110–11.

30. Ibid., 89–90, 104.

31. James L. Oschman, *Energy Medicine: The Scientific Basis* (Edinburgh, U.K.: Churchill Livingstone, 2000), 59–60.

32. Michael Shallis, *The Electric Connection* (New York: New Amsterdam Books, 1988), 118.

33. Ibid., 53–56.

34. Guy Brown, *The Energy of Life* (New York: The Free Press, 1999), 156.

35. Jamie Talan, "Tracking the Train of Thought," *Newsday,* May 6, 2003, A41.

36. James L. Oschman, *Energy Medicine: The Scientific Basis* (Edinburgh, U.K.: Churchill Livingstone, 2000), 28.

37. Ibid., 29.

38. Paul Pearsall, *The Heart's Code* (New York: Broadway Books, 1998), 55, 65.

39. Guy Brown, *The Energy of Life* (New York: The Free Press, 1999), 107–8.

40. J. Allan Hobson, *The Chemistry of Conscious States: How the Brain Changes Its Mind* (New York: Little, Brown and Company, 1994), 160–61.

41. Peter Levine with Ann Frederick, *Waking the Tiger, Healing Trauma* (Berkeley, Calif.: North Atlantic Books, 1997).

42. Ibid., 16.

43. Guy Murchie, *The Seven Mysteries of Life* (Boston: Houghton Mifflin Co., 1978), 227.

44. Peter Levine with Ann Frederick, *Waking the Tiger, Healing Trauma* (Berkeley, Calif.: North Atlantic Books, 1997), 19.

45. Ibid., 18.

46. Steven Johnson, "The Brain + Emotions: Fear," *Discover* (March 2003): 34.

47. Ibid., 20.

48. Paul Pearsall, *The Heart's Code* (New York: Broadway Books, 1998), 179.

49. Guy Murchie, *The Seven Mysteries of Life* (Boston: Houghton Mifflin Co., 1978), 229.

50. Paul Martin, *The Healing Mind* (New York: St. Martin's Press, 1997), 134.

51. Paul Pearsall, *The Heart's Code* (New York: Broadway Books, 1998), 207.

52. Peter Levine with Ann Frederick, *Waking the Tiger, Healing Trauma* (Berkeley, Calif.: North Atlantic Books, 1997), 38; Robert C. Scaer, "Observations on Traumatic Stress Utilizing the Model of the 'Whiplash Syndrome,'" *Bridges* (International Society for the Study of Subtle Energies and Energy Medicine) 8 (1) (Spring 1997): 4.

53. Robert Scaer, "The Neurophysiology of Dissociation and Chronic Disease," *Applied Psychophysiology and Biofeedback* 26 (1) (March 2001): 73–91, as reprinted in Trauma Information Pages, www.trauma-pages.com/a/scaer-2001.php.

54. Peter Levine with Ann Frederick, *Waking the Tiger, Healing Trauma* (Berkeley, Calif.: North Atlantic Books, 1997), 53–54.

55. Ibid., 54.

56. Ibid., 25.

57. Ibid., 68–71.

58. Daniel Goleman, ed., *Healing Emotions* (Boston: Shambhala, 1997), 114, 123–29.

59. Peter Levine with Ann Frederick, *Waking the Tiger, Healing Trauma* (Berkeley, Calif.: North Atlantic Books, 1997), 137.

60. Ashley Montagu, *Touching: The Human Significance of the Skin,* 2nd ed. (New York: Harper & Row, 1978), 194.

61. Pamela Oldham, "A Flight of Mind," *Washington Post*, February 18, 2003, F1.

62. Marlene Steinberg and Maxine Schnall, *The Stranger in the Mirror,* excerpt, www.strangerinthemirror.com/sim_synopsis.html.

63. Robert Scaer, "The Neurophysiology of Dissociation and Chronic Disease," *Applied Psychophysiology and Biofeedback* 26 (1) (March 2001): 73–91, as reprinted in Trauma Information Pages, www.trauma-pages.com/a/scaer-2001.php; Harvey J. Irwin, "Childhood Antecedents of Out-of-Body and Déjà Vu Experiences," *Journal of the American Society for Psychical Research* 90 (3) (1996): 157–72.

64. Marlene Steinberg and Maxine Schnall, *The Stranger in the Mirror,* excerpt, www.strangerinthemirror.com/sim_excerpt.html.

65. Marlene Steinberg and Maxine Schnall, *The Stranger in the Mirror,* www.strangerinthemirror.com/dissociative.html; Robert Scaer, "The Neurophysiology of Dissociation and Chronic Disease," *Applied Psychophysiology and Biofeedback* 26 (1) (March 2001): 73–91, as reprinted in Trauma Information Pages, www.trauma-pages .com/a/scaer-2001.php.

66. G. H. Gallup and F. Newport, "Belief in Paranormal Phenomena among Adult Americans," *Skeptical Inquirer* 15 (1991): 137–46; John Palmer, "A Community Mail Survey of Psychic Experiences," *Journal of the American Society for Psychic Research* 73 (3) (1979): 221–51; Colin A. Ross and Shaun Joshi, "Paranormal Experiences in the General Population," *Journal of Nervous and Mental Disease* 180 (6) (1992): 357–61.

67. Robert Scaer, "The Neurophysiology of Dissociation and Chronic Disease," *Applied Psychophysiology and Biofeedback* 26 (1) (March 2001): 73–91, as reprinted in Trauma Information Pages, www.trauma-pages.com/a/scaer-2001.php.

68. Mona Lisa Schulz, *Awakening Intuition* (New York: Harmony Books, 1998), 87.

69. Pamela Oldham, "A Flight of Mind," *Washington Post*, February 18, 2003, F1.

70. Mona Lisa Schulz, *Awakening Intuition* (New York: Harmony Books, 1998), 57.

71. Rhawn Joseph, *The Naked Neuron* (New York: Plenum Press, 1993), 347.

72. Ibid., 350.

73. Ibid., 352–53.

74. Ibid., 354.

75. Peter Levine with Ann Frederick, *Waking the Tiger, Healing Trauma* (Berkeley, Calif.: North Atlantic Books, 1997), 141, 147, 165.

76. Robert C. Scaer, "Observations on Traumatic Stress Utilizing the Model of the 'Whiplash Syndrome,'" *Bridges* (International Society for the Study of Subtle Energies and Energy Medicine) 8 (1) (Spring 1997): 6.

77. Ibid., 7.

78. Peter Levine with Ann Frederick, *Waking the Tiger, Healing Trauma* (Berkeley, Calif.: North Atlantic Books, 1997), 99–100.

79. Ibid., 181–87.

80. Ibid., 182.

81. Ibid., 183.

82. Ibid., 183–84.

83. Ibid., 260–61.

84. Ibid., 185.

85. Ibid., 184.

86. Paul Martin, *The Healing Mind* (New York: St. Martin's Press, 1997), 223.

87. Ibid., 283.

88. Ibid., 169.

89. Daniel Goleman, ed., *Healing Emotions* (Boston: Shambhala, 1997), 39.

90. Gabor Maté, "The Healing Force Within," *Vancouver Sun,* April 8, 2003, reprinted in *When the Body Says No,* www.whenthebodysaysno.ca/artvan.html.

91. Gabor Maté, *When the Body Says No* (Hoboken, N.J.: John Wiley & Sons, 2003), 201.

92. Ibid., 172–76.

93. Ibid., 201.

94. Ian Wickramasekera, "Secrets Kept from the Mind but Not the Body or Behavior: The Unsolved Problems of Identifying and Treating Somatization and Psychophysiological Disease," *Advances in Mind-Body Medicine* 14 (1998): 92–94.

95. Ronald Melzack, "Phantom Limbs," *Scientific American* 266 (April 1992): 120.

96. Eric Leskowitz, "Phantom Limb Pain: Subtle Energy Perspectives," *Subtle Energies & Energy Medicine* 8 (2) (2001): 126.

97. Ronald Melzack, "Phantom Limbs," *Scientific American* 266 (April 1992): 121.

98. Eric Leskowitz, "Phantom Limb Pain: Subtle Energy Perspectives," *Subtle Energies & Energy Medicine* 8 (2) (2001): 128.

99. Ronald Melzack, "Phantom Limbs," *Scientific American* 266 (April 1992): 120.

100. Ibid., 120.

101. Ibid., 123.

102. Ibid., 120.

103. Ibid., 124.

104. Ibid., 126.

105. Eric Leskowitz, "Phantom Limb Pain: Subtle Energy Perspectives," *Subtle Energies & Energy Medicine* 8 (2) (2001): 135–36.

106. Ibid., 136–37.

107. Ibid., 145.

108. Ibid., 147.

109. Center for the Advancement of Health, "PTSD: The Psychological Wounds of Terror," *Facts of Life* 6 (6) (October 2001).

110. Ibid.

111. Pamela Fitch and Trish Dryden, "Recovering Body and Soul from Post-Traumatic Stress Disorder," *Massage Therapy Journal* 39 (1) (Spring 2000), www.amtamassage .org/journal/soul.html (discussing Bessel van der Kolk).

112. Ibid.

113. Center for the Advancement of Health, "Child Abuse Can Last a Lifetime," *Facts of Life* 4 (2) (March 1999); "Brain Clue to Stress Disorder," BBC News, July 12, 2003, http://news.bbc.co.uk/1/hi/health/3051496.stm.

114. Sidran Institute, *Posttraumatic Stress Disorder* (fact sheet), www.sidran.org/ sub.cfm?contentID=66&sectionid=4 ; Pamela Fitch and Trish Dryden, "Recovering Body and Soul from Post-Traumatic Stress Disorder," *Massage Therapy Journal* 39 (1) (Spring 2000), www.amtamassage.org/journal/soul .html.

115. Center for the Advancement of Health, "PTSD: The Psychological Wounds of Terror," *Facts of Life* 6 (6) (October 2001).

116. Ibid.

117. Ibid.; Sidran Institute, *Posttraumatic Stress Disorder* (fact sheet), www.sidran .org/sub.cfm?contentID=66&sectionid=4.

118. Ibid.

119. Center for the Advancement of Health, "PTSD: The Psychological Wounds of Terror," *Facts of Life* 6 (6) (October 2001).

120. Neal A. Klein and Jeffrey Rausch, "Olfactory Precipitants of Flashback in Posttraumatic Stress Disorder: Case Reports," *Journal of Clinical Psychiatry* 67 (9) (September 1985): 383–84.

121. Rachel Yehuda, as quoted in Center for the Advancement of Health, "PTSD: The Psychological Wounds of Terror," *Facts of Life* 6 (6) (October 2001).

122. Pamela Fitch and Trish Dryden, "Recovering Body and Soul from Post-Traumatic Stress Disorder," *Massage Therapy Journal* 39 (1) (Spring 2000), www.amtamassage .org/journal/soul.html.

123. Michael A. Thalbourne and Bronwyn Fox, "Paranormal and Mystical Experience: The Role of Panic Attacks and Kundalini," *Journal of the American Society for Psychical Research* 93 (1999): 99–115.

124. Pamela Fitch and Trish Dryden, "Recovering Body and Soul from Post-Traumatic Stress Disorder," Massage Therapy Journal 39 (1) (Spring 2000), www.amtamassage .org/journal/soul.html.

125. Herbert Spiegel and David Spiegel, *Trance and Treatment: Clinical Uses of Hypnosis,* 2nd ed. (Washington, D.C.: American Psychiatric Publishing, 2004), 163.

126. James Trefil, *1001 Things Everyone Should Know About Science* (New York: Doubleday, 1992), 153.

127. Christopher Buckley, "Mr. Lincoln's Washington," *Smithsonian* (April 2003), 76–84, www.smithsonianmag.com/history-archaeology/lincoln.html.

128. Dennis William Hauck, *Haunted Places: The National Directory* (New York: Penguin Books, 1996), 116–17.

129. Gary Walters, quoted on White House website, www.whitehouse.gov/ghosts (page no longer current).

130. Bernard Grad, "The Healer Phenomenon: What Is It and How Might It Be Studied?" *Bridges* (International Society for the Study of Subtle Energies and Energy Medicine) 2 (2) (Summer 1991): 6.

131. Stanislov Grof, *Realms of the Human Unconscious* (New York: The Viking Press, 1975).

132. Ibid., 19.

133. Ibid., 46–47.

134. Ibid., 71.

135. Ibid., 76.

136. Benedict Carey, "The Afterlife of Near-Death," *New York Times*, January 18, 2009, www.nytimes.com/2009/01/18/weekinreview/18carey.html?_r=1.

137. Nandor Fodor, *Between Two Worlds* (West Nyack, N.Y.: Parker Publishing Co., 1964), 58.

138. Mental Health Channel, www.mentalhealthchannel.net/ocd/index .shtmlHealth; Steven Dubovsky, "Is OCD a Low-Serotonin Disorder?" Journal Watch Psychiatry, March 25, 2004, http://psychiatry.jwatch.org/cgi/ content/full/2004/325/4.

Chapter 6. Feeling and the Influence
of Atmosphere

1. David Abram, *The Spell of the Sensuous: Perception and Language in a More-than-Human World* (New York: Pantheon Books, 1996), 225.

2. Will Storr, *Will Storr vs. the Supernatural* (New York: Harper, 2006), 279.

3. D. Scott Rogo, ed., *Mind beyond the Body* (New York: Penguin Books, 1978), 187.

4. William Morris, ed., *American Heritage Dictionary of the English Language* (Boston: Houghton Mifflin Company, 1981), 775.

5. David Abram, *The Spell of the Sensuous: Perception and Language in a More-than-Human World* (New York: Pantheon Books, 1996), 237–39.

6. Ibid., 228–29, 237.

7. James Trefil, *1001 Things Everyone Should Know about Science* (New York: Doubleday, 1992), 182.

8. Ibid., 185–86.

9. Ibid., 152–53.

10. Ibid., 185–86.

11. Ibid., 124–25.

12. Ibid., 111.

13. Ibid.

14. Ibid., 112.

15. Ibid., 111, 186.

16. Ibid., 153.

17. Ibid., 155.

18. Ibid., 127.

19. Ibid., 121.

20. Ibid., 121–22.

21. Ibid., 16.

22. Ibid., 132–33.

23. Bijal Trivedi, "'Magnetic Map' Found to Guide Animal Migration," *National Geographic News* (October 21, 2001), http://news.nationalgeographic.com/news/2001/10/1012_TVanimalnavigation.html.

24. Rick Weiss, "Molecular Action May Help Keep Birds on Course," *Washington Post,* May 5, 2008, A8.

25. Philip MacEachron, personal correspondence with author, November 10, 2006.

26. Guy Murchie, *The Seven Mysteries of Life: An Exploration in Science and Philosophy* (Boston: Houghton Mifflin Co., 1978), 197.

27. Allen H. Frey and Rodman Messenger Jr., "Human Perception of Illumination

with Pulsed Ultrahigh-Frequency Electromagnetic Energy," *Science* 181 (July 27, 1973): 356–58.

28. Wikibooks, "Electronics/Frequency Spectrum," http://en.wikibooks.org/wiki/Electronics/Frequency_Spectrum.

29. Vic Tandy, "Ghost Sounds: A Review and Discussion of the Infrasound Theory of Apparitions," *International Journal of Parapsychology* 12 (2) (2001): 131–51.

30. Ibid., 133.

31. Ibid., 134.

32. Mary Roach, *Spook: Science Tackles the Afterlife* (New York: W. W. Norton & Company, 2005), 231.

33. Vic Tandy, "Ghost Sounds: A Review and Discussion of the Infrasound Theory of Apparitions," *International Journal of Parapsychology* 12 (2) (2001): 134.

34. Ibid., 135–36.

35. Ibid., 143.

36. Ibid., 136.

37. Ibid., 138.

38. James Trefil, *1001 Things Everyone Should Know about Science* (New York: Doubleday, 1992), 129–30.

39. Ibid., 129, 131.

40. Ibid., 131.

41. Ibid., 272–73; B. Blake Levitt, *Electromagnetic Fields* (New York: Harcourt Brace & Company, 1995).

42. James Trefil, *1001 Things Everyone Should Know about Science* (New York: Doubleday, 1992), 174.

43. B. Blake Levitt, *Electromagnetic Fields* (New York: Harcourt Brace & Company, 1995).

44. Ibid., 69.

45. Norman E. Rosenthal, "Diagnosis and Treatment of Seasonal Affective Disorder," *Journal of the American Medical Association* 270 (22) (December 8, 1993): 2717–20.

46. James W. Lance, *Migraines and Other Headaches* (East Roseville, New South Wales, Australia: Simon and Schuster, 1998), 62.

47. Lyall Watson, *Supernature: A Natural History of the Supernatural* (New York: Bantam Books, 1973), 84; David Jay Brown and Rupert Sheldrake, "Unusual Animal Behavior prior to Earthquakes: A Survey in Northwest California," http://animalsandearthquakes.com/survey.htm; Maryann Mott, "Can Animals Sense Earthquakes?" *National Geographic News* (November 11, 2003), http://news.nationalgeographic.com/news/2003/11/1111_031111_earthquakeanimals.html.

48. "Can Animals Predict Disaster?" *Nature,* PBS, May 13, 2005, www.pbs.org/wnet/nature/animalspredict/index.html; Ikeya Motoji, "Scientific Elucidation of Earthquake Precursors and Real Time Electromagnetic Monitoring for Disaster Prevention System," abstract at http://krf.or.jp/report/1997/english/ikeya-motoji%20b1.htm.

49. David Jay Brown, "Animals and Earthquakes: Interview with Dr. Motoji Ikeya," www.animalsandearthquakes.com/ikeya.htm.

50. Maryann Mott, "Can Animals Sense Earthquakes?" *National Geographic News* (November 11, 2003), http://news.nationalgeographic.com/news/2003/11/1111_031111_earthquakeanimals.html.

51. David Jay Brown, "Animals and Earthquakes: Interview with Dr. Motoji Ikeya," www.animalsandearthquakes.com/ikeya.htm.

52. Ibid.

53. David Jay Brown and Rupert Sheldrake, "Unusual Animal Behavior prior to Earthquakes: A Survey in Northwest California," http://animalsandearthquakes.com/survey.htm.

54. Maryann Mott, "Can Animals Sense Earthquakes?" *National Geographic News,* November 11, 2003, http://news.nationalgeographic.com/news/2003/11/1111_031111_earthquakeanimals.html.

55. Wikipedia, "Infrasound," http://en.wikipedia.org/wiki/Infrasound; "Can Animals Predict Disaster?" *Nature,* PBS, May 13, 2005, www.pbs.org/wnet/nature/animalspredict/infrasound.html.

56. Kate Ramsayer, "Infrasonic Symphony," *Science News Online* 165 (2) (January 10, 2004), Pearson Prentice Hall, www.phschool.com/science/science_news/articles/infrasonic_symphony.html.

57. Elephant Information Repository, http://elephant.elehost.com/About_Elephants/Senses/Hearing/hearing.html.

58. Katie Payne, review of *Silent Thunder: In the Presence of Elephants, Scientific American,* excerpted on www.amazon.com/SILENT-THUNDER-Elephants-Katy-Payne/dp/product-description/0684801086.

59. "Can Animals Predict Disaster: Eyewitness Accounts," *Nature,* PBS, www.pbs.org/wnet/nature/animalspredict/eyewitness.html.

60. "Can Animals Predict Disaster: "Tall Tales or True?" *Nature,* PBS, www.pbs.org/wnet/nature/animalspredict/talltales.html.

61. Maryann Mott, "Can Animals Sense Earthquakes?" *National Geographic News* (November 11, 2003), http://news.nationalgeographic.com/news/2003/11/1111_031111_earthquakeanimals.html; "Can Animals Predict Disaster: "Tall Tales or True?" *Nature,* PBS, www.pbs.org/wnet/nature/animalspredict/talltales.html.

62. Maryann Mott, "Can Animals Sense Earthquakes?" *National Geographic News,* November 11, 2003, http://news.nationalgeographic.com/news/2003/11/1111_031111_earthquakeanimals.html.

63. Elizabeth von Muggenthaler, quoted in "Tall Blondes," *Nature,* PBS, December 17, 2005, www.pbs.org/wnet/nature/tallblondes/infrasound.html.

64. Ned Rozell, "Straining to Hear the Voice of the Aurora," *Alaska Science Forum* (Article #1257), (October 19, 1995), www.gi.alaska.edu/ScienceForum/ASF12/1257.html.

65. Harriett Williams, "Sizzling Skies," *New Scientist,* January 6, 2001, 14–19.

66. Ibid.

67. Casey Grove, "Aural Auroral Encounters," pt. 2, Feb. 7, 2005, www.alaskascienceoutreach.com.

68. Michael Shallis, *The Electric Connection: Its Effects on Mind and Body* (New York: New Amsterdam Books, 1988), 173.

69. Casey Grove, "Aural Auroral Encounters," pt. 2, Feb. 7, 2005, www.alaskascienceoutreach.com/.

70. T. Neil Davis, "Auroral Sounds," *Alaska Science Forum* (Article #265) (November 2, 1978), www.gi.alaska.edu/ScienceForum/ASF2/265.html.

71. Wikibooks, "Electronics/Frequency Spectrum," http://en.wikibooks.org/wiki/Electronics/Frequency_Spectrum.

72. Harriett Williams, "Sizzling Skies," *New Scientist,* January 2001.

73. Kate Ramsayer, "Infrasonic Symphony," *Science News Online* 165 (2) (January 10, 2004), Pearson Prentice Hall, www.phschool.com/science/science_news/articles/infrasonic_symphony.html.

74. Mary Roach, *Spook: Science Tackles the Afterlife* (New York: W. W. Norton & Company, 2005), 216; Loyd Auerbach, *Ghost Hunting: How to Investigate the Paranormal* (Berkeley, Calif.: Ronin Publishing, 2003), 107–12.

75. Richard Wiseman and others, "An Investigation Into the Alleged Haunting of Hampton Court Palace: Psychological Variables and Magnetic Fields" *Journal of Parapsychology* 66 (December 2002): 389–409.

76. Ned Rozell, "Straining to Hear the Voice of the Aurora," *Alaska Science Forum* (Article #1257) (October 19, 1995), www.gi.alaska.edu/ScienceForum/ASF12/1257.html.

77. Mary Roach, *Spook: Science Tackles the Afterlife* (New York: W. W. Norton & Company, 2005), 218.

78. Wikibooks, "Electronics/Frequency Spectrum," http://en.wikibooks.org/wiki/Electronics/Frequency_Spectrum.

79. Bruno Leone, ed., *Paranormal Phenomena: Opposing Viewpoints* (San Diego: Greenhaven Press, 1997), 93.

80. Paul Devereux, *Earthmind: A Modern Adventure in Ancient Wisdom* (New York: Harper & Row, 1989), 83–84; Paul Devereux, *Earth Lights Revelation* (London: Blandford Press, 1990), 208.

81. Mary Roach, *Spook: Science Tackles the Afterlife* (New York: W. W. Norton & Company, 2005), 219.

82. Michael A. Persinger, "Increased Geomagnetic Activity and the Occurrence of Bereavement Hallucinations: Evidence for Melatonin-Mediated Microseizuring in the Temporal Lobe?" *Neuroscience Letters* 88 (1988): 271–74.

83. Ibid.

84. Paul Devereux, *Earth Lights Revelation* (London: Blandford Press, 1990), 208, 213–15.

85. Mary Roach, *Spook: Science Tackles the Afterlife* (New York: W. W. Norton & Company, 2005), 216.

86. Walter Randall and Steffani Randall, "The Solar Wind and Hallucinations— A Possible Relation Due to Magnetic Disturbances," *Bioelectromagnetics* 12 (1991): 67–70.

87. Paul Devereux, *Earthmind: A Modern Adventure in Ancient Wisdom* (New York: Harper & Row, 1989), 82–83.

88. Mary Roach, *Spook: Science Tackles the Afterlife* (New York: W. W. Norton & Company, 2005), 219–20.

89. Will Storr, *Will Storr vs. the Supernatural* (New York: Harper, 2006), 230.

90. Mary Roach, *Spook: Science Tackles the Afterlife* (New York: W. W. Norton & Company, 2005), 221.

91. Bruno Leone, ed., *Paranormal Phenomena: Opposing Viewpoints* (San Diego: Greenhaven Press, 1997), 98.

92. Darregh Johnson, "New Graves, Fresh Grief: Perennially Sedate Arlington Cemetery Adjusts to the Needs of Mourners of this War," *Washington Post,* May 20, 2007, A1.

93. Gordon Rattray Taylor, *The Natural History of the Mind* (New York: E. P. Dutton, 1979), 249.

94. George F. Mahl and others, "Psychological Responses in the Human to Intracerebral Electrical Stimulation," *Psychosomatic Medicine* XXVI (4) (1964): 337–68.

95. Michael A. Persinger, "Increased Geomagnetic Activity and the Occurrence of Bereavement Hallucinations: Evidence for Melatonin-Mediated Microseizuring in the Temporal Lobe?" *Neuroscience Letters* 88 (1988): 271–74.

96. Pierre Gloor and others, "The Role of the Limbic System in Experiential

Phenomena of Temporal Lobe Epilepsy," *Annals of Neurology* 12 (2) (August 1982): 129–44.

97. Ibid., 132.

98. Ibid., 134–35.

99. Ibid., 140.

100. Lyall Watson, *Supernature: A Natural History of the Supernatural* (New York: Bantam Books, 1973), 9.

101. Ibid., 222.

102. Carl Sagan, *Billions and Billions* (New York: Ballantine Books, 1997), 48.

103. Robert O. Becker, *Cross Currents* (Los Angeles: Jeremy P. Tarcher, 1985), 77.

104. Gary Farr, "The Pineal Gland," BecomeHealthyNow.com, June 28, 2003, www.becomehealthynow.com/article/bodyendocrine/737.

105. Wikipedia, "Pineal Gland," http://en.wikipedia.org/wiki/Pineal_gland.

106. Ibid.

107. Gary Farr, "The Pineal Gland," BecomeHealthyNow.com, June 28, 2003, www.becomehealthynow.com/article/bodyendocrine/737.

108. Robert O. Becker, *Cross Currents* (Los Angeles: Jeremy P. Tarcher, 1985), 77.

109. Ibid., 74–75.

110. B. Blake Levitt, *Electromagnetic Fields* (New York: Harcourt Brace & Company, 1995), 73.

111. Ibid., 78.

112. Kathy Quinn Thomas, "The Mind-Body Connection: Granny Was Right, After All," *Rochester Review* (University of Rochester), March 1997, www.rochester.edu/pr/Review/V59N3/feature2.html (human brain statistics).

113. Ibid.

114. Lawrence W. Fagg, *Electromagnetism and the Sacred* (New York: Continuum Publishing Co., 1999), 16.

115. Ibid., 154.

116. Ibid., 71.

117. Ibid., 123–24.

118. Ibid., 80–81.

119. Ibid., 81.

120. Ibid., 76; P. M. H. Atwater, *Beyond the Light* (New York: Birch Lane Press, 1994), 140–48.

121. Lawrence W. Fagg, *Electromagnetism and the Sacred* (New York: Continuum Publishing Co., 1999), 75.

122. James Trefil, *1001 Things Everyone Should Know about Science* (New York: Doubleday, 1992), 16.

123. Ibid., 163–64.

124. James L. Oschman, *Energy Medicine: The Scientific Basis* (Edinburgh: Churchill Livingstone, 2000), 59–60.

125. Andy Coghlan, "To Heal a Wound, Turn Up the Voltage," *New Scientist* (July 26, 2006), 15, www.newscientist.com/article/mg19125624.400.

126. Cass Decker and Mark Ratner, "Electronic Properties of DNA," *Physics World* 14 (8) (August 2001), http://physicsweb.org/articles/world/14/8/8.

127. William G. Roll, "Poltergeists, Electromagnetism and Consciousness," *Journal of Scientific Exploration* 17 (1) (2003): 75–86.

128. William G. Roll, "Recurrent Spontaneous Psychokinesis," *Bridges Magazine* (International Society for the Study of Subtle Energies and Energy Medicine) 10 (1) (1999): 8–12.

129. Ibid.

130. Remy Chauvin, *Parapsychology: When the Irrational Rejoins Science* (Jefferson, North Carolina: McFarland & Co., 1985), 120–23.

131. Paul Pearsall, *The Heart's Code: Tapping the Wisdom and Power of Our Heart Energy* (New York: Broadway Books, 1998) 55, 65.

132. Elmer E. Green and others, "Anomalous Electrostatic Phenomena in Exceptional Subjects," *Subtle Energies* 2 (3) (1991): 69–94.

133. Ibid., 79.

134. Remy Chauvin, *Parapsychology: When the Irrational Rejoins Science* (Jefferson, North Carolina: McFarland & Co., 1985), 101–5.

135. William G. Roll, "Poltergeists, Electromagnetism and Consciousness," *Journal of Scientific Investigation* 17 (1) (2003): 75–86.

136. Ibid., 81.

137. Johannes Mischo, "Personality structure of psychokinetic mediums," *Proceedings of the Parapsychological Association* 5 (1968): 35–37 as cited by William G. Roll, "Recurrent Spontaneous Psychokinesis," *Bridges Magazine* (International Society for the Study of Subtle Energies and Energy Medicine) 10 (1) (1999): 8–12.

138. Ruth Reinsel, "Physical Mediumship, Macro-PK, and the Autonomic Nervous System" (abstract of panel presentation submitted for the Parapsychological Association's forty-seventh annual convention, August 5–8, 2004, Vienna, Austria), citing two papers: William G. Braud, "Psi Performance and Autonomic Nervous System Activity," *Journal of the American Society for Psychical Research* 75 (1) (1981): 1–35; and William G. Braud, "ESP, PK, and Sympathetic Nervous System Activity," *Parapsychology Review* 16 (1985): 8–11.

139. William G. Roll and Michael A. Persinger, "Poltergeist and Nonlocality:

Energetic Aspects of RSPK," in *Proceedings of the Parapsychological Association* (forty-first annual convention, August 6–9, 1998, Halifax, Nova Scotia), 184–98.

140. Ibid., 188.
141. Ibid., 194.

Chapter 7. Anatomy of a Crisis

1. Rush W. Dozier, *Fear Itself: The Origin and Nature of the Powerful Emotion That Shapes Our Lives and Our World* (New York: St. Martin's Press, 1998), 4.
2. Ibid., 4–5.
3. Stephen Kiesling, "Wired for Compassion," interview with Daniel Goleman, *Spirituality and Health,* September/October 2006, 50.
4. Desmond Morris, *The Naked Ape: A Zoologist's Study of the Human Animal* (New York: McGraw-Hill, 1967), 169–70.
5. Helen Pearson, "Dying Leaves Its Mark on the Brain," *Nature,* Science Update, February 2, 2004, as reprinted in Chinese Medical & Biological Information, http://cmbi.bjmu.edu.cn/news/0402/3.htm.
6. Ibid.
7. Allen Spraggett, "Nandor Fodor: Analyst of the Unexplained," *The Psychoanalytic Review* 56A (1969): 128–37.
8. Rush W. Dozier, *Fear Itself: The Origin and Nature of the Powerful Emotion That Shapes Our Lives and Our World* (New York: St. Martin's Press, 1998), 64–66.
9. Ibid., 66.
10. Ibid., 67.
11. Ibid., 67–68.
12. Lyall Watson, *The Nature of Things: The Secret Life of Inanimate Objects* (Rochester, Vt.: Destiny Books, 1992), 168.
13. John Fuller, *The Ghost of Flight 401* (New York: Berkley Publishing Company, 1976), 60.
14. Ibid., 118.
15. Ibid., 82–83.
16. Ibid., 41.
17. Ibid., 130.
18. Ibid., 55.
19. Ibid, 164.
20. Ibid, 206.
21. Lyall Watson, *Supernature: A Natural History of the Supernatural* (New York: Bantam Books, 1973), 228.

22. David Henry Feldman, *Nature's Gambit: Child Prodigies and the Development of Human Potential* (New York: Basic Books, 1986), 196–97.

23. Ibid.

24. Alexander Lowen, *Pleasure: A Creative Approach to Life* (New York: Penguin Books, 1970), 157.

25. Ibid., 185–86.

26. Peter A. Levine with Ann Frederick, *Waking the Tiger: Healing Trauma* (Berkeley, Calif.: North Atlantic Books, 1997), 137.

27. Mona Lisa Schulz, *Awakening Intuition* (New York: Harmony Books, 1998), 106–7.

28. Larry Dossey, *Healing Beyond the Body* (Boston: Shambhala, 2001), 253 (telesomatic events); Mona Lisa Schulz, *Awakening Intuition* (New York: Harmony Books, 1998), 75 (clairsentience).

29. Larry Dossey, *Healing Beyond the Body* (Boston: Shambhala, 2001), 253.

30. Ibid.

31. Ibid., 253–54.

32. Ibid., 254.

33. Larry Dossey, *Reinventing Medicine* (New York: HarperSanFrancisco, 1999), 136–37.

34. Larry Dossey, *Healing Beyond the Body* (Boston: Shambhala, 2001), 254.

35. Larry Dossey, *Reinventing Medicine* (New York: HarperSanFrancisco, 1999), 93–94.

36. Jan Ehrenwald, *The ESP Experience: A Psychiatric Validation* (New York: Basic Books, 1978), 21–23.

37. Ibid., 26.

38. John Fuller, *The Ghost of Flight 401* (New York: Berkley Publishing Company, 1976), 312.

39. Diane Ackerman, *A Natural History of the Senses* (New York: Random House, 1990), 5, 43.

40. Morton Schatzman, "Ghosts in the Machine," *Psychology Today* (January 1981): 99.

41. Morton Schatzman, "Living with Apparitions," *New York Times Magazine,* April 27, 1980, 126.

42. Pamela Fitch and Trish Dryden, "Recovering Body and Soul from Post-Traumatic Stress Disorder," *Massage Therapy Journal* 39 (1) (Spring 2000), www.amtamassage.org/journal/soul.html (discussing Bessel van der Kolk); Daniel Goleman, *Emotional Intelligence* (New York: Bantam Books, 1995), 201–3.

43. Morton Schatzman, "Living with Apparitions," *New York Times Magazine,* April 27, 1980, 129–30.

44. William J. Cromie, "Hypnosis Found to Alter the Brain: Subjects See Color Where None Exists," *Harvard University Gazette,* August 21, 2000, www .news.harvard.edu/gazette/2000/08.21/hypnosis.html.

45. Michael Talbot, *The Holographic Universe* (New York: HarperCollins, 1991), 163.

46. Martin L. Rossman, "What Is Imagery, and How Does It Work?" excerpted from his book *Guided Imagery for Self-Healing* (Novato, Calif.: New World Library, 2000), HealthWorld Online, www.healthy.net/asp/templates/article .asp?pagetype=article&id=389; Martin L. Rossman, "Guided Imagery," in *Complementary and Integrative Medicine in Cancer Care and Prevention,* ed. Marc S. Micozzi (New York: Springer, 2007).

47. Victor Mansfield, Sally Rhine-Feather, and James Hall, "The Rhine-Jung Letters: Distinguishing Parapsychological from Synchronistic Events," *Journal of Parapsychology* 62 (1) (March 1998), 3–25.

48. John McCrone, *The Myth of Irrationality* (New York: Carroll & Graf Publishers, 1993), 165.

49. Ibid., 180–81.

50. Ibid., 184.

51. Robert L. Van de Castle, *Our Dreaming Mind* (New York: Ballantine Books, 1994), xix.

52. Ibid., xix, 400–401.

53. Ibid., ix.

54. Ibid., 364–65.

55. Ibid., 368–69.

56. Ibid., 409.

57. Michael Shallis, *On Time: An Investigation into Scientific Knowledge and Human Experience* (New York: Schocken Books, 1982), 174–75.

58. Andrew Nichols and William Roll, "The Jacksonville Water Poltergeist: Electromagnetic and Neuropsychological Aspects," in *Proceedings of Presented Papers, The Parapsychological Association* (forty-first annual convention, August 6–9, 1998, Halifax, Nova Scotia), 97–107.

59. Ibid., 105.

60. Ibid., 97.

61. Michael Talbot, *The Holographic Universe* (New York: HarperCollins, 1991), 149–50.

62. Gabor Maté, *When the Body Says No: Understanding the Stress-Disease Connection* (Hoboken, New Jersey: John Wiley & Sons, Inc., 2003), 172–76.

63. Cyril W. Smith and Simon Best, *Electromagnetic Man: Health and Hazard in the Electrical Environment* (New York: St. Martin's Press, 1989), 86–87, 93, 97.

64. F. David Peat, *Synchronicity: The Bridge between Matter and Mind* (New York: Bantam Books, 1987), 21.

65. Cyril W. Smith and Simon Best, *Electromagnetic Man: Health and Hazard in the Electrical Environment* (New York: St. Martin's Press, 1989), 100.

66. Michael Shallis, *The Electric Connection: Its Effects on Mind and Body* (New York: New Amsterdam Books, 1988).

67. Ibid., 22.

68. Ibid., 27–28.

69. James Houran and Rense Lange, "Diary of Events in a Thoroughly Unhaunted House," *Perceptual and Motor Skills* 83 (1996): 499–502; James Houran and Rense Lange, "Hauntings and Poltergeist-Like Episodes as a Confluence of Conventional Phenomena: A General Hypothesis," *Perceptual and Motor Skills* 83 (1996): 1307–16.

70. Harvey J. Irwin, "Childhood Antecedents of Out-of-Body and Déjà Vu Experiences," *Journal of the American Society for Psychical Research* 90 (3) (1996): 157–72; Harvey J. Irwin, "Origins and Functions of Paranormal Belief: The Role of Childhood Trauma and Interpersonal Control," *Journal of the American Society for Psychical Research* 86 (3) (1992): 199–208; Harvey J. Irwin "Childhood Belief and the Origins of Paranormal Belief: A Constructive Replication," *Psychological Reports* 74 (1994): 107–11; Sandra Stockenius and Peter Brugger, "Perceived Electrosensitivity and Magical Ideation," *Perceptual and Motor Skills* 90 (2000): 899–900; U. F. Malt and others, "Physical and Mental Problems Attributed to Dental Amalgam Fillings: A Descriptive Study of 99 Self-Referred Patients Compared with 272 Controls," *Psychosomatic Medicine* 59 (1997): 32–41.

71. Ulrich Frick and others, "Comparison Perception of Singular Transcranial Magnetic Stimuli by Subjectively Electrosensitive Subjects and General Population Controls," *Bioelectromagnetics* 26 (2005): 287–98; S. Liden, "Sensitivity to Electricity: A New Environmental Epidemic" *Allergy* 51 (1996): 519–24.

72. Gordon Rattray Taylor, *The Natural History of the Mind* (New York: E. P. Dutton, 1979), 218.

73. Joseph Chilton Pearce, *Magical Child: Rediscovering Nature's Plan for Our Children* (New York: Bantam Books, 1977), 196.

74. Matthew Manning, *The Link* (New York: Holt, Reinhart and Winston, 1975), 25.

75. Ibid., 98–99.

76. Cyril W. Smith and Simon Best, *Electromagnetic Man: Health and Hazard in the Electrical Environment* (New York: St. Martin's Press, 1989), 99.

77. Colin Wilson, *Poltergeist: A Study in Destructive Haunting* (New York: G. P. Putnam's Sons, 1982), 279.

78. D. Scott Rogo, *The Poltergeist Experience* (Wellingborough, Northampton-shire, England: The Aquarian Press, 1979), 225–29, 236–37.

79. Theresa Crenshaw, *The Alchemy of Love and Lust* (New York: G. P. Putnam's Sons, 1996).

80. Alice Park, "Sexual Healing," *Time* (January 19, 2004): 38–39.

81. Montagu, Ashley. *Touching: The Human Significance of the Skin,* 3rd ed. (New York: Perennial Library, 1986), 160.

82. Theresa Crenshaw, *The Alchemy of Love and Lust* (New York: G. P. Putnam's Sons, 1996), 82.

83. Alice Park, "Sexual Healing," *Time* (January 19, 2004): 38–39.

84. Suzi Landolphi, "Sexually Speaking," *Spa Magazine* (Fall 1998): 14.

Chapter 8. Sensitivity, Personality Traits, and Anomalous Perception

1. *Newsweek,* March 8, 2004, 19 (letter to the editor, name withheld).

2. Julie Robotham, "Riddle of the Quiet Killer," *Sydney Morning Herald,* May 4, 2002, 37, www.smh.com.au/articles/2002/05/03/1019441432740.html.

3. A. D. Cornell, "The Seen and Unseen Ghost," *International Journal of Parapsychology* XI (1) (2000): 143–48.

4. William Morris, ed., *American Heritage Dictionary of the English Language* (Boston: Houghton Mifflin Company, 1981), 1180.

5. Weiert Velle, "Sex Differences in Sensory Functions," *Perspectives in Biology and Medicine* 30 (4) (1987): 490–522.

6. Andy Coghlan, "How Sensitivity to Pain is Really All in the Mind," *New Scientist,* June 28, 2003, 17.

7. Richard Hollingham, "In the Realm of Your Senses," *New Scientist* (January 31, 2004): 40–43.

8. Jillyn Smith, *Senses and Sensibilities* (New York: John Wiley & Sons, 1989), 2–3; Lyall Watson, *Jacobson's Organ: And the Remarkable Nature of Smell* (New York: Plume, 2001).

9. Roxanne Khamsi, "Plastic Brains Help the Blind Place Sounds," January 25, 2005, *Chinese Medical & Biological Information,* http://cmbi.bjmu.edu.cn/news/0501/136.htm.

10. Anonymous, personal correspondence with author, September 19, 2000.

11. Dennis William Hauck, *Haunted Places: The National Directory* (New York: Penguin Books, 1996).

12. Paul Martin, *The Healing Mind* (New York: St. Martin's Press, 1997).

13. Richard Hollingham, "In the Realm of Your Senses," *New Scientist* (January 31, 2004): 40–43.

14. Lyall Watson, *Jacobson's Organ: And the Remarkable Nature of Smell* (New York: Plume, 2001).

15. Ibid.; Michael Schirber, "Women Suffer More Than Men," July 6, 2005, www .livescience.com/humanbiology/050706_pain_gender.html; University of California–Los Angeles, "Gender Differences in Response to Pain" (press release), November 5, 2003, www.sciencedaily.com/releases/2003/11/031105064626 .htm.

16. Elaine N. Aron, *The Highly Sensitive Person: How to Thrive When the World Overwhelms You* (New York: Carol Publishing Group, 1996).

17. Ibid., 7.

18. Ibid., 10–12.

19. Ibid., 14–15.

20. Jerome Kagan and Nancy Snidman, "Temperament and a Religious Perspective," *APS Observer* (Association for Psychological Science) 18 (10) (Oct. 2005), http://psychologicalscience.org/observer/getArticle.cfm?id=1862.

21. Elaine N. Aron, *The Highly Sensitive Person: How to Thrive When the World Overwhelms You* (New York: Carol Publishing Group, 1996), 20–21.

22. Ibid., xi.

23. Sharon Heller, *Too Loud, Too Bright, Too Fast, Too Tight: What to Do If You Are Sensory Defensive in an Overstimulating World* (New York: HarperCollins, 2002).

24. Ibid., 3.

25. Ibid., 9.

26. Ibid., 10.

27. Ibid., 95.

28. Ibid., 95.

29. Ibid., 152.

30. Ibid., 145–46.

31. Ibid., 146–47.

32. Ibid., 149–52.

33. Karen A. Smith and Karen R. Gouze, *The Sensory-Sensitive Child* (New York: HarperResources, 2005).

34. Ibid., 15.

35. Brock Eide and Fernette Eide, *The Mislabeled Child* (New York: Penguin, 2005), as quoted on The Sensory Processing Disorder Resource Center, www

.sensory-processing-disorder.com/autism-and-sensory-integration.html.

36. Sensory Processing Disorders Foundation, "Summary of Research Findings in Sensory Processing Disorder from KR1-07-06," http://209.169.7.42/library/kri.html.

37. Karen A. Smith and Karen R. Gouze, *The Sensory-Sensitive Child* (New York: HarperResources, 2005), 32–33.

38. Ibid., 36–38, 41–43.

39. Ibid., 16.

40. Occupational therapist Jane Koomar, personal communication with author, December 21, 2007.

41. Ibid.

42. Ernest Hartmann, *Boundaries in the Mind* (New York: Basic Books, 1991).

43. Ibid., 4–7.

44. Nicholas Humphrey, *A History of the Mind* (New York: Simon & Schuster, 1992), 204.

45. Ernest Hartmann, *Boundaries in the Mind* (New York: Basic Books, 1991), 34.

46. Ibid.

47. Ibid., 72.

48. Ibid., 7.

49. Ibid., 225.

50. Ibid., 233, 241.

51. Ibid., 15.

52. Paul Bergman and Sibylle K. Escalona, "Unusual Sensitivities in Very Young Children," *The Psychoanalytic Study of the Child* II (1949): 333–52.

53. Ibid., 333.

54. Ibid., 345–47.

55. Ian Wickramasekera, "Secrets Kept from the Mind but Not the Body or Behavior: The Unsolved Problems of Identifying and Treating Somatization and Psychophysiological Disease," *Advances in Mind-Body Medicine* 14 (1998): 81–132.

56. Ibid., 83.

57. Ibid., 84.

58. Ibid., 83–85.

59. Elizabeth Bogod, "Examining Sensitivity," www.ldpride.net/sensitivity.htm.

60. Stephanie S. Tolan, "Dabrowski's Over-excitabilities: A Layman's Explanation," www.stephanietolan.com/dabrowskis.htm.

61. Michael M. Piechowski, "Overexcitabilities," in *Encyclopedia of Creativity,* eds., Mark A. Runco and Steven R. Pritzker (Burlington, Mass., and St. Louis, Mo.: Academic Press, 1999), 325–33.

62. Positive Disintegration, "The Theory of Positive Disintegration by Kazimierz Dabrowski," www.positivedisintegration.com.

63. Sal Mendaglio, "Emotional Sensitivity in Gifted Children," Centre for Gifted Education, University of Calgary, www.ucalgary.ca/~gifted/resources/articles/Emotional%20SensitivitySM.pdf.

64. Stephanie S. Tolan, "Spirituality and the Highly Gifted Adolescent," www.stephanietolan.com/spirituality.htm.

65. Institute of Noetic Sciences, "Mapping Consciousness Through Research and Education: 2003/2004 Program Portfolio," www.noetic.org/research/files/folio.pdf, 9.

66. Auke Tellegen and Gilbert Atkinson, "Openness to Absorbing and Self-Altering Experiences ('Absorption'), a Trait Related to Hypnotic Susceptibility," *Journal of Abnormal Psychology* 83 (3) (1974): 268–77.

67. Ibid., 270.

68. "Why Streep Plays It Safe," *The Week,* August 13, 2004, People section, 10.

69. EncycloComedia, "David Frye," www.comedystars.com/bios/frye_david.shtml.

70. Auke Tellegen and Gilbert Atkinson, "Openness to Absorbing and Self-Altering Experiences ('Absorption'), a Trait Related to Hypnotic Susceptibility," *Journal of Abnormal Psychology* 83 (3) (1974): 276.

71. Ibid., 274–75.

72. Ibid., 275.

73. Paul Bergman and Sibylle K. Escalona, "Unusual Sensitivities in Very Young Children," *The Psychoanalytic Study of the Child* II (1949): 336.

74. Sheryl C. Wilson and Theodore X. Barber, "The Fantasy-Prone Personality: Implications for Understanding Imagery, Hypnosis, and Parapsychological Phenomena," in *Imagery: Current Theory, Research and Application,* ed. Anees A. Sheikh (New York: John Wiley & Sons, 1983), 340–87.

75. Ibid., 340.

76. Ibid., 354–55.

77. Ibid., 355.

78. Ibid., 381.

79. Elaine N. Aron, *The Highly Sensitive Person: How to Thrive When the World Overwhelms You* (New York: Carol Publishing Group, 1996), 161.

80. Sheryl C. Wilson and Theodore X. Barber, "The Fantasy-Prone Personality: Implications for Understanding Imagery, Hypnosis, and Parapsychological Phenomena," in *Imagery: Current Theory, Research and Application,* ed. Anees A. Sheikh (New York: John Wiley & Sons, 1983), 350.

81. Ibid., 350.

82. Ibid., 352–53.

83. Ibid., 354.

84. Ibid., 359.

85. Ibid., 379.

86. Steven J. Lynn and Judith W. Rhue, "Fantasy Proneness: Hypnosis, Developmental Antecedents, and Psychopathology," *American Psychologist* 44 (1988): 35–44.

87. Tracy R. Gleason, "Imaginary Companions and Peer Acceptance," *International Journal of Behavioral Development* 28 (3) (2004): 204–9.

88. Robert D. Friedberg, "Allegorical Lives: Children and Their Imaginary Companions," *Child Study Journal* 25 (1) (1995): 1–22.

89. Tracy R. Gleason, Raceel N. Jarudi, and Jonathan M. Cheek, "Imagination, Personality and Imaginary Companions," *Social Behavior and Personality* 31 (January 2003), 721–37; Paula Bouldin and Chris Pratt, "A Systematic Assessment of the Specific Fears, Anxiety Level, and Temperament of Children with Imaginary Companions," *Australian Journal of Psychology* 54 (2) (2002): 79–85.

90. Brett Laurson, ed., *Close Friendships in Adolescence* (San Francisco, Jossey-Bass Publishers, 1993), 75; Norma Estelle Cutts and Nicholas Moseley, *The Only Child: A Guide for Parents and Only Children of All Ages* (New York: G. P. Putnam, 1954), 96.

91. Marjorie Taylor, *Imaginary Companions and the Children Who Create Them* (New York: Oxford University Press, 1999), 70.

92. Ibid., 64.

93. Ibid., 115.

94. Brett Laurson, ed., *Close Friendships in Adolescence* (San Francisco, Jossey-Bass Publishers, 1993), 78.

95. Marjorie Taylor, *Imaginary Companions and the Children Who Create Them* (New York: Oxford University Press, 1999), 131.

96. Tracy R. Gleason, Raceel N. Jarudi, and Jonathan M. Cheek, "Imagination, Personality and Imaginary Companions," *Social Behavior and Personality* 31 (January 2003), 721–37.

97. Michael A. Thalbourne, "Transliminality: A Review," *International Journal of Parapsychology* 11 (2) (2000): 1–34.

98. Ibid., 5–7.

99. Michael A. Thalbourne and others, "Transliminality, Brain Function, and Synesthesia," *Journal of Nervous and Mental Disease* 189 (3) (2001): 190–92.

100. Gordon Rattray Taylor, *The Natural History of the Mind* (New York: E. P. Dutton, 1979), 220.

101. Ibid.

102. Ibid., 221–22.

103. James Houran and Rense Lange, "Diary of Events in a Thoroughly Unhaunted House," *Perceptual and Motor Skills* 83 (1996): 499–502.

104. James Houran and Carl Williams, "Relation of Tolerance of Ambiguity to Global and Specific Paranormal Experience," *Psychological Reports* 83 (1998): 807–18.

105. Rense Lange and James Houran, "The Role of Fear in Delusions of the Paranormal," *Journal of Nervous and Mental Disease* 187 (3) (1999): 159–66.

106. Richard Wiseman and others, "An Investigation into Alleged 'Hauntings,'" *British Journal of Psychology* 94 (2003): 195–211; Arran Frood, "Ghosts 'All in the Mind,'" BBC News, May 21, 2003, http://news.bbc.co.uk/2/hi/science/nature/3044607.stm; BBC News Scotland, "Castle Ghost Hunt's 'Curious' Findings," April 17, 2001, http://news.bbc.co.uk/2/hi/uk_news/scotland/1282114.stm.

107. Gordon Rattray Taylor, *The Natural History of the Mind* (New York: E. P. Dutton, 1979), 7–8.

108. Geoffery Schultz and Ronald Melzack, "The Charles Bonnet Syndrome: 'Phantom Visual Images,'" *Perception* 20 (6) (1991): 809–25.

109. Gene Weingarten, "Below the Beltway," *The Washington Post Magazine,* December 29, 2002, 3–5.

110. Jerry L. Carter, "Visual, Somatosensory, Olfactory, and Gustatory Hallucinations," *Psychiatric Clinics of North America* 15 (2) (1992): 347–58.

111. Ibid., 352.

112. Judy Foreman, "When Stopping to Smell Is a Problem," *Boston Globe,* May 8, 2001, www.myhealthsense.com/F20010508_stoppingSmell.html.

113. Simon Baron-Cohen, "Is There a Normal Phase of Synaesthesia in Development?" *Psyche* 2 (27) (1996), http://psyche.csse.monash.edu.au/v2/psyche-2-27-baron_cohen.html.

114. Brad Lemley, "Do You See What They See?" *Discover,* December 1999, 80–87.

115. Carol J. Schneider, "The Right Orbitofrontal Cortex—Master Regulator of the Brain and Body," *Bridges* (International Society for the Study of Subtle Energies and Energy Medicine) 8 (1) (1997): 8–10.

116. Michael Hopkin, "Brain Electrodes Conjure Up Ghostly Visions," *Nature News,* September 20, 2006, as reprinted on BioEd Online, Baylor College of Medicine, www.bioedonline.org/news/news-print.cfm?art=2805.

117. Peter McKellar, in *The Potential of Fantasy and Imagination,* Anees A. Sheikh and John T. Shaffer, eds. (New York: Brandon House, 1979), 189–97.

118. Ibid., 195–96.

119. Kevin R. Nelson and others, "Does the Arousal System Contribute to Near Death Experience?" *Neurology* 66 (2006): 1003–9.

120. Maurice M. Ohayon, "Prevalence of Hallucinations and Their Pathological Associations in the General Population," *Psychiatry Research* 97 (2–3) (December 27, 2000): 153–64.

121. Peter McKellar, in *The Potential of Fantasy and Imagination,* Anees A. Sheikh and John T. Shaffer, eds. (New York: Brandon House, 1979), 194.

122. Sheryl C. Wilson and Theodore X. Barber, "The Fantasy-Prone Personality: Implications for Understanding Imagery, Hypnosis, and Parapsychological Phenomena," in *Imagery: Current Theory, Research and Application,* ed. Anees A. Sheikh (New York: John Wiley & Sons, 1983), 365.

123. Celia Green, "Waking Dreams and Other Metachoric Experiences," *Psychiatric Journal of the University of Ottawa* 15 (2) (1990): 123–28.

124. Ibid., 125.

125. Sheryl C. Wilson and Theodore X. Barber, "The Fantasy-Prone Personality: Implications for Understanding Imagery, Hypnosis, and Parapsychological Phenomena," in *Imagery: Current Theory, Research and Application,* Anees A. Sheikh, ed. (New York: John Wiley & Sons, 1983), 352.

126. Ibid., 353–54.

127. Michaeleen C. Maher, "Quantitative Investigation of the General Wayne Inn," *Journal of Parapsychology* 64 (2000): 365–90.

128. Gertrude R. Schmeidler, "Quantitative Investigation of a 'Haunted House,'" *Journal of the American Society for Psychical Research* 60 (1966): 137–49.

129. William H. Philpott and Dwight K. Kalita, *Brain Allergies: The Psycho-Nutrient Connection* (New Canaan, Conn.: Keats Publishing, 1980), 18–19.

130. Temple Grandin and Catherine Johnson, *Animals in Translation* (New York: Scribner, 2005), 24.

131. Garry Cooper, "The Gorilla in the Living Room" (report from the 2005 Networker Symposium), *Psychotherapy Networker,* May 2005.

132. Elaine N. Aron, *The Highly Sensitive Person: How to Thrive When the World Overwhelms You* (New York: Carol Publishing Group, 1996), 7.

133. Temple Grandin and Catherine Johnson, *Animals in Translation* (New York: Scribner, 2005), 65.

134. Ibid., 51.

135. Ibid., 67.

136. Dan Olmsted, "The Age of Autism: More Sick Kids," United Press International, October 10, 2005.

137. Jill Neimark, "Autism: It's Not Just in the Head," *Discover*, April 2007, 33–38, 75 (quoting Martha Herbert).

138. Ibid.; Medical News Today, "Autistic Behaviors in Offspring Linked to Prenatal Exposure to Maternal Antibodies," February 12, 2008, www.medicalnewstoday.com/articles/97029.php.

139. Carrie Payton Dahlberg, "Study Explores Autism Link to Immune System," *Sacramento Bee*, January 25, 2008, B2.

140. Katerina Peshava, "Autism's Origins: Mother's Antibody Production May Affect Fetal Brain," *The Gazette* (Johns Hopkins University) 37 (2) (March 3, 2008), www.jhu.edu/~gazette/2008/03mar08/03autism.html.

141. William Stillman, *Autism and the God Connection* (Naperville, Ill.: Sourcebooks, 2006).

142. Donna Williams, *Autism and Sensing: The Unlost Instinct* (London: Jessica Kingsley Publishers, 1998).

143. Ibid., 55, 59.

144. Ibid., 35–36.

145. Baylor College of Medicine, "Poor Recognition of 'Self' Found in High Functioning People with Autism," news release, February 6, 2008, www.bcm.edu/news/item.cfm?newsID=1058.

146. "Mapping 'Self' and 'Other' in the Brain," *Science Daily*, May 19, 2006, www.sciencedaily.com/releases/2006/05/060519124614.htm.

147. Baylor College of Medicine, "Poor Recognition of 'Self' Found in High Functioning People with Autism," news release, February 6, 2008, www.bcm.edu/news/item.cfm?newsID=1058.

148. Claudia Wallis, "Inside the Autistic Mind, *Time* (May 7, 2006), 43–51, www.time.com/time/magazine/article/0,9171,1191843,00.html.

149. Centers for Disease Control and Prevention, "Autism Spectrum Disorders Fact Sheet," www.cdc.gov/ncbddd/autism/actearly/autism.html.

150. Matthew Manning, *The Link* (New York: Holt, Reinhart and Winston, 1975); Jan Ehrenwald, *The ESP Experience: A Psychiatric Validation* (New York: Basic Books, 1978), 185 (discussion of work by psychologist Peter Bander).

151. Ibid., 186–87.

152. Ibid., 188.

153. National Institutes of Health, "Asperger Syndrome," National Institute of Child Health and Development, www.nichd.nih.gov/health/topics/asperger_syndrome.cfm; Roy Richard Grinker, *Unstrange Minds* (New York: Basic Books, 2007), 60–61.

154. National Institute of Neurological Disorders and Stroke, "Autism Fact Sheet," www.ninds.nih.gov/disorders/autism/detail_autism.htm.

155. Roy Richard Grinker, *Unstrange Minds* (New York: Basic Books, 2007), 62–63.

156. Autism Society of America, "What is Autism: Facts and Stats," www.autism -society.org/site/PageServer?pagename=about_whatis_factsstats (figures quoted from 2001 report by the Centers for Disease Control and Prevention).

157. Miranda Hill, "Autism Spectrum Disorders More Common than Previously Believed, CDC Says after 14-State Study," MedicineNet.com, February 8, 2007, www.medicinenet.com/script/main/art.asp?articlekey=79371.

158. Roy Richard Grinker, *Unstrange Minds* (New York: Basic Books, 2007), 5.

159. Morton Ann Gernsbacher, review of *Unstrange Minds: Remapping the World of Autism,* by Roy R. Grinker, *Nature Medicine* 14 (3) (2008): 241.

160. Centers for Disease Control and Prevention, "Autism Spectrum Disorders Fact Sheet," www.cdc.gov/ncbddd/autism/actearly/autism.html.

161. Claudia Wallis, "Inside the Autistic Mind, *Time* (May 7, 2006), 43–51, www .time.com/time/magazine/article/0,9171,1191843,00.html.

162. American Association for the Advancement of Science, "Autistic Manner- isms Reduced by Sensory Treatment," EurekAlert!, April 25, 2008, www .eurekalert.org/pub_releases/2008-04/tu-amr042508.php.

163. Randolph E. Schmid, "Study: Brain May Have 'Blindsight,'" Associated Press, October 31, 2005, as reprinted on RedOrbit, www.redorbit.com/news/ science/290484/brain_may_have_blindsight/.

164. Elaine N. Aron, *The Highly Sensitive Person: How to Thrive When the World Overwhelms You* (New York: Carol Publishing Group, 1996), 4.

165. Temple Grandin and Catherine Johnson, *Animals in Translation* (New York: Scribner, 2005), 57–60, 285–287.

166. Ibid., 288.

167. Amy Tyberg and William H. Frishman, "Animal Assisted Therapy," in *Com- plementary and Integrative Medicine in Pain Management,* edited by Michael I. Weintraub, Ravinder Mamtani, and Marc S. Micozzi (New York; Springer, 2008), 115–24.

168. David M. Dosa, "A Day in the Life of Oscar the Cat," *New England Journal of Medicine* 357 (4) (July 26, 2007): 328–29; Associated Press, "Cat Plays Furry Grim Reaper at Nursing Home," July 27, 2007, MSNBC, www.msnbc.msn .com/id/19959718.

169. Temple Grandin and Catherine Johnson, *Animals in Translation* (New York: Scribner, 2005), 57.

170. Ibid., 63.

171. Kreskin, *Secrets of the Amazing Kreskin* (Buffalo, N.Y.: Prometheus Books, 1991), 149–50.

172. Ibid., preface.

173. Kreskin, personal interview with author, April 5, 2005.

174. Kreskin, *Secrets of the Amazing Kreskin* (Buffalo, N.Y.: Prometheus Books, 1991), 2.

Chapter 9. Environmental Sensitivity: Attesting to the Bodymind

1. Center for the Advancement of Health, "Fibromyalgia Syndrome: Improving the Treatment, Unraveling the Cause," *Facts of Life* 6 (8) (December 2001); Center for the Advancement of Health, "Migraine: Prevention and Treatment More Effective Than Most Realize," *Facts of Life* 7 (1) (February 2002).

2. Howard Mertz and others, "Regional Cerebral Activation in Irritable Bowel Syndrome and Control Subjects with Painful and Nonpainful Rectal Distension," *Gastroenterology* 118 (5) (May 2000): 842–48.

3. Andrew Cocke, "Men and Women Remember Things in Different Ways," *Brain Work* (Charles A. Dana Foundation), July–August 2002, 7.

4. Susan Hornik, "For Some, Pain is Orange," *Smithsonian* (February 2001): 48–56, www.smithsonianmag.com/science-nature/synesthesia-abstract.html.

5. Michael A. Thalbourne and others, "Transliminality, Brain Function, and Synesthesia," *Journal of Nervous and Mental Disease* 189 (3) (2001): 190–92; *The Diane Rehm Show,* National Public Radio (WAMU-FM), March 6, 2000, http://wamu.org/programs/dr/00/03/06.php; "A Sixth Sense," *60 Minutes II,* CBS News, August 14, 2002, www.cbsnews.com/stories/2002/01/08/60II/main323596.shtml.

6. Richard E. Cytowic, "Synesthesia: Phenomenology and Neuropsychology," *Psyche* 2 (10) (1995), http://psyche.csse.monash.edu.au/v2/psyche-2-10-cytowic.html.

7. Sean O'Neill, "A Striking Mystery," *Washington Post,* July 29, 2003, F1.

8. Institute of Noetic Sciences, "Donor Spotlight: David Ritchey—Sensitivity and the Transpersonal Experience," September 30, 2007, www.shiftinaction.com/node/5201; David Ritchey, personal correspondence with author, January 8, 2004; Dean Radin, personal correspondence with author, May 8, 2006.

9. Brandon Massullo, "Environmental Sensitivity and Paranormal Experience" Master's Dissertation, University of Edinburgh, 2008 (unpublished).

10. Helen Pearson, "Chronic Fatigue Has Genetic Roots," *Nature News,* April

21, 2006, as reprinted on BioEd Online, Baylor College of Medicine, www
.bioedonline.org/news/news.cfm?art=2487; Amanda Gardner, "Genetics May Drive Chronic Fatigue Syndrome," *HealthDay News,* April 20,
2006, as reprinted on HealingWell, http://news.healingwell.com/index.
php?p=news1&id=532266; Thomas H. Maugh II, "Chronic Fatigue Is in the
Genes, Study Finds," *Los Angeles Times,* April 21, 2006, A1; Emily See, "New
Evidence That Genetics are Responsible for Chronic Fatigue Syndrome," May
2, 2006, as reprinted on ProHealth, www.prohealth.com/library/showarticle
.cfm?id=7142&t=CFIDS_FM.

11. Weiert Velle, "Sex Differences in Sensory Functions," *Perspectives in Biology and Medicine* 30 (4) (1987): 490–522.
12. Ibid., 503–4.
13. Ibid., 504.
14. Ibid., 510.
15. Ibid., 509.
16. Society for Women's Health Research, "Sex Differences in Autoimmune Disease" (fact sheet), August 2004, www.womenshealthresearch.org/site/PageServer?pagename=hs_facts_autoimmune.
17. Paul Martin, *The Healing Mind: The Vital Links Between Brain and Behavior, Immunity and Disease* (New York: St. Martin's Press, 1997), 72.
18. University of California–Los Angeles, "Same Genes Act Differently in Males and Females" (press release), July 7, 2006, www.newswise.com/p/articles/view/521772/.
19. Larry Cahill, "His Brain, Her Brain," *Scientific American* (April 25, 2005), 40–47, www.sciam.com/article.cfm?id=his-brain-her-brain.
20. Jo Durden-Smith and Diane deSimone, *Sex and the Brain* (New York: Arbor House, 1983), 76.
21. Weiert Velle, "Sex Differences in Sensory Functions," *Perspectives in Biology and Medicine* 30 (4) (1987): 490–522.
22. Bjorn Carey, "Men and Women Really Do Think Differently," LiveScience, January 20, 2005, www.livescience.com/humanbiology/050120_brain_sex.html.
23. Jo Durden-Smith and Diane deSimone, *Sex and the Brain* (New York: Arbor House, 1983), 77–81.
24. Andrew Cocke, "Men and Women Remember Things in Different Ways," *Brain Work* (Charles A. Dana Foundation) (July–August 2002): 7.
25. Rhawn Joseph, *The Naked Neuron* (New York: Plenum Press, 1993), 382.
26. Ibid., 385.

510   *Notes*

27. Ibid., 386–87.

28. Thomas K. Connellan, *Bringing Out the Best in Others: 3 Keys for Business Leaders, Educators, Coaches and Parents* (Austin, Texas: Bard Press, 2003).

29. Wilfried Karmaus and others, "Does the Sibling Effect Have Its Origin In Utero? Investigating Birth Order, Cord Blood IgE Concentration, and Allergic Sensitization at Age Four," *American Journal of Epidemiology* 154 (2001): 909–15.

30. Brett Laurson, ed., *Close Friendships in Adolescence* (San Francisco: Jossey-Bass Publishers, 1993), 75.

31. David Wolman, "On the Other Hand," *New Scientist* (November 5, 2005): 36–39.

32. Ibid.; Stephen Christman, personal correspondence with author, November 18, 2005.

33. Julia Simner and others, "Synesthesia: the Prevalence of Atypical Cross-Modal Experiences," *Perception* 35 (8) (2006): 1024–33, abstract on PubMed, National Center for Biotechnology Information, www.ncbi.nlm.nih.gov/pubmed/17076063.

34. Evan Moreno-Davis, "Synesthesia: What Happens When Our Senses Get Their Wires Crossed?" www.neuroscience.pomona.edu/Evan/.

35. Sean Day, "Synaesthesia," http://home.comcast.net/~sean.day/html/types.htm.

36. Alison Abbott, "Ouch, I Saw That," *Nature News,* June 17, 2007, as reprinted on BioEd Online, Baylor College of Medicine, www.bioedonline.org/picks/news.cfm?art=3386; Charles Q. Choi, "Study: Some People Literally Feel Pain of Others," June 17, 2007, www.livescience.com/health/070617_touching_faces.html.

37. Richard Cytowic, cited in Synesthesia and the Synesthetic Experience, http://web.mit.edu/synesthesia/www/.

38. "A Sixth Sense," *60 Minutes II,* CBS News, August 14, 2002, www.cbsnews.com/stories/2002/01/08/60II/main323596.shtml.

39. Evan Moreno-Davis, "Synesthesia: What Happens When Our Senses Get Their Wires Crossed?" www.neuroscience.pomona.edu/Evan/.

40. "A Sixth Sense," *60 Minutes II,* CBS News, August 14, 2002, www.cbsnews.com/stories/2002/01/08/60II/main323596.shtml.

41. Shankar, Vedantam, "When Sound is Red: Making Sense of Mixed Sensations," *Washington Post,* October 14, 2002, A12.

42. Susan Hornik, "For Some, Pain is Orange," *Smithsonian* (February 2001), 48–56, www.smithsonianmag.com/science-nature/synesthesia-abstract.html.

43. Karen Patterson, "Psychosis Puzzle Pieces," *Dallas Morning News,* June 3, 2002, C1.

44. Simon Baron-Cohen and others, "Synesthesia: Prevalence and Familiality," *Perception* 25 (9) (1996): 1073–79, abstract on PubMed, National Center for Biotechnology Information, www.ncbi.nlm.nih.gov/pubmed/8983047.

45. Julia Simner and others, "Synesthesia: the Prevalence of Atypical Cross-Modal Experiences," *Perception* 35 (8) (2006): 1024–33, abstract on PubMed, National Center for Biotechnology Information, www.ncbi.nlm.nih.gov/pubmed/17076063.

46. Ibid.

47. *The Diane Rehm Show*, National Public Radio (WAMU-FM, Washington, D.C.), March 6, 2000, http://wamu.org/programs/dr/00/03/06.php.

48. Ibid.

49. Carol Steen, "Synesthesia: Hearing Colors, Tasting Shapes," Smithsonian Institute Resident Associates Program, Washington, D.C., October 15, 2001.

50. Roger Highfield, "Why Miles Davis Saw the Blues," *London Telegraph*, Oct. 27, 2004, www.telegraph.co.uk/scienceandtechnology/science/science-news/3334830/Why-Miles-Davis-saw-the-blues.html.

51. Jamie Ward, "Emotionally Mediated Synaesthesia," *Cognitive Neuropsychology* 21 (7) (2004): 761–72.

52. Pat Duffy and Ann Kennedy, meeting with author, May 28, 2006.

53. Unmesh Kher, "Ah, the Blue Smell of It!" *Time* (May 21, 2001), p. 64, www.time.com/time/magazine/article/0,9171,999926,00.html.

54. Tracey Lawson, "Truly Feeling Blue," *The Scotsman* (October 29, 2000), http://thescotsman.scotsman.com/ViewArticle.aspx?articleid=2373367.

55. Sean Day, "Famous Synesthetes," http://home.comcast.net/~sean.day/html/famous_synesthetes.html.

56. Unmesh Kher, "Ah, the Blue Smell of It!" *Time* (May 21, 2001), p. 64, www.time.com/time/magazine/article/0,9171,999926,00.html.

57. Simon Baron-Cohen, "Is There a Normal Phase of Synaesthesia in Development?" *Psyche* 2 (27) (1996), http://psyche.csse.monash.edu.au/v2/psyche-2-27-baron_cohen.html.

58. Ibid.

59. Ibid.

60. *The Diane Rehm Show,* National Public Radio (WAMU-FM, Washington, D.C.), March 6, 2000, http://wamu.org/programs/dr/00/03/06.php.

61. Richard E. Cytowic, "Synesthesia: Phenomenology and Neuropsychology." *Psyche* 2 (10) (1995), http://psyche.csse.monash.edu.au/v2/psyche-2-10-cytowic.html.

62. Sheryl C. Wilson and Theodore X. Barber, "The Fantasy-Prone Personality: Implications for Understanding Imagery, Hypnosis, and Parapsychological Phenomena," in *Imagery: Current Theory, Research and Application,* Anees A. Sheikh, ed. (New York: John Wiley & Sons, 1983), 350.

63. Michael Shallis, *The Electric Connection* (New York: New Amsterdam Books, 1988), 80–81.

64. Kenneth Ring, *Heading Toward Omega* (New York: William Morrow and Company Inc., 1984), 238.

65. Ibid., 236–37.

66. Weiert Velle, "Sex Differences in Sensory Functions," *Perspectives in Biology and Medicine* 30 (4) (1987): 515.

67. Jo Durden-Smith and Diane deSimone, *Sex and the Brain* (New York: Arbor House, 1983), 73.

68. Richard E. Cytowic, "Synesthesia: Phenomenology and Neuropsychology." *Psyche* 2 (10) (1995), http://psyche.csse.monash.edu.au/v2/psyche-2-10-cytowic .html.

69. Susan Hornik, "For Some, Pain is Orange," *Smithsonian* (February 2001), 48–56, www.smithsonianmag.com/science-nature/synesthesia-abstract.html.

70. Richard E. Cytowic, "Synesthesia: Phenomenology and Neuropsychology," *Psyche* 2 (10) (1995), http://psyche.csse.monash.edu.au/v2/psyche-2-10-cytowic .html.

71. Siri Carpenter, "Everyday Fantasia: The World of Synesthesia," *Monitor on Psychology* 32 (3) (March 2001), www.apa.org/monitor/mar01/synesthesia.html.

72. Carlos S. Alvarado, "Synesthesia and Claims of Psi Experience: An Exploratory Study" (presented at the 37th annual convention of the Parapsychological Association, August 7–10, 1994, Amsterdam, The Netherlands).

73. Center for the Advancement of Health, "Migraine: Prevention and Treatment More Effective than Most Realize," *Facts of Life* 7 (1) (February 2002).

74. Jayne Custred, "Migraines' Causes Only Partially Understood," *Houston Chronicle,* February 9, 2002, C1, as reprinted on Migraine Awareness Group, www .migraines.org/about_media/chrnical.htm.

75. James W. Lance, *Migraines and Other Headaches* (East Roseville, New South Wales, Australia: Simon and Schuster, 1998), 57.

76. Cynthia Lambert-Nehr, "Ease the Agony of Migraines," *Detroit News,* June 18, 2003, H6.

77. Blackwell Publishing, "New Data Reveals Weather Can Trigger a Migraine," July 2004 (news release), http://blackwellpublishing.com/press/pressitem .asp?ref=92.

78. "Curing an Ill Wind," *Time,* June 14, 1971, www.time.com/time/magazine/article/0,9171,909893,00.html?promoid=googlep.

79. James W. Lance, *Migraines and Other Headaches* (East Roseville, New South Wales, Australia: Simon and Schuster, 1998), 62.

80. L. J. Cooke, M. S. Rose, and W. J. Becker, "Chinook Winds and Migraine Headache," *Neurology* 54 (2) (2000): 302, www.neurology.org/cgi/content/abstract/54/2/302; January 25, 2000, "Is it All in Your Head? No, Weather Can Trigger Migraines," *Science Daily,* www.sciencedaily.com/releases/2000/01/000125052856.htm.

81. G. Matteis and others, "Geomagnetic Activity, Humidity, Temperature and Headache: Is There Any Correlation?" *Headache* 34 (1) (1994): 41–42.

82. American Academy of Family Physicians, "Migraine Headaches: Ways to Deal with the Pain," http://familydoctor.org/online/famdocen/home/common/brain/disorders/127.html; "Understanding Migraines," Excedrin, www.excedrin.com/headache_center/migraines_understanding.shtml.

83. Jane E. Brody, "Scientists Cast Misery of Migraine in a New Light," *New York Times,* August 8, 2006, D7, www.nytimes.com/2006/08/08/health/08brody.html.

84. Center for the Advancement of Health, "Migraine: Prevention and Treatment More Effective Than Most Realize," *Facts of Life.* 7 (1) (February 2002).

85. Marilyn Elias, "Acupuncture's Secret: Blood Flow to Brain." *USA Today,* March 3, 2004, www.usatoday.com/news/health/2004-03-03-acupuncture-blood-usat_x.htm.

86. Jayne Custred, "Migraines' Causes Only Partially Understood," *Houston Chronicle,* February 9, 2002, C1, as reprinted on Migraine Awareness Group, www.migraines.org/about_media/chrnical.htm.

87. Seymour Diamond, *The Hormone Headache* (New York: Macmillan, 1995), 66.

88. Ibid., 67.

89. James W. Lance, *Migraines and Other Headaches* (East Roseville, New South Wales, Australia: Simon and Schuster, 1998), 89.

90. Stephen Appel, "Notes on the Psychosomatic Element of Migraine," *Forum: The Journal of the New Zealand Association of Psychotherapists* 5 (3) (1998): 209–18.

91. Ibid.

92. Ibid., quoting Oliver Sacks.

93. John E. Sarno, *The Divided Mind: The Epidemic of Mindbody Disorders* (New York: Regan Books, 2006), 67–75.

94. Stephen Appel, "Notes on the Psychosomatic Element of Migraine," *Forum: The Journal of the New Zealand Association of Psychotherapists* 5 (3) (1998): 209–18.

95. Stephen Appel, personal correspondence with author, January 6, 2004.

96. Michael A. Thalbourne, "Transliminality: A Review," *International Journal of Parapsychology* 11 (2) (2000): 1–34; James Houran and Rense Lange, "Diary of Events in a Thoroughly Unhaunted House," *Perceptual and Motor Skills* 83 (1996): 499–502; James Houran and Rense Lange, "Hauntings and Poltergeist-Like Episodes As a Confluence of Conventional Phenomena: A General Hypothesis," *Perceptual and Motor Skills* 83 (1996): 1307–16; Sheryl C. Wilson and Theodore X. Barber, "The Fantasy-Prone Personality: Implications for Understanding Imagery, Hypnosis, and Parapsychological Phenomena," in *Imagery: Current Theory, Research and Application,* Anees A. Sheikh, ed. (New York: John Wiley & Sons, 1983), 340–87; Colin A. Ross and Shaun Joshi, "Paranormal Experiences in the General Population," *Journal of Nervous and Mental Disease* 180 (6) (1992): 357–61; Harvey J. Irwin, "Origins and Functions of Paranormal Belief: The Role of Childhood Trauma and Interpersonal Control," *Journal of the American Society for Psychical Research* 86 (3) (1992): 199–208; Harvey J. Irwin, "Childhood Antecedents of Out-of-Body and Déjà Vu Experiences," *Journal of the American Society for Psychical Research* 90 (3) (1996): 157–72.

97. Michael Shallis, *The Electric Connection* (New York: New Amsterdam Books, 1988), 32–33.

98. Ibid., 263.

99. Larry Dossey, personal correspondence with author, March 8, 2004.

100. Mircea Eliade, *Shamanism: Archaic Techniques of Ecstacy* (Princeton, N.J.: Princeton University Press, 1964).

101. Lyall Watson, *Lifetide: The Biology of the Unconscious* (New York: Simon and Schuster, 1979), 213; Douglas M. Stokes, *The Nature of Mind* (Jefferson, N.C.: McFarland & Company, 1997), 171.

102. Elaine N. Aron, *The Highly Sensitive Person: How to Thrive When the World Overwhelms You* (New York: Carol Publishing Group, 1996); Sharon Heller, *Too Loud, Too Bright, Too Fast, Too Tight* (New York: HarperCollins, 2002), 95; Paul Bergman and Sibylle K. Escalona, "Unusual Sensitivities in Very Young Children," *The Psychoanalytic Study of the Child* II (1949): 333–52.

103. Colin A. Ross and Shaun Joshi, "Paranormal Experiences in the General Population," *Journal of Nervous and Mental Disease* 180 (6) (1992): 357–61; Harvey J. Irwin, "Origins and Functions of Paranormal Belief: The Role of Childhood Trauma and Interpersonal Control," *Journal of the American Society for Psychical*

Research 86 (3) (1992): 199–208; Harvey J. Irwin, "Childhood Antecedents of Out-of-Body and Déjà Vu Experiences," *Journal of the American Society for Psychical Research* 90 (3) (1996): 157–72; Lenore C. Terr, "Childhood Traumas: An Outline and Overview," *American Journal of Psychiatry* 148 (1) (1991): 10–20.

104. Harvey Irwin, "Parapsychological Phenomena and the Absorption Domain," *Journal of the American Society for Psychical Research* 79 (1) (1985): 1–11.

105. Lenore C. Terr, "Time Sense Following Psychic Trauma: A Clinical Study of Ten Adults and Twenty Children," *American Journal of Orthopsychiatry* 53 (2) (1983): 244–61.

106. Lenore C. Terr, "Childhood Traumas: An Outline and Overview," *American Journal of Psychiatry* 148 (1) (1991): 10–20.

107. Daniel Goleman, "For Some People, Half of Day Is Spent in Fantasy," *New York Times,* December 15, 1987, C1, http://query.nytimes.com/gst/fullpage.html?sec=health&res=9B0DE7DC163BF936A25751C1A961948260.

108. Harvey J. Irwin, "Childhood Belief and the Origins of Paranormal Belief: A Constructive Replication," *Psychological Reports* 74 (1) (1994):107–11.

109. Sandra Stockenius and Peter Brugger, "Perceived Electrosensitivity and Magical Ideation," *Perceptual and Motor Skills* 90 (3) (2000): 899–900.

110. U. F. Malt and others, "Physical and Mental Problems Attributed to Dental Amalgam Fillings: A Descriptive Study of 99 Self-Referred Patients Compared with 272 Controls," *Psychosomatic Medicine* 59 (1) (1997): 32–41.

111. David Ruenzel, "Why Zebras Don't Get Ulcers," Brain Connection, www.brainconnection.com/topics/?main=fa/zebras; Jonah Lehrer, "The Reinvention of the Self," *Seed* (February/March 2006), http://seedmagazine.com/news/2006/02/the_reinvention_of_the_self.php?page=all&p=y.

112. Bruce D. Perry and others, "Childhood Trauma, the Neurobiology of Adaptation and Use-dependent Development of the Brain: How States Become Traits," *Infant Medical Health Journal* 16 (4) (1995): 271–91.

113. Ibid.

114. Lenore C. Terr, "Childhood Traumas: An Outline and Overview," *American Journal of Psychiatry* 148 (1) (1991): 10–20.

115. Kenneth Ring, *Heading Toward Omega* (New York: William Morrow and Company, 1984).

116. Kenneth Ring, *The Omega Project* (New York: Quill/William Morrow, 1992).

117. Ibid., 146.

118. Timothy T. Yates and James R. Bannard, "The 'Haunted' Child: Grief, Hallucinations, and Family Dynamics," *Journal of the American Academy of Child and Adolescent Psychology* 27 (5) (1988), 573–81.

119. Ibid.

120. Ernest Hartmann, *Boundaries in the Mind: A New Dimension of Personality* (New York: Basic Books, 1996), 119–20.

121. Ibid., 246.

122. Sara Goudarzi, "The Future of Science: A Conversation with Alan Lightman," Live Science, www.livescience.com/othernews/060215_alan_lightman .html.

123. Rabia Tuma, "Immune System Molecule Plays Essential Role in Brain Development," *Brain Work* (Charles A. Dana Foundation) 13 (1) (January–February 2003), 1.

124. Ibid.

125. Jo Durden-Smith and Diane deSimone, *Sex and the Brain* (New York: Arbor House, 1983), 170.

126. Faculty profile of Daniel Geschwind, UCLA Mental Retardation Research Center, www.mrrc.npi.ucla.edu/faculty.asp?param=&data=&faculty=467 (accessed January 22, 2009).

127. Bijal Trivedi, "How the Immune System Fine-Tunes the Brain," *New Scientist* (March 1, 2008): 44–47, www.newscientist.com/article/mg19726451 .900.

128. Ibid.

129. Jennifer Viegas, "My Genes Can't Stop Me Dancing," *Discovery News,* February 22, 2006, as reprinted in News in Science, Australian Broadcasting Corporation, www.abc.net.au/science/news/stories/s1576009.htm.

130. Kerri Smith, "Genes Influence Emotional Memory," news@nature.com, July 29, 2007, as reprinted on BioEd Online, Baylor College of Medicine, www .bioedonline.org/news/news.cfm?art=3488.

131. Lindsey Tanner, "Gene May Help Explain Stress Disorder," Associated Press, March 18, 2008, as reprinted on Newsvine, www.newsvine.com/_ news/2008/03/18/1374179-gene-may-help-explain-stress-disorder.

132. Constance Holden, "Seeds of PTSD Planted in Childhood," *ScienceNOW Daily News,* American Association for the Advancement of Science, March 18, 2008, as reprinted on Free Republic, www.freerepublic.com/focus/f-news/1989257/ posts; American Association for the Advancement of Science, "Past Child Abuse Plus Variations in Gene Result in Potent PTSD Risk for Adults," EurekAlert!, March 18, 2008, www.eurekalert.org/pub_releases/2008-03/ niom-pca031308.php.

Chapter 10. Psychosomatic Plasticity and the Persistence of Memory

1. Paul Martin, *The Healing Mind: The Vital Links Between Brain and Behavior, Immunity and Disease* (New York: St. Martin's Press, 1997), 2.

2. Mona Lisa Schulz, *Awakening Intuition: Using Your Mind-Body Network for Insight and Healing* (New York: Harmony Books, 1998), 204.

3. Richard O'Connor, *Undoing Perpetual Stress* (New York: Berkley Books, 2005), 350.

4. Paul Martin, *The Healing Mind: The Vital Links Between Brain and Behavior, Immunity and Disease* (New York: St. Martin's Press, 1997), 88–89; Daniel Goleman and Joel Gurin, eds., *Mind/Body Medicine: How to Use Your Mind for Better Health* (Yonkers, N.Y.: Consumers Union, 1993), 45.

5. Paul Martin, *The Healing Mind: The Vital Links Between Brain and Behavior, Immunity and Disease* (New York: St. Martin's Press, 1997), 91.

6. Daniel Goleman and Joel Gurin, eds., *Mind/Body Medicine: How to Use Your Mind for Better Health* (Yonkers, N.Y.: Consumers Union, 1993), 51–52.

7. Marilyn Elias, "Study: A Happy Marriage Can Help Mend Physical Wounds," *USA Today,* March 7, 2005, www.usatoday.com/news/health/2005-03-06-marriage-usat_x.htm.

8. Paul Martin, *The Healing Mind: The Vital Links Between Brain and Behavior, Immunity and Disease* (New York: St. Martin's Press, 1997), 42–43; Daniel Goleman and Joel Gurin, eds., *Mind/Body Medicine: How to Use Your Mind for Better Health* (Yonkers, N.Y.: Consumers Union, 1993), 35–38.

9. "Stress during Childhood Increases Risk of Allergies," *ScienceDaily,* June 18, 2008, www.sciencedaily.com/releases/2008/06/080618114728.htm.

10. Paul Martin, *The Healing Mind: The Vital Links Between Brain and Behavior, Immunity and Disease* (New York: St. Martin's Press, 1997), 92.

11. Ibid., 37.

12. Ibid., 88.

13. Ibid., 96–97.

14. Ibid., 167.

15. Daniel Goleman and Joel Gurin, eds., *Mind/Body Medicine: How to Use Your Mind for Better Health* (Yonkers, N.Y.: Consumers Union, 1993), 53.

16. Paul Martin, *The Healing Mind: The Vital Links Between Brain and Behavior, Immunity and Disease* (New York: St. Martin's Press, 1997), 230.

17. Ibid., 231–234.

18. Daniel Goleman and Joel Gurin, eds., *Mind/Body Medicine: How to Use Your Mind for Better Health* (Yonkers, N.Y.: Consumers Union, 1993), 53–54.

19. Chris Woolston, "How Writing Saved My Life," March 20, 2000, WebMD, www.webmd.com/balance/features/health-benefits-of-writing.

20. Stuart Wolpert, "Putting Feelings into Words Produces Therapeutic Effects in the Brain," University of California–Los Angeles (press release), June 21, 2007, www.universityofcalifornia.edu/news/article/9305.

21. Chris Woolston, "How Writing Saved My Life," March 20, 2000, WebMD, www.webmd.com/balance/features/health-benefits-of-writing.

22. "Depressing News for Diarists," *New Scientist,* September 11, 2004, 15.

23. Marion M. Jones, "Unconventional Wisdom: a Report on the Ninth Annual Convention of the American Psychological Society," *Psychology Today,* September 1, 1997, 34.

24. Rabiya S. Tuma, "Controlling Emotional Feedback Is Key to Depression," *BrainWork* (Charles A. Dana Foundation) (July–August 2005), 7, www.dana.org/news/brainwork/detail.aspx?id=678.

25. Miriam Greenspan, *Healing through the Dark Emotions: The Wisdom of Grief, Fear, and Despair* (Boston: Shambhala, 2003), 70.

26. Stefan Soltysik and Piotr Jelen, "In Rats, Sighs Correlate with Relief," *Physiology and Behavior* 85 (5) (August 7, 2005): 598–602.

27. G. A. Bradshaw and others, "Elephant Breakdown," *Nature* 433 (February 24, 2005): 807.

28. Ernest Hartmann, *Boundaries in the Mind* (New York: Basic Books, 1991), 236.

29. Sheryl C. Wilson and Theodore X. Barber, "The Fantasy-Prone Personality: Implications for Understanding Imagery, Hypnosis, and Parapsychological Phenomena," in *Imagery: Current Theory, Research and Application,* ed. Anees A. Sheikh (New York: John Wiley & Sons, 1983), 340–87.

30. Harris Dienstfrey, "The Aware Mind," *Noetic Sciences Review* 21 (1992): 17, as reprinted on Knowledge Center, http://66.201.42.16/viewitem.php3?id=205&catid=32&kbid=ionsikc.

31. Daniel Goleman, ed., *Healing Emotions* (Boston: Shambhala, 1997), 140.

32. Ashley Montagu, *Touching: The Human Significance of the Skin,* 3rd ed. (New York: Harper & Row, 1986), 272.

33. Ashley Montagu, *Touching: The Human Significance of the Skin,* 2nd ed. (New York: Harper & Row, 1978), 217.

34. Ibid., 3.

35. Hypnosis and Suggestion, "Measurement of Hypnosis and Hypnotisability," www.hypnosisandsuggestion.org/measurement.html.

36. Harris Dienstfrey, "The Aware Mind," *Noetic Sciences Review* 21 (1992): 17, as

reprinted on Knowledge Center, http://66.201.42.16/viewitem.php3?id=205& catid=32&kbid=ionsikc.

37. William J. Cromie, "Hypnosis Found to Alter the Brain: Subjects See Color Where None Exists," *Harvard University Gazette* (August 21, 2000), www .news.harvard.edu/gazette/2000/08.21/hypnosis.html.

38. Ibid.

39. Harris Dienstfrey, "The Aware Mind," *Noetic Sciences Review* 21 (1992): 17, as reprinted on Knowledge Center, http://66.201.42.16/viewitem.php3?id=205& catid=32&kbid=ionsikc.

40. John Sarno, *The Mindbody Prescription: Healing the Body, Healing the Pain* (New York: Warner Books, 1998), xx–xxi.

41. Peter A. Levine with Ann Frederick, *Waking the Tiger: Healing Trauma* (Berkeley, Calif.: North Atlantic Books, 1997), 141.

42. John Sarno, *The Mindbody Prescription: Healing the Body, Healing the Pain* (New York: Warner Books, 1998), 49.

43. Institute of HeartMath, "Science of the Heart: Exploring the Role of the Heart in Human Performance," www.heartmath.org/research/research-science-of-the-heart.html.

44. Ashley Montagu, *Touching: The Human Significance of the Skin,* 2nd ed. (New York: Harper & Row, 1978), 92.

45. Everett Gendler, commentary on the Hebrew Prayer "Nishmat Kol Chai," in *Kol Haneshamah* ("Voice of the Soul"), 2nd ed. (Wyncote, Pa.: The Reconstructionist Press 1995), 235.

46. Guy Brown, *The Energy of Life: The Science of What Makes Our Minds and Bodies Work* (New York: The Free Press, 1999), 190.

47. Ibid.

48. Harris Dienstfrey, "The Aware Mind," *Noetic Sciences Review* 21 (1992): 17, as reprinted on Knowledge Center, http://66.201.42.16/viewitem.php3?id=205& catid=32&kbid=ionsikc.

49. Kenneth Pelletier, "Between Mind and Body: Stress, Emotions, and Health," in *Mind-Body Medicine,* Daniel Goleman and Joel Gurin, eds. (Yonkers, N.Y.: Consumer Reports Books, 1993), 34.

50. Antonio R. Damasio, *The Feeling of What Happens: Body and Emotion in the Making of Consciousness* (New York: Harcourt, Brace & Co., 1999), 50.

51. Mona Lisa Schulz, *Awakening Intuition: Using Your Mind-Body Network for Insight and Healing* (New York: Harmony Books, 1998), xiv.

52. Ibid., 89–90.

53. Ibid., 101.

54. Ibid., 102.

55. Ibid., 103.

56. Ibid.

57. Brian Broom, *Somatic Illness and the Patient's Other Story* (New York: Free Association Books, 1997), 172.

58. Gordon Rattray Taylor, *The Natural History of the Mind* (New York: E. P. Dutton, 1979), 143.

59. Julie Motz, *Hands of Life* (New York: Bantam Books, 1998), 104.

60. Joseph Chilton Pearce, *Evolution's End: Claiming the Potential of Our Intelligence* (New York: HarperSanFrancisco, 1992), 103–4; Claudia Bierwolf and others, "Influence of Exogenous Atrial Natriuretic Peptide on the Pituitary-Adrenal Response to Corticotropin-Releasing Hormone and Vasopressin in Healthy Men," *Journal of Clinical Endocrinology and Metabolism* 83 (4) (1998): 1151–57.

61. Institute of HeartMath, "Science of the Heart: Exploring the Role of the Heart in Human Performance." www.heartmath.org/research/research-science-of-the-heart.html.

62. Paul Pearsall, *The Heart's Code: Tapping the Wisdom and Power of Our Heart Energy* (New York: Broadway Books, 1998).

63. Ibid., 8.

64. Paul Pearsall, Gary Schwartz, and Linda Russek, "Changes in Heart Transplant Recipients that Parallel the Personalities of Their Donors," *Journal of Near-Death Studies* 20 (3) (Spring 2002): 191–206, as reprinted on Paul Pearsall's website, www.paulpearsall.com/info/press/3.html.

65. Paul Pearsall, *The Heart's Code: Tapping the Wisdom and Power of Our Heart Energy* (New York: Broadway Books, 1998), 113.

66. Ibid., 89.

67. Paul Pearsall, Gary Schwartz, and Linda Russek, "Changes in Heart Transplant Recipients that Parallel the Personalities of Their Donors," *Journal of Near-Death Studies* 20 (3) (Spring 2002): 191–206, as reprinted on Paul Pearsall's website, www.paulpearsall.com/info/press/3.html.

68. Paul Pearsall, *The Heart's Code: Tapping the Wisdom and Power of Our Heart Energy* (New York: Broadway Books, 1998), 83.

69. Paul Pearsall, Gary Schwartz, and Linda Russek, "Changes in Heart Transplant Recipients that Parallel the Personalities of Their Donors," *Journal of Near-Death Studies* 20 (3) (Spring 2002): 191–206, as reprinted on Paul Pearsall's website, www.paulpearsall.com/info/press/3.html.

70. Ibid.

71. Ibid.

72. Ibid.

73. Ibid.

74. Ibid.

75. Paul Pearsall, *The Heart's Code: Tapping the Wisdom and Power of Our Heart Energy* (New York: Broadway Books, 1998), 7.

76. Bruce Greyson, Department of Psychiatric Medicine, University of Virginia Health System, personal correspondence with author, August 3, 2001.

77. Louisa Young, *The Book of the Heart* (New York: Doubleday, 2003).

78. Ibid., 92.

79. Ibid., 95–97.

80. Paul Pearsall, *The Heart's Code: Tapping the Wisdom and Power of Our Heart Energy* (New York: Broadway Books, 1998), 120.

81. Louisa Young, *The Book of the Heart* (New York: Doubleday, 2003), 93.

82. Ibid., 90.

83. Ibid., 88–89.

84. Paul Pearsall, *The Heart's Code: Tapping the Wisdom and Power of Our Heart Energy* (New York: Broadway Books, 1998), 111.

85. Ibid., 87.

86. Ibid., 95–97.

87. Louisa Young, *The Book of the Heart* (New York: Doubleday, 2003), 94–95.

88. Tri Giang Phan, et al., "Passive Transfer of Nut Allergy After Liver Transplantation," *Archives of Internal Medicine* 163 (2) (January 27, 2003): 237–39.

89. Mona Lisa Schulz, *Awakening Intuition: Using Your Mind-Body Network for Insight and Healing* (New York: Harmony Books, 1998), 88–89.

90. Ibid., 91.

91. Ian Stevenson, "The Phenomenon of Claimed Memories of Previous Lives: Possible Interpretations and Importance," *Medical Hypotheses* 54 (4) (2000): 652–59.

92. Ian Stevenson, "Phobias in Children Who Claim to Remember Previous Lives," *Journal of Scientific Exploration* 4 (2) (1991): 243–53.

93. William Falk, editorial in *The Week*, May 2, 2003, 5.

94. Ian Stevenson, personal correspondence with author, May 19, 2003.

95. David Henry Feldman, *Nature's Gambit: Child Prodigies and the Development of Human Potential* (New York: Basic Books, 1986), 193–94.

96. Ibid., 197.

97. Ibid., 199.

98. Ibid., 200.

99. Ibid., 201.

522   *Notes*

100. Ibid., 188, 191, 200.
101. Courtney Humphries, "Solving the Mystery of fMRI," *Technology Review*, Massachusetts Institute of Technology, June 20, 2008, www.technologyreview .com/Biotech/20986/?a=f; Deborah Halber, "MIT Unlocks Mystery Behind Brain Imaging" (MIT news release), June 19, 2008, http://web.mit.edu/ newsoffice/2008/astrocytes-0619.html; Nikhil Swaminathan, "Mysterious Brain Cells Linked to Blood Flow," *Scientific American,* June 20, 2008, www .sciam.com/article.cfm?id=mysterious-brain-cells-li; "Star-Shaped Brain Cells Make Scans Possible," June 19, 2008, HealthDay, www.healthday.com/Article .asp?AID=616613.
102. "Interview with Robert O. Becker, M.D.," *Bridges* (International Society for the Study of Subtle Energies and Energy Medicine) 1 (3) (Winter 1990): 5.
103. Gordon Rattray Taylor, *The Natural History of the Mind* (New York: E. P. Dutton, 1979), 45.
104. Guy Brown, *The Energy of Life: The Science of What Makes Our Minds and Bodies Work* (New York: The Free Press, 1999), 18.
105. Ibid., 20.
106. "Thinking with Blood: A New View of Information Processing in the Brain," McGovern Institute for Brain Research, Massachusetts Institute of Technology (news release), October 11, 2007, http://web.mit.edu/MCGOVERN/html/ News_and_Publications/2007_thinking_with_blood.shtml; Nikhil Swamnathan, "Blood Flow May Be Key Player in Neural Processing," *Scientific American,* January 24, 2008, www.sciam.com/article.cfm?id=blood-flow-may-be-key-player.
107. Ulrich Frick and others, "Comparison Perception of Singular Transcranial Magnetic Stimuli by Subjectively Electrosensitive Subjects and General Population Controls," *Bioelectromagnetics* 26 (2005): 287–98; S. Liden, "Sensitivity to Electricity: A New Environmental Epidemic," *Allergy* 51 (1996): 519–24.
108. Sandra Stöckenius and Peter Brugger, "Perceived Electrosensitivity and Magical Ideation." *Perceptual and Motor Skills* 90 (3) (2000): 899–900.
109. Paul Martin, *The Healing Mind: The Vital Links Between Brain and Behavior, Immunity and Disease* (New York: St. Martin's Press, 1997), 99–100.
110. Ibid., 102.
111. Ibid., 104–5.
112. Rachel Zelkowitz, "The Placebo Effect: Not All in Your Head," *ScienceNow Daily News,* American Association for the Advancement of Science, December 2, 2008; Andy Coghlan, "A Placebo Can Work if You Have the Genes for It," *New Scientist,* December 16, 2008, www.newscientist.com/article/mg20026854.900- first-placebo-gene-discovered.html?DCMP=OTC-rss&nsref=genetics.

Chapter 11. Time, Energy, and the Self

1. David Darling, *Soul Search: A Scientist Explores the Afterlife* (New York: Villard Books, 1995), 158.

2. Guy Brown, *The Energy of Life: The Science of What Makes Our Minds and Bodies Work* (New York: The Free Press, 1999), 67–68.

3. Malcom Gladwell, *Blink: The Power of Thinking Without Thinking* (New York: Little, Brown and Co., 2005), 225.

4. Ibid., 223–24.

5. Annabel Gillings, "Time Out of Mind," BBC News, February 23, 2006, http://news.bbc.co.uk/2/hi/uk_news/magazine/4741340.stm.

6. Guy Brown, *The Energy of Life: The Science of What Makes Our Minds and Bodies Work* (New York: The Free Press, 1999), 75.

7. Ibid., 68.

8. A. M. Joost Meerloo, "The Time Sense in Psychiatry," in *The Voices of Time,* J. T. Fraser, ed. (New York: George Brazillier, Inc., 1966), 250–51.

9. John Cohen, "Subjective Time," in *The Voices of Time,* J. T. Fraser, ed. (New York: George Brazillier, Inc., 1966), 257; Hudson Hoagland, "Some Biochemical Considerations of Time," in *The Voices of Time,* J. T. Fraser, ed. (New York: George Brazillier, Inc., 1966), 321–22.

10. Guy Brown, *The Energy of Life: The Science of What Makes Our Minds and Bodies Work* (New York: The Free Press, 1999), 72–73.

11. Cornelius A. Benjamin, "Ideas of Time in the History of Philosophy," in *The Voices of Time,* J. T. Fraser, ed. (New York: George Brazillier, Inc., 1966).

12. Ibid., 13–14.

13. Ibid., 13.

14. Ibid., 14.

15. Ibid., 22–23.

16. J. T. Fraser, "Comments on Time and the Uncanny," in *The Voices of Time,* J. T. Fraser, ed. (New York: George Brazillier, Inc., 1966), 254.

17. Cornelius A. Benjamin, "Ideas of Time in the History of Philosophy," in *The Voices of Time,* J. T. Fraser, ed. (New York: George Brazillier, Inc., 1966), 23.

18. Ibid., 23.

19. Ibid., 24.

20. Ibid., 25.

21. Robert D. Stolorow, *Trauma and Human Existence: Autobiographical, Psychoanalytic, and Philosophical Reflections* (New York: The Analytic Press, 2007), 19.

22. Ibid., 20.

23. Cornelius A. Benjamin, "Ideas of Time in the History of Philosophy," in *The Voices of Time,* J. T. Fraser, ed. (New York: George Brazillier, Inc., 1966), 25.

24. Ibid.

25. Guy Murchie, *Music of the Spheres,* vol. II, *The Microcosm* (New York: Dover Publications, Inc., 1967), 588.

26. Ibid., 589.

27. Cornelius A. Benjamin, "Ideas of Time in the History of Philosophy," in *The Voices of Time,* J. T. Fraser, ed. (New York: George Brazillier, Inc., 1966), 29.

28. Robert L. Van de Castle, *Our Dreaming Mind* (New York: Ballantine Books, 1994), 408.

29. Sy Safransky, "Sy Safransky's Notebook," *The Sun,* November 2001, 47.

30. Philip Kennicott, "The Home Movies of Hate: The Men Whose Dreams Create a World of Nightmares," *Washington Post,* December 14, 2001, C1.

31. Guy Brown, *The Energy of Life: The Science of What Makes Our Minds and Bodies Work* (New York: The Free Press, 1999), 114.

32. A. M. Joost Meerloo, "The Time Sense in Psychiatry," in *The Voices of Time,* J. T. Fraser, ed. (New York: George Brazillier, Inc., 1966), 247.

33. John Cohen, "Subjective Time," in *The Voices of Time,* J. T. Fraser, ed. (New York: George Brazillier, Inc., 1966), 270.

34. Ibid., 269.

35. A. M. Joost Meerloo, "The Time Sense in Psychiatry," in *The Voices of Time,* J. T. Fraser, ed. (New York: George Brazillier, Inc., 1966), 244.

36. Robert Ornstein, *The Psychology of Consciousness* (New York: Arkana Penguin, 1996), 90–91.

37. J. T. Fraser, "Comments on Time and the Uncanny," in *The Voices of Time,* J. T. Fraser, ed. (New York: George Brazillier, Inc., 1966), 254–55.

38. M. L. von Franz, "Time and Synchronicity in Analytic Psychology," in *The Voices of Time,* J. T. Fraser, ed. (New York: George Brazillier, Inc., 1966), 221.

39. Ibid., 229.

40. Ibid., 226.

41. Kenneth Ring, *Heading Toward Omega* (New York: William Morrow and Company, 1984), 105–7.

42. Jacob Needleman, *Time and the Soul* (New York: Currency/Doubleday, 1998), 116.

43. Stanislav Grof, *Realms of the Human Unconscious* (New York: The Viking Press, 1975), 46–47.

44. Robert Ornstein, *The Psychology of Consciousness* (New York: Arkana Penguin, 1996), 132.

45. A. M. Joost Meerloo, "The Time Sense in Psychiatry," in *The Voices of Time,* J. T. Fraser, ed. (New York: George Brazillier, Inc., 1966), 242.

46. Ibid., 243, 249.

47. Ibid., 246.

48. Ashley Montagu, *Touching: The Human Significance of the Skin,* 2nd ed. (New York: Harper & Row, 1978), 206.

49. John McCrone, "When a Second Lasts Forever," *New Scientist* (November 1, 1997): 52–56.

50. Rhawn Joseph, *The Naked Neuron: Evolution and the Languages of the Body and Brain* (New York: Plenum Press, 1993), 345.

51. Rachel Herz, "Emotion Experienced during Encoding Enhances Odor Retrieval Cue Effectiveness," *American Journal of Psychology* 110 (1997): 489–505.

52. Lyall Watson, *Jacobson's Organ and the Remarkable Nature of Smell* (New York: W. W. Norton & Company, 2000), 180–81.

53. Oliver Sacks, "When Music Heals Body and Soul," *Parade,* March 31, 2002, 5.

54. Rhawn Joseph, *The Naked Neuron: Evolution and the Languages of the Body and Brain* (New York: Plenum Press, 1993), 42.

55. Robert Lee Holtz, "The Song Remains the Same," *Washington Post,* December 13, 2002, A27.

56. Sue Goetinck, "Scientists Examine How the Brain Responds to Music," *The Greenville News,* September 4, 1998, 1E.

57. "Neuroscience: Music Plays to Brain's Emotional Side," Science Notebook, *Washington Post,* November 16, 1998, A2.

58. Michael Lemonick, "Music on the Brain," *Time,* June 5, 2000, 74–75; Thomas Verny, *The Secret Life of the Unborn Child* (New York: Dell Publishing Co., 1981), 186.

59. Robert Ornstein, *The Psychology of Consciousness* (New York: Arkana Penguin, 1996), 140–41.

60. John Pierrakos, *Core Energetics* (Menocino, Calif.: LifeRhythm, 1987), 27.

61. Jacob Needleman, *Time and the Soul* (New York: Currency/Doubleday, 1998), 23.

62. J. Andrew Ross, "The Self: From Soul to Brain," *Journal of Consciousness Studies* 10 (2) (2003): 67–85.

63. Ibid.

64. American Association for the Advancement of Science, "Unconscious Decisions in the Brain," EurekAlert!, April 14, 2008, www.eurekalert.org/pub_releases/2008-04/m-udi041408.php.

65. J. Andrew Ross, "The Self: From Soul to Brain," *Journal of Consciousness Studies* 10 (2) (2003): 67–85.

66. Ibid.

67. Susan Blackmore, *The Meme Machine* (New York: Oxford University Press, 1999).

68. David Darling, *Soul Search: A Scientist Explores the Afterlife* (New York: Villard Books, 1995), 134, 161–63, 172.

69. D. Alan Bensley, "Can Minds Leave Bodies? A Cognitive Science Perspective," *Skeptical Inquirer* 27 (4) (July-August 2003), 34–39 (citing work by James Gibson).

70. Edge, "A Self Worth Having: A Talk with Nicholas Humphrey," www.edge.org/documents/archive/edge142.html.

71. Jacob Needleman, *Time and the Soul* (New York: Currency/Doubleday, 1998), 132.

72. Edward Hoffman, *Visions of Innocence: Spiritual and Inspirational Experiences of Childhood* (Boston: Shambhala, 1992).

Chapter 12. Evidence for the Emotional Gateway

1. Marcia Angell, "Disease as a Reflection of the Psyche," *New England Journal of Medicine* 312 (24) (1985): 1570–72.

2. Gary Stix, "Ultimate Self-Improvement," *Scientific American,* September 2003, 45.

3. Barbara Strauch, *The Primal Teen: What New Discoveries about the Teenage Brain Tell Us about Our Kids* (New York: Doubleday, 2003), 140.

4. Richard A. Blasband, "The Ordering of Random Events by Emotional Expression," *Journal of Scientific Exploration* 14 (2) (2000): 195–216.

5. Gertrude R. Schmeidler and Lawrence LeSahn, "An Aspect of Body Image Related to ESP Scores," *Journal of the American Society for Psychical Research* 64 (2) (1970): 211–18.

6. Douglas Richards, "Boundaries in the Mind and Subjective Interpersonal Psi," *Journal of Parapsychology* 60 (September 1996): 227–40.

7. Caroline Watt, "What Makes a Good Psi Target?" *Journal of Parapsychology* 60 (March 1996): 25–41.

8. Rachel Sanders, Michael Thalbourne, and Peter Delin, "Transliminality and the Telepathic Transmission of Emotional States: An Exploratory Study," *Journal of the American Society for Psychical Research* 94 (1) (January–April 2000): 1–24; Jan Dalkvist and Joakim Westerlund, "Five Experiments on Telepathic Communication of Emotions," *Journal of Parapsychology* 62 (September 1998): 219–53.

9. Dean Radin, "Time-Reversed Human Experience: Experimental Evidence and Implications," Boundary Institute, July 31, 2000, www.boundary.org/articles/timereversed.pdf.

10. Theo de Graaf, Joop Houtkooper, and John Palmer, "Anticipatory Awareness of Emotionally Charged Targets by Individuals Who Went through Shocking Experiences: An Exploratory Study," *Journal of Parapsychology* 65 (4) (December 2001).

11. Rob Stein, "With New Findings, Neuroscientists Have a Hunch Intuition Makes Sense," *Washington Post,* February 28, 1997, A14.

12. Spacedog, "Infrasonic Experiment," www.spacedog.biz/Infrasonic/experiment.htm.

13. Jonathan Amos, "Organ Music 'Instills Religious Feelings,'" BBC News Online, September 8, 2003, http://news.bbc.co.uk/2/hi/science/nature/3087674.stm; Spacedog, "Infrasonic Experiment," www.spacedog.biz/Infrasonic/experiment.htm.

14. Chris Arnot, "Ghost Buster," *The Guardian,* July 11, 2000, www.guardian.co.uk/Archive/Article/0,4273,4038891,00.html.

15. J. L. Kirschvink, A. Kobayashi-Kirschvink, and B. J. Woodford, "Magnetic Biomineralization in the Human Brain," *Proceedings of the National Academy of Sciences* 89 (16) (August 15, 1992), 7683–87; R. Robin Baker, Janice G. Mather, and John H. Kennaugh, "Magnetic Bones in Human Sinuses," *Nature* 301 (January 6, 1983): 78–80, www.nature.com/nature/journal/v301/n5895/abs/301078a0.html.

16. Mark S. George, "Stimulating the Brain," *Scientific American,* September 2003, 67–73.

17. Paul Stevens, "Effects of 5-Second Exposure to a 50 mT, 20 Hz Magnetic Field on Skin Conductance and Ratings of Affect and Arousal," *Bioelectromagnetics* 22 (4) (2001): 219–23.

18. Paul Stevens, personal correspondence with author, March 12, 2001.

19. Marc Bekoff, *The Emotional Lives of Animals* (Novato, Calif.: New World Library, 2007), xiv.

20. Ibid., xiii–xiv.

21. Ibid., xviii.

22. Raymond Bayless, *Animal Ghosts* (New York: University Books, 1970), 123.

23. Sue Darroch, "Animal Apparitions," ParaResearchers of Ontario, www.pararesearchers.org/Ghosts/animalghosts/animalghosts.html.

24. Raymond Bayless, *Animal Ghosts* (New York: University Books, 1970), 103–4.

25. Ibid., 83.

26. Will Storr, *Will Storr vs. The Supernatural* (New York: Harper, 2006), 206–7, 210–11.

27. Raymond Bayless, *Animal Ghosts* (New York: University Books, 1970), 43.

28. Ibid., 105.

29. Sue Darroch, "Animal Apparitions," ParaResearchers of Ontario, www .pararesearchers.org/Ghosts/animalghosts/animalghosts.html.

30. Raymond Bayless, *Animal Ghosts* (New York: University Books, 1970), 149.

31. Matthew W. Fox, "The Nature of Compassion" in *The Smile of a Dolphin,* Marc Bekoff, ed. (New York: Discovery Books, 2000), 178.

32. Ibid.

33. Jeffrey Moussaieff Masson and Susan McCarthy, *When Elephants Weep* (New York: Delacorte Press, 1995), xiii.

34. Ibid., xvi.

35. Ibid., 222.

36. Ibid., 211, 223.

37. Ibid., xvii, 13, 99, 111.

38. Ibid., xiv, 7, 14, 91, 93–96, 104, 113, 190, 213; Barbara Smuts, "Child of Mine," in *The Smile of a Dolphin,* ed. Marc Bekoff (New York: Discovery Books, 2000), 151–53; Marc Bekoff, *The Emotional Lives of Animals* (Novato, Calif.: New World Library, 2007), 9, 11, 32, 41, 56; Jaak Panksepp, "The Rat Will Play," in *The Smile of a Dolphin,* Marc Bekoff, ed. (New York: Discovery Books, 2000), 146; Marc Bekoff, "Joy and Grief," 114; Marek Spinka, "They Just Wanna Have Fun," 157; Stephen M. Wise, *Drawing the Line: Science and the Case for Animal Rights* (Cambridge, Mass.: Perseus Books, 2002), 164–65.

39. Jeffrey Moussaieff Masson and Susan McCarthy, *When Elephants Weep* (New York: Delacorte Press, 1995), 179–82, 185, 191.

40. Ibid., 15, 16, 18; Marc Bekoff, *The Emotional Lives of Animals* (Novato, Calif.: New World Library, 2007), 57; Jaak Panksepp, "The Chemistry of Caring," in *The Smile of a Dolphin,* Marc Bekoff, ed. (New York: Discovery Books, 2000), 59.

41. Marc Bekoff, *The Emotional Lives of Animals* (Novato, Calif.: New World Library, 2007), 130.

42. Ibid., xx.

43. Raymond Bayless, *Animal Ghosts* (New York: University Books, 1970), 18.

44. Marc Bekoff, *The Emotional Lives of Animals* (Novato, Calif.: New World Library, 2007), 225.

45. Raymond A. Moody, *Life After Life: The Investigation of a Phenomenon— Survival of Bodily Death* (New York: Bantam Books, 1977).

46. D. Scott Rogo, "Analyzing the Phenomenon," in *Mind Beyond the Body*, D. Scott Rogo, ed. (New York: Penguin Books, 1978), 21–32.

47. Ibid., 31–32; John Palmer, "Consciousness Localized in Space Outside the Body," in *Mind Beyond the Body*, D. Scott Rogo, ed. (New York: Penguin Books, 1978), 37; Janet Mitchell, "Out of Body Vision" in *Mind Beyond the Body*, D. Scott Rogo, ed. (New York: Penguin Books, 1978), 155.

48. D. Scott Rogo, "Experiential Aspects of Out-of-Body Experiences," in *Mind Beyond the Body*, D. Scott Rogo, ed. (New York: Penguin Books, 1978), 45–48.

49. John Palmer, "Consciousness Localized in Space Outside the Body," in *Mind Beyond the Body*, D. Scott Rogo, ed. (New York: Penguin Books, 1978), 36.

50. Ibid., 35.

51. D. Scott Rogo, "Analyzing the Phenomenon," in *Mind Beyond the Body*, D. Scott Rogo, ed. (New York: Penguin Books, 1978), 24–25.

52. D. Scott Rogo, ed. "Experiments with Blue Harary," in *Mind Beyond the Body*, D. Scott Rogo (New York: Penguin Books, 1978), 187.

53. John Palmer, "Consciousness Localized in Space Outside the Body," in *Mind Beyond the Body*, D. Scott Rogo, ed. (New York: Penguin Books, 1978), 40.

54. Lucien Landau, "An Unusual Out-of-the-Body Experience," in *Mind Beyond the Body*, D. Scott Rogo, ed. (New York: Penguin Books, 1978), 307.

55. D. Scott Rogo, "Analyzing the Phenomenon," in *Mind Beyond the Body*, D. Scott Rogo, ed. (New York: Penguin Books, 1978), 21–22, 26–27.

56. D. Scott Rogo, "The Out-of-Body Experience: Some Personal Views and Reflections," in *Mind Beyond the Body*, D. Scott Rogo, ed. (New York: Penguin Books, 1978), 356.

57. D. Scott Rogo, "Analyzing the Phenomenon," in *Mind Beyond the Body*, D. Scott Rogo, ed. (New York: Penguin Books, 1978), 29.

58. John Palmer, "Consciousness Localized in Space Outside the Body," in *Mind Beyond the Body*, D. Scott Rogo, ed. (New York: Penguin Books, 1978), 36; Janet Mitchell, "Out of Body Vision" in *Mind Beyond the Body*, D. Scott Rogo, ed. (New York: Penguin Books, 1978), 158.

59. D. Scott Rogo, "Can We Explain the Out-of-Body Experience? Conceptual Models," in *Mind Beyond the Body*, D. Scott Rogo, ed. (New York: Penguin Books, 1978), 320.

60. D. Scott Rogo, "The Out-of-Body Experience: Some Personal Views and Reflections," in *Mind Beyond the Body*, D. Scott Rogo, ed. (New York: Penguin Books, 1978), 354.

61. Russell Targ and Harold Puthoff, "Remote Viewing of Natural Targets," in

Mind Beyond the Body, D. Scott Rogo, ed. (New York: Penguin Books, 1978), 219.

62. Janet Mitchell, "Out of Body Vision" in *Mind Beyond the Body,* D. Scott Rogo, ed. (New York: Penguin Books, 1978), 161.

63. American Association for the Advancement of Science, "Out-of-Body Experiences May Be Caused by Arousal System Disturbances in Brain," EurekAlert!, March 5, 2007, www.eurekalert.org/pub_releases/2007-03/uok-oem030507.php.

64. John Palmer, "ESP and Out-of-Body Experiences: An Experimental Approach," in *Mind Beyond the Body,* D. Scott Rogo, ed. (New York: Penguin Books, 1978), 193–94.

65. D. Scott Rogo, "Experiential Aspects of Out-of-Body Experiences," in *Mind Beyond the Body,* D. Scott Rogo, ed. (New York: Penguin Books, 1978), 47.

66. Michael Grosso, "Some Varieties of Out-of-Body Experience," in *Mind Beyond the Body,* D. Scott Rogo, ed. (New York: Penguin Books, 1978), 63–64.

67. Michael Shermer, "Demon-Haunted Brain," *Scientific American* (February 10, 2003); Sharon Begley, "Religion and the Brain," *Newsweek,* May 7, 2001, 51–57.

68. Ibid.

69. Tom Valeo, "Out-of-Body but in the Brain," *BrainWork* (Charles A. Dana Foundation) 16 (4) (July-August 2006): 8.

70. Mary Roach, *Spook: Science Tackles the Afterlife* (New York: W. W. Norton & Company, 2005), 266–67, 284.

71. Sarah Tippit, "Mind Over Matter," Reuters, June 28, 2001, as reprinted on "Sci-Tech," CBS News, www.cbsnews.com/stories/2001/06/28/tech/main298885.shtml.

72. Mary Roach, *Spook: Science Tackles the Afterlife* (New York: W. W. Norton & Company, 2005), 267 (Pim Van Lommel quote).

73. Sharon Begley, "Searching for the God Within," *Newsweek,* January 29, 2001, 59.

74. Sharon Begley, "Religion and the Brain," *Newsweek,* May 7, 2001, 51–57.

75. Shankar Vedantam, "Near Proof for Near-Death?" *Washington Post,* December 17, 2001, 11.

76. Jeffrey Long and Paul Bernstein, "Dutch NDE Study Attracts Worldwide Attention," International Association for Near-Death Studies, www.iands.org/research/important_studies/dutch_nde_study_attracts_worldwide_attention.html.

77. Ibid.

78. Shankar Vedantam, "Near Proof for Near-Death?" *Washington Post,* December 17, 2001, 11.

79. Sharon Begley, "Religion and the Brain," *Newsweek,* May 7, 2001, 56.

80. Kenneth Ring, *The Omega Project* (New York: Quill–William Morrow, 1992), 137, 144–46, 156–59; Melvin Morse, "A Layman's Summary of My Past Research," www.melvinmorse.com/e-pre.htm.

81. Kenneth Ring, *Heading Toward Omega* (New York: William Morrow and Co., 1984), 238; David Black, "Psychoanalytic and Psychophysiological Theories about the Out-of-Body Experience," in *Mind Beyond the Body,* D. Scott Rogo, ed. (New York: Penguin Books, 1978), 332.

82. P. M. H. Atwater, "Another Look at the Aftereffects of the Near-Death Experience," www.cinemind.com/atwater/anotherlook.html.

83. P. M. H. Atwater, "Brain Shift," www.cinemind.com/atwater/brainshift.html.

84. P. M. H. Atwater, *Beyond the Light* (New York: Birch Lane Press, 1994), 129–40.

85. Kevin Nelson, personal correspondence with author, July 12, 2007.

86. Kevin R. Nelson and others, "Does the Arousal System Contribute to Near Death Experience?" *Neurology* 66 (2006): 1003–9.

87. Jerry Adler, "Back from the Dead," *Newsweek,* July 23, 2007, 49; Mary Roach, *Spook: Science Tackles the Afterlife* (New York: W. W. Norton & Company, 2005), 263–91.

88. Oliver Sacks, "A Bolt from the Blue," *The New Yorker,* July 23, 2007, 38–42.

89. Michael Grosso, "Some Varieties of Out-of-Body Experience," in *Mind Beyond the Body,* D. Scott Rogo, ed. (New York: Penguin Books, 1978), 52–69.

90. Ibid., 54–56.

91. David Darling, *Soul Search: A Scientist Explores the Afterlife* (New York: Villard Books, 1995), 154–55, 167–68.

92. Michael Sabom, *Recollections of Death: A Medical Investigation* (New York: Harper & Row, 1982), 161; David Black, "Psychoanalytic and Psychophysiological Theories about the Out-of-Body Experience," in *Mind Beyond the Body,* D. Scott Rogo, ed. (New York: Penguin Books, 1978), 334.

93. Michael Sabom, *Recollections of Death: A Medical Investigation* (New York: Harper & Row, 1982), 161.

94. Bruce Greyson, "Increase in Psychic Phenomena Following Near-Death Experiences," *Theta* 11 (2) (Summer 1983): 26–29.

95. Michael Grosso, "Some Varieties of Out-of-Body Experience," in *Mind Beyond the Body,* D. Scott Rogo, ed. (New York: Penguin Books, 1978), 60.

96. Ibid., 66–67.

97. Ibid., 67.

98. Lynne Levitan and Stephen LaBerge, "Out-of-Body Experiences and Lucid Dreams," *Nightlight* 3 (2–3) (1991), www.lucidity.com/NL32.OBEandLD.html.

99. Emilio Tiberi, "Extrasomatic Emotions," *Journal of Near-Death Studies* 11 (3) (Spring 1993): 149–70.

100. Sarah Boseley, "Near-Death Visions Baffle Doctors," *The Guardian* (December 14, 2001), www.guardian.co.uk/uk/2001/dec/14/health.medicalscience.

101. Raymond Moody and Paul Perry, *Reunions: Visionary Encounters with Departed Loved Ones* (New York: Villard Books, 1993), 145.

102. P. M. H. Atwater, personal communication with author, July 25, 2007.

103. Oliver Sacks, "A Bolt from the Blue," *The New Yorker*, July 23, 2007, 38–42.

104. Mary Roach, *Spook: Science Tackles the Afterlife* (New York: W. W. Norton & Company, 2005), 204.

105. Oliver Sacks, "A Bolt from the Blue," *The New Yorker*, July 23, 2007, 41.

106. Michael Shallis, *The Electric Connection* (New York: New Amsterdam Books, 1988), 192.

107. Michael Shermer, "Demon-Haunted Brain," *Scientific American*, February 10, 2003.

Chapter 13. The Mind Reconsidered: A Meditation on Who We Are and Where We're Headed

1. Piero Scaruffi, Thymos: Studies on Consciousness, Cognition and Life, www.thymos.com/science/aab.html.

2. Nicholas Humphrey, *A History of the Mind* (New York: Simon & Schuster, 1992), 51.

3. Science Daily, "Rejection Really Hurts, UCLA Psychologists Find," October 10, 2003, www.sciencedaily.com/releases/2003/10/031010074045.htm.

4. Laura Nelson, "I Feel Your Pain," *Nature*, Feb. 20, 2004, as reprinted on BioEd Online, Baylor College of Medicine, www.bioedonline.org/news/news-print.cfm?art=790.

5. Louisa Young, *The Book of the Heart* (New York: Doubleday, 2003), 87.

6. Gabor Maté, "The Healing Force Within," *Vancouver Sun*, April 8, 2003.

7. Margaret Gunning, "January Interview—Gabor Maté," *January*, April 2003, www.januarymagazine.com/profiles/gmate.html.

8. Marc Kaufman, "A Meeting of Minds," *Washington Post*, September 21, 2003, D1.

9. Ibid.

10. Ibid.

11. Steven Johnson, "The Brain + Emotions: Fear," *Discover*, March 2003, 35.

12. Richard Dawkins, "Eulogy for Douglas Adams," September 17, 2001, www.edge.org/documents/adams_index.html.

13. John Horgan, *Rational Mysticism* (Boston: Houghton Mifflin Company, 2003), 103.

14. MacArthur Network on Mind-Body Interactions, "Vital Connections: Science of Mind-Body Interactions" (report on interdisciplinary conference, National Institutes of Health, March 26–28, 2001), 4.

15. Brain Connection, "Brain Facts," www.brainconnection.com/library/?main=explorehome/brain-facts.

16. Paul Pearsall, *The Heart's Code: Tapping the Wisdom and Power of Our Heart Energy* (New York: Broadway Books, 1998), 9, 15, 55.

17. Francis Crick, *The Astonishing Hypothesis: The Scientific Search for the Soul* (New York: Charles Scribner's Sons, 1994).

18. Rush W. Dozier, *Fear Itself: The Origin and Nature of the Powerful Emotion That Shapes Our Lives and Our World* (New York: St. Martin's Press, 1998), 31.

19. Carl Zimmer, *Soul Made Flesh: The Discovery of the Brain—and How It Changed the World* (New York: The Free Press, 2004), 265–66, 287.

20. Ibid., 7.

21. Louisa Young, *The Book of the Heart* (New York: Doubleday, 2003), 36.

22. Seven Johnson, "The Brain + Emotions: Love," *Discover,* May 2003, 72.

23. Daniel Amen, *Healing the Hardware of the Soul* (New York: The Free Press, 2002); Daniel Amen, *Change Your Brain, Change Your Life* (New York: Three Rivers Press, 1999), 4.

24. Alexander Lowen, *Pleasure: A Creative Approach to Life* (New York: Penguin Books, 1970), 120–21.

25. Diane Ackerman, *A Natural History of the Senses* (New York: Random House, 1990), xix, 307.

26. Malcolm Jeeves, "Neuroscience and the Soul," *Woodstock Report,* no. 53, March 1998, http://woodstock.georgetown.edu/publications/report/r-fea53a.htm (from a forum cosponsored by the Woodstock Theological Center and the Georgetown University Center for the Study of Science and Religion).

27. Paul Shepard, *Nature and Madness* (Athens, Ga.: University of Georgia Press, 1982), xiii.

28. Richard Louv, *The Diane Rehm Show,* National Public Radio, January 2, 2006, http://wamu.org/programs/dr/06/01/02.php (a discussion of Louv's book, *Last Child in the Woods: Saving our Children from Nature-Deficit Disorder*).

29. Edward O. Wilson, *Biophilia* (Boston: Harvard University Press, 1984).

30. Andrew I. Wolff and William H. Frishman, "Animal-Assisted Therapy and Cardiovascular Disease," in *Complementary and Integrative Therapies for Cardiovascular Disease,* 3rd ed., William H. Frishman, Michael I. Weintraub,

and Marc S. Micozzi, eds. (St. Louis, Mo.: Elsevier Mosby, 2005), 362–68; Emory University Health Sciences Center, "Emory Scientist Reports Nature Contact May Heal Humans," Science Blog, March 2001, www.scienceblog .com/community/older/2001/B/200112037.html.

31. Stephen R. Kellert, *Kinship to Mastery: Biophilia in Human Evolution and Development* (Washington, D.C.: Island Press, 1997), 116–17 (discussing work of Roger Ulrich).

32. Howard Frumkin and Richard Louv, "The Powerful Link between Conserving Land and Preserving Health," Land Trust Alliance Special Anniversary Report, Children & Nature Network, July 1, 2007, www.childrenandnature .org/news/detail/the_powerful_link_between_conserving_land_and_ preserving_health.

33. Emory University Health Sciences Center, "Emory Scientist Reports Nature Contact May Heal Humans" March 2001, www.scienceblog.com/community/ older/2001/B/200112037.html.

34. American Institute of Architects, "Biophilia in Practice: Buildings that Connect People with Nature," www.aia.org/nwsltr_cote.cfm?pagename=cote_a_ 200608_biophilia (originally printed in *Environmental Building News,* July 1, 2006).

35. Ibid., quoting office design researcher Judith Heerwagen.

36. Howard Frumkin and Richard Louv, "The Powerful Link between Conserving Land and Preserving Health," Land Trust Alliance Special Anniversary Report, Children & Nature Network, July 1, 2007, www.childrenandnature .org/news/detail/the_powerful_link_between_conserving_land_and_ preserving_health.

37. David Schneider, review of *The Biophilia Hypothesis,* Edward O. Wilson and Stephen Kellert, eds. *Whole Earth Review,* Spring 1994, as reprinted on BNET Business Network, http://findarticles.com/p/articles/mi_m1510/is_n82/ ai_15297572.

38. Elizabeth Cohen, "Exposure to Nature May Make People Healthier," CNN.com/Health, March 23, 2001, http://archives.cnn.com/2001/ HEALTH/03/23/nature.health/index.html (Howard Frumkin quote).

39. Marc Bekoff, *The Emotional Lives of Animals* (Novato, Calif.: New World Library, 2007), 24.

40. David Schneider, review of *The Biophilia Hypothesis,* Edward O. Wilson and Stephen Kellert, eds. *Whole Earth Review,* Spring 1994, as reprinted on BNET Business Network, http://findarticles.com/p/articles/mi_m1510/is_n82/ ai_15297572.

41. Antonio R. Damasio, *Descartes' Error: Emotion, Reason, and the Human Brain* (New York: G. P. Putnam's Sons, 1994), xvi.

42. David Lauterstein, "What Is Zero Balancing?" Zero Balancing Health Association, www.zerobalancing.com/article2.shtml.

43. Edward O. Wilson, *Biophilia* (Boston: Harvard University Press, 1984), 139.

44. Stephen R. Kellert, *Kinship to Mastery: Biophilia in Human Evolution and Development* (Washington, D.C.: Island Press, 1997), 1.

45. James Hillman, "A Psyche the Size of the Earth: A Psychological Foreword," in *Ecopsychology: Restoring the Earth, Healing the Mind,* ed. Theodore Roszak, Mary E. Gomes, and Allan D. Kanner (San Francisco: Sierra Club Books, 1995), xvii–xxiii.

46. Chellis Glendinning, "Technology, Trauma, and the Wild," in *Ecopsychology: Restoring the Earth, Healing the Mind,* Theodore Roszak, Mary E. Gomes, and Allan D. Kanner, eds. (San Francisco: Sierra Club Books, 1995), 45.

47. Anita Barrows, "The Ecopsychology of Child Development," in *Ecopsychology: Restoring the Earth, Healing the Mind,* Theodore Roszak, Mary E. Gomes, and Allan D. Kanner, eds. (San Francisco: Sierra Club Books, 1995), 101–10; Laura Sewell, "The Skill of Ecological Perception," in *Ecopsychology: Restoring the Earth, Healing the Mind,* ed. Theodore Roszak, Mary E. Gomes, and Allan D. Kanner (San Francisco: Sierra Club Books, 1995), 201–15.

48. Miriam Greenspan, *Healing through the Dark Emotions: The Wisdom of Grief, Fear, and Despair* (Boston: Shambhala, 2003), 219, 231.

49. Laura Sewall, "The Skill of Ecological Perception," in *Ecopsychology: Restoring the Earth, Healing the Mind,* Theodore Roszak, Mary E. Gomes, and Allan D. Kanner, eds. (San Francisco: Sierra Club Books, 1995), 214.

50. Miriam Greenspan, *Healing Through the Dark Emotions: The Wisdom of Grief, Fear, and Despair* (Boston: Shambhala, 2003), 231.

51. Ibid., 211–13.

52. David Abram, "The Ecology of Magic," in *Ecopsychology: Restoring the Earth, Healing the Mind,* Theodore Roszak, Mary E. Gomes, and Allan D. Kanner, eds. (San Francisco: Sierra Club Books, 1995), 315.

53. "A Vote for Neuroethics," *Scientific American,* September 2003, 13 (introduction to special issue).

54. Nicholas Carr, "Is Google Making Us Stupid?" *The Atlantic,* July/August 2008, 56–63.

55. Margaret Wertheim, "Philosophy in the Flesh—A Talk with George Lakoff," Reality Club (online forum), April 12, 1999, www.edge.org/discourse/lakoff .html.

56. James J. Lynch, *The Language of the Heart: The Body's Response to Human Dialogue* (New York: Basic Books, 1985), 309.

57. Stacey Burling, "More Talk, Fewer Pills, Says Local Psychiatrist," *Philadelphia Inquirer,* June 3, 2002.

58. Joseph Chilton Pearce, *Evolution's End* (New York: HarperSanFrancisco, 1992), xix.

59. P. M. H. Atwater, *Children of the New Millennium* (New York: Crown Publishing Group, 1999); William Stillman, *Autism and the God Connection* (Naperville Ill.: Sourcebooks, 2006).

60. Robert Ornstein, *The Psychology of Consciousness* (New York: Penguin/Arkana, 1996), 2–3.

61. Susan Blackmore, "Why Psi Tells Us Nothing about Consciousness," www.susanblackmore.co.uk/conferences/tucson96.html (address given at the second "Toward a Science of Consciousness" conference, Center for Consciousness Studies, University of Arizona–Tucson, April 13, 1996).

62. Louisa Young, *The Book of the Heart* (New York: Doubleday, 2003), 98.

63. "Kathleen Noble: Interview by Douglas Eby," Talent Development Resources, http://talentdevelop.com/interviews/KNoble.html.

64. Jerre Levy, personal correspondence with author, April 2, 2003.

65. Francis Crick, *The Astonishing Hypothesis: The Scientific Search for the Soul* (New York: Charles Scribner's Sons, 1994), 263.

Bibliography

———◆———

Abram, David. *The Spell of the Sensuous: Perception and Language in a More-than-Human World.* New York: Pantheon Books, 1996.

Ackerman, Diane. *A Natural History of the Senses.* New York: Random House, 1990.

———. *An Alchemy of Mind: The Marvel and Mystery of the Brain.* New York: Scribner, 2004.

Allman, William F. *The Stone Age Present.* New York: Simon and Schuster, 1994.

Amen, Daniel. *Change Your Brain, Change Your Life.* New York: Three Rivers Press, 1999.

———. *Healing the Hardware of the Soul.* New York: The Free Press, 2002.

Aron, Elaine. *The Highly Sensitive Child: Helping Our Children Thrive When the World Overwhelms Them.* New York: Broadway Books, 2002.

Atwater, P. M. H. *Beyond the Light.* New York: Birch Lane Press, 1994.

———. *Children of the New Millennium.* New York: Crown Publishing Group, 1999.

Auerbach, Loyd. *Ghost Hunting: How to Investigate the Paranormal.* Berkeley, Calif.: Ronin Publishing, 2003.

Barasch, Marc Ian. *Healing Dreams: Exploring the Dreams That Can Transform Your Life.* New York: Riverhead Books, 2000.

———. *The Healing Path: A Soul Approach to Illness.* New York: Putnam's Sons, 1993.

Bauer, Henry H. *Science or Pseudoscience: Magnetic Healing, Psychic Phenomena, and Other Heterodoxies.* Urbana, Ill.: University of Illinois Press, 2001.

Bayless, Raymond. *Animal Ghosts.* New York: University Books, 1970.

Becker, Robert O. *Cross Currents.* Los Angeles: Jeremy P. Tarcher, 1985.

537

Bekoff, Marc, ed. *The Emotional Lives of Animals.* Novato, Calif.: New World Library, 2007.

———. *The Smile of a Dolphin: Remarkable Accounts of Animal Emotions.* New York: Discovery Books, 2000.

Blackmore, Susan. *The Meme Machine.* New York: Oxford University Press, 1999.

Broom, Brian. *Somatic Illness and the Patient's Other Story.* New York: Free Association Books, 1997.

Broughton, Richard S. *Parapsychology: The Controversial Science.* New York: Ballantine Books, 1991.

Brown, Chip. *Afterwards, You're a Genius: Faith, Medicine, and the Metaphysics of Healing.* New York: Riverhead Books, 1998.

Brown, Guy. The *Energy of Life: The Science of What Makes Our Minds and Bodies Work.* New York: The Free Press, 1999.

Carter, Rita. *Mapping the Mind.* Berkeley/Los Angeles, Calif.: University of California Press, 1998.

Chauvin, Remy. *Parapsychology: When the Irrational Rejoins Science.* Jefferson, N.C.: McFarland & Co., 1985.

Chin, Richard M. *The Energy Within: The Science Behind Oriental Therapy from Acupuncture to Yoga.* New York: Marlow & Company, 1995.

Combs, Allan, and Mark Holland. *Synchronicity: Science, Myth, and the Trickster.* New York: Marlowe & Company, 1996.

Connellan, Thomas K. *Bringing Out the Best in Others: 3 Keys for Business Leaders, Educators, Coaches and Parents.* Austin, Tex.: Bard Press, 2003.

Crenshaw, Theresa L. *The Alchemy of Love and Lust.* New York: G. P. Putnam's Sons, 1996.

Crichton, Michael. *Travels.* New York: Ballantine Books, 1988.

Crick, Francis. *The Astonishing Hypothesis: The Scientific Search for the Soul.* New York: Charles Scribner's Sons, 1994.

Cytowic, Richard. *The Man Who Tasted Shapes.* New York: Jeremy P. Tarcher/Putman, 1993.

Damasio, Antonio R. *Descartes' Error: Emotion, Reason, and the Human Brain.* New York: G. P. Putnam's Sons, 1994.

———. *The Feeling of What Happens: Body and Emotion in the Making of Consciousness.* New York: Harcourt, Brace & Co., 1999.

Darling, David. *Soul Search: A Scientist Explores the Afterlife.* New York: Villard Books, 1995.

Davidson, Jonathan, and Henry Dreher. *The Anxiety Book: Developing Strength in the Face of Fear.* New York: Riverhead Books, 2003.

Devereux, Paul. *Earth Lights Revelation.* London: Blandford Press, 1990.

———. *Earthmind: A Modern Adventure in Ancient Wisdom.* New York: Harper & Row, 1989.

Diamond, Seymour. *The Hormone Headache: New Ways to Prevent, Manage, and Treat Migraines and Other Headaches.* New York: Macmillan, 1995.

Dossey, Larry. *The Extraordinary Healing Power of Ordinary Things.* New York: Harmony Books, 2006.

———. *Healing Beyond the Body: Medicine and the Infinite Reach of the Mind.* Boston: Shambhala, 2001.

———. *Reinventing Medicine: Beyond Mind-Body to a New Era of Healing.* New York: HarperSanFrancisco, 1999.

Downer, John. *Lifesense: Our Lives through Animal Eyes.* London: BBC Books, 1991.

Dozier, Rush W. *Fear Itself: The Origin and Nature of the Powerful Emotion That Shapes Our Lives and Our World.* New York: St. Martin's Press, 1998.

Dreher, Henry. *Mind-Body Unity: A New Vision for Mind-Body Science and Medicine.* Baltimore, Md.: The Johns Hopkins University Press, 2003.

Duff, Kat. *The Alchemy of Illness.* New York: Pantheon Books, 1993.

Durden-Smith, Jo, and Diane deSimone. *Sex and the Brain.* New York: Arbor House, 1983.

Dychtwald, Ken. *Bodymind.* Los Angeles: Jeremy P. Tarcher, Inc., 1977.

Edelman, Gerald. *Bright Air, Brilliant Fire: On the Matter of the Mind.* New York: Basic Books, 1992.

Ehrenwald, Jan. *The ESP Experience: A Psychiatric Validation.* New York: Basic Books Inc., 1978.

Eide, Brock, and Fernnette Eide. *The Mislabeled Child.* New York: Penguin, 2005

Eigen, Michael. *The Sensitive Self.* Middletown, Conn.: Wesleyan University Press, 2004.

Eisenbud, Jule. *The World of Ted Serios: Thoughtographic Studies of an Extraordinary Mind.* Jefferson, N.C.: McFarland & Company Publishers, 1989.

Ekman, Paul. *Emotions Revealed: Recognizing Faces and Feelings to Improve Communication and Emotional Life.* New York: Times Books/Henry Holt & Co., 2003.

Eliade, Mircea. *Shamanism: Archaic Techniques of Ecstasy.* Princeton, N.J.: Princeton University Press, 1964.

Fagg, Lawrence W. *Electromagnetism and the Sacred: At the Frontier of Spirit and Matter.* New York: Continuum Publishing Co., 1999.

Feldman, David Henry. *Nature's Gambit: Child Prodigies and the Development of Human Potential.* New York: Basic Books, 1986.

Fodor, Nandor. *Between Two Worlds.* West Nyack, N.Y.: Parker Publishing Co., 1964.

Ford, Clyde W. *Compassionate Touch: The Body's Role in Emotional Healing and Recovery.* Berkeley, Calif.: North Atlantic Books, 1999.

Fraser, J. T., ed. *The Voices of Time.* New York: George Brazillier Inc., 1966.

Frattaroli, Elio. *Healing the Soul in the Age of the Brain: Becoming Conscious in an Unconscious World.* New York: Viking Penguin, 2001.

Freud, Sigmund. *Studies in Parapsychology.* Edited by Philip Rieff. New York: Collier Books, 1963.

Frey, William H., with Muriel Langseth. *Crying: The Mystery of Tears.* Minneapolis, Minn.: Winston Press Inc., 1985.

Frishman, William H., Michael I. Weintraub, and Marc S. Micozzi, eds. *Complementary and Integrative Therapies for Cardiovascular Disease.* 3rd ed. St. Louis, Mo.: Elsevier Mosby, 2005.

Fuller, John. *The Ghost of Flight 401.* New York: Berkley Publishing Co., 1976.

Gallagher, Winifred. *The Power of Place: How Our Surroundings Shape Our Thoughts, Emotions, and Actions.* New York: Poseidon Press, 1993.

Gaylin, Willard. *The Rage Within: Anger in Modern Life.* New York: Simon and Schuster, 1984.

———. *On Being and Becoming Human.* New York: Penguin Books, 1990.

Gershon, Michael. *The Second Brain: The Scientific Basis of Gut Instinct.* New York: HarperCollins, 1998.

Gersten, Dennis. *Are You Getting Enlightened or Losing Your Mind?* New York: Harmony Books, 1997.

Gladwell, Malcolm. *Blink: The Power of Thinking Without Thinking.* New York: Little, Brown & Co., 2005.

Goleman, Daniel. *Destructive Emotions.* New York: Bantam Books, 2003.

———. *Emotional Intelligence: Why It Can Matter More than IQ.* New York: Bantam Books, 1995.

———, ed. *Healing Emotions.* Boston: Shambhala Publications, 1997.

Goleman, Daniel, and Joel Gurin, eds. *Mind/Body Medicine: How to Use Your Mind for Better Health.* Yonkers, N.Y.: Consumers Union, 1993.

Grandin, Temple, and Catherine Johnson. *Animals in Translation: Using the Mysteries of Autism to Decode Animal Behavior.* New York: Scribner, 2005.

Greenfield, Susan. *The Private Life of the Brain: Emotions, Consciousness, and the Secret of the Self.* New York: John Wiley & Sons, 2000.

Greenspan, Miriam. *Healing through the Dark Emotions: The Wisdom of Grief, Fear, and Despair.* Boston: Shambhala, 2003.

Greenspan, Stanley, and Stuart Shanker. *The First Idea: How Symbols, Language, and Intelligence Evolved from Our Primate Ancestors to Modern Humans.* New York: Da Capo Press, 2006.

Griffin, Susan. *What Her Body Thought: A Journey Into the Shadows.* New York: HarperSanFrancisco, 1999.

Grinker, Roy Richard. *Unstrange Minds: Remapping the World of Autism.* New York: Basic Books, 2007.

Grof, Stanislav. *Realms of the Human Unconscious.* New York: The Viking Press, 1975.

Groopman, Jerome. *The Anatomy of Hope: How People Prevail in the Face of Illness.* New York: Random House, 2004.

Hartmann, Ernest. *Boundaries in the Mind: A New Dimension of Personality.* New York: Basic Books, 1996.

———. *Dreams and Nightmares: The New Theory of the Origin and Meaning of Dreams.* New York: Plenum Trade, 1998.

Hauck, Dennis William. *Haunted Places: The National Directory.* New York: Penguin Books, 1996.

Heller, Sharon. *Too Loud, Too Bright, Too Fast, Too Tight: What to Do if You Are Sensory Defensive in an Overstimulating World.* New York: HarperCollins, 2002.

Hillman, James. *The Soul's Code: In Search of Character and Calling.* New York: Warner Books, 1996.

Hobson, J. Allan. *The Chemistry of Conscious States: How the Brain Changes its Mind.* New York: Little, Brown and Company, 1994.

Hoffman, Edward. *Visions of Innocence: Spiritual and Inspirational Experiences of Childhood.* Boston: Shambhala Books, 1992.

Horgan, John. *Rational Mysticism: Spirituality Meets Science in the Search for Enlightenment.* Boston: Houghton Mifflin Company, 2003.

———. *The Undiscovered Mind: How the Human Brain Defies Replication, Medication, and Explanation.* New York: The Free Press, 1999.

Humphrey, Nicholas. *A History of the Mind: Evolution and the Birth of Consciousness.* New York: Simon & Schuster, 1992.

———. *Leaps of Faith: Science, Miracles, and the Search for Supernatural Consolation.* New York: Basic Books, 1996.

Huxley, Aldous. *The Doors of Perception and Heaven and Hell.* New York: Harper & Row, 1963.

Johnson, Mark. *The Meaning of the Body: The Aesthetics of Human Understanding.* Chicago: The University of Chicago Press, 2007.

Joseph, Rhawn. *The Naked Neuron: Evolution and the Languages of the Body and Brain.* New York: Plenum Press, 1993.

Jung, Carl. *Memories, Dream, Reflections.* Edited by Aniela Jaffe. New York: Random House, 1971.

———. *On Psychic Energy.* Princeton, N.J.: Princeton University Press, 1969.

Kagan, Jerome. *Galen's Prophesy: Temperament in Human Nature.* New York: Basic Books, 1994.

Kagan, Jerome, and Nancy Snidman. *The Long Shadow of Temperament.* Cambridge, Mass.: Belknap Press, 2004.

Karpf, Anne. *The Human Voice.* New York and London: Bloomsbury, 2006.

Kegan, Robert. *The Evolving Self: Problem and Process in Human Development.* Cambridge, Mass.: Harvard University Press, 1982.

Kellert, Stephen R. *Kinship to Mastery: Biophilia in Human Evolution and Development.* Washington, D.C.: Island Press, 1997.

Klaus, Marshall H., John H. Kennell, and Phyllis H. Klaus. *Bonding: Building the Foundations of Secure Attachment and Independence.* Reading, Mass.: Addison-Wesley Publishing Co., 1995.

Knaster, Mirka. *Discovering the Body's Wisdom.* New York: Bantam Books, 1996.

Kreskin. *Secrets of the Amazing Kreskin.* Buffalo, N.Y.: Prometheus Books, 1991.

Lance, James W. *Migraines and Other Headaches.* East Roseville, New South Wales, Australia: Simon and Schuster, 1998.

Lee, John. *Facing the Fire: Experiencing and Expressing Anger Appropriately.* New York: Bantam Books, 1993.

Leonard, Brian E., and Klara Miller, eds. *Stress, the Immune System and Psychiatry.* West Sussex, England: John Wiley and Sons, 1995.

Leone, Bruno, ed. *Paranormal Phenomena: Opposing Viewpoints.* San Diego: Greenhaven Press, 1997.

LeVay, Simon. *The Sexual Brain.* Cambridge, Mass.: The MIT Press, 1993.

Levine, Peter A., with Ann Frederick. *Waking the Tiger: Healing Trauma.* Berkeley, Calif.: North Atlantic Books, 1997.

Levitt, B. Blake. *Electromagnetic Fields: A Consumer's Guide to the Issues and How to Protect Ourselves.* New York: Harcourt Brace & Co., 1995.

Lightman, Alan. *A Sense of the Mysterious: Science and the Human Spirit.* New York: Pantheon Books, 2005.

Louv, Richard. *Last Child in the Woods: Saving our Children from Nature-Deficit Disorder.* Chapel Hill, N.C.: Algonquin Books, 2005.

Lowen, Alexander. *Bioenergetics.* New York: Penguin Books, 1975.

———. *Pleasure: A Creative Approach to Life.* New York: Penguin Books, 1970.

———. *The Spirituality of the Body: Bioenergetics for Grace and Harmony.* New York: Macmillan Publishing Company, 1990.

Lynch, James J. *The Language of the Heart: The Body's Response to Human Dialogue.* New York: Basic Books, 1985.

Madow, Leo. *Anger.* New York: Charles Scribner's Sons, 1972.

Manning, Matthew. *The Link.* New York: Holt, Reinhart and Winston, 1975.

Martin, Paul. *The Healing Mind: The Vital Links between Brain and Behavior, Immunity and Disease.* New York: St. Martin's Press, 1997.

Masson, Jeffrey Moussaieff, and Susan McCarthy. *When Elephants Weep: The Emotional Lives of Animals.* New York: Delacorte Press, 1995.

Maté, Gabor. *When the Body Says No: Understanding the Stress-Disease Connection.* Hoboken, N.J.: John Wiley & Sons, Inc., 2003.

Mayer, Elizabeth Lloyd. *Extraordinary Knowing: Science, Skepticism, and the Inexplicable Powers of the Human Mind.* New York: Bantam/Random House, 2007.

McCrone, John. *The Myth of Irrationality: The Science of the Mind from Plato to Star Trek.* New York: Carroll & Graf Publishers, 1993.

McDougall, Joyce. *Theaters of the Body: A Psychoanalytic Approach to Psychosomatic Illness.* New York: W. W. Norton & Company, 1989.

Micozzi, Marc S., ed. *Complementary and Integrative Medicine in Cancer Care and Prevention.* New York: Springer, 2007.

———, ed. *Fundamentals of Complementary and Alternative Medicine.* 3rd ed. St. Louis, Mo.: Elsevier, 2006.

Montagu, Ashley. *Touching: The Human Significance of the Skin.* 2nd ed. New York: Harper & Row, 1971 (3rd ed. New York: Perennial Library, 1986).

Moody, Raymond A. *Life After Life: The Investigation of a Phenomenon—Survival of Bodily Death.* New York: Bantam Books, 1977.

Moody, Raymond A., and Paul Perry. *Reunions: Visionary Encounters with Departed Loved Ones.* New York: Villard Books, 1993.

Moore, Pete. *Being Me: What It Means to Be Human.* Chichester, West Sussex, England: Wiley, 2003.

Morris, Desmond. *The Human Animal: A Personal View of the Human Species.* New York: Crown Publishers, 1994.

———. *Intimate Behavior.* New York: Random House, 1971.

———. *The Naked Ape: A Zoologist's Study of the Human Animal.* New York: McGraw-Hill, 1967.

Morris, Richard. *Time's Arrows: Scientific Attitudes toward Time.* New York: Simon and Schuster, 1985.

Motz, Julie. *Hands of Life.* New York: Bantam Books, 1998.

Murchie, Guy. *Music of the Spheres, Vol. II: The Microcosm.* New York: Dover Publications, Inc., 1967.

———. *The Seven Mysteries of Life: An Exploration in Science and Philosophy.* Boston: Houghton Mifflin Co., 1978.

Murphy, Michael. *The Future of the Body: Explorations into the Further Evolution of Human Nature.* Los Angeles: Jeremy P. Tarcher, 1992.

Nathanielsz, Peter W. *Life in the Womb: The Origin of Health and Disease.* Ithaca, N.Y.: Promethean Press, 1999.

Needleman, Jacob. *Time and the Soul.* New York: Currency/Doubleday, 1998.

Northrup, Christiane. *Women's Bodies, Women's Wisdom: Creating Physical and Emotional Health and Healing.* New York: Bantam Books, 1998.

O'Connor, Richard. *Undoing Perpetual Stress: The Missing Connection between Depression, Anxiety, and 21st Century Illness.* New York: Berkley Books, 2005.

Ornstein, Robert. *The Psychology of Consciousness.* New York: Arkana Penguin, 1996.

Oschman, James L. *Energy Medicine: The Scientific Basis.* Edinburgh, United Kingdom: Churchill Livingstone, 2000.

Payne, Katy. *Silent Thunder: In the Presence of Elephants.* New York: Penguin, 1999.

Pearce, Joseph Chilton. *The Crack in the Cosmic Egg.* New York: The Julian Press, 1971.

———. *Evolution's End: Claiming the Potential of Our Intelligence.* New York: HarperSanFrancisco, 1992.

———. *Magical Child: Rediscovering Nature's Plan for Our Children.* New York: Bantam Books, 1977.

Pearsall, Paul. *The Heart's Code: Tapping the Wisdom and Power of Our Heart Energy.* New York: Broadway Books, 1998.

Peat, F. David. *Synchronicity: The Bridge Between Matter and Mind.* New York: Bantam Books, 1987.

Persinger, Michael A., and Gyslaine Lafrenier. *Space-Time Transients and Unusual Events.* Chicago: Nelson-Hall, 1977.

Pert, Candace B. *Molecules of Emotion: Why You Feel the Way You Feel.* New York: Scribner, 1997.

Philpott, William H., and Dwight K. Kalita. *Brain Allergies: The Psycho-Nutrient Connection.* New Canaan, Conn.: Keats Publishing, 1980.

Poland, Janet. *The Sensitive Child*. New York: Skylight Press, 1995.

Pierrakos, John. *Core Energetics*. Mendocino, Calif.: Life Rhythm, 1987.

Ramachandran, V. S., and Sandra Blaskeslee. *Phantoms in the Brain: Probing the Mysteries of the Human Mind*. New York: William Morrow, 1998.

Raymo, Chet. *Skeptics and True Believers: The Exhilarating Connection between Science and Religion*. New York: Walker & Company, 1998.

Reeves, Paula. *Women's Intuition: Unlocking the Wisdom of the Body*. Boston: Conari Press, 1999.

Ring, Kenneth. *Heading Toward Omega: In Search of the Meaning of the Near-Death Experience*. New York: William Morrow & Co., 1984.

———. *The Omega Project: Near-Death Experiences, UFO Encounters, and Mind at Large*. New York: William Morrow & Co., 1992.

Roach, Mary. *Spook: Science Tackles the Afterlife*. New York: W. W. Norton & Company, 2005.

Rogo, D. Scott, ed. *Mind beyond the Body: The Mystery of ESP Projection*. New York: Penguin Books, 1978.

———. *The Poltergeist Experience*. Wellingborough, Northamptonshire, United Kingdom: The Aquarian Press, 1979.

Root-Bernstein, Robert and Root-Bernstein, Michele. *Sparks of Genius: The Thirteen Thinking Tools of the World's Most Creative People*. New York: Houghton Mifflin, 2000.

Roszak, Theodore, Mary E. Gomes, and Allan D. Kanner, eds. *Ecopsychology: Restoring the Earth, Healing the Mind*. San Francisco: Sierra Club Books, 1995.

Rothschild, Babette. *The Body Remembers: The Psychophysiology of Trauma and Trauma Treatment*. New York: W. W. Norton & Company, 2000.

Rubenfeld, Ilana. *The Listening Hand: Self-Healing through the Rubenfeld Synergy Method of Talk and Touch*. New York: Bantam Books, 2000.

Runco, Mark A., and Steven R. Pritzker, eds. *Encyclopedia of Creativity*. Burlington, Mass. and St. Louis, Mo.: Academic Press, 1999.

Sabom, Michael. *Recollections of Death: A Medical Investigation*. New York: Harper & Row, 1982.

Sacks, Oliver. *The Man Who Mistook His Wife for a Hat*. New York: HarperCollins Publishers, 1987.

———. *Migraine*. Berkeley, Calif.: University of California Press, 1992.

———. *Musicophilia: Tales of Music and the Brain*. New York: Alfred A. Knopf, 2007.

Sagan, Carl. *Billions and Billions*. New York: Ballantine Books, 1997.

Sarno, John. *The Divided Mind: The Epidemic of Mindbody Disorders.* New York: Regan Books, 2006.

———. *The Mindbody Prescription: Healing the Body, Healing the Pain.* New York: Warner Books, 1998.

Schatzman, Morton. *The Story of Ruth.* New York: G. P. Putnam's Sons, 1980.

Schulz, Mona Lisa. *Awakening Intuition: Using Your Mind-Body Network for Insight and Healing.* New York: Harmony Books, 1998.

Shallis, Michael. *The Electric Connection: Its Effects on Mind and Body.* New York: New Amsterdam Books, 1988.

———. *On Time: An Investigation into Scientific Knowledge and Human Experience.* New York: Schocken Books, 1982.

Sheikh, Anees A., ed. *Imagery: Current Theory, Research and Application.* New York: John Wiley & Sons, 1983.

Sheikh, Anees A., and John T. Shaffer, eds. *The Potential of Fantasy and Imagination.* New York: Brandon House, 1979.

Sheldrake, Rupert. *Dogs That Know When Their Owners Are Coming Home: And Other Unexplained Powers of Animals.* New York: Three Rivers Press, 2000.

———. *The Rebirth of Nature: The Greening of Science and God.* New York: Bantam Books, 1991.

———. *The Sense of Being Stared At (and Other Aspects of the Extended Mind).* New York: Crown Publishers, 2003.

Shepard, Paul. *Nature and Madness.* Athens, Ga.: The University of Georgia Press, 1982.

Shermer, Michael. *Why People Believe Weird Things: Pseudoscience, Superstition, and Other Confusions of Our Time.* New York: W. H. Freeman and Co., 1997.

Shinoda Bolen, Jean. *Close to the Bone: Life-Threatening Illness as a Soul Journey.* Boston: Conari Press, 2007.

Shroder, Tom. *Old Souls: The Scientific Evidence for Past Lives.* New York: Simon & Schuster, 1999.

Siegel, Ronald. *Fire in the Brain: Clinical Tales of Hallucination.* New York: Dutton, 1992.

Skynner, Robin, and John Cleese. *Families and How to Survive Them.* New York: Oxford University Press, 1983.

Smith, Cyril W., and Simon Best. *Electromagnetic Man: Health and Hazard in the Electrical Environment.* New York: St. Martin's Press, 1989.

Smith, Jillyn. *Senses and Sensibilities.* New York: John Wiley & Sons, 1989.

Smith, Karen A., and Karen R. Gouze. *The Sensory Sensitive Child: Practical Solutions for Out-of-Bounds Behavior.* New York: HarperResource, 2005.

Starylanyl, Devin, and Mary Ann Copeland. *Fibromyalgia and Chronic Myofascial Pain.* 2nd ed. Oakland, Calif.: New Harbinger Publications, 2001.

Steiger, Brad. *Real Ghosts, Restless Spirits, and Haunted Places.* Detroit: Visible Ink Press, 2003.

Steinberg, Marilyn, and Maxine Schnall. *The Stranger in the Mirror: Dissociation— the Hidden Epidemic.* New York: Cliff Street Books, 2000.

Sternberg, Esther M. *The Balance Within: The Science Connecting Health and Emotions.* New York: W. H. Freeman & Co., 2000.

Stillman, William. *Autism and the God Connection.* Naperville Ill.: Sourcebooks, 2006.

Stokes, Douglas M. *The Nature of Mind: Parapsychology and the Role of Consciousness in the Physical World.* Jefferson, N.C.: McFarland & Company, Inc., 1997.

Stolorow, Robert D. *Trauma and Human Existence: Autobiographical, Psychoanalytic, and Philosophical Reflections.* New York: The Analytic Press, 2007.

Stolorow, Robert D., George E. Atwood, and Donna M. Orange. *Worlds of Experience: Interweaving Philosophical and Clinical Dimensions in Psychoanalysis.* New York: Basic Books, 2002.

Storr, Anthony. *Music and the Mind.* New York: The Free Press, 1992.

Storr, Will. *Will Storr vs. the Supernatural.* New York: HarperCollins Publishers, 2006.

Strauch, Barbara. *The Primal Teen: What New Discoveries about the Teenage Brain Tell Us about Our Kids.* New York: Doubleday, 2003.

Talbot, Michael. *The Holographic Universe.* New York: Harper Collins, 1991.

Taylor, Gordon Rattray. *The Natural History of the Mind.* New York: E. P. Dutton, 1979.

Time-Life Books. *Phantom Encounters.* Alexandria, Va.: Time-Life Books, 1988.

———. *Psychic Powers.* Alexandria, Va.: Time-Life Books, 1987.

Tompkins, Peter, and Christopher Bird. *The Secret Life of Plants.* New York: Harper & Row, 1973.

Trefil, James. *1001 Things Everyone Should Know about Science.* New York: Doubleday, 1992.

Van de Castle, Robert L. *Our Dreaming Mind.* New York: Ballantine Books, 1994.

Verny, Thomas, and John Kelly. *The Secret Life of the Unborn Child.* New York: Dell Publishing Co., 1981.

Vickerstaff Joneja, Janice M., and Leonard Bielory. *Understanding Allergy, Sensitivity, and Immunity.* New Brunswick, N.J.: Rutgers University Press, 1990.

Wallace, Daniel J., and Janice Brock Wallace. *All About Fibromyalgia: A Guide for Patients and Their Families.* New York: Oxford University Press, 2002.

Watson, Lyall. *Jacobson's Organ: And the Remarkable Nature of Smell.* New York: W. W. Norton & Company, 2000.

———. *Lifetide: The Biology of the Unconscious.* New York: Simon and Schuster, 1979.

———. *The Nature of Things: The Secret Life of Inanimate Objects.* Rochester, Vt.: Destiny Books, 1992.

———. *Supernature: A Natural History of the Supernatural.* New York: Bantam Books, 1973.

Weintraub, Michael I., Ravinder Mamtani, and Marc S. Micozzi, eds. *Complementary and Integrative Medicine in Pain Management.* New York: Springer, 2008.

Williams, Donna. *Autism and Sensing: The Unlost Instinct.* London: Jessica Kingsley Publishers, 1998.

Wilson, Colin. *Poltergeist: A Study in Destructive Haunting.* New York: G. P. Putnam's Sons, 1982.

Wilson, Edward O. *Biophilia.* Cambridge, Mass.: Harvard University Press, 1984.

Wise, Stephen M. *Drawing the Line: Science and the Case for Animal Rights.* Cambridge, Mass.: Perseus Books, 2002.

Young, Louisa. *The Book of the Heart.* New York: Doubleday, 2003.

Zimmer, Carl. *Soul Made Flesh: The Discovery of the Brain—and How it Changed the World.* New York: The Free Press, 2004.

Index

Massullo, Brandon, 292–93, 294
Maté, Gabor, 134–35, 226–27, 437
Maudsley, Henry, 64
Maurer, Daphne, 303
McCrone, John, 218–19
Mead, Margaret, 281
medical conditions, 287–89
meditation, 125, 269
Melzack, Ronald, 139–41, 145
memes, 391-392
memory
 emotional, 50–51
 emotions integral to, 27–28
 genetic basis for, 321
 heart carrying, 341
 past-life, 256, 350–54
 self and, 391
 smell as cue for, 46–47, 385–86
 transplanted organs and, 348–50
mental felt perceptions, 51–52
mental senses, 18
Merker, Bjorn, 45
Mesmer, Franz, 113
metabolic rate, 363–64, 366, 382
metabolism, 66–67, 113, 364, 366
metachoric experiences, 265–66, 424
migraine, 60, 283, 305–10, 423
mind, 56–57, 436, 453–54
mindfulness, 125, 269
mirror neurons, 95–97, 301, 414
mitochondria, 112-113
Monro, Jean, 227
Montagu, Ashley, 71–72, 85, 86, 332, 335
Montague, P. Read, 272–73
Moody, Raymond, 415, 416, 419
Moore, Christopher, 357
Morris, Desmond, 35–36, 201–2
Motz, Julie, 339
multiple sclerosis, 134
Murchie, Guy, 18–19, 170, 188, 280, 373–74

music, 21–22, 63, 386, 404, 405, 432, 433
Myers, Richard, 202–3

Nadal, Rafael, 64
Nathanielsz, Peter, 76, 88
natural disasters, 176–78, 325
nature, 445, 447–48
nature and nurture, 60, 101–2, 313
near-death experiences (NDEs), 189–90, 304, 316, 419, 423, 424–25, 427, 432–33
Needleman, Jacob, 381
Nelson, Kevin, 424
Nemeroff, Charles, 87
neocortex, 47–49, 53, 92, 201
neuroscience, 1–4, 442–44, 450–51
neurosignature, 140, 141
Newberg, Andrew, 421
Nichols, Andrew, 222–23
Noble, Kathleen, 457

obsessive-compulsive disorder (OCD), 161–62
olfactory lobe, 45–46, 48f
orbitofrontal cortex, 53–54, 94–95, 99–100, 159, 201
Ornstein, Robert, 387, 455–56
out-of-body experience (OBE), 13–14, 127, 380–81, 415–34
overexcitabilities, 255–56

pain, 39, 40, 90, 138–46, 334
panic attacks, 150–51
Panksepp, Jaak, 414
parasympathetic nervous system, 40, 41f
past lives, 256, 350–54
Pauli, Wolfgang, 227
Payne, Katy, 177
Pearce, Joseph Chilton, 340, 454–55
Pearsall, Paul, 17, 340–44, 346, 347, 353, 443